European Takeovers
The Art of Acquisition

European Takeovers

The Art of Acquisition

Author and Editor
Jeremy Grant

Published by
Euromoney Books
Nestor House, Playhouse Yard
London EC4V 5EX
United Kingdom

Telephone: +44 020 7779 8544

Copyright © 2005 Euromoney Institutional Investor PLC, Jeremy Grant and individual contributors

ISBN 1 84374 216 0

This publication is not included in the CLA Licence and must not be copied without the permission of the publisher.

All rights reserved. No part of this publication may be reproduced or used in any form (graphic, electronic or mechanical, including photocopying, recording, taping or information storage and retrieval systems) without permission by the publisher.

The views and opinions expressed in this book are solely those of the authors. Although Euromoney Books has made every effort to ensure the complete accuracy of the text, neither it nor the editor or authors can accept any legal responsibility whatsoever for consequences that may arise from errors or omissions or any opinions or advice given.

Typeset by Julie Foster.
Printed by Hobbs the Printers.

Contents

Author biographies		xiii
Foreword *Geoffrey Owen*		xxi
Editor's preface *Jeremy Grant*		xxiii
Introduction *Jaap Winter*		xxv

Part I:	**Inside the takeover regulation and tactics**	1
Chapter 1:	Takeovers and the market for corporate control *Jeremy Grant*	3
	Introduction	3
	The role of takeovers in a market economy and the Continental/Anglo–American divide	4
	A brief history of hostile takeovers	20
Chapter 2:	Takeover regulation and the balancing of interests *Jeremy Grant*	34
	Introduction	34
	A brief history of takeover regulation	35
	Major components of takeover regulation	37
	Derivatives transactions and contracts for differences	38
Chapter 3:	The European Takeover Directive *Jeremy Grant*	53
	Background to the Directive	53
	The European Takeover Directive – amended, with commentary	56
Chapter 4:	Takeovers in Europe – shareholder decisions and open markets – a UK perspective *Jonathan Rickford*	66
	Introduction: regulating takeovers – property rights and wider objectives	66
	Breakthrough: restrictions and threshold	68

	Breakthrough – compensation, jurisdiction and mandatory bids	71
	Operating the Directive: optionality	75
	Afterword	87

Chapter 5: 'Acting in concert' – first conclusions drawn from two recent takeovers and the Takeover Directive — 92
Erik Bomans and Charles Demoulin

Introduction	92
The Fondiaria takeover by SAI	92
The Beiersdorf takeover by a consortium led by Tchibo	94
The need for a clear and common definition of persons 'acting in concert'	96
The definition of 'acting in concert' under the Takeover Directive	97
Persons acting in concert and shareholder activism	99
Conclusion	101

Chapter 6: Optionality arrangements and reciprocity in the Takeover Directive — 103
Matteo Gatti

Optionality and reciprocity combined	104
An assessment of optionality	106
The uncertain case for reciprocity in takeovers	110
Conclusion	112

Chapter 7: The mandatory bid rule and the sell-out right in the Takeover Directive: harmonisation for its own sake? — 119
Luca Enriques

Provisions on mandatory bids and the sell-out right	120
General principles	120
The mandatory bid rule	120
The sell-out right	122
Why the provisions on mandatory bids and the sell-out right are trivial	123
Conclusion	124

Part II: European jurisdictions — 127

Chapter 8: United Kingdom City Code — 129
Simon Jay and Stuart Banks

Evolution and present status of the Panel and the Takeover Code	129
General principles	131
Types of offer	132
Basic structure and timetable of offer	133
Market purchases	136

	Conduct during an offer	137
	Disclosure of dealings – contracts for differences and proposals for changes to the Code	140
	Proposed changes to disclosure rules	140
	Key points for a potential bidder for a UK plc	141
	Case studies	142

Chapter 9: Austria 149
Max Becker, Phillip Dubsky and Dieter Buchberger

Conditionality of offers	149
Timing and revision	150
Mandatory bid rule	151
Consideration	153
Anticipated mandatory offer	153
Squeeze-out and sell-out	153
Target's response	153
Reform of the Takeover Act	154

Chapter 10: Belgium 156
Paul Van Hooghten and Philippe Remels

Disclosure of important shareholdings	156
Voluntary public takeover bids and counterbids	157
Mandatory public offers and maintaining of the market price	162
Public squeeze-out bids	164
Special topics on takeover practice in Belgium	166
Potential impact of the Takeover Directive	172
Summary of some of the key elements in the Belgian takeover regulation	173

Chapter 11: Denmark 175
Peter M. Andersen and Regina M. Andersen

Basis of the takeover regime	175
Applicability of Danish takeover rules and definition of 'control'	176
Structuring a takeover of a company listed in Denmark	177
Squeeze-out and delisting	180
Defences against a hostile takeover	181
Impact of the Takeover Directive	183

Chapter 12: Finland 184
Dimetrios Himonas, Carla Wallgren, Paula Lima and Elisa Heinonen

Mandatory offers	185
Offer consideration – the concept of equitable price	187

CONTENTS

Competing offers	188
Implications for target companies	188
Special topics on takeover practice in Finland	190
Conclusion	191

Chapter 13: France — 193
Valérie Lemaitre and Sophie de Beer

Types of takeover bids	193
Main terms of takeover bids	195
Typical bid procedure	196
Board neutrality and defensive measures	200
Market purchases	202
Main impact of the Takeover Directive	203
Ten most important points for acquirers in France	204

Chapter 14: Germany — 207
Klaus Riehmer

Important aspects of the German Takeover Act	207
Impact of the Takeover Directive	211
Case studies	212

Chapter 15: Greece — 217
Alexander Metallinos

Conditionality of offers	218
Procedure	218
Voluntary offers	219
Mandatory offers – the implied concept of control	219
The position of the board of directors of the target company	221
Purchase of minority shareholdings	222
Major considerations for bidders	223

Chapter 16: Hungary — 224
András Posztl

Nature of the takeover rules and enforcement	225
Definition of 'control'	225
Disclosure of acquisition of control	226
Mandatory takeover bids	226
Voluntary takeover bids	229
The takeover procedure	229
Squeeze-out and sell-out rights	232
Defensive tactics	232
Sanctions for non-compliance	233

	Special topics	233
	Impact of the Takeover Directive	235
	Practical thoughts	236

Chapter 17: Ireland — 238
Adrian Benson

Relevant statutes and regulations	238
'Control' and other definitions	240
Methods of acquiring control	240
Timing of offers and revisions	241
Extensions and revisions of offers	241
Sample timetable for a takeover	242
Conditionality of offers	243
Break fees and irrevocables	244
Disclosure	245
Mandatory offers	246
Acquisition of minority shareholdings	248
Conversion of a public limited company to a private limited company	248
Board neutrality and defensive measures	249
Impact of the Takeover Directive	251

Chapter 18: Italy — 255
Fabio Labruna and Roberto Tallarita

The Financial Act 1998	255
Participation in listed companies	256
Tender offers	257
Mandatory tender offers	257
Mandatory tender offers: exemptions	261
The tender offer process	263
Key rules on the conduct of the offer	264
The European Takeover Directive	267
Case studies	268

Chapter 19: Luxembourg — 272
Laurent Schummer

Regulatory authorities and statutory provision	272
Conditionality of offers	273
Timing and revisions	273
Equal treatment of shareholders not mandatory	274
Offer consideration	274
Target securities	275
Offeree neutrality	275

	Squeeze-out and sell-out	276
	Impact of the Takeover Directive	277

Chapter 20: The Netherlands — 279
Martin van Olffen, Jaap W. Winter and Michael Ch. Schouten

Introduction	279
Methods of acquisition	280
Regulatory framework	281
Public offers	282
Takeover defence	286
Impact of the Takeover Directive	288

Chapter 21: Poland — 292
Roman Rewald, Dr. Lukasz Gasinski and Anna Iwaszkiewicz

Significant changes in prospect	292
Conditionality of bids	293
Timing	293
Disclosure of the bid	294
Mandatory bid rule and definition of 'control'	294
Squeeze-out	296
Sell-out	296
Protecting minority shareholders	297
Board neutrality and shareholders' consent	297
Exemptions	298
Impact of the Takeover Directive	298

Chapter 22: Portugal — 300
Manuel Costa Salema with the assistance of Ana Bebiano

Laws and regulations	300
Bidder and target	300
Public offer versus private placement	301
Recommended versus hostile offers	301
General versus partial offers	301
Compulsory versus optional offers	302
Price	302
Conditional takeover offers	303
Defence mechanisms preceding a takeover offer	304
Documentation	304
Assistance of a financial intermediary	305
Timetable and actions	305
Revision	307
Post-bid neutrality	307
Squeeze-out and sell-out rights	308

	Successive takeover offers	308
	Competing offers	309
	Impact of the Takeover Directive	309
	Important considerations for bidders	310

Chapter 23: Russia — 311
Scott C. Senecal, Murat N. Akuyev and Yulia A. Solomakhina

Anti-takeover provisions of the Joint Stock Companies Law	312
Anti-monopoly clearance	316
Disclosure requirements of the Securities Law	317
Specific requirements applicable to takeovers of credit organisations	318

Chapter 24: Spain — 320
Alejandro Fernández de Araoz

The mandatory bid rule	320
Procedural aspects and timetable	322
Exemptions	324
Defensive tactics and the role of the target company's board	327
Analysis of the competing bid system	327
Taking the company private: mandatory bids in 'public to private' context	328
Potential impact of the Takeover Directive on the Spanish regime	330
Special topics in takeover practice in Spain	330
Further case studies	334
Some practical thoughts on takeovers in Spain	336

Chapter 25: Sweden — 337
Thomas Wallinder and Patrick Marcelius

Bid preparation, timing of offers and revisions	337
Conditionality of offers	339
Stake building	341
Mandatory bids	342
Consideration	342
Hostile bids	343
Acquisitions of minority shareholdings and delisting	347
Impact of the Takeover Directive	348
Important points for offerors to keep in mind	349

Part III: United States — 351

Chapter 26: An ocean of difference on takeover regulation — 353
John Armour and David A. Skeel, Jr

The content of takeover regulation in the United Kingdom and the United States	353

CONTENTS

        The divergent modes of regulation   355
        Conclusion   357

Chapter 27: US takeover law and practice   360
        Introduction   360
        US takeover preparedness and responding to unsolicited offers   362

Appendix I: Directive 2004/25/EC of the European Parliament and of the Council of 21 April 2004 on Takeover Bids   377

Appendix II: Comparison of national takeover provisions   391

Author biographies

The editor

Jeremy Grant is on academic sabbatical based at the Graduate Institute of International Studies in Geneva and the London School of Economics. He holds a law degree from the LSE, and MSc degrees in Management and International Relations from the same institution. His research focuses on corporate governance, M&A, takeover defences and anti-trust regulation of mergers. He has worked for JP Morgan in corporate finance and equity research. He is also co-author of a forthcoming book *Corporate Governance in the US and Europe*.

The contributors

Murat N. Akuyev is a senior attorney based in the Moscow office of Cleary Gottlieb Steen & Hamilton LLP. His practice focuses on corporate and financial transactions, particularly securities offerings, joint ventures and mergers and acquisitions. Murat also has extensive experience in cross-border transactions involving businesses in Russia. He joined the firm in 1995. In 1996 and 1997 he was resident in the London office. Murat is a member of the Bar of New York and is a Russian-qualified lawyer.

Peter M. Andersen is a partner in the leading Danish law firm Bech-Bruun's capital markets department. He holds a Master's Degree in Law from the University of Copenhagen, was admitted to the bar in 1997 and has the right of audience before the Supreme Court. From 1998 to 2001 Peter conducted courses in international commercial law at the University of California, Davis and Berkeley and has authored and co-authored various articles in Danish and international publications on mergers and acquisitions, Danish business entities, private and international law. He was an external lecturer at the University of Copenhagen in commercial law from 1999 to 2001 and now lectures in business entities/company law at the Danish Bar Association's mandatory bar education. Peter specialises in medium- and large-sized M&A transactions involving both listed and unlisted corporations and in corporate restructurings, partnerships and joint ventures, company law in general and litigation.

Regina M. Andersen is a senior associate in the capital markets department of Bech-Bruun. She holds a Master's Degree in Law from the University of Copenhagen and was admitted to the bar in 2001. She has authored and co-authored a number of articles on Danish stock exchange laws. Regina specialises in stock exchange laws, company law and various regulatory matters regarding financial undertakings.

John Armour is senior lecturer in the Faculty of Law and research associate in the Centre for Business Research at Cambridge University. He studied at Oxford University (BA, BCL) and Yale Law School (LL.M.). He has held visiting positions at the University of Pennsylvania Law School and the University of Amsterdam. His research focuses on corporate law, corporate insolvency law and corporate finance, in which areas he has published widely. He has carried out empirical research projects on the economic impact of changes in legal rules, including insolvency law and company law, and has been involved in policy-related projects commissioned by the DTI, the FSA, and the Insolvency Service.

Stuart Banks has been an associate at Cleary Gottlieb Steen & Hamilton LLP since April 2000. His practice areas include public and private mergers and acquisitions, transactions for private equity funds and venture capital investments. Stuart also advises on general corporate and commercial matters including joint ventures. From 2002 to 2004, he was seconded to the Panel on Takeovers and Mergers, the regulatory body responsible for takeovers of UK public companies, thereby gaining substantial experience of the regulation of bids for public companies. He was responsible for a number of noteworthy cases including several competitive and hostile takeovers. Stuart was also the secretary to the Code Committee of the Panel and, as such, was involved in the development of new policy relating to public takeovers.

Max Becker has been a partner in the Vienna office of DLA Weiss-Tessbach Rechtsanwälte GmbH since 2001. He is responsible for the firm's M&A practice in Central and Eastern Europe (CEE). He has handled several multi-jurisdictional M&A transactions in CEE and advises clients on any related issues, including takeover procedures and merger control cases. Further main areas of practice include corporate law including restructuring.

In addition to his law degree at the University of Vienna, Max obtained a MBA degree at the Vienna University of Business Administration and a LL.M. at the University of San Diego.

Max teaches corporate law at the University of Vienna. He has published several articles on competition law in CEE and is responsible for the Austrian section of a major loose leave collection on corporate law in Europe.

Adrian Benson has a Bachelor of Business and Legal Studies (BBLS) degree from UCD where he graduated in 1995. Adrian qualified as a solicitor in April 1999 and is qualified to practise in the Republic of Ireland. Adrian is an associate solicitor in the corporate and commercial department of Dillon Eustace where he advises on company and commercial law queries and transactions including drafting joint venture agreements, asset purchase agreements, share purchase agreements and share subscription agreements. His experience includes advice on and negotiating domestic and international transactions including mergers and acquisitions, asset sales, share sales, investments, employee share schemes, and matters relating to all aspects of corporate governance.

Erik Bomans has a law degree from the University of Leuven (Belgium) where he graduated in 1991. In 1993 he graduated from The Johns Hopkins University (Washington, D.C.) as a Master of Arts in international politics and economics. He was admitted to the Brussels Bar in 1996 and is qualified to practise in Belgium. After three years of practice at the corporate law department of Linklaters De Bandt in Brussels, Erik joined Deminor International as a consultant in 1995. Erik became a partner of Deminor in 2000 where he advises investors on corporate finance transactions, special situations and investor protection.

AUTHOR BIOGRAPHIES

Dieter Buchberger is senior associate in DLA Weiss-Tessbach Rechtsanwälte GmbH's Vienna-based Corporate M&A group. His main areas of practice include acquisitions and disposals of public and private companies, corporate restructuring, joint ventures, anti-trust and merger law. He obtained his law degree and doctorate at the University of Vienna and a Master's Degree in European and International Law (LL.M.) at the University of Bremen/Germany.

Phillip Dubsky is a partner in the corporate, M&A team of DLA Weiss-Tessbach Rechtsanwälte GmbH. He is a qualified Austrian solicitor and member of the New York Bar. Phillip specialises in (cross border) mergers and acquisitions as well as capital market transactions, in particular in Central and Eastern Europe. In addition, he has been involved in some of the most prominent private equity transaction of the last few years, primarily advising international and national private equity funds on their investments in Austria and the CEE region. Phillip heads the venture capital/emerging markets and private equity group for the CEE region.

Luca Enriques is a professor of business law at the University of Bologna Faculty of Law, where he teaches courses in corporate law, corporate governance and securities regulation. Before entering into academia, Luca worked for the Bank of Italy in Rome. He has published two books, the leading treatise on Italian securities regulation (with Renzo Costi) and several articles in Italian as well as international law reviews on topics relating to corporate governance, takeovers, and EC company law. He is an adviser to the Italian Ministry of Economy and Finance and an independent consultant to the Rome and Milan offices of Cleary Gottlieb Steen & Hamilton LLP.

Alejandro Fernández de Araoz is a partner of Araoz y Rueda Abogados and has been qualified to practise in Spain since 1986. He holds a PhD from Universidad Complutense of Madrid, as well as an LL.M. from the London School of Economics and Political Science and an LL.M. from New York University School of Law. He has been a visiting researcher at Harvard Law School and at the Ludwig-Maximilian Universität of Munich. Alejandro is an associate professor of commercial law at Universidad Complutense of Madrid. He has written extensively on corporate and securities and his professional experience includes advice on and negotiation of domestic and international transactions, particularly in the areas of corporate acquisitions, private equity and joint venture agreements.

Matteo Gatti is assistant professor of commercial law at the Università degli Studi di Milano-Bicocca. Matteo graduated with honours from the Law School of the University of Milan in 1997, received an LL.M. degree from Harvard Law School in 2002 and a Ph.D. in commercial law at the University of Brescia in 2003. He has published several articles about corporate and M&A law in major Italian law reviews and published a book in 2004 entitled *Opa e struttura del mercato del controllo societario* (Tender Offers and the Structure of the Market for Corporate Control).

Dr Lukasz Gasinski is a US-qualified attorney. He graduated from the Faculty of Law and Administration of Warsaw University in 1997 and received an LL.M. degree from Columbia University (2001) where he studied thanks to the Kosciuszko Foundation Scholarship. He received his PhD degree in 2003. He also received the Vontobel Foundation prize for the best Master's thesis written at the Faculty of Law and Administration of Warsaw University. Lukasz joined Weil, Gotshal & Manges in 2002. He specialises in corporate law and the law on public trading in securities. He lectures on commercial law at Warsaw University and has authored many publications on corporate law.

Elisa Heinonen is a senior associate at Roschier Holmberg. She is a member of Roschier Holmberg's transactions and finance practice group, specialising in public company transactions and capital markets.

Dimitrios Himonas is a partner at Roschier Holmberg's transactions and finance practice group and co-head of the public company transactions stream, specialising in capital markets and public company transactions. Dimitrios has broad experience gained from domestic and international capital market and corporate transactions.

Anna Iwaszkiewicz graduated from the Faculty of Law and Administration of Warsaw University in 2001, and completed a course in English and European law co-organised by Warsaw University and Cambridge University. Prior to joining Weil, Gotshal & Manges in 2005, Anna worked for the Legal Office of the International Atomic Energy Agency in Vienna. She specialises in international public and civil law, including commercial law with a special focus on corporate and IP law.

Simon Jay has been a partner at Cleary Gottlieb Steen & Hamilton LLP since 1999. Simon's practice focuses on corporate transactions, in particular mergers and acquisitions (public and private), representing both corporate acquirers and sellers, as well as private equity institutions. He also has substantial capital markets' experience representing both issuers and underwriters on IPOs involving UK listings. Simon is a solicitor of the Supreme Court of England and Wales.

Fabio Labruna has been a partner in Gianni, Origoni, Grippo & Partners in Rome since 2003. He works in corporate law, specialising in mergers and acquisitions. Fabio was admitted to practice in 1993, and admitted to the bar in Italy in 1995. He studied at the University of Naples, (J.D., *maxima cum laude*, 1991); holds a Master's Degree in European Legal Studies (LL.M.) from the College of Europe, Bruges; and a scholarship from the Italian Ministry of Foreign Affairs, 1992–93. Fabio completed a Stage in the Legal Service of the Commission of the European Communities in 1993 and was a visiting foreign lawyer at the Brussels office of Skadden, Arps, Slate, Meagher & Flom in 1995 and 1997.

Valérie Lemaitre has been a partner of Cleary Gottlieb Steen & Hamilton LLP since 2002, having joined the firm in 1994. Based in the Paris office, her practice focuses on corporate and financial matters, including acquisition transactions involving public companies, structured financings, leveraged transactions and securities offerings. She received an LL.M. degree from Columbia Law School in 1994, a Diplôme d'Etudes Supérieures Spécialisées en Droit des Affaires et Fiscalité and a Diplôme du Magistère de Juristes d'Affaires from the Université de Paris II in 1990. Valérie is a member of the bars in New York and Paris.

AUTHOR BIOGRAPHIES

Paula Linna is a senior associate at Roschier Holmberg. She is a member of Roschier Holmberg's transactions and finance practice group, specialising in public company transactions, corporate advisory and corporate law.

Patrik Marcelius is a senior associate at Mannheimer Swartling and specialises in public takeovers and equity capital markets. He received an LL.M. from Stockholm University in 1998 and an LL.M. from the University of Cambridge in 2000.

Alexander Metallinos is a partner at Karatzas & Partners in Athens. He holds a Master of Laws from Yale University and a doctorate from the Westfällische Wilhelms Universität Münster. He is the author of *Die europarechtskonforme Auslegung*, Münster 1994, (*Insurance Contracts in Private International Law* (in Greek)), Athens 1997 and numerous articles. Alexander has been involved in a number of significant equity offerings and mergers and acquisitions in Greece, including the first leveraged buyout of a major Greek company (the first acquisition by international private equity firms in Greece) and many tender offers in Greece. He has advised ISDA and numerous banks and other financial institutions on the enforceability of the ISDA Master Agreement where Greek parties are involved and on other derivatives issues.

Martin van Olffen, a civil law notary and partner with the Dutch law firm De Brauw Blackstone Westbroek, is a specialist in corporate law and mergers and acquisitions, including corporate governance. He has advised a large number of listed companies on their corporate structure and corporate governance. He has also advised on the development and implementation of defence strategies as well as the negotiation of settlement agreements in a number of recent contested takeovers in the Netherlands. A professor of corporate law at the University of Nijmegen, he is also a member of the Joint Committee on Corporate Law of the Dutch Bar Association.

András Posztl, a partner at DLA Weiss-Tessbach Horváth & Partners, has been involved in numerous international cross-border and domestic finance and corporate transactions including competition law matters (merger clearance procedures). With more than eight years' experience, he has been involved in major international M&A and corporate finance transactions with special focus on public equity deals. András studied at Eötvös Loránd University, Faculty of Law (Degree in Law: summa cum laude, 1994); completed EU and competition law studies at Universität Trier (1994) and postgraduate corporate law studies between 1997 and 1999. András was admitted to practise in Hungary in 1997.

Roman Rewald is a US-qualified attorney and a partner at Weil, Gotshal & Manges. He graduated from the Faculty of Law and Administration of the Nicolaus Copernicus University with Master's Degrees in both Public Administration and Law, and from the University of Detroit Law School with a Juris Doctor degree. He has acted as counsel in corporate, energy law and real estate matters. He has also extensive experience in foreign joint ventures, banking and real estate acquisitions in Poland. Roman advised the World Bank on the legal issues of housing and mortgage finance in Poland, and the Polish Ministry of Finance on the banking system's privatisation. Roman is the chairman of the American Chamber of Commerce in Poland.

AUTHOR BIOGRAPHIES

Jonathan Rickford CBE is a solicitor and independent consultant on regulation and European law and policy. He is also a Visiting Professor at the London School of Economics. Jonathan was Director of Corporate Strategy at BT from 1993 to 1996, having previously held posts with BT since 1987 as their Director of Government Relations and solicitor and chief legal adviser. He was also a member of the CBI's Europe Committee, Companies Committee and City Panel, and was the Project Director of the Government's independent Review of Company Law (1998–2001).

In 2002 Jonathan was a member of the EU High Level Group on Corporate Law and Visiting Professor in International Commercial Law at the University of Leiden in The Netherlands.

Klaus Riehmer is a lawyer at Cleary Gottlieb Steen & Hamilton LLP's Frankfurt office. His practice focuses on public and private mergers & acquisitions as well as corporate transactions and corporate restructurings. He has advised on various milestone transactions in Germany, such as the Vodafone/Mannesmann takeover, which was the first successful hostile takeover in Germany. Klaus also advised on the UniCredito/HVB merger, the largest cross-border banking merger in Europe and the largest public transaction under the new German Takeover Act of 2002. He is also widely published, in particular on public takeovers in Germany.

Manuel Costa Salema is a partner of Carlos Aguiar, P. Pinto & Associados since 2002 and specialises in financial and capital market law, banking law, business and corporate law and mergers and acquisitions. Manuel completed a postgraduate degree in Financial Markets, Institutions and Instruments from the Universidade Nova de Lisboa, Porto Derivative Exchange and Securities Market Commission in 2000. He has been a member of the Portuguese Bar (*Ordem dos Advogados*) since 1996 and is a member of the International Bar Association.

Michael Ch. Schouten, an attorney, is a law associate in mergers and acquisitions with the Dutch law firm De Brauw Blackstone Westbroek in Amsterdam. A University of Amsterdam graduate, he has also researched corporate law issues at Fordham Law School in New York City and Université Paris 1 Panthéon – Sorbonne in France. Michael publishes regularly on developments in EU corporate law.

Laurent Schummer joined Linklaters Loesch's corporate and M&A practice in 1998 after completing his studies at Université Catholique de Louvain and at the University of Chicago. He specialises in general company law, mergers and acquisitions, joint ventures and group restructurings, equity offerings, listings and takeover bids. Laurent is also very active in private equity (upstream and downstream) and unregulated real estate structures. He is the author of several articles in the area of securities laws.

Scott C. Senecal has been the head of Cleary Gottlieb Steen & Hamilton LLP's Moscow office since 1996. His practice focuses on financial and corporate law. Scott has extensive experience in mergers and acquisitions, capital market transactions and syndicated loans. His Russian M&A work has included advising western and Russian acquirers and sellers in the oil and gas, electricity, engineering, real estate, fast food and beer sectors. Scott is consistently cited as one of the leading lawyers in Russia by various publications. He is a member of the bar in New York.

David Skeel is the S. Samuel Arsht Professor of Corporate Law at the University of Pennsylvania Law School. He is the author of *Icarus in the Boardroom: The Fundamental Flaws in Corporate America and Where They Came From* (Oxford: Oxford University Press, 2005); *Debt's Dominion: A Political History of Bankruptcy Law in America* (Princeton: Princeton University Press, 2001); and numerous articles on corporate law and corporate insolvency. Professor Skeel has also written commentaries on corporate law and related issues for the *New York Times*, *Financial Times*, *Los Angeles Times*, *Philadelphia Inquirer*, and a variety of other publications.

Yulia A. Solomakhina is an associate based in the Moscow office of Cleary Gottlieb Steen & Hamilton LLP. Her practice focuses on corporate and financial transactions, particularly securities offerings, mergers and acquisitions and cross-border transactions involving businesses in Russia. Yulia joined the firm as an associate in 2002 after working as a *stagiaire* of the firm in 2000 and 2001. She is a qualified Russian lawyer.

Roberto Tallarita has been a partner in Gianni, Origoni, Grippo & Partners in Rome since 2003. He works in Corporate Law, specialising in mergers and acquisitions. He studied at the University of Rome (J.D., *maxima cum laude*, 2003). Roberto is the author of two publications on civil rights and is currently specialising in acquisitions of private and public companies.

Carita Wallgren is a partner at Roschier Holmberg's transactions and finance practice group and head of the public company transactions stream, specialising in public company transactions, corporate advisory and corporate law. Carita has been involved in a great number of domestic and cross-border mergers and acquisitions as well as public company transactions.

Thomas Wallinder is a partner at Mannheimer Swartling and specialises in public takeovers and equity capital markets. Thomas is a member of the Swedish Bar Association, the Bar in New York and the International Bar Association. He received an LL.M. from University of Stockholm in 1990 and an LL.M. from Duke University in 1991.

Jaap W. Winter, an attorney and partner with the Dutch law firm De Brauw Blackstone Westbroek, advises corporate clients and institutional investors on corporate law and on corporate governance developments in the Netherlands and the EU. As chairman of the EU High Level Group of Company Law Experts, member of the Dutch Corporate Governance Committee, member of the European Corporate Governance Forum and chairman of the Committee Modernising Collective Investment Schemes, he plays a prominent role in developments in corporate law in Europe. Jaap is also a professor of international company law at the University of Amsterdam and a visiting professor at Columbia Law School in New York City.

Foreword

Geoffrey Owen
Senior Fellow at the Institute of Management, London School of Economics

How can greater dynamism be injected into the European economy? This is the question which has preoccupied member governments of the European Union over the last few years. Productivity growth has been sluggish; unemployment – in most though not all member states – is high; and there has been a persistent failure to foster new, fast-growing firms in high-technology industries. On all these fronts the US record is superior, and part of the explanation seems to be the existence in the United States of a set of policies and institutions, including large and well-organised financial markets, which makes possible the rapid transfer of resources from declining to growing sectors of the economy.

The most obvious US advantage is the size of its domestic market, and the European Union has sought to match that, first through the Single Market Programme, designed to remove barriers to the cross-border flow of goods and services, and then through the introduction of the single currency. These policies, especially the first, have had beneficial effects in promoting competition, not least through the liberalisation of sectors such as telecommunications and electricity which had previously operated as national monopolies. But market-opening measures of this sort are only part of what is needed if Europe is to catch up with the United States. No less important is an integrated financial market, one that is as effective as that of the United States in channelling funds to new enterprises, in dealing promptly with under-performing companies, and in facilitating the restructuring of industries.

In this context mergers and acquisitions have an important role to play, and here, as several contributors to this book make clear, Europe still has a long way to go. While there has been an increase in M & A activity in Europe in recent years, much of it has taken place on a national basis, and most of the large cross-border amalgamations – such as the creation of Arcelor through the combination of three steel companies in France, Spain and Luxembourg – have been agreed transactions. Despite a few well-known cases such as Vodafone's acquisition of Mannesmann, hostile take-overs are rare in most of Europe. While British quoted companies, in particular, are entirely open to hostile bids (even more open, in some respects, than their American counterparts), there is no Europe-wide market for corporate control comparable to that which exists in the United States.

Why this should be, and what can be done about it, are among the issues discussed in this book. Much attention is rightly focused on the saga of the European take-over directive, ending in a compromise measure that, arguably, may do nothing to promote cross-border take-over activity and could even impede it. The background to this disappointing outcome is the lack of consensus about whether more hostile takeovers are in the best interests of the European economy and European society.

To some extent the unease in Europe about the market for corporate control stems from an attachment on the part of powerful interest groups – including community leaders, trade unions and even some corporate executives – to the status quo. Companies which have long been associated with particular cities or regions are often regarded as part of the social fabric, committed to the area in a way which would not be matched by a new owner, especially if that owner comes from a different country and has a different corporate culture. The idea that companies have social responsibilities that go beyond obligations to shareholders is deeply entrenched in parts of Continental Europe.

There is also a political dimension, demonstrated most clearly in recent statements from the French government that it would seek to bar foreign take-overs of companies deemed to be operating in 'strategic' sectors. Coming not long after the Sanofi-Aventis affair, when the French authorities effectively discouraged a Swiss company, Novartis, from entering the take-over battle, these pronouncements show that the 'national champion' mindset is far from dead in France. (This does not, of course, prevent French 'national champions' from making hostile take-over bids in other countries.)

A more fundamental obstacle to the emergence of a genuinely open take-over market is the prevalence in most European countries of an ownership structure which is far more concentrated than in the United Kingdom or the United States. Most public companies have a single shareholder – a family, a financial institution, perhaps another industrial company – which regards its investment as semi-permanent and is in a strong position to block an unwelcome take-over bid. In some countries, notably Germany, these holdings are beginning to be unwound, as the dominant shareholders (especially banks) find better use for their capital, and there may be a trend towards a more diffuse shareholding pattern. But the process is bound to be gradual, and it will not necessarily lead to a surge in hostile take-over activity.

How much does this matter? It may be that Europe can regain its economic dynamism without drastically reorganising its financial system on American lines; as Enron and other scandals have shown, there is a downside to shareholder-based capitalism, just as there is with the stakeholder version. What is clear, though, is that efficient financial markets are a necessary ingredient in a thriving modern economy, and that such markets must include clear and consistent rules for the conduct of take-overs, whether friendly or hostile. The precise balance between national and European regulation is bound to be a subject for debate, but at both levels investors and managers need predictability and transparency in the way the rules are interpreted and applied. Such a system is still missing in Europe.

This book provides a comprehensive guide to the current state of take-over regulation in different European countries, as well as useful comparisons with the United States; especially valuable are the detailed case studies which point up serious deficiencies either in the rules themselves or in the way they are implemented. It is a notable contribution to the cause of European financial market reform.

Editor's preface

Jeremy Grant

This volume was conceived as a road map to the shifting M&A environment in Europe. This arena is subject to two major forces – the economic drive for Pan-European consolidation across sectors, and the increasingly complex set of M&A regulations which shape firm's takeover tactics. The latter obviously differ across each jurisdiction, but are now subject to a degree of harmonisation due to the introduction of the European Takeover Directive. However, the ability of member states to opt out of certain articles has added a further layer of complexity across national regimes. Therefore, as Chapter 1 states, we attempt to 'trace the contours of the emerging Pan-European jurisdiction created by the Directive'. To this end we present a number of chapters giving an overview of the Directive, and a chapter on the current merger regulation regime in most member states and the likely impact of the Directive on it.

The book was a by-product of a research project undertaken by myself and Dr Tom Kirchmaier into European corporate governance at the London School of Economics while I was on academic sabbatical. Therefore, I must thank both Tom and Geoffrey Owen for hosting me while I completed the manuscript – a process that took rather longer than expected.

I would also like to thank all the contributors for their excellent work – almost every one contacted responded positively and with enthusiasm. There would have been no book without their willingness to share expertise. Also a special note of thanks to Simon Jay for coordinating the project at Cleary Gottlieb, to Sarah Nash for her initial support at JPMorgan and to Marty Lipton for his help with the US section.

At Euromoney Books thanks to Elizabeth Gray and Charles Harris for their hard work and patience in coordinating so many diverse contributors and negotiating various bumps along the road to publication.

I would also like to thank family and friends – my father and sister, Gabriella Saracino, Raj Panasar, Ginevra Rossi, Thomas Paulmichl, Gianluca Leotta and Selman Ansari for help in various ways. Also to Andy Cohen for his hospitality in Geneva. Finally, to Daniela, B.B.

Introduction

The good, the bad and the ugly of the European Takeover Directive

Jaap Winter
Chairman of the EU High Level Group of Company Law Experts

As of May 2006, takeover bids in the European Union will be governed by the rules of the 13th Directive on Takeover Bids. These rules in their final form are as astonishing as the legislative genesis of the Directive. There are some good rules in the Directive, particularly those on minority protection; some bad, such as the jurisdiction clauses; and some which can only be described as ugly, such as the rules on defence against takeovers. As usual, the ugly provides for the most interesting debate, and there is a risk that these 'ugly' clauses obscure other parts of the Directive. Mr Bolkestein, the European Commissioner in charge of securing agreement on the Directive in the Council and Parliament, has suggested that the Directive is not worth the paper on which it is printed. This is a very clear, but may be too severe judgement.

The minority protections afforded by the Directive, the mandatory bid rule, and the squeeze-out and sell-out rules do make sense. Thirteen of the then fifteen member states agreeing on the Directive already had mandatory bid systems in place. There is some concern among economists that the mandatory bid rule is in fact counterproductive in that it creates a disincentive to make takeover bids, and that in general the economic basis for the rule may be weak. On the other hand, the practice in the United States in the 1980s with coercive partial bids followed by squeeze-out mergers, provides some evidence that minority shareholders need some degree of protection when control is sought in ways other than through a full bid on the share capital of the company. The squeeze-out facility is both an efficient tool for the bidder who has acquired a very substantial part of the share capital (90 to 95 per cent according to the Directive) to acquire the remaining shares and avoid having to deal with minority shareholders, as well as a protection for minority shareholders who have not tendered their shares in the offer, ensuring they can still sell their shares at a fair price. This is reinforced by the sell-out right that can be used by the minority shareholders themselves to force the acquirer of the 90 to 95 per cent share capital to buy their shares for a fair price.

The elements of the Directive that can be considered 'bad', are, however, necessary. One of the objectives of the Directive is to provide a regulatory framework that can deal with cross-border bids, involving target companies with multiple listings or with listings in a jurisdiction other than where they were incorporated. The rules of the Directive are complex and yield different results in different cases. Maintaining the distinction of regulatory powers between company law and securities law is difficult. National political defensiveness, similar to discussions surrounding which national regulator should be involved in approving a prospectus, prevented

INTRODUCTION

more efficient and clear rules being agreed. Nevertheless, rules on these issues needed to be made, and although improvement is certainly possible, there is now a framework with which European regulators can work : they should therefore be able to reach sensible solutions.

What then are the 'ugly' provisions of the Directive? The discussions over various drafts of the Directive focused primarily on what model Europe should adopt for dealing with defence against takeover bids. As Jonathan Rickford sets out in Chapter 4: 'Takeovers in Europe – shareholder decisions and open markets – a UK perspective', there were, in essence, two models available. The United Kingdom model is based on shareholder decision-making with full information and target board neutrality. The United States model is based on decision-making by the board to exercising normal operational powers, which allows them, in principle, to defend against a bid. Shareholders and bidders rely on the courts to secure protection against conflicts of interest of directors. The various drafts of the Directive have always been based on the UK model. This is in line with key features of European company law which provides for shareholder decision-making on important structural decisions. In Spring 2001, fourteen of the fifteen member states agreed to the Directive based on this model, with Article 9 prescribing board neutrality. The European Parliament rejected the Directive, with an unprecedented hung vote. The basic objection was that the Directive did not create a level playing field. It did not do so within the EU, because, in many member states, so-called pre-bid defence structures could be applied and are, in fact, applied widely. Similarly, it did not create a level playing field with the United States, as US boards are able to deploy poison pills and other defence tactics. The High Level Group was then asked to come up with a solution. We recommended that the Directive be based on two guiding principles: shareholder decision making and proportionality. Article 9 of the Directive confirmed the shareholder decision-making principle, thus preventing post-bid defences by boards which are not specifically authorised by shareholders. A new Article should provide for a breakthrough of pre-bid structures that would disallow a bidder to exercise control if the bidder has acquired at least 75 per cent of the share capital of the company.

Based on these recommendations the Commission published a new draft of the Directive, including Article 9 and a new Article 11, providing a breakthrough of only a limited number of pre-bid structures. With this draft, the Commission was very provocative. For some, this still did not sufficiently level the playing field; for others, the field was far too flat. The need to secure some form of compromise prior to ten new member states joining made reaching agreement take priority over concerns of consistency and feasibility. The result is a new Article 12, laying down a compromise in which both the board neutrality rule and the breakthrough rule have become optional: member states have the option not to impose these rules on the listed companies in their jurisdiction (opt out) but must offer the ability to companies to apply these rules voluntarily (opt in). In addition, even companies that apply Articles 9 and/or 11 do not have to do so when faced with a bidder who itself does not apply Articles 9 and/or 11, the so-called reciprocity rule. This optionality makes for an enormously complex situation in practice (see, for an example, the various alternatives for the United Kingdom described again by Jonathan Rickford in his chapter). The final result is a Directive bulging with paradoxes. Here are four of the most pertinent below.

Level playing field

The objective of the Directive was to ensure a level playing field for takeover bids in the EU. The core of the debate was the concern that a level playing field could not be created by dealing only with post-bid defences (Article 9) and not with pre-bid defences. The optionality of the core rules, however, creates precisely the opposite of a level playing field. Each member state may decide to impose the rules, or not do so and whether to apply the reciprocity provision. This certainly does not create a level playing field for takeover bids in all member states. Calling for a level playing field may have been a political figleaf for protecting national interests: many member states did not want to give up defensive mechanisms protecting their core industry from takeovers if other member states were unwilling to do so. When it appeared that all member states may have needed to give up both post-bid and pre-bid defences, they agreed that none of this would be mandatory. It seems like 'we all want to go to heaven but nobody wants to die'.

Agreed but optional board neutrality

Fourteen of the fifteen member states in 2001 agreed to the shareholder decision-making principle, as reflected in the board neutrality rule of Article 9. If the Directive had been adopted in its 2001 form, this principle would now have been mandatory across the EU. The final Directive also makes this principle optional. All member states can opt-out of imposing Article 9. The Dutch government has announced its intention to do so (see Chapter 20: 'The Netherlands') and Germany is expected to follow suit (see Chapter 14: 'Germany'). Others may follow.

Emmenthaler breakthrough

The breakthrough rule of Article 11 covers only a limited number of pre-bid defences that may limit the control of a bidder: share transfer restrictions, voting right restrictions (including multiple voting rights) and special rights to appoint directors. Pyramid structures by their nature could not be made subject to the rule. Therefore, the High Level Group recommended dealing with pyramids separately by not allowing stock exchange listing for holdings companies whose sole activity was to hold shares in another listed company. It remains to be seen whether this recommendation will at some point be implemented. In any event, many control devices remain outside the scope of the breakthrough rule, including: non-voting shares and non-voting depository receipts of shares; special rights to initiate or veto resolutions; and transfer and voting right restrictions in shareholder agreements entered into before 21 April 2004. Many companies could voluntarily accept Article 11 and still maintain rigorous defences.

The illusory fairness of reciprocity

Article 12 Part 3 allows for member states to exempt a company applying Articles 9 and/or 11 from applying these against a bidder who is not subject to Articles 9 and/or 11 itself. It is difficult to understand why the European politicians insisted on this reciprocity rule to be included in the Directive, as member states would not be required to impose either Article 9 or 11 and each company could individually then opt-in if it felt it would make sense to do so. Any member state could allow any company that did not want to be subject to a takeover to shield itself against it. Who then is in need of this reciprocity rule? It resembles an attempt to have one's cake and eat it as well. It has everything to do with the perceived unfairness of US companies being able to defend themselves against takeover bids where European companies cannot do so. The High Level Group went to some length to clarify that the US model is not

INTRODUCTION

as black and white in favour of defensive measures as many in Europe believe. The situation in the United States, even with the ability to defend the board, is still much more favourable to takeovers than that in many European jurisdictions. In any case, allowing member states the discretion not to impose Articles 9 and 11 would have removed that perceived unfairness. The result is a rule of which the exact meaning is not clear. For example, does it only apply to target companies who have voluntarily opted into Article 9 or 11 or also to companies who are subject to these rules by force of their member state law? Does it work against bidders who could have made the opt-in choices for Articles 9 and 11 but did not, or does it also work against bidders who did not have that choice? If the intention was to create the possibility to defend against a US bidder, then certainly the latter interpretation seems to be correct. In that case, the rule can also be applied against all non-listed companies (whether EU or non-EU) who bid for EU-listed companies.

There are serious concerns whether this discriminatory effect of the reciprocity rule is acceptable under the rules providing for freedom of establishment and free movement of capital rights under the EU treaty and under the the World Trade Organisation's obligations for EU member states. In addition, the reciprocity rule may cause unworkable situations when competing bids are made for the same target company which could then defend against one but not against the other. The rule may also be abused in practice. Finally, and interestingly, the reciprocity rule creates an unintended incentive for those EU-listed companies that want to be players in consolidating markets rather than targets, to apply Articles 9 and 11 voluntarily.

There will be many more difficulties, both for member states trying to implement this part of the Directive in their national laws, for companies trying to apply them, and for regulators and courts asked to enforce them. In terms of law making and what people may expect from clear law, the end result is poor. Is this to say that aside from the good and bad elements of the Directive, it is not worth the paper on which it is printed? I am not so sure. It may be that giving member states and companies options to choose their decision-making model and the requirement to be transparent about those choices (Article 10 of the Directive) will help the capital markets to better decide what model they favour. The need for all member states at least to incorporate both the rules on shareholder decision-making and the rules on breakthrough as rules that companies must be able to apply may set some a benchmark against which companies' boards will have to account for their choices and will be judged on the results. Institutional investors, their advisors and investment banks may feature this in their analyses of the value of companies. If so, it will become a relevant element that determines the cost of capital for companies and therefore their financial strength. Those who have always said that markets can, and should be left to, sort the good from the bad themselves (and therefore that legislation is not necessary) should welcome this result. It is an experiment that is about to begin. We will have to wait and see what will happen in practice and what impact the Directive will have.

Part I:

Inside the takeover regulation and tactics

Chapter 1

Takeovers and the market for corporate control

Jeremy Grant

> 'Hostile takeovers are but gangsterism and the law of the strongest'
> François Mitterrand, former President of France, 14 February 1989

> 'Can it even be unfriendly when someone wants to have influence over that which he owns?'
> Meite Thiede (cited by Gordon, 2003)

The first section of this chapter examines the theory behind takeovers, the distinctions between agreed and hostile bids, and how practices and markets differ between the United States and Europe. The second section presents a brief history of hostile takeovers in the United States and Europe, and a series of case studies of hostile bids.

Introduction

Corporate takeovers, particularly hostile transactions, are traditionally an Anglo–American phenomenon. However, in recent years they have become increasingly important in Continental Europe, driven by technological change, the creation of the single market and the introduction of the euro. In 2004, after over a decade of debate and revision, the European Parliament finally passed the 13th Directive on Takeover Bids, with the aim of standardising takeover regulation across the EU and encouraging more cross-border hostile deals. Although the final draft of the directive has critics who view it as ineffectual and/or too complex (see Enriques, Gatti and Rickford in this volume), it will undoubtedly have a significant influence on the European takeover battles of the next decade.

The aim of this volume is comprehensively to explore the current state of takeover regulation across Europe and to begin to trace the contours of the emerging pan-European jurisdiction created by the directive. To this end, we present a chapter on most member states of the EU and Russia. However, we also devote significant coverage to the US mergers and acquisitions (M&A) regulations, both in this introductory chapter and in the chapter on the United States. This is because the United States has had the most active takeover market in the world and consequently, along with the United Kingdom, has had arguably the most sophisticated regulatory regime, although it is significantly different from the emerging European one due to its emphasis on judge-made law. The United States is presented here both to give readers an insight into it in isolation and to help them to understand the similarities and differences between the two regimes.

In this opening chapter we give an overview of European/US similarities and differences. However, it concludes with two European case studies of failed cross-border hostile takeovers: Pirelli's bid for control of Continental in 1990 and the attempt by Louis Vuitton Moët Hennessey (LVMH) to seize control of Gucci in 1999. Both bids took place against a background of inadequate takeover regulation, with great uncertainty as to the legality of the tactics deployed by the raider and the targets. Moreover, minority shareholders were subject to decisions that were often against their interests in relation to a device whose *raison d'être* is to protect their interests. Consequently, the cases illustrate the necessity of effective takeover regulation to protect the interests of all shareholders, which is one of the underlying themes of this book as a whole.

The role of takeovers in a market economy and the Continental/Anglo–American divide

Takeovers are an important external corporate governance mechanism that facilitates effective corporate restructuring. In a seminal article published in 1965, Henry Manne described the market for corporate control, in which management teams compete for the right to manage corporate resources of public firms.[1] Competition between firms and management teams ensures that shareholders' capital is put to its highest value-added usage and that returns are maximised. As Hannah (1972) describes it, 'the carrot of private profit for the bidder thus provides an admonitory stick for a sleepy management'.

Effective corporate governance mechanisms, such as takeovers, also lower the cost of capital, ultimately making firms more competitive.[2] As such, the market for corporate control is an important complement to product market competition. Product market competition can help to ensure the efficient use of capital within the firm, but it has little influence on the distribution of profits back to the investor. This is one of the paradoxes at the heart of the corporate governance debate.

Principals and agents

The underlying problems of corporate governance in a world where contracts between managers and shareholders are incomplete have been well documented. The separation of ownership and control of the public corporation gives rise to a classical principal–agent problem, which can result in the sub-optimal use of capital and a failure to return excess capital to shareholders.

As early as 1932, Adolph Berle and Gardiner Means[3] pointed out the fundamental principal–agent conflict in the United States in relation to the modern public corporation. Firms had transformed themselves from privately owned and entrepreneur-driven entities into widely held public companies, in order to reap the benefits of scale and scope available in the domestic market of the time (Chandler, 1990; Kirchmaier, 2001). In an environment of highly dispersed ownership, as in the United States and the United Kingdom, the individual shareholder has little or no incentive to monitor management in relation to the efficient use of capital. As monitoring is a costly procedure, the marginal cost of monitoring often exceeds the marginal benefits of improved performance. As the Nobel laureate economist Joseph Stiglitz has pointed out, monitoring becomes a public good, as every shareholder benefits from the monitoring activities of others (Stiglitz, 1982). The *ex-ante* threat of a takeover, whether hostile or agreed by the board, strongly incentivises managers to take account of shareholders' interests against this background.

M&A value drivers

There are several other drivers of M&A value. Transactions enabled talented managers, such as Jack Welch at General Electric (GE), Sandy Weil at Citigroup or Warren Buffet at Berkshire Hathaway, to increase the assets under their control. Acquisitions allow for the transfer of organisational structures and procedures. A number of case studies have highlighted these organisational and knowledge-based techniques as intangible assets at GE (see for example Bruner, 2004, on corporate development as a strategic capability in GE Power Systems[4] or Ashkenas, DeMonaco and Francis, 1998, on acquisition integration at GE Capital).[5] It is clear from these case studies that GE has made large investments in its intangible assets, even in industrial businesses, and has been successful in scaling these assets in multiple acquisitions in all its business lines. It is equally clear that the deployment of intangible assets is a strong source of value in its acquisitions. Therefore, the firm can be seen as adding unique value to a deal.

More traditionally, takeovers also facilitate industrial consolidation where there is overcapacity, and the creation of economies of scope and scale, by reorganising business units into configurations that maximise vertical and horizontal efficiencies.

The European Commission highlighted all of these factors when drafting the Takeover Directive. As the Commission stated, its goal was to increase the number of hostile takeovers in Continental Europe, in order to improve the quality of European management, and to allow firms to take advantage of EU-wide economies of scope and scale:

> European-wide rules for takeover bids are considered vital to the objective of improving Europe's competitiveness, notably facilitating cross-border consolidation of industry. The Commission's aim is to create a vibrant takeover market, providing mechanisms for takeovers and changes in the management of poorly run firms, and reducing the scope for management to extract private benefits.[6]

Hostile and agreed takeovers

Ultimately, a hostile offer allows the bypassing of the incumbent management and a direct appeal to the target's shareholders on efficiency and/or strategic grounds. In the United States, such an offer usually requires the target's board approval, as it does to varying degrees across Europe. Therefore, the distinction between a hostile takeover and an agreed takeover can often become a subtle one. To make a broad distinction, hostile bids are those that are launched without the agreement of the directors of the target firm. However, boards may initially reject offers, even when they ultimately intend to sell the firm, as part of a bargaining strategy to increase the price received by the target's shareholders or to attract other bidders to the process. On the other hand, the public announcement of a deal may come as a surprise to the market and be perceived as friendly even when the confidential negotiations preceding the announcement have been adversarial.

Empirical research by G. William Schwert[7] demonstrates that the majority of deals that are perceived as hostile by the media are not distinguishable from friendly deals, except that hostile bids deploy more publicity as part of the bargaining process. He concludes that strategic bargaining by the target's board of directors is the primary reason for the rejection of takeover offers in the first instance, which causes the markets and the media then to classify them as hostile.

Takeovers in the United States and the United Kingdom

Hostile deals seemingly represent only a small percentage of all the M&A transactions that take place each year. In the 1990s, 239 hostile takeovers were announced in the United States and 158 in the United Kingdom, representing 2.3 per cent and 6.5 per cent, respectively, of the total number of announced tender offers. Even in the 1980s, the number of hostile bids was less than 100 each year in the United States, against hundreds of tender offers launched (Coates, 1999). In the United Kingdom, the percentage of hostile bids in the 1980s was higher. Jenkinson and Mayer (1994) estimate that between 1984 and 1988 approximately 26 per cent of bids for UK public companies were hostile.

The degree of hostility in UK bids is driven by the well-defined duties of directors to shareholders. Unlike US firms (see Exhibit 1.1), British firms do not have post-bid defences available, such as 'poison pills' (selective issuance of stock to dilute the raider's stake). They must adhere to strict rules, which are contained in the City Code, on post-bid neutrality in terms of frustrating actions aimed at the raider. Their primary post-bid defence is to find a 'white knight', which may only offer an increased counter-bid, since partial bids are forbidden. Most other common defences, such as issuances of new shares, share buy-backs, sale of major assets ('crown jewels'), 'Pac-man defences' or 'golden parachutes', require shareholder approval. Meanwhile, institutional investors have forced many UK firms to dismantle their pre-bid defences. For example, in 2001 British Telecom was forced by shareholders to withdraw a 15 per cent voting ceiling. Pressure from UK institutional investors has also prevented firms from deploying other pre-bid devices, such as dual share classes.[8]

As stated above, a deal is usually defined as hostile when the target's board publicly rejects the bidder's offer. However, in the United States what would once have been hostile

---

Exhibit 1.1

Taxonomy of pre- and post-bid defences available

Ordinary business:	*Pre-bid*	*Post-bid*
Pure defence	Dual share classes	Poison pill
	Voting ceiling	Pac-man defence
	Poison pill	
	Corporate charter amendments	
	Staggered board	
Embedded defence	Change of control provisions in joint venture, debt, customer and employment contracts	Spin-offs (crown jewels)
		White knight/squire
	Strategic acquisitions	Anti-trust litigation
	Golden parachutes	Strategic acquisitions
	Tin parachutes	Share buy-backs
		Special dividends

Source: Adapted from Arlen and Talley (2003).

deals have become agreed ones thanks to the design of incentive contracts that strongly align the interests of senior managers with shareholders. This alignment of interests has been facilitated through the increase in the options component of remuneration and the accelerated vesting of these options on a change of control.[9] The average salary of an S&P 500 CEO rose from US$3.5 million in 1992 to US$14.8 million in 2000 (Owen, Kirchmaier and Grant, 2005). This dramatic increase can be explained primarily by the increase in the options component.

Therefore, US managers are far less likely to reject a value-enhancing acquirer's overtures for self-interested reasons than two decades ago, because they are likely to be well-rewarded for their efforts in building the business initially. They are also incentivised to use defensive devices, such as poison pills, for strategic bargaining to increase the premium received by all shareholders. Conversely, the acquirer can also turn 'hostile' if managers and directors attempt to thwart their advances for self-interested reasons.[10]

Unlike their UK counterparts, US directors are not bound by a doctrine of strict board neutrality on presentation of a takeover bid and can take broader stakeholder constituencies into account. Theoretically, a US firm that employs both a poison pill and a staggered board, which prevents shareholders undertaking a proxy contest to remove it in one go, is reasonably bid-proof and can 'just say no' to an offer (see Bebchuk and Hart, 2002, and Bebchuk *et al.*, 2002).[11]

However, the strength of an independent director's fiduciary responsibilities to shareholders in the United States, and the ability of shareholders to enforce these via the courts and the introduction of adaptive devices (such as stock options discussed above), entail that in practice it is rare for senior managers and directors to continue blocking a value-enhancing transaction (see Kahan and Rock, 2002, on these issues). Although the Delaware courts[12] have yet to rule on the issue following this line of argument, it is likely that they will take a tough stance in future where the board retains both a poison pill defence and a staggered board structure if it continues to reject a value-enhancing takeover offer, against the wishes of shareholders.[13] As Kahan and Rock point out, 'there have been remarkably few cases where incumbents have held on after losing the first round of a proxy contest'. The Oracle Peoplesoft case study below offers an overview of these issues in relation to a particularly dramatic case.

Case study: Oracle vs. Peoplesoft Softwar.[14]

In June 2003, Oracle's CEO, Larry Ellison, launched an US$8.8 billion hostile takeover offer for Peoplesoft, a rival manufacturer of enterprise resource planning (ERP) software. Ellison's strategic aim was to compete more effectively with SAP, a larger German software maker, in the US$22 billion global ERP market. However, Peoplesoft's CEO, Craig Conway, rejected the bid, calling it 'atrociously bad behaviour' and labelling Ellison a 'sociopath'. The case is particularly interesting because Peoplesoft employed multiple defences in its efforts to thwart Ellison.

The firm had both a poison pill in its corporate charter and a staggered board. The former defence allowed Peoplesoft to issue new discounted equity to selected shareholders, in order to dilute Oracle's stake in the event that it breached a 20 per cent ownership threshold. The latter meant that not all the members of the board of directors were elected each year, so a potential raider would be unable to mount a proxy contest to remove the entire board at the same time. In response, Ellison launched a lawsuit against the board, asking the courts to review the legality of all Peoplesoft's defences.

> Peoplesoft also initiated anti-trust complaints with both the US and European authorities. The US Department of Justice originally blocked the transaction on competition grounds in February 2004. However, this prohibition was overturned by the courts in September the same year.
>
> In the period before the deal received anti-trust clearance, Conway of Peoplesoft undertook an ambitious programme of 'embedded defences' against Oracle. These defences are contracts that may be logical in the ordinary course of business, but also significantly raise the costs of acquisition and stretch the bounds of takeover defences. Such provisions in this case included a customer assurance programme that offered refunds of over US$2 billion in total if Peoplesoft was subject to a change of control, golden parachutes for senior executives and tin parachutes for employees who faced being downsized. However, these were to lead to Conway's eventual downfall. It is likely that the board of directors began to view their sanctioning of them as potential violations of their fiduciary duties to shareholders, as the defences were essentially transfers of wealth from shareholders to managers and customers. The directors could thus have faced the threat of shareholder litigation.[15] This would obviously have mattered far less if Conway's anti-trust strategy had worked. In October 2004, Conway was removed by the board, despite the release of very strong financial results. Peoplesoft was eventually acquired by Oracle in December 2004.

Mergers of equals

It should also be noted that in the United States friendly 'mergers of equals' (MOE) between strategically complementary firms, with structures that theoretically create roughly equal influence between partners, often end up as takeovers, with one firm's senior management ultimately replacing the other's.[16] Again, it is likely that early vesting of the options component of executive remuneration has incentivised managers to risk entering into such transactions. It can also be argued that target shareholders end up paying these extra costs, as studies show that premiums paid under MOE structures are significantly lower than for hostile deals or plain vanilla acquisitions. Ultimately, the reality is often, as GE's former CEO Jack Welch states (Welch, 2005):

> People at equal companies are probably less well-equipped than anyone to merge. They may claim during the deal heat to be entering into a perfect and equivalent union, but when the integration rolls around who is taking charge must be established quickly. Someone has to lead and someone has to follow, or both companies will end up standing still.

> ### Case study: Daimler Chrysler (1998) – who is in the driving seat?
> An excellent example of an MOE structure that concealed the underlying dynamics of a takeover is the cross-border acquisition of Chrysler by Daimler-Benz in 1998. The car manufacturer selected a structure agreeable to both sets of management and aimed at

gaining the necessary approvals of regulators, shareholders and trade unions on both sides of the Atlantic. However, the deal structure gave clues as to who was ultimately in the driving seat:

- Daimler-Benz, with revenues of US$69 billion versus US$61 billion at Chrysler, was the larger firm. Despite this, an MOE structure was developed for the transaction. At the time Daimler-Benz was constrained by German law from shifting its state of incorporation;[17]
- a dual CEO structure was adopted, with both Jürgen Schrempp of Daimler and Bob Eaton of Chrysler sharing management control. However, the two men had an understanding that Eaton would remain with the firm for only two years. Eaton was pushed out by Schrempp in 2000 and a German executive, Dieter Zetsche, was sent from Stuttgart to take control of Chrysler operations in the Detroit area;
- due to German law, the combined company was required to adopt a two-tier board structure. Chrysler executives were given half the seats on the management board, but Chrysler directors only gained one third of the seats on the supervisory board, which continued to be presided over by Daimler's Chairman, Hilmar Kopper.

The ultimate result of the merger was that within two years most of Chrysler's senior executives had departed. These executives received approximately US$96 million in benefits over this period, including golden parachutes.

In 2000, Chrysler's largest shareholder, Kirk Kerkorian, filed a lawsuit against Daimler Chrysler, claiming that the senior management had committed fraud by presenting the deal as an MOE when in fact it was an acquisition of Chrysler by Daimler-Benz.

Case study: Chase Manhattan/JP Morgan (2000)

The acquisition of JP Morgan by Chase Manhattan is another example of an MOE. However, in this case it was obvious that JP Morgan was being acquired by Chase from day one. The majority of JP Morgan's senior management departed the firm within a short period of the deal being announced, while its CEO, Sandy Warner, stayed on as Chairman before later leaving the institution. A similar situation arose after the merger of Citicorp and Travelers, which lead to the exit of John Reed (see the account in Rubin, 2004).

A final category of takeover defences are those embedded in the terms of a friendly deal once a firm is 'in play', to raise the cost of competing offers or make the target less attractive to other acquirers. These include:

Break up fees: This is a fee paid upon termination of deal, usually because the target has received a higher bid. The rational is the fee covers the costs incurred by the bidder in mounting a contest in which it has ultimately lost out. However, they can be used to deter competing bidders. Coates and Subramaniam (2000) find an increasing use of such fees in the United States from one third of deals from 1988 to 1998, to two thirds in 1999/2000. Such devices are becoming increasingly common in Europe (see CVC/Cortifiel case study in Chapter 24 on Spain).

Stock lock up options: These enable the acquirer to purchase more of the target's shares at a discounted price, thus diluting a rival bidder and possibly creating a blocking minority. This device is used on occasions in the United States and is normally structured as a right to buy a 19.9 per cent stake in the target. At 20 per cent, the target firm would be required to seek shareholder approval under exchange listing rules. In the United States, stock lock up options are deployed in a smaller number of deals than break up fees. Coates and Subramaniam (2000) found them in 13 per cent of deals from 1988 to 1998.[18] In contrast, strict adherence to pre-emption rights in Europe would make similar options very difficult.

The legal responsibilities of a board of directors in the United States faced with both an outright acquisition offer or a friendly MOE, and the defensive actions they can take, are discussed in detail in Chapter 27.

Takeovers in Europe

In contrast to the United States and the United Kingdom, hostile deals in Continental Europe are much rarer. There were only 67 hostile bids in the (then) 15 EU member states in the 1990s. This was equal to 1.3 per cent of all tender offers. However, there were variations between countries. For example, hostile advances have now become quite common in France, primarily among French companies, and include a number of recent high-profile deals.[19] In contrast, until the deal between Vodafone and Mannesmann, in 1999, Germany had witnessed only a handful of attempted hostile deals in the whole post-war period, none of which succeeded. Exhibit 1.2 shows an estimate of the number of attempted hostile bids in European countries as a percentage of domestic traded companies (in the 1990s).

The low incidence of hostile bids in Continental Europe can be explained primarily by structural barriers related to the way in which companies are owned and financed. A secondary factor is the historically more permissive attitude toward the regulation of technical barriers, such as pre- and post-bid defences. In contrast to the US Williams Act 1968 and the UK City Code, also issued in 1968, takeover regulation began to emerge on the Continent only in the 1980s and until the mid-1990s much of it was voluntary in nature.

Structural barriers

Shareholdings in Continental Europe are much more concentrated, with families often retaining control of firms long after they

Exhibit 1.2

Estimate of the number of attempted hostile bids in European countries

Country	Hostile bids (as a % of domestic traded companies)
Belgium	0.5
Denmark	0.8
Finland	0.9
France	1.7
Germany	0.3
Italy	3.4
Netherlands	1.3
Portugal	1.9
Spain	0.2
Sweden	3.7
United Kingdom	4.4
United States	6.5

Source: Rossi and Volpin (2003).

Exhibit 1.3
Ownership distribution of the top 100 public companies in Germany, Italy, France and Spain, 2002 (%)

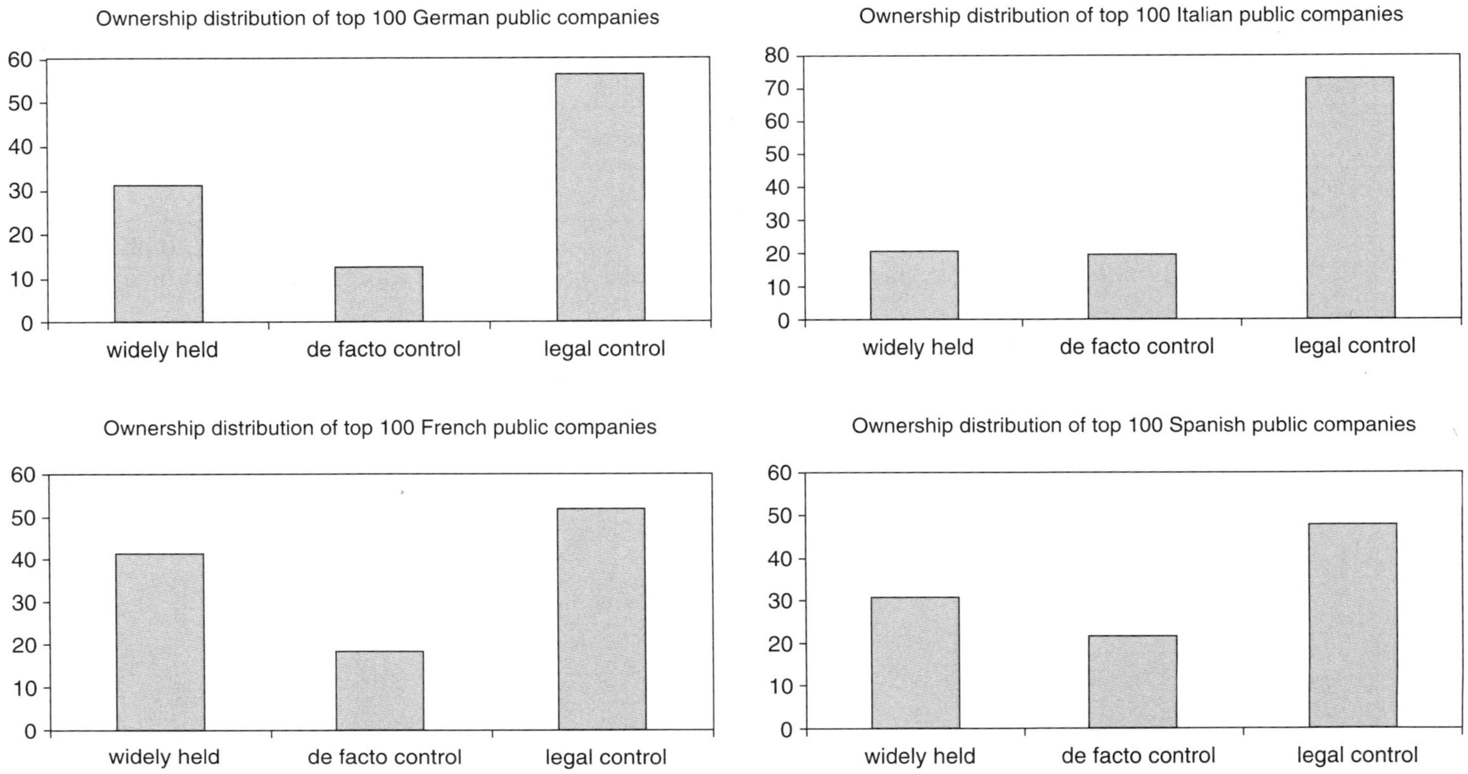

Sources: Grant and Kirchmaier (2004).

PART I: INSIDE THE TAKEOVER REGULATION AND TACTICS

have been taken public. Moreover, until recently the state has been a significant shareholder in many European firms. Exhibits 1.3 and 1.4 show the ownership structures and identities of the largest shareholders in the top 100 public firms in each of four major Continental European economies. Ownership structures are divided into three categories:

- legal control, where either one shareholder or a shareholder group controls over 50 per cent of the votes at the annual general meeting;
- de facto control, the level of ownership of voting shares at which local regulators have concluded that a shareholder will have significant influence on the outcome of decisions at the annual general meeting; and
- widely held, where no single shareholder or tied group of shareholders owns a percentage of voting share capital above the mandatory bid threshold.

Legal control is the dominant ownership category in every country surveyed, with 50 per cent or more of the sample. Firms in this category are essentially bid-proof. The most important type of owners are families, except in Spain.

Academic surveys argue that higher ownership concentration in Continental Europe, as opposed to the Anglo–American world, is a response to lower degrees of minority shareholder protection under civil law systems (see La Porta *et al.*, 1996, 1997 and 1999). Concentrated ownership can, to an extent, mitigate the principal–agent problem. This is because it can provide for better control of management, as the size of the ownership stake and the incentive to monitor are positively correlated. In turn, this should improve firm performance and equally benefit minority shareholders. On the other hand, it can come with costs for minority

Exhibit 1.4

Identities of the largest shareholders in the top 100 public companies in Germany, Italy, France, Spain and the United Kingdom, 2002

	Largest shareholder			Second largest shareholder		
	I	II	III	I	II	III
France	Family (37)	Corporate (22)	Institutional (12)	Institutional (24)	Miscellaneous (18)	Corporate (15)
Germany	Family (31)	Financial (19)	Corporate (17)	Institutional (41)	Financial (15)	Family (12)
Italy	Family (30)	State (15)	Institutional (15)	Institutional (38)	Family (16)	NA (16)
Spain	Corporate (25)	Financial (23)	Institutional (11)	Institutional (31)	Financial (17)	Corporate (12)
United Kingdom	Institutional (81)	Family (8)	Corporate (6)	Institutional (86)	Miscellaneous (6)	Family (5)

Source: Grant and Kirchmaier (2004).

shareholders, as the controlling owners may expropriate from them, while the board of directors, which should protect the interests of minorities, is likely to be captured by the controlling shareholders.[20]

Minority shareholder expropriation is one of a number of private control benefits enjoyed by large-block holders at the expense of firm value (Jensen and Meckling, 1976; Grossman and Hart, 1988). These include pecuniary benefits, such as straightforward asset expropriation, termed 'tunnelling' (Johnson et al., 2000) and 'financial tunnelling', in which the controlling shareholder engages in complex financial transactions to the disadvantage of minority shareholders. However, private control benefits also come in non-pecuniary forms. Jensen and Meckling (1976) describe these as:

> the utility generated by ... the physical appointments of the office, the attractiveness of office staff, the level of employee discipline, the kind and amount of charitable contributions, personal relations (friendship, respect, and so on) with employees, a larger than optimal computer to play with, or purchase of production inputs from friends.

Holmen and Högfeldt (2000) view these in terms of the social prestige of running a firm, the ability to promote relatives and the feeling of power from 'doing it my way'.

A number of surveys have attempted to measure private control benefits at the country level (see Exhibit 1.5). For example, Nenova (2000) documents differing levels of private control benefits across a large cross section of countries, reflected in premiums paid for voting shares.[21] Dyck and Zingales (2004) document similar control premiums paid in Continental European block trades.

Moreover, large owners such as families, governments or corporates may have strategic goals that differ from the maximisation of shareholder value. For example, family owners receive private control benefits and therefore place a high premium on retaining control of the firm; hence they are likely to be more risk averse and capital constrained. They also face potential problems of nepotism, succession and family conflict (see Thomsen and Pedersen, 2000). Corporate owners may be ineffectual monitors, while governments pursue political goals and provide managers with protection from market discipline.

Exhibit 1.5
Measures of private control benefits

	Nenova (2000) – premium paid for shares with voting right attached (%)	Dyck and Zingales (2003) – premium paid to acquire a controlling block of equity (%)
United States	2.0	1.0
United Kingdom	N/A	1.0
Germany	9.5	10.0
France	28.0	2.0
Italy	29.0	37.0
Spain	N/A	4.0
Portugal	N/A	20.0
Sweden	1.0	7.0
Poland	N/A	13.0
Czech Republic	N/A	58.0

Accordingly, the drivers of value destruction are not just the expropriation of private control benefits, but may also include a macrolevel misalignment of ownership preferences with optimal corporate strategy. For example, M&A strategies based on the creation of economies of scale and scope, and funded via equity issuance, are better suited to firms with widely diversified shareholder bases, rather than firms that are family controlled.[22]

Technical barriers

Control by large shareholders or shareholder blocks in Continental Europe is often enhanced via devices that distort the distribution of voting rights and hence separate the strategic control of a company from the distribution of shares and cash flow rights. These mechanisms also distort the relationship between ownership and risk bearing and ultimately ensure that the firm is bid proof.

Multiple share classes, pyramids and cross-shareholdings are the three main control devices employed in Continental Europe to create the distinction between voting rights and cash flow rights.

- **Multiple share classes** confer percentages of votes that are disproportionate to cash flow rights on certain classes of equity (see Exhibit 1.6). Traditionally, companies issued shares with no or low voting rights, in order to allow a controlling shareholder to maintain control while issuing equity to which they did not subscribe.

  Golden shares (a subset of multiple share classes not represented in Exhibit 1.6) generally allow governments to maintain special control rights. They are often used in newly privatised industries:

  > Governments have claimed that this is necessary when they see their strategic interests at stake and they fear that those interests would be compromised

Exhibit 1.6

Dual share structures in firms surveyed in selected EU member states, 2002

	Number of firms surveyed	Number of firms with dual share structures
Belgium	130	0
Portugal	87	0
Spain	632	1
France	607	16
Germany	704	124
Austria	99	23
Ireland	69	16
Denmark	210	70
Italy	208	86
Finland	129	47
Sweden	334	185
Total:	5,162	1,035

Source: Faccio and Lang (2002).

Exhibit 1.7

A stylised pyramid structure

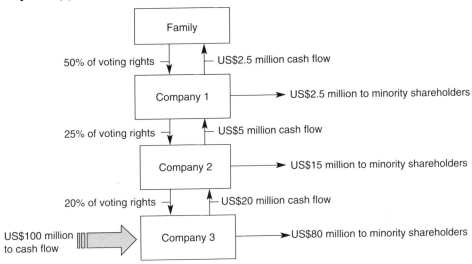

Family has 20% voting control, but 2.5% of the cash flow rights. Their voting rights are eight times cash flow rights.

Source: Author's own.

if some outside shareholder gained control of the business. An alternative to actual shares are laws that are passed to limit the number of shares or votes any one outside shareholder can control (Gaughan, 2002, p. 190).

However, in three judgements delivered in June 2002 the European Court of Justice declared most such measures illegal, due to their incompatibility with the free movement of capital in the EU (Adolff, 2002).[23]

- **Pyramids** are a form of corporate control structure whereby a company holds shares in another company, which in turn holds shares in another one (see Exhibit 1.7). Control of the corporation at the top of the pyramid combines with the stakes all the way down to achieve outright control of the chain. Dividends, transfer pricing and management fees (often used for tax purposes) are employed to funnel cash up the control chain. Collectively these are 'tunnelling' devices, inter-company dealings whose terms benefit the controlling shareholder at the top of the pyramid, often at the expense of minority shareholders (Johnson *et al.*, 2000).

  The corporate structure of L'Oréal up to 2004, when the structure was dissolved in order to improve transparency and corporate governance, provides an example of a simple pyramid structure (see Exhibit 1.8).[24]

- **Cross-shareholdings** are defensive arrangements whereby two companies buy stakes in each other and senior managers/owners sit on each other's boards and vote their shares together defensively. For example, Bianchi (1998) found that circular holdings of over 2 per cent connected 20 groups of Italian companies equal to 36 per cent of the capitalisation of the Milan Stock Exchange (see Exhibit 1.9).

PART I: INSIDE THE TAKEOVER REGULATION AND TACTICS

Exhibit 1.8

Ownership structure of L'Oréal up to February 2004*

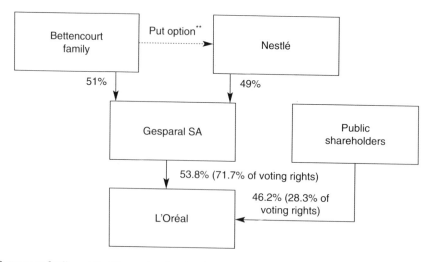

Notes
* The Bettencourt family and Nestlé agreed to dissolve Gesparal and cancel double voting rights in February 2004.
** This allows the Bettencourt family to put its control stake in Nestlé. This would trigger a mandatory bid to minority shareholders under the French takeover law of 1989.

Sources: L'Oréal Annual Report, JP Morgan Research, *Financial Times*.

In addition, there are a number of other control devices and defence mechanisms that are widely used in Europe.

- **Partnerships limited by shares** are used in France (*sociétés en commandite par actions*), Italy (*accomandita per azioni*) and Germany (*Kommanditgesellschaft auf Aktien*).[25] Such partnerships (exemplified in Exhibit 1.10) function with a small number of unlimited liability partners exerting control, while outside shareholders provide the majority of the capital, but have little influence over the strategic direction of the business.

- **Corporate charter provisions** have as their primary purpose to ward off interference from outsiders and, ultimately, hostile takeover bids. In the United States, such devices are known as 'shark repellent'. Provisions common in Continental Europe include staggered boards and voting caps. Corporate charters can also contain share transfer restrictions. For example, in Germany Allianz and Munich Re retain the right via their corporate statutes to block any share transfers, although for practical purposes they have restricted this right to 'extraordinary circumstances when considered essential for the company'. Several national airlines in Europe, such as Lufthansa, also have share transfer restrictions in order to comply with European aviation regulations. It should be noted that French corporate charters can also impose voting caps and double the voting rights of 'faithful' shareholders who hold the stock for over two years.[26] These rights relate to ordinary shares and are not defined legally as a special class of share. According to Faccio and Lang (2002, p. 384), 'in France most firms grant two votes for each ordinary share' (see the corporate structures of LVMH and L'Oréal presented in this chapter).

Exhibit 1.9
Cross-share holdings among major Italian companies

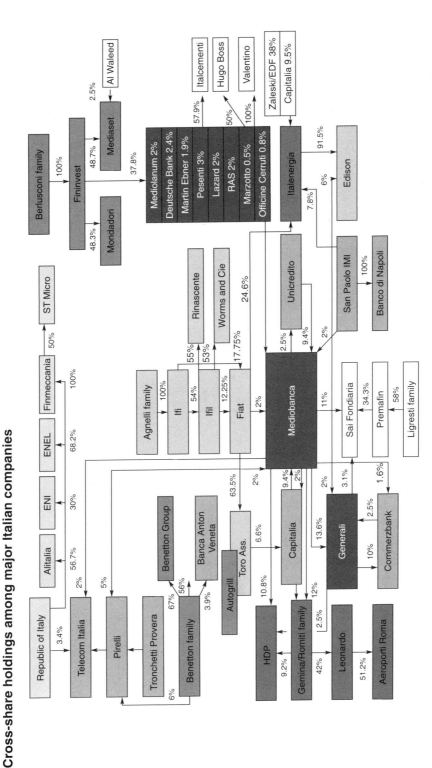

Sources: *La Repubblica*, Mediobanca, JP Morgan, Consob, Bloomberg, 2003.

Exhibit 1.10
An example of a limited partnership: Michelin's ownership structure as of 31 December 2002

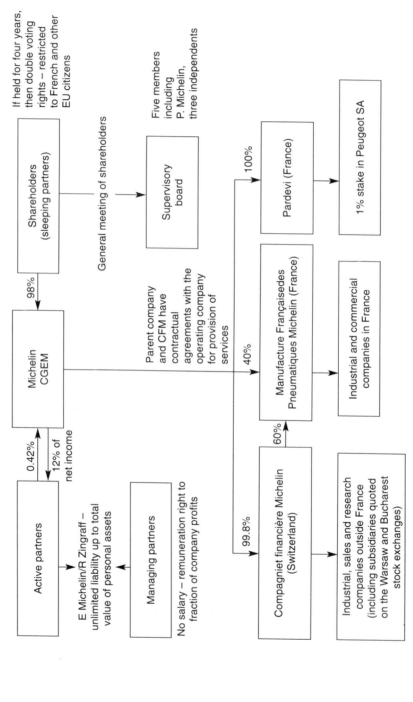

Source: Annual Report (2002).

Exhibit 1.11
Ownership structure of Donna Karen International, 2000

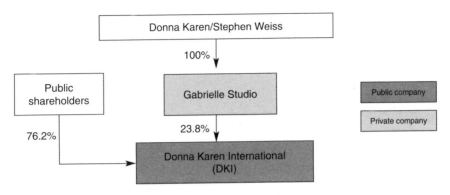

Licensing agreement between Gabrielle Studio and DKI:
- fixed licensing fees paid to Gabrielle Studio at 1.75% on first US$250 million of revenue, 2.5% on next US$250 million and 3% on next US$750 million;
- change of control termination clauses related to Ms Karen's employment and the licensing of 'Donna Karen' and 'DKNY' trademarks.

Sources: Arlen and Talley (2003).

- **Embedded defences** are company/industry-specific devices, as defined by Arlen and Talley (2003), which may have legitimate business purposes. Such defences include change of control provisions in leases, licences, joint venture agreements, employment contracts or debt instruments, as well as the issuance of preferred stock with puts. Examples include LVMH, which is owned by Bernard Arnault through the holding company Christian Dior. LVMH's major assets, its brands, are owned at the holding company level (see the Gucci case study at the end of this chapter for more details). When LVMH purchased Donna Karen in 2001, it acquired a firm with similar embedded defences (see Exhibit 1.11).

  The array of embedded defences has never been fully catalogued, so it is difficult to determine how far they have been deployed. However, Arlen and Talley conclude that embedded defences have not been used extensively for the purpose of defending incumbent managements against hostile takeovers.

In conclusion, where a significant investor or group of investors, particularly a family, controls a large proportion of the stock, exerts a dominant influence on the board and receives considerable private control benefits from the firm, a bidder, whether hostile or not, has little chance of success.[27] Even when European corporations are widely held, the options compensation of senior managers' remuneration significantly lags that of the United States and it rarely vests on a change of control.[28] This ensures that managers are far more averse to value increasing takeovers. In turn, these factors impede the creation of companies with pan-European scope and scale, and are partly the reason why the European Commission introduced the Takeover Directive in the first place.

PART I: INSIDE THE TAKEOVER REGULATION AND TACTICS

A brief history of hostile takeovers

Siegmund Warburg is credited with devising the first cross-border hostile takeover of the modern era when he helped the US firm Reynolds Metal to acquire British Aluminium in 1958. Traditionally in Britain, 'the loyalty of shareholders to directors was strong and the directors of other companies had a natural aversion to challenging it,' but 'by the 1960s the divorce of ownership and control had proceeded sufficiently to leave a wide range of quoted companies vulnerable to takeover offers' (Hannah, 1974). The case of British Aluminium illustrates these points well.

> ### Case study: The aluminium war of 1958[29]
>
> In 1958, the US metals firm Reynolds was interested in acquiring British Aluminium (BA). Although BA was undervalued and traded at approximately the cost of one of its many plants, it was 'an exclusive, inbred company which didn't welcome intruders' (Chernow, 1993, p. 674). Siegmund Warburg, with his US allies, built a 10 per cent stake in the firm, but their offer for the company, of three pounds and 18 shillings (equivalent to £3.90) per share, was firmly rebuffed. BA had instead decided to sell a 30 per cent stake to Alcoa for £3.00 per share. BA's Chairman, Lord Portal, pointedly refused to put the higher Reynolds offer before his shareholders and dismissed Warburg and his allies as 'carpetbaggers'.
>
> Warburg then decided to appeal directly to minority shareholders via a series of press conferences. BA had rising institutional ownership and the portfolio managers were dismayed by Portal's failure to bring the alternative offer to them. BA continued to marshal its defences, including a syndicate of UK banks that offered to purchase a 50 per cent stake in the company for four pounds and two shillings (now £4.10) per share. Warburg himself was called in by the Governor of the Bank of England and told to abandon his hostile takeover bid. Instead, Warburg raised his offer to four pounds and five shillings (now £4.25) per share. By January 1959, Reynolds had majority control of BA.
>
> This deal represented a major break with the past. Previously, mergers had been 'negotiated on the backs of envelopes,' but 'henceforth corporate battles would be fought in the open and not behind closed doors' (Chernow, 1993, p. 652).

Hostile takeovers in the United States

The United States had to wait rather longer for its first blue chip hostile takeover.[30] The 1960s witnessed the rise of conglomerates, multi-business organisations that were supposed to allocate capital more efficiently than the market. By the 1970s, however, investors had become disillusioned with conglomerates' value-destroying deals and their internal capital markets, which allocated capital inefficiently, often on the basis of political criteria rather than effective hurdle rates (see Scharperstein, 1997). Investors also realised that diversification of risk could be more efficiently created through a balanced portfolio of individual securities than via conglomerate structures. Therefore, hostile takeovers began to gain respectability as a way of releasing value from moribund corporate structures. Conglomerates were taken over and split into component firms, which were then sold to competitors in the same industry. Other firms were encouraged to sell off non-core businesses and concentrate on their core competences.

Following Reynolds/BA in the United Kingdom, the watershed hostile deal in the United States was International Nickel of Canada's successful bid for EBS in 1974. This was partly due to the fact that the deal involved two blue chip firms, but also because Morgan Stanley, one of the corporate establishment's main investment banks, agreed to advise the predator. This transaction was soon followed by hostile takeovers of Otis Elevators by United Technologies and of Garlock Industries by Colt Industries.[31]

The 1970s also saw the rise of junk bonds (or sub-investment-grade/high-yield bonds). These allowed 'creative' entrepreneurs to go after established firms, often with the intention of breaking them up to release shareholder value.[32] In a significant strategic move, Michael Milken of Drexel, Burnham, who had resuscitated the junk bond market in the 1970s and early 1980s, set up an M&A business within Drexel's junk bond division to advise and underwrite takeover entrepreneurs such as Ron Perelman, Boon Pickens and Carl Icahn. Milken's annual conference at the Beverly Hills Hotel came to be dubbed the 'Predators' Ball' (see Bruck, 1988). These raiders saw their potential fund pools swell as many states channelled their public employees' pension funds to a wider range of asset classes, including junk bonds and leveraged buyout investment funds. Many of the institutions managing such pension and mutual fund money declared a change of policy on defensive charter amendments, which had protected firms from hostile bids, and began to vote against them.

While individual states had evoked anti-takeover corporate statutes, the US Supreme Court declared many of these unconstitutional in Edgar vs. MITE Corporation (1982), declaring that the Williams Act, passed by Congress in 1968, should be the primary legislation regulating the takeover process in the United States. The Act gave corporate boards just a 20-day respite to consider an offer and organise post-bid defences against a raider.

However, an increasing number of the bids forwarded by raiders were 'two-tier' or 'front-loaded': the raider offered a higher premium for the shares he needed to gain control than for the rest of the outstanding share capital.[33] These offers often unfairly induced shareholders to tender quickly rather than lose out on a significant premium.[34] This mechanism also prevented boards from searching for better offers. In turn, many of the deals were financed via junk bonds on the assets of the firm being taken over, which clearly had important ramifications for other stakeholders, including legacy creditors, suppliers, customers and employees, who, it was argued, should be given consideration by the board in its deliberations.

In 1982, Martin Lipton, a prominent M&A lawyer, found his services called upon by El Paso Electric, which had received a takeover offer from General American Oil. He advised management to defend the firm by issuing a warrant dividend plan (preferred stock) to the current shareholders of record, excluding the raider. As a dividend target, shareholders would receive preferred stock convertible into shares of the acquirer on a change of control. The ultimate effect of this would be to dilute the raider's ownership stake in their own firm. This became known as a 'first-generation poison pill' or 'flip-in poison pill'.

In 1983, this device was deployed again to defend Lennox, a manufacturer of china, from a hostile bid from Brown Foreman, a distiller whose brands included Jack Daniels. The effects of the poison pill would have significantly diluted the founding Brown family's 60 per cent controlling position, thereby making Lennox a far less attractive proposition.[35]

In this initial incarnation, the poison pill displayed some disadvantages. It was redeemable only after a long time period, usually more than 10 years. This would have negative consequences for the firm if it later wanted to enter into an agreed merger. It also had consequences for the target's leverage position, as the ratings agencies counted preference shares towards the firm's debt burden, because they are fixed-income securities, thus making the firm a riskier proposition from the perspective of investors.

In 1985, Lipton came up with a 'second-generation' or 'flip-over' poison pill. This entailed a rights offering that permitted target shareholders to buy stock in the acquiring firm at a discount for a specific period. Beyond this a 'third-generation' or 'flip-in/flip-over' poison pill was also developed, which was triggered by a single step, such as an unsolicited tender offer.[36]

Legal challenges were constantly made against poison pills, particularly in the Delaware court system. In two landmark cases in 1985, the legality of poison pills was upheld. First, in Unocal (1985) the Delaware Supreme Court declared that more general defensive tactics were 'reasonable in relation to the threat that the board rationally and reasonably believed was posed by [the raider] Mesa's inadequate and coercive two-tier tender offer'.[37] In justifying the decision, the court stated that the business judgement rule applied to directors' duties in relation to takeover defences. In essence this meant that directors would not incur liability in taking the decision to reject a takeover bid as long as there were no conflicts of interest on their part and they discharged their duty of care. However, the court subjected directors to an enhanced duty of care and a test of reasonableness in relation to the threat faced.

In the Household case (1985), the Delaware Supreme Court upheld the legality of the defendant's poison pill.[38] This landmark decision set the poison pill up as a common defence in corporate America. A survey in 2000 found that 56 per cent of surveyed firms had poison pills in their corporate charters (Rosenbaum, 1999).

The Delaware courts set up a 'comprehensive legal framework for corporate control contests and [this] has led to predictability in corporate governance' (Lipton and Rowe, 2001). Far from preventing value-enhancing M&As, the court takes a flexible, 'fact-intensive, case-by-case examination with directors bearing the burden of proof of the reasonableness of their decisions' (Lipton and Rowe, 2001). The subtle balancing of the interests of shareholders and those of other constituencies can be illustrated in the Delaware Supreme Court's decision to emphasis the necessity of the proxy mechanism for shareholders ultimately to remove the board if they disagree with its decision to reject a takeover bid.[39] The balance has been furthered through the deployment of bilateral adaptive devices (Kahan and Rock, 2002). These include increased options-based remuneration, which more effectively aligns the interests of managers and shareholders as discussed above.

Hostile takeovers in Continental Europe

As discussed earlier, hostile takeovers have been comparatively rare in Continental Europe and numbers differ between countries. One of the first took place in 1988. Carlo De Benedetti, the Italian raider, made a hostile bid for a stake in Société Générale de Belgique, a finance, property and media group. With an initial holding of 18.6 per cent, he undertook a tender offer for a further 15 per cent to create a blocking minority. This failed when the French conglomerate Suez was brought in as a white knight. France has witnessed a number of hostile takeovers, subject to government guidance and pressure to create 'national champions', for example, Sanofi Synthelabo's recent successful bid for Aventis.

However, there were only a small number of hostile bids in Europe's largest economy, Germany, in the entire post-war period up to 2000 (Gordon, 2003). Most foundered on political opposition.

- *Feldmuhle Noble (1988):* The company received an offer for 51 per cent of the share capital. However, Deutsche Bank voted 55 per cent of the shares, mostly through proxy voting, thereby defeating the bid. The bank then voted the shares in favour of a 5 per cent voting ceiling. However, not surprisingly, this was one that did not apply to proxy votes held by banks.
- *Pirelli/Continental (1990):* The Italian tyre manufacturer Pirelli made an ill-fated hostile offer for its rival Continental, based in the German state of Lower Saxony. This was defeated by a German management support group of shareholders with a blocking majority of 25 per cent plus one vote, including Allianz (5 per cent), Deutsche Bank (5 per cent), BMW, Volkswagen and Daimler Benz (7 per cent combined), Dresdner Bank (3 per cent) and various Landesbanks with a combined 3 per cent. A group of firms from Lower Saxony then purchased a portion of Pirelli's stake in Continental with state support (for further details see the case study below).
- *Thyssen/Krupp Hosech (1997):* Krupp Hosech's hostile bid for a rival steelmaker, Thyssen, was the first Anglo–American-style tender offer in Germany. It included a 25 per cent premium and was offered to all shareholders. Under pressure from the German industrial union IG Metall, which attacked the bid as an example of 'Wild West capitalism', politicians brokered a 'friendly' merger.

In Italy, hostile bids were very rare before Olivetti's takeover of Telecom Italia in 1999 and the subsequent change of control to Pirelli. This was followed by a number of other deals, including Generali/INA, SAI/Fondaria (see case study in Chapter 2) and the French utility EDF's attempt to acquire the electricity-generating assets of Montedison.

The following case studies examine a number of these transactions in more detail.

Case study: Vodafone/Mannesmann (2000) – day of the locusts

'Every Mann knows: If you want to grow, you need a good mother.' – Tagline from an ad, showing a baby breast feeding, issued by Vodafone to persuade shareholders to vote in favour of its offer.

Unlike the previous examples, Vodafone's bid for Mannesmann[40] was the first hostile takeover to succeed in Germany. Mannesmann's CEO, Klaus Esser, adhered to the principles of shareholder choice and did not pursue post-bid defences or attempt to marshal the help of German politicians or the house bank.

Mannesmann was a traditional German industrial conglomerate whose divisions included machine tools, automotive products and metal tubes. In the 1990s, two thirds of Mannesmann's investments went into the telecommunications industry as it built a German mobile phone network, D2, and took stakes in other European telecom services companies. In 1999, in an unusual step for a German industrial firm, Esser, a lawyer by training, was promoted from CFO to CEO. Esser wished to restructure the conglomerate into two focused divisions.

Mannesmann's ownership structure was different from that of most German corporations. Sixty per cent of its share capital was owned by foreign investors and 40 per cent was with UK and US institutions. Due to the acquisition of Orange plc, the Hong Kong conglomerate Hutchison Whampoa owned 10.2 per cent.

In October 1999, Vodafone's CEO, Sir Chris Gent, approached Esser with a friendly merger offer, valuing Mannesmann at US$106 billion. Gent was turned down, but then stated that he would take the offer directly to the shareholders. In December 1999, Gent launched an all-share offer for the German firm, valued at US$131 billion. Astutely, Gent went to great lengths to assure the German establishment of the industrial logic of the deal, declared that the company's headquarters would remain in Düsseldorf and promised that there would be no layoffs.

Esser made the counter-arguments equally strenuously. He never resorted to traditional defensive tactics. For example, Mannesmann still had a 5 per cent voting ceiling in its articles of incorporation, which was not scheduled to expire (under the Kontrag laws) until July 2000. Esser made his case purely on its economic merits, stating, 'poison pills and white knights are detrimental to the shareholders' interests ... we have to subject ourselves to public opinion, whether we are better than Vodafone's management'. Ultimately, while Esser was unsuccessful in securing Mannesmann's independence, he managed to increase the offer price to US$199 billion.

However, the question remains whether Mannesmann/Vodafone was an exception, given the influence of foreign investors and Esser's principled adherence to shareholder choice, rather than a sign of major changes in attitude. Chancellor Gerhard Schröder was reported to have concluded 'never again'. Subsequently, foreign acquirers have again faced political opposition when approaching German firms, as Proctor & Gamble did in the case of Beiersdorf (see case study in Chapter 2).

Case study: Pirelli's hostile bid for Continental (1990)[41]

'Not like this Mr Pirelli' – Continental CEO's response to Pirelli's offer

Pirelli's offer for Continental is particularly noteworthy because Pirelli faced the wrath of 'Deutschland, Inc.', via a consortium of German banks, firms and politicians, and was nearly driven into financial ruin. This can be contrasted with the events surrounding Vodafone's acquisition of Mannesmann.

In September 1990, Pirelli approached the management of Continental with a convoluted takeover offer. Pirelli claimed that it had held talks with both the board of Continental and Gerhard Schröder, then the Premier of the state of Lower Saxony, and had received the consent of both. The proposed transaction entailed a complex reverse merger whereby Continental would undertake a capital increase to purchase Pirelli's Netherlands-based holding company's assets. Pirelli would then use the proceeds of this transaction to buy a controlling stake in Continental. A group of Italian investors with over 50 per cent of Continental's stock, later identified as including Mediobanca and Fiat, and acting in concert, would then tender their shares to Pirelli, allowing the Italians to restructure the supervisory board to represent their interests.

A few days later, Continental rejected the offer, on the grounds that the price demanded by Pirelli for the assets of its holding company was excessive. In December, Continental received a request from Alberto Vicari, an Italian shareholder with 5 per cent of the voting capital, for the calling of an extraordinary general meeting. Vicari proposed several resolutions to be voted on at the meeting, including the removal of the 5 per cent voting ceiling from the articles of incorporation. This amendment to the articles required a 75 per cent supermajority. In turn, the removal of the 5 per cent limit would facilitate the Pirelli transaction.

In response, Continental and its investment banking advisers, Deutsche Bank, sought to create a management support group of shareholders with a blocking majority of 25 per cent plus one vote. In February 1991, the German press reported that such a group had been formed. This included Allianz (5 per cent), Deutsche Bank (5 per cent), BMW, Volkswagen and Daimler-Benz (7 per cent combined), Dresdner Bank (3 per cent), and various Landesbanks (with a combined 3 per cent). However, at the extraordinary general meeting shareholders voted to repeal the voting ceiling, but rejected all other proposals related to the Continental takeover.

In March 1991, the district court of Hanover striped Pirelli and its allies of their voting rights, on the grounds that they were engaged in a pooling arrangement. Such arrangements needed to be disclosed to the firm at the 20 per cent threshold before the voting rights could be used. As part of the concert party agreement, Pirelli had undertaken to compensate its allies for any decline in the share price of their stakes in Continental. In return, Pirelli had a call option to buy out the stakes and prevent transfer to any third party.

With its takeover attempt at a standstill and Continental's share price in decline, Pirelli was under financial pressure, as it was contractually bound to compensate its allies for any losses suffered on their holdings. It was later calculated that these losses stood at US$280 million. Pirelli was forced to undertake a rights issue and a divestiture, while its CEO, Leopold Pirelli, was forced to resign by the Italian banks.[42]

Skirmishes between Pirelli and Continental continued over the next year, as the Italians were again prevented from voting their shares at the annual general meeting of Continental in 1992 and Continental demanded that they pay back the dividends received. Pirelli launched a legal appeal, hoping to be re-enfranchised.

In 1993, a conclusion was reached with Pirelli agreeing to sell its stake in Continental back to a consortium of German firms based in Lower Saxony, including the state's Landesbank and the local electricity utility, in a deal that was underwritten by the state through guaranteed bonds. This stake was purchased at a 30 per cent premium after Pirelli threatened to sell it to the Japanese. Despite this, Pirelli still suffered substantial losses.

Case study: Gucci vs. Louis Vuitton (1999)[43] – battle of the handbags

'(Bernard) Arnault is trying to steal this company' – Domenico De Sole, President of Gucci (Gay Forden, 2001)

'I invited him (De Sole) to lunch, and he invited me to Morgan Stanley' – Bernard Arnault, Chairman of LVMH (Gay Forden, 2001)

The saga of the ill-fated attempt by LVMH to seize control of Gucci illustrates the importance of regulating the takeover process to protect shareholders' interests and allow them to realise a fair return on their investments when a change of corporate control transaction takes place. It is particularly interesting because the case was fought out in the

PART I: INSIDE THE TAKEOVER REGULATION AND TACTICS

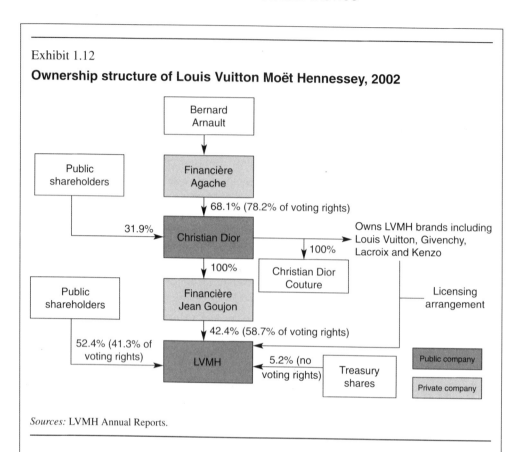

Exhibit 1.12

Ownership structure of Louis Vuitton Moët Hennessey, 2002

Sources: LVMH Annual Reports.

Netherlands, a jurisdiction that did not have a takeover code in place at the time. Therefore, mandatory bid requirements did not apply and board directors' duties when faced with a bid were far from clear. This was also true of the legality of the poison pill defence deployed by Gucci to ward off LVMH. Ultimately, the Dutch courts had to rule *ex post* on various takeover manoeuvres under general corporate laws relating to the fair treatment of shareholders.

The Italian leather goods company Gucci was founded in Florence by Guccio Gucci in 1923. After World War II, the business and the brand's cachet grew strongly. In the 1970s and 1980s, the founding family capitalised on the brand's value via multiple licensing deals. However, by 1993 the company was close to bankruptcy. LVMH's Chairman, Bernard Arnault, was approached as a potential rescuer, although he balked at the price tag of US$400 million. Eventually the private equity firm Investcorp, which already owned 50 per cent of Gucci, came through with a cash injection in return for the other half of the equity and reincorporated the company in The Netherlands for tax purposes. With Investcorp fully in control, and under the leadership of CEO Domenico De Sole and designer Tom Ford, a dramatic turnaround began, with Gucci's sales growing from US$264 million in 1994 to over US$1 billion in 1999. Investcorp realised a significant return on its investment when Gucci went public in 1995, listing its shares on the Amsterdam Stock Exchange (because Milan had turned down its application) and American depositary receipts in New York. In the initial public offering, Investcorp sold 48 per cent of the firm. The next year Investcorp sold its remaining stake in a secondary offering, leaving Gucci a widely held stock, primarily owned by institutional investors.

Meanwhile, LVMH had originally been a public company jointly controlled by the Moët, Hennessey and Vuitton families, but had fallen into the hands of Bernard Arnault. He had inherited from his father a French construction firm whose main business was building public housing, but in 1984 he had acquired the bankrupt textile firm Boussac, which owned the Christian Dior fashion house, from the French government. He had sold off the majority of Boussac's other assets at a significant profit while retaining Dior. He then deployed a portion of the proceeds to target other luxury goods companies, using Dior as an acquisition vehicle. Arnault was, in fact, invited to buy a stake in LVMH by the Vuitton family, although he later sided with the Moët and Hennessey families against them, and took control of LVMH through a 37 per cent stake. Arnault was able to do this because France did not have a mandatory bid threshold in place at the time. He became known in the French press as 'the Terminator' and the 'wolf in cashmere'. Subsequently, Arnault built up a powerhouse of global luxury brands across markets, including Givenchy, Lowe, Dom Perignon and TAG-Heuer, as well as retail outlets such as DFS and Sephora.

The LVMH pyramid of companies was structured to make them virtually takeover-proof (see Exhibit 1.12). The Arnault family holds the controlling stakes in both the publicly listed entities LVMH and Christian Dior through private companies, and in addition LVMH's major assets, its brands, are owned at holding company level by Dior, over which Arnault has total control with 78.2 per cent of the voting rights, and are licensed back to LVMH. This licensing agreement acts as an effective poison pill, because it can be revoked on a change of control at LVMH, destroying the value of the company.

In 1998, Arnault started acquiring Gucci shares through a phantom corporation. By the beginning of January 1999, LVMH had acquired 5 per cent of Gucci's shares in the open market. By the end of the month, it had acquired 34 per cent of the company, at a cost of US$1.4 billion, including the purchase of a 9.5 per cent stake from Prada. This was 1 per cent above the French mandatory bid threshold of 33 per cent, where an owner of a company is regarded by the regulators as having control. However, The Netherlands, where Gucci was incorporated and had its main listing, did not have a mandatory bid threshold in place.

Arnault informed Gucci's CEO, Domenico De Sole, that as the largest shareholder he expected to be able to appoint directors to the board. De Sole replied that this would be unacceptable unless Arnault were to bid for the outstanding share capital of Gucci, at an approximately 50 per cent premium[44] to the share price prior to Arnault's buying spree, as it would give LVMH, a competitor firm, access to Gucci's confidential deliberations and strategy. However, Arnault was not obliged to launch a tender offer for all outstanding shares and could control the firm through his stake. De Sole believed that LVMH 'never intended to make a full and fair offer for the company'.

De Sole's suspicions were confirmed when Arnault rejected the invitation to bid for the company, claiming that both firms would benefit from the synergies that cooperation would bring at the current level of ownership. De Sole commented:

> We don't believe in his synergies. I find it preposterous that he thinks he can come here and help us. He should fix his own brands. Except for Vuitton his

> fashion brands are doing terribly. The only synergy that would exist would be for myself and Mr Ford to come over and fix Christian Dior.
>
> However, Gucci's corporate by-laws at the time of the offering had been drafted to facilitate a takeover. An attempt at the annual general meeting in 1997 to impose a voting ceiling of 20 per cent on any single investor was defeated by shareholders. The only initial defensive measure Gucci's lawyers could come up with was an employee share ownership plan (ESOP) including issuances of stock options to De Sole and Ford, as a poison pill.[45] This at least would give the management time to look for a white knight.
>
> In July 1999, shareholders at an extraordinary general meeting authorised the issuance of 1.5 million new shares and another 6 million in June 2000, which significantly diluted LVMH's stake. PPR, a French retail conglomerate headed by François Pinnault, who was a business rival of Arnault, was brought in as a white knight. Eventually PPR ended up with 42 per cent of Gucci for US$3 billion, diluting LVMH's stake down from 34 per cent to 21 per cent. PPR would have four members on a nine-member board and would also contribute the Sanofi Beauté business, which it had recently acquired for US$1 billion, including the design house Yves Saint-Laurent. The deal was approved by independent shareholders at the annual general meeting, despite LVMH's opposition.
>
> The deal represented a US$3 billion cash injection into the firm, although not to shareholders. However, it was clearly justified to defend against a partial bid and raised the premium at which Gucci was trading. The deal strengthened the company and benefited shareholders. As De Sole said, 'what took Gucci to the US$1 billion mark wasn't going to get it to the US$2 billion mark' (quoted by Gay Harden, p. 322). With its cash pile and Yves Saint-Laurent, Gucci could pursue its ambitions as a multi-brand luxury goods group in direct competition with LVMH.
>
> In return, Arnault launched a number of lawsuits against Gucci in the Dutch courts, alleging mismanagement of the company and unfair shareholder treatment. This presented the Dutch courts with a series of legal issues for which there were no precedents. Realising that he would be a minority shareholder in a firm controlled by a hostile major shareholder and management, Arnault also finally launched a full bid for Gucci at US$85 per share, including the PPR stake, or US$91 per share if the PPR deal was rescinded. However, by then it was far too late.
>
> In March 1999, the Dutch court ruled that Gucci's supervisory board was required to consider LVMH's offer without the influence of PPR. However, it refused to grant LVMH's request for an independent overseer of the board. It also refused to reverse the sale to PPR and upheld the ESOP and the issuance of stock options to the senior managers.
>
> The case then went to the Enterprise Chamber of the Court of Appeals. This ruled that the share capital increase via the ESOP violated Dutch corporate law on the fair treatment of shareholders and ordered the ESOP annulled. However, this defence had served its purpose in allowing Gucci time to find a white knight. On the more important question of the issuance of shares to PPR, the court refused to annul the arrangement.
>
> In October 1999, Gucci counterattacked, asking the court to force LVMH to divest its stake. Eventually, on appeal, the Dutch court also upheld the ESOP.

> A negotiated solution was reached between PPR and LVMH in 2001, driven by pressure from the Dutch authorities, which were struggling to find solutions to the issues posed. PPR bought out LVMH's stake for US$2 billion, netting Arnault a profit of US$700 million. At the same time, PPR launched a forward tender offer for all outstanding shares in 2004.

References

Adolff, J., 'Turn of the Tide? The Golden Share Judgements of the European Court of Justice and the Liberalisation of European Capital Markets', *German Law Journal – European and International Law* (August 2002).

Arlen, J., and E. Talley, 'Unregulated Defenses and the Perils of Shareholder Choice', *University of Pennsylvania Law Review* (2003).

Ashkenas, R.L., L.J. DeMonaco, *et al.*, 'Making the Deal Real: How GE Capital Integrates Acquisitions', *Harvard Business Review* (January/February 1998).

Baums, T., 'Hostile Takeovers in Germany: A Case Study on Pirelli vs. Continental', *Arbeitspapier* 3/93, (1993).

Bebchuk, L.A., *et al.*, 'The Powerful Anti-Takeover Force of Staggered Boards: Theory, Evidence and Policy', *Stanford Law Review*, No. 887 (2002).

Bebchuk, L.A., and O.D. Hart, 'Takeover Bids vs. Proxy Fights in Contests for Corporate Control', *Harvard Law and Economics Discussion Paper*, No. 336 (2002).

Berle, A.A., and G.C. Means, *The Modern Corporation and Private Property* (New York: MacMillan, 1932).

Bianchi, M., 'La Proprieta Circolare Nei Gruppi Quotati Italiani', *Rapporto IRS Sul Mercato Azionario* (1998).

Bruck, C., *The Predators' Ball: The Inside Story of Drexel Burnham and the Rise of the Junk Bond Raiders* (New York: Random House, 1988).

Bruner, R., *Corporate Development as a Strategic Capacity: The Approach of GE Power Systems Applied Mergers & Acquisitions* (London: John Wiley & Sons, 2004).

Bruner, R.F., *Deals From Hell* (London: John Wiley & Sons, 2005).

Chandler, A., 'Scale and Scope: The Dynamics of Industrial Capitalism', (Cambridge, Massachusetts: Belknap Press, 1990).

Chernow, R., *The Warburgs: The Twentieth-Century Odyssey of a Remarkable Jewish Family* (London: Random House, 1993).

Coates, J.C., 'Measuring the Domain of Mediating Hierarchy: How Contestable are US Public Corporations', *Journal of Corporate Law* (1999).

Coates, J.C., 'Ownership, Takeovers and EU Law: How Contestable Should EU Corporations Be?', Harvard – John M. Olin Centre For Law, Economics and Business Discussion Paper, No. 450 (2003).

Dyck, A., and L. Zingales, 'Private Benefits of Control: An International Comparison', *Journal of Finance* (2004).

Faccio, M., and L. Lang, 'The Ultimate Ownership of Western European Corporations', *Journal of Financial Economics* (2002).

Gaughan, P., Mergers, *Acquisitions and Corporate Restructuring* (London: John Wiley & Sons, 2002).

Gilson, R.J., 'Unocal 15 Years Later (And What We Can Do About It)', *Delaware Journal of Corporate Law*, No .26.

Gordon, J.N., 'An American Perspective on the New German Anti-Takeover Law', *Die Aktiengesellschaft*, No. 12 (2002).

Gordon, J.N., 'An International Relations Perspective on the Convergence of Corporate Governance: German Shareholder Capitalism and the European Union 1990–2003', European Corporate Governance Institute Law Working Paper, No. 406 (2003).

Grant, J., and T. Kirchmaier, 'Corporate Ownership Structure and Performance in Europe', Centre for Economic Performance, Discussion Paper 631, London School of Economics (2004).

Grossman, S., and O. Hart, 'One Share, One Vote and the Market for Corporate Control', *Journal of Financial Economics* (1987).

Hannah, L., 'Takeover Bids in Britain Before 1950: An Exercise in Business Prehistory', *Business History* (1972).

Harden, S.G., *The House of Gucci: A Sensational Story of Murder, Madness, Glamour and Greed* (New York: Harper Collins, 2001).

Holmen, M., and P. Hogfeldt, 'A Law and Finance Analysis of Initial Public Offerings', Stockholm School of Economics Working Paper (2000).

Holmstrom, B., and S. Kaplan, 'Corporate Governance and Merger Activity in the US: Making Sense of the 1980s and 1990s', University of Chicago Working Paper (2001).

Jensen, M., and W. Meckling, 'Theory of the Firm: Managerial Behavior, Agency Costs and Agency Structure', *Journal of Financial Economics* (1976).

Johnson, S., *et al.*, 'Tunnelling', *American Economics Review* (2000).

Kahan, M.B., and E.B. Rock, 'How I Learned to Stop Worrying and Love the Pill: Adaptive Responses to Takeover Law', *University of Chicago Law Review*, No. 69 (2002).

Kirchmaier, T., 'Merger, Demerger and Corporate Performance', PhD Thesis, Management Department, London School of Economics (2001).

Klein, M., *The Life and Legend of Jay Gould* (Maryland:Johns Hopkins University Press, 1986).

LaPorta, R., F. Lopez-de-Silanes, *et al.*, 'Law and Finance', NBER Working Paper, No. 5661 (1996).

LaPorta, R., F. Lopez-de-Silanes, *et al.,* 'Corporate Ownership Around the World', *Journal of Finance* (1999).

LaPorta, R., and R. Vishny, 'Legal Determinants of External Finance', *Journal of Finance* (1997).

Lipton, M., and P.K. Rowe, 'Pills, Polls and Professors: A Reply to Professor Gilson', *Delaware Journal of Corporate Law*, No. 27 (2001).

Manne, H.G., 'Mergers and the Market for Corporate Control', *Journal of Political Economy* (1965).

Mayer, C., and T. Jenkinson, *Hostile Takeovers: Defence, Attack and Corporate Governance* (London: McGraw Hill, 1994).

Monks, R., and N. Minow, *Corporate Governance* (London: Blackwell Publishing, 2003).

Nenova, T., 'The Value of Corporate Votes and Control Benefits: A Cross Country Analysis', Harvard University Working Paper (2000).

Owen, G,T., Kirchmaier and J. Grant, *Corporate Governance in the US and Europe: Where Are We Now?* (Basingstoke: Palgrave MacMillan, 2005).

Rosenbaum, V.K., 'Corporate Takeover Defences 2000', Working Paper, Investor Responsibility Research Centre (1999).

Rossi, S., and P. Volpin, 'Cross Country Determinants of Mergers and Acquistions', *ECGI Working Paper*, No. 25, (2003).

Rubin, R., and J. Weisberg, *In an Uncertain World* (New York: Random House, 2004).

Schaferstein, D., and J. Stein, 'The Dark Side of Internal Capital Markets: Divisional Rent Seeking and Inefficient Investments', NBER Working Paper, No. 6539, (April 1998).

Schreiber, J.J.S., *Le Defi American – (The American Challenge)* (London: Hamish Hamilton, 1968).

Schwert, G.W., 'Hostility in Takeovers: In the Eyes of the Beholder', *Journal of Finance* (December 2000).

Stiglitz, J., *Ownership, Control and Efficient Markets: Some Paradoxes in the Theory of Capital Markets*, Economic Regulation (1982).

Thomsen, S., and T. Pedersen, 'Ownership Structure and Economic Performance in the Largest European Companies', *Strategic Management Journal*, No. 21 (2000).

Ward, V., 'Betting the Bank', *Vanity Fair* (September 2005).

Wasserstein, B., *Big Deal: Mergers and Acquisitions in the Digital Age* (New York: Time Warner Books, 2000).

Welch, J., and S. Welch, *Winning* (New York: Harper Collins, 2005).

Yergin, D., and J.Stanislaw, *The Commanding Heights: The Battle for the World Economy* (New York: Simon and Schuster, 2002).

PART I: INSIDE THE TAKEOVER REGULATION AND TACTICS

[1] See H.G. Manne (1965).

[2] One of the major criticisms of M&A is that on average they destroy value. Unfortunately, this perspective is not well-grounded in scientific fact and a recent meta-study by Bruner (2005), of over 130 surveys of the performance of mergers and transactions across geographies and timeframes, and using different methodologies, finds the opposite. On average, M&A transactions create significant value for the shareholders of the target firm, the shareholders of the target and the acquirer combined earn a positive return, and shareholders of the acquirer receive the market rate of return. More broadly, M&A transactions release capital to be efficiently shifted across sectors and geographies, moving it from 'sunset to sunrise industries' (Holstrom and Kaplan, 2001) and aiding funding of entrepreneurs with new ideas. As former US Treasury Secretary, Lawrence Summers has stated, 'it was impatient, value-focused, shareholders who did America a great favour by forcing capital out of its traditional companies and thereby making it available to find venture capitalists and the Ciscos and Microsofts that are now in position to propel our economy very rapidly forward'.

[3] Berle and Means (1932).

[4] In 2001, GE Power Systems acquired 17 other firms.

[5] The authors summarise that GE's organisational innovations stem from 'dozens of experiments until they crystallised to form a methodology others could follow' (p. 165).

[6] Press release, European Commission, Statement No. 13, 2002.

[7] Schwert (1999).

[8] There remain a few exceptions to this rule in the FTSE 100, including the Daily Mail General Trust, which has two classes of shares.

[9] Options grants are often structured to vest over a manager's tenure with a firm, for example, a 10-year period. However, upon a change of control they will all vest at once, allowing the manager to realise multiple years' compensation and to sell the underlying shares to the acquirer at a premium.

[10] See Gordon (2002).

[11] A number of US firms also have dual share classes. A survey of the 1,900 largest firms in 1999 found that 11.5 per cent had dual shares. These included Berkshire Hathaway, Dow Jones, Ralph Lauren, Viacom and Comcast.

[12] Delaware, partly due to the fact that it has the most developed body of corporate law, is the state of choice for incorporation of corporate America. Almost two thirds of the S&P 500 are incorporated there. As Coates (2003) points out, Delaware, 'through mimicry, writes most law for the rest'.

[13] See a discussion of the Delaware regime in the second section of this chapter, particularly the court's subtle balancing of interests.

[14] This is based on 'Oracle vs. Peoplesoft: The Next Round', in *ISS Governance Weekly*, 10 August 2004.

[15] There is emerging evidence that US boards are becoming increasingly concerned about the threat of shareholder litigation. See Ward (2005) on the deliberation of the Morgan Stanley board on the future of the firm.

[16] MOEs are mergers between firms of roughly equal size. Deal structures do not usually involve a large premium for the target shareholders and consideration is via an exchange of shares. Although small in number, MOE structures have been used in significant high-value, high-profile deals including Daimler Chrysler, BP/Amoco, Citicorp/Travelers and Hewlett Packard/Compaq.

[17] No such legal constraints exist in the United States. Subsequently, this German constraint has been relaxed by a number of rulings of the European Court of Justice that allow EU firms to separate their seat of incorporation from their real seat (headquarters location and physical production facilities) within the EU: see, for example, the Centros case (1999).

[18] However, they have been deployed in some very high profile deals including Paramount/Viacom, Conrail/CSX and GE/Honeywell.

[19] Recent hostile French deals include Soc-Gen, BNP/Paribas, TotalFina/ELF, Sanofi Synthelabo/Aventis and Alcan/Pechiney.

[20] Parmalat was an extreme example of the phenomena of European board capture. Of the 13 members of its board, the chairman was Calisto Tanzi, the founder, and the other 12 were either members of the Tanzi family, employees of Parmalat or business associates of the family.

[21] These are calculated as the percentage of market capitalisation captured by dominant shareholders beyond their equity stake.

[22] Families are likely to prefer organic growth as it presents lower risk and there is less danger of their losing control of the firm with the dilution of their stake.

[23] Case C-438/99: Commission vs. France, Case C-367/98: Commission vs. Portugal and Case C-503/99 Commission vs. Belgium.

[24] L'Oréal's corporate structure made it bid-proof. However, it was not originally created to ward off raiders, but rather to halt the advances of government plans for nationalisation. It should also be noted that, despite its corporate structure, L'Oréal has had a stellar record in creating shareholder value under its CEO Lindsay Owen Jones.

[25] This device is common, for example, in the European tyre industry, having been deployed by both Michelin and Pirelli (although Pirelli changed its corporate structure in May 2003). The German consumer goods company Henkel also uses this structure.

[26] These measures were introduced to limit the influence of foreign shareholders (see Servan-Schreiber, 1967). Ironically, the California State Employees Retirement Fund (CalPERS) has held as much as 5 per cent of France's equity market (Yergin and Stanislaw, 2002), while Anglo–American institutions hold over 40 per cent of the CAC 40 (Monks and Minow, 2003).

[27] It should be noted that this is not a phenomenon just applicable to Continental Europe. For example, a UK government study of the lack of takeovers in the domestic market in the 1930s found that 'the personal feelings of aged family proprietors were often the major reason for the rejection of merger proposals' (Hannah, 1974).

[28] In Germany, the awarding of an ex-pat golden parachute to Mannesmann CEO Klaus Esser led to criminal charges being levied against both himself and the firm's board members who approved it, including the CEO of Deutsche Bank.

[29] This case study is based on Chernow (1993).

[30] This is discounting the hostile raids made by railroad robber baron, Jay Gould, in the 19th century (Klein, 1996).

[31] In the late 1960s, a number of hostile bids had been made for US blue chips, but all had failed.

[32] Entrepreneurs such as Ted Turner, Craig McCraw and Steve Wynn deployed them to build their early empires in cable, wireless communications and Las Vegas respectively, while others, such as Ronald Perelman, went after established targets, such as Revlon, and became known as takeover entrepreneurs.

[33] Ie, the raider would pay more for the first 51 per cent of the share capital than for the remaining 49 per cent.

[34] The Securities and Exchange Commission (SEC) later prevented selective/two-tier tender offers.

[35] For an account of the Lennox takeover battle see Gaughan (2002).

[36] This was in relation to Sir James Goldsmith's success in circumventing the second-generation poison pill in the takeover of Crown Zellerbach by buying control of the firm in the market with just over 50 per cent of the stock. While this action activated the rights at the 20 per cent threshold, they did not become exercisable until the raider acquired 100 per cent of the firm's stock. See Gaughan (2002) for further details.

[37] Quote from Wasserstein (2000, p. 239).

[38] This was despite the fact that the SEC filed a brief with the court arguing that the poison pill should be overturned.

[39] The emphasis on elections over market transactions has been subsequently criticised by some legal scholars (see Gilson, 2001).

[40] This case study is based on Gordon (2003).

[41] This case study is based on Baums (1993).

[42] Management of the company was taken over by Pirelli's son-in-law, Marco Tronchetti Provera, while Leopoldo became Chairman. A decade later, Tronchetti Provera launched a hostile bid for control of Telecom Italia.

[43] This case study is based on Gay Harden (2001).

[44] This premium was in line with both average premiums in the industry and for all M&A deals at the time. *Source:* author access to Morgan Stanley's valuation model.

[45] In fact, 83 per cent of the ESOP was reserved for De Sole and Ford. This was not revealed to shareholders at the time, although there was no obligation to do so under Dutch law. Gucci subsequently argued that the ESOP needed to be controlled by senior management if it was to serve as an effective takeover defence. Moreover, this European poison pill differed from the US variety in that in the United States pills are so powerful that one has never actually been triggered.

Chapter 2

Takeover regulation and the balancing of interests

Jeremy Grant

> *'The value of the shares is not important because people are not interested in buying our shares and we are not interested in trying to promote the value of our shares'*
> Vincent Bollore, French corporate raider, on his family's publicly listed company (Simmons and Silver, 2003)

We ended Chapter 1: 'Takeovers and the market for corporate control' with two case studies of ill-fated takeovers to illustrate the problems and costs that arise for firms (and ultimately shareholders) without an effective merger regulation framework to facilitate a market for corporate control. Chapter 2 provides an overview of the major components of such a framework in more detail by examining the nature and rationale of concepts including mandatory bid thresholds, disclosure requirements and squeeze-out/sell-out rules. We include in this chapter a number of case studies, including Tchibo's acquisition of control of Beiersdorf. This highlights the issues and costs that arise where there is an adequate regulatory framework for takeovers, however, there are issues with enforcement and parties are allowed to exploit loopholes which go against the fundamental principles of takeover regulation.

Introduction

There is broad agreement in principle that takeovers should be regulated to protect the interests of all shareholders. The OECD Principles of Corporate Governance (1999/2004) state that:

> Markets for corporate control should be allowed to function in an efficient and transparent manner.
>
> 1. The rules and procedures governing the acquisition of corporate control in the capital markets, and extraordinary transactions such as mergers, sales of substantial portions of corporate assets, should be clearly articulated and disclosed so investors understand their rights and recourse. Transactions should occur at transparent prices and under fair conditions that protect the rights of all shareholders according to their class.
> 2. Anti-takeover devices should not be used to shield management and the board from accountability.

There are two main policy considerations of takeover regulation (which can sometimes conflict):

- *Facilitation of mergers and acquisitions*: For the purposes of restructuring corporate assets for their highest value-added usage and lowering the transaction costs of such control changes. These ends are primarily achieved through the imposition of board neutrality which prevents the use of post-bid defences and the utilisation of devices such as squeeze-out provisions.
- *Investor protection*: In particular, the protection of minority investors through disclosure requirements and the provision of a valuable exit opportunity for minority investors at the same price as controlling shareholders.

Takeovers are regulated, as are most markets hallmarked by information and bargaining power asymmetries, to ensure that they function effectively by minimising market imperfections and increasing efficiency. Therefore, information asymmetries between the raider and the target firm and its shareholders are minimised via stringent disclosure requirements. Asymmetries of bargaining power and conflicts of interest are regulated via provisions such as mandatory bid rules, fair pricing provisions and sell-out rights, which protect the interests of minority shareholders and ensure that they collect a fair price for their shares on exit.

However, there is a balance to be achieved between encouraging efficient corporate restructuring and mitigating conflicts of interest. Regulatory requirements which protect minority shareholders can increase the price of a bid for a potential acquirer by distributing more of the gains from the takeover to the target's shareholders. This could make some bids less attractive, thus discouraging value-increasing transactions. However, the effective balancing of interests of acquirers and target shareholders should not prevent value-increasing transactions. It should be noted that the markets which have the strongest protections for minority investors, the United States and United Kingdom (see La Porta *et al.*, 1996, 1997 and 1999), also have the most active M&A markets. A cross-country study by Rossi and Volpin (2003) finds there are significantly higher volumes of M&A activity (and consequently more hostile deals) in countries with better accounting standards and stronger shareholder protection.

Overall, takeover regulation should facilitate entry for effective acquirers and provide a fair exit opportunity for minority investors. The regulatory regime should also provide a high degree of legal certainty, which in turn lowers transaction costs and facilitates a more efficient market for corporate control, while retaining a degree of flexibility to encompass changes in the market. To maximise efficiency in the takeover market, the regulator must balance these competing objectives.

A brief history of takeover regulation

In Europe, the United Kingdom has been at the forefront of takeover regulation since the introduction of the City Code on Takeovers in 1968 by the Bank of England in light of a number of abuses that were arising in the domestic takeover market. The Code is administered by the Takeover Panel, which is part of the self-regulatory structure of the City of London. Until recently, it did not have the force of law.[1] In contrast to this unified approach, the United States has developed a complex regulatory framework reflecting the federal nature of its legal system. This consists of federal legislation (for example, the Williams Act 1968 and subsequent SEC rulings which deal with disclosure requirements and timing), as well as state statutes and case law which focus on directors' duties when faced with a takeover bid (for example, the Unocal and Household decisions in 1985, and Paramount in 1991). As discussed in Chapter 1, the decisions of the Delaware courts have very effectively ordered the takeover process by defining directors' duties and the legality of takeover defences in the United States. Both regimes also provide a high degree of certainty, thus facilitating a more efficient takeover market.

On the other hand, Continental Europe has lacked effective takeover regulation. Only in the 1970s/1980s did takeover regulation begin to emerge. At first this was of a self-regulatory nature, eventually replaced by binding rules in the late 1990s. For example, in Germany, Europe's largest economy, a voluntary takeover code was introduced in 1995 to protect shareholder interests during takeover bids. This code was developed by a small committee within the Ministry of Finance and was issued without any major input from companies and business associations such as the Federation of German Industry. While the takeover code was strongly influenced by the UK Takeover Code and was monitored by an Office of the Takeover Commission, its institutional context was quite different from that of the United Kingdom. Unsurprisingly, compliance with the code was weak. Only 540 of 933 listed companies complied, although 79 of the DAX-100 corporations did (Bundesministerium der Finanzen, 2000). In 2002, Germany introduced a statutory Takeover Code.

Exhibit 2.1
Types of takeover regulation in the EU

Country	Type of regulation
Austria	1998: Legislation
Belgium	1964: Self Regulatory Guidelines Issued by the Banking Commission
	1989, 2003: Legislation
Denmark	1979: Self Regulation
	1995, 2005: Legislation
Finland	1989: Legislation
France	1970s: Self Regulation
	1989: Legislation
Germany	1995: Self Regulation
	2002: Legislation
Ireland	1997, 2001: Legislation
Italy	1970s: Self Regulation – Stock Exchange Code
	1998: Legislation
The Netherlands	1970s: Self Regulation
	1995: Legislation (general corporate law)
Spain	1991, 2003: Legislation
Sweden	1971: Self Regulation
United Kingdom	1968: Self Regulation
	2000: Statutory Underpinning
United States	1968: Federal Legislation
	Also State Legislation

Source: Adapted from Berglof and Burkart (2003).

As Exhibit 2.1 demonstrates, in recent years, most EU members have also moved to introduce statutory takeover codes. This has been driven both by the significantly increased number of takeovers in Europe and also by the European Commission's introduction, after long negotiations with the Parliament, of a European Takeover Directive. The Directive was modelled on the UK City Code, and both it and the national codes which transcribe it into domestic legislation, contain significant common features.

Major components of takeover regulation

Disclosure requirements

In the EU, the Large Holdings Directive 1988 (88/627/EEC) sets disclosure thresholds for voting and cash flow rights which must be reported to national market regulators. Each acquirer of a company's stock has to give due notice within seven days to that company if his or her amount of shares equals, surmounts or falls below certain thresholds (10 per cent, 20 per cent, one-third, 50 per cent and two-thirds, respectively). Shares which are held by a third party on the account of the acquirer have to be added to his own holdings.

In almost all cases, the Directive has significantly lowered national disclosure thresholds to a minimum of 10 per cent.[2] The average prior to its implementation was 10 per cent in the early 1990s and has been lowered to 5 per cent now, with a duty to report each increase in the stake in multiples of 5 per cent up to 50 per cent. In many countries, this disclosure must be accompanied by a statement on 'strategic intentions'. This facilitates the free flow of information and requires acquirers to state their intentions in relation to a future tender offer. It also allows for easier monitoring and enforcement of European directives on insider trading and facilitates the role of M&A arbitrageurs in pricing and bearing risk. Arbitrageurs allow target shareholders to exit their positions prior to the deal closing and bear the risk that the deal will not close in exchange for a spread. This can be measured as the difference between the current share price of the target and the offer price of the bidder. The size of the 'arb' spread indicates the market's perspective on the likelihood that the deal will close. If the arb spread is negative, this indicates that the market believes that another bidder will top the current offer. Therefore, by transmitting information and providing liquidity to institutional investors who do not wish to wait for a takeover contest or an anti-trust clearance, arbitrageurs facilitate an effective market in corporate control.

However, disclosure can increase the cost of a bid as it limits the raider's ability to gain a significant toehold in the company before the market prices in a bid through the M&A arbs, thus increasing the price he must pay for the target as a whole (see Grossman and Hart, 1980). Aside from the level of the disclosure threshold itself, the number of days the raider has to report this after breaching the threshold can be important. The average in the EU is five working days.[3] Gaining a toehold is often an effective way to ward off rival bidders. Thus, the acquirer has a head start on rivals and may be able to build up a blocking majority.

In the United States, Section 13(d) of the Williams Act 1968 requires disclosure through the filing of the form Schedule 13D with the SEC when a 5 per cent ownership threshold is passed. However, this must be done within 10 days of exceeding the threshold. This gives acquirers a 10-day window to aggressively buy more shares in the open market without necessarily having to pay the full takeover premium. See Shleifer and Vishny (1986) and Burkart (1999).

PART I: INSIDE THE TAKEOVER REGULATION AND TACTICS

Derivatives transactions and contracts for differences

There is currently significant controversy surrounding the use of derivatives in takeover contests. These make economic sense as the purchaser only has to put up a small fraction of the cost of the underlying shares for an economic exposure to movements in the share price, for example, with a contract for differences (CFD). Traditionally, holders of derivative contracts did not have voting rights, however, this is changing and they could be used to disguise the holding of significant stakes in companies. They can also have very beneficial effects in helping acquirers to fine tune financing and manage exposure to risk and volatility.

> **Case study: Northern Electric/Trafalgar House (1995)**
>
> This transaction is one of the first recorded instances of derivatives, in this case CFD, being used in a takeover deal. In 1995, Trafalgar House bid to take over Northern Electricity. As part of the deal, the acquirer entered into CFDs with its investment banking adviser based on the share price movements of other UK regional electricity companies, as these would benefit from a re-rating of the entire sector. Trafalgar House aimed to cover its bid costs through this mechanism. At the time these transactions did not have to be disclosed. The UK Takeover Panel subsequently changed the City Code's disclosure provisions.

> **Case study: Mylan Laboratories/King Pharmaceuticals (2004)[4]**
>
> Derivatives products have also been used in the United States in takeover contests. In December 2004, Mylan Laboratories, a pharmaceutical company, made a bid for King Pharmaceuticals, a manufacturer of generic drugs. Corporate raider Carl Icahn owned a 10 per cent stake in Mylan and tried to block the acquisition. Perry Corporation, a New York M&A arbitrage hedge fund, owned 7 million shares in King. At the same time, it entered into a swaps contracts with two investment banks giving it 10 per cent of the voting rights in Mylan, with limited exposure to changes in its share price. This was achieved by Perry buying a stake in Mylan, while having the investment banks short the same number of shares. The transaction could have negated Icahn's ownership stake, although ultimately he was able to block the takeover. However, this was the first time such a transaction had been reported and it is rumoured that similar transactions were entered into in other high-profile deals in the United States.

Article 10 of the Takeover Directive requires the disclosure of all takeover defences and devices adopted for commercial purposes which could be utilised as defences (embedded defences). Again, this clause facilitates the free flow of information, lowers transaction costs and increases the efficiency of the takeover market.

Principle of equal treatment of all shareholders

This principle requires management and directors to treat all shareholders within each class of shares, where there are dual share classes, equally. In a takeover, the terms and conditions of sale should be the same for minorities. As for large shareholders selling the control block, the bidder is required to keep the offer open to all shareholders for a minimum period of time and allow all target shareholders to withdraw under certain conditions. The principle underpins requirements on offer pricing and the mandatory bid rule (see below). It is widely accepted in Europe in principle, not always adhered to in practice, and is enshrined in the European Directive on Takeover Bids. Although the United States does not have a mandatory bid rule, acquirers are required to purchase shares tendered into an offer pro rata.

In relation to counter arguments to the principle, some empirical evidence demonstrates that control premiums are higher in countries that use concentrated ownership as a corporate governance device (and have high private control benefits) than in others with widespread ownership. These facts may impede a market in corporate control based on equal treatment of all shareholders, as the raider will have to extend the high premium paid for the private control benefits of the controlling shareholder to all shareholders.[5] More compellingly, evidence also shows that where private control benefits are low, concentrated ownership can lower the costs of control, thus facilitating changes in control. For example, in Sweden where the premiums on multiple voting shares are small or even negative (see Exhibit 2.2), the transfer of control blocks would facilitate control transfers at a lower cost, which, if transactions are value enhancing, could benefit minority shareholders and would speed up corporate restructuring. (See Hughes/News Corp case study below for an example of a value-enhancing acquisition of a control stake.)

Exhibit 2.2

Major dual-class stock companies – Sweden

Company	Share price* (SEK)		NOSH (MM)		Market cap (SEK BN)		Vote value			
	A Shares	B Shares	A Shares	B Shares	A Shares	B Shares	SEK	SEK BN	Voting premium	% Price B + vote value
Atlas Copco	154.50	143.50	140	70	21.6	10.0	12.22	1.8	9	7
Electrolux	135.00	140.00	10	329	1.4	46.0	–5.56	–0.2	–4	–4
Ericsson	4.14	3.37	656	14,819	2.7	49.9	0.77	0.5	23	19
Holmen	212.00	202.50	23	57	4.8	11.6	10.56	0.3	5	4
Industrivarden	84.50	79.50	134	59	11.3	4.7	5.56	0.8	7	6
Investor	45.40	45.30	312	455	14.2	20.6	0.11	0.0	0	0
SCA	288.00	287.00	42	190	12.2	54.5	1.11	0.1	0	0
SEB	79.00	72.00	674	31	53.2	2.2	7.78	5.3	11	9
SHB	115.50	111.50	650	65	75.1	7.2	4.44	2.9	4	3
SKF	210.00	209.50	43	70	9.1	14.7	0.56	0.0	0	0
Stora Enso	87.50	89.50	184	722	16.1	64.7	–2.22	–0.6	–2	–2
Tele2	137.50	138.00	22	126	3.0	17.3	–0.56	0.0	0	0
Volvo	127.50	134.50	139	303	17.7	40.7	–7.78	–1.3	–6	–5
Mean:									3	3
Median:									0	0

* At 30 September 2002

Sources: JPMorgan M&A Research, Bloomberg, Thomson Financial.

Despite the widespread acceptance of equality of treatment, disputes can still arise in a takeover over the treatment of minority shareholders who have been issued a different class of shares.

> **Case study: Wella/Proctor & Gamble (2003)**
>
> In 2003, P&G acquired control of Wella, a German hair care company. Wella had two classes of shares outstanding – ordinary voting shares held by the controlling family and preference shares held by minority shareholders. P&G offered €92.25 for the ordinary shares and €65 for the preference shares, creating a control premium of 42 per cent, although both classes of shares had traded broadly within the same price range. Disgruntled minority shareholders sued P&G. However, they had limited legal ground to stand on as the offer complied with the German Takeover Code and the European Directive. Both state that equality of treatment for all shareholders does not extend to dual share classes.
>
> This case can be contrasted with Schneider/Legrand (2001). Here, the French courts overturned the approval of the regulator in relation to a differentiated offer to the holders of ordinary and preferred shares, despite the fact that the ordinary shares traded at a significant premium. See the case study in Chapter 13: France for more details.

It is arguable that differentiated treatment of dual share classes is a violation of the principle of equality of treatment. In the future, dual share class recapitalisations could be deployed to deprive minority shareholders of a control premium.[6]

Offer pricing

Regulation of the offer price is a vital element of equality of treatment. It is standard practice to require the offer to all shareholders at least to equal the highest price paid or agreed to by the bidder, or any party acting in concert with him, in a set number of months prior to the bid. If the bidder subsequently purchases shares in the target at a higher price, he must extend this to all shareholders. This is the criteria laid down in Article 5 of the Takeover Directive. For example, it is also the criteria set in Germany.[7] However, other countries' approaches differ. Italy requires that the bidder offer not less than the weighted average of the average price of the last 12 months and highest price paid by the bidder. Therefore, in Italy, a bidder is not required to pay the same premium to all shareholders. This would seem to run contrary to the intentions of the directive.

Many states in the United States require that all shareholders receive the same price when they tender. It is also common for US corporate charters to contain fair price provisions for the same effect.

Mandatory bid thresholds (MBT)

This mandates the acquirer to make a tender offer to all shareholders once he has accumulated sufficient shares to exercise control over the target. In practice, it allows shareholders a fair exit option with minority shareholders able to participate in the control premium, and adds to legal certainty, because bidders can predict their costs. It also prevents the controlling shareholder from extracting private control benefits *ex post* a takeover.

Historically, prior to the introduction of MBT, large shareholders in Europe were able to flip control stakes between each other without having to buy out minority shareholders at a premium. Critics of the MBT argue that it decreases the likelihood of value-enhancing transactions because it increases the cost and it closes down the market in control block trades. However, these are costs that have to be borne if the principle of equality of treatment of all shareholders is to be adhered to.

Of course, there are certain situations where the trading of control blocks with no extension of the premium to minority shareholders is beneficial, for example, in a system which has concentrated ownership, but low private control, such as Sweden. However, the benefits depend primarily on the characteristics of the purchaser (that is, do they bring superior management skills and expertise as well as complementary assets to the table?). Alternatively, is the purchaser just going to extract private control benefits at the expense of minority shareholders (see Bebchuk, 1994)?

In the United States, where there is no federal mandatory bid threshold and the sale of control blocks is theoretically allowed, such transactions are nevertheless rare. This is partly due to the increased regulatory burden and openness to minority shareholder litigation at the 10 per cent and 20 per cent ownership thresholds. The recent example of the acquisition of a control stake in Hughes Electronics by News Corp is examined below to highlight the differences between efficient and inefficient control stake transactions.

Case study: Hughes/GM/News Corp (2003)[8]

In 2003, General Motors (GM) sold a controlling stake (20 per cent) in Hughes Electronics to Rupert Murdoch's News Corp, which also purchased a further 14 per cent from other shareholders for a combined consideration of US$6.6 billion. Both GM and public shareholders received US$14 per share, although GM received its consideration in cash, while other shareholders were paid in cash and News Corp stock.

Murdoch wished to take control of Hughes' satellite TV business, DirecTV, the largest provider in the United States and Latin America, and fold it into his television empire, Sky Global Networks division, which included BSkyB and Sky Italia in Europe and Star TV in Asia. The seller, GM, clearly transferred control to a stronger management team with greater revenue synergies including complementary technology, content and willingness to invest in the business to the benefit of all shareholders. However, even this transaction was controversial. Hughes stock fell on announcement of the merger and the two major proxy voting services, ISS and Glass Lewis, gave differing recommendations. The board of Hughes was restructured to allay investor concerns. Six of the 11 seats went to independent directors, who would also compose the Audit, Compensation and Corporate Governance Committees. Any amendments to corporate charter provisions would require board approval and a 75 per cent supermajority of shareholders.

Cross-country variations

In Europe, the MBT differs between countries and now averages around one-third of the share capital (see Exhibit 2.3 for levels in the major European economies). Previously, it was often set at majority control (50 per cent plus). Requirements for an MBT are contained in the European Directive. As stated above, it also requires that the bid be made at a price no lower than that paid to any other shareholder over a set timeframe.

Most European countries have adopted mandatory bid thresholds. The exceptions as at mid-2005 are Luxembourg and The Netherlands. However, both thresholds and offer price differ across jurisdictions. Thresholds differ between 20 per cent and two-thirds of the voting capital, while the average is around one-third. Some countries have multiple thresholds. For example, Hungary sets it at 33 per cent, but also retains a lower threshold of 25 per cent for widely held companies. Other countries do not spec-

Exhibit 2.3
MBT in Europe

Country	%
France	33.3
Italy	30
Germany	30
Spain	25
United Kingdom	30

Source: Grant and Kirchmaier (2004).

ify a threshold, rather they require a bid when 'control' is gained. For example, Belgium defines control as 'power to exercise a decisive influence on the board and managers'.

The Spanish MBT is graduated and the Takeover Code also applies a broader definition of control. If a shareholder acquires, or intends to acquire, above 25 per cent of a company, he must launch a bid for at least 10 per cent of the capital. If he holds a stake of between 25 per cent and 50 per cent, and wishes to increase this by more than 6 per cent in the following 12 months, again he must bid for at least 10 per cent of the capital. To increase a holding above 50 per cent, he must bid for 100 per cent of a firm. If a shareholder acquires below 25 per cent of the share capital of a firm, but has the power to appoint more than one-third of the directors, he must launch an offer for 10 per cent of the capital. If the acquirer has the power to appoint over 50 per cent of the directors, he must bid for 100 per cent of the share capital. The extra criteria relating to directors was introduced in 2003 after a number of controversial cases in which acquirers were able to gain control of Spanish companies by buying in below the MBT (see Chapter 8 on Spain for more details).

However, this is not a phenomena confined to Spain. There are other examples across Europe. For example, in Italy, Pirelli acquired control of Telecom Italia in 2001 through the purchase of a 28 per cent control stake in Olivetti (at an 80 per cent premium). The control stake in the widely held Olivetti was 2 per cent below the Italian MBT and therefore the premium received by the controlling shareholders did not have to be shared with other minority shareholders.

Ignoring the MBT

There are exceptions to the MBT. For example, if the stake was held before the Takeover Code was introduced, then the owner may be exempt. However, this concept can often be ambiguous and open to abuse. Interpretations of this 'grandfathering' provision have allowed the party to act in concert where it does not want to pay for its full stake increase itself. See the Beiersdorf case study below.

> **Case study: the acquisition of control of Beiersdorf by Tchibo (2003)[9]**
>
> In the early 2000s, Allianz, the German insurer, wanted to release value from its US$50 billion portfolio of industrial holdings. This included a stake in Beiersdorf, a Hamburg-based manufacturer of skin-care products. In the interests of maximising returns to its

shareholders, Allianz approached Proctor & Gamble (P&G) about acquiring the 43.6 per cent stake in 2002.

However, P&G was not the only potential buyer. Tchibo, a coffee retailer privately held by the Herz family, had increased its stake in Beiersdorf to just above 30 per cent in 2002 and made it clear that they would also be interested in taking control of the company. The strategic rationale for Tchibo to increase its stake to 30.3 per cent was to take advantage of a grandfathering provision in the 2002 German Takeover Code. On one interpretation, this exempts existing shareholders from making a mandatory bid to buy out all minorities when increasing their stake. On the other hand, if P&G had acquired Allianz's 43.6 per cent stake, it would have been required under German law to extend this offer to all Beiersdorf shareholders.

At the same time, the Herz family was beset by a family feud. Tchibo was forced to buy out two of the Herz siblings 40 per cent stake for approximately €4 billion. Having undertaken this transaction, Tchibo made it clear that it would not put up all the money needed to buy out Allianz at the price demanded, let alone make a bid for the outstanding minorities. Yet, Tchibo wanted control of Beiersdorf without having to pay the full cost and decided that it could get what it wanted by siding with Beiersdorf's employees and Germany's politicians. Hamburg's Christian Democrat mayor, Ole von Beust, feared the loss of employment as well as tax revenue to the City. Facing an election, he was highly motivated to defend local employment. Von Beust contacted the office of the German chancellor, Gerhard Schröder, in Berlin and other national politicians to successfully enlist their support.

Subsequently, the Chairman of Tchibo, Dieter Ammer, sent a letter to Allianz, telling it that a consortium, including Tchibo, was prepared to purchase most of Allianz's stake. At the time, Allianz was continuing negotiations with P&G. There then occurred an extraordinarily complex and opaque series of transactions to minimise the costs to Tchibo, while delivering them control over Beiersdorf and rewarding Allianz with a significant premium to the current share price (itself reflecting a prospective takeover premium) that was not extended to minority shareholders. Losses were immediate with Beiersdorf's share price plummeting 13.5 per cent with the announcement of the deal on 23 October 2003.

Mechanics of the deal

Under the deal, Allianz sold a majority of its 43.6 per cent stake to a consortium consisting of Tchibo, a holding company for the assets of the City of Hamburg[10] and Beiersdorf's own pension fund (TROMA). Tchibo took a 19.6 per cent stake, Hamburg a 10 per cent stake and the pension fund 4 per cent. The consortium paid an average price of €133.69 per share, a 33.5 per cent premium to the closing price on 31 October 2003. Additionally, in December, Beiersdorf's own cash (and debt capacity) was deployed in a share buyback offer to support the Tchibo deal. The offer itself was effectively 80 per cent reserved for Allianz's shares, thus leaving minority shareholders out in the cold. Subsequently, in a side deal, Allianz purchased 4 per cent of the founding Claussen family's 10 per cent stake at an average price of €135 per share (a 40 per cent premium), indicating that the Claussens were party to agreements between the consortium and Allianz.

Exhibit 2.4
Beiersdorf's ownership structure

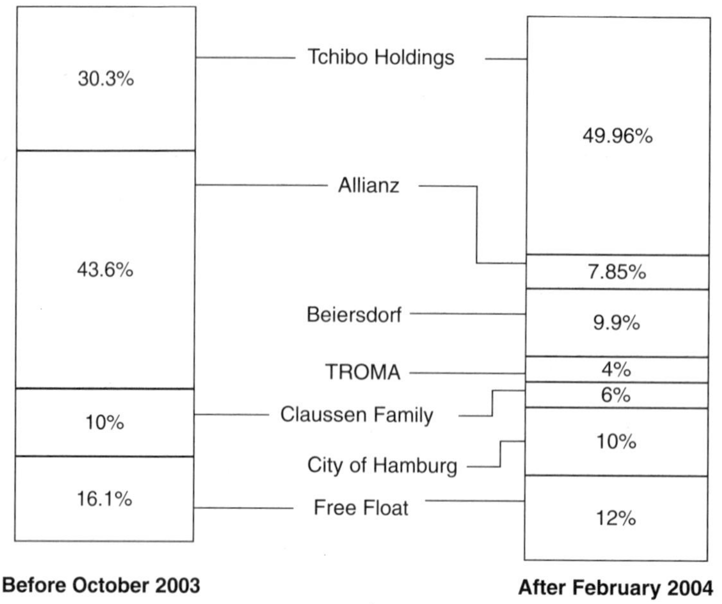

Before October 2003	After February 2004
Tchibo Holdings: 30.3%	Tchibo Holdings: 49.96%
Allianz: 43.6%	Allianz: 7.85%
	Beiersdorf: 9.9%
	TROMA: 4%
Claussen Family: 10%	Claussen Family: 6%
	City of Hamburg: 10%
Free Float: 16.1%	Free Float: 12%

Sources: Company Reports, *Wall Street Journal* (2004).

Exhibit 2.4 depicts the ownership structure before and after the deal. The nature of the deal highlights a number of issues, outlined below.

Minority shareholder protection

The Tchibo/Beiersdorf deal provides an example of minority shareholder exploitation through circumvention of the German Takeover Code 2002, particularly its provisions requiring an acquirer to make a mandatory bid for all outstanding minorities. As stated, Tchibo increased its stake in Beiersdorf to just above the MBT of 30 per cent before the Takeover Code came into force. It argued that it was exempt from the mandatory bid provisions that would require P&G, as well as any other investor, to extend its offer to all shareholders at the same price. However, the Takeover Code itself does not mention this grandfathering provision. Rather, there is a reference to grandfathering in the explanatory notes to the code, which were not ratified by the Bundestag. This means that the concept of grandfathering, which is one of Tchibo's main arguments in the case, is legally ambiguous.

Moreover, the first principle of the German Takeover Code states, 'holders of securities of the target company of the same class must be treated equally'. Since Beiersdorf only has one class of shares, the Tchibo offer clearly discriminated against minorities. The acquiring consortium argued that there was no change in control as Tchibo was increasing an existing stake from 30 per cent to approximately 50 per cent. However, this ignores the fact that Allianz was previously the largest shareholder with 43.5 per cent of

> the shares. At best, Tchibo was a blocking minority shareholder. The new shareholder structure left Tchibo as the largest shareholder in a consortium with at least 63 per cent of the stock. This is more than enough to trigger a mandatory bid for the minorities. Finally, the consortium contained two new parties that acted in concert with Tchibo, namely TROMA and the City of Hamburg, and together the consortium acquired a stake of 33.6 per cent, well over the MBT.
>
> Following complaints from Beiersdorf's minority shareholders, BaFin, Germany's federal financial regulator, examined the deal and subsequently cleared it. In a brief statement (in German) released on its website on 23 January 2004, the regulator stated that although there had been a joint acquisition, there was no evidence that the parties had acted in concert. It went on to argue that the parties had no continued common strategic interests or voting interests, despite the fact that these had been extensively detailed by the parties in the buyback prospectus issued by Beiersdorf.
>
> A further issue relates to support for the bid from Beiersdorf's own cash pile via its share buyback offer in December 2003. Here the consortium was able to use changes in Germany's financial regulations to its advantage. Share buybacks have only been legal in Germany since the 'Kontrag' laws of 1998, as a way of returning cash to minority shareholders. However, shareholders' funds were deployed to support a transaction that is against their interests. Free cash flow should be returned to shareholders or otherwise be deployed in developing marketing and distribution channels. Therefore, the buyback was a further exploitation of minority shareholders. At its June 2004 annual general meeting, Beiersdorf gained support for another buyback programme, which could be deployed in the future to buy out the remaining stake of Allianz or buy back Hamburg's shares. Again, this would increase the ownership percentages and hence cash flow rights of the remaining shareholders with Tchibo as the prime beneficiary. However, such a buyback would have to be conducted at a large premium to prevent Hamburg from making a loss on its dealings with the firm. Therefore, in conclusion, Tchibo was able to seize control of Beiersdorf via a series of transactions which allowed it to circumvent the mandatory bid rule.

In a number of recent cases, parties acting in concert have attempted to circumvent MBTs by ignoring them and secretly acting in concert. This seems to be a particular problem in Italy (see the SAI/Fondiaria case study).

> **Case study: SAI/Fondiaria (2001) – hidden control**
>
> In July 2001, two publicly listed Italian insurance firms, SAI and Fondiaria, announced a merger. SAI was controlled by a Sicilian property developer – Salavatore Ligresti – through Premafin, a leveraged financial holding company. One of Fondiaria's largest shareholders, both directly and indirectly, was Mediobanca, Italy's premier merchant bank. Since SAI did not have enough cash to make a full offer for Fondiaria, it acquired a 29 per cent stake from Montedison, a holding company controlled by Mediobanca, at a 56 per cent premium. The size of the premium indicated that substantial private control benefits were being conferred. This stake was 1 per cent below the MBT of the Draghi Decree.

PART I: INSIDE THE TAKEOVER REGULATION AND TACTICS

Since Mediobanca also directly owned 14 per cent of Fondiaria, Consob, Italy's stock market regulator, decreed that Mediobanca and SAI were acting in concert, requiring a full tender offer for all minority shareholders. This would have cost SAI €1.7 billion, an amount that it could not afford. Therefore, in a clever move, SAI parked 22 per cent of its stake with a consortium of five banks. They paid the same price for the stake as SAI had in the original transaction with Montedison (that is, each paid a control premium despite the fact that individually none would have control). However, the separate agreements with the banks each contained a call option for SAI to repurchase the stake if a merger between SAI and Fondiaria was agreed. Despite each agreement containing the same terms, the banks claimed that they were acting independently, because again, a finding of acting in concert would trigger a mandatory tender offer. Moreover, the syndicate included the bank that was advising SAI on its offer. In May 2002, Consob capitulated and found that the consortium of banks were not acting in concert with SAI and Mediobanca, therefore depriving minority shareholders of the acquisition premium.

With the aid of the five banks, SAI now had *de facto* control of Fondiaria with 22 per cent held by the banks, 14 per cent held by Mediobanca and its remaining stake of 7 per cent, for a combined total of 43 per cent of the stock. Under pressure from the banks, Fondiaria's board was forced to accept SAI's hostile deal, which involved a share exchange on terms far less attractive to minority shareholders than a tender offer. See Exhibit 2.5 for the new corporate structure.

Exhibit 2.5

SAI/Fondiaria's post-merger structure

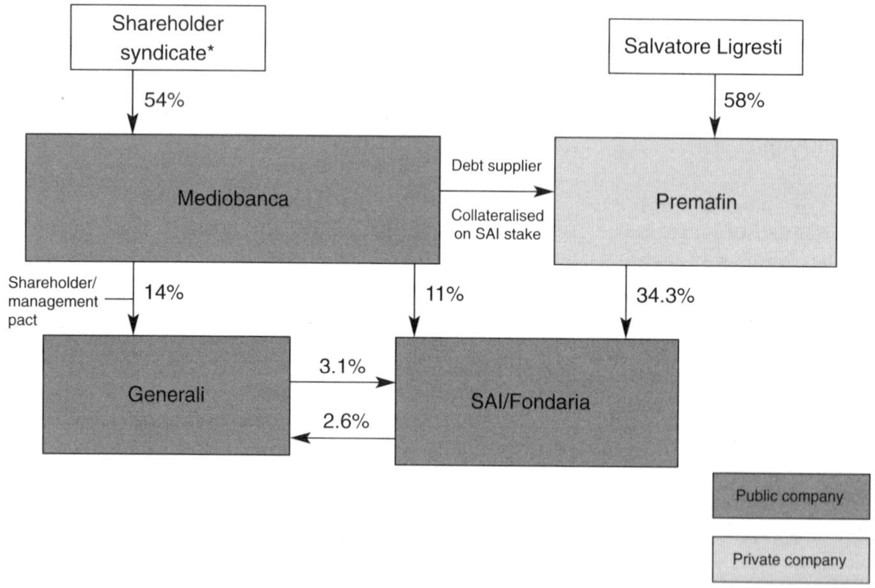

* Includes CapItalia and Unicredito

Sources: *La Repubblica* (2003), Mediobanca (2003), *Financial Times* (2003).

However, a serious problem remained. The deal also needed the consent of Italy's anti-trust authorities as it essentially gave Mediobanca control of both Assicurazioni Generali, Italy's largest insurer and Europe's third largest, and the combined SAI Fondiaria, Italy's largest casualty insurer. Mediobanca was effectively in a dominant position in the Italian insurance market and so in violation of both Italian law and pan-European regulations.

After an extensive investigation, the Italian anti-trust authorities accused Mediobanca of misrepresenting its role in SAI's takeover. It found that Mediobanca had control of Generali, in which it had a 14 per cent stake, and joint control of SAI Fondiaria. Moreover, in its investigation, it discovered a secret accord between Mediobanca and Generali, giving the bank oversight of the insurer's strategic decisions. This finding, along with a ruling of the administrative court of Lazio against it, led Consob to reopen its investigation.

In late December 2002, the anti-trust authorities officially ruled against Mediobanca. By way of remedy, it required the freezing of 2 per cent of Mediobanca's voting rights in Generali and prevented SAI Fondiaria voting its 2.4 per cent stake in Generali and from participating in shareholders' meetings. This was an attempt to push Mediobanca's weight in shareholder meetings to less than 50 per cent of shares present. This decision was immediately followed by a Consob ruling that Mediobanca and SAI had made illegal secret pacts. It ordered the bank and SAI to reduce their combined stake of 43 per cent to below 30 per cent and imposed fines.

However, from the minority shareholder perspective, the ruling did little to improve their position. Since Mediobanca had already pushed through the merger of SAI and Fondaria, it needed a far smaller stake to exert combined control over the new entity. More importantly, Consob did not require a mandatory tender offer for all minority shareholders of Fondaria, despite finding the parties in violation of the Italian Takeover Code.

In conclusion, the controlling shareholders of SAI, illegally acting in concert, were able to push through a merger with Fondaria on terms which were not beneficial to minority shareholders.

Case study: Banca Antonveneta (2005) – hidden control 2[11]

'Come as you usually do, through the back door'
Antonio Fazio, Governor of the Italian Central Bank, to Banca Popolare Chief Executive Gianpiero Fiorani

At the beginning of 2005, the Italian bank, Banca Antonveneta, was approaching a transformational period. It was controlled by a syndicate of shareholders, who combined held 31 per cent of the equity. These included the Dutch bank ABN Amro, the Benetton family and the financier Emilio Gnutti. However, the shareholder pact which bound the syndicate together was set to expire in April 2005. ABN Amro declared its interest in taking control of Antonveneta. This would entail raising its 12.7 per cent stake. However, this required the permission of the Bank of Italy. The Governor, Antonio Fazio, notoriously opposed foreigners controlling Italian banks. As it later became clear, he preferred an 'Italian solution'.

> To this end emerged Banca Popolare di Lodi (BPL), a small regional Italian bank, lead by CEO Gianpiero Fiorani. It was highly acquisitive having spent over €6 billion on acquisitions in the previous four years to create a national branch network. BPL, in concert with other parties, including Emilio Gnutti, Stefan Ricucci, a property developer, and other associates, began buying Antonveneta shares between December 2004 and February 2005 with money lent to them by BPL. The aim was to gain control of the board in time for the annual general meeting at the end of April 2005 after the shareholder pact had expired. BPL disclosed its own stake in Antonveneta, but denied any agreements with other parties.
>
> After the pact expired on 15 April, ABN announced a cash offer for the entire share capital at €25 per share. BPL hoped to block the offer and arranged a new concert party including Gnutti and Ricucci. Between 15 April and 22 April, they acquired a further stake bringing their combined holdings up to 46.7 per cent, of which BPL held 29.3 per cent directly. Clearly, they had breached the MBT and were required under Italian law to make a cash bid for the entire share capital of Antonveneta. Unfortunately, BPL did not have the money to do this, would damage its capital adequacy ratios and fall seriously short of mandatory levels.
>
> At the same time, the Bank of Italy withheld permission for ABN's bid until BPL was able to make its own (all paper) offer. However, the Italian securities market regulator, Consob, ruled that BPL was in breach of the MBT and must make an all cash offer. BPL disposed of various minority interests, although the sale contracts contained call options which allowed BPL to re-acquire the assets at a later date for the same price. It was also given a debt facility by a syndicate of 10 international banks secured on the Italian bank's stake in Antonveneta.
>
> However, these manoeuvres were to little avail as, in July, Italian magistrates impounded the BPL concert party's stake based on evidence from wiretaps on CEO Fiorani's phone, including conversations with Bank of Italy Governor Fazio. Consob then froze its offer for Antonveneta. In August, a judge ordered Fiorani and BPL's finance director be suspended pending further investigation.
>
> At the time of writing (September 2005), it looked as though ABN Amro was poised to take control of Banca Antonveneta.

Squeeze-out and sell-out rules

Squeeze-out rules

These give the acquirer the right to force minority shareholders to sell their shares to him at (or even below) the tender offer price. To enjoy this right, the bidder must acquire a high percentage of the share capital, usually over 90 per cent. In some countries, the threshold is set at 95 per cent (Belgium, Germany, France and The Netherlands) and Ireland has the lowest at 80 per cent. The Takeover Directive states that squeeze-out thresholds should be between 90 and 95 per cent.

The rule is aimed at allowing a bidder to gain 100 per cent of the equity to simplify accounting and administration because there is no obligation to deal with minority shareholders. Otherwise, the acquirer has to incur costs of not being able to fully integrate the acquisition in relation to the assets and financial and organisational infrastructure. The cost of maintaining an administrative infrastructure to discharge minority rights (that is, call general and extraordinary meetings) would have to be borne and the acquirer could be at risk of obstructive behaviour by minority shareholders. Ultimately, the acquirer could have to incur the greater costs of delisting the firm.

From an efficiency perspective, squeeze-out should make the M&A process more efficient as it may lead to a decrease in the tender price. However, this depends on the fair value of the shares in the squeeze-out, that is, can the squeeze-out price be below the tender offer price? If so, then there is an inducement for minority shareholders to tender which benefits the raider. However, if it can be above, this acts as a disincentive to tender (see Maug, 2004).

The Takeover Directive (Article 15) presumes that the tender offer price, based on the fact that the vast majority of shareholders have accepted it, shall be presumed to be a fair price. However, the wording of the article leaves some room for the setting of a different price. This opens up issues of how an independent assessment could be undertaken to come up with an alternative price. Another major issue to consider is whether the legal regime allows statutory mergers or delistings which can be used as a *de facto* squeeze-out at higher costs, but lower valuations than the tender offer (for example, see Deutsche Telecom and T-Online case study below).

Case study: Deutsche Telecom/T-Online (2004) – squeeze-out alternatives

In October 2004, T-Online (TOI), the German internet services provider, and its parent company Deutsche Telecom (DT), entered into merger discussions. DT intended to reintegrate its partially floated internet unit to bolster its fixed line business and reap cost savings of up to €1 billion. To achieve these ends, DT made a *de facto* two-tier offer to TOI's minority shareholders. Up until 4 February 2005, investors could sell their shares back to DT in a tender offer for €8.99 in cash, a sum considerably below the 2000 IPO price of €27 and independent estimates of the fundamental value of the firm.

Issues of the adequacy of the offer were raised by independent valuations prepared for TOI by the German audit firm Warth & Klein and a fairness opinion commissioned from the investment bank Rothschild. Based on this analysis, the board of TOI stated that, 'the offered purchase price per TOI share is significantly below the per share company value of TOI established by performing a discounted future earnings valuation or on the basis of other internationally recognised valuation methods'. Therefore, the management board was neither able to recommend or reject the offer, although none of the board members tendered their own shares.

Despite the issues relating to the adequacy of the offer, DT pushed ahead with the cash offer, stating that shareholders who did not tender would be subject to a statutory merger under German law compelling them to tender TOI shares for DT shares at an exchange ratio of between €0.45 and €0.55 a DT share. This range valued TOI shares below the €8.99 cash offer and left considerable uncertainty for the investor about the effective merger price.

Prior to the tender offer, DT held 73.93 per cent of TOI, Lagardere, the French family-controlled defence contractor and media group, owned 5.69 per cent and minority

> investors approximately 20 per cent. By the end of December, DT had increased its stake to 73.98 per cent, as investors were expecting – wrongly – an improvement of DT's offer. Therefore, only by securing a portion of the Lagardere stake could it be absolutely certain of its ability to force through a statutory merger against the will of minority shareholders. Under German law, statutory mergers allow a parent to buy out minority shareholders in a subsidiary at a value set by an independent expert, while taking the share price as the lower boundary.
>
> On 7 February 2005, Lagardere announced that it had sold the majority of its stake back to DT at an undisclosed price. This placed the German company in a position to acquire minority stockholder's shares, through the statutory merger process, at a discount to the cash offer already rejected by most minority shareholders, and the advisers of TOI, as inadequate.

Sell-out rules

These protect minority shareholders by giving them the right to demand that the acquirer buys out their shares on fair terms, that is, at the tender offer price. However, the rule may reduce the pressure to tender, particularly if investors can hold up firms to increase the sell-out price. The Takeover Directive (Article 16) requires member states to institute sell-out rights, based on fair pricing provisions similar to Article 15 on squeeze-outs. Currently, a number of European countries do not have sell-out rights including Italy, Belgium and Spain.

Board neutrality and takeover defences

Because takeovers are an external corporate governance mechanism, managers and directors can be faced with a conflict of interest. Whilst the transaction may increase shareholder value, it is also likely to endanger their jobs and status. Therefore, they may undertake behaviour that discourages value-creating takeovers. Often this can take the form of pre-bid defences (which discourage bids) and post-bid takeover defences. See Chapter 1 for an extensive discussion on the array of defences available both pre- and post-bid.

Board neutrality is an important principle of the European Takeover Directive. A number of European jurisdictions, such as the United Kingdom, adhere to the principle of strict board neutrality in the face of a takeover bid. This prevents either the management or the board of directors undertaking frustrating actions. In the United Kingdom, the principle applies to all frustrating actions without the approval of shareholders.

In other European jurisdictions, it often applies only to certain devices. For example, poison pills are illegal in most European countries due to strong pre-emption rights. Dual-share classes are not legal or frowned upon by institutional investors in the United Kingdom, Belgium and Germany. However, this ban only applies to publicly listed stock in Germany. Dual shares can also be capped at a proportion of the equity capital (25 per cent in France, 50 per cent in Italy, Spain and Portugal). However, other countries have no restrictions (Austria, Ireland, Luxembourg, Greece and The Netherlands). Most importantly, if a firm has a dominant shareholder with over 50 per cent plus of the voting rights, he can afford to 'just say no'.

> ### Germany
> Allows post-bid defences with the consent of the supervisory board. There is a duty of neutrality, but it does not apply to acts undertaken in the ordinary course of business (such as looking for competing offers) or approved by the supervisory board. Firms have an array of pre- and post-bid defences open to them. Those that require shareholder approval include: issuance of new shares if the firm does not already have authorisation for new share capital, share buy-backs (limited to 10 per cent) and sale of major assets.
>
> Those that do not require shareholder approval include: issuance of new shares if capital has been approved, sale of some assets and distribution of some proceeds in the form of a dividend, counter offers (Pac-man defence) as acquisitions do not require shareholder approval, pursuit of alternative offers, acquiring another firm to create anti-trust issues and extending loans to management and board members.
>
> ### Italy
> Requires 30 per cent shareholder approval to create post-bid defences. If a firm is widely held, then it can be hard to get 30 per cent. However, as we saw in Chapter 1, most firms have a dominant shareholder (or shareholder syndicate) effectively making them takeover proof.

This chapter has highlighted the basic elements of a merger regulation framework including the conflicts and complementarities between the components and the underlying principles of regulation. It also began to highlight some of the divergences between EU member states' current takeover regulation and the Takeover Directive. These issues are explored in more detail in Chapter 3: The European Takeover Directive.

References

Bebchuk, L.A., 'Efficient and Inefficient Sales of Control', *Quarterly Journal of Economics* (November 1994).

Berglof, E., and M. Burkart., 'European Takeover Regulation', *Economic Policy* (April 2003).

Grant, J., and T. Kirchmaier., 'It's All Cosmetic: Reform in Germany is Only Skin Deep', *Wall Street Journal Europe* (28 July 2004).

Grant, J., and T. Kirchmaier, 'Corporate Ownership Structure and Performance in Europe', Centre for Economic Performance, Discussion Paper 631, London School of Economics (2004).

Grossman, S., and O. Hart, 'Takeover Bids, the Free Rider Problem and the Theory of the Corporation', *Bell Journal of Economics* (1980).

LaPorta, R., F. Lopez-de-Silanes *et al.,* 'Law and Finance', NBER Working Paper, No. 5661 (1996).

LaPorta, R., F. Lopez-de-Silanes *et al.*, 'Corporate Ownership Around the World', *Journal of Finance* (1999).

PART I: INSIDE THE TAKEOVER REGULATION AND TACTICS

LaPorta, R., and R. Vishny, 'Legal Determinants of External Finance', *Journal of Finance* (1997).

Maug, E.G., 'Efficiency and Fairness in Minority Freezeouts: Takeovers, Overbidding and the Freeze-In Problem', SSRN Working Paper (2004).

Rossi, S., and P. Volpin, 'Cross-Country Determinants of Merger and Acquisitions', ECGI Finance Working Paper No. 25 (2003).

Ross Sorkin, A., 'Nothing Ventured, Nothing Gained', *New York Times* (2 December 2004).

Shleifer, A., and R. Vishny, 'Larger Shareholders and Corporate Control', *Journal of Political Economy* (1986).

Simmons, J., and V. Silver, 'Vincent Bollore: Banking Provocateur', *Bloomberg Markets* (August 2003).

Taylor, E., and S. Ellison, 'With Nivea at Risk, Old German Club Swings into Action', *Wall Street Journal* (19 February 2004).

---

[1] However, the City Code is now recognised by the Financial Services and Markets Act 2000. The United Kingdom's financial markets regulator, the Financial Services Authority, can bring disciplinary procedures based on the recommendations of the Panel. The Code and the Panel will have statutory footing when the European Directive on Takeover Bids is transcribed into UK law. See Chapter 8 on the United Kingdom for more details.

[2] The exception was the United Kingdom where the threshold was 3 per cent. At the other end of the spectrum was Germany, with a threshold of 25 per cent.

[3] At the lower end of the scale, Italy requires the acquirer to report two days after the breach of the threshold.

[4] Based on Sorkin (2004).

[5] Although this begs the question of why a controlling shareholder who enjoys private control benefits (both pecuniary and non-pecuniary) would be motivated to sell control in the first place and how you would value these benefits going forward.

[6] In the late 1980s, the United States witnessed a wave of dual share class recapitalisations to make firms bid proof. However, the SEC issued Rule 19c-4 to prohibit the reduction of voting rights of current shareholders. This was initially fought by the Business Roundtable, however, the SEC required the major exchanges to incorporate the restrictions in their listing rules.

[7] Germany also has a second criteria – the price must also be at least equal to the weighted-average stock price in the three months prior to the offer.

[8] Based on Hughes Investor Roadshow Presentation, September 2003.

[9] This case study is based on Grant and Kirchmaier (2004) and Taylor and Ellison (2004).

[10] HGV Hamburger Gesellschaft für Vermögens- und Beteiligungsverwaltung mbH.

[11] This case study is based on 'Brothers in Arms', *The Economist*, 13 August 2005.

Chapter 3

The European Takeover Directive

Jeremy Grant

> *'We all want to go to Heaven, but nobody wants to die'*
> Jaap Winter, Chairman of the High-Level Group of Company Law
> Experts, on the passage of the European Takeover Directive

This chapter examines the background to the European Takeover Directive, particularly the major changes between the original drafts and the final version, and presents an amended version of the Directive itself, with commentary on the most important and controversial clauses.

Background to the Directive

In July 2001, after 12 years of consultation and the rejection by member states of various prior proposals, the European Commission put forward the 13th European Directive on Takeover Bids (DTB) to the European Parliament for approval. The proposal had become part of the Financial Services Action Plan (1999) following the introduction of the single European currency and was later endorsed by the member states as part of the Lisbon Agenda of March 2000, initiated to increase European competitiveness. The aim of the directive was to create an active market in corporate control and encourage further consolidation, creating firms with pan-European scope and scale. As the Commission stated in a later press release (European Commission Statement No.13, 2002):

> European-wide rules for takeover bids are considered vital to the objective of improving Europe's competitiveness, notably facilitating cross-border consolidation of industry. The Commission's aim is to create a vibrant takeover market, providing mechanisms for takeovers and changes in the management of poorly run firms, and reducing the scope for management to extract private benefits.

However, the directive was rejected by the European Parliament in a hung vote of 273 to 273 (see Exhibit 3.1). The primary objection of opponents of the directive, led by Germany, was the proposed ban on the enactment of post-bid defences, such as corporate restructurings or debt issuance, by managers and boards on the receiving end of a hostile offer. Other objections stated at the time were the perceived lack of a level playing field with the United States, due to the widespread availability of poison pills under US corporate law, and the lack of provision for employee consultation and protection. However, the issues in relation to the US were more imaginary than real as EU firms were acquiring far more in the United States at the time than vice versa (see Exhibit 3.2).

In response to the rejection, the Commission convened the High-Level Group (HLG) of Company Law Experts, chaired by Jaap Winter, to provide independent advice. In January 2002, the group issued its report, endorsing the Commission's attempt to adopt regulation of European M&A on the basis of the UK City Code on Takeovers and certain fundamental principles, many of which were contained in the original proposal. These included the following:

- there should be equality of treatment of all shareholders;
- partial bids for control should be banned through the use of mandatory bid thresholds;
- shareholders' decision making in relation to a tender offer should be made primary, through the requirement that all post-bid defences enacted by the board be subject to shareholder approval. The only frustrating

Exhibit 3.1

Outcome of the European parliamentary vote on the Takeover Directive

Countries	Votes for	Votes against
Germany	1	95
France	45	26
Italy	32	36
United Kingdom	72	6
Spain	26	31
Netherlands	9	22
Belgium	5	16
Greece	2	21
Portugal	19	1
Sweden	19	0
Austria	4	14
Denmark	13	0
Finland	11	2
Ireland	10	2
Luxembourg	5	1
Total:	273	273

Source: Adapted from 'The EU's 13th Directive on Takeover Bids: Unlucky for Some', Harvard Business School Case Study (2002).

Exhibit 3.2

Cross-border M&A

Foreign acquisitions of US firms (2000)

Country of origin of acquirer	Value of transaction (US$ billion)	Number of transactions
United Kingdom	78	313
Germany	48	138
Netherlands	39	71
France	28	87

Foreign acquisitions of EU firms by non-EU firms (2000)

Country of origin of acquirer	Value of transaction (US$ billion)	Number of transactions
United States	98.7	1,035
Japan	8.6	47
Canada	3.1	78
South Africa	2.5	32

Source: Adapted from 'The EU's 13th Directive on Takeover Bids: Unlucky for Some', Harvard Business School Case Study (2002).

measure boards should be able to undertake without shareholder approval would be to seek out competing bids;
- where there existed a separation of cash flow rights and voting rights through control devices such as dual-class shares, golden shares or voting ceilings, these should be reunified for the purposes of deciding the outcome of a takeover contest. This should be achieved by allowing the bidder to break through such devices when he had acquired 75 per cent of the cash flow rights of a firm. This was known as the 'breakthrough rule' (BTR); and
- squeeze-out and sell-out rules should be implemented.

Overall, the HLG endorsed the Commission's approach and called for a harmonisation of European takeover regulation and the creation of a level playing field between member states.

In October 2002, the Commission presented a new proposal based on the recommendations of the HLG. The proposal again provided for strict board neutrality when faced with a tender offer. It also added a breakthrough provision and rules on squeeze-outs and sell-outs. The revised version of the directive again met significant hostility, led by Germany, which, this time, was backed up by the Nordic member countries and France, where multiple share classes are common. These countries argued that they would be disproportionately penalised by the breakthrough clause. This was because the directive did not cover certain other devices that separate cash flow and voting rights, such as pyramids or non-voting shares. On the other hand, public dual-share classes are outlawed in Germany and German representatives in the European Parliament argued that the ban on post-bid defences would leave German firms particularly vulnerable to raiders, as many were protected only by cross-holdings, which were in the process of being unwound. Earlier legislation in Germany, the Control and Transparency Act (Kontrag, 1998), had outlawed most pre-bid defences, including voting ceilings and public multiple voting shares.

Eventually, the Commission was forced to introduce a series of exemptions as a political compromise to ensure that the directive was passed by the European Parliament. Member states are not required to adopt Article 9 (board neutrality) or Article 11 (breakthrough). They can also enact reciprocity provisions, thus denying firms from member states that have opted out from using Articles 9 and 11 the opportunity to take over firms that have opted in. If a state does not adopt them, firms within that state can go ahead and opt in. However, they would also have the option to opt out again if faced with a raider from a state that has opted out and the raider himself has not opted back in. Therefore, if a firm has opted out, it cannot use the breakthrough provision to acquire a firm that has opted in. Thus, every member state is faced with four choices:

- whether or not to implement the board neutrality rule (Article 9);
- whether or not to implement the reciprocity provisions in relation to board neutrality in cases where either the member state has opted in, or the state has opted out, but certain firms have opted in;
- whether or not to implement the BTR; and
- whether or not to implement reciprocity provisions in relation to the BTR, which can be opted into by both member states and individual firms.

These four options give member states 16 different regimes to choose from. Ultimately, it is argued that the DTB creates even greater variation and complexity in the market.

PART I: INSIDE THE TAKEOVER REGULATION AND TACTICS

The European Takeover Directive – amended, with commentary

DIRECTIVE 2004/25/EC OF THE EUROPEAN PARLIAMENT AND OF THE COUNCIL, 21 APRIL 2004, ON TAKEOVER BIDS

Article 1: Scope

1. This Directive lays down measures coordinating the laws, regulations, administrative provisions, codes of practice and other arrangements of the Member States, including arrangements established by organisations officially authorised to regulate the markets (hereinafter referred to as 'rules'), relating to takeover bids for the securities of companies governed by the laws of Member States ...

Article 3: General principles

1. For the purpose of implementing this Directive, Member States shall ensure that the following principles are complied with:

    (a) all holders of the securities of an offeree company of the same class must be afforded equivalent treatment; moreover, if a person acquires control of a company, the other holders of securities must be protected;

    Note – This clause exempts dual-share classes from equal pricing provisions. However, it establishes a general principle of equality among shareholders of the same class and protection from expropriation for minority shareholders.

    (b) the holders of the securities of an offeree company must have sufficient time and information to enable them to reach a properly informed decision on the bid; where it advises the holders of securities, the board of the offeree company must give its views on the effects of implementation of the bid on employment, conditions of employment and the locations of the company's places of business;
    (c) the board of an offeree company must act in the interests of the company as a whole and must not deny the holders of securities the opportunity to decide on the merits of the bid;

    Note – Establishes the principle of shareholder decision making; that the board should not create post-bid defences without shareholder consent. However, circumstances could arise in which there would be a divergence between an interpretation of 'the interests of the company', and the principle of shareholder decision-making which gives the owners the ultimate word on whether to accept a takeover bid or not. Article 9 was drafted to clarify the target firm's duties in such a situation by outlawing any frustrating actions by the target's board of directors, and therefore upholding the principle of shareholder decision making.

    (d) false markets must not be created in the securities of the offeree company, of the offeror company or of any other company concerned by the bid in such a way that the rise or fall of the prices of the securities becomes artificial and the normal functioning of the markets is distorted;

(e) an offeror must announce a bid only after ensuring that he/she can fulfil in full any cash consideration, if such is offered, and after taking all reasonable measures to secure the implementation of any other type of consideration;

(f) an offeree company must not be hindered in the conduct of its affairs for longer than is reasonable by a bid for its securities.

2. With a view to ensuring compliance with the principles laid down in paragraph 1, Member States:

(a) shall ensure that the minimum requirements set out in this Directive are observed;

(b) may lay down additional conditions and provisions more stringent than those of this Directive for the regulation of bids.

Note – Indicates that the Directive lays down only minimum requirements. Further national regulation may be necessary to regulate takeovers effectively.

Article 4: Supervisory authority and applicable law

1. Member States shall designate the authority or authorities competent to supervise bids for the purposes of the rules which they make or introduce pursuant to this Directive. The authorities thus designated shall be either public authorities, associations or private bodies recognised by national law or by public authorities expressly empowered for that purpose by national law. Member States shall inform the Commission of those designations, specifying any divisions of functions that may be made. They shall ensure that those authorities exercise their functions impartially and independently of all parties to a bid.

Note – Establishes the principles of impartiality and equality of treatment between domestic constituencies and foreign investors.

Article 5: Protection of minority shareholders, the mandatory bid and the equitable price

1. Where a natural or legal person, as a result of his/her own acquisition or the acquisition by persons acting in concert with him/her, holds securities of a company as referred to in Article 1(1) which, added to any existing holdings of those securities of his/hers and the holdings of those securities of persons acting in concert with him/her, directly or indirectly give him/her a specified percentage of voting rights in that company, giving him/her control of that company, Member States shall ensure that such a person is required to make a bid as a means of protecting the minority shareholders of that company. Such a bid shall be addressed at the earliest opportunity to all the holders of those securities for all their holdings at the equitable price as defined in paragraph 4.

2. Where control has been acquired following a voluntary bid made in accordance with this Directive to all the holders of securities for all their holdings, the obligation laid down in paragraph 1 to launch a bid shall no longer apply.

PART I: INSIDE THE TAKEOVER REGULATION AND TACTICS

3. The percentage of voting rights which confers control for the purposes of paragraph 1 and the method of its calculation shall be determined by the rules of the Member State in which the company has its registered office.

Note – This clause allows for variances in the MBT at the member state level. These vary at the national level from 20 per cent to 66 per cent. Luxembourg and The Netherlands have yet to introduce MBTs at the time of writing (summer 2005). However, the majority of member states, including the United Kingdom and Germany, set the MBT at 30 per cent. It has been argued that this level is too high and that control of a widely held firm can be gained at a lower threshold. In contrast, the SEC has a rebuttable presumption of control at 10 per cent of a widely held firm, although there is no federal MBT.

4. The highest price paid for the same securities by the offeror, or by persons acting in concert with him/her, over a period, to be determined by Member States, of not less than six months and not more than 12 before the bid referred to in paragraph 1 shall be regarded as the equitable price. If, after the bid has been made public and before the offer closes for acceptance, the offeror or any person acting in concert with him/her purchases securities at a price higher than the offer price, the offeror shall increase his/her offer so that it is not less than the highest price paid for the securities so acquired.

Note – The clause allows for flexibility at the member state level. For example, Germany and the United Kingdom require that the price be equal to the highest pre-bid price paid by the acquirer, while Italy sets the price as at least equal to the average of the share price in the 12 months prior to the bid and the highest price paid by the raider for any shares he has purchased.

Provided that the general principles laid down in Article 3(1) are respected, Member States may authorise their supervisory authorities to adjust the price referred to in the first subparagraph in circumstances and in accordance with criteria that are clearly determined. To that end, they may draw up a list of circumstances in which the highest price may be adjusted either upwards or downwards, for example where the highest price was set by agreement between the purchaser and a seller, where the market prices of the securities in question have been manipulated, where market prices in general or certain market prices in particular have been affected by exceptional occurrences, or in order to enable a firm in difficulty to be rescued. They may also determine the criteria to be applied in such cases, for example the average market value over a particular period, the break-up value of the company or other objective valuation criteria generally used in financial analysis. Any decision by a supervisory authority to adjust the equitable price shall be substantiated and made public.

Note – This clause gives substantial discretion to regulatory authorities at the national level, allowing a multi-criteria approach similar to that employed in France.

Article 9: Obligations of the board of the offeree company

1. Member States shall ensure that the rules laid down in paragraphs 2 to 5 are complied with.

2. During the period referred to in the second subparagraph, the board of the offeree company shall obtain the prior authorisation of the general meeting of shareholders given for this purpose before taking any action, other than seeking alternative bids, which may result in the frustration of the bid and in particular before issuing any shares which may result in a lasting impediment to the offeror's acquiring control of the offeree company. Such authorisation shall be mandatory at least from the time the board of the offeree company receives ... the bid and until the result of the bid is made public or the bid lapses. Member States may require that such authorisation be obtained at an earlier stage, for example as soon as the board of the offeree company becomes aware that the bid is imminent.

Note – Reinforces the earlier principle contained in Article 3(1c), that the target's board should not create post-bid defences without the consent of shareholders, and thus firmly entrenches the principle of shareholder decision making. Outlawed post-bid defences include corporate restructurings (major asset disposals: crown jewels, increased leverage), white knights/squires (who purchase a large block of stock to thwart the raider, but do not take control), poison pills (dilutive stock issuances) and Pac-man defences (where the target launches a bid for the raider).

3. As regards decisions taken before the beginning of the period referred to in the second subparagraph of paragraph 2 and not yet partly or fully implemented, the general meeting of shareholders shall approve or confirm any decision which does not form part of the normal course of the company's business and the implementation of which may result in the frustration of the bid.
4. For the purpose of obtaining the prior authorisation, approval or confirmation of the holders of securities referred to in paragraphs 2 and 3, Member States may adopt rules allowing a general meeting of shareholders to be called at short notice, provided that the meeting does not take place within two weeks of notification being given.

Note – The clause places decision making regarding an offer firmly with the general meeting of shareholders. However, significant discretion is retained by the member states in terms of process and levels of approval. For example, Italian corporate law requires the approval of one third of shareholders, while the UK City Code virtually prohibits all post-bid defences without majority shareholder approval. The divergence is further heightened when the regulation is put into the context of national ownership structures. For example, large publicly held firms in Italy have a dominant shareholder with at least 30 per cent of voting rights; conversely, most large listed UK firms are widely held.

5. The board of the offeree company shall draw up and make public a document setting out its opinion of the bid and the reasons on which it is based, including its views on the effects of implementation of the bid on all the company's interests and specifically employment, and on the offeror's strategic plans for the offeree company and their likely repercussions on employment and the locations of the company's places of business as set out in the offer document.

Note – Requires the directors of the target company to issue a public opinion on the offer to advise shareholders and employees.

PART I: INSIDE THE TAKEOVER REGULATION AND TACTICS

Article 10: Information on companies as referred to in Article 1(1)

Note – Article 10 requires disclosure of all takeover defences and devices that have been adopted for commercial purposes and could be used as defences (embedded defences).

1. Member States shall ensure that companies as referred to in Article 1(1) publish detailed information on the following:

    (a) the structure of their capital, including securities which are not admitted to trading on a regulated market in a Member State, where appropriate with an indication of the different classes of shares and, for each class of shares, the rights and obligations attaching to it and the percentage of total share capital that it represents;
    (b) any restrictions on the transfer of securities, such as limitations on the holding of securities or the need to obtain the approval of the company or other holders of securities, without prejudice to Article 46 of Directive 2001/34/EC;
    (c) significant direct and indirect shareholdings (including indirect shareholdings through pyramid structures and cross-shareholdings) within the meaning of Article 85 of Directive 2001/34/EC;
    (d) the holders of any securities with special control rights and a description of those rights;

    Note – Refers primarily to government-held 'golden shares', which have special rights attached.

    (e) the system of control of any employee share scheme where the control rights are not exercised directly by the employees;
    (f) any restrictions on voting rights, such as limitations of the voting rights of holders of a given percentage or number of votes, deadlines for exercising voting rights, or systems whereby, with the company's cooperation, the financial rights attaching to securities are separated from the holding of securities;
    (g) any agreements between shareholders which are known to the company and may result in restrictions on the transfer of securities and/or voting rights within the meaning of Directive 2001/34/EC;
    (h) the rules governing the appointment and replacement of board members and the amendment of the articles of association;
    (i) the powers of board members, and in particular the power to issue or buy back shares;
    (j) any significant agreements to which the company is a party and which take effect, alter or terminate upon a change of control of the company following a takeover bid, and the effects thereof, except where their nature is such that their disclosure would be seriously prejudicial to the company; this exception shall not apply where the company is specifically obliged to disclose such information on the basis of other legal requirements;

    Note – Requires disclosure of embedded defences.

    (k) any agreements between the company and its board members or employees providing for compensation if they resign or are made redundant without valid reason or if their employment ceases because of a takeover bid.

    Note – Requires disclosure of golden and tin parachutes.

Article 11: Breakthrough

1. Without prejudice to other rights and obligations provided for in Community law for the companies referred to in Article 1(1), Member States shall ensure that the provisions laid down in paragraphs 2 to 7 apply when a bid has been made public.

2. Any restrictions on the transfer of securities provided for in the articles of association of the offeree company shall not apply vis-à-vis the offeror during the time allowed for acceptance of the bid.

    Any restrictions on the transfer of securities provided for in contractual agreements between the offeree company and holders of its securities, or in contractual agreements between holders of the offeree company's securities entered into after the adoption of this Directive, shall not apply vis-à-vis the offeror during the time allowed for acceptance of the bid.

    Note – This clause outlaws share transfer restrictions contained in either the target's articles of association or via subsequent contract with shareholders in relation to a takeover offer.

3. Restrictions on voting rights provided for in the articles of association of the offeree company shall not have effect at the general meeting of shareholders which decides on any defensive measures in accordance with Article 9. Restrictions on voting rights provided for in contractual agreements between the offeree company and holders of its securities, or in contractual agreements between holders of the offeree company's securities entered into after the adoption of this Directive, shall not have effect at the general meeting of shareholders which decides on any defensive measures in accordance with Article 9. Multiple-vote securities shall carry only one vote each at the general meeting of shareholders which decides on any defensive measures in accordance with Article 9.

    Note – Applies the principle of one share, one vote to the general meeting of shareholders convened to approve post-bid defences, invalidates ceilings on voting rights and limits multiple-voting shares to one vote each in this meeting.

4. Where, following a bid, the offeror holds 75 per cent or more of the capital carrying voting rights, no restrictions on the transfer of securities or on voting rights referred to in paragraphs 2 and 3 nor any extraordinary rights of shareholders concerning the appointment or removal of board members provided for in the articles of association of the offeree company shall apply; multiple-vote securities shall carry only one vote each at the first general meeting of shareholders following closure of the bid, called by the offeror in order to amend the articles of association or to remove or appoint board members. To that end, the offeror shall have the right to convene a general meeting of shareholders at short notice, provided that the meeting does not take place within two weeks of notification.

    Note – The highly controversial BTR allows a raider who has acquired 75 per cent of the cash flow rights of a firm to 'break through' certain other voting rights restrictions at the first general shareholders' meeting following bid closure. These restrictions on voting rights include share transfer restrictions, ceilings on voting rights, extraordinary powers of certain shareholders to appoint directors and securities with multiple-voting rights. The aim of the clause is to facilitate control by the raider of the firm through the removal of the incumbent board and the alteration of the articles of association at the shareholders' meeting. However, the clause was subsequently criticised for excluding from the BTR certain other devices that separate cash flow from voting rights, such as pyramid ownership structures (prevalent in France, Germany and Italy), non-voting shares and French double voting shares for long-term shareholders. It has also been pointed out that this provision could be evaded by European firms shifting their state of incorporation, exchanging dual-class shares for pyramid structures or issuing non-voting shares.

5. Where rights are removed on the basis of paragraphs 2, 3, or 4 and/or Article 12, equitable compensation shall be provided for any loss suffered by the holders of those rights. The terms for determining such compensation and the arrangements for its payment shall be set by Member States.

Note – The report of the HLG, upon which Article 11 is based, did not provide for compensation to shareholders who lost multiple voting rights. This clause allows member states great latitude in determining compensation, but it also invites a host of problems as to its quantification.

6. Paragraphs 3 and 4 shall not apply to securities where the restrictions on voting rights are compensated for by specific pecuniary advantages.

Note – Exempts preferred shares and certain other hybrid securities from the BTR on the basis of their position over ordinary shares in the hierarchy of dividend payouts. It is not clear, however, whether these are to be counted towards the 75 per cent threshold of cash flow rights or not.

7. This Article shall not apply either where Member States hold securities in the offeree company which confer special rights on the Member States which are compatible with the Treaty, or to special rights provided for in national law which are compatible with the Treaty or to cooperatives.

Note – This clause exempts golden shares held by governments of member states from the BTR. However, the exemption applies only where such golden shares are 'compatible' with member states' treaty obligations. This is particularly important point because the European Court of Justice has found that such arrangements are incompatible with the free movement of capital within the EU (see, for instance, Case C-438/99: Commission vs. France).

Article 12: Optional arrangements

Note – The following article allows member states to opt out of the provisions relating to: (1) the necessity to acquire shareholder approval for post-bid defences (Article 9(2) and (3)); and (2) the BTR (Article 11). These protectionist measures were inserted into the Directive primarily at the insistence of Germany, in return for not blocking the passage of the Directive itself in the European Parliament.

1. Member States may reserve the right not to require companies as referred to in Article 1(1) which have their registered offices within their territories to apply Article 9(2) and (3) and/or Article 11.

   Note – Allows member states to opt out of Article 9 and 11.

2. Where Member States make use of the option provided for in paragraph 1, they shall nevertheless grant companies which have their registered offices within their territories the option, which shall be reversible, of applying Article 9(2) and (3) and/or Article 11, without prejudice to Article 11(7). The decision of the company shall be taken by the general meeting of shareholders, in accordance with the law of the Member State in which the company has its registered office in accordance with the rules applicable to amendment of the articles of association. The decision shall be communicated to the supervisory authority of the Member State in which the company has its registered office and to all the supervisory authorities of Member States in which its securities are admitted to trading on regulated markets or where such admission has been requested.

   Note – Firms within member states that have opted out of Articles 9 and 11 can opt back into either Article 9 or Article 11, or both. The decision to opt back in, and to which of these Articles, is to be taken by the general meeting of shareholders during the 18-month period before the bid (see Article 12, section 5, below).

3. Member States may, under the conditions determined by national law, exempt companies which apply Article 9(2) and (3) and/or Article 11 from applying Article 9(2) and (3) and/or Article 11 if they become the subject of an offer launched by a company which does not apply the same Articles as they do, or by a company controlled, directly or indirectly, by the latter, pursuant to Article 1 of Directive 83/349/EEC.

   Note – This is a reciprocity clause: if a firm that has opted back into Articles 9 and/or 11 is subject to a takeover offer from another firm from a member state that has opted out and that firm itself has not opted back in, then the acquirer cannot use Articles 9 and 11 in relation to its bid. Again, this decision to apply reciprocity has to be taken by the member state and by the firm – in the latter, specifically by the general meeting of shareholders in the 18-month period before the bid (see Article 12, section 5, below).

4. Member States shall ensure that the provisions applicable to the respective companies are disclosed without delay.
5. Any measure applied in accordance with paragraph 3 shall be subject to the authorisation of the general meeting of shareholders of the offeree company, which must be granted no earlier than 18 months before the bid was made public in accordance with Article 6(1).

Article 13: Other rules applicable to the conduct of bids

Member States shall also lay down rules which govern the conduct of bids, at least as regards the following:

(a) the lapsing of bids;
(b) the revision of bids;
(c) competing bids;
(d) the disclosure of the results of bids;
(e) the irrevocability of bids and the conditions permitted.

Note – Allows member states significant autonomy in dealing with these issues, for example in relation to the revision of bids.

Article 15: The right of squeeze-out

1. Member States shall ensure that, following a bid made to all the holders of the offeree company's securities for all of their securities, paragraphs 2 to 5 apply.
2. Member States shall ensure that an offeror is able to require all the holders of the remaining securities to sell him/her those securities at a fair price. Member States shall introduce that right in one of the following situations:

   (a) where the offeror holds securities representing not less than 90 per cent of the capital carrying voting rights and 90 per cent of the voting rights in the offeree company; or
   (b) where, following acceptance of the bid, he/she has acquired or has firmly contracted to acquire securities representing not less than 90 per cent of the offeree company's capital carrying voting rights and 90 per cent of the voting rights comprised in the bid.
   In the case referred to in (a), Member States may set a higher threshold that may not, however, be higher than 95 per cent of the capital carrying voting rights and 95 per cent of the voting rights.

   Note – This clause allows for some variance at the member state level in the squeeze out threshold between 90 per cent and 95 per cent. Most states set the threshold at either 90 per cent or 95 per cent, but some differ substantially. For example, the threshold in Ireland is 80 per cent and in Italy it is 98 per cent, while some member states, such as Spain, do not have squeeze-out rights, but other devices that function to similar effect.

3. Member States shall ensure that rules are in force that make it possible to calculate when the threshold is reached. Where the offeree company has issued more than one class of securities, Member States may provide that the right of squeeze-out can be exercised only in the class in which the threshold laid down in paragraph 2 has been reached.
4. If the offeror wishes to exercise the right of squeeze-out he/she shall do so within three months of the end of the time allowed for acceptance of the bid.
5. Member States shall ensure that a fair price is guaranteed. That price shall take the same form as the consideration offered in the bid or shall be in cash. Member States may provide that cash shall be offered at least as an alternative. Following a voluntary bid, in both of the cases referred to in paragraph 2(a) and (b), the consideration offered in the bid shall be presumed to be fair where, through acceptance of the bid, the offeror has acquired securities representing not less than 90 per cent of the capital carrying voting rights comprised in the bid. Following a mandatory bid, the consideration offered in the bid shall be presumed to be fair.

Note – Minority shareholders being squeezed out are to be offered a fair price. Where the threshold has been met, the tender offer price is presumed to be fair. However, the wording of this clause leaves room for setting a price different from the tender offer price. In some member states, such as Germany, a statutory merger can achieve the same squeeze-out effect. However, this can be initiated at a much lower threshold (75 per cent in Germany) than a squeeze-out and without strict fair pricing provisions.

Article 16: The right of sell-out

1. Member States shall ensure that, following a bid made to all the holders of the offeree company's securities for all of their securities, paragraphs 2 and 3 apply.
2. Member States shall ensure that a holder of remaining securities is able to require the offeror to buy his/her securities from him/her at a fair price under the same circumstances as provided for in Article 15(2).
3. Article 15(3) to (5) shall apply *mutatis mutandis*.

Note – Many member states, including Spain, Italy and Austria, do not currently have sell-out rights.

Article 17: Sanctions

Member States shall determine the sanctions to be imposed for infringement of the national measures adopted pursuant to this Directive and shall take all necessary steps to ensure that they are put into effect. The sanctions thus provided for shall be effective, proportionate and dissuasive. Member States shall notify the Commission of those measures no later than the date laid down in Article 21(1) and of any subsequent change thereto at the earliest opportunity.

Article 21: Transposition

Member States shall bring into force the laws, regulations and administrative provisions necessary to comply with this Directive no later than 20 May 2006.

Note – This is the deadline for compliance by all 25 member states.

Chapter 4

Takeovers in Europe – shareholder decisions and open markets – a UK perspective[1]

Jonathan Rickford[2]
The Company Law Centre, British Institute of International and Comparative Law, London

Introduction: regulating takeovers – property rights and wider objectives

This chapter offers a perspective from a UK point of view on the 'breakthrough' provisions of the European Directive on Takeovers[3] and their relation with the provisions on shareholder decision making and board neutrality. These provisions sit at the centre of a highly charged policy debate about the desirable shape and structure of the markets for capital, corporate control and corporate management services within the EU.

The policy considerations supporting the regulation of mergers[4] fall into two sets: the protection of investors and the facilitation (or impeding) of mergers. The case for the former is largely uncontroversial, but the latter raises rival imperatives. On the one hand, regulators may favour industrial restructuring and liquid markets in corporate control and management services, but, on the other, rival policies are in play. These include mercantilist and protectionist policies (misguided or not) favouring company continuity of management and ethos, conservation of control of corporate resources (whether at management, shareholder or political level) and conservation of employment, within national or state jurisdictions.[5]

The relevant market failures to be addressed by regulation are not controversial in the case of investor protection. These are primarily: inadequate information and time leading to pressured and ill-judged decisions by target shareholders, preferential bidding excluding weaker investors/outsiders, harassment of company operations by bidders and interference with the market process by conflicted managers in both bidders and targets.

Opinions may differ on what market failures are to be addressed in the case of policies impeding or facilitating mergers. In particular, national economic objectives may require protection of claimed legitimate externalities. A degree of obstruction, or at least slowing, of market processes may thus be regarded as necessary to achieve a legitimate public good, but these arguments are open to serious objections based on the Treaty provisions on free movement of capital and establishment, which are designed precisely to oppose many such assertions of national (and nationalist) economic policy.[6]

All these conflicting considerations underlie the new EU merger regime.

The two main models of merger regulation are described below. Both tend to be characterised by reference to the investor protection objective. While the facilitation dimension is inevitably addressed by all systems and there is a trade-off between it and investor protection, that dimension tends to be less specifically addressed.[7] However, in the case of the European regime it is explicitly stated as an objective.[8] It was recognised as such throughout the development of the Directive and in particular from the revival of the financial services and corporate law action plans, which were triggered by the Lisbon Council declaration on competitiveness in 2000.[9]

The two possible existing models of merger regulation available to Europe were the UK ('City Code') model and the US model; Europe opted for the former. This relies on continuous *a priori* regulation of mergers by an expert, hands-on regulator, shareholder freedom of decision making with full information, within a regulated timetable, and its necessary correlative, target board neutrality. The US model, on the other hand, relies, for target shareholder protection, on the exercise by boards of essentially their normal operational powers. Shareholders and other investors and bidders must intervene through the courts to discipline these boards' activities and in particular to secure protection against the inevitable conflicts of interest for directors seeking to protect their own position or extract rents from the transaction.

The UK emphasis on shareholder decision making has much in common with the traditional Continental European approach to the governance of restructuring, through consensual mergers, which is also based on strong versions of such decision making rules.[10] On the other hand, the UK emphasis on freedom of property and contractual rights for target company shareholders conflicts with widespread, if perhaps vague, Continental theories favouring the stakeholder orientation of company governance. These regard such governance as in part designed to serve a wider public good. Such theories are also, perhaps surprisingly, reflected in US theory, which regards the company board as in some sense an independent mandatory of the state with a wider stakeholder-oriented remit.[11]

The Directive is perhaps somewhat ambiguous on this critical question, in that it incorporates, as a key overriding principle ('General Principle (c)'), that:

> the board of an offeree company must act in the interests [sic] of the company *and* must not deny the holders of securities the opportunity to decide on the merits of the bid.[12]

The overall investor protection philosophy of the Directive is clearly based on the first principle, shareholder decision making, set out in the Report of the Commission's advisory High Level Group (known as the 'Winter Report' after its chairman),[13] from which these Directive provisions derive, and thus on freedom of contract and freedom of property rights for shareholders. This principle emerges both in General Principle (c) and in the neutrality rule in Article 9 of the Directive. That Article provides that boards may, during a bid period, only take actions which may result in frustration of the bid with the prior authorisation of a general meeting of shareholders, often referred to as the meeting to authorise 'defensive measures'.

However, the Winter Report was also animated by the need to achieve takeover facilitation,[14] which required that where contractual and property rights were exercised in ways which inhibited 'legitimate' bids these rights should be broken through. Thus the breakthrough provision embodies an enhanced, idealised, or paternalistically imposed, freedom of shareholders based on a defined optimal redistribution of rights, described as a breaking through of 'restrictions'. This is intended to achieve, in takeover situations, the second Winter principle of proportionality (sometimes simplistically described as 'one share, one vote'). Thus the 'successful' bidder (defined broadly as a bidder who has, wholly or in part by virtue of the bid, achieved a 75 per cent holding)[15] should be able to exercise the rights over the company which would have accrued to him if the cash flow rights, or risk, which he has acquired were reflected in proportionate control. This in its ideal form requires that all 'disproportionate restrictions' should therefore be broken, or rather replaced with proportionate provisions. These must operate both during the takeover period (to ensure that defensive measures are only authorised on the basis of a proportionate authority) and after the threshold of success has been achieved by the bidder. At this stage a special meeting (the 'post-breakthrough meeting') can be called by the bidder to put in place his preferred control mechanisms.

This principle, proportionality, even in its pure form as proposed by Winter, raises a number of fundamental difficulties.[16] It is also adopted in the Directive in a severely curtailed form and made optional, giving rise to further difficulties and uncertainties. Both the curtailment and the optionality show less than full commitment by the EU legislature to takeover facilitation and the Winter principles.

Thus the investor-protection mechanisms, of shareholder decision making and board neutrality, and the merger-facilitating, breakthrough policy emerge in the Directive against an ambivalent background. There is ambivalence not only on company purposes and the legitimacy of ultimate shareholder control, but also on the facilitating of mergers in open, state and inter-state, markets.

The remainder of this chapter examines the effects of this modified implementation of the breakthrough principle (sometimes called 'mini-breakthrough') and its inter-play with the neutrality, or shareholder decision making, component of the new EU regime.

Breakthrough: restrictions and threshold

We have noted that breakthrough is characterised as the breaking of the target's restrictions on proportionality of cash flow rights and control rights when a certain threshold of success has been achieved by the bidder.

The definitions of the restrictions to be broken and of the threshold when they are fully broken are found in Article 11. Some restrictions are to be broken for any meeting called to authorise defensive measures, some for the post-breakthrough meeting when the successful bidder is empowered to reorder the company, some for the whole of the offer period and some for that period and thereafter. Article 11 also indicates the threshold of success, when ongoing breakthrough is to be achieved.

'Restrictions'

As for restrictions, broadly speaking (Article 11(2)–(4)):

- restrictions on free transfer (including, apparently, limits on holdings) of target company securities, whether incorporated in the articles or in certain contracts[17] are all suspended 'vis-à-vis the offeror',[18] both during the offer period and thereafter if the offeror has achieved the threshold (Article 11(2) and (4));
- 'restrictions on voting rights', included in the articles, or such contracts, are also suspended and 'multiple voting securities' carry one vote only, for the relevant meetings, in other

words, the defensive measures authorisation and post-breakthrough meetings (Article 11(3) and (4)); and
- 'extraordinary rights'[19] of shareholders to appoint, or remove, board members are not to apply at any time after the bidder achieves the threshold (Article 11(4)).

Various anomalies emerge in the way these provisions relate to multiple voting securities, non-voting securities and securities carrying preferential rights.

Multiple voting securities

'Multiple voting securities' are to carry only 'one vote each'[20] at both defensive and post-breakthrough meetings, but it seems that only a limited range of voting distortions is covered by this provision. To qualify as 'multiple voting securities' securities must be of a 'distinct and separate' (sic) class – an unexpected result, achieved not in Article 11, but in the definitions in Article 2(1)(g). Thus, for example, the typical French 'ceiling' or 'time lapse voting' shares, which are only fully enfranchised after a holding period, are not caught, because while the voting rights of such shares will vary from time to time, according to the contingency of the duration of a holding, they remain of the same class.[21] This device is sometimes justified on the grounds that it rewards 'loyal' or 'long-term' shareholders, but the effect is to entrench boards and incumbent shareholders. It clearly infringes the proportionality principle and inhibits takeovers, rendering them more costly and commercially unattractive (typically ensuring that the bidder acquiring such a share obtains a diluted control right unless he is able to wait for up to four years for the shares to be fully enfranchised).

However, separate classes of multiple voting shares of the kind common in Scandinavia and not unknown in the United Kingdom (often referred to as Class A and Class B shares) are broken.[22] It is not entirely clear how multiple vote shares of different classes are to be enfranchised, for example suppose that there are two classes of share of £1 nominal with one vote and of £3 nominal with six votes are the latter to carry one vote, or three? The proportionate approach seems clearly right in principle, but it is not consistent with the language of the directive ('one vote each').

Non-voting securities

Non-voting shares are apparently not subject to the breakthrough principle. It is clear that non-voting equity contravenes proportionality. To satisfy the principle it needs both to count as risk capital for assessing the bidder's achievement of the threshold and it needs to be appropriately enfranchised to carry its proper weight at both meetings, both in the hands of the offeror and in the hands of others, whether sympathetic to the offeror or not. Threshold issues are considered below, but as to the second of these needs, enfranchisement, it is reasonably clear that it is not met.

There are a number of reasons for this conclusion. First, as a matter of language, it is hard to regard the absence of a vote as a 'restriction on voting rights' to be overridden under Article 11(3). Voting rights on non-voting securities are not 'restricted', they are just absent (and have never arisen). Secondly, if it was intended to include non-voting securities, provision would be needed to indicate how many votes non-voting shares should get if, as will normally be the case, they are of a different class from voting shares. Perhaps, however, this deficiency could be remedied by adopting a proportionate approach, as suggested above for multiple voting securities. Thirdly, and most conclusively, such an outcome seems impossible to reconcile with the Directive definition of 'securities' as limited to voting securities in Article 2(1)(e). The Directive is full of provisions providing protection only to holders of such 'securities'. Most significantly in the context of breakthrough, restrictions on transfer, including limits on holdings, are broken through only for such 'securities', that is, such restrictions on non-voting securities are not overridden. The restrictions on voting rights in the articles appear at first sight possibly (the language point apart) to be breakable whether the securities in question are voting or not, because there is no express linkage to 'securities' in Article 11(3), first sentence, which governs this, but those in contracts are quite clearly broken only if they are on voting securities: see Article 11(3), second sentence, which requires the contracts in question to be with 'holders of securities'. The inevitable (for the sake of consistency), though surprising, conclusion seems to be that 'restrictions on voting rights' can, as the language indeed suggests, only arise on voting securities. The combination of these three arguments seems conclusive. Non-voting securities do not, therefore, get the benefit of the breakthrough provision in the sense of having votes conferred upon them, even though they may carry cash flow risk.

Thus non-voting securities are not enfranchised in the hands of the offeror in the post-breakthrough meeting, nor can the offeror, or others sympathetic to the offer, exercise votes on such shares in the meeting called to authorise defensive measures. A company which renders itself bid-proof by keeping voting shares in the hands of the board and its supporters and issuing non-voting equity to others is not vulnerable to breakthrough in that respect.

I understand that securities that are not shares, and therefore can carry no votes, but carry equity risk, through a right to participate in profits, are common in some countries. Thus 'enjoyment rights' (*Genussrechte*)[23] are increasingly used in Germany and constitute a means of avoiding the one share, one vote principle which applies now to almost all German public companies.[24] These too are apparently, because they are not voting securities, not subject to breakthrough though they may require annual disclosure under the special control disclosure regime in Article 10.[25]

Securities with preferential rights
Article 11(6) excludes certain preference-type securities from certain breakthrough provisions. It provides that securities to which breakthrough rules on voting restrictions apply – that is, for the purpose of adjusting rights during the offer period and/or removing restrictions once the breakthrough threshold has been achieved – do not include 'securities where the restrictions on voting are compensated for by specific pecuniary advantages'. It seems that a company can, in this sense, continue to be bid-proofed by issuing equity with limited voting rights and with, for example, a dividend preference, however small.[26] It is less clear whether acceptances of an offer for such preferential equity will count towards the breakthrough threshold; however I am now inclined (in agreement with the UK government's announced intentions on the threshold, see below) to believe that it will.[27]

Threshold

There are also problems on the definition of the threshold for breakthrough and the concept of risk capital in that connection. Article 11(4) merely provides that 'where the offeror holds 75 per cent of the capital carrying voting rights' this allows the offeror to call the post-breakthrough meeting. This makes it quite clear that acceptances of offers for non-voting shares do not count towards achievement of the breakthrough threshold (consistently with the analysis of restrictions above), but it is not clear how the 75 per cent share of voting capital is to be determined where there are more than one class of voting share.

Perhaps the most obvious possible criteria are nominal value or voting power. A third, less objective and orthodox, criterion is market value. As to the first two possibilities, if multiple voting shares and single voting shares have the same nominal value, is the achievement of 75 per cent to be assessed by reference to their aggregate nominal value or rather to the aggregate of voting rights acquired? Presumably, it would not be consistent with the Directive for member states to implement it by treating '75 per cent of the capital carrying voting rights' as meaning either (i) 'capital carrying 75 per cent of the voting rights', or perhaps even (ii) 'capital carrying 75 per cent of the voting rights at the post breakthrough meeting'. Yet weighting the capital acquired by reference to nominal value seems to lead to the anomaly that in determining whether the 75 per cent threshold has been achieved a French 'ceiling' share can be treated as weighted according to its nominal value, but at the post-breakthrough meeting its actual voting power is to remain restricted, because it is not a 'multiple voting right' share. Arguments of consistency point towards interpretation (ii) above, but it is probably unsustainable.

This is amongst the issues to be resolved by member states when they come to implement. The UK government proposes to adopt the third possible approach mentioned above, that is, to define the threshold by the value of the voting securities acquired (including shares such as preference shares, which carry the right to vote only in certain circumstances, such as when a preferential dividend is in arrears).[28] This seems to be permitted by the Directive.[29] It is arguably also the interpretation most consistent with the theory underlying the proportionality principle (on the basis that market values reflect future cash flow rights). It will, however, give rise to valuation problems at the margin, at least where a class of voting shares is not quoted. It will also again produce the anomalous result, mentioned above for the nominal value approach, in some cases, that is, where voting preference shares count towards the threshold, but do not count towards the votes available to the bidder, whether at the defensive measures or at the post-threshold meetings.

Conclusions on restrictions and threshold

By way of conclusion on the Directive definitions of the restrictions to be broken through and the threshold to be achieved to allow such breakthrough, it seems fair to reflect that the rules seem to be complex, arbitrary, obscure and highly imperfect in achieving the desired result.[30] Arguably, they discriminate unfairly between different devices with equivalent effect which operate in different member states. A cynic might conclude that the larger states, France, Germany and the United Kingdom, successfully exempted their national practices – delayed ceiling voting, preferential and non-voting shares respectively – while Scandinavian countries, where multiple voting shares in separate classes are common, failed to achieve a similar escape. The proposed UK implementing measures do not generally adopt a position on the difficulties of interpretation mentioned above. They simply require that before a UK company can opt in to breakthrough, its constitution must satisfy the Directive requirements, either in all circumstances, or at least in circumstances where the Directive disapplies them.[31]

Breakthrough – compensation, jurisdiction and mandatory bids

The other main issues on the content of the breakthrough regime relate to compensation for loss of restriction rights, the implications of the Directive rules on jurisdiction, that is, which national authority is to regulate the various aspects of a takeover with international characteristics, and the effect of the enhanced rights of bidders as a result of breakthrough on the mandatory bid regime, which is a central part of the investor protection provisions of the Directive.

Compensation

Article 11(5) provides a right to 'equitable compensation' for removal of rights as a result of the breakthrough rules (including the voluntary adoption by companies of breakthrough as the result of the optional provisions in Article 12, discussed below). This gives rise to issues about quantum and timing.

Compensation – quantum

First, how is this compensation to be assessed? Is it to reflect the private benefits achievable by exercising block-holder power – arguably a price for insiders' looting opportunities and not a basis to be recognised in law? It is sometimes argued, as an alternative, that shares with enhanced control rights carry a premium to reflect the benefit to outsiders of such block-holder governance, but it is not clear that these two arguments are really distinct. Special rights holders may indeed be regarded as entitled to a preferential share of the enterprise value at the outsiders' expense to reflect the benefits to outsiders of 'block-holder' control, but if the market attaches a premium to special rights shares, this can only be because the market expects cash-flow advantages (in the shape of private benefits) to flow from their holding. Whatever the merits of that debate, the bidder's passing of the threshold surely indicates that in the judgement of the members the incumbent management has failed to achieve a competitive performance. This would indicate that the insiders/controllers have failed to secure any advantages to the company as a whole which were envisaged as the *quid pro quo* for dilution of the outsiders' control. If so, any such implicit bargain to reward block-holders for governance advantages has failed and no compensation is justified, or 'equitable' in Directive terms. Market valuations may perhaps reflect either of these considerations, private benefits to block-holders or benefits conferred by block-holders on outsiders. Perhaps there is merely a less precise recognition that control confers benefits at the expense of outsiders, which are permissible within the overall flexible framework of discretionary operational control and business judgement, but it should be noted that this is hardly consistent with the overall philosophy of the Directive: a control premium is denied under the mandatory bid rule,[32] which seems inconsistent with recognition of a premium for control blocks.

Whatever the merits of these arguments and their implications for quantifying compensation (if any), compensation is now mandatory for 'any loss suffered' under Articles 11 and 12. The terms and modalities are to be set by member states.

Compensation – timing

There appear also to be problems about timing of the fixing of such compensation. Because of the difficulties of quantifying it the member states are likely to set up some mechanism of arbitration, appraisal or adjudication. This will have the additional attraction of avoiding the need to settle quantum issues at the implementation stage, but such processes are likely to be controversial and time consuming. Are they to take place before the offer can proceed, in which case the delays are likely to kill the viability of the breakthrough mechanism, or after the event?

Article 6(3)(e) indicates that a bidder who wishes to rely on breakthrough must make an offer of compensation in advance. This provision requires the offer document to state, *inter alia*, 'the compensation offered for the rights which might be removed as a result of the breakthrough rule', with particulars of how it is to be paid and the method to be employed in determining it, but it is difficult to understand how this provision for an offer of compensation in the offer document is intended to work.

The legislative objective is that the shareholders whose shares are not acquired should have their rights broken through and it is difficult to follow how the level of compensation to be given to them can be made the subject of a contractual offer. Where an offer is addressed to shareholders whose rights might be broken through, and such shareholders accept the offer, no issue of equitable compensation for them can arise. Moreover, since the Directive requires equivalent treatment of shareholders of the same class, it is difficult to see how one set of shareholders with special rights could be awarded compensation for breakthrough while another set achieves merely the offer price for voluntary surrender of their rights.[33]

On the other hand, where such an offer is made, the costs of compensating the shareholders whose rights are to be broken through will depend on how many of them accept the offer. General Principle (e) in Article 2(1) of the Directive, which corresponds to General Principle 3 in the City Code, requires that the offeror should be sure that he has access to the finances needed to complete the offer. How can this be achieved with no certainty as to the cost of breakthrough? Although the offer of compensation is required in the offer document, this may not be accepted. Some form of ex post-adjudication or appraisal will still be required to achieve an equitable measure of compensation. Indeed, what that measure is may depend in part on the extent to which shareholders with special rights, and perhaps others who are not shareholders, have accepted the offer in the offer document.

Compensation and class rights

As we shall see below, member states are free to opt out of the breakthrough rule, but if they do companies are to be given the option to opt back in, so as to subject themselves voluntarily to the regime. This is to be done by resolution in general meeting in accordance with the law applicable to amendment of the articles of association.[34] Many, but not all of the necessary changes, which will be required to remove special rights which are to be overridden by the adoption of the breakthrough regime, will be rights attaching to a class of shares. Variations of companies' articles in most systems require special majorities of the class affected to authorise such alterations of their rights.

So in the case of such rights, if the member state in question adopts the optional approach to breakthrough, the problems of compensation can, arguably, be solved in advance by consent. Special resolutions of meetings of the classes affected will be required and if these are carried then there is no longer a case for equitable compensation in respect of the rights waived or modified. The UK government proposes to adopt this route.[35] It is an elegant solution, but open to objection on two possible scores. The first objection is that the Directive is intended to facilitate mergers by creating favourable conditions for bidders and the imposition of an additional resolution over and above the standard resolution required for altering the articles is an impermissible additional impediment. The second objection is that the Directive requires that all rights holders should be allowed equitable compensation and the solution proposed may not be equitable for the minority dissentients in the class meetings. These arguments deserve consideration,[36] but they are not persuasive. First, the reference in

Article 12 to the rules for varying the articles must include all the relevant rules, including special rules in class rights cases and, secondly, a qualified majority acceptance of whatever terms have been set for the variation of rights may legitimately be regarded as providing an indication of the equitability of those terms, satisfying the Directive test of equitable compensation for all. General company law provisions protect minorities from unfair treatment at the hands of the majority.

However, unfortunately, even if this conclusion is correct, this solution to the problem both of quantum and of timing of compensation for loss of rights through breakthrough is incomplete. It does not deal with rights which are not class rights of shareholders. Parties to agreements with rights restricting the transfer of shares will not necessarily be shareholders and their rights are normal contractual ones, rather than rights under the articles. They are not, therefore, protected by the class rights provisions. For this reason, the UK government's proposal includes special provisions allowing the holders of such rights to apply to the court for compensation for the breakthrough of their rights.[37] Unfortunately, a scheme providing for the consent of such rights holders, similar to the regime for class rights holders, does not look consistent with the Directive.[38]

The implementation of the provisions for compensation for breakthrough looks likely to present formidable problems for the member states, particularly for those which do not opt out of Article 11. As we shall see below, all member states have an inescapable obligation to make such provision as a result of the provisions of Article 12 on options.

Jurisdiction

The Directive rules on jurisdiction may also raise issues in the breakthrough context.

Article 4(2) provides, to simplify somewhat, that where a company is formed[39] in one member state, but only listed in another or others, the member state of listing is to have jurisdiction in such matters as the bid price, bid procedure, the offer document and disclosure of the bid, but the state of formation is to have jurisdiction on employee matters and 'company law' matters, such as the definition of control and the conditions under which frustrating board action is to be allowed. In such dual jurisdiction cases, who is to have authority for setting and regulating the breakthrough process?

As to compensation, the answer appears to be the place of listing, because this relates to the price. Moreover, as we have seen, the compensation must be disclosed in the offer document – a matter for the state of listing – but as to whether the threshold is achieved and what restrictions are to be treated as broken through and the effects of this at the various stages in the process, there seems to be more difficulty. Is each of these a 'matter relating to company law' under Article 4(2)(e)? Arguably, the issue is analogous to the percentage of voting rights required for control for mandatory bid purposes, or the conditions under which management may take action to frustrate the bid, and is therefore a matter for the law of the target company's incorporation.[40] If this is correct, then particularly close cooperation between the authorities concerned will be required in such cases.[41] The UK government in draft clauses implementing the Directive recently published treats compensation matters as a matter for the law of the registered office, applying the relevant provisions to UK registered companies,[42] but when the UK Takeover Panel makes rules about the offer document to implement Article 6(3) these will need to extend to companies incorporated elsewhere in the EEA, but not listed there and listed in the United Kingdom.

Mandatory bids

Finally, there may be questions on the relationship of the breakthrough rule with Article 5, which requires a mandatory bid on the acquisition of control. If breakthrough would apply if a bid were to be made, should the potential for breakthrough change the threshold for determining control on the grounds that if the target is subject to the rule acquisition of control is easier? Since the Directive is silent on this, it is presumably for member states to resolve. The short and simple answer appears to be that a company is subject to the mandatory bid rule because it is in a position to exercise control now, without the need to acquire more shares or exercise breakthrough powers in consequence. So the fact that breakthrough might become possible in relation to the target should be treated as irrelevant. It may also not be possible to say with certainty whether, if a bid were to be made, the breakthrough rule would apply, as this may depend on a company's use of optionality.

Operating the Directive: optionality

The preceding section examined some aspects of the breakthrough regime in Article 11 of the Directive and its relationship with the neutrality or 'no frustration' rule in Article 9. However, the effect of these provisions is complicated by the compromise solution on neutrality and breakthrough adopted in the Directive. This was designed to meet the opposition in the European Parliament and in some member states on a number of grounds. The respectable argument was that the Directive imposed neutrality, but could only achieve a 'level playing field' for operation of neutrality through a breakthrough provision which was incomplete and interfered with property rights. The less respectable argument, which undoubtedly had a role to play, was that the directive neutrality regime, even in its modified form, would allow national structures of control and political and economic influence to be broken down by cross-frontier bids.

The solution was to confer both member state and company options on the application of both neutrality and breakthrough. This solution was so far reaching that it met all these arguments.

This section examines some aspects of how those options are likely to play out. The ground rules for the use of the options will be identified first. The section then turns to the likely outcomes from a UK perspective:[43]

- first, in terms of the choice by the UK government on whether to opt out of Article 9 (neutrality), or 11 (breakthrough), or both;
- next, the implications of such choice for the decisions of companies under the likely UK regime will be examined; and
- finally, the likely use by the UK government of the reciprocity option (Article 12) and the consequences for UK companies, first as targets and then as bidders, will be assessed.

Neutrality/breakthrough options – ground rules

There are three basic ground rules for the exercise of the options open in respect of neutrality and breakthrough:

(i) member states may opt out of Articles 9 (neutrality) and/or 11 (breakthrough) (hereafter for simplicity '9 and/or 11') – Article 12(1). If a member state retains 9 and/or 11, companies incorporated in that state are bound by it/them, and have no options (probably, however, subject to their being permitted by the relevant member state under ground rule (iii) below to opt out when faced with a bid from a company which does not apply the same articles – the 'reciprocity power', see below);

(ii) in relation to an article which a member state opts out of in this way, it must allow its companies to opt back in. This decision is reversible by the company and is to be taken by the shareholders in general meeting by enhanced majority – Article 12(2). It was argued that even though companies might be permitted by member states to adopt the less open position of rejecting neutrality and/or breakthrough, they should be given the opportunity to choose, or be thrust by market forces into, a more liberal or open stance; and

(iii) member states clearly have an option to allow any company opting back in again under Article 12(2) in this way, to decide to opt out again in certain circumstances (the reciprocity power already mentioned which is provided for by Article 12(3)). Key rules for those circumstances are: there must be a bid by a company (or an associate of such a company) which does not apply the 'same' articles, as a consequence of the optional arrangements. This decision (the reciprocity opt out) may be taken by a company board, but it must have been authorised by the general meeting to do so no more than 18 months before the bid was announced.[44]

Tiresome, but potentially important, questions of interpretation arise on the scope of this reciprocity power.

There is no doubt from the text that it may be conferred on target companies which have been exempted from 9 and/or 11 by the relevant member state implementing provision under Article 12(1), but have chosen to opt back in under Article 12(2) (in other words, companies voluntarily subject to 9 and/or 11), but it is more doubtful whether Article 12(3) also allows member states to enable a company to exercise this reciprocity power where 9 and/or 11 apply to it involuntarily. This will be because the company has not opted back in under Article 12(2), but because the member state has not opted out of those articles under Article 12(1) in the first place.

The relevant texts are the substantial provision in Article 12(3) and the explanatory words in the preamble, Paragraph (21).

Article 12(3) allows member states to exempt '*companies which apply* Articles 9(2) and (3) and/or 11 from applying Articles 9(2) and (3) and or 11 if they become subject to *an offer launched by a company which does not apply the same articles* as they do...' Paragraph (21) of the preamble expands this by stating, 'Without prejudice to international agreements... Member States should be allowed not to require *companies which apply these provisions in accordance with the optional arrangements* to apply them when they become subject to an offer launched by a company *which does not apply the same provisions as a consequence of the use of these optional arrangements*' [emphasis added].

The natural meaning of these texts, read together, seems on a first impression to be that they enable member states to confer the reciprocity power *only on companies which have opted back in under Article 12* (in other words, which 'apply these provisions in accordance with the optional arrangements') and that the reciprocity power is only exercisable against bidding companies to which the same articles do not apply as a result of the use of the same opting arrangements (in other words, they have decided not to opt back in under Article 12(2), or conceivably have done so, but then reversed that decision).

However, this strict interpretation is very arguably absurd, at least in relation to target companies.

As for such targets, why should the position of a target company be different where it is a subject to Article 9 and/or 11 by operation of member state law, as opposed to where it has exercised its own option to adopt 9 and/or 11? Why should the decision by a member state to apply 9 and/or 11 to all its companies preclude it from conferring on them a power which it could confer if it did not take that arguably stricter and more desirable position? This would be an incentive for member states to opt out of those articles. Only then could companies secure the benefit of reciprocity by voluntarily adopting them.

This argument from the merits can be accommodated in the texts in two steps. First, on the substantive provision in Article 12(3), it is reasonable to argue that target companies that are subject to 9 and/or 11 involuntarily (in other words, because member states have not opted out) nevertheless do 'apply' those articles. The language of Article 12(1), which allows member states 'not to require companies ... to *apply*' 9 and/or 11, confirms this use of the word. Such companies therefore fall within Article 12(3) consistently with the use of language in the Directive text.

As for the preamble provision, it can then be argued that the language should not be read as restricting this effect, that is, such a target company is a company that applies 9 and/or 11 'in accordance with the optional arrangements' in the sense that the member state has failed to exercise the option to opt out of them. This is admittedly a somewhat more stretched use of language, particularly bearing in mind that the Article 12 regime is an exception and reciprocity an exception to the exception, normally requiring strict construction.[45]

To my mind, however, the argument on the merits supported by this textual analysis is on balance reasonably convincing. This view of the scope of Article 12(3) – the 'liberal view' – (allowing the benefits of reciprocity to be conferred on companies that are subject to 9 and/or 11 involuntarily as a result of a member state decision not to opt out) is the preferable one. The rest of this chapter adopts that view, but, because the conclusion cannot be claimed as certain, at appropriate points it refers to the implications of the stricter view.[46] (The two views are referred to below as the 'liberal' and 'strict' view.)

UK government options on Articles 9 and 11

Adopting the UK perspective, how will the United Kingdom exercise the options? As to Article 9, the United Kingdom was always very unlikely to contemplate an opt out from neutrality. This would require a complete rewrite of the City Code, with the discarding of the fundamental General Principle 7 on board neutrality, and undermine the common law Proper Purpose doctrine which provides that directors are not to use their powers for purposes which subvert the overall control over the ownership of the company, which lies with shareholders.[47] It would even call into question the basic loyalty duty which requires directors to act in the best interest of the company, by which is meant that of the members as a whole. The UK government has now announced its intention to opt in to Article 9 and takeover rules implementing that decision as part of the implementation of the Directive are expected to be announced shortly.[48]

However, the position is very different for Article 11. As we have seen above, there are powerful objections to applying the breakthrough regime to UK listed companies. These objections are based on three main considerations:

PART I: INSIDE THE TAKEOVER REGULATION AND TACTICS

- First, there are cases where breakthrough will override arguably wholly legitimate property rights. These fall into three main classes.

    - The first comprises a small minority of listed companies entrench block-holder, often family-holding, structures through equity shares with differentiated voting rights. Many of these have reached the point where an increasingly diffuse, perhaps second or third-generation, family holding may allow bidders to acquire sufficient of the family shares to achieve the threshold (however it is to be defined – see above). Typically, these companies are of minor economic and political importance (for example, family-owned breweries which are fast disappearing), but some are significant. For example, one is a major media group – Daily Mail and General Trust plc. (But note that the Daily Mail share structure is a two-class one, of voting and non-voting shares. The discussion above suggests that probably, because the absence of a vote is not a breakthrough restriction, Daily Mail is immune from Article 11.) Newly listed companies may well wish to retain family-holding structures or existing control structures of this kind and to outlaw them might deter legitimate new entry to the listed market. It is uncertain how many UK companies may be in this position.
    - A second class of such companies involves structures designed to protect a particular company ethos inherent in the value of the company. An example is Reuters plc, another major listed media and technology company, whose share structure includes a voting trust designed to prevent damaging changes of control or company policy. The Reuters structure resembles state golden share provisions, but the interest designed to be protected – editorial independence – is not such as could be protected by a member state golden share. The exemption for state special rights under Article 11(6) very arguably extends to such provisions. However, without activation of that article, which is not currently intended by the UK government,[49] the Reuters structure would apparently, in its present form, be broken by the Directive breakthrough mechanism if Reuters were to opt in.[50]
    - The third class of such companies are the so-called 'double-headed' companies. These are enterprises usually formed from companies incorporated in two jurisdictions and bound together by articles' provisions designed to ensure an indissoluble link of management and ownership. This would, for example, prevent control of one company being acquired without control of the other. Typical such mechanisms require common board membership and that shares in both companies are held in the same hands. This involves special rights of board appointment and dismissal and restrictions on transfers of shares (for example, requiring that acquisition of shares in one company must be accompanied by acquisition of shares in the other or that directors must be appointed to both boards). These restrictions would clearly be subject to breakthrough, allowing one company to be taken over without the other, destroying the dual character of the enterprise.[51]

- A second group of objections to adopting Article 11 centre on the uncertainties and inconsistencies of the restriction and threshold components of the rule and the obscurity and apparent unworkability of the compensation regime, discussed above.
- Thirdly, related to these considerations, if the limits of the restrictions broken through have been correctly identified above, then adoption of Article 11 will provide a powerful incentive to companies to adopt those defensive structures which escape the provision – mainly non-

voting and time-lapse voting shares and possibly non-share equity rights. In this way, they can retain disproportionate voting structures while gaining the benefits of technical Article 11 conformity – closed company wolves in open company sheeps' clothing so to speak.

While UK institutional investors favour Article 11 (see above), as government consultations have shown, even if the United Kingdom opts out of Article 11, companies are nevertheless free to opt in to it under Article 12(2) and institutional investors are free to exercise their influence to bring this about.

It may be objected that this very right to opt back in means that the difficulties identified with Article 11 will have to be addressed anyway. This is true. However, the problems will be smaller in practical effect if they need only be addressed for companies which opt back in.

The UK government has now announced that it proposes to opt out of Article 11, citing many of the arguments above together with fears that imposing one share, one vote structures on companies may lead them to seek listing outside the EU or in an EU state which had opted out.[52]

UK company opt ins to Article 11

If the UK government does not opt out of Article 9, but does of Article 11, as currently proposed, it must provide for companies to opt to reapply Article 11; see Article 12(2). Provision will therefore have to be made in any event to address all the problems of the breakthrough regime set out above.

Will UK companies opt for 'reapplying'[53] Article 11 in this way? For the typical one share, one vote company this will make no difference to their current vulnerability to bids, but may enhance their powers as bidders, because of consequent immunity to reciprocal action; see below. Even if the United Kingdom decides not to exercise the option to confer reciprocity powers on UK companies, such immunity will still be an advantage. Although it will, in that case, make no difference to UK bidders for UK targets, the immunity will be available against target companies in other member states. Few such open-structured UK companies are likely to be deterred from opting in by the concern that they might wish at some later stage to change their constitution into a more 'closed' or disproportionate form. Even if they were, they are reasonably free by special resolution to opt out again.[54] Such companies will, therefore, very probably opt in under Article 12(2). They have nothing of significance to lose and an immunity against reciprocal defensive measures in some cases to gain. What those cases are is discussed below.

There will also be a number of UK companies which are not one share, one vote companies, but which have share structures which are not vulnerable to breakthrough, particularly those which rely on non-voting shares to achieve restricted control, such as Daily Mail and General Trust plc. These companies too will have nothing to lose by opting back in to Article 11. Moreover, they will have something to gain, because by doing so they will render themselves immune to reciprocity measures under Article 12(3) by any company for which they may choose to make a bid. They thus become 'wolves in sheeps' clothing' as already described. This is a particularly outrageous effect of the limits on the restrictions subject to breakthrough which is likely to deter many community companies from opting back in under Article 12(2). The reciprocity regime is very far from achieving 'equality of arms'.

For other companies, the decision will be more balanced. It will be possible to opt in in a way which retains existing control structures for general purposes, leaving the company open only in relation to successful (that is, threshold achieving) bidders. The decision to reverse the 'reapplication' of Article 11 (opting out again) must be in general meeting by qualified majority, but the closed structures may operate in relation to this decision.[55] Evidently, existing control structures will operate in such meetings.

However, it seems unlikely that the decision to opt back in to Article 11 will be attractive to UK block-holders and holders of special rights who are rendered vulnerable by Article 11.

UK government option on reciprocity

If, as is now very likely, the United Kingdom finally decides to apply Article 9, but to opt out of Article 11, the next question is whether to allow companies which are subject to either article (in the first case whether they like it or not, but in the second because they have opted back in) the benefit of the reciprocity power under Article 12(3).

Application of Article 9 to the UK target

We have assumed that the United Kingdom will subject all UK registered companies to Article 9 neutrality. Will a UK company ever be able to opt *out of* Article 9?

The answer to this question depends in part on whether the liberal or strict view is taken of Article 12(3), discussed above. On the strict view, the United Kingdom could not enable UK companies to disapply Article 9 when faced with a bidder who does not apply the same articles because such companies are not 'applying the article in accordance with the optional arrangements'.[56]

However, even if the liberal view is correct, it has always been very unlikely that the United Kingdom will exercise the option to allow UK companies to opt out of Article 9 neutrality in reciprocity cases for the same reasons (discussed above) as it seems likely that it will not opt out of the article under Article 12(1). (If these arguments are not enough, there are also objections in principle to allowing company boards to exercise reciprocity powers, which are discussed in the context of Article 11, below.)

The UK government has also now announced that it does not intend to allow reciprocity in relation to Article 9 (or indeed 11, but the arguments on this are perhaps more open and are discussed separately below).[57] It will, therefore, be assumed below that UK companies will not be free to opt out of Article 9.

Application of Article 11 to the UK target

Will the United Kingdom exercise its power under Article 12(3) to allow companies which have opted back in to Article 11 to engage in reciprocity? What are the merits of such reciprocity in principle? Vulnerability to breakthrough creates a stronger discipline on management and controlling shareholders by strengthening the hand of outsiders. Is there any case for allowing this discipline to be diluted where the bidder is not subject to the same discipline?

There are a number of arguments against doing so:

- first, the bidder's structure is normally irrelevant to offeree shareholders. There may be an argument that in a share-for-share offer, the offerees stand to be locked into a company with a less open structure than their own, but, so long as they are properly informed, as they should be under Article 10, they can express their wishes on this by not accepting and/or demanding a higher price;

- secondly, the reciprocity power is to be exercised by the board, though on the basis of a shareholder authority.[58] To confer such a power on a board in a bid seems inconsistent with the neutrality principle and raises all the dangers of conflict of interest which led the United Kingdom, and more recently the EU, to adopt the shareholder decision model; and
- thirdly, the resolution conferring the power can be achieved on the basis of pre-breakthrough majorities. It will be likely to be exploited to achieve the special interests of those benefiting from disproportionate restrictions.

However, the most important objections are more general and fundamental ones. The purpose which the power serves raises fundamental issues of legal principle and economic policy at both national and community law level.

At national level, the main argument in favour of the provision appears to be that it is somehow legitimate for directors of a target company to inhibit a commercial transaction which would otherwise properly proceed, because the constitution of a bidder is objectionable, in the sense that the bidder would not be open to a similar bid itself. This is a mercantilist, or international trade policy, argument about the conditions of international establishment and the risks of the companies from one member state (or perhaps a third country, but as to this see below) taking over those from another without the possibility of reciprocal vulnerability. There is a fear of 'one way traffic' in corporate control with 'national assets' being 'stolen'. This general policy argument is likely to be completely irrelevant to the merits of the bid and not a matter which should be of concern to the target board. Indeed, such a consideration is ruled out by the Directive itself, which, by the overriding principle in Article 3(1)(c), requires the target board 'to act in the interests of the company as a whole'. Making target boards the instruments of such international policy objectives is wholly inappropriate so far as the interests they are constituted to serve are concerned.

Moreover, at the level of community law (these objections to allowing company boards to sacrifice the interests of their shareholders on the altar of national interest apart), the adoption by a member state of this mechanism is contrary to well-recognised treaty principles on freedom of establishment and free movement of capital. The reciprocity power as it operates for cross-frontier bids is a restriction on freedom of establishment and free movement of capital which requires to be justified in accordance with the 'rule of reason'. General economic objectives, such as the desire to achieve equality in the conditions of establishment between one state and another cannot justify member state action of this kind, '... economic grounds can never serve as justification for obstacles prohibited by the Treaty'.[59]

There are also difficulties with the detail of the reciprocity option which suggest that it is unattractive, see below.

On the other hand, allowing companies to opt back out again for reciprocity reasons may be something of an incentive to their opting in. The merits of the option for the member state and for companies also depend on its practical effect, which is discussed in detail below.

However, on balance – and on the basis of the argument so far – it has always seemed unlikely that the United Kingdom would exercise the member state option in favour of allowing a UK target, which has chosen to opt back in to Article 11, the reciprocity power to disapply the provision when faced by a bidder which does not apply the same articles as the UK target does. The UK government has now announced that it does not intend to allow reciprocity to UK company targets in such cases, on anti-protectionist grounds and for reasons of simplicity.[60] However, this decision is perhaps the one most likely to come under pressure as

PART I: INSIDE THE TAKEOVER REGULATION AND TACTICS

the UK legislation progresses and is also the form of reciprocity likely to be most attractive to other member state governments. It therefore seems worthwhile to examine the implications of allowing such reciprocity.

Reciprocity options at company level

If the United Kingdom were to make the option available for Article 11, would it be used? This depends on the benefits of the option for UK companies as targets. Reciprocity is also relevant at company level for UK companies as bidders because (regardless of the UK government's final decision) the threat of the invocation of reciprocity against them may affect their decisions on whether to opt back in to Article 11. The issues are similar and can be conveniently dealt with sequentially, beginning with UK targets.

Reciprocity: issues for UK targets

If the United Kingdom decides to apply Article 9 (and not to allow reciprocity in relation to it), but to opt out of Article 11, as suggested, and (contrary to the UK government's current intention) to allow reciprocity in relation to Article 11 under Article 12(3), in what circumstances (if any) will UK companies as targets be able to disapply Article 11 against a bidder?

It should first be noted for the sake of completeness that (obviously) if the UK target company does not reverse the application of the opt out from Article 11 conferred by the United Kingdom under Article 12(1), its exemption from Article 11 is clearly always available.

However, if it opts *back into* Article 11 under Article 12(2), in what circumstances could it opt back out again ('reciprocate') under Article 12(3), if the United Kingdom were to allow this by conferring the reciprocity power in all the relevant circumstances under that article?

To repeat, we are assuming a UK target company which is involuntarily subject to Article 9 and is not permitted to disapply that article in any circumstances, but which is voluntarily subject to Article 11 as a result of having opted back in under Article 12(2). That is to say, it applies both articles – 9 mandatorily and 11 voluntarily.

Article 12(3), taken with preamble paragraph (21), provides that the target may opt back in again where the bidder does not apply the 'same articles' as it does, as a consequence of the use of the relevant optional arrangements.

There are seven cases,[61] that is, where such a bidder is subject to:

(i) both Articles 9 and 11 (that is, as a mandatory requirement under the home law). Here there can be no reciprocation (the bidder is subject to the same articles as the target);[62]
(ii) Article 9 (so mandatory), but not 11. Here reciprocation is allowed, because the articles the bidder applies are not the same as those applied by the target and the bidder has done this by use of an option (that is, an option not to opt back into Article 11);
(iii) Article 11(so mandatory), but not 9. This seems a doubtful case. On the one hand, the articles applied by the bidder are not 'the same' as those applied by the target. On the other hand, the target, by opting out of Article 11, will make itself exempt from an article which does apply to the bidder. This might be thought anomalous (and it might be argued that the bidder applies 'the same' article). However, very arguably, it makes

sense to allow a company subject to neutrality, targetted by a company which is immune from neutrality, to block breakthrough even though the bidder is subject to breakthrough. (This conclusion is supported by the detailed text – the provision applies where the bidder does not apply 'the same articles [plural]');

(iv) both Articles 9 and 11 (as a result of the bidding company having opted back in under Article 12(2)). No reciprocation is allowed (the articles applied by bidder and target are the same);

(v) neither article (by a decision to opt out of both). Yes, reciprocation is permissible. The bidder is subject to different provisions by company option;

(vi) Article 9, but not 11 (by bidder's option in both cases). Yes, for the same reason; and

(vii) Article 11, but not 9 (by bidder's option in both cases). Arguably, again yes; compare case (iii).[63]

In sum, if this analysis is correct, the UK target may opt out of Article 11 in all cases, except where the bidder is bound, by member state law or company option, into both Articles 9 and 11. This is (probably) true *even where the bidder is subject to Article 11*.

This analysis does not seem to affect the merits for the United Kingdom of denying the reciprocity option to UK companies, unless the policy merits of allowing opt out of 11 where a bidder applies 11 (but not 9) are disputed while the legal analysis is accepted.

Nor does it seem to affect the merits of the UK decision to apply Article 9, but not 11. Those UK companies which opt back in to Article 11 will (probably) not be subject to reciprocity as bidders, see below. There is no need for the United Kingdom to immunise UK companies against reciprocity by opting in to Article 11.

Reciprocity against third-country, unlisted and unincorporated bidders

The power to engage in reciprocal action under Article 12 arises for member state companies where the offer is by a company which 'does not apply the same articles as they do' (Article 12(3)) 'by the use of these optional arrangements' (preamble paragraph (21)) (or the offer is by a seventh directive subsidiary of such a company).

Whatever the ambiguity of these words, they apparently exclude offers by individuals, companies not listed within the community (wherever incorporated), which are not subsidiaries of community-listed companies (such subsidiaries are expressly within Article 12(3)) and, remarkably, third-country companies, because these do not fail to apply the 9 and/or 11 'by use of the optional arrangements'. They are in that position irrespective of any option under Article 12 of the Directive, which simply does not apply to them.[64] It applies only to companies listed within the community with registered offices within the territories of the member states.

The effect in relation to third-country companies is particularly surprising as the preamble says that the provision is 'without prejudice to international agreements', words apparently intended to ensure that where companies from third countries are entitled to national treatment in connection with takeover bids, their rights are not affected. Moreover, one of the main preoccupations of those arguing for a level playing field was the alleged immunity of third-country, particularly US, companies to contested bids as the result of a lack of board neutrality.[65]

This third-country point was never likely to influence the United Kingdom's decision to apply Article 9, since the position described already exists, but one might expect many member states to opt out of Articles 9 and 11 to take care of the point. Company boards too, concerned at the prospect of vulnerability to third-country takeovers may be unlikely to propose to their general meetings that they should resolve to reapply these articles. If this is indeed the effect of the Directive, it is particularly unfortunate.

A final point in this connection is that if this argument is correct the effect of the Article 12 reciprocity power is to discriminate against community bidders in favour of third-country bidders.[66] This may be a further argument for regarding the Directive as treating third-country and community company bidders not applying the articles alike.

Reciprocity: issues for UK bidders

Now consider the vulnerability of a UK registered company bidding for an EU target where the United Kingdom has exercised (as indeed it is now expected to do) the member state option to apply Article 9 and not Article 11. This offeror will be unaffected for this purpose by whether the United Kingdom allows reciprocal action under Article 12(3), since this decision does not affect the vulnerability of UK bidders to reciprocal action by the target. However, the vulnerability of the UK bidder to possible reciprocal action (assuming such action is permitted by the target's member state) will depend (under the 'same articles' test) on whether it retains its opted out status from Article 11 under Article 12(2) or opts back in. What difference will it make in practice? Let us consider first the position where the UK company retains the opt out from Article 11.

If the UK bidder retains its opt out from Article 11

On this first scenario, the six cases can be considered,[67] that is, where the target is:

(i) bound by both Articles 9 and 11 (by mandatory member state law) – on the 'liberal' view, reciprocation is possible since the articles applied are not the same; it may even be possible for the target to repudiate *both Articles 9 and 11*, if the governing member state law allows this, since no limitation is imposed by Article 12(3) on the scope of the action allowed.[68] Arguably the text is defective or perhaps the Directive is to be interpreted as only allowing opting out of an article, where that same article is not applied, but the argument has been made for allowing opting out of both articles in similar cases involving a UK target, above;

(ii) bound by Article 11 only (mandatory), but opted out of 9 – on the liberal view, the target may opt out of 11 because the articles applied by the bidder are not the same. On the strict view, there can be no retaliation. On any view, the target keeps the benefit of the disapplication of Article 9;

(iii) bound by Article 9 only (mandatory), but opted out of 11 – no reciprocation is possible on Article 9 (whether on a strict or a liberal view, since the articles applied are the same), but of course the target keeps the benefit of 11;

(iv) opted in to both – yes, reciprocation is possible on any view. The target can certainly opt out of Article 11 and apparently also 9 (the offeror satisfies the 'not the same' test). This is perhaps a surprising result, but see (i) above;

(v) opted in to 9, not 11 – no reciprocation by the target is permitted (the articles applied are the same); or

(vi) opted in to 11, not 9 – yes. The target may take reciprocal action and opt out of 11 (the articles applied are not the same; the bidder operates by use of the company option).

If the UK bidder opts back in to Article 11

On the second scenario, where the UK bidder has opted back in to Article 11, one can consider the same six cases, that is, where target is:

(i) bound by both articles (mandatory) – no reciprocation is allowed as the articles applied are the same (this, on the liberal view, produces a different result for the UK bidder than his position on retaining the opt out, but the same on the strict view);

(ii) bound by 11 only (mandatory) – on the liberal view, the target is free to retaliate on 11 because the articles applied are not the same, but this is an absurd result because the bidder is bound more strictly than the target; on the strict view the target is not free to retaliate on 11 which applies to him as a result of a member state option; on any view he remains exempt from 9 (here again whether the result is the same for the bidder depends on whether one adopts the liberal view);

(iii) bound by 9 only (mandatory) – on the liberal view, similarly, the target is free to retaliate on Article 9, but not so on the strict one, and remains exempt from 11 (here again, whether the result is the same for the bidder depends on whether one adopts the liberal view);

(iv) opted in to both – no retaliation (same articles applied) (with a different result for the bidder from that on the first scenario);

(v) opted in to 9, not 11 – arguably the target can 'reciprocate' by opting out of Article 9, although it applies to the UK bidder. The articles applied are not 'the same' because the bidder applies both, but this is perverse. The bidder does apply what the target applies and more; or

(vi) opted in to 11, not 9 – arguably, similarly, the target can 'reciprocate' by opting out of Article 11, for similar reasons. The articles applied are not the same because the bidder applies both. The same comment applies as for the previous case.

Arguably, cases (ii), (iii), (v) and (vi) produce a perverse result. The target is allowed to retaliate because there is a mismatch between the provisions applied, but this is because of an exemption of the target not enjoyed by the bidder.[69] Case (v), for example, seems particularly outrageous – the UK bidder is worse off after opting in to 11 than he would be if he had remained opted out! Compare case (v) in the first scenario above.

Should UK companies opt back in to block reciprocal action?

One would expect that where the UK bidder has been exempted from, but opted back in to, Article 11 and is bound by 9 there would be no case where reciprocation would be allowed. This result can be achieved by adopting a purposive construction of the 'not the same' provision to the effect that it only allows reciprocation where the restrictions applied by the bidder are both not the same as the target's restrictions and the result is the target being subject to a restriction to which the bidder is not subject. On that basis, one would conclude that the case for the UK company opting in to Article 11 on reciprocity grounds will depend on the merits of being immune from reciprocity in cases (iv) and (vi) and, if one takes the liberal view, cases (i) and (ii). Whether this is likely to happen seems to depend on the facts, but it seems entirely possible, indeed probable, given that, as indicated above, most UK companies have little if anything to lose by opting in to 11.

PART I: INSIDE THE TAKEOVER REGULATION AND TACTICS

Reversibility of Article 12(2) opt ins: tactical considerations

As noted above, under Article 12(2), the option which member states must give to companies to reapply Articles 9(2) and (3) and/or 11 is reversible. There are serious dangers that companies will be tempted to make tactical use of this decision. For bidders, this allows temporary immunisation from reciprocal action by opting in to both, or one, of these articles again, bearing in mind that in due course they can reverse the position. For targets, it seems to allow them to immunise themselves from the consequences of opting back in by reversing their Article 11(2) option, but both decisions have to be taken by a qualified majority in the general meeting, so they are relatively 'sticky' and are likely to take place in the full glare of publicity. The UK government proposes to deal with the risks of tactical opting out by requiring a 12-month interval after an opt in before this can be done.[70] There is no equivalent interval to deal with tactical opting in by bidders.

Conclusions on reciprocity

The member state reciprocity option looks deeply unattractive. Its merits for companies and its legality at company and community level look very questionable. It raises apparently difficult and complex questions as to the effect in particular cases, which will complicate and add expense to control transactions. The United Kingdom has managed without it hitherto and is now very unlikely to exercise the reciprocity power. In the new environment, UK companies may choose to subject themselves to breakthrough even though the United Kingdom rejects it. It may therefore be argued that they should be allowed the means to mitigate the consequences of doing so, but that argument seems unlikely on balance to change the calculus.

If reciprocity is to be allowed, a simple and rational scheme could be argued for as follows:

- where a bidder does not apply Article 9 and/or Article 11, then a target which does apply Article 9 and/or 11 may opt out of either such article or, as the case may be, both;
- the case for allowing a target to opt out of an article only if that same article is not applied by the bidder, needs to be considered carefully. While omitting such a restriction may be regarded as unreasonable in that it allows targets to opt out of articles applied by bidders, since Articles 9 and 11 will bear differently on different kinds of company it makes some sense to allow a target to remove both if either is not adopted by the bidder. On the other hand, this argument should not be taken too far; and
- certainly, where the bidder applies both articles, targets should not be allowed to opt back out of either or both.

This regime, while arguably not strictly required by the Directive, is not inconsistent with it. Member states are explicitly entitled to apply the reciprocity regime under conditions determined by national law. They should do so in this sense, if at all.

However, the case for this approach rests on the legitimacy of allowing target company boards to seek to achieve a kind of equality of arms with companies making public offers to their shareholders. As explained, these arguments have no merit. If member states wish to restrict the free movement of capital and establishment for this purpose, this is a matter for member state action, not one to be entrusted to company boards at the expense of shareholders. For this reason, it is hoped and expected that the United Kingdom at least will maintain its intention not to exercise its option under Article 12(3) to confer reciprocity powers on UK registered companies even in relation to breakthrough. Indeed, the policy arguments against any member state applying the reciprocity regime at all are very strong and its legality in community law is in the highest degree dubious.

Afterword

This chapter has examined the interplay of the European neutrality and breakthrough rules from a UK perspective. It now seems very likely that the UK government will retain the neutrality principle in its absolute form, with no room for UK companies to escape it. The position on breakthrough is different. Companies will remain free to adopt 'one share, one vote' constitutions or not as they please, although for market reasons and the need to reduce the cost of capital, the process of alignment of all UK listed companies on that model can be expected to continue.

Whatever their constitutions, all UK listed companies will in future have the right under EU law as implemented in the United Kingdom to adopt such open structures to apply when they are involved in takeovers as targets. The effects of doing so are regrettably unclear, both in terms of the implications for their own governance, and in terms of their position as bidders for companies in other member states. The prospects of UK companies being permitted to engage in 'reciprocal' action on this front (by reapplying restrictions on voting and ownership rights when faced with a bidder with a closed constitution from a closed member state regime) now look remote. The implications of this possibility have, however, been examined above. Such examination may have helped to illustrate the implications of the alternative approach both for the United Kingdom and more widely within the EU. It is to be hoped that it is academic.

---

[1] This chapter covers part of the ground first reviewed in a paper for the Oxford Roundtable on Corporate Governance in March 2003 (before EU Directive adoption) published as J Rickford, 'The Emerging European Takeover Law from a British Perspective' (2004) 15 *EBLR*, p. 1379 ('Rickford 2004 EBLR'), which discusses these issues in a wider perspective.

[2] Director, The Company Law Centre, British Institute of International and Comparative Law. Visiting Professor, London School of Economics and Political Sciences.

[3] Directive 2004/25/EC of 21.4.04 on takeover bids, OJ L142/12, 30.4.2004 ('the Directive'). The Directive is to be brought into force through implementing domestic legislation in each EU and EEA state by 20 May 2006, Article 21(1). Articles referred to without attribution are articles of this Directive.

[4] 'Merger' is usually used in English to denote business combinations both by takeover (that is, offers by one company – the bidder – for the shares, or sufficient shares to confer control, in another – the target) and by transactions with similar effect (such as by agreed transfer of the target's undertaking). Core policy considerations are the same for both types; UK takeover regulation applies to both, but the Directive, and proposed UK implementing provisions on breakthrough (see below), only apply to takeovers.

[5] What connecting factors 'locate' corporate control for this purpose is a debatable question, normally lost in the nationalist rhetoric, but it lies beyond the scope of this chapter.

[6] See, for example, the 'golden share' cases such as Commission vs. Portugal, referred to in more detail below.

[7] See P Davies and K Hopt, in Chapter 7 of *The Anatomy of Corporate Law*, ed R Kraakman *et al.* (OUP: 2004) making a similar point and drawing a similar distinction and P Davies, 'The Notion of Equality in European Takeover Regulation', in J Payne (ed.), *Takeovers in English and German Law*, Hart (OUP: 2002), p. 9, pp. 26–27.

[8] Though only in the preamble, (3), (19), (20), (24), but cf. (25) rather than the body of the text.

[9] Lisbon European Council, Presidency Conclusions, 23–24 March 2000, paragraphs 20–22.

[10] For example, 3rd Directive on mergers of public companies 78/885/EEC, Article 7, 6th Directive on divisions of public companies 82/891/EEC, Article 5, European Company Statute Council Regulation 2157/2001, Articles 17, 32, 37.

PART I: INSIDE THE TAKEOVER REGULATION AND TACTICS

[11] See, for example, L Bebchuk and A Ferrell, 'Federalism and Corporate Law, The Race to Protect Managers from Takeovers' (1999) 99 *Col LR*, p. 1168. The US 'stakeholder statutes' are designed to allow, or even oblige, boards to obstruct bids at the expense of shareholders where, in the directors' view, it is necessary to protect, for example, employees or local community interests. The statutes were enacted through a combination of local political, trades union and management interests to obstruct the perceived damage to state interests from restructuring and relocation of assets, employment and corporate control. Even in states with no stakeholder statute, such as Delaware and other states with laws based on the Model Business Corporations Act (MBCA), the directors' fidelity duty, to serve the interests of 'the company', can be invoked to similar purpose – see, for example, MBCA, ABA 1999 edition, Section 8.30 and commentary at 8–41(2).

[12] Article 3(1)(c), emphasis added. Does the article imply that the two things cannot conflict? Cf. Article 9(5): the board is to publish its opinion of the bid and its effects 'on all the Company's interests and specifically employment'. Article 3(1)(c) governs implementation of the whole of the Directive, including Articles 9 (neutrality), 11 (breakthrough) and, crucially, 12 (optionality).

[13] This group, appointed by the Commission in September 2001 to recommend a way forward after the deadlock in the European Parliament in July 2001, based itself on two principles – shareholder decision making, which requires board neutrality, and proportionality of risk and control, which leads to a breakthrough regime for disproportionate governance rules. See High Level Group of Company Law Experts, Report on Issues Relating to Takeover Bids (EC: Brussels, 10 January 2002), pp. 20–23.

[14] *Ibid*. p. 19.

[15] Acquisition of 'control' by other means requires a mandatory general bid – see Article 5.

[16] For detailed discussion see Rickford, 2004 *EBLR* above, 1385 and ff.

[17] That is, any contract to which the company and the security holder is a party and any other contract between securities holders entered into after adoption of the Directive (21.4.2004) – Article 11(2), 2nd sentence.

[18] This seems to leave such restrictions enforceable *inter partes*, but the effect must presumably be to disapply the restrictions in relation to transfers to the offeror. Apparently even if the threshold is not achieved, the bidder remains entitled to securities acquired in this way.

[19] Not defined. Presumably these are rights which depart from normal default rules. Under UK standard default articles (Table A 1985, Article 73), the board is first appointed in the constitution, the board itself fills casual vacancies, the whole board is replaced at the first annual general meeting by ordinary resolution and one-third retire and are similarly replaced at each subsequent AGM. This can be overruled by a special resolution (75 per cent majority). Special rights to appoint directors are sometimes conferred by the articles and they could apparently be by contract with the company (both, I believe, unheard of for listed companies). The ordinary rule on dismissal is in the Companies Act 1985, Section 303 – any director is always dismissable without cause by ordinary resolution.

[20] Article 12(3), 3rd paragraph and (4), second phrase.

[21] Confirmed by the Commission position in its proposal of 2 October 2002, see Explanatory Memorandum, OJ C45E 25.2.2003, at 9. For a description of such 'actions à droit de vote double du droit français' see J Simon, 'OPA: Divine Surprise ou Faux Semblant?', *EUREDIA*, 2003/3, p. 329, p. 340.

[22] See U Bernitz, 'The Attack on the Nordic Multiple Voting Rights Model' (2004) 15 *EBLR*, p. 1423, and R Skog, 'The Takeover Directive, the "Breakthrough" Rule and the Swedish System of Dual Class Common Stock', *ibid*., p. 1439.

[23] Article 221(3) Aktiengesetz.

[24] See Article 12(2) prohibiting 'multiple voting rights' and Article 134(1), (2), prohibiting a ceiling of votes in listed companies. Both provisions were introduced by the Gesetz zur Kontrolle und Transparenz im Unternehmensbereich, 6 March 1998 (Kontrag), BGBl I 1998 786.

[25] Article 10(1)(f) requires disclosure of 'systems whereby, with the company's co-operation, the financial rights attaching to securities are separated from the holding of securities'. This seems designed to deal with cases where securities and votes are vested in depositary banks and depositary receipts carry cash flow rights. *Quaere* whether *Genussrechte* are to be disclosed under this provision.

[26] Such 'preference' shares need not necessarily be excluded from equity exposure. Similarly, the German provision in AktienGesetz Article 139, for departure from one share/one vote for preference shares, allows substantial departure from the proportionality principle. Restrictions on transfer of such securities in the articles or in relevant agreements are broken through during the bid period, but (apparently) not post-breakthrough – Article 11(6) disapplies (3) and (4), but not (2).

[27] Cf. J Rickford (2004) *EBLR*, above, at p. 1392. Article 11(6) provides that (3) and (4) shall not apply to 'securities where the restrictions on voting rights are compensated for...', etc. (4) defines the threshold as where the offeror

'holds 75 per cent or more of the capital carrying voting rights'. If (6) is construed narrowly and literally, as is appropriate for an exception, it does not exclude preference shares from the general reference to 'capital', but only from 'securities' in (4). This means, anomalously, as with the French case above, successful bidders may pass the threshold, but not command 75 per cent of the votes at the post-threshold meeting, but this objection is hardly conclusive, particularly given that precedent.

[28] See clauses R26(2) and R29(1) in the DTI Company Law Reform announcement, 19 July 2005 at www.dti.gov.uk/cld/clauses.htm ('DTI Announcement').

[29] See the discussion of the preference shares exception, above.

[30] For completeness, it should be added here that Article 11(6) disapplies Article 11 from securities which confer special rights on member states where 'compatible with the Treaty' and for other such rights (including, presumably, special rights conferred on states otherwise than as shareholders and on others, whether as shareholders or not). This exempts lawful 'golden shares' and the like. European Court of Justice jurisprudence substantially reduces the scope for such internal market distortions. See cases C-367/98, C-483/99, C-503/99, C-463/00, C-98/01 and C-174/04 (Commission vs. Portugal, France, Belgium, Spain, UK and Italy, respectively). Member states may take advantage of this provision to treat such companies as conforming with the breakthrough regime, that is, disregarding such offending provisions (with consequent benefits as bidders as well as targets – see below, but the UK clauses, DTI Announcement, above, simply prevent such companies 'opting in' to Article 11 – clause R24(4)).

[31] See DTI Announcement, clause R24(3). Non-constitutional constraints are, however, specifically addressed in clause R26, which removes restrictions on the transfers of shares to the offeror during the offer period and to any person thereafter (although Article 11(2) (offer period) refers to 'securities' and to agreements vis-à-vis the offeror and is invoked by Article 11(4) (post-threshold)).

[32] Article 5.

[33] Article 3(1)(a) – equivalent treatment. Article 6(3)(e) also appears to require the offer document to offer the compensation not only to shareholders, but also to other holders of rights to be broken through. Is the offer document to be addressed to them?

[34] Article 12(2), 2nd.

[35] See DTI Announcement 2005, above, explanatory notes, 16, 17. Companies Act 1985, Sections 125–129.

[36] Not least because, if they are correct, some rights holders have individual rights and some only class rights, see below.

[37] Ibid., clause R26(5). Quaere whether this provision needs to extend further to cover contractual rights as against the company for the appointment or dismissal of directors. These too need not be contained in articles nor be conferred on shareholders.

[38] There is a case for Directive amendment if only for consistent treatment of rights holders. After five years, the Commission is to review the operation of the Directive and make proposals for revision – Article 20. Compare the facility under a Companies Act 1985, Section 425 scheme of arrangement.

[39] Strictly speaking 'has its registered office' there, which may raise complications for countries that apply the 'real seat' doctrine. These are problems beyond the scope of this chapter.

[40] Whether reciprocity action is available to the target and under what conditions is apparently a matter for the member state of the registered office, but the circumstances in which it can be invoked and its relationship with the board's duties under General Principle (c) in Article 2(1) are less clear – see Article 12 and the discussion below.

[41] Such cooperation is required under Article 4(4).

[42] See DTI Announcement July 2005, above, clause R26(5), providing compensation for loss resulting from the overriding of agreements restricting the transfer of shares relating to UK registered companies. Other restrictions are dealt with under the UK opt out regime by class protection rights at the company opt in stage – see above.

[43] The reader who regards this as parochial may draw comfort from the fact that it makes for simplicity, by excluding many permutations.

[44] Article 12(3) and (5), read with preamble, paragraph (21).

[45] Some assistance might be gained from the similar (though not identical) language used in the preamble to describe the offeror company against which reciprocity can be invoked. This is described there as a company that 'does not apply the same provisions as a consequence of the use of these optional arrangements'. Unfortunately, however attractive a contrario argument, that companies which do apply such provisions involuntarily must be immune from reciprocity and therefore cannot be companies which 'do not apply the same provisions as a consequence of the use of these optional arrangements' does not run. All offeror companies that fail to apply 9 and/or 11 will do so voluntarily by use of the optional arrangements, in the sense that they will have failed to opt back in.

[46] This 'more liberal' view is taken by J Simon, above, 'OPA: Divine Surprise ou Faux Semblant?', *EUREDIA* 2003/3, p. 329, p. 340 (with slight hesitation) and S Maul and A Kouloridas, 'The Takeover Bids Directive' (2004) 5 *German Law Journal* No 4, at [12] (without discussion).

[47] Hogg vs. Cramphorn [1967] Ch 254, Howard Smith vs. Ampol [1974] AC 821 PC.

[48] See 'Implementation of the Directive on Takeover Bids – A Consultative Document', DTI, London, January 2005 URN 05/511, 3.6 and DTI Announcement 2005, above, draft clauses R24. I have argued elsewhere – see note 16 above – that there is one possible counter-argument – that a UK opt out of Article 9 would allow companies to opt back in under Article 12(2), thus giving such companies the advantage of invoking the reciprocity power to opt out again under Article 12(3), when faced with a bidder not applying 'the same' articles, but this depended on the stricter view of Article 12(3), rejected above. In any event, this argument never seemed likely to have any weight in the United Kingdom. UK companies are already subject to this alleged handicap and the objections to enabling them to empower their boards to engage in such tactics are overwhelming. There are also major objections in principle to the reciprocity power and the United Kingdom appears firmly to have decided not invoke it – see below.

[49] See the DTI Announcement July 2005, above, and draft clauses.

[50] It involves a ceiling on shareholdings of 15 per cent in the articles and a special share with enhanced voting powers enabling override of resolutions proposed by anyone controlling Reuters or which threaten its editorial independence, see http://about.reuters.com/aboutus/overview/independence.asp. The government proposes to opt out of Article 11 – see below, but the failure to invoke Article 11(6) prevents Reuters from opting in without changing its constitution (assuming that the Reuters provisions' justification by reference to editorial independence renders them consistent with community law).

[51] See, for example, the account of Unilever's structure in F Barca and M Becht eds, *The Control of Corporate Europe* (OUP: 2001), p. 35.

[52] See the DTI 2004 consultation document, note 48 above, 3.7–3.9.

[53] There is a minor awkwardness in speaking of companies which already comply with the one share, one vote open structure embodied in the breakthrough conditions as 'opting in' to Article 11. They are already 'in'. This problem is resolved in the UK draft clauses by providing that such companies may pass a resolution to opt in. See clause R24 referred to above. There is no doubt that this is legitimate under the Directive.

[54] Article 12(2). The proposed UK clauses will, however, require that this is not done for 12 months to prevent abuse by short-term opting in and out to achieve tactical advantage during bids, see DTI Announcement 2005, above, clause R25(6) and explanatory notes, 16.

[55] Article 12(2). The UK clauses allow a company to opt in to Article 11 either by altering the company's constitution to remove the restrictions entirely or by adopting measures which ensure that they only operate consistently with Article 11 – see clause R24(3)(a)(i) and (ii).

[56] Preamble (21), 3rd sentence – discussed above.

[57] See DTI consultation document 2004, note 48 above.

[58] The authority must have been conferred a maximum of 18 months before the bid announcement (creating a recurring shareholder discipline), but an ordinary resolution is sufficient for community purposes – Article 12(5).

[59] See in particular the golden share cases, for example, Commission vs. Portugal ECJ C-367/98, especially at 52 and now Commission vs. Italy C-174/04.

[60] DTI consultation document 2004, at note 48 above, 28. The document also argues that the provision ought not to operate against third-country company bidders for fear of retaliation and in the interests of international trade. However, the provision is probably not applicable against third-country companies anyway – see below.

[61] If one were completely satisfied with the liberal view, above, on the availability of Article 12(3) to companies involuntarily bound by 9 and/or 11, there would only be four cases where reciprocity could arise. These are where the bidding company is bound – in whatever way, (i) by both 9 and 11, (ii) by 9, but not 11, (iii) by 11, but not 9, and (iv) by neither. (There are seven cases and not eight above because being bound by one or both may be voluntary or involuntary, but being bound by neither will always be voluntary.) However, it seems useful to extract all seven cases in order to illustrate the different effect of the strict view.

[62] On a very strict interpretation of Article 12(3), the bidder does not 'apply the same provisions as a consequence of the use of those optional arrangements' – see preamble 21, but see the discussion above.

[63] The first three possible cases involve the member state imposing Article 9 and/or 11 and companies not opting in to the articles not imposed. Cases (iv) to (vii) are those where the member state leaves the company free to opt back into 9 and/or 11 as a result of disapplying both.

[64] Article 12(1) applies to companies referred to in Article 1(1) (that is, governed by the law of a member state with securities admitted to listing on a community-regulated market) with registered office within a member state. Articles 9 and 11 themselves only apply to such companies (Article 9 via the definition of offeree company, takeover bid and Article 1(1), Article 11 explicitly). A possible contrary argument is that third-country companies are always open to reciprocity because all such companies (whether or not subject to their own national neutrality/breakthrough provisions) are not such companies as apply the same articles 'as a consequence of the use of those optional arrangements' because they could not make such use. This displacement of a negative might be regarded as a minor violence to an obscure text. The *travaux* are ambiguous – see the European Parliament proceedings, referred to below.

[65] The European Parliament recognised this problem. See the Report of 8 December 2003, FINAL A5 0469/2003, at pp. 80–82 and 91–92, where the Committee on Industrial, External Trade, etc matters proposed a special reciprocity article (new Article 17a) addressing bids from third-country companies. However, this article was not adopted in the final agreed text.

[66] Very arguably unlawful under Article 12 (discrimination on grounds of nationality) of the Treaty Establishing the European Community.

[67] If we were wholly satisfied that the liberal view applied, we would need to consider only three cases. The missing seventh case, as compared with the analysis of the position of UK companies as targets, is the case where neither article applies. Obviously, the question of reciprocal action cannot arise where the target is already opted out of both articles.

[68] On the strict interpretation of Article 12(3), however, no reciprocation is possible because the target's status is not the company's option.

[69] It may be asked why the converse case – where the UK company is the target – does not raise similar problems. I believe the answer is that the UK company will always be bound by Article 9 on our scenario. It will never be in a position where it applies one of the articles by not opting out and disapplies another as a result of opting out and not having opted back in. So it can never be a target within cases (v) or (vi).

[70] DTI July 2005 Announcement, above, clause R25(6).

Chapter 5

'Acting in concert' – first conclusions drawn from two recent takeovers and the Takeover Directive

Erik Bomans and Charles Demoulin
Denimor, Brussels

Introduction

Two recently contested takeover transactions regarding Fondiaria (in Italy) and Beiersdorf (in Germany) illustrate the need for a clear and uniform definition of 'acting in concert' under the takeover regulations of the EU member states. As this chapter shows, legal uncertainty regarding such definition has led to important losses for minority shareholders. Now that the Takeover Directive provides for a definition of 'persons acting in concert', market regulators throughout the EU should issue clear and uniform rules about their interpretation of 'acting in concert'. They should also issue specific rules in order to address the specificities of a coordinated exercise of voting rights by (institutional) shareholders, often referred to as 'shareholder activism'.

The Fondiaria takeover by SAI

On 18 February 2002, SAI SpA, an Italian insurer, acquired a 29 per cent stake in La Fondiaria Assicurazioni SpA, another insurance company, from Montedison. Montedison was on the verge of being taken over by Italenergia, a company controlled by the Fiat group. Right before the takeover of Montedison, Mediobanca, a reference shareholder of both Montedison and Fondiaria, orchestrated an arrangement with Montedison aimed at keeping Fondiaria in friendly hands. Mediobanca wanted to secure control over Fondiaria, since the latter had an important stake in Generali and in Mediobanca itself.

According to the arrangement, SAI, an insurance company friendly to Mediobanca (through SAI's controlling shareholder Premafin), undertook to acquire the 29 per cent stake in Fondiaria from Montedison at a price of €9.5 per share, offering a premium of between 40 and 60 per cent towards the then prevailing market price (depending on the reference period). The shares were bought in two steps: SAI immediately acquired a 6.7 per cent stake directly from Montedison and undertook to acquire the remaining 22.2 per cent on 28 February 2002 at the latest. To overcome objections from the regulator overseeing insurance companies (ISVAP) against the acquisition of the 29 per cent stake,[1] SAI was forced to find other investors who were willing to acquire the 29 per cent stake in Fondiaria.[2] In February 2002, five investors (among them JP Morgan and Commerzbank) bought the 6.7 per cent stake in Fondiaria from SAI and bought an additional stake of 22.2 per cent directly from Montedison. It later emerged that these investors had bought the shares under put and call arrangements and that they were holding the shares on behalf of SAI. SAI exercised its call option on the shares later in 2002.

Since the stake acquired from Montedison was below 30 per cent (even if the shares acquired by the five white knights were attributed to SAI), SAI argued that it was not under an obligation to launch a bid on all of the outstanding shares of Fondiaria. In accordance with Italian law, a bidder who, individually or by acting jointly with other buyers, acquires 30 per cent or more of the shares of a listed company, is under an obligation to launch a bid on all of the outstanding shares. The price of the mandatory bid equals the average of the highest price paid for the acquisition of the shares and the six months' average stock market closing price.

Minority shareholders argued that control over Fondiaria had changed hands in favour of a new group, composed of Mediobanca (13.8 per cent shareholder of Fondiaria) and SAI (29 per cent shareholder, directly and indirectly, through the put and call arrangements). In their view, SAI and Mediobanca acted 'in concert' and should thus be regarded as one single entity for the purpose of calculating the 30 per cent threshold triggering a mandatory bid under Italian law. According to these minority shareholders, Mediobanca and SAI were under an obligation to launch a mandatory bid on all outstanding Fondiaria shares.

It later emerged from evidence produced by Italy's competition authority,[3] that Mediobanca had orchestrated the entire transaction, from negotiating the deal with Montedison to finding white knights who were willing to acquire the 29 per cent stake in lieu of SAI. It also appeared that Mediobanca had master-minded the subsequent merger between SAI and Fondiaria,[4] which was the ultimate transaction aimed at consolidating Premafin's and Mediobanca's control over SAI and Fondiaria. Mediobanca had pledged financial support to Premafin and SAI allowing the latter to realise the takeover. Finally, Mediobanca had actively intervened in discussions about SAI–Fondiaria's future governance.

Consob, Italy's market regulator, issued three different statements on the issue of the mandatory bid. When conducting a preliminary review of the Fondiaria takeover, Consob initially said that it had found certain indications of the existence of a concert party action between SAI and Mediobanca. On 17 May 2002, Consob however communicated that it had not found any evidence of such concert party action between SAI and Mediobanca.

Consob was forced to review its May 2002 ruling after it was annulled by the administrative court of Lazio (Rome) on 26 November 2002, at the request of a minority shareholder. At the time of the Lazio court ruling, the Italian competition authority had already found evidence of a concert party action between Mediobanca and SAI.

Yet, Consob's final ruling of 18 December 2002, confirming the existence of a concert party action between Mediobanca and SAI, provided no relief to minority shareholders. Consob imposed administrative fines and forced Mediobanca and SAI to reduce their joint stake in the merged company to below 30 per cent, but stopped short of imposing a mandatory bid on all of Fondiaria's outstanding shares. Consob argued it was too late to impose such a bid, since many shares had changed hands between the takeover (February 2002) and Consob's final decision (December 2002).

Certain minority shareholders went to court to claim compensation for the losses they had suffered as a result of the buyers' failure to launch a bid on their shares at the mandatory bid price. A first court judgement was rendered in the case by the Court of Milan on 26 May 2005, awarding damages to minority shareholders.

The Beiersdorf takeover by a consortium led by Tchibo

In September–October 2003, rumours circulated about a possible takeover of Beiersdorf AG, the Hamburg-based cosmetics company owner of the Nivea brand. It was no secret that Allianz, a 43.6 per cent shareholder of Beiersdorf, wanted to dispose of its stake. Various media reported that Allianz was discussing with Procter & Gamble about a sale of its stake at a price valuing Beiersdorf at between €9 billion and €10 billion (€110–120 per share). The stock market price of Beiersdorf went up on expectations that Procter & Gamble would buy Allianz's stake, which would automatically lead to a mandatory bid on all of Beiersdorf's outstanding shares.

As from September 2003, however, various newspapers reported that Tchibo, a 30.3 per cent shareholder of Beiersdorf, would envisage taking control over Beiersdorf. Since Tchibo had distributed a substantial part of its cash reserves during the summer of 2003 to buy out some of its family shareholders, it would not have been able to take over Allianz's entire stake, let alone to launch a bid for all outstanding Beiersdorf shares. When local Hamburg politicians, who were facing an election, were alerted about a possible takeover of Beiersdorf by Procter & Gamble and the problems Tchibo was facing to acquire Allianz's stake, they started conducting discussions with all parties concerned to find a 'Hamburg solution'. Local Hamburg politicians feared that a takeover by Procter & Gamble would lead to job losses, to asset sales and to a loss of tax income for the City of Hamburg (estimated at €200 million per year).

The City of Hamburg first tried to broker a solution by finding other investors, such as the state-owned HSH Nordbank, to acquire part of Allianz's stake. When this seemed impossible, the City of Hamburg said it would consider acquiring a stake in Beiersdorf itself. The discussions between Tchibo and the City of Hamburg were reported in the press and representatives of the City made no secret of the fact that they wanted to keep Beiersdorf in local hands.

On 22 October 2003, Tchibo, Beiersdorf and Allianz issued press releases stating that Allianz had sold a 32.6 per cent stake to a 'consortium led by Tchibo', consisting of Tchibo (buying 19.6 per cent), HGV (a City of Hamburg investment fund, buying 10 per cent), and Beiersdorf's own pension fund (buying 3 per cent). In addition, Beiersdorf said it would repurchase 10 per cent of its own shares and that Allianz would sell at least 7.4 per cent of Beiersdorf's shares under the share repurchase programme, which Allianz was able to represent thanks to the buyers' transfer of rights under such programme to Allianz. In total, Allianz was therefore able to sell an aggregate stake of 40 per cent to the Tchibo consortium and to Beiersdorf. Allianz kept a stake of about 3.6 per cent.

On the day following the closing of the transaction, the City of Hamburg stated in a press release:

> The negotiating partners are happy that they have succeeded in preserving Beiersdorf AG as an independent and listed company based in Hamburg. It is our goal to provide long-term security to the company, its employees and partners and to continue the company's successful development. Furthermore, it is the purpose that Beiersdorf will be the first Hamburg company to be part of the DAX index.

Representatives of Tchibo and of Beiersdorf itself made similar statements. Allianz said in its own press release that it had sold its shares at an 'average' price of €130 per share (versus a closing stock market price of €114.8 on 21 October 2003, the date preceding the announcement of the transaction and a one-month average closing price of €110.2). The 'average' price of the transaction meant that the various buyers had agreed on a price adjustment mechanism depending on the price at which Beiersdorf would repurchase its own shares. As Beiersdorf repurchased its own shares in December 2003 at a price of €113 per share, some other buyers must have made up the difference in order for Allianz to receive an average price of €130 per share for its 40 per cent stake.

Tchibo argued it was not under an obligation to launch a tender offer on Beiersdorf shares, since it already owned more than 30 per cent of the shares of the company when the new German Takeover Code entered into force. BaFin, Germany's market regulator, in its initial reaction to the takeover, said that if Tchibo was acting in concert with the other buyers, it could be forced to launch a tender offer on all of Beiersdorf's shares.

Under German law, when a person acquires 30 per cent or more of the shares with voting rights of a listed company, it is obliged to launch a bid on all of the shares with voting rights of that company. The voting rights held by other persons with whom the buyer acts in concert are added to the buyer's voting rights for the purpose of calculating the 30 per cent threshold. The fact that Tchibo already held 30 per cent of the voting rights when the German Takeover Act entered into force was not relevant to the extent that the buyers' consortium could be considered as a new entity controlling more than 30 per cent of the voting rights. The German Takeover Code does not provide for an exception for parties acting in concert if one of those parties already owned 30 per cent or more of the voting rights of the target company when the Takeover Code entered into force.

When some minority shareholders, descendants of the founders of Beiersdorf, started complaining about their treatment under the deal, Allianz bought half of their stake (5 per cent of Beiersdorf's shares) at an estimated price of €135 per share. Allianz's stake therefore increased again to 9 per cent.

On 23 January 2004, BaFin issued a press release stating that it had not found any evidence of the existence of a concert party action between the various buyers. BaFin said:

> there were no indications that the buyers were coordinating their voting rights or that they had agreed materially to influence the target company

Bafin said it could not determine that the three buyers had agreed on common objectives beyond the acquisition of shares, such as securing Beiersdorf's local anchorage ('Sicherung des Standortes Hamburg'). As possible examples of pursuing common objectives beyond the acquisition of shares, BaFin mentioned the aim to divide the company up, to transfer the registered office or to have an understanding about the future board composition.

Certain minority shareholders, who were less lucky than the founders' descendants, filed a law suit aimed at getting damages. They argued that Tchibo and the other buyers were acting in concert and therefore were under an obligation to launch a tender offer at the mandatory bid price such as provided for by German law. As at mid-2005, the court case was still pending before the Landsgericht of Hamburg.

PART I: INSIDE THE TAKEOVER REGULATION AND TACTICS

The need for a clear and common definition of persons 'acting in concert'

The above-described cases illustrate well the importance of having a clear definition of what can be regarded as 'acting in concert' since this definition can have far-reaching consequences under the mandatory bid rule. In order to achieve the objective to create an integrated European financial market, it is also necessary to rely on a common definition, as well as on common criteria in order to know when a cooperation can qualify as a concert party action.

Minority shareholders of Beiersdorf and Fondiaria legitimately expected an offer on their shares at the mandatory bid price, as a coordinated acquisition of shares had clearly occurred with the view of acquiring control over their company. The coordinated behaviour of the buyers and the aim to acquire control were obvious to any outside observer. Yet, in both cases, the market regulators failed to find evidence of the existence of a concert party action.[5]

When it became clear that the investors' expectations would not be met, the share price of Fondiaria and Beiersdorf started falling sharply. Interestingly, the share price fell even below the level at the time the expectations of a mandatory bid started to occur.

In the case of Fondiaria, the strong share price depreciation can certainly be explained by the merger with SAI which the new controlling shareholders imposed on Fondiaria's minority shareholders after the change of control.[6] Under the merger, Fondiaria was valued at €4.5 per share (taking the date preceding the board decision approving the merger as a reference), far below the price of €9.5 per share that SAI paid to acquire control over Fondiaria.

In the case of Beiersdorf, less positive results were released by the company (and its competitors) in the six-month period following the takeover, leading to investors doubting whether the company would be able to realise its future growth ambitions as an independent company. In contrast to the Fondiaria case, where the Italian stock market regulatory authority initially indicated that it had found evidence of 'acting in concert',[7] the market did not believe that the German market regulator would sanction the highly politically supported Beiersdorf transaction.[8]

Apart from these specific circumstances, it is clear that investors dumped both companies' shares, disappointed as they were about the companies' (and their controlling shareholders') treatment of minority shareholders.

The lack of a clear and common definition may thus lead to legal uncertainty and to law suits, the outcomes of which are difficult to predict. Market regulators or local courts can come to different interpretations. In case a court confirms the existence of a concerted action, considerable time may have elapsed between the time of the change of control and the court decision. One may then question whether the court should sanction the concert party action by imposing a tender offer on all of the outstanding shares, or whether damages are the only possible remedy. If damages are awarded, who will be entitled to the damages[9] and how will the damages be calculated?[10]

These numerous questions and uncertainties surrounding the sanctioning of mandatory bid rules through court action underline the need for a clear definition of 'acting in concert' in order to prevent disputes and discussions from arising.

In addition, more and more investors are starting to actively exercise their shareholders' rights and to coordinate such exercise in order to strengthen their position. As will be examined further below in the section entitled 'Persons acting in concert and shareholder activism', it has therefore become necessary to address this issue, with regard to the definition of 'acting in concert' and the mandatory bid rule, in order to remove obstacles against the development of shareholder activism which is often considered as a positive evolution and a strong contribution to the implementation of good corporate governance standards.

The definition of 'acting in concert' under the Takeover Directive

There was so far no uniform European or international concept of 'acting in concert'. Most takeover regulations that refer to this concept do not contain clear and comprehensive definitions, leaving ample scope for liberal or conservative interpretations by courts and/or market regulators.

After almost 15 years of endless debate, a European directive on takeovers (the 'Takeover Directive') has finally been approved.[11] The Takeover Directive provides for a list of definitions (Article 2), including a definition of 'persons acting in concert'.

The Takeover Directive defines 'persons acting in concert' as follows:

> 'persons acting in concert' shall mean natural or legal persons who cooperate with the offeror or the offeree company on the basis of an agreement, either express or tacit, either oral or written, aimed either at acquiring control of the offeree company or at frustrating the successful outcome of a bid (Article 2.1(d)).[12]

Since the Takeover Directive provides for a definition of 'persons acting in concert', it seems difficult to admit that member states, while implementing the Takeover Directive in their own national legislation, still have the possibility to use another definition.[13] The Takeover Directive can be seen as an important step towards a common definition (and a common interpretation) of 'acting in concert' throughout the EU.

One key element of the Takeover Directive definition that deserves attention is where the definition requires a cooperation aimed at 'acquiring control of the offeree company'.

Based on the provisions of the Takeover Directive relating to the mandatory bid (Article 5), one could assume that the Takeover Directive has, at least indirectly, specified what is considered as an 'acquisition of control'. Article 5.1 provides that a mandatory bid must be launched as soon as one or more persons acting in concert acquire(s) shares that, directly or indirectly, give them a specified percentage of voting rights in that company, giving them control of that company.

The Takeover Directive further specifies:

> The percentage of voting rights which confers control for the purposes of paragraph 1 and the method of its calculation shall be determined by the rules of the Member State in which the company has its registered office (Article 5.3).

This means that, under the Takeover Directive, shareholders do not need to demonstrate that the percentage of voting rights held by one or more persons acting in concert actually gives the control of the company. The Takeover Directive provides for a presumption of control as soon as a certain percentage of voting rights is held by one or more persons acting in concert.[14]

The Takeover Directive does not require that the persons acting in concert effectively exercise their control over the company following the acquisition of shares (which gives them a controlling stake). This is one of the most disputed issues in the two cases discussed in the first section of this chapter.

In both cases, the main question is whether the cooperation between several parties with the objective to acquire a controlling stake constitutes a concert party action in itself, or whether the concept of 'acting in concert' also requires an agreement among these parties to coordinate their conduct beyond the acquisition of shares (for example, by exercising their voting rights).

If parties cooperate jointly to acquire a stake that is defined as a 'controlling stake' under the applicable law, it seems irrelevant to verify whether or not these parties are coordinating their conduct with regard to the target company following this acquisition. Some of them may elect to remain passive shareholders in the future and not to intervene in the target company's affairs, leaving the task of effectively controlling the company to one or more other parties.

For instance, SAI would not have been capable of buying the Fondiaria stake from Montedison without the active coordinating role and financial help of Mediobanca. Actually, Mediobanca did not enter into an agreement with SAI regarding future control over Fondiaria. There had, however, been various discussions to which Mediobanca participated and from which Mediobanca's willingness to play an active role in the merged entity could be derived. The Court of Milan, in its 26 May 2005 ruling, referred to these facts as evidence that Mediobanca and SAI were acting in concert.[15] It is however not clear whether Consob and the Court of Milan would have come to the same conclusion if the evidence had not been uncovered by the Italian competition authority.

In the Beiersdorf case, Tchibo would not have been able to buy out Allianz's stake in Beiersdorf without the City of Hamburg's coordinated acquisition of a 10 per cent stake. The City of Hamburg undeniably played a role in bringing about the transaction and in transferring control.

There is no doubt that the various buyers have pursued a common objective beyond the acquisition of shares: keeping Beiersdorf in local, friendly hands. For the City of Hamburg, the realisation of this objective may have been sufficient to justify a €1 billion investment in the company. Even without an agreement on some kind of future joint control, the City of Hamburg's conduct should be qualified as 'acting in concert'.[16]

Yet Bafin said there was no 'acting in concert' in the Beiersdorf matter, since it, surprisingly, could not find evidence that the buyers had a common objective beyond the acquisition of shares. Courts have so far taken an even more restrictive view, according to which the concept of 'coordinated behaviour regarding the target company'[17] requires that the concert parties are coordinating their *voting rights* beyond the acquisition of shares. In one of the first test cases involving the concept of 'acting in concert', the Higher Court of Frankfurt interpreted the concept as follows:

> It is required that the third party coordinates its *voting behaviour* with the bidder and thereby strengthens the power of the bidder. The third party must consciously cooperate with the bidder with the goal *to coordinate shareholder rights and to exercise them jointly in a continuous way.*[18]

However, is it relevant, for the definition of a concert party action, to demonstrate that the City of Hamburg and Mediobanca had the objective of exercising control over the respective target companies? In the end, both had reached their objective through the coordinated acquisition of shares: keeping the target company out of third parties' hands.

When a single buyer acquires a participation in a listed company that is defined as a 'controlling stake' under the applicable takeover law, it is not necessary to verify whether this party effectively has the objective of exercising control over the target company. We do not see why several parties, who have coordinated their behaviour with the view of acquiring a controlling stake, would only be under an obligation to launch a bid if they have agreed jointly to exercise control. Why should the application of the mandatory bid rule be subject to additional requirements when the acquisition of the controlling stake (which triggers a mandatory bid) is the objective of several parties cooperating together instead of one person alone?

By requiring evidence of an agreement on the future joint exercise of control, courts and stock market regulators unnecessarily restrict the concept of 'acting in concert', making it easier to circumvent the mandatory bid rule. The Takeover Directive provides for a presumption of control, whether or not there is an objective effectively to exercise such control. This presumption will have to be part of the national implementing legislations.

Since such additional requirement – the exercise of control following the acquisition of a controlling stake – is not provided for by the Takeover Directive, we do not believe that member states may introduce or keep similar requirements in their national legislation that would narrow the scope of the mandatory bid rule under the Takeover Directive.

Persons acting in concert and shareholder activism

It may be questioned whether the rules described above should also apply to a coordination among persons who are actively defending their rights as shareholders of a listed company. Shareholders may participate to conference calls and have other informal contacts with a view to analysing and preparing their voting policy at a shareholders' meeting. Such contacts are frequent and necessary for shareholders to be able actively to defend their shareholder rights. They may occur while these shareholders are buying and selling shares of the company.

The circumstances under which such coordination occurs are quite different from a cooperation in order to acquire a controlling stake in a company as discussed in the preceding section. Such cooperation mostly involves the purchase of shares through one or more block trades or through a purchase out of the market.

The mere fact that persons come together to act in concert (for instance, by entering into an agreement), without any acquisition of shares taking place, will not normally lead to a mandatory bid under Article 5 of the Takeover Directive, even if they hold an aggregate percentage of voting rights considered to be conferring control over the company for the purposes of the mandatory bid rule. Article 5 of the Takeover Directive requires an 'acquisition'.[19]

According to the City Code:

> when a party has acquired shares without the knowledge of other shareholders or potential shareholders but subsequently comes together with other shareholders to cooperate as a group to obtain or consolidate control or a company and their existing shareholdings amount to 30 per cent or more of that company, the Panel will not normally require a general offer to be made under this Rule (Note 1 under Rule 9).

In other words, an acquisition of shares that precedes the start of a concert party action will not, normally, lead to a mandatory bid.

Yet, it is not enough to have the acquisition of shares preceding the start of a concert party action to prevent a mandatory bid from being triggered. The prior acquisition of shares must not be linked in any way to the subsequent concert party action.[20] Otherwise, it would become too easy to circumvent the mandatory bid rule.

The obligation to launch a bid will normally apply, under the City Code, when any person who has once come together with other parties subsequently acquires shares.[21]

Such situation may be dramatic for active institutional shareholders who would agree to act together in order to push for reforms and corporate governance improvements in a listed company, for instance by filing proposals at a general meeting of shareholders (removal of directors, and so on). If such action qualifies as a concert party action, an acquisition of shares by any of its members may lead to all of them having to launch a mandatory bid if it is demonstrated that they hold an aggregate percentage of voting rights that is considered to confer control of the company.

Confronted with the risk of having to launch a takeover bid, active institutional shareholders would be left with two options: either they no longer take active and coordinated measures to push for corporate governance reforms (which would be the end of efficient shareholder activism) or they limit their ability to invest in shares. Neither solution is, of course, satisfactory.

In order to prevent the mandatory bid rule from being an obstacle against shareholder activism, a more realistic and pragmatic approach is therefore required for the definition of 'persons acting in concert'. Inspiration may be found in the City Code which provides for a specific solution when persons who are deemed to be acting in concert engage into what can be described as 'shareholder activism' and they do not to seek the control of the company.

Note 2 under Rule 9 specifies that:

> the Panel does not normally regard the action of shareholders voting together on a particular resolution as action which of itself indicates that such parties are acting in concert. However, the Panel will normally presume shareholders who requisition or threaten to requisition the consideration of a board control-seeking proposal either at an annual general meeting or at an extraordinary general meeting, in each case together with their supporters as at the date of the requisition or threat, to be acting in concert with each other and with the proposed directors. Such parties will be presumed to have come into concert once an agreement or understanding is reached between them in respect of a board control-seeking proposal with the result that subsequent purchases of shares by any member of the group could give rise to an offer obligation.

It is therefore essential to verify whether a shareholder proposal at a general meeting is 'board control-seeking'. The City Code offers several factors to make such assessment. The main factor is the existence of a relationship between the proposed directors and the shareholders proposing or supporting them (agreement between the activist shareholders and the directors with respect to their proposed appointment, remuneration of the proposed directors by the activist shareholders, and so on).

The City Code provides that if there is no relationship between any of the proposed directors and any of the activist shareholders, or if the relationship is insignificant, the proposal is not considered to be board control-seeking and the parties will not be presumed to be acting in concert without it being necessary to consider other factors.

If, however, it is demonstrated that there is a relationship which is not insignificant, the analysis of whether the proposal is board control-seeking will depend on the application of other factors (the number of directors to be appointed or replaced compared with the total size of the board, the board positions held by the directors, the nature of the mandate of the proposed directors, and so on). The Code further proposes additional factors to determine whether parties no longer act in concert.

The main practical consequences of the solution proposed by the City Code is that active shareholders acting together to exercise their voting rights may represent on aggregate a high percentage of voting rights – which is often necessary in order to make sure that their proposal(s) get(s) the approval of the general meeting – without necessarily being considered to be acting in concert for the purpose of the mandatory bid rule.

However, such solution must be applied with caution in order to prevent any circumvention of the mandatory bid rule by persons who, 'disguised' as shareholder activists, would actually be seeking the control of the company.

Conclusion

As we conclude our analysis, we believe that it becomes increasingly necessary, within an integrated European financial market, to rely on common concepts and definitions in order to identify, with the required legal certainty, concert party actions which may, under certain circumstances, lead to the obligation to launch a bid on all shares of a listed company.

It is also important that this definition is applied in a harmonised way throughout the EU and that the same criteria are used in all member states. This is the best way to increase legal certainty.

The Takeover Directive definition should therefore be accompanied by a comprehensive set of implementing guidelines and criteria in order to have a common interpretation of the definition within the EU. This may probably be one of the first tasks for the 'contact committee' set up by the Takeover Directive.[22]

The mandatory bid rule is seen as a protection of minority shareholders (Article 5 of the Takeover Directive is headed 'Protection of minority shareholders, the mandatory bid and the equitable price'). However, we have explained that situations such as a coordinated exercise of voting rights at the general meeting of shareholders may fall within the scope of the mandatory bid rule. As shareholder activism is commonly regarded as benefiting all (minority) shareholders, it is therefore necessary to make sure that a rule aiming at protecting minority shareholders (the mandatory bid rule) does not deprive these minority shareholders from another protection (the possibility to coordinate the exercise of voting rights in order to improve the corporate governance structure of a company without the intention to acquire the control of this company).

We believe that the solutions proposed by the UK Takeover Panel may be a source of inspiration in order to achieve this objective at the European level. As we are probably heading to an increase of cross-border shareholder activism, the need to rely on a pragmatic approach that is applied in a harmonised way throughout the EU seems greater than ever.

---

[1] On 27 December 2001, ISVAP had refused to grant an authorisation to SAI to acquire a stake of 29 per cent in Fondiaria, on the basis of the existence of cross-shareholdings between SAI and Fondiaria (in violation of Italian law) and the negative impact of the acquisition on SAI's solvability ratio.

[2] Pursuant to the contract with Montedison, SAI had committed to buy the 29 per cent stake or, were it not to be authorised to buy the shares, to find other investors who were willing to acquire the shares, under the penalty of paying a sum of €258 million. The sum of €258 million was paid as a guarantee to Montedison.

PART I: INSIDE THE TAKEOVER REGULATION AND TACTICS

[3] Autorità Garante della Concorrenza e del Mercato, 10 October 2002.

[4] The merger was approved by the shareholders' meetings of SAI and Fondiaria on 19 December 2002.

[5] In the Fondiaria case, Consob's third communication of 18 December 2002 (confirming the existence of a concert party action) relied on evidence found by the Italian competition authorities.

[6] The merger was approved by the board of the two companies on 30 May 2002. The merger was voted by the shareholders' meetings of the two companies on 19 December 2002.

[7] Consob communication of 10 August 2001.

[8] Various newspaper articles reported about political intervention, up to the Chancellor's level, at various stages of the transaction.

[9] Questions arise as to whether only shareholders who held the shares at the time of change of control are entitled to damages, and whether only shareholders who kept the shares (but not those who sold them) are entitled to damages.

[10] As explained above, the failure to launch a tender offer has led to a substantial stock market price fall below the stock market price when speculation about a possible bid started. Should damages only compensate the loss suffered as a result of the failure to launch a bid or equally the loss following a subsequent fall of the stock market price after the change of control?

[11] Directive 2004/25/EC of the European Parliament and of the Council of 21 April 2004 on takeover bids, *OJ*, 30 April 2004, L 142, p.12.

[12] Article 2.2. further provides that, 'For the purposes of paragraph 1(d), persons controlled by another person within the meaning of Article 87 of Directive 2001/34/EC (2) shall be deemed to be persons acting in concert with that other person and with each other.'

[13] The UK Takeover Panel has already indicated that it would have to change the definition of the City Code on Takeovers and Mergers (the 'City Code') of 'persons acting in concert' to come into line with the Takeover Directive definition (see Statement 2005/10 of the Takeover Panel on the Issue of Explanatory Paper about DTI Consultation Document on the Takeovers Directive, 20 January 2005, p.21).

[14] Takeover regulations of several EU member states already provide for a presumption of 'control' when a certain percentage of voting rights is reached (for example, in Italy and Germany, the threshold is 30 per cent).

[15] There were various 'contacts' to discuss the future of the future merged entity, such as the future registered office and the name of the merged company; Mediobanca had clearly indicated that it wanted to be part of these discussions. There were also indications that Mediobanca wanted to participate in (informal) decisions about the composition of the future board of the merged entity (Tribunale di Milano, Sezione VIII Civile, 26 May 2005).

[16] It is useful to remember that the Takeover Directive provides that persons who jointly acquire shares with the objective of frustrating the successful outcome of a bid are also considered to be acting in concert, without requiring evidence of any future joint control over the target company.

[17] 'Abgestimmtes Verhalten in Bezug auf die Zielgesellschaft' as set forth in §30, Al. 2 of the German Code on Securities and Takeovers (WpÜG).

[18] OLG Frankfurt/M., 25 August 2003, 'Pixelpark'; authors' emphasis.

[19] 'Where a natural or legal person, as a result of his/her own acquisition or the acquisition by persons acting in concert with him/her' (Article 5.1 of the Takeover Directive).

[20] This is why the UK Takeover Panel requires that the prior acquisition takes place 'without the knowledge of other shareholders or potential shareholders'.

[21] Note 1 under Rule 9 of the City Code further provides that, 'Such parties having once come together, however, the provisions of the Rule will apply so that: (a) if the combined shareholdings amount to less than 30 per cent of that company, an obligation to make an offer will arise if any member of that group acquires further shares so that the total shareholders reach 30 per cent or more, or (b) if the combined shareholdings amount to between 30 per cent and 50 per cent of that company, no member of that group may acquire shares which would increase the total percentage shareholding of the group without incurring a similar obligation'.

[22] 'A contact committee shall be set up which has as its functions: (a) to facilitate, without prejudice to Articles 226 and 227 of the Treaty, the harmonised application of this Directive through regular meetings dealing with practical problems arising in connection with its application; (b) to advise the Commission, if necessary, on additions or amendments to this Directive' (Article 19.1).

Chapter 6

Optionality arrangements and reciprocity in the Takeover Directive

Matteo Gatti
Università degli Studi di Milano – Bicocca[1]

The recently adopted European Directive on Takeover Bids (the 'Takeover Directive')[2] has created broad dissatisfaction among European policymakers and the financial community in general because of its cautious approach to the regulation of takeover defences. The core of this feeling stems from the fact that two key features of the Takeover Directive, the board neutrality (or passivity) rule set forth in Article 9 and the breakthrough rule (BTR) set forth in Article 11, are not mandatory, since member states have the option to choose whether or not to implement such provisions.

The board neutrality rule compels a target company's directors to obtain a prior shareholders' authorisation when engaging in defensive actions to preserve the company's independence – 'any action, other than seeking alternative bids, which may result in the frustration of the bid'.

The BTR is a device aimed at making certain pre-bid defences, such as differential share structures (multiple voting shares, capped or time-phased voting restrictions, non-voting shares) or restrictions on transfers of shares, ineffective *vis-à-vis* a bidder.

Since both are considered to be important devices for increasing takeover activity, the fact that their adoption will depend upon choices by national legislatures puts into question whether the ultimate outcome of the Takeover Directive will indeed be the promotion of a vibrant and efficient pan-European market for corporate control.

The debate regarding the appropriate regulation of anti-takeover devices has always been extremely controversial. Historically, reaching an agreement among member states has never been considered a straightforward task. This is why it eventually became necessary for all parties to reach a compromise, which resulted in failure to meet the Commission's ambitious goal of harmonising European takeover laws through a strong shareholder-oriented approach. In fact, Article 12 of the Takeover Directive, endorsing a proposal by the Italian presidency in late 2003 aimed at granting some flexibility to member states and companies, allows member states to opt out of the board neutrality rule and/or the BTR. At the same time, Article 12 allows companies having their offices in a member state that has opted out of Articles 9 and/or 11 to opt into such rules.

Such an optionality device ends up setting forth or, better, tolerating a Babel-like system for takeover defences across the various national jurisdictions. Moreover, since companies can nevertheless opt into any of the two regimes and such decision(s) can always be reversed by their shareholders, the number of possible combinations and, hence, of possible regimes increases.

Optionality is not the only factor thwarting harmonisation in the field of takeover defences. The European law-makers have also introduced a reciprocity feature, which was proposed in the midst of the negotiations during the first half of 2003 by the Portuguese presidency. Member states can decide whether to relax the prohibitions and restrictions arising out of the board neutrality rule and/or the BTR in the event that a bid is made by a company that is not subject to the same prohibitions and restrictions, because it is not compelled to obey, or has decided not to opt into, the board neutrality rule and/or the BTR. Mixing optionality rules (Article 12(1) and (2)) with the reciprocity rule (Article 12(3)) gives rise to several combinations that member states and/or companies can adopt to regulate the regime of pre-bid and post-bid defensive tactics.

The degree of flexibility resulting from the optionality and reciprocity regimes has provided member states with several ways to escape from imposing strict regulation on takeover defences.

The Takeover Directive has clearly failed to achieve the long-term policy goal of promoting a strong takeover market by limiting the availability of defensive tactics. Meanwhile, the optionality and reciprocity features represent an intriguing test of how member states address the underlying policy choices and of how companies react to the possibility of deciding to opt into the pro-takeover EU default regime.

This chapter argues that optionality may very well be a sound approach with regard to the BTR, as the beneficial impact of the rule is still being hotly debated among commentators, and that it represents an acceptable compromise for the gradual implementation of the board neutrality rule. Quite plausibly, an abrupt introduction of a mandatory board neutrality rule would have generated, at least in some member states, a backlash in both national politics and corporate practice. The next section of the chapter discusses the failure of the Takeover Directive to harmonise the regime of takeover defences throughout Europe; the following section addresses the optionality feature, highlighting the ultimate reasons why the Italian/Portuguese compromise was, at this stage, unavoidable in order to have the Takeover Directive approved; the chapter will then conclude with an analysis of the reciprocity clause and the problems that it is most likely to raise.

Optionality and reciprocity combined

Several combinations versus complete freedom for member states

Pursuant to Article 12 of the Takeover Directive, each member state must make four choices in connection with the board neutrality rule and the BTR. Each member state must decide:

- whether or not to implement the board neutrality rule;
- whether or not to implement the reciprocity clause in relation to the board neutrality rule (which, if not opted into by the member state, can always be opted into at the company level);
- whether or not to implement the BTR; and
- whether or not to implement the reciprocity clause in relation to the BTR (given that, like the board neutrality rule, if the BTR is not implemented by a member state, it can always be opted into at the company level).

Given these four binary choices and, hence, all the possible combinations thereof, theoretically the Takeover Directive gives member states the possibility of choosing among 16 different regimes. The actual number of possible combinations increases dramatically[3] if two more possibilities are added:

- where a member state has opted out, making opt ins at the company level with regard to choices about the board neutrality rule and/or the BTR (Article 12(2)); and
- where a member state has adopted the reciprocity clause, deciding, again at the company level, whether or not to exploit reciprocity (Article 12(5)).[4]

Further, as Professor Winter has shown, where a reciprocity clause has been enacted the rules relevant to a bid for a company subject to either the board neutrality rule or the BTR or both will thus vary depending on whether or not the bidder is a company subject to any of the rules.[5]

In any case, given that the system arising out of Articles 9, 11 and 12 of the Takeover Directive compels member states to implement specific rules with regard to takeover defences, defences will no longer be left to the complete freedom of national systems, which, could have chosen not to provide any specific regulation. Given that member states must take an express position with regard to the board neutrality rule and the BTR, even the most takeover-sceptical member state, assuming that it opts out of both of the rules, is at least bound to enact the regimes set forth by Articles 9 and 11 for the benefit of companies that decide to opt into them pursuant to Article 12(2) of the Takeover Directive.

At a minimum, when member states opt out of Articles 9 and 11, such rules represent a 'take it or leave it' package that European public companies must be provided with in relation to takeover defences. If Article 9 and/or Article 11 is/are not mandatory, the 'leave it' alternative will consist of embracing national rules. The bottom line is that companies, at best, can decide between national and EU regulation only, but cannot shape their own regime in their by-laws as they wish, unless, of course, national legislation allows them to do so.[6]

Another important difference between the availability of different combinations and a silent approach leaving member states with a blank cheque on whether (and how) to regulate defences is that Article 12 requires national systems to clearly state their positions on the board neutrality rule and the BTR. It also requires member states to decide whether or not to enact the reciprocity clause. Both such decisions will lead to an outcome that cannot be deemed to be politically neutral. Instead of leaving things as they are, the Takeover Directive not only contains the minimum requirements that European law sets forth in the field of takeover defences, but also and, arguably, more notably, it represents an important observation point from which to analyse the policy evolution in the regimes of takeover defences.

Was harmonisation the ultimate goal for European policy-makers?

The alleged political failure of the Takeover Directive is ascribed to the fact that the board neutrality rule is not binding, as member states can opt out of it. It is no mystery that such a rule gave rise to major disagreement in the course of negotiations and made a previous directive proposal fail.

It is noteworthy that the alleged failure of the Takeover Directive is not simply ascribed to its inability to achieve harmonisation through national legislation and practices. What bothers the Directive's critics most is that the Directive falls short of imposing a precise policy approach: the board neutrality principle. The European Commission's aim was to open up the EU market for corporate control through the adoption of measures that could facilitate such a market, rather than merely to level the playing field.

It is well known that harmonisation does not necessarily imply a reduction of barriers in the market. In fact, harmonisation serves the purpose of simplifying certain practices and makes the given market more accessible to the relevant players, on the assumption that it reduces the transaction costs generated by different regulations. However, uniform rules might well go in the direction of increasing the obstacles to creating a strong single market. This is particularly true when the benefits of regulations are not the same for all firms and when such firms might instead take advantage of some regulatory competition, or when over-inclusive rules lead to regulatory capture.

Moreover, in the market for corporate control, the advantages of uniformity in the rules governing targets should not be overestimated, given that market participants are sufficiently sophisticated and well advised to assess, from a structural and legal standpoint, the strengths and weaknesses of the given target, and that the number of transactions is very low as compared to the market for commodities other than corporate control. Standardisation and uniformity are crucial when the number of transactions that market players perform every day is high, or when such players lack the time, skills or experience to properly evaluate in detail all the aspects of the underlying transaction. In contrast, corporate control transactions are planned long before they are eventually announced and by that later point bidders know, or should know, all about the ownership structure of their targets, including the applicable regime for pre-bid and post-bid defences. Given that the intricacies in connection with ascertaining applicable regulation are just one of the many issues that a bidder must solve before stepping into a takeover battle, it seems quite odd to believe that a 'one size fits all' regime for targets would have generated a material cost reduction in connection with takeover planning. If, at the end of the bidder's preliminary analysis, it turns out that the given target is impenetrable because of the anti-takeover regime that such target is ultimately subject to, market players will stop seeing it as a viable candidate for acquisition. Conversely, if it turns out that the control of the target is contestable, the prospective bidder will be more likely to decide to go further. In sum, the possible reduction in transaction costs resulting from a uniform regime appears to be a secondary aspect for takeover policy-making.[7]

Instead of harmonisation, which often leads to overreaching regulation and regulatory capture, the European Commission's goal is to enact provisions facilitating trade and business in the relevant market. In the market for corporate control, this means rules aimed at thwarting any managerial attempt to frustrate takeovers.[8] Given the ambitious nature of such a goal, the eventual defeat of the Commission's agenda was all but unavoidable. Resistance to the UK approach to takeover defences, together with scepticism about the 'saviour effects' of hostile takeovers and contestability of corporate control in general,[9] all contributed to that defeat. The final outcome can thus hardly be considered outrageously protectionist, or another piece of evidence that the Commission is 'a good example of a regulatory body which is unable to translate policy into legislation'.[10] More simply, the time was not ripe for getting so many constituencies to agree on such a controversial policy.

An assessment of optionality

An assessment of the merits of the optionality rules set forth by Article 12 of the Takeover

Directive requires a distinction between optionality in respect of the board neutrality rule and optionality in respect of the BTR.

Optionality and the BTR

One cannot ignore the fact that the advantages of the enactment of the BTR are still being hotly debated by experts.[11] Not only does the BTR contain a heterogeneous package of provisions, each of which *per se* would require a separate analysis of its desirability,[12] but its allegedly favourable impact on the contestability of EU firms is not considered particularly significant[13] or, in any event, sufficient to outweigh the costs related to the restraints that it would impose on flexibility and freedom of contract among companies and investors in the market,[14] and related to the incentives that it would create for replacing differential voting structures with functionally equivalent pyramidal structures.[15] Given the scarce evidence of real advantages or disadvantages brought about by the BTR, the policy choice to leave member states (and companies) free to implement it cannot raise serious criticism, at least at this early stage.

Optionality and the board neutrality rule

Evaluating whether optionality represents a sound policy with respect to the board neutrality rule is a more complex task. Before coming to the conclusion that the choice of an optional board neutrality rule is bad policy, as critics of the Takeover Directive stress, one should first demonstrate that a uniform policy approach with regard to takeover defences, notwithstanding political, structural and cultural differences in national markets for corporate control, better promotes the interests of investors, and that such uniform policy should consist of the board neutrality rule. Both questions require a preliminary evaluation of the advantages and disadvantages of the board neutrality rule.

Advantages of the board neutrality rule

Proponents of this provision emphasise that board neutrality prohibits conflicted incumbent management from raising obstacles to hostile takeovers, which in turn are considered allocatively beneficial to the economic system, as they promote synergies and better economies of scale/scope, sanction inefficient management teams and put pressure on managers to work harder in order to keep stock prices high, thus avoiding, or limiting, the risk of the firm's becoming a target in the future. According to this view, hostile takeovers are an effective and spontaneous market device for the reduction of agency costs between shareholders and managers in widely held firms.[16]

Further, in the context of the pan-European market, the board neutrality rule has always been considered to be not only a technical device to facilitate takeovers, but also a sort of crucial political precondition, given its underlying signalling effect, for the creation of a thick cross-border market for corporate control, helping EU enterprises to grow and to capture the benefits of the potential economies of scale generated by the bigger dimension of the market in which they operate.

Objections to board neutrality

Criticism of the takeover phenomenon historically represents a long-standing argument against board neutrality. In fact, some authors are opposed to the philosophy of board neutrality, as they deny its underlying basis. According to opponents of hostile takeovers, synergies and spontaneous market-generated reactions against mismanagement only partially explain the phenomenon. According to these commentators, the ultimate reasons for takeovers are inherently redistributive, as takeovers generate wealth transfers at the expense of certain stakeholders (creditors, employees, local communities, investors, the bidder's shareholders and so forth).[17] Denying directors veto powers with respect to unsolicited takeovers, the argument goes, would leave firms and the market as a whole incapable of countering corporate raiders.

Notwithstanding the endorsement of the argument that takeovers are beneficial and should be promoted, or at least not thwarted, by policy-makers, other commentators believe that a board neutrality rule, due to the strong pressure it puts on incumbents, can end up promoting anti-takeover reactions, both at the company level, via pre-bid defences,[18] and/or at the legislative level, possibly leading to the imposition of various regulatory obstacles,[19] which would ultimately result in a decrease in takeover activity.

Providing shareholders with the final say in an acquisition procedure, by way of any voting or similar device, is said to give rise to several drawbacks, particularly from an *ex ante* perspective. Considering that an incumbent management, which by definition retains a specific investment in the firm, has a natural predisposition to reject any hostile acquisition,[20] a tender offer regulation based on board neutrality and shareholders' choice would lead to the adoption of several pre-bid barriers, which in turn could harm shareholders even more than standard post-bid defences can.[21] In fact, if the inconvenience of an approach allowing management to defend the company's independence during the course of the bid is represented by the risk that managers would use their powers to entrench themselves, then pre-bid defences raise a two-fold concern. Not only is it quite complicated to identify a defence mechanism in an action taken in the ordinary course of the company's life, but it is also problematic to demonstrate that such a mechanism constitutes the prevailing and thus pathological component of an action that the management has taken within its full powers. Therefore, pre-bid defences, in particular where they are appropriately covered by complex corporate transactions, can be considered to be as dangerous as post-bid defences.[22]

Board neutrality would not only create arbitrages between post-bid and pre-bid defences, but also stimulate incumbent shareholders and managers to lobby for certain regulatory obstacles against prospective bidders. Even if such regulatory obstacles may eventually be deemed to be contrary to the EU treaties and struck down by competent European bodies, foreign prospective bidders could nevertheless be dissuaded from launching a bid if they consider the obstacles as symptoms of national resistance to cross-border mergers in the given member state.

Similarly, pro-takeover legislation may well result in fewer firms being eager to go public, which is something that contradicts the goal of having a thick European takeover market, as, self-evidently, the presence of public firms represents a necessary precondition for the growth of such a market.

Opponents of board neutrality have also made the case that empowering a board to say no to certain coercive bids, such as partial bids, non-cash bids or bids that are not fully-funded and so on, or to creeping acquisitions, or to low-value bids might represent an important device for a target's shareholders, who would otherwise run the risk of being forced to tender reluctantly to low-value two-tier acquisitions.[23] Impeding board responses would reduce the usefulness of an important tool for countering inefficient acquisitions.[24,25]

Another argument raised by opponents of board neutrality lies in the fact that the rule would make European firms juicier targets for the appetites of foreign companies, most notably US companies, which in turn can benefit from management-friendly regimes on takeover defences and, hence, can hardly ever be taken over by EU firms. It should be noted that the inability to achieve a level playing field with the United States was one of the three political considerations that motivated the European Parliament's decision to strike down the old proposal for the 13th Directive.[26]

Optionality in the light of objections to the board neutrality rule

Frontal opposition to hostile takeovers was precisely what the European Commission was trying to counter with its approach against takeover defences. In this respect, the Takeover Directive effectively fails to fulfil the Commission's agenda of removing such biases against a free takeover market.

However, given the risk that the board neutrality rule could have ended up promoting some protectionist backlashes, the optionality feature, instead of being dismissed as factual proof of the failure of the Commission's policies, can rather be considered as a first, gradual step toward the goal of an open European market for corporate control. In the absence of an adaptive device such as optionality, an abrupt imposition of board neutrality could have led to unpredictable reactions from companies, as well as from national legislatures and/or regulators. The optionality device will instead help those national legislatures that have not yet introduced any board neutrality rule to slowly test the impact of board neutrality on their systems, through the observation of the use that companies make of the opt in device.[27] The advantage of the adaptive optional system provided for by the Takeover Directive is that it limits shocks at the national level caused by the sudden vulnerability of targets.

Moreover, the adaptive system set forth under Article 12(1) allows member states to grant companies a more effective regime to counter inefficient acquisitions. For example, a national legislature could decide to apply the board neutrality rule only to bids that are all-cash, fully funded and in respect of any and all shares,[28] thus giving directors the possibility of responding to partial or exchange offers.[29]

As to the argument emphasising the lack of reciprocity with the United States, notwithstanding the persuasive criticism it has raised,[30] the vulnerability of EU firms was one of the main factors that led to the introduction of the reciprocity clause, although it is far from clear whether such a protection can be enforced *vis-à-vis* non-EU firms.

The mechanics of optionality under the Takeover Directive

Articles 9, 11 and 12 of the Takeover Directive together set forth a pro-takeover default system that member states can reverse. While it is not easy to make predictions about the choices of member states with respect to the BTR,[31] one should expect that the policy choice of whether or not to opt out of the board neutrality rule is going to be path-dependent. In fact, it is implausible that, after all the efforts that have been made to resist the board neutrality rule, a country such as Germany would eventually adopt it. On the other hand, it is difficult to see any reasons – other than mere political retaliation or protectionism, which can in any event be pursued by enacting the reciprocity device – why a member state that has previously embraced board neutrality would decide to undo such a policy.

A member state opting out of any of the rules must nevertheless give the option to companies with offices in its territory to voluntarily make themselves subject to such restrictions.

As to the mechanics of the opt out/opt in scheme set forth in Article 12(1) and (2), it is questionable whether such a scheme is superior to an easier and functionally equivalent one in which a member state that does not impose the board neutrality rule as mandatory would be required to set such a regime as the default rule with the possibility for companies to opt out of it.[32] It should be noted that this latter system, if compared with the opt out/opt in mechanism of Article 12(1) and (2), would have the virtue of clearly signalling to the market which issuers intend to depart from the pro-shareholders standard provided for by the board neutrality rule. In other words, a pro-takeover default is preferable, as it requires targets to take steps to reverse it, which is something that may have a negative impact on share prices and would shine a spotlight on targets that try to hide. In case of adoption of a pro-incumbents default, the market would quite certainly not expect that many 'virtuous' targets would take actions to reverse it and targets would certainly not bother to make the market change its mind.[33] Further, since the default rule set forth in Article 12(1) of the Takeover Directive is board neutrality, it appears strange that, when regulating the default for member states that opt out of board neutrality, the European law-makers have allowed member states to impose an opposite default.[34] In any case, given that the system described above – board neutrality rule as default, with a possibility for companies to opt out – does not seem to substantially depart from the one provided for in the Takeover Directive – the possibility for member states to set forth a default other than the board neutrality rule with the option for companies to opt into such rule. Member states could always impose the latter default without breaching the Takeover Directive.

The uncertain case for reciprocity in takeovers

According to Article 12(3) of the Takeover Directive:

> Member States may, under the conditions determined by national law, exempt companies which apply Article 9(2) and (3) and/or Article 11 from applying Article 9(2) and (3) and/or Article 11 if they become the subject of an offer launched by a company which does not apply the same Articles as they do, or by a company controlled, directly or indirectly, by the latter.

Reciprocity represents a peculiar way to achieve a 'level playing field' in the takeover market.[35]

The first tool that European policy-makers conceived when required to attain that goal was actually the BTR. One of the main criticisms that the European Parliament raised in 2001 against the rejected proposal for the 13th Directive and, particularly, the board neutrality rule that it provided for rested upon the fact that such a policy approach would have had a significantly different impact in the various national jurisdictions, due to the diversities within company laws, practices and structures across the EU. Given the unbalanced effects of the board neutrality rule among potential target companies,[36] the Commission gave a mandate to the High-Level Group (among other things) to identify a technical device to ensure a level playing field while maintaining the policy goal of the board neutrality rule. The device envisaged by the High-Level Group was indeed the BTR, the ultimate goal being that of transforming companies that had erected certain pre-bid barriers into firms with control that would be contestable in the market.

Hence, the first strategy pursued by European policy-makers in order to reach a level playing field was to promote an increase in the number of potential targets by allowing the breaking through of certain pre-bid anti-takeover devices.[37] However, as pointed out above, the BTR failed to be approved by member states and was softened through the optionality rule in Article 12(1) of the Takeover Directive.

The reciprocity feature provided for in Article 12(3) of the Takeover Directive is probably the most radical device to reach a level playing field. National legislatures that are unable or unwilling to force companies to become more contestable may introduce a system in which a bidder is excluded from certain advantages in taking over another company (the applicability to the target of Articles 9 and/or 11) if the bidder itself is not subject to such rules. Reciprocity pursuant to Article 12(3) of the Takeover Directive does not set forth any actual prohibition of a bidder from taking over a target subject to such rules: it simply creates a disincentive for a company not having similar characteristics. It makes it impossible for that type of company to avail itself of rules eliminating certain obstacles to takeovers.

Reciprocity has two significant drawbacks.[38] First, from a practical standpoint, the rule is under-inclusive in pursuing a level playing field, as the mere fact that a company is subject to the board neutrality rule and/or the BTR does not automatically make it contestable. In fact, for full reciprocity to be effective, both companies would need to have the same degree of contestability, which is technically impossible to define and would render very few companies subject to the rules. Secondly, reciprocity would restrict the group of potential bidders to listed companies that are themselves open to hostile bids, which would be at odds with the promotion of a vibrant market for corporate control, as it would impose a large demand-side restriction.[39] This would result in both fewer takeovers and lower premiums.

Article 12(3) of the Takeover Directive requires member states to decide whether or not to adopt reciprocity: only if it has been adopted by the national legislature can companies choose whether or not to apply Article 9 and/or 11 *vis-à-vis* bidders that are not subject to such rules.[40] This means that, similarly to their inability to autonomously opt out of Articles 9 and/or 11, companies alone cannot introduce reciprocity. Therefore the alleged 'pro-choice' approach stemming from the Takeover Directive is put into play only if member states decided to enact anti-takeover rules. It does not allow companies to escape from pro-takeover legislation that contemplates both the board neutrality rule and the BTR, and that does not provide for any reciprocity rule.

Given the broad powers that member states have been granted with respect to reciprocity,[41] it would be premature to try to assess its final impact, as much will depend on the way in which each member state introduces the rule. The issues to be solved are many and include the following:

- Can reciprocity work outside the EU, such that the bans on defensive actions can be relaxed if the bidder is, for example, a US corporation?[42] What if a non-contestable US corporation were to opt into the two regimes?
- Would reciprocity also apply *vis-à-vis* limited liability companies? What if those companies introduced the board neutrality rule and/or the BTR into their own by-laws, with the obvious purpose of benefiting from the application of such rules to their target?
- Will reciprocity also apply between companies in the same jurisdiction?

- Can national legislatures expand the scope of reciprocity by, for example, exempting target companies from applying the board neutrality rule and/or the BTR when the bid is launched by a company with a controlling shareholder?
- How would reciprocity work if the BTR were only partially implemented in a given member state, for example if national regulation prescribes the rule on share transferability set forth by Article 11(2) only and not the remainder of Article 11? Can a company subject to Article 11(2) only and thus not embracing the full BTR be exempted from applying the rule if the bid were made by a bidder that is not subject to it?

Considering the typical degree of freedom with which national legislatures enact European directives and the lack of any effective enforcement of sanctions for failure to implement them appropriately,[43] there is a substantial risk that reciprocity, instead of levelling the playing field, could end up jeopardising the Takeover Directive, by driving national legislatures to introduce cumbersome and overly protectionist caveats to the applicability of Articles 9 and/or 11.

Finally, reciprocity is in general characterised by two main aspects:

- it is inherently a protectionist measure – not as drastic as a barrier, but still a limitation on the prerogatives of foreigners; and
- it generates an incentive for the national legislature to provide foreigners with certain rights so that its citizens can take advantage of the same rights abroad, in those countries where reciprocity applies too.

Both of these characteristics are present with respect to the system provided for in Articles 9, 11 and 12 of the Takeover Directive.[44] While the protectionist aspect is, as anticipated, in line with the agenda of those who oppose takeovers, the incentive aspect goes in the opposite direction. Thus, in member states that opt out of Article 9 and/or Article 11, companies having acquisition plans will most probably opt into Article 9 and/or Article 11.[45] Such member states should therefore carefully consider whether or not to introduce reciprocity, as this would, paradoxically, result in more firms becoming subject to board neutrality and/or the BTR.

Conclusion

Given the difficulties that member states had in reaching a uniform policy with respect to the regulation of takeover defences, it was necessary for European law-makers to adopt a compromise text allowing each member state to choose among many different combinations. Irrespective of whether or not this outcome leads to the conclusion that European policy-making in the field of corporate law has once again shown its limits – particularly when very crucial issues, such as the protection of corporate control, are at stake – the actual implementation of the Takeover Directive by both member states and, where applicable, companies will provide legal and economic commentators with a very interesting observation point for analysing, on the one hand, the policy choices on takeover defences that national legislatures embrace and, on the other hand, the ways in which companies use their powers to reverse or embrace such choices.

Given that, at this stage, any forecast of the ultimate decisions would be pretty naïve and possibly useless, the only member state that has taken a position thus far is the United

Kingdom, which has made it clear that it will maintain the board neutrality rule and will opt out of the BTR, without enacting any reciprocity provisions,[46] all there is to do is to wait and see what happens after the 'big bang' of 20 May 2006.

References

Ayres, I., and R. Gertner, 'Filling Gaps in Incomplete Contracts: An Economic Theory of Default Rules', *Yale Law Journal*, Vol. 94, No.87 (1989).

Bainbridge, S.M., *Mergers and Acquisitions* (New York: Foundation Press, 2003).

Bebchuk, L.A., 'The Case Against Board Veto in Corporate Takeovers', *University of Chicago Law Review*, Vol 973, No. 69 (2002).

Bebchuk, L.A., and A. Hamdani, 'Optimal Defaults for Corporate Law Evolution', *Northwestern University Law. Review,* Vol. 489, No. 96 (2002).

Bebchuk, L.A., and O. Hart, 'A Threat to Dual-Class Shares', *Financial Times* (31 May 2002), p. 11.

Becht, M., 'Reciprocity in Takeovers', in G. Ferrarini *et al.* (eds), (2004), cited below.

Berglöf, E., and M. Burkart, 'European Takeover Regulation', *Economic Policy* (2003).

Black, B.S., and R. Kraakman, 'Delaware's Takeover Law: The Uncertain Search for Hidden Value', *Northwestern University Law Review*, Vol. 521, No. 96 (2002).

Blair, M., and L.A. Stout, 'A Team Production Theory of Corporate Law', *Virginia Law Review*, Vol. 247, No. 85 (1999).

Carney, W., 'Shareholder Coordination Costs, Shark Repellents, and Takeout Mergers: The Case Against Fiduciary Duties', *American Bar Foundation Research Journal*, Vol. 341, No. 2 (1983).

Cioffi, J.W., 'Restructuring "Germany Inc.": The Politics of Company and Takeover Law Reform in Germany and the European Union', *Law and Policy*, Vol. 355, No. 24 (2002).

Coates, J.C., IV, 'Ownership, Takeovers and EU Law: How Contestable Should EU Corporations Be?', in G. Ferrarini *et al.* (eds), 2004, cited below.

DeAngelo, H., and E. Rice, 'Anti-Takeover Charter Amendments and Stockholder Wealth', *Journal of Finance and Economics* 11 (1983).

Easterbrook, F.H., and D.R. Fischel, *The Economic Structure of Corporate Law* (Cambridge, MA: Harvard University Press, 1991).

Edwards, V., 'The Directive on Takeover Bids – Not Worth the Paper it's Written On?', *European Company and Financial Law Review* (1991), pp. 416–39.

Enriques, L., 'In tema di difese contro le opa ostili: verso assetti proprietari più contendibili o più piramidali?', *Giur. comm.*, Vol. 108, No. 1 (2002).

Enriques, L., 'The Mandatory Bid Rule in the Proposed EC Takeover Directive: Harmonization as Rent-Seeking?', in G. Ferrarini *et al.* (eds), (2004), cited below.

Enriques, L. 'EC Company Law Directives and Regulations: How Trivial Are They?', forthcoming in *University of Pennsylvania Journal of International Economic Law*.

Ferrarini, G., 'Takeover Defences and the New Proposal for European Directive', Working Paper (2002) downloadable at www.cedif.org.

Ferrarini, G., K.J. Hopt, J. Winter, and E. Wymeersch (eds), *Reforming Company Law and Takeover Law in Europe* (Oxford and New York: Oxford University Press, 2004).

Gatti, M., *Opa e struttura del mercato del controllo societario* (Milan: Giuffre, 2004).

Godden, R., 'Why the Takeover Directive will be a Non-Event', *Financial News* (25 January 2004).

Gordon, J.N., 'An American Perspective on Anti-Takeover Laws in the EU: The German Example', in G. Ferrarini *et al.* (eds), (2004), cited above.

Haddock, D.D., J.R. Macey, and F.S. McChesney, 'Property Rights in Assets and Resistance to Tender Offers', *Virginia Law Review*, Vol. 701, No. 73 (1973).

Hertig, G., and J.A. McCahery, 'Revamping the EU Corporate and Takeover Law Agenda – and Making It a Model for the US', Working Paper (2004) posted at www.repositories.cdlibe.org.

Kahan, M., and E.B. Rock, 'Corporate Constitutionalism: Anti-takeover Charter Provisions as Precommitment', *University of Pennsylvania Journal of International Economic Law*, Vol. 473, No. 153 (2003).

Lipton, M., and P.K. Rowe, 'Pills, Polls and Professors: A Reply to Professor Gilson', *Delaware Journal. of Corporate Law*, Vol.27, No. 1 (2002).

Maul, S., and A. Kouloridas, 'The Takeover Bids Directive', *German Law Journal*, Vol. 355, No. 5 (2004).

McDaniel, M., 'Bondholders and Corporate Governance', *Business. Law*, Vol. 413, No. 41 (1986).

Morck, R., A. Schleifer, and R. Vishny, 'Do Managerial Objectives Drive Bad Acquisitions?', *Journal of Finance*, No. 45 (1990).

Painter, R., and C. Kirchner, 'Takeover Defences under Delaware Law, the Proposed Thirteenth EU Directive and the New German Takeover Law: Comparison and Recommendations for Reform', Illinois Law and Economics Working Papers, Series Paper No. 02-006 (2002), downloadable at http://papers.ssrn.com/pape.tar?abstract_id=311740.

Roe, M.J., *Political Determinants of Corporate Governance* (Oxford and New York: Oxford University Press, 2003).

Shleifer, A., and L.H. Summers, 'Breach of Trust in Hostile Takeovers', in A.J. Auerbach (ed.), *Corporate Takeovers: Causes and Consequences* (Chicago: University of Chicago Press, 1988).

Siems, M.M., 'The Rules on Conflict of Laws in the European Takeover Directive', *European Company and Financial Law Review* (2004), pp. 458–76.

Subramanian, G., 'Bargaining in the Shadow of Takeover Defences', *Yale Law Journal*, Vol. 621, No. 113 (2003).

Vella, F., 'La passivity rule nella legge italiana sulle offerte pubbliche di acquisto e gli effetti sul mercato del controllo societario', *Banca, impresa e società* (1993), p. 259 *et seq.*

Wachter, M.L., 'Takeover Defence when Financial Markets are (Only) Relatively Efficient', *University of Pennsylvania Journal of International Economic Law*. Vol. 787, No. 151 (2003).

Winter, J., 'EU Company Law at the Crossroads', in G. Ferrarini *et al.* (eds), 2004, cited above.

---

[1] This chapter originated as a paper prepared for a seminar, 'Il Nuovo Diritto Societario Europeo', held in Padua on 20 May 2005. I am grateful to Luca Enriques, Benjamin Faulkner, Jeremy Grant and seminar participants for useful comments on earlier versions. I wish also to thank Denise Filauro for research assistance. All errors are mine.

[2] Directive 2004/25/EC of the European Parliament and of the Council of 21 April 2004 on takeover bids, O.J. L 142/12 of 30 April 2004.

[3] In fact, for each of the eight combinations in which a member state provides for a single opt out (either from the board neutrality rule or from the BTR) companies can opt into the relevant rule, which adds eight other possible combinations to the 'menu'. One could make the point that, since the set of choices to be made at the company level is the same as the set occurring at the member state level (whether or not to adopt the board neutrality principle and/or the BTR), opt ins at the company level will not add any new combinations. However, since choices at the company level are reversible, they are intrinsically different from the choices made by a national legislature. Moreover, the possibility of opting in at the company level also implies that different regulations may be encountered within the same jurisdiction. Further, given that, for each of the four combinations in which member states opt out of both rules, companies can decide to (i) opt into the board neutrality rule only; (ii) opt into the BTR only; or (iii) opt into both rules, there are 12 additional possibilities. The reason why there would be four possible combinations if member states opted out of both the board neutrality rule and the BTR lies in the fact that such member states might (i) implement no reciprocity clauses with respect to any of the rules; (ii) implement the reciprocity clause with respect to the board neutrality rule only; (iii) implement the reciprocity clause with respect to the BTR only; or (iv) implement the reciprocity clause for both rules. Given that there is also an optional element when reciprocity is enacted, as companies can decide whether or not to authorise the relevant measure (Article 12(5)), the overall number of possible combinations increases further.

[4] 'Any measure applied in accordance with paragraph 3 shall be subject to the authorisation of the general meeting of shareholders of the offeree company, which must be granted no earlier than 18 months before the bid was made public'.

[5] See J. Winter (2004), p. 18. For instance, in the event that, in a member state that has enacted the reciprocity feature for both Articles 9 and 11, Company X is subject to both Articles 9 and 11 (and has authorised the measure pursuant to Article 12(5)), and Company X is potentially subject to four different regimes, depending on the rules to which a potential bidder is subject, then (i) if the bid is made by Bidder A, which is subject to both, Company X will be subject to both; (ii) if the bid is made by Bidder B, which is subject to Article 9 and not Article 11, Company X will be subject to Article 9 only; (iii) if the bid is made by Bidder C, which is subject to Article 11 and not Article 9, Company X will be subject to Article 11 only; and (iv) if the bid is made by Bidder D, which is not subject to any of the two rules, Company X will not be subject to either of them.

[6] According to Professors M. Kahan and E.B. Rock (2003), this latter adaptive approach would be the optimal policy choice for the regulation of takeover defences.

[7] Notwithstanding this, it should be acknowledged that the Babel-like regime that has finally been approved is too chaotic.

[8] As emphasised in the text, harmonisation could, theoretically, have been achieved through a rule allowing directors to erect barriers to takeovers. There is no doubt that such a rule would level the playing field, but, at the same time, it would have contrasted, at least in the Commission's view, with the promotion of a vibrant and strong market.

[9] For a discussion, see below.

[10] G. Hertig and J.A. McCahery (2004), p. 3.

[11] The proposal to introduce the BTR was advanced in the Report of the High-Level Group of Experts on Issues Related to Takeover Bids as a device with which to create a 'level playing field' for shareholders across the different legal systems in the EU. However, as reported by the Commission itself, in the Proposal of 2 October 2002 that followed the Report and formally reopened the preparations for the Takeover Directive, the rule found widespread opposition 'from virtually all member states and interested parties, notably because of the legal problems to which they may give rise (application threshold, concept of risk-bearing capital, compensation for right foregone)': Proposal for a Directive on Takeover Bids COM (2002) 534, O.J. 45 E of 25.02.2003, p. 4.

[12] Most of the criticism surrounding the BTR has entailed the imposition of a 'one share, one vote' principle over dual-class share structures (see footnote 15 below), while less concern has been raised with respect to the rule set forth under Article 11(2) that limits restrictions to the transfer of securities (for a critique on the latter provision, see V. Edwards (2004), p. 437, which stresses that the rule is both redundant, as listing requirements already provide for free transferability of shares, and over-inclusive, as it may catch some normal market arrangements such as sale agreements with deferred settlements and irrevocable undertakings to accept a takeover when bundled with a restriction on the sale of the underlying securities).

[13] See J.C. Coates IV (2004), which emphasises that only a trivial fraction (3–4 per cent) of European listed firms would be subject to the rule.

[14] See the Consultative Document issued by the UK Department of Trade and Industry on 20 January 2005, p. 27, which argues that there are some cases in which differential share structures may provide advantages.

[15] See, among others, L.A. Bebchuk and O. Hart (2002), and L. Enriques (2002).

[16] For this approach, see, among others, F.H. Easterbrook and D.R. Fischel (1991), pp. 162 *et seq.*

[17] See, albeit with different approaches in relation to the optimal solution for tackling such redistributions, among others, M. Lipton and P.K. Rowe (2002), M. McDaniel (1986); A. Shleifer and L.H. Summers (1988); M. Blair and M.A. Stout (1999); R. Morck, A. Shleifer and R. Vishny (1990).

[18] J. Arlen and E. Talley (2003).

[19] See R. Painter and C. Kirchner (2002), which mentions anti-trust and other regulatory barriers.

[20] Compare J.C. Coates IV (2004), p. 689, 'if US takeover experience has any lessons, it is that top managers worry about few things more than preserving the control of their firms', with M. Kahan and E.B. Rock (2002) and J.N. Gordon (2004): the conflict of interest problem should be revisited, in the light of the alignment between shareholders and directors due to executive compensation systems based on stock option plans.

[21] If effective post-bid remedies, such as poison pills in the US context, are banned, the management will seek to make the company takeover-proof by resorting to other remedies that can be easily adopted before a bid. One may think of defences hidden by some plausible financial or industrial justification, such as the insertion of change-of-control provisions in the company's most important contracts (joint ventures, contracts with the management, credit agreements and so forth). Such provisions could raise several costs for a potential acquirer and thus constitute a substantial burden for any non-solicited change of control. See J. Arlen and E. Talley (2003); M.L. Wachter (2003); F. Vella (1993).

[22] Note that post-bid defences can at least be easily recognised and become subject to judicial scrutiny. Pre-bid defences might be preferable precisely because a judge might never be able to second-guess decisions made long before the bid was launched.

[23] See H. DeAngelo and E.M. Rice (1983), W. Carney (1983), D.D. Haddock, J.R. Macey and F.S. McChesney (1987), J. Arlen (2002), S.M. Bainbridge (2003). For an opposite approach, see G. Subramanian (2003).

[24] For a critique, see L.A. Bebchuk (2002), which argues that granting boards veto powers is an undesirable solution to the problem of inefficient acquisitions.

[25] Given the restrictions stemming from the implementation of the Second Directive, it is debatable whether board response would be a useful device to prevent coercive bids, as European directors would lack sufficient powers to adopt effective defensive tactics (see, among others, G. Ferrarini (2002), at 17). Accordingly, board neutrality might also be considered an inadequate means to counter takeover defences and thus to promote a vibrant market for corporate control. In fact, board neutrality alone does not impede target companies from engaging in frustrating actions, if incumbents can count on a sufficient number of votes to authorise frustrating actions against the bid. Note that, if the private benefits of control are sufficiently high, a decision to reject the bid will be undertaken even if the bid is a value-increasing one.

[26] See the Proposal for a Directive on Takeover Bids COM (2002) 534, *O.J.* 45 E of 25.02.2003, p. 2.

[27] Such a result cannot be considered as a non-event (for this conclusion, see R. Godden (2004)) if it is borne in mind that 'opt in provisions are not trivial if they introduce a regime previously unavailable in one of the member states and if companies in this state do opt into the new regime in significant numbers' (L. Enriques (2005), pp. 17–18).

[28] Cf. L. Enriques (2004), p. 793 n. 105.

[29] A counter-argument could be that the problem of coercive acquisitions in Europe is minimised by the mandatory bid rule and, hence, board response would be redundant. For a critical view with respect to the effectiveness of the mandatory bid as a remedy against coercive acquisitions, see M. Gatti (2004), pp. 67 n. 63 and 268: the mandatory bid makes a partial bid or a street sweep more expensive, but does not impede these types of acquisitions from succeeding.

[30] See, among others, J.N. Gordon (2004), which argues that poison pills do not in practice impede a takeover market because, unlike European-style defences, they are not irreversible and, moreover, given the vesting of stock options upon a change of control and the ensuing alignment with shareholders' interests, managers carefully evaluate the profitability of a bid before deciding not to redeem a poison pill.

[31] It should be noted that a decision to impose the BTR will have a different impact on the legislation of each member state, depending on whether the contractual provisions to be broken through represent common practice or, at least, are legally feasible in the given member state. Where dual-class share structures are not common in a given national system, the enactment of the BTR will not result in a major risk for potential targets. Moreover, introducing the BTR, particularly where such a rule, as mentioned above, would make only a small impact on potential targets, might help in overcoming a reciprocity device set forth in another member state (see below).

[32] The system described in the text was initially proposed by Portugal during the legislative work on the Takeover Directive. In fact, the Portuguese proposal envisaged a system in which member states could elect to impose the application of Article 9 and/or 11, but with the possibility of allowing their companies to opt out of any of the rules.

[33] The underlying assumption is that setting the board neutrality rule as a default would be preferable, as this would need firms to require the market to approve a departure from such a pro-investor standard, with all the consequences that this effort may generate, notably a potential drop in the stock price. This would not necessarily mean that companies would find it much harder to derogate from the default, particularly when they can count on a non-trivial number of shareholders backing their agenda. However, it seems quite clear that such a default rule would be superior to an opposite pro-incumbents default, in which the status quo favours managers, and which requires investors to activate in order to obtain the desired arrangements. Cf. I. Ayres and R. Gertner (1989). Note that if national company law contemplates in the rules governing shareholders' meetings a system of blocking minorities, there would be a further reason to prefer a pro-investor default, as, self-evidently, in such case a minority of incumbents can block a majority from endorsing the pro-takeover rule. Cf. also L.A. Bebchuk and A. Hamdani (2002), which discusses asymmetries in reversibility of the default.

[34] Given that the European law-makers showed some preference for board neutrality, it would have made more sense to impose an identical default at the company level.

[35] See note 11 above.

[36] According to some commentators, Germany's biases against the board neutrality rule were not necessarily caused by the underlying neo-liberal approach of the rule, but rather because domestic reforms (notably, the Control and Transparency Law 1998) modernised and liberalised the corporate governance structures of German firms to a degree that rendered such firms more contestable. See J.W. Cioffi (2002).

[37] As is pointed out below, while the BTR seeks to promote the level playing field by increasing the number of potential targets, the reciprocity feature does that by ultimately reducing the number of potential bidders.

[38] See M. Becht (2004).

[39] It can also be legitimately questioned whether the concept of reciprocity in itself makes sense in a capitalist economy. Unless one makes the case that being takeover-proof unduly helps prospective bidders in prevailing *vis-à-vis* their competitors in the market for corporate control (all other potential buyers) that do not have the same characteristics, the argument that a non-contestable company should not be allowed to take over a contestable one sounds merely evocative.

[40] When reciprocity is enacted in the given member state, Article 12(5) substantially requires that companies be authorised to use the reciprocity feature by their general meeting, 'Any measure applied in accordance with paragraph 3 shall be subject to the authorisation of the general meeting of shareholders of the offeree company, which must be granted no earlier than 18 months before the bid was made public'.

[41] Article 12(3) requires national legislators to determine the conditions according to which the exemptions from the applicability of the board neutrality rule and/or the BTR would work pursuant the reciprocity feature.

[42] Compare J. Winter (2004), pp. 18–19, and S. Maul and A. Kouloridas (2004), pp. 359–60, both of which stress that excluding non-EU companies from the benefits of Article 9 and/or 11 would be in breach of the international legal

117

obligations of the EU and member states, with V. Edwards (2004), p. 430, which argues that reciprocity provisions would also apply *vis-à-vis* US bidders.

[43] See L. Enriques (2005), p. 8 *et seq*.

[44] For an evaluation of the advantages and disadvantages of reciprocity, see the Consultative Document issued by the UK Department of Trade and Industry on 20 January 2005, p. 28, which concludes that the drawbacks of reciprocity – protectionism, risks of retaliation for UK businesses abroad and complexity – largely outweigh its sole advantage, which is the incentive for companies to adopt open takeover regimes.

[45] See M.M. Siems (2004), p. 460 n. 8.

[46] See the Consultative Document issued by the UK Department of Trade and Industry on 20 January 2005, p. 25 *et seq*.

Chapter 7

The mandatory bid rule and the sell-out right in the Takeover Directive: harmonisation for its own sake?

Luca Enriques
University of Bologna and ECGI Research Associate

In April 2004, almost 15 years after the European Commission issued the first proposal for a directive on takeovers,1 the EC succeeded in adopting the Takeover Directive.2 This was possible only after the Council and the European Parliament had agreed not to harmonise target companies' defensive tactics, by making the rules on the obligations of the board of the target company (Article 9) and on breakthrough (Article 11) optional for member states (Article 12).

This compromise solution has deprived the directive of much of its bite. Arguably, most of the remaining provisions are little more than 'housekeeping rules', clarifying matters such as the competent authority and the applicable law in cross-border takeovers (Article 4), providing procedural rules on how to conduct a bid and what to disclose (Articles 6, 7 and 8), or laying down broad and vague general principles on takeovers (Article 3).

The only remaining rules that appear to potentially affect the structure of bids and therefore more directly have an impact upon the functioning of the market for corporate control within the EU are those regarding mandatory bids, squeeze-outs and the sell-out right (Articles 5, 15 and 16 respectively). However, a closer look at two of these provisions, those on mandatory bids and the sell-out right, justifies a more sceptical view of their impact on the market for corporate control and, by implication, of the Takeover Directive as a whole. In fact, these provisions are easily avoidable, whether by members states at the implementation stage or, later on, by private parties, with the help of smart lawyers and, possibly, supervisory authorities. In other words, the provisions are drafted in such a way as to leave it to the member states whether such investor protection tools will indeed have some bite or whether they make it possible, if not easy, for acquirers to avoid the extra costs imposed by them.

To support this argument, the chapter proceeds as follows. The next section describes in detail the provisions on mandatory bids and the sell-out right. The section following shows that the directive leaves plenty of room for member states and acquirers of control wishing to avoid the requirement, depending on the choice made by the member states at the implementation stage and/or by their supervisory authorities later on. The final section concludes that these provisions are trivial and attempts to provide an answer to the question why such trivial rules were adopted at all. In doing so, it also argues that the EU mandatory bid rule will complicate and petrify the regulatory environment, leading to higher rents for lawyers, and that it will grant wide discretion to securities agency officials, allowing them also to extract higher rents.

Provisions on mandatory bids and the sell-out right

The Takeover Directive grants member states wide discretion, both at the time of implementation and in the practical administration of the rules as implemented, to set the mandatory bid price and, more importantly, to decide whether a bid must be made once the relevant threshold has been crossed. The provision on the sell-out right operates only when the acquirer so wishes.

General principles

Essential to an understanding of the directive's framework of rules are the definitions and broad principles set forth in Articles 2–4 of the Takeover Directive.

Article 2(e) defines 'securities' as those 'carrying voting rights in a company' (in its general meeting). When the directive uses this expression it does *not* cover non-voting shares. The term 'bid' includes both mandatory and voluntary offers (Article 2(a)). Article 3 lays down a series of fundamental principles that member states must follow in implementing the directive, at least one of which is worth citing (section 1, letter (a)), 'if a person acquires control of a company, the other holders of securities must be protected'.

Member states 'may lay down additional conditions and provisions more stringent than those of this directive for the regulation of bids' (Article 3(2)), meaning both voluntary and mandatory bids. The directive provides only minimum safeguards for minority shareholders, leaving member states free to devise further protections.[3] The Preamble[4] expressly states that member states may decide to apply rules on mandatory bids to other types of securities, such as non-voting shares.

Finally, according to Article 4(5):

> Provided that the general principles laid down in Article 3(1) are respected, Member States may provide in the rules that they make or introduce pursuant to this directive for derogations from those rules: (i) by including such derogations in their national rules, in order to take account of circumstances determined at national level and/or (ii) by granting their supervisory authorities, where they are competent, powers to waive such national rules, to take account of the circumstances referred to in (i) or in other specific circumstances, in which case a reasoned decision must be required.

The mandatory bid rule

Article 5 contains the mandatory bid rule provisions, under which, according to section 1:

> Where a natural or legal person, as a result of his/her own acquisition or the acquisition by persons acting in concert with him/her [as defined in Article 2(d)], holds securities of a company ... which, added to any existing holdings of those securities and the holdings of persons acting in concert with him/her, directly or indirectly give

him/her a specified percentage of voting rights in that company, giving him/her the control of that company [a concept to be defined by each member state: section 3], Member States shall ensure that such a person is required to make a bid as a means of protecting the minority shareholders of that company. Such a bid shall be addressed at the earliest opportunity to all the holders of those securities for all their holdings at the equitable price as defined in section 4.
According to the first sub-section of section 4:

The highest price paid for the same securities by the offeror, or by persons acting in concert with him/her, over a period, to be determined by Member States, of not less than six and not more than 12 months before the bid referred to in section 1 shall be regarded as the equitable price. If, after the bid has been made public and before the offer closes for acceptance, the offeror or any person acting in concert with him/her purchases securities at a price higher than the offer price, the offeror shall increase his/her offer so that it is not less than the highest price paid for the securities so acquired.

According to the second and third sub-sections of section 4:

Provided that the general principles laid down in Article 3(1) are respected, Member States may authorise their supervisory authorities to adjust the price referred to in the first subsection in circumstances and in accordance with criteria that are clearly determined. To that end, they *may* [author's emphasis] draw up a list of circumstances in which the highest price may be adjusted either upwards or downwards, for example [and hence not exhaustively] where the highest price was set by agreement between the purchaser and a seller [reasonably, in case of collusion], where the market prices of the securities in question have been manipulated, where market prices in general or certain market prices in particular have been affected by exceptional occurrences, or in order to enable a firm in difficulty to be rescued. They may also determine the criteria to be applied in such cases, for example the average market value over a particular period, the break-up value of the company or other objective valuation criteria generally used in financial analysis. Any decision by a supervisory authority to adjust the equitable price shall be substantiated and made public.

According to section 5:

By way of consideration the offeror may offer securities, cash or a combination of both. However, where the consideration offered by the offeror does not consist of liquid securities admitted to trading on a regulated market it shall include a cash alternative. In any event, the offeror shall offer a cash consideration at least as an alternative where he/she, or persons acting in concert with him/her, over a period beginning at the same time as the period determined by the Member State in accordance with section 4 and ending when the offer closes for acceptance, has purchased for cash securities carrying 5 per cent or more of the voting rights in the offeree company. Member States may provide that a cash consideration must be offered, at least as an alternative, in all cases.

Where there is an acquisition through a voluntary bid to all holders of securities for all their holdings, there is no obligation to launch a bid (section 2):

> Finally, in addition to the protection provided for in section 1, Member States may provide for further instruments to protect the interests of the holders of securities provided that those instruments do not hinder the normal course of the bid.

The sell-out right

According to Article 16:

> Member States shall ensure that, following a bid made to all the holders of the offeree company's securities for all of their securities ...[,] a holder of remaining securities is able to require the offeror to buy his/her securities from him/her at a fair price under the same circumstances as provided for in Article 15(2).

The circumstances are the following (Article 15(2)):

> (a) where the offeror holds securities representing not less than 90 per cent of the capital carrying voting rights and 90 per cent of the voting rights in the offeree company, or (b) where, following acceptance of the bid, he/she has acquired or has firmly contracted to acquire securities representing not less than 90 per cent of the offeree company's capital carrying voting rights and 90 per cent of the voting rights comprised in the bid. In the case referred to in (a), Member States may set a higher threshold that may not, however, be higher than 95 per cent of the capital carrying voting rights and 95 per cent of the voting rights.

Article 16(3) provides that 'Article 15(3) to (5) shall apply *mutatis mutandis*'. This means that 'Member States shall ensure that rules are in force that make it possible to calculate when the threshold is reached' (Article 15(3). Further, '[w]here the offeree company has issued more than one class of securities, Member States may provide' that the sell-out right 'can be exercised only in the class in which the threshold laid down in section 2 has been reached' (see Article 15(3), second section). If the holder of securities wants to exercise his/her right, 'he/she shall do so within three months of the end of the time allowed for acceptance of the bid referred to in Article 7' (see Article 15(4)). Finally (see Article 15(5)):

> Member States shall ensure that a fair price is guaranteed. That price shall take the same form as the consideration offered in the bid or shall be in cash. Member States may provide that cash shall be offered at least as an alternative. Following a voluntary bid, in both of the cases referred to in [Article 15,] section 2(a) and (b), the consideration offered in the bid shall be presumed to be fair where, through acceptance of the bid, the offeror has acquired securities representing not less than 90 per cent of the capital carrying voting rights comprised in the bid. Following a mandatory bid, the consideration offered in the bid shall be presumed to be fair.

Why the provisions on mandatory bids and the sell-out right are trivial

The mandatory bid rule and the sell-out right provision are trivial, because it will be easy for private parties to avoid them with the help of national policy-makers and supervisory authorities.

Anyone familiar with national mandatory bid rules and practices will notice that these provisions leave plenty of room to avoid the mandatory bid requirement, depending on how national implementing rules are drafted and enforced.

For instance, in order to make the mandatory bid rule meaningful, member states will have to supplement the provisions of Article 5 with more specific rules on matters, such as the treatment of control acquisitions of companies controlling a listed company, which do not appear to be covered.[5]

The directive provides for only one explicit derogation from the mandatory bid requirement: when the threshold is crossed following a 100 per cent bid. However, it is well known that legal systems imposing a mandatory bid upon change of control routinely identify a much broader set of derogations. For instance, in France a bid is not mandatory following the acquisition of a stake higher than the relevant threshold in cases of:

- gratuitous acquisitions;
- acquisitions following a *pro-rata* distribution by a corporation;
- acquisitions through a capital increase in case of financial difficulty;
- mergers or divisions approved by the general meeting of the relevant company;
- a reduction in the number of shares or votes;
- a third party owning the majority of shares, alone or in concert with other persons; or intra-group transfers of shares.[6]

Some of these exemptions follow logically from the requirement in the directive that the holding acquired must confer control. Some do not. In any event, in implementing the directive, member states already providing for a mandatory bid rule will most likely confirm the variable range of derogations that they presently have in place. Member states introducing it for the first time will also provide for more or less far-reaching derogations.

Article 4(5) grants member states and national supervisory authorities wide discretion in the administration of national mandatory bid regimes. Member states may allow their supervisory authorities to decide, case by case, that the mandatory bid rule does not apply in certain special circumstances, whether specified by the national rules or not ('in other special cases'). Unjustified or over-frequent use of this power may constitute a breach of Article 3(1)(a) – protection of minority shareholders in case of control transfer – unless some other equivalent form of protection is provided. In any event, the grey area in which a reasoned decision may be judged to be consistent with the directive is broad enough to leave member states and national supervisory authorities considerable influence over whether and how to enforce the mandatory bid rule.

Member states and their supervisory authorities will also have wide discretion, with respect to the equitable price, in determining the circumstances and the criteria justifying a discount.

As member states are able to carve out exceptions to the mandatory bid rule, and because the supervisory authorities may derogate from the highest price paid rule, this framework will leave plenty of room to design transactions in such a way as to minimise the acquirer's cost.

The sell-out right, in turn, is granted only where 'a bid [is] made to all the holders of the offeree company's securities for all of their securities'. This can be either a voluntary bid or a mandatory bid. As seen above, mandatory bids may turn out to be easily avoidable, depending on the choices made by member states and national supervisory authorities. Where this is the case, the right to sell will depend crucially on the acquirer's willingness to let minority shareholders exercise it. In any event, by setting a sufficiently low price for a voluntary bid for all the shares the acquirer may succeed in holding securities representing less than 90 per cent of the capital carrying voting rights and 90 per cent of the voting rights in the offeree company, thus preventing minority shareholders from exiting the company by way of the sell-out right.[7]

Conclusion

The Takeover Directive provides for a very generic, vague rule that control transfers must be followed by a mandatory bid, but entrusts EU and national policy-makers, and, to an even greater extent, national supervisory agencies with wide powers to grant partial and total exemptions, thus leaving it to member states whether to take the mandatory bid rule seriously. It also introduces a sell-out right, but basically makes it conditional upon the willingness of the bidder to let minority shareholders exit.

One may wonder why the EU should adopt rules that are easily avoidable and therefore trivial.[8] Of course, it is often the case that vague and therefore easily avoidable rules are the only possible outcome of lengthy and difficult negotiations among member states, which are far from happy to lose control over sensitive areas such as ownership structures and the market for corporate control, as the compromise on defence measures shows even more vividly. Further, as Paul Stephan has noted with regard to international agreements:[9]

> the people who negotiate international agreements, as well as the people who serve the institutions that promote these negotiations, have powerful incentives to achieve some kind of agreement regardless of substantive outcome. Association with a concluded agreement brings prestige ...

This is also true with regard to the negotiation of EU directives and regulations.

Finally, with specific regard to the mandatory bid rule, an interest group perspective may help to explain why it took the shape it did in the directive. It is in fact certain that some interest groups will gain from it. Chief among these are the policy-makers and securities agency officials to whom so much power and discretion are granted in deciding whether the rule applies and what the mandatory bid price should be. Further, those providing advisory services in the market for corporate control and, above all, lawyers specialising in mergers and acquisitions[10] stand to gain from having in place a mandatory bid rule such as that designed in the directive. Their services will in fact be available to buyers and sellers who want to evade the mandatory bid, or at least to obtain a discount.

One may object that mandatory bid regimes very similar to the one in the directive are already in place in most member states, so that there should be no increase in the rents that securities agency officials and lawyers can extract, leaving them indifferent to its approval. The point, of course, is not that government officials and lawyers in countries with no mandatory bid rule yet in place will also be able to extract such rents following its transposition.[11] Much more significantly, the directive would increase rents for government officials and lawyers across the EU in at least three ways.

First, the mandatory bid rule in the directive is more flexible in terms of price discounts, which are left to national supervisory authorities, than at least some of the member state mandatory bid regimes now in place.[12] To put it bluntly, this greater flexibility would allow supervisory authority officials to make decisions that may be of great value to the powerful people involved in acquisitions, whether as sellers or as buyers, while at the same time providing lawyers with a wider range of tools with which to earn fees and seek to please their clients.

Secondly, the petrification effect typical of all directives[13] would keep member states from scrapping their own mandatory bid rules, unless they agree to scrap the one in the Takeover Directive.

Finally, like any directive, at least in the area of company law,[14] the Takeover Directive would add another layer of complexity to a regulatory picture that is already highly technical and complex in all jurisdictions. Questions of consistency between national provisions or decisions and the directive can be raised, which is a highly pleasing prospect from the point of view of at least one of the interest groups mentioned.

Note: This chapter is based on a paper originally presented at the conference 'A Modern Regulatory Framework for Company and Takeover Law in Europe', held on 29–31 May 2003 in Syracuse, Italy; papers presented at the conference have been published in G. Ferrarini, K.J. Hopt, E. Wymeersch and J. Winter (eds), *Reforming Company and Takeover Law in Europe* (Oxford University Press, 2004).

[1] The original proposal for a takeover directive was published in *O.J.* 1989, C 64/8.

[2] Directive 2004/25/EC of the European Parliament and of the Council of 21 April 2004 on takeover bids, *O.J.* 30 April 2004, L142/12.

[3] Compare Preamble, n. (9).

[4] Preamble, n. (11).

[5] Compare B. Dauner Lieb and M. Lamandini, *The New Proposal for a Directive on Company Law Concerning Takeover Bids and the Achievement of a Level Playing Field,* European Parliament Working Paper (2003), p. 57.

[6] See, for example, A. Viandier, *OPA, OPE et autres offres publiques* (Levallois: Éditions Francis Lefebvre, 1999), pp. 288–98. Other legal systems provide for similar derogations. On the UK's City Code, see, for example, C. Pearson, 'Mandatory and Voluntary Offers and Their Terms', in M. Button and S. Bolton (eds), *A Practitioner's Guide To The City Code on Takeovers and Mergers* (Old Woking: City & Financial Publications, 1999), pp. 97, 104–107; on Italy see, for example, L. Enriques, *Mercato del controllo societario e tutela degli investitori* (Bologna: Il Mulino, 2002), pp. 147–210.

[7] As a matter of fact, it is far from clear why the sell-out right should be granted only where a takeover bid is highly successful. See L. Enriques, 'The Mandatory Bid Rule in the Proposed EC Takeover Directive: Harmonization As Rent-Seeking?', in G. Ferrarini *et al.* (eds), *Reforming Company and Takeover Law in Europe* (Oxford University Press, 2004), pp. 767, 783.

[8] I have argued elsewhere that the provisions of most EU company law directives and regulations are trivial, so that the conclusion here is far from an exception in the EU company law framework: see L. Enriques, 'EC Company Law Directives and Regulations: How Trivial Are They?', forthcoming in *University of Pennsylvania Journal of International Economics and Law*, and available as ECGI Working Paper No. 39/2005 at http://papers.ssrn.com/sol3/papers.cfm?abstract_id=730388.

[9] P.A. Stephan, 'The Political Economy of Choice of Law', in 90 *Geo. L.J.* 957, 961 (2002).

[10] The inclusion of investment bankers among relevant interest groups would be more controversial, because the mandatory bid rule may increase their fees, due to the greater complexity of the transactions, but it also reduces the number of takeovers. It is far from certain that the net effect is favourable to investment bankers. Intuitively, the increase in fees and power respectively for lawyers and supervisory agency officials is of such magnitude as to offset the negative effect of fewer takeovers.

[11] When the directive was finally approved, 12 of the then 15 member states already had a mandatory bid rule in place. See L. Enriques, 'The Mandatory Bid Rule in the Proposed EC Takeover Directive: Harmonization As Rent-Seeking?', in G. Ferrarini *et al.* (eds), *op.cit.*

[12] For instance, in Italy, no price discount can be granted by the supervisory authority.

[13] See, for example, R.M. Buxbaum and K.J. Hopt, *Legal Harmonization and the Business Enterprise* (Berlin and New York: de Gruyter, 1988), p. 243.

[14] See, for example, B.R. Cheffins, *Company Law: Theory, Structure and Operation* (Oxford: Clarendon Press, 1997), p. 448; H. Halbhuber, 'National Doctrinal Structures and European Company Law', 38 *CML Rev.* (2001) pp. 1385, 1407–08; L. Enriques, 'EC Company Law Directives and Regulations: How Trivial Are They?', forthcoming in *University of Pennsylvania Journal of International Economics and Law*, and available as ECGI Working Paper No. 39/2005 at http://papers.ssrn.com/sol3/papers.cfm?abstract_id=730388, pp. 38–39.

Part II:

European jurisdictions

Chapter 8

United Kingdom City Code

Simon Jay and Stuart Banks
Cleary Gottlieb Steen & Hamilton LLP, London

Evolution and present status of the Panel and the Takeover Code

The Panel on Takeovers and Mergers (the 'Panel') is the United Kingdom's takeover regulator, administering the City Code on Takeovers and Mergers (the 'Code') and the Rules Governing Substantial Acquisitions of Shares (the 'SARs').[1] The Panel was formed at the initiative of the Bank of England in 1968 in response to the development of various abusive practices in the market to create a self-regulatory body with no formal legal status or powers responsible for takeovers of UK public companies. The Panel has experienced a considerable degree of change since its inception and will shortly become a statutory body with enforcement powers of its own, but one of its great successes has been to retain its self-regulatory model against the backdrop of increasingly formal financial regulation, enabling it to respond rapidly and flexibly to meet the needs of a dynamic market.

The modern Panel comprises a number of different organs:

The Panel Executive:	is responsible for the day-to-day administration of the Panel's functions;
The 'Full Panel':	hears appeals from decisions of the Panel Executive;
The Appeal Committee:	hears appeals from certain decisions of the Panel;
The Code Committee:	reviews Code rules and undertakes public consultation on proposed rule changes.

A greater degree of structural and procedural formalism was introduced by the Panel in 2001 to address concerns arising under the Human Rights Act 2000: a more complete separation of powers as between the Panel Executive, the 'Full Panel' and the Appeal Committee, and the Code Committee resulted. The creation of the Code Committee was accompanied by a new consultation procedure for gathering the market's views on proposed rule changes.

While the recently adopted EU Takeover Bids Directive (the 'Directive') can be expected to increase the level of formalism of some aspects of the Panel's operations, it should not have a significant impact on the Panel's flexible and responsive approach to regulation. As expected, the UK government has indicated its intention to implement Article 9 (the 'board passivity rule', which is already represented by General Principle 7 and Rule 21 of the Code) and to opt out of Article 11 (the 'breakthrough rule') of the Directive; the Directive is, therefore, unlikely to result in major changes to the text of the Code, although

PART II: EUROPEAN JURISDICTIONS

the General Principles are to be replaced by the Directive principles. The Directive's main consequences will be:

- *Structural:* A limited review of the Panel's structures and procedures to bolster the internal separation of functions (for example, the Panel intends to introduce nomination and remuneration committees) to accompany the transition in its status to a body exercising statutory powers. In addition, the judicial functions of the Panel will become known as the Hearings Committee and the Appeals Tribunal.
- *Enforcement-related:* Under the implementing legislation, the Panel will be granted limited enforcement powers. These powers will include the ability to compel the disclosure of information, the power to make compliance and compensation rulings, the ability to seek court orders to compel compliance with the Code, and the power to impose sanctions.

Historically, the Panel has enjoyed a privileged relationship with the courts following precedent set in the 1987 case of *ex parte Datafin*, in which a party attempted to obtain judicial review of a Panel decision. The judge concluded that the courts should decline to intervene in the course of a takeover and should generally limit themselves to reviewing the Panel's decision-making processes after the conclusion of the bid. The UK government has stated that it does not wish to interfere with the Datafin principle when implementing the Directive, although it does intend to confer upon the Panel limited immunity from suit and to include provisions to reduce the prospects of tactical litigation in takeover bids.

At present, the Panel and the Financial Services Authority (the 'FSA', the United Kingdom's principal regulator of providers of financial services and markets) cooperate closely in relation to a number of areas such as market abuse and the UKLA's listing rules. The FSA also endorses the Code (pursuant to Section 143 of the Financial Services and Markets Act 2000 (the 'FSMA')) and provides in its rules (MAR 4) that an authorised person (broadly speaking, financial firms authorised to conduct investment business) must comply with the Code and must cease to act where its client will not so comply. As it is generally difficult to effect a UK takeover without an authorised UK adviser, this provision amounts to 'statutory underpinning' of the Code. When the Directive is transposed into UK law, the UK government intends to repeal Section 143 of the FSMA as the Code will, by that stage, be on a statutory footing with the Panel having its own direct enforcement powers.

Due to the breadth of the FSMA provisions on market abuse and the principles-based approach of the Panel, there is considerable scope for overlap between the two regulators' jurisdictions. To address this issue, the Panel and the FSA adopted Operating Guidelines, a protocol covering inter-regulator communications and process in circumstances where both regulators have jurisdiction. These guidelines recognise that the Panel is the principal regulator in relation to public takeovers and clarify that the FSA will not normally intervene using its market abuse powers during the course of a takeover bid except where there is a concern that there has been market abuse by misuse of information, or in certain other specified circumstances.

Application of the Code

At present, the Code applies to all public companies and certain private companies resident in the United Kingdom (which, for these purposes, includes the Channel Islands and the Isle of Man). A company is considered to be resident in a jurisdiction if it is incorporated in and has its place of central management in the United Kingdom.²

Following the transposition of the Directive into UK law, the position will become more complicated. The Panel will have jurisdiction in relation to offers for companies that have any of their securities admitted to trading on a UK regulated market, irrespective of its place of management. For other public and private companies (including, as at the time of writing, companies admitted to AIM and OFEX, which are not regulated markets), the Code will apply as it does now, with the residency test to be satisfied before the Panel will take jurisdiction of an offer.

Significant practical uncertainty will arise where a person makes an offer for a company which falls to be regulated jointly by two different authorities. This can occur in a number of different ways (for example, where a company is admitted to trading on a regulated market outside of its jurisdiction of incorporation). In cases where the company is incorporated in the United Kingdom, the Panel will retain jurisdiction for 'matters relating to company law' (that is, the mandatory bid threshold and restrictions on frustrating action), with the authority in the member state of listing taking responsibility for the procedural aspects, such as the bid timetable. Where a company is incorporated outside of the United Kingdom, but is admitted to trading on a UK regulated market, the roles are reversed with the Panel taking control of procedural aspects only.

General principles

The Code is based on 10 General Principles, with more detailed provisions contained within 38 rules. However, the General Principles are a pervasive theme and the Panel has a broad discretion to interpret the detailed rules to give effect to the 'spirit of the Code' represented by these General Principles.³ The key General Principles are as follows:

- *Requirement for an offer:* The General Principles require that, where control is acquired or consolidated, a general offer to all other shareholders is required. 'Control' for these purposes means a holding of 30 per cent or more of the issued voting rights of the company in question.
- *Equality of treatment and information:* A fundamental tenet of the Code is that shareholders are treated equally in terms of the offer terms and the provision of information (in terms of both content and timing).
- *Avoidance of false markets:* Another key General Principle of the Code is the requirement to avoid the creation of false markets. In the rules of the Code, this General Principle is reflected in the requirements for confidentiality, the obligation to make an announcement where a leak about the possibility of a takeover offer has occurred and the obligation to give timely updates on the progress of an offer. The Code's requirement for transparency of dealings through dealing disclosures under Rule 8 is also a reflection of this important General Principle.
- *Provision of, and accuracy of, information:* The Code requires that target company shareholders are provided with sufficient information to enable them to reach a decision in relation to the offer. The General Principles state that this information must be prepared to the highest standards of care and accuracy.
- *Advice to shareholders by target boards:* The General Principles require the board of a target company to obtain independent advice on the terms of an offer and to publish the substance of that advice, as well as their own views.

- *Frustrating action*: The board of a target company is prohibited from taking action which could frustrate an offer from the time it becomes aware that a *bona fide* offer might be imminent. This does not amount to a blanket prohibition of the use of 'poison pills' (which, in any event, are likely to be inconsistent with UK company law), but does severely restrict their use.

Most rules of the Code apply not only to the offeror and target themselves, but also to any persons 'acting in concert' with those parties. The application of rules to concert parties – for example, financial advisers of the offeror or target – is intended to ensure that the rules cannot be circumvented by the parties entering into arrangements with others to assist in securing control of a target or defending against an unwelcome offer.

Types of offer

It is possible to implement a takeover of a UK plc through several different routes. In practice, one of the following two routes is used in the vast majority of transactions:

- *Offer:* The first is the contractual offer, in which the bidder posts a document containing the terms and conditions of its offer to the shareholders of the target company. If accepted by a target shareholder, a binding, conditional contract is formed between the shareholder and the bidder. The offer conditions must include the so-called 'acceptance condition', the effect of which is to entitle the bidder to walk away from its offer unless acceptances are received representing 90 per cent of the shares to which the offer relates (although this level is normally waivable at the option of the bidder to a minimum level of 50 per cent).[4] Upon the attainment of the 90 per cent acceptance level, the bidder can invoke the statutory compulsory acquisition provisions of Sections 428–430F of the Companies Act 1985, thereby acquiring the remaining shares and obtaining 100 per cent ownership of the target.[5]
- *Scheme:* A scheme of arrangement under Section 425 of the Companies Act 1985 is the second commonly used route. To be successful, this process, which is supervised by the court, requires the approval of a majority in number representing three-quarters by value of the target shareholders attending and voting at specially convened meetings of each class of shareholder. The sanction of the court is also required and is sought at a hearing in which the court evaluates the overall fairness of the transaction.

A scheme of arrangement has the advantage of allowing the bidder to reach absolute control in a single step and at a 'lower' approval threshold than an offer. However, a scheme is implemented by the target company (as opposed to the bidder, as in the case of an offer) and, as such, introduces a greater risk of target or third-party disruption. In addition, since shareholders representing 25 per cent or more of the votes represented at the meeting will be able to vote down the scheme, low turn out at the meeting will enhance the power of dissenting shareholders to block the transaction.

Types of offer consideration

Bidders may offer a wide variety of forms of offer consideration to target company shareholders, with the principal constraint being the commercial desirability of that type of consideration.

Each form of consideration must be made available to all shareholders (a reflection of the General Principle requirement for equal treatment) and an independent valuation must be published in the offer document in relation to any unlisted consideration.

Full cash offers are common in the UK market, as are offers involving listed company securities or a combination of the two. Bidders often provide for a significant degree of choice for target shareholders by offering full or partial 'alternatives' (for example, the bidder might allow target shareholders to elect for cash in lieu of all or some of their entitlement to shares in the bidder). A further refinement involves a 'mix and match' facility under which target shareholders can elect to receive a different blend of, for example, shares or cash, with the final determination depending on the elections of other shareholders. In cash offers, an unlisted loan note alternative is often used as this assists certain types of shareholder to defer and, ultimately, minimise tax charges on sale. It is also possible to offer deferred or contingent consideration in UK public M&A transactions (see, for example, the offer by First Group for GB Railways in which some payments were contingent on the awards of certain rail franchises to the target group).

A number of bids in the early 2000s have seen the use of relatively complex forms of offer consideration: the successful bid by Songbird for Canary Wharf Group saw the use of a listed 'stub-equity' alternative, and the offer for Chelsfield by Duelguide utilised similar securities in an unlisted form.

Partial offers

With the consent of the Panel, it is possible for a bidder to offer to acquire less than the whole of the target company. In such bids, if shareholders tender acceptances in excess of the bidder's desired ownership threshold, acceptances are scaled back. Where the offeror is seeking to increase its shareholding via a partial offer to a level below 30 per cent of the target's issued share capital, the Panel will normally grant consent. However, where the desired ownership level is more than 30 per cent of the target company, the Panel will be more reluctant to grant consent given that it will be effectively waiving the requirement for the offeror to make a mandatory offer under Rule 9. For this reason, any such offer must be expressed to be conditional on shareholders (excluding the offeror and persons acting in concert with it) holding more than 50 per cent of the voting rights of the target consenting to the making of the offer. Although partial offers are relatively rare, there were several partial offers during the early 2000s including HBOS's offer for St. James' Place Capital, and Guinness Peat Group's hostile partial offer for De Vere Group.

Basic structure and timetable of offer

The takeover process will commence via an approach by the bidder to the board of the target company (Rule 1). In the case of a hostile offer, this 'approach' will be by way of information only and will be shortly followed by a unilateral announcement of an offer by the bidder. In the case of a friendly approach, the bidder will be seeking to obtain information on the target in order to satisfy its due diligence requirements (but note the issues raised by the 'equality of information' requirement of Rule 20.2 discussed below). If a deal can be agreed, the bidder will expect the board of the target to recommend its offer and may seek irrevocable undertakings from shareholders of the target prior to announcement of the offer.

During this period, the Code demands that both parties maintain absolute secrecy prior to any announcement being made (Rule 2.1). Once the bidder has formed a firm intention to make an offer, it must announce that intention. However, an announcement may also be required at an earlier stage in a number of circumstances, including the following:

- when discussions are about to be extended to include more than a very restricted number of people; this is often an issue where financing commitments from third parties are required;
- where the target company is the subject of rumour and speculation or there is an untoward movement of its share price and there is reason to attribute that rumour or movement to the bidder's actions; and
- where (following an approach) the offeree company is the subject of rumour and speculation or there is an untoward movement in its share price.

Once the board of the target has received an approach, the responsibility for making an announcement will primarily rest with the target (unless the approach is rejected by the target, in which case it will revert to the bidder). Prior to that time, it will be for the bidder to make an announcement.

As a result of these requirements, an announcement of a possible offer under Rule 2.4 will often be made by bidder or by target. The content of such an announcement may range from a simple indication that discussions are taking place to a more detailed description of possible terms – there are no prescribed content requirements. Detailed possible offer announcements were used in the cases of Marks & Spencer and The London Stock Exchange. However, while the announcement of a possible offer (unlike the announcement of a firm intention to make an offer – a so-called 'Rule 2.5 announcement') will not bind the bidder to proceed with an offer, it may have significant consequences as to the terms of any subsequent offer, if made. For example, where an announcement of a possible offer includes an indication of price, then the potential bidder will not be allowed subsequently to make an offer at a lower price unless there has occurred an event which the bidder specified in the announcement as an event which would enable the indicative price to be set aside; the Panel would not normally allow such a reservation to be based upon the bidder's subsequent due diligence. In addition, the announcement of a possible offer will trigger the commencement of an 'offer period'; see further below. At any time after the announcement of a possible offer has been made, the target board will be entitled to seek from the Panel a 'put up or shut up' notice (Rule 2.4(b)) requiring the potential bidder either to announce a firm intention to make an offer or to withdraw within a specified period, normally six to eight weeks from the date of the commencement of the offer period where the target seeks a ruling to this effect in the early stages. If the potential bidder does not announce its firm intention to make an offer within that period, it will normally be precluded from doing so for a further period of six months (Rule 2.8).

Once a bidder has formed a firm intention to make an offer (Rule 2.5), it must make an announcement to that effect, including all principal terms and condition of the offer. Such an announcement may only be made once the bidder has every reason to believe it can implement the offer. Committed financing in respect of any cash component must therefore be in place at this time. Having made such an announcement, the bidder is bound to proceed with the offer and must post a formal offer document to shareholders of the target within the next 28 days, at which point a fairly rigid timetable will govern the offer process (see below).

If the offer requires anti-trust or other regulatory clearances in order to proceed, it may be possible to structure the transaction as a pre-conditional offer. Here, the bidder commits to make an offer only once the relevant pre-conditions have been satisfied, for example, the clearances have been obtained, thereby avoiding the possibility of the offer lapsing as a result of failure to obtain clearances within the timetable permitted.

The conditions of an offer will normally include the following:

- *Acceptance condition:* In a takeover offer, the bidder will normally condition its offer on the receipt of acceptances representing 90 per cent (as to the significance of this, see 'Types of offer' above).
- *Anti-trust, regulatory and shareholder approvals:* The bidder will be able to include receipt of all relevant approvals as a condition of the offer. In any event, the offer must include a term that it will lapse if a second stage EU or UK anti-trust investigation is instigated (Rule 12).
- Most offers will also include standardised conditions as to the absence of third-party actions, material adverse change, and so on.

The Code prescribes that an offer may not normally be subject to conditions which depend solely on subjective judgements by the directors, the principal exception being as to the terms on which regulatory consents are granted (Rule 13). Even then, a bidder will only exceptionally be permitted to invoke a condition (other than the acceptance condition or approvals condition) in order to terminate its offer. Conditions relating to the financing of a bid or completion of satisfactory due diligence are generally prohibited.

The offer, once made by posting of the offer document, must initially remain open for acceptances for a period of at least 21 days (Rule 31.1). Within 14 days of posting, the target board must make its views on the offer, and those of an independent financial adviser, known to shareholders (Rule 30.1). If the acceptance condition has not been satisfied by the first closing date, the offer period may be extended at the discretion of the offeror, but the offer will normally lapse if the acceptance condition has not been satisfied by the 60th day after posting (Rule 31.6). Once the acceptance condition has been declared satisfied, all other conditions must be satisfied within a further 21 days (Rule 31.7). The bidder may also revise its offer up until the 46th day after posting of the offer document (Rule 32.1). Conversely, the target is required to provide all relevant information to its shareholders no later than the 39th day after posting (Rule 31.9).

Acceptances, once made, are normally irrevocable. However, an offer must provide that acceptances become revocable should the acceptance condition not have been satisfied by the 42nd day after posting (Rule 34).

If a third party subsequently announces a competing offer, then both bids will normally switch to the timetable of the subsequent competing offer upon the posting of the second bidder's bid documents. In extreme cases where the presence of competing offerors runs the risk of the offer timetable running over an extended period of time, the Panel may impose an auction process in order to foreclose the timetable, as in the cases of Canary Wharf Group and Debenhams.[6]

Where an offer is referred for a second stage anti-trust investigation in the United Kingdom or at EU level, it will automatically lapse (Rule 12). If the offer is subsequently cleared, then the bidder will normally be required to decide whether or not to reinstitute its offer (which may be on different terms from its original offer) within 21 days of clearance (Note (a)(iii) to Rule 35.1). If, however, the offer has been structured as a pre-conditional offer, the bidder will be bound to proceed on the terms of the original terms announced.

Market purchases

A bidder may consider making market purchases either during the currency of an offer or prior to its announcement for a number of reasons. Securing a significant shareholding may improve the bidder's chance of successfully acquiring control of the target particularly in a contested situation. Furthermore, it may present an opportunity for the bidder to 'insure' itself against failed bid costs should a third party successfully outbid it. However, before making market purchases, a bidder will need to consider both whether there are any obstacles to such purchases and the consequences of effecting them.

Can market purchases be made?

The bidder will need to consider not only the provisions of the Code, but also the insider dealing regime contained in the Criminal Justice Act 1993 ('CJA') and the market abuse regime under Section 118 of the FSMA.

Both the insider dealing regime and the market abuse regime make it unlawful for a person to deal in securities while in possession of price sensitive information ('PSI'). In a takeover situation, the bidder may have PSI either because (prior to any announcement) he is aware of his own intention to make a bid or because he has business information relating to the target as a result of having been given access to its books and records.

The bidder's knowledge of his own intention to make a bid will not prohibit his making market purchases of target securities either under the CJA or FSMA (see Schedule 1, CJA, paragraph 3 and the Code of Market Conduct at MAR 1.4.28 C). However, the defences/exemption available will not extend to permit the bidder to enter into derivatives positions which give it an economic exposure only to the target's securities.

Business information on the target will, however, prevent a bidder making market purchases if that information constitutes PSI since the CJA provides no exemption in these circumstances.

The SARs restrict the speed with which a person may increase his holding of shares to an aggregate of between 15 per cent and 30 per cent of the voting rights of a company. Subject to certain exemptions, a person may not in any period of seven days acquire shares representing 10 per cent or more of the target voting rights if such acquisition would bring his total holding to more than 15 per cent, but less than 30 per cent of such rights. The SARs will, however, cease to apply once a bidder has announced a firm intention to make an offer.

Rule 5 of the Code prohibits a person from acquiring shares which would increase his total holding to more than 30 per cent of the target unless (among other exceptions) that acquisition is from a single shareholder and is the only such acquisition within seven days or the acquisition immediately precedes the announcement of a firm intention to make an offer which is recommended by the board of the target.

The bidder will also need to consider the impact of market purchases on its ability to apply the 'squeeze-out' provisions of Section 428 of the Companies Act 1985.

In addition, the bidder will need to be aware of any regulatory constraints which would either prohibit, or require filings to be made in respect of, the acquisition of a shareholding in the target.

Is public disclosure required?

Under the provisions of Sections 198–210A of the Companies Act 1985, any person who acquires a material interest in 3 per cent or more of the share capital of a UK public company is required to notify that interest to the company concerned within two business days of the acquisition. If the target company is listed, it is required to announce any interest notified to it via a regulatory information service. Further acquisitions which break through percentage points above 3 per cent must also be notified. The Act contains provisions requiring the aggregation of parties acting in concert.

Separately, Rule 8 of the Code contains a regime for the public notification of dealings by parties to a takeover bid once an 'offer period' has commenced, and by other persons including shareholders holding 1 per cent or more of the relevant company's securities. For this purpose, an 'offer period' will commence once an announcement of an offer or possible offer has been announced by any person. The Panel's website contains a running list of companies currently deemed to be in an offer period. Where a cash offer only is in contemplation, disclosures are required only in relation to the target's securities. If a securities exchange offer is contemplated, then disclosures are required in relation to both bidder and target securities.

What consequences may flow from market purchases?

Rule 6 of the Code requires that where a bidder, or a person acting in concert with a bidder, has made market purchases within the three-month period prior to the commencement of the offer period, or during the offer period, but before the announcement of a firm intention to make an offer, or prior to that three-month period in certain circumstances, then any offer to target shareholders must be on no less favourable terms, that is, the price paid for market purchases will set a 'floor' to the offer consideration.

Similarly, market purchases made after an offer has been announced above the offer price will require an immediate increase in the offer price to not less than the highest price paid.

Rule 11 of the Code requires that a bidder who (or whose concert parties) purchase target shares during an offer period, or who has acquired 10 per cent or more of the target's shares during the period commencing 12 months before the offer period and during the offer period, must include a cash offer at not less than the highest price paid in any subsequent takeover offer.

Under Rule 9 of the Code, any person who (alone or with persons acting in concert with him) acquires shares in a target carrying 30 per cent or more of the voting rights (or who, already holding 30 per cent, increases his holding (any increase will trigger Rule 9)) is required to make an unconditional cash offer for the remaining shares.

Conduct during an offer

The parties to a takeover must observe strict guidelines during the course of an offer so as to avoid falling foul of the Panel's requirements for clear and accurate information and the

PART II: EUROPEAN JURISDICTIONS

avoidance of false markets. In addition, the Panel proactively monitors announcements and communications made in the course of an offer to ensure that the important General Principle regarding the equality of information is observed. Rules 19 and 20 of the Code contain detailed provisions in this regard.

Public statements, press briefings and analysts' meetings all present particular dangers, some of which are described below:

- *Dealing with the press:* The Panel requires that advisers take responsibility for the release of information during a bid, and recommends particular care when giving media interviews. In effect, the Panel regards statements made in media reports as made by the interviewee even if there is an element of misreporting. Although some statements are capable of retraction, a public statement denying the truth of the unintended statement may have tactical implications and is unlikely to be desirable.

    Planned public statements should be prepared to 'prospectus standards' as the Code requires the highest standards of care and accuracy. The sanctions for making misleading statements contained in Section 397 of the FSMA are further reasons to take extreme care in the drafting of press releases (as well as other offer-related documentation and communications).

- *No increase/no extension statements:* Statements which suggest that a bidder has no intention of increasing or extending its offer are binding on the bidder such that the bidder will be prevented from revising or extending its offer. Accordingly, a bidder should avoid being drawn into discussions about its offer strategy for fear that it will be held to observe its stated strategy at the expense of flexibility in the future.[7]

- *Unacceptable statements:* Rule 19.3 states that a party must not make factually correct but potentially misleading statements. For example, a bidder must take care not to lead the market to conclude that a revision to its offer might be imminent, unless it is prepared to commit itself to make that revision. Failing to observe this rule is likely to create a false market in breach of the Code, and, where parties have contravened this provision, it has tended to draw a swift public rebuke from the Panel (for example, in the case of Wembley).[8] In addition, the parties must take extreme care in making statements regarding the level of support that their offer (or defence) has obtained. Given the potential impact of such statements,[9] the Panel now requires that such statements be verified to its satisfaction under an onerous procedure.

- *Profit forecasts and merger benefits:* There is a risk that statements made by a target company, or a bidder in the case of a securities exchange offer, could be construed as a profit forecast. Profit forecasts are not prohibited under the Code, but Rule 28 requires a public report by the accountants and financial advisers to the party making the forecast, resulting in significant expense and distraction, potentially at a critical moment in the offer process. The Panel adopts an expansive definition of the term 'profit forecast' such that almost any statement which implies a floor or ceiling on the profits (or losses) for a particular period is treated as a forecast. By way of illustration, a statement regarding revenues alone cannot amount to a forecast, but a statement referring to both revenue enhancements and cost savings might.

    In securities exchange offers, it is also important to avoid reference to the potential synergies that are expected to result from the combination. Such 'merger benefits statements' are also subject to the requirement for a public report in certain circumstances under Note 8 on Rule 19.1 of the Code.

- *Meetings with analysts and shareholders:* Rule 8.1 sets out detailed rules for the monitoring of meetings between a party to an offer with shareholders and analysts by representatives of the financial adviser to the party to the offer. This monitoring process is intended to ensure that material information and opinions are not released selectively. An example of this process failing occurred in the hostile offer by BIL for Thistle Hotels, in which the bidder was forced by the Panel to publish an analysts' presentation which it had made privately, and which contained new arguments relating to its offer. Had this presentation contained profit forecasts or merger benefits statements, full reporting obligations could have followed.
- *Telephone and media campaigns:* In hostile or difficult offers, the parties occasionally wish to use telephone campaigns in which shareholders are contacted directly to reinforce the messages contained in the bid documentation. Telephone calls must be conducted by the staff of a financial adviser to the bid or, where this is not possible, under the supervision of the financial adviser using a pre-prepared script approved by the Panel in advance.

    Parties to offers are sometimes tempted to participate in television and radio interviews in connection with their offer. Generally, this is not recommended unless the conditions are controlled and the interview is tightly scripted, as there is a risk that unintended consequences of the type described above could flow from an unclear or unplanned statement in a live interview situation.
- *Advertisements:* The use of media advertisements in connection with an offer is, generally, prohibited. The Panel regards it as essential that the contest for control takes place through the use of properly detailed shareholder documentation.
- *Equality of information to competing bidders:* Rule 8.2 requires that any information given by a target to one offeror or potential offeror must, on request, be given to another even if that offeror is less welcome. This means that, in practice, a UK target will be reluctant to provide a bidder with sensitive non-public information for fear of it having to be provided to, for example, a competitor.
- *Frustrating action:* In addition to the above, the actions which a target may take during the course of an offer or, prior to that, when the board of the target has reason to believe that an offer may be imminent, will be constrained by the restrictions on 'frustrating action' set out in Rule 21 (which represents the detailed application of General Principle 7). During this period, the target board may not, without the prior approval of shareholders in general meeting (except pursuant to a contract previously entered into) issue shares (or options to acquire or securities convertible into shares), agree to acquire or dispose of assets of a material amount or enter into contracts otherwise than in the ordinary course of business (which will include amending or entering into a new service contract with a director).[10] In addition to Rule 21, company law requirements – in particular the requirement that directors' powers are not exercised with an improper purpose – are likely to restrict the extent to which a UK plc is able to put in place defensive measures without shareholders' approval. The board of a UK plc defending against a hostile bid will therefore be prevented from taking action which removes the decision as to whether to accept the bid from its shareholders. 'Defensive measures' will normally be limited to seeking alternative offers for the company or seeking approval from shareholders for a capital restructuring of the company, or simply seeking to persuade shareholders not to accept the offeror's bid. However, Rule 21 will not normally apply so as to prevent the board of a target from

seeking to persuade a regulator to refuse clearance for a transaction. See, for example, the 1989 case involving a bid by Holake for BAT.

Disclosure of dealings – contracts for differences and proposals for changes to the Code

As referred to above, Rule 8 of the Code governs the disclosure of dealings in the course of an offer or possible offer. During an offer period,[11] a bidder, the target company and their respective associates[12] are required, under Rule 8.1 of the Code, to disclose all dealings in 'relevant securities'.[13] This includes dealings in derivatives referenced to shares in any such company and options in respect of such shares.

Under Rule 8.3, persons who own or control 1 per cent or more of any class of relevant securities of the target company or, if appropriate, the bidder (or who will so own or control 1 per cent or more as a result of a transaction) must disclose publicly all dealings in such relevant securities of that company carried out during an offer period. However, Note 7 on Rule 8 provides that:

> Under Rule 8.3, a disclosure of dealings in options or derivatives is only required if the person dealing in such options or derivatives owns or controls 1 per cent or more of the class of securities which is the subject of the option or to whose price the derivative is referenced.

As a result, persons whose only interests are in the form of derivatives referenced to, or options in respect of, shares of a target company (or, if appropriate, a bidder), no matter how large, have no obligation to disclose their dealings under Rule 8 (as long as they are not also associates of the bidder or target company).

A counterparty to a large derivative or option might acquire more than 1 per cent of a company's shares as a hedge and, as such, would *prima facie* have a disclosure obligation under Rule 8.3. However, where the counterparty to the derivative or option is a recognised market-maker or principal trader under the Code, it will generally benefit from an exemption from disclosure. As a result, many counterparties to derivative and option transactions do not disclose either the derivative or option business which they write or the transactions which they enter into to hedge those derivative or option positions, even when their shareholding is above 1 per cent.

Proposed changes to disclosure rules

In 2005, the panel published proposals for consultation under which Rule 8.3 would be extended such that a person would be required to disclose where he holds a long position in respect of 1 per cent or more of any class of relevant securities. So-called 'naked' short positions (that is, short positions without any additional holding in the physical securities) would not fall to be disclosed under the new regime.

How is 1 per cent interest determined?

Interests held by way of physical long positions, call options, long derivative interests and written put options would be aggregated to determine whether a person holds a long position of 1 per cent or more, and the aggregation would be performed on a class-by-class basis. Out-of-the-money instruments cannot be ignored for the purpose of these calculations, and short positions cannot be netted-off against long positions to reduce a person's holding below the disclosure threshold (although any short positions must be disclosed, as to which see 'What must be disclosed?' below).

Who must disclose?

The obligation to make a disclosure lies with the investor acquiring the interest in the derivative contract or option, and not with the counterparty. Disclosure obligations are triggered not just by the acquisition of new derivative or options, but also by the disposal of, entering into of, closing out of, exercise (by either party) of any rights under or variation of the terms of the derivative.

When is ownership determined?

For the purposes of determining a person's aggregate interest, the relevant cut-off time is 12 midnight (London time) each day. Interests must be disclosed by 12 noon (London time) on the next following London business day.

What must be disclosed?

All material information relating to the derivatives or options contract must be disclosed to ensure full transparency and avoid market confusion. It is expected that, following the implementation of the proposals, the Panel will require disclosure of dealings and resulting positions in all classes of relevant securities (and derivatives referenced to and options in respect of such relevant securities) held once the 1 per cent threshold has been crossed in any class of relevant security.

Key points for a potential bidder for a UK plc

- If offering cash, ensure that unconditionally committed funding is available prior to announcement of a firm offer.
- Do not expect access to extensive non-public information from the target.
- Do not make any statements which are publicly accessible which give an indication of willingness to bid or level of price to be offered without seeking prior advice.
- Do not deal in securities of the target (or related derivative instruments) without seeking prior advice.
- Ensure that any information relevant to the bid which is made public is (a) accurate and not misleading and (b) made available to all shareholders of the target simultaneously.
- Treat all shareholders of the target equally.
- Do not enter into agreements or arrangements relating to the bid which you would not be prepared to see publicly disclosed.
- Do not expect to be able to rely on conditions to an offer other than those relating to acceptance levels, regulatory approvals and shareholder approvals.
- Maintain absolute secrecy prior to announcement of an offer.
- Be prepared to deal openly and honestly with the Panel.

PART II: EUROPEAN JURISDICTIONS

Case studies

> ### Case study: Canary Wharf plc
>
> The long-running competitive bid process for Canary Wharf Group plc demonstrated a number of important Code principles. The case, involving actual bids (in contrast to the case of Marks & Spencer Group plc, described below), also shows the flexible approach taken by the Panel to resolve novel issues arising in the course of the takeover process. In this case, there were also a number of Panel appeals, one of which is described below.
>
> The key events in the takeover process were as follows:
>
> | | |
> |---|---|
> | June 2003 | Canary Wharf announces that it has received a number of approaches in relation to a possible offer for Canary Wharf and has formed an independent committee of the board in order to deal with bids. |
> | | Offer period commences in relation to Canary Wharf. |
> | 5 December 2003 | Silvestor UK Properties Limited (a company formed by Simon Glick and the Morgan Stanley Real Estate Fund (MSREF)) announces bid, to be implemented by way of a scheme of arrangement, at 265p per Canary Wharf share. |
> | 15 January 2004 | Deadline imposed for other potential bidders to announce firm proposals by 13 February 2004.[14] |
> | 5 February 2004 | CWG (a company formed by a Canadian company, Brascan) announces a takeover offer at 270p per Canary Wharf share. |
> | | Silvestor announces an increased offer of 275p per Canary Wharf share. |
> | 12 February 2004 | CWG announces an increased offer also of 275p per Canary Wharf share. |
> | 7 April 2004 | Panel announces that Silvestor, CWG and Canary Wharf have agreed a procedure under Rule 32.5 of the Code, under which Silvestor and CWG would be able to revise their offers through an auction procedure, intended to provide an orderly framework for resolution of the competitive situation. |
>
> **Code framework**
>
> The announcement made by Canary Wharf on 6 June 2003 commenced an offer period, at which point associates of Canary Wharf and connected exempt market-makers and fund managers would have begun to make disclosures under Rules 8 and 38 of the Code.
>
> Silvestor's announcement of 5 December 2003 of a firm intention to make a takeover bid for Canary Wharf was made under Rule 2.5 of the Code, and created an obligation for a circular (in this case, a scheme of arrangement proposal) to be posted to the shareholders of Canary Wharf within 28 days. The competing bid from CWG announced on 5 February 2004 itself commenced a 28-day timetable for the posting of an offer document.

The auction procedure

One of the principal aims of the Code is to ensure that takeover bids are conducted within an orderly framework. There was a danger, in the case of Canary Wharf, that the bidding war between CWG and Silvestor could continue indefinitely, and the Panel chose to invoke Rule 32.5 of the Code,[15] under which it is able to impose an auction procedure to bring the competitive process to a head.

The auction comprised three bidding stages, with the bidders able to bid on each day. The final offers for Canary Wharf following the auction procedure (which were not capable of further revision without Panel consent) were as follows:

- *Songbird* (a new bid vehicle backed by the same parties as Silvestor). On the final day of the auction procedure, it was announced that the Silvestor scheme of arrangement would be withdrawn and that Songbird would make a takeover offer of 238p in cash and 57p in quoted shares for each Canary Wharf share.

    Under a mix and match election, Canary Wharf shareholders could elect to receive either 295p in cash per Canary Wharf share or additional quoted Class B shares or unlisted Class C shares.

- *CWG*. CWG offered 275p in cash per Canary Wharf share. However, shareholders could elect to receive quoted Class A shares or unlisted Class B shares in respect of up to 29.2p of the cash consideration.

    There was also an additional share election under which Canary Wharf shareholders could elect to receive a greater proportion of their consideration in the form of Class A shares or Class B shares subject to other shareholders not electing to receive such shares.

The Committee announced, on 19 April, that it intended to recommend the Songbird offer to Canary Wharf shareholders. On 21 May, Songbird announced that it had received acceptances in respect of 60.9 per cent of the issued Canary Wharf shares. Its offer therefore became unconditional as to acceptances and was declared wholly unconditional at the same time. CWG made an immediate announcement that its offer had lapsed. The auction process was a success insofar as it brought the protracted battle for control of Canary Wharf to an orderly conclusion although some commentators observed that the auction was more akin to a sealed bid process similar to that used by the Panel to bring to an end the competitive process in St David Capital/WPD Limited/Hyder plc.[16] However, the structure of the auction allowed the bidders to make relatively trivial revisions to their offers at each of the stages; some observers felt that the process had failed in so far as it did not result in a true 'competitive' auction arising until the final stage. Arguably, this is unfair criticism: the Code's function is not to maximise value for the target's shareholders.

Appeal on General Principle 1

The first appeal related to General Principle 1 as applied to Simon Glick, who was an existing shareholder in Canary Wharf. CWG claimed that the participation of Simon Glick in the MSREF consortium amounted to a breach of General Principle 1 because Canary Wharf shareholders were not being afforded an opportunity to participate in the equity of CWG. The Panel Executive had determined that the intended participation of

Glick in the MSREF consortium did not amount to a breach of General Principle 1 because his participation in the consortium was so significant as to confer upon him 'joint offeror status', that is, that he was effectively a bidder jointly with the MSREF bid vehicle such that he fell outside the scope of General Principle 1 (because a bidder is in a wholly different position to a simple target shareholder). CWG were not satisfied with the Panel Executive's ruling on this point and appealed the decision to the full Panel.

In its published decision, the Panel confirmed the validity of joint offeror status and determined that a number of factors had to be considered when deciding whether a person was a joint offeror:

Factors in favour of joint offeror status
- Ownership of a high proportion of the equity share capital in the bid vehicle after completion of the acquisition.
- The ability to exert a significant influence over the future management and direction of the bid vehicle.
- Making a significant, non-financial contribution to the consortium (e.g. management or industry-specific expertise).
- The ability to influence or direct the conduct of the bid itself.

Factors against joint offeror status
- Arrangements enabling the proposed joint offeror to obtain an accelerated exit from the consortium.
- The absence of the factors set out above.

Although the decision in this appeal was an important development in Panel precedent, the example it provides illustrates the speed and responsiveness afforded by the Panel system as well as the Panel's ability to review the substance of a case, focusing on the Code's general principles amd without undue regard to rigid precedents or rules.

Case study: Marks and Spencer plc

In contrast to the bids for Canary Wharf, each of which involved the posting of an actual takeover offer to shareholders, the recent takeover proposal for Marks and Spencer Group plc made by Revival Acquisitions Limited (a vehicle promoted by the entrepreneur, Philip Green) involved only possible offer announcements. It is, therefore, a good illustration of the operation of the Panel rules, updated in 2004, on so-called 'virtual' bids. As is common in virtual bids, the potential bidder announced its interest and shortly thereafter published its indicative offer terms in a press announcement.

The facts of the case were as follows:

27 May 2004	Revival Acquisitions announces that it is considering a cash and share offer for Marks & Spencer.
3 June 2004	Revival Acquisitions announces a pre-conditional possible offer for Marks & Spencer at between 290p and 310p per Marks & Spencer

	share plus a 25 per cent interest in the equity share capital of Revival Acquisitions. Possible offer conditional on the receipt of a recommendation of the board of Marks & Spencer and access to limited due diligence information.
	Later in the day, the board of Marks & Spencer rejects the proposal as it '… significantly undervalues the Marks & Spencer Group …'.
16 June 2004	Revival Acquisitions announces a revised pre-conditional possible offer for Marks & Spencer of 370p per Marks & Spencer share, indicating that it would be prepared to offer a partial share alternative. Revival reiterates that the making of its offer would be conditional on the receipt of a recommendation of the board of Marks & Spencer and access to limited due diligence information.
	The board of Marks & Spencer immediately rejects the proposal as it '… significantly undervalues the Marks & Spencer Group and its prospects…'.
28 June 2004	Marks & Spencer issues an announcement rebutting allegations regarding certain share dealings carried out by its chief executive prior to the commencement of the offer period.
2 July 2004	Revival Acquisitions issues an announcement in the form of an open letter to Marks & Spencer's pension fund trustees requesting a meeting.
6 July 2004	Panel announces that Revival Acquisitions must, by 6 August 2004, either announce a firm intention to make an offer for Marks & Spencer or announce that it will not proceed with an offer for Marks & Spencer.
7 July 2004	Revival Acquisitions announces a revised final pre-conditional possible offer for Marks & Spencer at 400p per Marks & Spencer share or a cash and share alternative. Revival again reiterates that the making of its offer would be conditional on the receipt of a recommendation of the board of Marks & Spencer and access to limited due diligence information.
	At the same time, Revival Acquisitions announces that it has received the support (in the form of an irrevocable undertaking to accept an offer) of Brandes Investment Partners LLC in respect of 11.7 per cent of the issued share capital of Marks & Spencer, such support to fall away in the event of an offer valuing a Marks & Spencer share at 430p or more.
8 July 2004	The board of Marks & Spencer announces that it continues to reject the Revival Acquisitions proposal.
	Revival Acquisitions announces that it has obtained further support from Schroder Investment Management, through a non-

	binding letter of intent to accept an offer at 400p per Marks & Spencer share.
9 July 2004	Revival Acquisitions announces that holders of Marks & Spencer shares (and derivatives contracts referenced to those shares) have confirmed that they believe that Marks & Spencer should allow Revival Acquisitions to access due diligence information.
	Revival Acquisitions also publishes, in the form of an open letter, further correspondence with the trustee of the Marks & Spencer pension fund reiterating its request for due diligence.
12 July 2004	Marks & Spencer announces its defence strategy, an operational review, and capital restructuring and divestment of a division to HSBC.
	Marks & Spencer holds investors' conference to deliver operational review.
13 July 2004	Revival Acquisitions holds conference call for its supporters.
	Later in the day, Revival Acquisitions announces that it has received further support from holders of Marks & Spencer shares (and derivatives contracts referenced to those shares) that have confirmed that they believe that Marks & Spencer should allow Revival Acquisitions to access due diligence information.
14 July 2004	Revival Acquisitions announces that is has received further indications of support.
15 July 2004	Revival Acquisitions withdraws its possible offer for Marks & Spencer.

Code framework

Bidders normally prefer to conduct negotiations to obtain a recommendation for their proposed takeover bid in private, as this allows negotiations to take place without external pressures such as press speculation and share price volatility resulting from speculation about the prospects of an offer (which can make the offer terms difficult to assess). In circumstances where the parties desire privacy but there is evidence that a leak has occurred, the Panel can require the bidder or the target to announce the possibility of an offer under Rule 2.2 of the Code (a manifestation of General Principle 6 and the desire to avoid the creation of false markets). However, unsolicited bidders occasionally wish to publicise their interest in acquiring a company (and, possibly, the terms upon which they propose to make an offer) without committing themselves to bid. This is permitted under the Code, enables the interested party to test the market's reaction to its proposed offer and any terms that are announced and is often a tactic to pressurise the board of the target company. The use of such announcements is a classic 'virtual bid' tactic and is, as a result of the desire to pressurise the target, known as a 'bear hug'.

In the case of Marks & Spencer, Revival Acquisitions initially made a short-form possible offer announcement (of the type used in cases where there has been a leak). None of the announcements of proposed offers made by Revival Acquisitions amounted to a firm commitment to launch a takeover offer for Marks & Spencer: on three separate occasions, Revival Acquisitions made a very specific form of possible offer announcement – a 'pre-conditional possible offer' announcement – which, whilst not committing the maker to an offer, includes a list of items (in the form of pre-conditions) which the potential bidder wishes to address prior to formalising its bid. In Marks & Spencer, the conditions included the provision of certain due diligence information and access to the M&S pension fund trustees.

As mentioned above, in 2004 the Panel undertook an extensive consultation exercise relating to the treatment of virtual bids and the problems of regulating such offers. This consultation exercise was launched against a backdrop of an increasing number of public takeover transactions funded by private equity houses. One of the key elements of this consultation exercise was to codify and improve Panel practice on the treatment of statements of the terms upon which a possible offer might be made by a bidder.

The Panel's revised approach to such situations involved the potential bidder being held to the terms of any possible offer announced by it (except in certain limited circumstances).

'Put up or shut up'
As another key component of the changes to the Code proposed in connection with virtual bids, the Panel codified the existing practice of imposing so-called 'put up or shut up' deadlines. This is a mechanism for bringing proposed offer situations to a conclusion at the request of the offeree company. Without the framework of put up or shut up, there would be no mechanism for offeree companies to bring to an end possible offer situations (as the formal Code timetable does not commence until the announcement of a firm intention to bid under Rule 2.5 of the Code). The Panel had previously justified the imposition of such deadlines under what was Rule 35.1(b) of the Code, but practices had developed over time that necessitated certain revisions to the Code itself. The Panel assumes that target companies are damaged by the distraction caused by an offer or possible offer and that protracted distraction will harm shareholders' interests. In imposing a deadline (following a request by the target company), the Panel attempts to balance the interests of shareholders in receiving an offer to consider against the damage that is caused by the possible offer hanging over the company. In Marks & Spencer, the 'state of siege' caused by Revival Acquisition's interest was intense and had certainly resulted in the senior management of the retailer devoting significant amounts of time and effort to defending the approach.

Typically, the Panel imposes a deadline between six and eight weeks from the date of the commencement of the offer period if the request is made at the earliest possible stage. If the request is made at a later stage, the Panel seeks to balance the timing considerations to produce a fair result. In the case of Revival Acquisitions/Marks & Spencer the deadline fell only four weeks after the date of the Panel Statement but more than eight weeks after the commencement of the offer period. Revival Acquisitions withdrew voluntarily from the offer process prior to the deadline.

Statements of support and the growing importance of derivatives
As demonstrated by the chronology of events set out above, a key tactic of the Revival Acquisitions camp was the use of statements of shareholder support. The Panel closely

> regulates the making of such statements as a result of the potential for misleading the market as to the level of support obtained. In particular, in such situations, the Panel requires a detailed verification exercise to be conducted under Note 2 on Rule 19.3 prior to the release of any statements of the level of support achieved.
>
> The M&S situation was one of the first high-profile transactions in which the influence of stakeholders with interests held by way of derivative instruments was critical.
>
> As a result of the M&S situation and other cases in which derivatives holders were influential, the Panel's Code Committee commenced a major consultation exercise on the treatment of derivatives dealings under the Code. In summary, the Panel's stated preference for the treatment of derivatives dealings was that such dealings should, for most purposes under the Code, be treated as dealings in the securities to which the derivatives are referenced. This is likely to be a controversial proposal and it remains to be seen whether the Panel will succeed in gaining widespread acceptance of the concept.

---

[1] A detailed discussion of the SARs is beyond the scope of this chapter, but, in summary, the SARs restrict the speed at which a person can build a stake of between 15 to 30 per cent of the issued voting rights of a listed company.

[2] The Panel will not take jurisdiction in other cases. See Panel Statement 2002/7 relating to Xstrata, a UK public company with its place of central management in Switzerland.

[3] Implementation of the Directive in the United Kingdom will result in the existing 10 General Principles being replaced by the six General Principles set out in the Directive.

[4] This is true of the acceptance condition in a voluntary offer. In a mandatory offer, the condition is somewhat different and does not allow the bidder to ensure that it will attain the level of acceptances necessary to exercise compulsory acquisition rights.

[5] Normally, compulsory acquisition rights are used as a tool to overcome shareholder apathy and 'sweep up' the remaining shareholders who have not responded to the bid documentation. However, by their nature, compulsory acquisition rights can also be used to force a sale by a dissenting minority, as in the 2005 case of Manchester United.

[6] See Panel Statements 2004/11 and 2003/33.

[7] For similar reasons, prior to making an offer, a potential bidder should avoid making any statement that implies that it may be unlikely to bid. The Panel will construe such a statement as a 'no intention to bid' statement and, under Rule 2.8 of the Code, the bidder will be prevented from bidding for six months from the date of its statement unless an exception applies.

[8] See Panel Statements 2004/10.

[9] See, for example, Panel Statement 2000/1, regarding an unverified statement of support made near to the conclusion of the bitterly fought battle for control of National Westminster Bank.

[10] Upon implementation of Article 9 of the Directive in the United Kingdom, Rule 21 will be amended so as to be consistent with that Article.

[11] An offer period commences in relation to a target company at the time of the first public announcement by any party of an offer or possible offer. The offer period ends when an offer becomes or is declared unconditional as to acceptances or when all announced potential bidders have made public that they are no longer interested in making a bid.

[12] The definition of an 'associate' is detailed and captures a broad category of connected persons. The definition of 'associates' is broader than the definition of 'concert parties'.

[13] Disclosures are required in relation to the 'relevant securities' of the target company and, in a securities exchange offer, a bidder. The term 'relevant securities' covers all equity and convertible debt securities, as well as rights to subscribe, options in respect of, and derivatives referenced to, such securities.

[14] Panel Statement 2004/1.

[15] See Panel Statement 2004/11. This was the first example of an auction process being followed by the parties to the bid, although the Panel had previously invoked Rule 32.5 in connection with the competitive bidding process surrounding the Laragrove and Baroness bids for Debenhams plc).

[16] See Panel Statement 2000/10.

Chapter 9

Austria

Max Becker, Phillip Dubsky and Dieter Buchberger
DLA Weiss-Tessbach Rechtsanwälte GmbH, Vienna

The Austrian Takeover Act (*Übernahmegesetz*) came into force on 1 January 1999. It was based on the proposal of 7 November 1997 for the 13th Company Law Directive. The Takeover Act is essentially divided into three parts: regulating voluntary bids, mandatory bids and the procedure for takeover bids before the Takeover Commission (*Übernahmekommission*). The Commission is an independent 12-member panel that enforces the takeover regime and supervises public tender offers.

The Takeover Act is guided by five general principles:

- equal treatment of all shareholders;
- adequate time and sufficient information to shareholders;
- neutral and unbiased behaviour of the board of a target company;
- avoidance of market distortions; and
- expedient completion of takeover procedures.

The Takeover Act applies only to companies that have their corporate seats in Austria and whose securities are listed on the official market (*amtlicher Handel*) or the semi-official market (*geregelter Freiverkehr*) of the Vienna Stock Exchange.

The restricted scope of the Takeover Act will need to be amended under the Parliament and Council Directive (EC) No. 25/2004 (the Takeover Directive). Under the new regime of the Takeover Directive, in the event of a difference between the place of listing and the corporate seat of the target, the law of the corporate seat will apply on all issues in connection with corporate law and the provision of information to employees. On the other hand, the law of the marketplace of the target company will apply on all issues with regard to the procedure of the mandatory bid, such as the offering documentation, consideration issues and the notification of the offer.

Conditionality of offers
General approach
The Takeover Act allows the attachment of conditions to tender offers only under limited circumstances. In addition, the Takeover Commission is generally reluctant to approve offers that are subject to conditions and rights of withdrawal.

Voluntary offers and anticipated mandatory offers may be rendered subject to certain conditions and rights of withdrawal if such conditions are objectively justified – in particular, if they are based on a legal obligation of the bidder – or if the right of withdrawal is not at the exclusive discretion of the bidder. Any conditions need to be explicitly mentioned in the offer document and are, therefore, subject to approval by the Takeover Commission. The Commission has approved conditions relating, for example, to regulatory approvals, in particular merger control clearance; approvals by the shareholders' meeting of the bidder; the non-occurrence of certain events, such as insolvency; and material changes in the target company.

With regard to mandatory offers, the Takeover Act allows only conditions relating to regulatory approvals rendered by the appropriate authority, whether for competition matters, banking supervision or insurance supervision.

Recent decisions

In one recent decision, Jenbacher/GE Holding (2003), the Takeover Commission approved a condition relating to a material adverse change in the target's commercial status, given that such material adverse change was clearly defined, was not at the bidder's discretion and was to be verified by an independent third party within the offer period.

In another recent decision, Siemens/VA-TECH (2004), the Commission approved the introduction of a new condition, not previously mentioned in the offer documents, which allowed the bidder to withdraw from the bid if the offer was not accepted by shareholders representing 90 per cent of the voting rights. However, in a subsequent and related ruling, the Commission confirmed that the introduction of this new condition was allowed only because, in turn, the bidder waived a condition requiring the elimination of a maximum voting right restriction (*Höchststimmrecht*).

Timing and revision

A takeover offer must be announced by the bidder without delay if the board of directors and the supervisory board have made a decision to make a tender offer, or if the acquisition of a controlling interest has occurred, requiring the bidder to make a mandatory tender offer.

In addition, the bidder has to make a public announcement beforehand if there is a substantial movement in the price of securities or rumours; speculation arises concerning the bid; and there are reasonable grounds for concluding that these originate in the preparation of the bid, in the bidder's plans to make such a bid or in the purchase of shares by the bidder (creation of false markets).

The announcement must be made either through publication in a daily newspaper or through electronic media throughout Austria.

After disclosing its intention to make a bid, the bidder must notify the Takeover Commission within 10 trading days. The Commission may, at the request of the bidder, extend this period to a maximum of 40 trading days. If the bidder does not comply with this notification requirement, the bidder is prohibited from making another bid for one year, starting 40 days from the public announcement.

The offer document must include:

- the terms of the bid;
- the particulars of the offer;

- the securities that are subject to the bid;
- the consideration offered for each security;
- the offeror's intentions regarding future business policy;
- the period for acceptance of the bid; and
- the terms and conditions of the financing of the bid.

The offeror is also obliged to appoint a qualified independent expert to provide advice throughout the proceedings and to examine the documents. The expert must ascertain that the offer documents are in compliance with the law, in particular with regard to the consideration offered. The offer documents and the expert's findings must be published no earlier than the 12th and no later than the 15th trading day after their receipt by the Takeover Commission, unless the Commission has prohibited the publication of the bid.

The period for accepting the bid should not be less than 20 and not more than 50 trading days. However, this period may be extended by the Takeover Commission under certain circumstances, in particular if the bid is a mandatory bid or is subject to the condition that a specified acceptance threshold is reached. In any event, the acceptance period cannot expire before the end of 15 working days after the target's board has reported on the terms of the bid and, in particular, on the consideration offered, and has made a recommendation to the shareholders as to whether or not to accept the offer.

Mandatory bid rule

Definition of 'controlling shareholding'

Anyone obtaining a controlling shareholding in a (listed) target company is obliged to launch a mandatory bid for all the securities of that company and to notify such bid to the Takeover Commission within 20 trading days: this is the 'mandatory bid rule'. A controlling shareholding is deemed to be ownership in the target enabling the bidder, solely or together with other natural persons or legal entities, to exercise dominant influence directly, indirectly or contractually, for instance through a syndicate agreement. The Takeover Act does not specify a threshold for dominant influence, but it does provide guidance by stipulating specific factors that have to be taken into account for the assessment of dominant influence:

- the number of voting shares acquired;
- the number of voting shares in public hands;
- the voting stock usually represented at the general meeting of shareholders; and
- specific control related provisions in the articles of association.

All these factors have to be considered when assessing the existence of dominant influence.

The Takeover Commission has issued a regulation giving additional guidance on the definition of a controlling shareholding (*1. Übernahmeverordnung* of 9 March 1999). The regulation provides for certain facts that would constitute a controlling shareholding:

- the majority of the voting rights; or
- the right to appoint or to dismiss the majority of either the managing board or the supervisory board; or
- the right to exercise dominant influence over the company.

There are two other facts that may be taken as indications of the existence of a controlling shareholding, although either indication can be rebutted. First, where a shareholder, either solely or in concert with other parties, has acquired at least 30 per cent of the voting rights, the indication can be rebutted by demonstrating that at least one other shareholder holds the same or a higher number of voting rights. Secondly, where a shareholder, either solely or in concert with other parties, has acquired at least 20 per cent, but less than 30 per cent, of the voting rights – provided that this amount would have represented more than half of the voting rights present at the last three consecutive shareholders' meetings – the indication can be rebutted by demonstrating that at least one other shareholder holds 10 per cent of the voting rights or that at least three other shareholders each hold at least 5 per cent of the voting rights of the company.

'Creeping in'

If somebody who holds a controlling share, but not the majority, of the voting rights of the offeree company acquires, within a period of 12 months, shares representing more than 2 per cent of the voting rights of the company, he/she is obliged to make a bid: this is known as 'creeping in'.

Articles of association

Notwithstanding the statutory provisions on the definition of a 'controlling shareholding', the target itself may stipulate provisions in its articles of association that lower the threshold for the launch of a mandatory bid, provided that the threshold does not go below 20 per cent of the voting rights. In addition, the articles may provide for a clause that determines a partial 'opt out' from the mandatory bid rule, which means that the mandatory bid comprises only ordinary shares and preference shares that have already been floated, as well as convertible bonds and options.

Exemptions

The Takeover Act provides for various exemptions from the mandatory bid rule:

- the restructuring of a shareholding without an effective change in the persons who exercise control, as, for example, through the assignment of shares to a different entity with the same persons owning the entity in the same proportions;
- the assignment of shares between family members by way of a gift, succession by heritage or the splitting of a legal estate following a divorce;
- the assignment of shares to a private trust, provided that the beneficiaries are previous owners or relatives of the company.

Further exemptions are available for financial institutions that acquire voting rights in connection with their securities business, such as investment fund business, share deposit or share commission business or market-making activities. Such acquisitions do not trigger the obligation for a mandatory offer if the respective transactions do not affect the financial interests of the shareholders and are appropriate for the realisation of the business in question.

Notification procedure

Instead of making a bid, it is sufficient to notify the relevant facts to the Takeover Commission if:

- the number of voting rights necessary to give rise to a controlling shareholding is exceeded insignificantly and only temporarily or unintentionally;
- shares are transferred within a group of shareholders acting in concert and affect the composition of the group only insignificantly;
- in the event of an acquisition of an indirect holding, the book value of the direct holding in the target company amounts to less than 25 per cent of the book value of the net assets of the party through which the indirect holding is acquired; or
- shares are acquired purely for reorganisation purposes or as security for claims.

In these cases, the Takeover Commission may order a mandatory bid if it deems it necessary, especially in the case of a possible negative impact on the financial interests of the shareholders. Further, instead of ordering a mandatory bid, the Commission may impose other appropriate conditions for the execution of the transaction.

Consideration

In a voluntary bid, every kind of consideration, such as cash or a share swap, is allowed. For a mandatory bid, however, the bidder has to make a cash offer, since a lone share swap offer is not allowed.

In a mandatory bid, the consideration must not be less than the average market price during the last six months and must not provide for a higher discount than 15 per cent as compared to the highest consideration granted by the bidder during the last 12 months.

Anticipated mandatory offer

If a voluntary bid might result in the acquisition of a controlling shareholding, the rules for a mandatory bid apply. Such an anticipated mandatory offer requires that the bidder has no controlling shareholding prior to the offer and intends to acquire more than 50 per cent of the voting rights in the target before the end of the acceptance period.

Squeeze-out and sell-out

The Takeover Act does not contain specific provisions regarding squeeze-out procedures. However, the Transformation Act (*Umwandlungsgesetz*) and the Demerger Act (*Spaltungsgesetz*) allow any shareholder holding a minimum of 90 per cent of the shares of a company to squeeze-out the minority shareholders against payment of an appropriate cash consideration.

Current law in Austria does not provide for sell-out rights as provided for in Article 16 of the Takeover Directive.

Target's response

The Takeover Act stipulates the principle of neutrality for the reaction of the target company to takeover offers. Accordingly, neither the management board nor the supervisory board may take any action that might influence the free decision of the shareholders or frustrate the entire offer. Any actions taken in order to defend the company from hostile bids are legitimate insofar as they are based on obligations of the management board that have been incurred before the bid or have been approved by shareholders' resolutions adopted after the bidder's intention to make a bid has been announced.

After a public bid has been announced, the target's management board must, and the supervisory board may, respond to the bid. According to the principle of neutrality, their responses must reflect a free and neutral view of the bid, especially highlighting facts that might violate the interests of shareholders, employees, creditors and the public. In their responses, the boards must produce arguments for and against the acceptance of the bid. Further, the target must appoint an external expert who must establish a written assessment of the offer, the response of the management board and any (optional) comments by the supervisory board.

The response of the management board, the optional comments of the supervisory board and the assessment of the expert must be submitted to the Takeover Commission and the workers' council within 10 trading days from the announcement of the bid.

Reform of the Takeover Act

The Ministry of Justice is currently working on a reform of the Takeover Act, not only in order to implement the Takeover Directive, but also to revise the Act in the light of the experience gained in applying it since its entering into force on 1 January 1999. The main topics for the reform are the following.

Definition of 'controlling shareholding'

Unlike in most EU member states, Austrian takeover law does not provide for a clear-cut threshold with respect to the shareholding in the target company law that would trigger the obligation to make a bid. If the acquired shares represent between 20 per cent and 30 per cent of the voting rights of the target, the decision whether this constitutes a controlling shareholding is taken on the basis of an individual assessment of the respective case. It has been suggested that the results under this flexible system are not sufficiently predictable for a potential investor. Accordingly, industry representatives in particular have demanded the introduction of a clear-cut threshold of 30 per cent of the voting rights, meaning that the acquisition of less than 30 per cent would not trigger the obligation to make a bid. However, the Takeover Commission favours the retention of a more flexible system.

Acquisition of a controlling shareholding due to measures of a third party

Under current law, the 'passive' acquisition of a controlling shareholding, for example through the sale of shares by another major shareholder, would trigger the obligation to make a bid unless a statutory exemption applies. It is currently being discussed whether, in the event of such a passive acquisition of control, the controlling shareholder should have the right to choose either to sell the shares above the threshold for a controlling shareholding or to waive the voting rights for the shares exceeding the threshold.

Securities instead of cash consideration

Under the current Takeover Act, it is not admissible to offer securities instead of a cash consideration in a mandatory offer. There is strong support for an amendment that would allow the offeror to offer liquid securities instead of cash.

Board neutrality

The current rules of the Takeover Act require the management board and the supervisory board of the offeree company to refrain from any act liable to frustrate the bid, unless such act is based on a prior obligation of the administrative organs of the offeree company or on resolutions passed by the general meeting of shareholders after the intention of the offeror to make a bid has become known.

The Takeover Directive also contains an exception from the neutrality requirement in the event of a prior obligation of the administrative organs. Article 9, sections 2 and 3 of the Takeover Directive provides for the possibility of opting out of the obligation to implement rules about board neutrality.

Nevertheless, it is expected that board neutrality will remain in the Takeover Act, although there might be a need to adapt the provision in the Act to the requirements of the Takeover Directive.

Breakthrough

The current Takeover Act does not contain breakthrough provisions as provided for in Article 11 of the Takeover Directive. Contractual agreements between shareholders providing for restrictions on the transfer of securities or for restrictions on voting rights can frequently be found in Austrian companies. It is not yet clear whether Austria will make use of the possibility of opting out of the obligation to implement breakthrough provisions. If it does so, Austrian companies will be granted the option to implement a breakthrough provision in their articles of association. Consequently, there is a need for legislative provision in this context.

Equitable price in the event of a mandatory bid

In the event of a mandatory bid, the Takeover Act allows for a 15 per cent discount from the highest price paid for the respective securities by the offeror, or entities acting in concert, over a period of 12 months before the bid. As such a discount is not covered by the Takeover Directive, it will have to be abolished.

Information on companies

The publication requirement of Article 10 of the Takeover Directive addressing, among other things, restrictions on voting rights and 'change of control' clauses in any significant agreements, will have to be implemented in the revised Takeover Act.

Squeeze-out and sell-out

Provisions regarding the rights of squeeze-out and sell-out, as provided for in Articles 15 and 16 of the Directive, are not contained in the current Takeover Act. Here too the necessary amendments to the Act will have to be made.

Chapter 10

Belgium

Paul Van Hooghten and Philippe Remels
Linklaters De Bandt, Brussels

In Belgium, public takeovers and changes of control are regulated by the Law of 2 March 1989 on the disclosure of important participations in listed companies and the regulations on public takeover bids (the 'Law of 2 March 1989'); the Law of 22 April 2003 relating to the public offer of securities (the 'Law of 22 April 2003'); and the Royal Decree of 8 November 1989 on public takeover bids and changes in the control over companies (the 'Takeover Decree').

The Takeover Decree is divided into three main sections, setting out what are commonly referred to as the Chapter II, Chapter III and Chapter IV procedures:

- Chapter II sets out the procedure for the conduct of voluntary public takeover bids and counterbids;
- Chapter III deals with mandatory public takeover bids and the maintenance of the market price following the acquisition of a controlling interest in a public company; and
- Chapter IV regulates public bids to squeeze-out minority shareholders in public companies.

The potential impact of the European Directive 2004/25/EC of the European Parliament and of the Council of 21 April 2004 on takeover bids (the 'Takeover Directive') on Belgian takeover regulation is discussed below.

The Banking, Finance and Insurance Commission (BFIC) is the administrative body entrusted with the control of compliance with the Takeover Decree. The BFIC can also grant derogations from the Takeover Decree in specific cases. Following the changes brought about by the Law of 2 August 2002 regarding the supervision of the financial sector and financial services, all disputes relating to takeover bids must be submitted to the Court of Appeal of Brussels, which has exclusive jurisdiction in these matters.

Disclosure of important shareholdings

Pursuant to Article 1 of the Law of 2 March 1989, as implemented by the Royal Decree of 10 May 1989 on the disclosure of important participations in listed companies, and Article 514 of the Belgian Companies Code, any natural or legal person acquiring securities of a Belgian company listed in a regulated market in the European Economic Area, in such a way that the proportion of the voting rights held, directly or indirectly, would reach at least 5 per cent, must disclose this fact to the BFIC and the relevant company within two business days after the acquisition. The target company must disclose the notification to the public on the next business day at the latest. Any person increasing a holding above a level of 10 per cent, 15 per cent, 20 per cent and so on in increments of five percentage points must likewise disclose this fact to the BFIC and the relevant company. These thresholds may be lower, but not lower than 3 per cent, if there are provisions to that effect in the by-laws of the relevant company. The notification duty also applies when securities are transferred and the seller's participation drops below one of the thresholds.

Voluntary public takeover bids and counterbids

Scope

Chapter II of the Takeover Decree applies to public takeover bids to acquire voting securities or securities that confer the right to subscribe to, acquire or convert into voting securities.

For the purposes of Chapter II, a bid is considered to be a 'public' bid if it meets any of the following conditions:

- any advertising means are used either by the bidder or on its instruction in order to announce or recommend the bid to more than 50 persons in Belgium, other than certain professional investors. Adverting means include, among other techniques, spreading information in the written press, in periodicals, or through radio, television or other audiovisual means; spreading circulars or other standardised documents relating to the bid, even when personally addressed to the recipient; and spreading information by telephone or through electronic means of communication;
- a financial intermediary other than one authorised in Belgium is involved;
- more than 50 persons in Belgium, other than certain professional investors, are solicited by the bidder or on his behalf.

Certain exceptions apply, where, for example, the shareholders of the target are all institutional investors acting on their own behalf.

Whether or not the target company is listed or registered as a public company is irrelevant to the determination of whether a transaction falls within the scope of Chapter II of the Takeover Decree.

Notification to the BFIC and requirements for the bid

Any person intending to launch a public takeover bid for voting securities of a company or their equivalent must give the BFIC prior notice. This notification must include the price, the terms and conditions of the bid, and evidence that all the following requirements have been met:

- the bid must relate to all the voting securities or their equivalent not yet owned by the bidder, unless it is a bid that, when successful, will leave the bidder, taken together with its directors, its affiliated persons and other persons acting in concert with the bidder, with a maximum of 10 per cent of the votes attached to the securities issued by the target company. It is nevertheless possible to make the bid conditional upon obtaining a minimum number of acceptances, such as 50 per cent of all the securities issued by the target company;

- in a cash bid, the bidder must demonstrate that it has the funds necessary to carry out the public takeover bid, either in an account opened with a Belgian credit institution or in the form of an unconditional and irrevocable credit facility granted by such a credit institution;
- in an exchange bid, the bidder must demonstrate that it holds the securities necessary to carry out the public takeover bid, or has the power to issue, to cause the issue of, or to acquire a sufficient number of the offered securities within the payment term;
- the terms and conditions of the bid must be in compliance with the Takeover Decree and such terms and conditions, in particular the price, must be such that the bidder is normally able to obtain the desired result;
- the bidder must commit itself to seeing the bid through;
- an authorised credit institution or stockbroking company located in Belgium must be appointed as paying agent, and be responsible for receiving the acceptance forms and paying the price to the securities-holders of the target company.

The bidder must attach to its notification to the BFIC a detailed file including the draft prospectus, an overview of the target securities already held by the bidder and the draft forms of acceptance to be used by the securities-holders accepting the bid.

No later than on the banking day following the receipt of the bidder's notification, the BFIC must publicly announce that it has received such a notification. A copy of this announcement must be sent to the bidder, the target company and, if the target company's securities are listed in a Belgian regulated market, the Belgian market authority. Prior to the BFIC's announcement, no one may announce the bid (except if the BFIC so requires in particular circumstances).

The BFIC can suspend its public announcement for a maximum of three days if it is of the opinion that the Takeover Decree is not being complied with, or that any of the terms and conditions of the bid, in particular the price, is not credible. If the bidder is still not in compliance at the end of the three days, the BFIC can urge the bidder to comply, impose a prohibition on the bidder's use of the rights or benefits acquired pursuant to the breach and impose a penalty. The bidder can file an appeal with the Court of Appeal of Brussels against such a decision of the BFIC.

Conditional bids

Unlike a mandatory bid, which must be unconditional (see below), a voluntary public takeover bid can be conditional, provided that the conditions were included in the notification of the bid by the bidder to the BFIC and that the BFIC has accepted such conditions.

According to the BFIC, if a condition is not satisfied, the bid does not automatically lapse, but the bidder is given the option to withdraw the bid. If the bidder does not notify the BFIC that it wants to withdraw the bid, the BFIC assumes that the bidder maintains the bid.

In principle, a bidder must make a bid for all securities issued by the target that the bidder does not yet hold, except where, after the bid, the offeror, together with its directors, affiliated persons, and the natural and legal persons acting in concert with it, owns not more than 10 per cent of the voting rights attached to the securities issued by the target.

Notwithstanding this obligation, and except in the event of a mandatory takeover bid, the offeror may condition its bid on the acquisition at the end of the bid period of a determined percentage of the securities issued by the target. If this threshold is not reached, the bidder is not obliged to purchase the securities offered for sale. However, in such an event, a bidder may nevertheless decide to pursue the bid if it has reserved this right in the bid prospectus.

The bidder may also condition its bid on a material adverse change clause, with clear and verifiable conditions, or on the approval of the relevant competition or other regulatory authorities.

The obtaining of sufficient financing cannot constitute a condition, since, pursuant to Article 3 of the Takeover Decree, before making the bid the bidder must either place the required funds in a bank account with a credit institution registered in Belgium, or ensure an irrevocable and unconditional credit facility with any such institution. Likewise, in the event of an exchange bid the bidder must prove that it holds, or has the power to acquire, to issue or to have issued in a timely manner a sufficient number of securities as consideration if the bid is completed.

Once the bid has been launched, the bidder may amend or withdraw its bid only in a limited number of circumstances.

Changing the terms of the bid and withdrawal of the bid

As mentioned above, a public takeover bid must in principle be irrevocable. Once it has been notified to, and announced by, the BFIC, the bidder can change the terms of the bid only in order to improve them from the point of view of the holders of securities in the target company. Further, the bid can be withdrawn by the bidder only in the following circumstances:

- where the shareholders' meeting or the board of directors of the target company has taken any of the defensive measures referred to in Article 12 of the Takeover Decree (see below);
- where there is a counterbid or a higher bid;
- if any required administrative authorisations, such as clearance from the competition authorities, have not been obtained;
- where any of the conditions set out in the notification of the bid to the BFIC and approved by the BFIC is not satisfied for reasons beyond the bidder's control; or
- with the BFIC's approval, in exceptional circumstances that prevent the bid from being completed for reasons beyond the bidder's control.

The bidder must notify the BFIC of its decision to withdraw the bid. The BFIC publicises such withdrawal.

Prospectus, target board's statement and approval by the BFIC

The bid document, commonly known in Belgium as the prospectus, must be drafted according to the provisions of the Takeover Decree and the BFIC's guidelines. It aims at providing information to the securities-holders of the target company in order to allow them to decide whether or not they should sell their securities. Detailed information must be supplied regarding the bidder, the target company, the securities to be acquired, the consideration, and the terms and conditions of the bid.

Within a period of five banking days after the receipt of the draft prospectus through the BFIC, the board of directors of the target company may forward its remarks and comments regarding the draft bid document to the BFIC and the bidder. If the board of directors of the target is of the opinion that the draft prospectus is incomplete or misleading, it must inform the bidder and the BFIC.

The board of directors of the target company must also prepare a statement regarding its views on the bid. In formulating its statement, which is published either in the prospectus or separately, the board of directors must take into account the interests of the holders of securities, the creditors and the employees of the target company. The statement must also indicate, *inter alia*, whether the board will apply certain transfer restrictions provided for in the company by-laws, such as clauses requiring prior board approval for certain transfers of securities, and whether the directors of the company intend to sell their securities to the bidder. The directors must also request the shareholders whom they *de facto* represent on the board to communicate their intentions regarding the securities they hold. Finally, the board of directors' statement must refer to the opinion of the works council of the target company. The bid must be submitted to the target company's works council, which may formulate an opinion regarding the intended bid.

The BFIC must decide, within 15 business days following receipt of the complete file from the bidder, whether or not to approve the prospectus.

Publication of the prospectus

The prospectus may be made public only after it has been approved by the BFIC. The prospectus must mention that it has been approved by the BFIC, but that such approval does not imply an assessment as to the advisability and quality of the bid, nor of the situation of the bidder.

The prospectus is to be made freely available to the public through at least one Belgian credit institution or stockbroking company. The fact that a prospectus has been issued and the location(s) where it can be obtained must be published in one or more Belgian newspapers.

Bid period, counterbids and higher bids, and reopening of the bid

The period during which the public takeover bid is open starts from the date of publication of the prospectus and must last for at least 10 banking days, but no longer than 20 banking days.

A counterbid can be made up to two banking days before the expiration of the original public takeover bid. The counterbidder must propose a consideration at least 5 per cent higher than that proposed by the first bidder and the conditions of the counterbid may not be more stringent than those of the initial public takeover bid. The same procedure and requirements as apply to a public takeover bid apply to any counterbid.

In the event of a counterbid, the first bidder may in turn make a second counterbid, with consideration higher by at least 5 per cent than that in the first counterbid, but is not required to submit a new notification or prospectus.

Holders of securities who accepted a public takeover bid are no longer bound by their acceptance in the case of a valid counterbid. Each increase in the bid consideration also applies for the holders of securities who accepted the bid prior to such increase.

The results of the public takeover bid must be made public, at the latest, on the fifth banking day following the closing of the bid. The BFIC must be informed of the total number of securities acquired and held by the bidder in the target company. If the acquisition of a certain number of the securities was a condition of the bid and the number of securities effectively introduced in the bid is lower, the bidder can still accept the acquisition of such lower number of securities if it has provided for this option in the announcement of the bid to the BFIC.

If, following the closing of the bid, the bidder holds at least 90 per cent of the target company's securities, the bidder must reopen the bid within one month following the publication of the results of the bid, for a period of at least 15 banking days.

When no reopening of the bid is necessary on the aforementioned ground, because the bidder did not acquire 90 per cent of the target company's securities, but within three months following the closing of the bid the bidder requests that the securities of the target company be delisted from a Belgian regulated market, the bidder must reopen the bid within one month following such delisting request, for a period of at least 15 banking days.

If the bidder, following the closing of a public bid or following the reopening of such bid, holds, alone, directly or indirectly, or acting in concert, at least 95 per cent of the voting securities of the target company, the bidder can reopen the bid with the same conditions during a period of at least 15 banking days following the publication of the results of the bid, in order to launch a squeeze-out under Article 513 of the Belgian Companies Code (Chapter IV of the Takeover Decree does not apply). Such reopening of the bid is possible only if the bidder has explicitly provided for this option in the prospectus. Further, if the bidder, alone, directly or indirectly, or acting in concert, already controlled the target company before launching the public takeover bid, it can reopen the bid as a squeeze-out bid only where through the reopened bid it has acquired not only 95 per cent of the voting securities, but also at least 66 per cent of the voting securities that it did not yet hold when launching the bid. The squeeze-out bid must be for a cash consideration.

Case studies

Fairness of consideration offered

A takeover bid by the Dutch company Ford Capital BV for its subsidiary Ford Motor Company (Belgium) NV was announced on 24 March 2000. The target company distributed Ford products in Belgium and Luxembourg. The Ford group intended to introduce a new transfer-pricing system for its European distribution companies that would result in a material decrease in the results of Ford Motor Company (Belgium). According to the prospectus, the intention was to give the minority shareholders the possibility of selling their shares before the new transfer-pricing system was introduced. The prospectus also announced that the bidder would launch a squeeze-out bid if the relevant thresholds were reached following the opening or reopening of the takeover bid.

In a fairness opinion requested by the target board, an investment bank concluded that the offered price was fair when taking into account the fact that the transfer-pricing system was to be changed. The target board followed this conclusion in its statement on the bid.

The BFIC had the impression that the future decrease in results had already been taken into account in the bid price, which it considered to be an unacceptable situation, and informed the bidder of its concerns.[1] In the end, Ford Capital BV gave in to pressure from the BFIC and increased its bid considerably. In addition, the justification of the price in the prospectus was modified, and new versions of the fairness opinion and the target board's statement were issued, stating, without qualification, that the price was fair.

In this respect, it should be mentioned that under current legislation the BFIC cannot force a bidder to increase its bid price as was demonstrated in the BNP Paribas/Cobepa

> case where BNP refused the request of the BFIC to increase its bid price for the shares in Cobepa. This may change pursuant to the implementation of the Takeover Directive.
>
> **Level of acceptance thresholds**
> As mentioned above, a bidder may condition its bid on the acquisition by the end of the bid period of a determined percentage of the securities issued by the target. For a long time, the BFIC seemed not to accept acceptance thresholds as high as the threshold for launching a squeeze-out bid, which is 95 per cent. However, it has become clear that the BFIC no longer objects to such high acceptance thresholds, following such bids as that by NV Bank Degroof for NV de Buck Vermogensbankiers, announced on 20 May 2003; the bid by Korfinco NV for Koramic Building Products NV, announced on 6 June 2003; and the bid by United Services Group NV for Solvus NV, announced on 17 June 2005.
>
> **Target board's statement and conflict of interest**
> On 19 August 1999, a takeover bid for Tractebel NV was announced by the French company Suez Lyonnaise des Eaux SA and the Belgian company Generale Maatschappij van België NV. Before the prospectus could be approved, minority shareholders started legal proceedings against Tractebel. One of their arguments was that the target board's statement on the bid was in breach of Articles 60 and 60bis of the (former) Coordinated Laws on Commercial Companies, now Articles 523 and 524 of the Belgian Companies Code providing for a specific procedure in the event of a conflict of interests of the directors. In a decision of 19 January 2001, the Brussels Court of Appeal finally held that Articles 523 and 524 do not apply to the advice on the bid that the board must give pursuant to Article 15 of the Takeover Decree and that the directors who *de facto* represent the bidder on the target board must not abstain when the target board decides on the statement to be issued regarding the bid.

Mandatory public offers and maintaining of the market price
Scope

Chapter III of the Takeover Decree applies only to changes of control in Belgian public companies. For the purposes of Chapter III, a Belgian company is considered to be a 'public' company if:

- its securities, whether voting securities or securities that confer the right to subscribe to, acquire or convert into voting securities, are listed in a Belgian regulated market or are regularly traded in auctions periodically organised by a stock exchange company; or
- its securities, whether voting securities or securities that confer the right to subscribe to, acquire or convert into voting securities, are held by the Belgian public, meaning by more than 50 Belgian holders of securities.

The relevant criterion is not a specific shareholding threshold, but the concept of control. 'Control' is defined as the power to exercise a decisive influence on the appointment of the majority of the directors or managers of a company, or on the orientation of its management.

There is joint control where shareholders of a company have agreed that decisions regarding the orientation of the management of the company must be taken by mutual agreement. Under certain circumstances, the law also provides for legal presumptions of control and joint control.

Notification to the BFIC prior to acquiring control

When a person wants to acquire sole or joint control over a Belgian public company, that person must notify the BFIC of the intention to do so and file with the BFIC at least five banking days before acquiring such control, except where:

- the securities are to be acquired through a voluntary public takeover bid for the securities of the target company; or
- the relevant securities are to be subscribed to in a capital increase decided by the shareholders' meeting of the target company, or by exercising conversion rights or warrants.

Sale of securities by remaining securities-holders

Chapter III of the Takeover Decree provides that, where exclusive or joint control of a public company is acquired other than by means of a voluntary public takeover bid or securities subscribed in a capital increase, and where the price or consideration paid for such an acquisition of securities exceeds the market price at the time of acquisition, the remaining holders of securities must unconditionally have the opportunity to transfer all their securities either:

- at the same price or consideration, if the relevant securities giving the buyer the controlling interest have been acquired in one transaction; or
- at the highest price or consideration paid by the buyer during the 12 months preceding the acquisition of control, if the relevant securities have been acquired over several transactions.

The remaining holders of securities must be offered such opportunity to sell their securities to the person who has acquired control – whose bid can be replaced by a bid from a third party offering the same terms and guarantees – through one of two procedures.

On the one hand, the buyer can launch a public takeover bid, basically in accordance with the rules explained above. If the buyer who has acquired control holds, alone, directly or indirectly, or acting in concert, at least 95 per cent of the voting securities of a public company within the meaning of Article 438 of the Belgian Companies Code, the buyer can make its public takeover bid into a squeeze-out bid within the meaning of Article 513 of the Belgian Companies Code (Chapter IV of the Takeover Decree does not apply). The fact that the bidder wants to make it a squeeze-out bid must be mentioned when announcing the bid and in the bid prospectus. The squeeze-out bid must be for a cash consideration.

On the other hand, the remaining holders of securities may be offered the opportunity to sell to the buyer who has acquired control by way of maintaining the market price of the securities of the target company at a level equal to the price or consideration for the acquisition of the controlling interest for at least 15 banking days.

In either case, the procedure adopted must be made public within three banking days after the acquisition of control and must be implemented, at the latest, 30 banking days after such acquisition.

> **Case study: Acquiring indirect control**
>
> In the Royal Vendôme case,[2] the BFIC decided, although Article 41 of the Takeover Decree does not explicitly provide for this, that acquiring indirect control of a Belgian public company by acquiring control of an intermediary holding company[3] also falls also within the scope of Article 41.
>
> However, the BFIC's Royal Vendôme doctrine can no longer be upheld following the judgements of the Antwerp Court of Appeal of 13 March 2000 and the Court of Cassation of 22 November 2002 in the Super Club case. From these judgements, the following can be concluded:
>
> - the fact that a holding company's main asset and main source of income is a controlling interest in a Belgian public company is not sufficient for Article 41 of the Takeover Decree (mandatory takeover bid in case of change of control) to apply;
> - the fact that control is acquired over the holding company is in itself not sufficient for Article 41 to apply to the Belgian public company that is controlled by the holding company;
> - in principle, acquiring control over a foreign (non-Belgian) company falls outside the scope of Article 41, even when, as a result, (indirect) control is acquired over a Belgian public company. It will be up to the court to decide, in view of the 'real seat' doctrine that applies in Belgium (in contrast to the 'seat of incorporation' doctrine that applies in some other jurisdictions), whether the target holding company is indeed a foreign company really managed from abroad.
>
> The above conclusions are to be regarded as nuanced. Under certain circumstances, the court could hold, on the basis of fraud, simulation, circumvention of the law or abuse of right, that acquiring control over a holding company that controls a Belgian public company is tantamount to a change of control of the Belgian public company to which Article 41 of the Takeover Decree applies.

Public squeeze-out bids

Scope

Minority shareholders in Belgian companies, public or private, can be squeezed-out, but it should be noted that the squeeze-out procedures for public and private companies are different. This section describes only the squeeze-out procedure for public companies, which is set forth in Article 513 of the Belgian Companies Code and Chapter IV (Articles 45 and following) of the Takeover Decree.

The squeeze-out rules set out in Chapter IV of the Takeover Decree apply to public squeeze-out bids launched by a person holding, alone, directly or indirectly, or acting in concert, at least 95 per cent of the voting securities of a public company (within the meaning of Article 438 of the Belgian Companies Code) and aiming at acquiring all the voting securities of the target company in accordance with Article 513 of the Belgian Companies Code.

Procedure

Although the procedure set out in Chapter IV of the Takeover Decree is rather similar to a squeeze-out following a voluntary takeover bid, there are differences in the specific nature of the separate public squeeze-out bid.

If a person holding at least 95 per cent of the voting securities of a public company wants to acquire all the remaining shares, that person must give prior notice to the BFIC and submit a file including:

- a draft prospectus containing an opinion from an independent expert as to the fairness of the price offered;
- the statement of the board of directors of the target company, giving the board's view on the independent expert's opinion and the fairness of the price offered; and
- a report (fairness opinion) by an independent expert, containing, among other things, the expert's assessment as to whether, given the valuation methods that are generally used, the valuation methods used by the bidder are pertinent to value the target company and to justify the price offered, as well as the expert's assessment as to whether the price offered does or does not safeguard the interests of the securities-holders.

Such squeeze-out bid must be in cash and either the funds must be placed in a bank account with a financial institution registered in Belgium or the bidder must ensure an irrevocable and unconditional credit facility with any such institution.

On or before the banking day following receipt of the bidder's notification, the BFIC must announce the public squeeze-out bid and indicate whether a copy of the independent expert's opinion can be obtained. During a period of 15 banking days following the announcement, the holders of the remaining securities can file any complaints about the bid with the BFIC, in particular regarding the valuation of the target company. After those 15 banking days, the BFIC has 15 banking days in which to communicate its comments on the bid to the bidder, the target company, the relevant market authorities and those holders of securities that filed complaints. However, if the BFIC feels that no comments on the bid are necessary, it can immediately make a decision on the approval of the prospectus.

If the BFIC does comment on the bid, the bidder has 15 banking days from the communication of such comments to react and, as the case may be, improve the terms of the bid. After those 15 banking days, the BFIC will make its decision on the approval of the bid.

Following the closing of the bid period, which must last for at least 10 banking days and at most 20 banking days, the securities that have not been offered are deemed to have been transferred by operation of the law to the bidder. The price relating to such securities must be deposited with a government institution, the *Deposito en Consignatiekas/Caisse des Dépôts et Consignations*, for the benefit of the previous owners.

Following the closing of the public squeeze-out bid, the executive committee or relevant market authority of the regulated markets must, on their own initiative, delist any of the target company's securities that were listed in their markets.

Simplified squeeze-out

The procedure set out in Chapter IV of the Takeover Decree does not apply when a squeeze-out is linked to the reopening of a voluntary public takeover bid or to a mandatory public takeover bid.

> **Case study: Constitutionality of the squeeze-out procedure**
>
> On 9 November 1991, the BFIC announced the intention of the French company Total Chimie, a subsidiary of Total Fina Elf SA, to launch a public squeeze-out bid for the remaining shares of NV PetroFina. This bid gave rise to several disputes regarding the valuation of the target, but, more importantly, it also raised the issue of whether the squeeze-out principle is unconstitutional.
>
> Two requests for a preliminary ruling were made to the Court of Arbitration regarding the conformity of Article 513 of the Belgian Companies Code with the principles of equality and non-discrimination set out in Articles 10 and 11 of the Belgian Constitution. Two questions were raised:
>
> - is Article 513 of the Belgian Companies Code unconstitutional because it differentiates between securities-holders in a public company, who cannot prevent the automatic transfer of their securities at the end of the squeeze-out bid, and securities-holders in a private company, who can prevent their securities from being transferred at the end of the squeeze-out bid?
> - is Article 513 of the Belgian Companies Code unconstitutional because it differentiates between securities-holders holding, alone, directly or indirectly, or acting in concert, at least 95 per cent of the voting securities of a public company, who can launch a public squeeze-out bid, and minority securities-holders in the same company, who do not have a sell-out right?
>
> On 14 May 2003, the Court of Arbitration answered both questions in the negative.

No 'reverse squeeze-out'

Under Belgian law, there is no 'reverse squeeze-out' according to which a minority shareholder can demand that the majority shareholder starts a squeeze-out procedure.

Special topics on takeover practice in Belgium

Defensive measures and the role of the target board of directors

Role of the target board of directors

The basic principle is that the board of directors of a Belgian company must act in the best interest of the company. The directors may not use their powers in the interest of themselves or of third parties. Failure to act in the best interest of the company can lead to the liability of the directors, which, subject to certain conditions, can be triggered by either the company, (minority) shareholders or third parties.

In addition, in the context of a public takeover bid, the prohibition on frustrating action by the board of directors of the target company as from receipt of the notification of a public bid is one of the principles of takeover regulation in Belgium.

Conflicts of interest

The Belgian Companies Code provides for specific procedures in the event that the directors, when making any decisions, have a conflict of interest. Two different procedures need to be distinguished.

Under Article 523 of the Belgian Companies Code, if a director has a direct or indirect patrimonial conflict of interest regarding a decision within the competence of the board, he/she must inform the other directors prior to taking any decision and also needs to fulfil certain formalities. In a public listed company, the director having a conflict may not participate in deliberations concerning the conflict issue and may not cast any vote on such decision. This restriction does not apply in a private company.

Article 524 of the Belgian Companies Code applies, subject to certain exceptions, to each decision that relates to transactions between a listed company and any of its affiliated companies other than its subsidiaries, or to transactions between a subsidiary of the listed company and a company affiliated to such subsidiary other than the latter's own subsidiary. All such decisions or transactions need to be reviewed beforehand by a committee of three independent directors, assisted by one or more experts. Such committee reports to the board of directors, but the latter is not obliged to follow the committee's recommendations. A director is deemed independent when he/she complies with a series of conditions set out in the Belgian Companies Code.

In the event of a violation of Articles 523 or 524, the company can demand the nullity of the transaction or decisions. In addition, the Belgian Companies Code provides for particular directors' liability.

In a takeover situation, the above articles often apply when a director is a shareholder or the representative of a shareholder of the target company.

Statement of the target board of directors on the bid

Under Article 15 of the Takeover Decree, the board of the target company must prepare a statement regarding its views on the bid. The Takeover Decree provides that, in formulating such statement, the board must take into account the interest of all holders of securities, creditors and employees of the target company. In addition, this statement must contain certain other information (see above).

In a decision of 19 January 2001, the Brussels Court of Appeal held that Articles 523 and 524 of the Belgian Companies Code do not apply to the advice on the bid that the board must give pursuant to Article 15 of the Takeover Decree.

Pre-bid defences

Belgian companies may insert transfer-blocking clauses into their by-laws, provided that such clauses are limited in time and are at all times in the company's interest.

The by-laws may also provide for first-refusal clauses and prior-approval clauses, subject to the condition that the entire procedure of approval or first refusal by the board may not delay the transfer of securities for more than six months. In addition, if, pursuant to such clauses, the transfer of the securities is not approved or the first-refusal clause is applied in the event of a bid, Article 511 of the Belgian Companies Code provides that, within five banking days after the closing of the bid, it must be proposed to the securities-holders that their securities be purchased by one or more persons approved by the board or against whom the first-refusal clause will not be exercised. In such case, the price offered to the securities-holders must be at least equal to the price offered in the bid.

However, there is an exception to Article 511 of the Belgian Companies Code. Pursuant to Article 512 of the Belgian Companies Code, the target board can enforce the approval clauses provided for in the by-laws to the extent that the refusal is justified on the basis of a consistent and non-discriminating application of the approval criteria determined by the board of directors and communicated to the BFIC before the announcement of the bid.

It is also possible for a company to grant rights to third parties that could influence the assets of the target company or could create a liability or obligation of the latter ('poison pills'), dependent on the launching of a takeover bid for the securities of the target company, or a change of control in the latter. However, Article 556 of the Belgian Companies Code requires prior shareholders' approval for such agreements and, in addition, such shareholders' resolution needs to be filed with the clerk's office of the competent commercial court before the target company is notified of a takeover bid. Failure of such filing entails the nullity of the shareholders' resolution.

Defences after the launching of the bid

The most common defence techniques after the launching of the bid are the redemption of shares and the use of authorised capital.

Article 557 of the Belgian Companies Code authorises the board of directors, subject to the conditions set out in Article 620 of the Belgian Companies Code, after having been notified of a bid, to redeem its shares or profit certificates 'to prevent serious and imminent damage to the company'. Such redemption is limited to 10 per cent of the total issued share capital.[4] This possibility must be expressly stated in the by-laws of the company, which must also specify the maximum number of shares, profit certificates or other certificates to be acquired, the duration for which the authorisation is granted to the board of directors, which may not exceed three years, and the minimum and maximum consideration to be paid for the redeemed shares. The law allows the board to finish transactions that are sufficiently advanced before the receipt of the bid notification, including the redemption of shares pertaining thereto. In addition, certain other conditions and publicity formalities are set out in Article 620 of the Belgian Companies Code.

As to authorised capital, in principle, the capital in a Belgian company can be increased only by a decision of the shareholders' meeting deciding with a special quorum and majority. Subject to certain conditions and restrictions, however, the by-laws can provide that the board can also decide to increase the capital without a shareholders' resolution in an 'authorised capital' procedure. However, as from the time the board has been informed by the BIFC of a bid, the board may not proceed any longer with any of the following actions:

- an increase in the company's capital through a contribution in kind or in cash with limitation or abolition of the preferential right of shareholders; or
- the issuance of any voting securities, whether or not they represent capital, or of securities giving rights to subscribe to or acquire voting securities, unless the securities are first offered to the shareholders *pro rata* with their shareholding in the company.

Notwithstanding the above principle, the board – even after having been notified of a bid – may increase the share capital of the target company via the authorised capital procedure if the shareholders, deciding with special attendance and majority requirements, specifically approved such procedure not more than three years before the receipt of the notification of the bid. This possibility must be expressly stated in the by-laws of the company and this authorised capital procedure is allowed only to the extent that:

- the shares issued are fully paid up as from their issuance;
- the issuance price is not less than the price offered by the bidder; and
- the number of shares issued does not exceed 10 per cent of the issued capital prior to the capital increase.

The board may also complete the implementation of obligations validly contracted before the receipt of the bid notification (Article 607 of the Belgian Companies Code). The BFIC must be notified of such decisions, which also need to be made public.

The so-called 'crown jewel defence' is not widespread in Belgium. Article 557 of the Belgian Companies Code provides that, as from the receipt of a bid announcement, only the shareholders' meeting may make decisions or engage in any actions that would significantly change the composition of the assets or liabilities of the company, or enter into obligations for no real consideration. There is also a prohibition on making such decisions or engaging in such actions under the condition precedent of the success or failure of the bid.

The law allows the board to complete transactions that are sufficiently advanced before the receipt of the bid announcement.

Fairness opinions

Strictly speaking, there does not exist under Belgian law a legal requirement to issue fairness opinions in the framework of public takeover bids, except in the event of a public squeeze-out bid (see above). In such event, Article 47 of the Takeover Decree requires that the bidder files with the BFIC, among others, the report of an independent expert on the pertinence, given the valuation methods that are generally used, of the methods used by the bidder to value the company and to justify the price offered. The independent expert also has to indicate whether he/she is of the opinion that the price offered does or does not safeguard the interests of the securities-holders.

Notwithstanding the above, fairness opinions are becoming increasingly common in Belgium. In the first place, they are used by the bidder, who, in valuing the target and determining the corresponding bid price, is often assisted by an investment bank. However, when a majority shareholder is bidding to acquire the other securities of the target company that it does not yet hold, it is a practice of the BFIC to require that an additional and separate fairness opinion be issued by an expert who is independent of the bidder and has been appointed by the board of directors of the target. This requirement is not provided for in the law, but results from the BFIC's exercise of its discretionary power to monitor public takeover bids. The BFIC may also require fairness opinions in other complex or delicate situations.

Although there is no legal requirement for the board of directors to do so, except in the situations already mentioned, it has become increasingly common for boards of directors of the target to instruct financial institutions to render fairness opinions to assist them with the statement they need to issue in connection with a takeover bid (Article 15 of the Takeover Decree). Although it is not legally required in the context of a public takeover bid, in the event of discussion, such a fairness opinion can be helpful in reducing the risk of legal challenge to board members by holders of securities, as a result of the board's acceptance of an allegedly insufficient bid price. However, the fairness opinion does not exempt the directors from stating their personal opinion regarding the takeover bid. Fairness opinions in such situations typically comment on the valuation methods used and the merits of the bid.

The prospectus includes either the conclusion of the fairness opinion or the full text. If the fairness opinion was requested by the bidder, the conclusion of such opinion is often published in the prospectus after the justification of the price by the bidder. If the fairness opinion was requested by the board of directors of the target, the conclusion of such opinion is often incorporated in the board's advice in accordance with Article 15 of the Takeover Decree. In recent transactions, not only the conclusion, but the entire text, of the fairness opinions was published in the prospectus.

It should be noted that, although the financial institution issuing a fairness opinion is appointed by either the bidder or the board of directors of the target, its independence can be an issue and should be considered.

Although it is more general in nature, Article 524 of the Belgian Companies Code (as mentioned above) can also be mentioned in this respect.

Break-up fees

Break-up fees are fees to be paid by the target company to the bidder if the transaction with the bidder does not take place. In Belgium, break-up fees are not commonly used. Although they are not illegal *per se,* their validity depends on such fees being in the company's best interest. Given the nature of such break-up fees, this assessment is often not easy to make. In the absence of the company's best interest, the director's liability can be at stake. We do not have knowledge of any Belgian case law in respect of break-up fees.

Exclusivity and due diligence

If, in principle, a bidder wants exclusivity, he needs to obtain it from the reference or majority shareholders and not from the board of directors. However, there is no legal impediment for the bidder to enter into other agreements with the board of directors of the target. Possible agreements pertain to the undertaking by the board to support the bidder's bid, including the giving of positive advice pursuant to Article 15 of the Takeover Decree, subject to its right to give comments on the prospectus and subject to the opinion of the works council. When giving its advice on the bid, the board must take into account the interest of the holders of securities, creditors and employees of the target company (Article 15, paragraph 2 of the Takeover Decree).

Whether a bidder can proceed with due diligence before launching its bid remains a difficult question because of the various laws involved and the various conflicting interests, including, most notably:

- the obligation of confidentiality versus the obligation to make public certain information that could affect the stock price;
- the principle of equal treatment of all shareholders;
- the duty of directors to act in the interest of the company; and
- the right of securities-holders to sell their shares.

The current situation can be summarised as follows:

- neither (majority/reference) shareholders nor directors may divulge confidential information in respect of the target company without the approval of the board of directors;
- if shareholders want to allow due diligence, they need to ask the permission of the board of directors of the target company;
- when considering such a request, the board needs to take into account the interest of the company; the identity of the candidate acquirer, which may be an issue if, for instance, the candidate acquirer is a competitor of the company; and the nature of the information to be disclosed. The board should authorise due diligence only if the candidate purchaser is sufficiently serious, as can be demonstrated by the fact that it has shown a clear interest in acquiring the securities through or followed by a public takeover bid, but even then the board should take the company's interest into account;
- before the candidate purchaser is allowed to gain access to the data room, it should sign a confidentiality undertaking as well as a standstill obligation;
- the due diligence period should be kept as short as possible; and
- it is generally recommended that the BFIC be notified.

There remains the difficult question as to the timing of the public announcement of such due diligence. It seems generally accepted now that such due diligence needs to be made public only when a firm bid has been made and has a reasonable chance of resulting in a sale, even when subject to certain conditions, such as the approval of the competition authorities. Although the existence of a firm bid can also give rise to discussions, it is generally accepted that a bid is firm if there is a clear bid price. It should be noted that such announcement should be made in concert with the BFIC. As set out above, no announcement of a public takeover bid may be made before the BFIC has announced it. However, during the course of due diligence and before a firm bid, an announcement may be authorised by the BFIC in particular circumstances, for example, in the event of a serious change in the stock price.

Obligatory squeeze-out procedures

Currently, Belgian law does not have a sell-out procedure as set forth in Article 16 of the Takeover Directive, according to which a holder of remaining securities is able to require the bidder to buy his/her securities at a fair price. Within the framework of the implementation of the Takeover Directive, the Belgian legislature will need to work out such a procedure.

However, the current Article 32 of the Takeover Decree provides for a similar obligation: if the bidder has acquired 90 per cent or more of the target's securities, it must offer to purchase the remaining securities at the same price as under the bid, within one month of the publication of the bid's outcome, and such bid must remain open for at least 15 banking days.

A similar obligation exists in the event of a delisting. If a bidder who has acquired less than 90 percent of the target's securities wishes to delist such securities within three months after the closing of the bid, it must offer to purchase the remaining securities at the same price as under the bid. Such bid must be made within one month after the delisting request and must remain open for at least 15 banking days. This obligation to reopen the bid in the event of a delisting does not apply, however, if the bidder has acquired at least 90 per cent of the securities and has already reopened its bid pursuant to Article 32, paragraph 1 of the

Takeover Decree. In such case, it is not obliged to reopen a second time when requesting a delisting.

Through the above procedures, those securities-holders who did not offer their securities in the initial bid still have the possibility of selling their securities at the bid price.

It should be noted that Article 642 of the Belgian Companies Code provides for a procedure pursuant to which any shareholder may, for 'justified reasons', demand that the competent court order the other shareholder(s) to which such reasons pertain to acquire its shares. However, this 'dispute procedure' does not apply to public companies as defined in Article 438 of the Belgian Companies Code.

Market manipulation and insider dealing

The Law of 2 August 2002 on the supervision of the financial sector and financial services prohibits market manipulation and insider dealing, and provides for both criminal and administrative sanctions in respect of them.

Administrative supervision of market manipulation and insider dealing is carried out by the BFIC, which also applies the administrative penalties. The judicial authorities carry out the criminal investigations.

Potential impact of the Takeover Directive

In many respects, Belgian takeover regulation is already in line with the Takeover Directive. Nevertheless, several changes remain necessary. However, as at 31 July 2005, no draft implementation text was available.

Threshold

As set out above, in Belgium the criterion triggering a mandatory offer is not the acquisition of a specific shareholding threshold, but a combination of the acquisition of 'control' and a price exceeding the market price. The requirement in Article 5.1 of the Takeover Directive to provide for a specific threshold at which a bid will be required will lead to the most dramatic change in Belgian takeover regulation. At present, it is not known which threshold will be applied by Belgium.

Articles 9 and 11 of the Takeover Directive

Although no text is available yet, Belgium may very well opt out from the breakthrough rules provided by Article 11 of the Takeover Directive.

Belgium will probably not opt out from Article 9 of the Takeover Directive, since the principles laid down in Article 9 correspond to the principles of Belgian takeover regulation. Nevertheless, since the present legislation allows certain defence techniques, certain changes will be required to bring the Belgian legislation completely into line with Article 9, in particular with respect to Articles 557, 607, 620 and 928 of the Belgian Companies Code.

Articles 557, 928 and 607 of the Belgian Companies Code provide for exceptions pursuant to which a board of directors can still proceed with certain defensive measures even after having been informed of a bid. Under Articles 557 and 928 of the Belgian Companies

Code (which have the same text, except that Article 928 relates to a European company), the board of directors is authorised to 'complete actions that are sufficiently advanced at the time of the receipt of the notification by the BFIC of a bid'. Article 607 of the Belgian Companies Code provides that the prohibitions set out in the article (see above) do not apply to 'obligations validly contracted prior to the receipt of the notification by the BFIC of a bid'. Neither of these exceptions is in line with the Takeover Directive, since its Article 9.3 allows the board to continue to implement those decisions that have been made before the notification of the bid and not yet partly or fully implemented at that time only if they form part of the normal course of the target company's business and their implementation may not result in the frustration of the bid. If these conditions are not fulfilled, the approval or confirmation of the shareholders' meeting is required.

Since the redemption of shares may deprive the bidder of up to 10 per cent of the target company's shares, or even up to 20 per cent if used in combination with authorised capital, it falls within the scope of Article 9.2 of the Takeover Directive, referring to 'actions that may result in the frustration of the bid'. Accordingly, it will no longer be allowed for companies not benefiting from the opt out exemption.

The 'authorised capital' procedure clearly falls within the scope of Article 9.2 of the Takeover Directive – '... issuing any shares which may result in a lasting impediment to the bidder's acquiring control of the target company' – and will no longer be allowed for companies not benefiting from the opt out exemption.

Other changes

Other changes will be required, including:

- the modification of certain definitions;
- amendment of the rules regarding the competent supervisory authority and applicable law;
- the introduction for the first time of the possibility that the supervisory authority may adjust the equitable price (optional price); and
- the introduction of a requirement for certain additional information to be included in the bid document as well as in the company's annual report.

As set out above, Belgian takeover regulation does not provide for a sell-out right, which will now have to be provided for.

Summary of some of the key elements in the Belgian takeover regulation

A bidder must notify the BFIC before launching a public takeover bid, acquiring control of a Belgian public company or launching a public squeeze-out bid.

Where exclusive or joint control over a public company is acquired other than by means of a voluntary public takeover bid or securities subscribed in a capital increase, and where the price or consideration paid for such an acquisition of securities exceeds the market price at the time of the acquisition, the acquirer must launch a public takeover bid or maintain the market price to offer the remaining holders of securities the opportunity to transfer all their securities on the same conditions.

A voluntary public takeover bid can be conditional, but mandatory takeover bids must be unconditional.

Once a takeover bid has been notified to, and announced by, the BFIC, the bidder can change the terms of the bid only in order to improve them from the point of view of the holders of securities in the target company and the bid can be withdrawn by the bidder only in specific circumstances.

The bidder must draw up a prospectus regarding the bid and the prospectus must be approved by the BFIC. The target board must issue a statement regarding the bid.

Even though there is no legal requirement under Belgian law to issue fairness opinions within the framework of public takeover bids, except in the event of a public squeeze-out bid, fairness opinions are becoming increasingly common in Belgium.

Several defence mechanisms can be used before and after the launch of a public takeover bid, but Belgian law prohibits the target board from taking certain actions after it has been informed of the bid by the BFIC.

A person holding, alone, directly or indirectly, or acting in concert, at least 95 per cent of the voting securities of a public company can launch a public squeeze-out bid (cash consideration) on the remaining securities. The remaining securities that have not been offered by the time the bid is closed are deemed to have been transferred by operation of the law to the bidder.

Minority securities-holders in a public company do not have a sell-out right.

Several changes in takeover regulation in Belgium have become necessary in view of the need to implement the Takeover Directive.

---

[1] See the BFIC's annual report for 1999–2000, p. 85.

[2] See the BFIC's annual report for 1990–91, pp. 76-78.

[3] In the Royal Vendôme case, the only asset of the intermediary holding company Royal Vendôme was a 50 per cent participation in the Belgian public company Royal Belge. This participation was Royal Vendôme's only source of income.

[4] Article 620, §1, 2^c of the Belgian Companies Code.

Chapter 11

Denmark

Peter M. Andersen and Regina M. Andersen
Bech-Brunn, Copenhagen

Danish laws and regulations applying to takeovers have existed for a number of years. The implementation of the Takeover Directive into Danish law in July 2005 has amended the rules significantly. Some of the more significant amendments are the following:

- the shareholders of the target company are now vested with the power to control the management of the company so that they do not take any measures impeding the takeover bid;
- any rights attached to all or some of the shares of the target company that may hinder or impede a takeover bid ('defensive measures') may be suspended for as long as the takeover offer runs;
- public listed companies are now under an obligation to provide information in their annual reports about measures that may impede a takeover of the company.

The new rules are all designed to facilitate takeovers of public listed companies in accordance with the scope of the Directive. Given the rather significant changes, there is reason to believe that the new rules will in fact have a facilitating effect on attempts to take over Danish listed companies.

Basis of the takeover regime

The Danish rules and regulations regarding takeovers are found in Sections 31 and 32 of the Danish Securities Trading Act (Consolidated Act No. 171 of 17 March 2005, as subsequently amended; here referred to as the 'STA') and Executive Order No. 618 of 23 June 2005 (the Takeover Order) issued by the Danish Financial Supervisory Authority (FSA).

The STA underwent a significant overhaul during the spring of 2005 in order to implement, *inter alia*, the Prospectus Directive (Directive 2003/71 of 4 November 2003), the Market Abuse Directive (Directive 2003/6 of 28 January 2003) and the Takeover Directive (Directive 2004/25 of 21 April 2004). The rules implementing the latter directive came into force on 2 July 2005. The previous takeover rules in the STA were thus significantly amended, with consequential significant amendments of the Danish Companies Act (DCA) and the Danish Accounting Act.

In addition to the black-letter law, the practice of the Copenhagen Stock Exchange (CSE) also plays an important role in the continued development and interpretation of the rules related to securities trading, including the takeover rules. A number of statements and decisions by the CSE on matters related to securities trading, including takeovers, have been published on the CSE's website (www.cse.dk). The CSE has also prepared a set of guidelines that sums up current practice and interpretation of the takeover rules.

Applicability of Danish takeover rules and definition of 'control'

The STA takeover rules and the rules promulgated under it apply when a controlling interest in a company listed or traded on the CSE, in an authorised marketplace or in another regulated market is transferred directly or indirectly.

Controlling influence

Section 31 of the STA provides that if a controlling influence in the target company is obtained, the acquirer has to offer the remaining shareholders of the target company the opportunity to dispose of their shares to the acquirer within a period of four weeks on identical terms.

Under Section 31, the acquirer is considered as having obtained a controlling influence in the target company if the acquirer:

- holds the majority of voting rights in the target company;
- becomes entitled to appoint or dismiss a majority of the target company's members of the board of directors;
- has obtained the right to exercise a controlling influence over the target company according to the articles of association or otherwise in agreement with the target company;
- will control the majority of voting rights in the target company according to an agreement with other shareholders; or
- is able to exercise a controlling influence over the target company and will hold more than one-third of the voting rights in the target company.

Direct and indirect transfers

The takeover rules may be triggered by direct transfers of shares as well as by indirect transfers. By including indirect transfers, a transfer of shares in a company, whether it is listed or not, that holds a controlling stake in a listed company may also lead to the applicability of the takeover rules.

Mandatory and voluntary offers

The STA and the Takeover Order apply to both mandatory and voluntary offers. If control over the target company has been obtained by the acquirer by way of acquisitions in the market or by private transactions with one or more shareholders, this will trigger an obligation for the acquirer to make a mandatory offer to the minority shareholders in accordance with the takeover provisions set forth in the STA and the Takeover Order. Likewise, if the acquirer seeks to obtain a controlling influence by way of making a public voluntary offer to the shareholders, such a voluntary offer also has to be made in accordance with the takeover provisions set out in the STA and the Takeover Order. The rules applying to voluntary offers do, however, offer the acquirer more flexibility, for example in the adding of conditions to the offer, which is not permitted in a mandatory offer, and in setting the price to be offered.

Before the implementation of the Takeover Directive, Danish takeover rules stipulated that a public voluntary offer had to be followed up by a mandatory offer, provided that the acquirer obtained a controlling influence over the target company as a result of the voluntary offer. Although the elimination of this requirement does not appear explicitly in the new takeover provisions, such a requirement no longer exists. Thus, if a controlling influence has been obtained as a result of a voluntary offer made in accordance with the Takeover Order, no mandatory offer needs to be submitted subsequently.

Exemptions

The Takeover Order itself provides for four specific exemptions from the takeover rules when control is obtained by way of:

- inheritance;
- gift;
- the taking over of the shares by an unsatisfied pledgee; or
- inter-group transfers.

The main rationale for these exemptions is that no intended change of control within the meaning of the STA has been made.

Further, a number of other instances that in fact bring a person above the control level usually triggering the takeover rules may also qualify for an exemption in accordance with current CSE practice. Disregarding the obvious situations where the takeover rules are deliberately circumvented, the following instances have, in previous instances dealt with by the CSE, been considered outside the scope of the takeover rules:

- control obtained by way of a passive change in a person's shareholding, for example by way of a share capital reduction in the listed company or by way of the listed company's acquiring treasury shares;
- control obtained by way of private placement or a merger; and
- transfer of listed shares among shareholders acting in concert.

Structuring a takeover of a company listed in Denmark

Obtaining a controlling influence in the target company

A controlling influence in the target company may be obtained either through acquisitions in the market, or in private transactions with one or more shareholders, or by launching a voluntary offer for the shares in the target company. Most takeovers in Denmark are initiated by launching a public voluntary takeover offer in accordance with the STA and the Takeover Order.

The documentation required

Pre-offer announcement

A new concept in the form of a pre-offer announcement has been introduced in Danish law as a result of implementing the Takeover Directive. Thus, a decision or duty to make a mandatory or voluntary offer has to be communicated to the market through the relevant marketplace.

Accordingly, in the case of listed companies, the pre-offer announcement has to be made through the CSE.

The Takeover Order provides that such a pre-offer announcement shall be made as soon as a decision to launch an offer has been made. The pre-offer announcement may, however, be made only after the acquirer has ensured that it is in fact able to satisfy any demand for consideration in the form of cash and has taken all reasonable measures to ensure that any other form of consideration, such as shares, can be satisfied.

Since the acquirer's preparation of the takeover offer as such – including negotiating the finance documentation, conducting due diligence investigations, preparing the offer document and, potentially, negotiating with the board of directors of the target company on the offer price – is often not finalised until immediately before the scheduled launch date, it is unlikely that the pre-offer announcement of a voluntary offer will be made before the date when the offer document is published.

Offer document and offer advertisement
Irrespective of whether the acquirer is making a mandatory or a voluntary offer, the acquirer is under an obligation to prepare and submit an offer document to the shareholders in the target company containing, *inter alia*:

- the offer price and consideration (cash and/or shares and so forth);
- the offer period;
- the terms and conditions of the offer; and
- other information allowing the shareholders to make an informed decision as to whether to tender their shares.

The Takeover Order sets out in detail the information required in the offer document and provides that the offer document has to be approved by the CSE.

The offer document must be published through the CSE and sent to registered shareholders in the target company. In addition, an offer advertisement providing a brief account for the offer must be submitted to the CSE, published in a major Danish newspaper and sent to all registered shareholders.

Statement by the board of the target company
Pursuant to the Takeover Order, the board of directors of the target company prepares and publishes a statement to the shareholders of the target company on the advantages and disadvantages of the takeover offer, including the expected development of the company.

The statement must be published through the CSE by the board of directors of the target company before the expiry of the first half of the period during which the offer is open. Likewise, an advertisement including all or part of the board's statement must be published in a major Danish newspaper and sent to the registered shareholders.

In recent years, a market practice has developed in Denmark whereby, in offers that are not contested, the board of directors' recommendation of the offer is published concurrently with, or even as an integral part of, the public offer document.

If the offer is amended during the offer period, the board of directors of the target company must, within seven days after the publication of an altered offer submitted by the acquirer, prepare and publish an additional statement for the shareholders of the target company on the alterations compared to the original offer document. This must include a statement of the advantages and disadvantages of the alterations made to the offer document.

Main characteristics of offer document

Equal treatment of shareholders/identical terms

Takeovers have to be carried out in accordance with general Danish law principles on equal treatment of shares. In both mandatory and voluntary offers, shareholders within the same class of shares must be accorded equal treatment. Further, if the acquirer is under an obligation to submit a mandatory offer, the acquirer must offer the minority shareholders the right to dispose of their shares on 'identical terms'. This means that the minority shareholders in a mandatory offer must receive the same consideration as paid by the acquirer for the majority holding. In addition, all other terms must, to the extent practicable, be identical. However, if the acquirer has obtained the majority holding by way of a share exchange offer, the acquirer is nevertheless entitled to offer a cash consideration to the remaining shareholders.

The minimum cash consideration offered to the minority shareholders has to be based on the highest price paid by the acquirer within the last six months before the submission of the offer. If the acquirer has acquired shares at a higher price within 12 months before the offer, the FSA may under special circumstances decide that this higher price shall apply to the offer.

The 'identical terms' requirement gives rise to particular problems in connection with the existence of dual or multiple classes of shares. If the target company has several classes of shares, an offer price must be fixed for each class of shares. For the share classes in which the acquirer has acquired shares, the principle of the highest price must be applied. Where all share classes are listed, an offer price based on the stock market prices, and proportionately equal to the highest price in the share class or classes in which the acquirer has acquired shares, must be fixed for the share classes in which the acquirer has not acquired shares. Where one or more of several share classes are listed and others are unlisted, the price fixed for the unlisted share classes may not be more than 50 per cent higher than the price offered to the minority shareholders.

The equal treatment principle also implies that, if the acquirer has reserved the right to acquire shares in the market during the course of the takeover offer, the acquirer is restricted from acquiring such shares on better terms than those offered in the context of the takeover offer, unless the acquirer improves the offer to match the price agreed to outside the context of the takeover offer.

Offer period

An offer, whether mandatory or voluntary, has to remain open for a period of at least four weeks and at most 10 weeks.

Any amendment made within the last two weeks of the offer period extends the offer period by two weeks. Waiving of conditions attached to the offer does not extend the offer period. Any prolongation of the offer period must be made before the expiry of the offer period.

Offer and acceptance mechanisms

The shareholders in the target company can freely decide whether or not to accept a public offer. However, once a shareholder has accepted the offer, such acceptance may not be withdrawn unless otherwise provided for in the offer document. In practice, shareholders are granted an option to withdraw only if a competing offer is launched. Although their shares have been tendered before the expiry of the offer period, the acquirer has to offer all shareholders the benefit of an increased offer price offered by the acquirer.

Unless the acquirer has reserved the right to revoke the offer in the offer document, the acquirer is obliged to keep the offer open throughout the entire offer period and is bound by acceptances from shareholders within the offer period, subject to satisfaction of the conditions attached to the offer, if any.

Once it is clear that conditions made in the offer, if any, have been fulfilled, or waived, and the acquirer has made an announcement to that effect, the acquisition becomes binding.

Conditions

The basic position regarding any voluntary (non-mandatory) bids is that it is possible for the acquirer to make the offer conditional. However, the CSE does not generally allow conditions that the acquirer is able to control itself or that are too far reaching. The rationale behind this is that the launching of a public offer may have an impact on the share price and there is a risk that overly broad conditions would increase the possibility that offers are made merely for the purpose of influencing the stock price.

In addition to the condition of obtaining at least 90 per cent of the shares and votes of the target company, which is almost always included in the offer since that offer will allow the acquirer to redeem the remaining minority shareholders pursuant to the DCA, the offer document typically includes conditions stipulating:

- no changes in the target company's capital structure or articles of association during the offer period;
- the obtaining of anti-trust clearances and other necessary regulatory approvals;
- no new legislation, court orders and so forth obstructing the offer; and
- no material adverse changes during the offer period and no public announcement of an adverse nature from the target company.

Under current CSE practice, an offer may not be conditional upon the acquirer obtaining the required financing of the acquisition. Such financing must be in place by the time the voluntary offer is launched and, under the new provisions, even earlier, since a pre-offer announcement is required before the publication of the offer document and such a pre-offer announcement may not be made before securing the cash or share consideration in full. A brief statement on how the offer is financed and the main conditions (if any) attached to the financing must be included in the offer document.

Further, the CSE is unlikely to accept a condition stipulating 'due diligence satisfactory to the acquirer'. The CSE has, however, accepted conditions including due diligence investigations when benchmarked against, for instance, specific published financial or business-related information.

The offer ordinarily includes a right for the acquirer to waive any or all of the conditions.

Squeeze-out and delisting

After completion of the takeover bid period, the usual next step in a public-to-private takeover process is to initiate a compulsory redemption of the remaining shareholders' shares and effect a delisting of the target company. A prerequisite for initiating such processes is, however, that the acquirer has obtained a control level of at least 90 per cent, which is why a voluntary takeover bid always contains a 90 per cent control level condition.

A redemption process following a takeover may be effected either by following the route described in the DCA or by adopting a resolution at a general meeting to the effect that the shares of the target company become redeemable. The latter route is the fastest way of obtaining 100 per cent control.

In brief, the DCA sets forth that in situations where a shareholder holds more than 90 per cent of the shares in a company and a corresponding proportion of the voting rights, such a shareholder may require the company's remaining shareholders to allow their shares to be acquired by that shareholder. Subject to such a decision being made, the minority shareholders are requested to transfer their shares to the majority shareholder within a period of four weeks. In the event that not all the shares are transferred pursuant to such a transfer request, another transfer request has to be published in the Danish *Official Gazette*, allowing any remaining shareholder to transfer their shares within a period of three months. Any non-transferred shares still remaining may subsequently be redeemed by way of the majority shareholder depositing the redemption price. Any disagreement on the part of minority shareholders in relation to the redemption price may be conferred to independent experts. A squeeze-out conducted pursuant to the DCA may thus take up to six or seven months.

The other route available to a majority shareholder holding a minimum of 90 per cent of the share capital and votes is to adopt a resolution by the required 90 per cent majority at a general meeting, which may typically be convened with at least eight days' and at most four weeks' notice, to the effect that the company's shares are to become redeemable by the majority shareholder. The majority shareholder is free to set a redemption period shorter than the required four-week period pursuant to the DCA and no subsequent notice period is required. Immediately after the expiry of the redemption period, the majority shareholder may redeem any non-transferred shares still remaining by payment or deposit of the redemption price. Such a squeeze-out may thus be completed in about two months.

To effect a delisting, the target company has to submit an application to the CSE. The CSE allows the delisting unless, in the opinion of the CSE, a delisting is not in the reasonable interest of the shareholders, the target company's financiers or the securities market. In practice, the CSE is unlikely to allow a delisting of the target company if the acquirer holds less than 90 per cent of the shares and the votes in the target company following the completion of the tender offer.

Defences against a hostile takeover

So far, Denmark has experienced few hostile or contested takeovers. Accordingly, there are only limited amounts of practice and case law regarding this subject.

Until Denmark implemented the Takeover Directive, there was no specific regulation concerning defences against a takeover, other than general corporate and company law principles that had to be adhered to. Except for the obligation of the board of directors to publish a statement regarding a public offer, there were previously no provisions in Danish statutory law or in Danish regulations setting forth the duties of the board of directors and the management of a company when faced by a takeover attempt.

PART II: EUROPEAN JURISDICTIONS

However, the implementation of the Takeover Directive has led to the amendment of the DCA to provide the following:

- the shareholders in the target company may resolve to introduce procedures pursuant to which the board of directors must obtain shareholder approval before taking measures that may hinder or impede a takeover bid, other than deciding to analyse other potential offers, provided that the country where the acquirer or the acquirer's parent company is incorporated has introduced similar procedures – the principle of reciprocity;
- the shareholders in the target company may resolve to introduce procedures pursuant to which special shareholders' rights included in the company's articles of association, in shareholders' agreements and similar, including disparate voting rights, voting caps, ownership caps or rights of first refusal, are suspended in the event of a takeover bid – the principle of reciprocity applies here too;
- in companies that have introduced suspension of shareholder rights as provided above, the acquirer must, subject to the completion of the takeover bid, pay compensation to those shareholders that may suffer a loss due to suspension of shareholder rights, and the offer documents must include information on the compensation to such shareholders.

Typical defensive devices open to Danish companies are:

- disparate voting rights (a 10:1 ratio is allowed);
- voting caps;
- ownership caps;
- limited negotiability of shares, although to a large extent this is contrary to maintaining a listing on the CSE; and
- the target company's purchase of its own shares.

A significant number of the major companies listed on the CSE, as well as a number of financial institutions, have included such defensive devices in their articles of association.

A hostile shareholder's shareholding may also be diluted by increasing the target company's share capital by subscription for cash or contribution in kind for special shareholders. However, the issue of new shares to, for instance, a more 'friendly' investor, with or without pre-emptive rights for the existing shareholders against cash or against contribution in kind, gives rise to various company law issues.

Under the new takeover rules, these defensive devices can effectively be suspended in connection with a public offer, thus facilitating such an offer, if the shareholders so wish. However, the new rules do not apply to defensive devices included in an agreement, normally a shareholders' agreement, entered into before 31 March 2004.

As mentioned above, there are no specific provisions in Danish statutory law or in Danish regulations setting forth the duties of the board of directors and the management of a company when faced by a takeover attempt. Some guidance with respect to the applicable duties may, however, be derived from the general principles of governance found in the DCA and – although this is not binding – a report on prudent corporate governance prepared by an expert group for the CSE in 2003.

The DCA imposes on the board of directors a duty to act loyally towards all shareholders. This prohibits the board and the management from acting in a fashion that is clearly likely to provide certain shareholders or others with an undue advantage at the expense of other shareholders or the company. Thus, for instance, when considering whether the board of a company that faces a hostile takeover attempt is entitled to allocate new shares to a friendly shareholder, as described above, it must be considered whether the board thereby creates undue advantages for others at the expense of the shareholders.

It is expressly stated in the report on prudent corporate governance that the shareholders should be given the opportunity to decide whether to accept a potential takeover offer. Hence, the board of directors should refrain from taking any measures on its own initiative – increasing the share capital if authorised to do so by the shareholders or acquiring treasury shares – which in reality prevent the shareholders from receiving the offer.

Under the new takeover rules, however, the shareholders can actively hinder or limit the management's defensive actions in connection with a public offer.

Impact of the Takeover Directive

The implementation of the Takeover Directive has introduced a number of new features into the Danish takeover and corporate law environment, of which those described above are the most significant. What all these new features have in common is that they are all designed to facilitate takeovers of listed companies in accordance with the scope of the Takeover Directive.

The first takeover bid pursuant to the new rules was made public by the CSE on 12 July 2005, only 10 days after the rules came into force. New takeover bids are undoubtedly to be seen in the months and years to come.

The FSA has stated that a working group will be established in order to review and, if required, update the provisions of the Takeover Order before the expiry of the implementation deadline set forth in the Takeover Directive (May 2006), taking into consideration experience in Denmark in the interim. Thus, Danish takeover provisions may be further amended before then.

Chapter 12

Finland

Dimetrios Himonas, Carla Wallgren, Paula Lima and Elisa Heinonen
Roschier Holmberg, Helsinki

In April 2004, the Finnish Ministry of Finance appointed a working group with a mandate to prepare for the implementation of the directive of the European Parliament and the Council on takeover bids (the Takeover Directive) into Finnish law (the 'Working Group'). The Working Group published its report in May 2005 with the intention that the amendments proposed by the Working Group be made and enter into force as of 1 January 2006 (provided that the reform of the Finnish Companies Act, which is currently in preparation, will become effective as of the same date) or, alternatively, as of 20 May 2006.

As a general comment, the Takeover Directive does not seem to necessitate any major legislative amendments in Finland. The key principles of the directive are already part of Finnish law. The most important of such key principles are probably the equal treatment of all shareholders and the ensuring of an equitable offer price; the obligation of the board of directors of the target company to act in the interests of the company and all its shareholders, while not denying shareholders the opportunity to decide on the merits of any bid; adequate disclosure; and the right of shareholders to make an informed decision on the offer. Also, the main features of the directive, such as the obligation to make a mandatory offer, or the squeeze-out right and obligation, are already now in place.

While many of the main features of the directive are left to the regulatory discretion of member states, the implementation also provides a good opportunity to deal with issues that the market has identified as being in need of reassessment or reform. Although the main task of the Working Group has consisted of ensuring detailed consistency with the provisions of the directive and reviewing existing features, it seems that the implementation of the directive will also, to a certain extent, result in a more extensive rewriting of the Finnish law provisions relating to takeover bids.

Currently, the main provisions relating to takeovers are found in the Finnish Securities Market Act. The duties of the board of directors of the target company and squeeze-out rights are regulated by company law. Major amendments to this allocation of the relevant provisions are not anticipated, as the directive is proposed to be implemented mainly through revised provisions of the Securities Market Act and through self-regulation. The following overview outlines the principal amendments to be introduced through the revised and new regulations proposed, including amendments regarding mandatory offers, offer consideration and competing offers, as well as the position of the target company and its board of directors.

Mandatory offers

Obligation to make a mandatory offer

One of the main considerations that the Working Group has had to address is the threshold for the requirement to make a mandatory offer. The mandatory offer rule in the directive does not necessitate any material amendments to Finnish law, as the concept of a mandatory offer is already in place. However, market practice and international trends have indicated a need to reassess the threshold triggering the obligation to launch a mandatory offer. The directive leaves it to member states to determine the definition of 'control' triggering a mandatory offer. According to the Securities Market Act as currently in force, the requirement to make a mandatory offer arises when a shareholder's holding or certain joint holdings exceed(s) two-thirds of the total voting rights of a listed company. This threshold is high compared to that in other member states.

In addition, Finnish market practice could be argued to support a need for a lower mandatory offer threshold. Many Finnish-listed companies have already chosen to adopt a redemption threshold of one-third and/or one-half by introducing such a lower mandatory offer requirement in their articles of association (often referred to as a 'poison pill'). Among the companies that have elected to voluntarily opt for a lower mandatory offer level are leading Finnish companies known as 'trendsetters' in the field of corporate governance, including Nokia, the banking and insurance group Sampo, forest industry companies such as UPM-Kymmene, and the energy company Fortum.

The Working Group proposes that the current provisions of the Securities Market Act be revised in this respect. The threshold triggering an obligation to launch a mandatory offer is proposed to be reduced to 30 per cent of the total votes in the target company, or, where the offeror already holds more than 30 per cent of the votes, to 50 per cent. As regards current holdings that already exceed this threshold, certain exemptions would apply. Thus, the obligation to launch a mandatory offer is not triggered if the respective threshold of 30 per cent or 50 per cent has been exceeded before the amendments to the Securities Market Act have become effective, provided that the respective holding decreases below the threshold during the three years following the entry into force of the proposed amendments. However, the requirement to reduce one's holding below the threshold in order to avoid the obligation to launch a mandatory offer is not applicable if the respective threshold has been exceeded prior to the date of the government bill introducing the amendments. Further, if a shareholder's holding in the target company already exceeds the relevant threshold of 30 per cent or 50 per cent, another shareholder will not be under an obligation to launch a mandatory offer until its holding exceeds the holding of the other shareholder.

Offer procedures

The efficiency of the different redemption procedures as a whole and their coordination has also been assessed by the Working Group. Currently, the offeror is obliged to proceed through a number of different, partly parallel redemption procedures when acquiring control of a listed company, often increasing transaction costs quite substantially. When acquiring control, the voluntary offer will be followed by a mandatory offer under the Securities Market Act. In addition, the offeror may be required to launch a mandatory offer under a redemption obligation according to the target company's articles of association. Such offer is often run parallel to the mandatory (or voluntary) offer under the Securities Market Act and shall, as applicable, be conducted in accordance with the rules on voluntary offers. Finally, in order to gain 100 per cent of the shares, a squeeze-out procedure under the Companies Act will follow. Where, for example, the offeror first acquires more than 90 per cent of the shares and votes in the target company by a voluntary offer, the offeror will then be obliged to launch both a mandatory offer under the Securities Market Act and to pursue the redemption procedure according to the target company's articles of association, if applicable, and, in order to gain 100 per cent of the shares, to initiate squeeze-out proceedings under the Companies Act. All procedures have their own particular requirements and their particular (differing) price definitions. As a consequence of all this, the takeover will involve three or four different offer/redemption procedures and at least three different price definitions, with possible recourse to courts or arbitral tribunals as an interim or final remedy. Bearing in mind that, under the current Rules of the Helsinki Stock Exchange, the delisting of a company requires 100 per cent ownership by the bidder, the target company will have to continue to comply with, for instance, the reporting and disclosure requirements imposed on listed companies throughout a large part of squeeze-out proceedings until the bidder has reached 100 per cent ownership through the arbitral proceedings. In practice, the obtaining of 100 per cent ownership always requires arbitral proceedings, as a number of minority shareholders will typically challenge the redemption price offered in a squeeze-out.

In order to simplify the current procedures, it is now proposed that a voluntary offer would no longer need to be followed by a mandatory offer under the Securities Market Act where the threshold triggering the mandatory offer has been exceeded by means of a voluntary offer made for all shares and securities that entitle to shares in the target company (shares and other securities the offer is made for are referred to as 'target securities'). Squeeze-out proceedings under the Companies Act would, however, still need to be initiated in order to acquire 100 per cent of the shares in the target company, unless (though this is probably highly unlikely in practice) all shares have already been tendered in the offer. No amendments are proposed with respect to the current partly parallel offering procedures in situations where the offeror is also required to launch an offer under the target company's articles of association. However, as the threshold triggering the obligation to launch a mandatory offer is proposed to be reduced, it is likely that the number of different offering procedures will in practice be further reduced, as the need for an additional redemption obligation under the articles of association will diminish. In any event, as long as a target company has a 'poison pill' clause in its articles of association, it will remain a possibility that several offer thresholds, with different offering procedures, will continue to apply with respect to the target company.

As regards the different price definitions under the different offer/redemption procedures, the Working Group proposes that the current regulations of the Securities Market Act and the Companies Act be harmonised, so that the price offered in a mandatory offer should also constitute the equitable price in a squeeze-out, unless there are specific reasons for any other conclusion. As mentioned above, the current practice is that the price offered in a squeeze-out is challenged by a number of minority shareholders and in certain squeeze-out cases the price awarded by the arbitral tribunal has indeed been higher than the mandatory offer price. An interesting development is a recent decision by the District Court of Helsinki, where the court ruled that the dividend declared and paid out by the target company while the squeeze-out proceedings were pending could be deducted from the redemption price payable by the acquirer to the remaining minority shareholders in the target. However, the decision has been appealed and it remains to been seen whether it will be upheld by the higher courts or not.

Offer consideration – the concept of equitable price

Mandatory offers

The Working Group has also reassessed the concept of the 'equitable price' to be offered in mandatory offers. The current Finnish rule refers to the market value of the target security, defined generally as the volume-weighted average price paid for the securities in public trading during the 12 months preceding the triggering of the redemption obligation, or any higher price paid by the offeror during such 12-month period. Considering that the corresponding time period in those member states of the EU where such period is defined currently ranges from three to 12 months, Finland is at the higher end. As there is a risk that the offer consideration in mandatory offers may be quite high, this fairly strong protective mechanism has, in practice, probably stood in the way of takeovers that might otherwise have taken place, due to the price fluctuations on the market and especially the fall in share prices during certain periods, as, for example, following the IT boom.

The Takeover Directive determines the equitable price as the highest price paid by the offeror during not less than six and not more than 12 months before the offer, subject to possible adjustment by the national supervisory authority, pursuant to defined principles. As a result of the reassessment of the current provisions of the Securities Market Act, the Working Group proposes, in accordance with the requirements of the directive, that the price to be determined as the highest price paid by the offeror during the six months preceding the date when the obligation to make a mandatory offer was triggered, or, in the absence of such purchases, as the volume-weighted average price paid in public trading during the three months preceding the date.

The Working Group does not propose any amendments to the current requirement according to which the offer consideration in a mandatory offer must always be offered to be paid in cash, while other forms of consideration may be offered as an alternative to cash payment.

Voluntary offers

Although not required by the directive, a new provision with respect to the offer consideration in voluntary offers for all shares and securities that entitle to shares is also proposed to be introduced. Reflecting the corresponding proposal regarding mandatory offers, the concept of market value would be the basis for determining the consideration. The proposal refers again to the highest price paid by the offeror during the six months immediately preceding the announcement of the offer. Also, the requirement to offer a cash alternative, as currently required in connection with mandatory offers, would also be extended to voluntary offers under certain circumstances.

Obligation to increase offer consideration

In addition to the above, one further obligation deriving from the concept of equal treatment of all addressees of the offer is proposed to be introduced with respect to the offer consideration. According to the Working Group's proposal, the current general obligation to treat holders of target securities equally would be supplemented with a more specific obligation. Accordingly, the offer terms would need to be adjusted during the offer period if the offeror, or any certain related parties, acquires target securities for a higher price than the initial offer price after the announcement of the respective voluntary offer, or after triggering the obligation to launch a mandatory offer, and before the expiry of the offer period. The respective adjustment would need to reflect any such higher price paid. The Working Group has also proposed a top-up obligation, to be effective during the nine months following the expiry of the offer period, which is largely similar to a corresponding obligation currently in force with respect to certain conditional offers.

Competing offers

A phenomenon in Finnish takeovers during the past few years has been the increased number of competing offers. However, the Securities Market Act lacks specific regulations in this respect. The Working Group also proposes specific provisions with respect to competing offers protecting, in particular, the rights of the initial offeror and holders of target securities. Where a competing offer is launched, the initial offeror would be entitled to amend the terms and conditions of its offer and to extend the offer period (irrespective of the statutory maximum duration described below). Further, shareholders that have accepted the initial offer would be entitled to cancel their acceptance. The initial offeror would also have a right to cancel its offer.

Implications for target companies
Board statement

Currently, the obligations of the board of directors of the target company are regulated by the generic provisions on the duties of boards of directors in the Companies Act. The Working Group does not propose specific amendments in this respect. However, in line with the Takeover Directive, the Working Group proposes, as an explicit addition to the provisions currently in force, a statutory requirement for a statement by the board of directors of the target company regarding the offer. A similar statement has been the market practice so far, based on the currently applicable recommendation by the Financial Supervision Authority, although this recommendation only requires the offeror to request such a statement and does not directly impose an obligation on the board to issue one. A proposed further requirement for the board of directors of the target company specifically to inform the holders of target securities, and to assess the impact of the offer on the operations and employees of the target company, would clearly be an addition to the current regulations. Also, deriving from the requirements of the directive, a specific obligation to instruct employees of the target company of the offer is proposed to be imposed on the board of directors.

Board passivity and breakthrough rule – voluntary implementation through self-regulation

As indicated above, the position of the target company or its corporate bodies is not currently addressed by the Securities Market Act, but is governed by Finnish company law. Accordingly, the board of directors of the target company has a general obligation to act in the interest of the target company, with particular regard to the interest of the shareholders. Any act by the board of directors should be assessed against this general obligation, which prevents the board from acting in the interest of one or some shareholders only, whether a majority or minority. The board of directors also has a fiduciary duty towards the company and its shareholders collectively, which may involve a duty to act and require the board to take an active stand in connection with industrial reorganisations.

Implementation of the extensively debated breakthrough rule and board passivity rule found in Articles 9 and 11, respectively, of the directive is at the discretion of member states, according to the opt in and opt out system applied by the directive. Irrespective of the fact that the Working Group does not directly support an opt in solution with respect to the rules, except for a partial opt in regarding Article 9, it seems that a target company may nevertheless opt in, as the rules are proposed to be introduced in Finland through self-regulation and voluntary incorporation in target companies' articles of association. For such purposes, a new 'Takeover Panel', which would operate in connection with the Central Chamber of Commerce, is proposed to be introduced. The 'Takeover Panel' would be vested with powers to issue recommendations of a general nature as well as, upon application, recommendations, on a case by case basis, on issues that may arise under Articles 9 and 11. Also, the reciprocity provision included in Article 12 of the directive is proposed to be covered in recommendations of the 'Takeover Panel'.

Currently, Finland has no self-regulatory body, nor does it have any authority specifically assigned to the supervision of takeover bids. The Financial Supervision Authority exercises general supervision of compliance with the Securities Market Act by approving offer documents and overseeing generally the conduct of takeover bid procedures, but it does not have power conclusively to decide on substantive issues, such as the offer price (though it has sometimes published its divergent view on an offer price). These issues have to be resolved by the courts, which in these situations risks being too cumbersome and time consuming. Legal precedent is, in consequence, scarce. Although the proposed 'Takeover Panel' would be entitled to issue recommendations, on a case by case basis, regarding a specific takeover situation, it is in practice not proposed to be vested with more extensive powers than the Financial Supervision Authority. Consequently, as the preparations regarding the implementation of the directive proceed, the necessary considerations in connection with the establishing of the 'Takeover Panel' may be expected to concern the extent of its powers.

With respect to the breakthrough rule found in Article 11 of the directive, it is proposed that the rule may be voluntarily adopted by listed companies in their articles of association. As the issuance of further guidelines is also in this respect left to the proposed 'Takeover Panel', the practical implementation of the rule still remains to be resolved. In relation to the breakthrough rule, the question of multiple voting rights in particular has been largely discussed. While considered in general a Nordic issue, the question increasingly seems to be considered a non-event by Finnish market participants. Even though many listed companies have a dual share system, whereby the shares of one class may have a higher voting right (maximum 20 times) than the shares of another class, the trend seems to be a gradual move towards a 'one share, one vote' system. Companies that can be said to represent best practice in the Finnish market have in fact already removed their dual share systems. (Dual share classes are further discussed below.)

Further prospective amendments from the target company's perspective

One further proposal of the Working Group implicitly relates to the target company's position in connection with a takeover situation. While the Working Group proposes a new statutory minimum offer period duration of three weeks and a maximum duration of 10 weeks, it is also proposed that, at the target company's request, the Financial Supervision Authority could, without a requirement to consult the offeror, decide to extend the offer period, in order for the target company to convene a general meeting of shareholders to assess the offer. Although the content or purpose of the assessment is not discussed in the Working Group's proposal, it seems that the board passivity rule found in Article 9 of the directive is reflected to a certain extent in the provision, which can be interpreted to protect the right of the target company's shareholders to assess the offer at a general meeting of shareholders. The Financial Supervision Authority would also be vested with powers to grant permission on special grounds for the offer period to exceed the maximum duration of 10 weeks provided that this would not impede the target company's operations for an unreasonably long time.

Finally, in line with the directive's requirements, an obligation to present information in the annual report on factors that are likely to materially affect a public tender offer for the company's securities is proposed to be imposed on all listed companies.

Special topics on takeover practice in Finland

Break-up fees

The question of break-up fees – where the target company may undertake, typically in a combination or similar agreement, to pay a certain amount to an offeror if the target company's board of directors withdraws its recommendation relating to the offer due to a subsequent higher offer being launched – is not regulated under the Finnish takeover regime, has not been tested in a court of law in Finland and is not addressed by the Working Group. It therefore remains open to interpretation.

Some consider break-up fees to be against the fiduciary duties of the board of directors, as it would in general be difficult for the target board to act in a way that could deprive the shareholders of the possibility of considering a second offer, if such a competing offer is made at a higher price and is otherwise realistic as to its conditions. According to a more pragmatic view, a reasonable break-up fee could be accepted as a necessary step in the process of ensuring that an agreement is reached with a bidder, if the target board considers this to be in the best interests of the company and the shareholders collectively, as, for example, where a significant premium is being offered. In general, a break-up fee arrangement could be justified where the bidder makes it a precondition to launching an offer and it would therefore be in the interests of the company and its shareholders to accept it. In the event of a subsequent competing offer, the target board would be required to reassess what is in the best interests of the company and the shareholders under the changed circumstances, and, depending upon the merits of the competing offer, the target board could decide to withdraw its support for the first offer and pay the break-up fee, if this was considered to be in the best interests of the company and its shareholders.

The question of break-up fees remains highly debatable. In general, a target board should be very cautious in entering into any agreement that could prevent the board from acting in accordance with its fiduciary duty at all times without risking a breach of prior contracts.

Defensive measures

Generally, takeover bids may range from friendly to competitive and hostile situations. At the outset of a takeover situation, it is not always possible to say how a takeover will develop.

For instance, an agreed combination can turn into a competitive situation if a competing offer is subsequently launched, ultimately resulting in another takeover, friendly or hostile.

A recent phenomenon in the Finnish market has been the increased number of competing offers in takeovers. Generally, it could be argued that the Finnish takeover environment has become more aggressive. In the case of Hackman, Nordic Capital first went public with its bid for Hackman, but was outbid by the Italian ALI Group. In the case of Novo Group, a Finnish IT services firm, another Finnish IT services firm, SysOpen, launched a public tender offer, only to be outbid by the Swedish firm WM-Data. Most recently, in June 2005, the Icelandic investor Thor Björgólfsson launched a tender offer for the Finnish virtual telecommunications operator Saunalahti Group, which was followed by a competing offer by the Finnish operator Elisa Corporation in July 2005.

Alternative corporate restructuring, as a reaction to a tender offer, has also recently been seen in the Finnish market, in the case of the Finnish media group Alma Media, whose broadcasting division was sold to the Swedish publishing company Bonnier and the Swedish investment company Proventus after a bid for Alma Media had been launched by the Norwegian media group Schibsted.

To conclude, although not all the cases of competing offers seen in the Finnish market may be characterised as defences against a hostile takeover, competing bids seem to have become a trend in the Finnish market.

Traditionally, dual share classes have been relatively common in Finnish and other Nordic listed companies. Although different share classes can be seen as a means of defence in a takeover situation, the background to dual share classes in many Finnish companies lies in the fact that the companies were family-owned and the dual share class system was used as a means of retaining control within such families. During the past 10 years, no significant premium has generally been paid on the market for the voting rights attached to multiple-vote listed shares. In fact, it is often considered that there is more power in liquidity than in multiple voting rights and that, as a rule, ordinary shares are more liquid. It is also argued that there may be little extra pay for voting rights in the future, due to modern governance and transparency, whereby any such votes cannot be exercised for particular interests not shared by the minority shareholders. It has been suggested that market forces may soon remove the remaining multiple voting rights from the Finnish market. The consolidation of classes of shares has in practice been undertaken by decision of the shareholders' meeting, either against no compensation at a ratio of 1:1, when no premium has been paid for the voting rights in public trading, or, in some cases, against additional compensation of newly issued shares of the remaining class.

Another typical phenomenon in the Finnish takeover environment has been the insertion of 'poison pill' clauses into the articles of association of listed companies, stating that a party acquiring a specific portion, typically one-third or one-half, of the company's shares and votes is obliged to make an offer for the remaining shares in the company. However, the significance of such clauses is likely to diminish if the Working Group's proposal to reduce the threshold for mandatory offers under the Securities Market Act to a corresponding level is realised.

Conclusion

It seems fair to conclude that the implementation of the Takeover Directive is unlikely to result in an extensive reform of the Finnish takeover regime, although certain amendments of a material nature are proposed to be introduced, in particular in order to simplify the current partly parallel takeover procedures.

To summarise, the principal amendments to the Finnish takeover regime due to the implementation of the directive include the following:

- the threshold for mandatory offers is proposed to be reduced to 30 per cent and 50 per cent of the total votes in the target company;
- the main rule for pricing in both voluntary and mandatory offers would be based on the highest price paid by the offeror during the six months preceding the offer and the price offered in a mandatory offer would also constitute the equitable price in a squeeze-out, unless there are specific reasons for any other conclusion;
- new rules regarding competing offers are proposed to be introduced, including the initial offeror's right to amend the terms and conditions of its offer, or cancel the offer, and the shareholders' right to cancel their acceptance of the initial offer;
- a top-up obligation would apply in cases where the offeror acquires target securities for a higher price than the initial offer price after the announcement of the respective voluntary offer, or after triggering the obligation to launch a mandatory offer, as well as for a period of nine months following the expiry of the offer period;
- implementation of the extensively debated breakthrough rule and board passivity rule found in Articles 9 and 11 of the directive are proposed to be introduced through self-regulation by a new 'Takeover Panel' and voluntary incorporation in target companies' articles of association, although the practical implications still remain to be resolved.

Finally, the following summarises some of the main features of the takeover regime in Finland under the regulations currently in force:

- from the offeror's point of view, acquiring control of a listed company requires a number of different, partly parallel offer/redemption procedures, and all procedures have their own particular requirements and their particular (differing) price definitions;
- delisting of the target company is only possible once the bidder has acquired 100 per cent ownership through a squeeze-out, which means that the obligations imposed on listed companies need to be observed throughout the offer/redemption procedures;
- from the target board's point of view, the most important key principles to bear in mind in a takeover situation include equal treatment of all shareholders and the ensuring of an equitable offer price;
- in competing offers, it would in general be difficult for the target board to act in a way that could deprive the shareholders of the possibility of considering a second offer, if such a competing offer is made at a higher price and is otherwise realistic as to its conditions, and the legality of break-up fees is debatable.

Chapter 13

France

Valérie Lemaitre and Sophie de Beer
Cleary Gottlieb Steen & Hamilton LLP, Paris

The foundations of the current French takeover regulations were laid by Law No. 89-531, on the Security and Transparency of the Financial Market, dated 2 August 1989. Pursuant to this law, the Autorité des marchés financiers (AMF) is the authority responsible for the regulation and supervision of takeovers, including clearing and overseeing the orderly conduct of takeovers, reviewing and approving offer documents, and investigating and sanctioning violations of its regulations. Title III of Book II of the General Regulations (*Réglement général*) of the AMF contains the bulk of French takeover regulations, although there are a few provisions relating to takeover bids in the French Monetary and Financial Code.[1]

French takeover regulations apply only to companies whose registered office is located in France and that have securities admitted to trading on a French regulated market.[2] In addition, however, any takeover bid made in France for securities admitted to trading on a French regulated market, whether or not the issuer of such securities is a French company, must be made on the basis of an offer document approved by the AMF.[3]

It is expected that the Takeover Directive (Directive 2004/25/EC) will have a limited impact on French takeover regulations, with limited changes, for example, to pricing rules and the rules concerning defensive measures (see the section 'Main impact of the Takeover Directive' below).

Types of takeover bids

In principle, a takeover bid must cover all securities giving access to the target company's share capital, such as shares, convertible or exchangeable bonds or warrants.[4] A few exceptions to this general rule exist, notably when the bidder is acquiring up to a maximum of 10 per cent of the voting rights of the target company and, under certain conditions, when the issuer is launching a bid to buy back its own shares or other equity securities.

Voluntary versus mandatory takeover bids

French takeover regulations distinguish between voluntary and mandatory takeover bids. A bidder must generally launch a mandatory bid when it has acquired, through the acquisition of existing securities or subscription to newly issued securities, a significant interest in the target company. A mandatory bid is triggered:

- when the bidder increases its interest above 33.33 per cent of the shares or voting rights of the target company;[5]

- if the bidder holds between 33.33 and 50 per cent of the shares or voting rights of the target company, when the bidder increases its interest by more than 2 per cent over a 12-month period; or
- when, as a result of an acquisition of a block of securities, the bidder holds, taking into account the securities and voting rights held by it prior to such acquisition, 50 per cent or more of the shares or voting rights of the target company – in this last case, the bid is referred to as a 'standing offer'.

In addition, a controlling shareholder is required to launch a mandatory bid if it makes certain material decisions with respect to the target company, such as a decision to materially amend the articles of association of the target company; to merge or to transfer all or most of the assets of the target company; to amend the target company's business operations significantly; or not to allow the target company to declare dividends for several years.

Finally, if the bidder holds 95 per cent or more of the voting rights of the target company, a mandatory bid must be launched upon the minority shareholders' request to be bought out.

Under French regulations, all securities and voting rights held by persons acting in concert must be aggregated in order to determine whether the thresholds mentioned above (and below) are met. Under the French Commercial Code, persons are acting in concert when they have entered into an agreement relating to the acquisition or sale, or the exercise, of voting rights of, and with a view to implementing a common strategy *vis-à-vis,* an issuer.

The AMF may, upon the bidder's written application and in certain circumstances, exempt the bidder from the obligation to make a mandatory bid. The AMF's General Regulations contain detailed rules concerning such exemptions,[6] which may be granted, for example, in connection with mergers and other transactions approved by the general meeting of the target company's shareholders.

If a bidder fails to make a mandatory bid when increasing its interest above 33.33 per cent or by more than 2 per cent (as indicated above), the securities held by the bidder in excess of these thresholds lose their voting rights until the bidder complies with its obligation to make a mandatory bid. The failure to file a mandatory bid with the AMF may in any case result in a significant penalty being levied against the defaulting shareholder[7] and/or in the AMF enjoining the shareholder from filing a bid.

Squeeze-out

Under French takeover regulations, a bidder may carry out a squeeze-out of the minority shareholders of a target company, provided that the bidder holds 95 per cent or more of the share capital and voting rights of the target company. Upon completion of the squeeze-out, the shares of the target company are automatically delisted.

In a report issued in April 2005, a working group appointed by the AMF to make certain recommendations regarding independent financial valuation recommended that, pursuant to the Takeover Directive, the squeeze-out threshold be reduced to 90 per cent of the share capital and voting rights of the target company. Such a reduction would facilitate certain transactions, such as public-to-private transactions,[8] and reduce the incidence of minority shareholders being stuck with illiquid securities.

Main terms of takeover bids

Conditions

Under French takeover regulations, a bid becomes irrevocable upon filing with the AMF and the bidder is bound to acquire the securities tendered. The bid may be subject to limited conditions, in particular the following.

First, with respect to exchange offers, the authorisation of a general meeting of the bidder's shareholders is required to issue the securities offered as consideration.

Secondly, a minimum number of securities and/or voting rights of the target company must be obtained, generally representing 50.01 per cent of the target's share capital and voting rights. However, mandatory takeover bids may not be subject to such a minimum tender condition.

Thirdly, if clearance from the anti-trust authorities of the EU, any EU member state or the United States is not obtained in Phase I (preliminary review) and a Phase II (in-depth review) is initiated, the takeover bid automatically becomes null and void. This condition may not be waived during the bid period.

Fourthly, other regulatory approvals, such as from banking and insurance authorities, may be made conditions only for the opening of a bid. Once such approvals have been obtained, the bid is opened and the bidder is bound to acquire the securities tendered, regardless of the conditions to which the regulatory approvals are subject.

Takeover bids cannot be subject to conditions relating to financing, due diligence or third-party approvals other than the regulatory approvals indicated above.

Consideration

Other than squeeze-outs, which must be made for cash,[9] the consideration offered in a takeover bid may consist of a cash payment in euros, liquid securities admitted to trading on a regulated market, or a combination of cash and securities. The AMF generally requires that securities offered as consideration be admitted to trading on a French regulated market, or that the bidder undertakes to have the securities admitted to trading on such a market shortly after the closing of the bid.[10] Bidders often provide a significant degree of choice to target shareholders by offering full or partial alternatives. It is also possible to offer deferred or contingent consideration.

In general, the bidder freely determines the consideration offered, subject to approval by the AMF. In the event of a standing offer, however, the consideration to be offered to minority shareholders must be equal to that paid to the majority shareholders.

Other than in the case of standing offers, where (as stated) the consideration must be equal to that paid to majority shareholders, the AMF evaluates the consideration offered by the bidder on the basis of 'commonly used objective valuation criteria' and the 'characteristics of the target company'. In practice, the bidder is required to justify the consideration offered under a 'multi-criteria analysis', in which it benchmarks the consideration offered to results under several valuation methods. The AMF conducts its review on a case by case basis, which varies depending on the context of the offer and the specificities of the target company. The most commonly used valuation methods include:

- the volume-weighted average trading price of the securities over several reference periods (for example, 12 months, six months, three months and one month ending before the announcement of the bid);

- the purchase price paid by the bidder for securities of the target company in the months preceding the bid;
- the net asset value of the target company, reassessed to take undervalued assets into account;
- the discounted cash flows of the target company;
- the return or profit-earning ratios of comparable companies; and
- the price paid in previous comparable market transactions.

Following the Schneider Electric/Legrand case, the prudent approach is to use the same valuation criteria for the target company whatever the securities concerned and to justify differing consideration primarily on the respective characteristics of such securities.

In the exchange offer by Schneider Electric for Legrand's securities in 2001, the consideration offered to holders of Legrand's ordinary shares and preferred shares (shares with no voting rights and a preferred dividend right attached) were not only different,[11] but were also based on different valuation criteria. The Paris Court of Appeals[12] decided to cancel the AMF's approval of the bid because it did not appropriately justify why different valuation methods should be used for the purpose of justifying the consideration paid for the ordinary shares on the one hand and for the preferred shares on the other, or why the characteristics of the preferred shares should result in lower consideration for them compared to that for the ordinary shares.

In the context of a squeeze-out, the bidder must also provide a fairness opinion from an independent expert.[13]

Typical bid procedure

Exhibit 13.1 sets out the timetable for a takeover bid in France, based on the assumptions that the takeover bid is for cash only, and that the bidder and the target company do not prepare a joint offer document. A joint offer document would result in a reduction of the length of the bid by approximately 10 trading days.

Filing of the bid and approval by the AMF

Under French takeover regulations, one or several financial intermediaries that are licensed to carry out firm underwriting in France file(s) the takeover bid with the AMF on behalf of the bidder. Such intermediaries guarantee the 'content and irrevocable nature of the bidder's commitments' and, in particular, that tendering security-holders of the target company will receive payment for their securities upon settlement.

Upon the filing of the bid and the draft offer document with the AMF, the bidder must publish a press release describing the main terms of its bid. Trading in the securities of the target company is generally suspended from the time of the filing until the AMF approves the bid.

The AMF has five trading days to review the terms and conditions of the bid and the draft offer document. The AMF may, however, suspend the running of this time period with a request for information or supporting documentation. Once the bid has been approved, the bidder must promptly publish the offer document and send it to the management and the works council of the target company.

When the AMF approves the terms and conditions of the bid, it issues a notice of approval (*avis de recevabilité*). The AMF's approval of the offer document is also formalised

Exhibit 13.1

Timetable of a takeover bid in France

D − 1	D	D + 5	D + 7	D + 8
Meeting of the bidder's board of directors	Filing of the bid and of draft offer document with the AMF	Clearance of the bid by the AMF	Publication of the offer document	Opening of the acceptance period
	Suspension of trading by Euronext	Approval of the offer document by the AMF		Publication of the timetable for the bid by the AMF and Euronext
	Publication by the AMF of the main terms of the offer; publication by the bidder of the main terms of the offer in a newspaper with a national circulation	Filing of offer document with the target		Meeting of the target's board of directors
	Beginning of applicable trading restrictions			
	Meeting of the bidder's and target's works councils to inform them of the bid			

D = trading days

(*Continued*)

Exhibit 13.1 *(Continued)*

Timetable of a takeover bid in France

D + 10	D + 13	D + 15	D + 17	D + 39
Filing with the AMF of the draft response document by the target	Approval of the target's response document by the AMF	Publication of the target's response document	Second meeting of target's works council to discuss offer and hear CEO of bidder if so convened	Last day to file an increased bid or a competing offer with the AMF
Filing of offer document with the target's works council	Filing of the target's response document with the bidder			
	End of the 10-day period during which the AMF's decisions on clearance of the offer and approval of the offer document may be challenged			

D + 43	D + 47	D + 52	D + 55
Closing of the acceptance period	Centralisation of the tendered securities of the target by Euronext	Publication of the final results of the bid by the AMF	Settlement of the bid

D = trading days

Source: Author's own.

by a decision (*visa*). These decisions may be challenged before the Paris Court of Appeals within 10 days from their date of publication. A challenge to the AMF's decisions does not, however, automatically suspend the enforceability of such decisions; a freeze order would need to be sought to this effect.[14]

Content of the offer document

The offer document must be in the French language and is to be prepared either solely by the bidder or jointly with the target company. Certain information must be provided in the offer document, including the following:

- a description of the bidder's corporate organisation, articles of association, business, assets and financial situation, including, in certain circumstances, *pro-forma* financial statements. In the event that the bidder's securities are to be used as consideration, this description should contain a high level of detail and comply with the content requirements of a French listing prospectus. A foreign bidder's financial statements must be translated into French, but need not be presented according to International Financial Reporting Standards;
- a description of the bidder's intentions for the coming 12 months with respect to the industrial and financial policy of the target company, its management and its workforce (including as a result of any contemplated restructuring), as well as with respect to the listing of the target company's securities;
- a description of the terms and conditions of the bid, including the number of target securities that the bidder offers to acquire and the number of securities already held by the bidder, the consideration offered, any conditions attached to the offer and the financing of the offer;
- the provisions of agreements to which the bidder is a party, or of which it is aware, and that are likely to have an impact on the valuation or the outcome of the bid,[15] as well as the names of the persons with whom the bidder is acting in concert.

The target company is also required to prepare and file a document with the AMF, providing substantially the same information as the bidder's offer document – except for the description of the main terms and conditions of the offer, and intentions for the coming 12 months – as well as a description of the board of directors' decision to recommend, or not to recommend, the offer and the conditions under which this decision was made. The target company may provide this information either in a separate French offer document or in a joint offer document with the bidder.

Duration of the bid

Other than in the case of standing offers or offers subject to the simplified procedure, which remain open for 10 trading days, bids remain open for 25 trading days from the date of publication of the bidder's offer document, subject to an extension of up to 35 trading days if the document was not prepared jointly by the bidder and the target company. This period may also be extended due to the filing of an increased bid or the submission of a competing bid by a third party.

PART II: EUROPEAN JURISDICTIONS

If competing bids are made, the AMF may either set a deadline for the filing of increased bids or require that competing bidders make a final bid when the bid has been open for more than 10 weeks. This rule was adopted following the battle between BNP and Société Générale for the acquisition of Paribas in 1999, when the bids extended over a period of almost seven months.

Modifications during the bid period

Bids may be modified only in a limited number of circumstances and to a limited extent. Bidders may always improve their bids by filing an increased bid, which may typically consist of an increase in the bid price[16] or a waiver of the minimum tender condition. Whenever a bidder increases its bid, the AMF may decide that prior tenders by security-holders of the target company are cancelled. In any case, increased bids must be filed no later than five trading days prior to the end of the period in which the bid remains open.

In the recommended takeover offer for GrandVision in 2003, the bid, which was subject to a minimum tender condition of 66.66 per cent, failed when investors considered that the price offered was too low, with GrandVision's stock trading price being higher than the bid price. A third party, Hal Holding, acquired 32 per cent of GrandVision's shares on the market during the last five trading days of the bid and, barred by the above-mentioned five trading days period, the bidder was unable to increase its bid.

Bidders may also modify their bid in the event of a competing bid. In this case, they may withdraw their bid; change the terms and conditions of their bid, for example by switching from cash consideration to consideration in securities; or make an increased bid. The opening of a competing bid results in the cancellation of tenders by security-holders of the target company in the prior bid.

Finally, bidders are entitled to withdraw their bid if:

- the target company takes unconditional actions that result in a modification of the target company's substance, such as capital increases, an acquisition or disposal of assets and share buy-backs; or
- the bid becomes without purpose, for example when competitors agree to jointly acquire the target company, superseding their initial bids on a stand-alone basis.[17]

Board neutrality and defensive measures

The target company's board of directors is required to analyse the terms and conditions of the bid, and then to issue an opinion on the bid and its consequences, both for the target company, and for its shareholders and employees. The works council of the target company also has the right to issue a statement on the bid.

Under French law, the management of the target company is subject to a 'duty of neutrality' in takeover bids, which limits its ability to take defensive measures. First, managers and directors are company fiduciaries. They must therefore always act in furtherance of the corporate interest of the target company (which is distinct from the interest of the target's shareholders) and may not take defensive measures contrary to such corporate interest. In addition, and more importantly, once a bid has been filed for the target company, all actions taken by the target company must be in the ordinary course of business, unless such actions have been expressly authorised by a general meeting of the shareholders of the target company held after the filing of the bid, or have been submitted to the AMF for review and disclosure to the public. In particular, authorisations to issue new securities that were granted to the board of directors by a general shareholders' meeting held prior to the filing of the bid may not be used unless the issuance is in the ordinary course of business.

Finally, defensive measures must comply with the takeover principles set forth in French takeover regulations, including the principles of free competition among bidders and free determination by bidders of the consideration offered.

In the context of the hostile takeover bid launched by Sanofi-Synthélabo for Aventis in 2004, Aventis's management decided to call a general shareholders' meeting to authorise the issuance of free warrants to existing Aventis shareholders. Such warrants, which were highly dilutive, were to be exercisable if two conditions were met: (i) Sanofi-Synthélabo's bid remained hostile; and (ii) Sanofi-Synthélabo lost its rights on the Plavix® patent in the United States and a generic version of Plavix® was marketed in the United States before the end of 2007. If these two conditions were met, the warrants would have resulted in a massive issuance of Aventis shares and therefore have significantly increased the consideration paid by Sanofi-Synthélabo for 100 per cent of Aventis's share capital. In order for this issuance of warrants to comply with the principle of free competition among bidders and not to disadvantage Sanofi-Synthélabo in a competition with another bidder, the warrants were to be cancelled upon the filing of a competing bid for Aventis. However, before Aventis was able to hold the general shareholders' meeting, the AMF issued an opinion in which it indicated that the issuance of such warrants would be contrary to (i) the principle of free determination by bidders of the consideration offered, to the extent that such warrants would force Sanofi-Synthélabo to increase the consideration to be paid for all Aventis shares; and (ii) the orderly conduct of public bids. As a result, Aventis did not proceed with the issuance of the warrants. Aventis was no more successful with the 'white knight' defensive measure, as the potential white knight, the Swiss company Novartis, did not make any offer in the context of the French government's strong support for the merger of Aventis and Sanofi-Synthélabo combination, and the emergence of a French leader.

Defensive measures may be roughly divided into the following four categories: white knights; measures resulting in a reduction in the target company's attractiveness; measures resulting in an increase in the number of shares that must be acquired in order for the takeover bid to be successful; and other measures including the Pac-man defence.

White knights

The management of the target company may seek a white knight to launch a competing bid. They do not need shareholders' approval to proceed, but the choice of, and the combination with, the white knight must be in the corporate interest of the target company. In addition, the white knight cannot benefit from any actions taken by the target company, such as a transfer of treasury shares, that violate the free competition principle.

Measures resulting in a reduction in the target company's attractiveness

The target company may have agreed to a change of control provision in certain key agreements; to put options on certain assets that are triggered upon a change of control of the target company; to break-up fees in exchange for exclusivity in the context of a friendly transaction; or to the payment of golden parachutes to certain key managers. In order to be valid, all such measures must be in the corporate interest of the target company, and also comply with the principles of free competition among bidders and board neutrality, which basically depend on whether the amount and/or asset at stake in the measure is significant and whether the measure would effectively prevent a competitor from launching a bid.

For example, the US joint subsidiary of Bénédictine and Whitbread had the option to acquire either party's shareholding in the event of the change of control of that party. In the context of the bid launched by Rémy et Associés for Bénédictine in 1988, the COB (the predecessor of the AMF) requested that such option be inapplicable during the bid, as Bénédictine's shareholding in the US subsidiary constituted a material asset and application of the option would be contrary to the principle of free competition among bidders.

Break-up fees are also strictly scrutinised. Break-up fees have been used on occasion in France in order to secure the tendering of shares by shareholders to a particular bidder's offer.[18] Break-up fees raise significant issues with respect to the principles of free competition among bidders and board neutrality if their amount is such as to bar, or to significantly disfavour, any competing bid.

Measures resulting in an increase in the number of shares to be acquired

The bidder must acquire more securities in order to gain control of the target company when the by-laws of the target company provide for voting ceilings[19] or double voting rights; or the target company has issued several classes of securities, such as both ordinary shares and preferred shares without voting rights; or the shareholders' meeting of the target company decides, after the commencement of a takeover bid, to issue new securities.

Share buy-backs may also act as a defensive measure, in that the target is in competition with the bidder in acquiring shares on the market.[20]

The Pac-man defence

The Pac-man defence is one of a number of other types of defensive measure that have also been used in France. For example, in 1998, Elf Aquitaine launched a bid for TotalFina after the commencement of TotalFina's offer for Elf Aquitaine. The offer for the bidder must be made early in the offer process for the Pac-man defence to be effective, such that the timetables of the two bids run parallel. This defence also raises serious issues under French corporation law, which prohibits reciprocal shareholdings between two companies.

Market purchases

Before launching a bid

Following the Zodiac case, the acquisition of shares of a target company prior to the launch of a bid raises serious concerns under French insider trading rules. In the Zodiac case (Court of Appeals of Paris, 15 November 1994), Zodiac, which held more than one-third of the share capital of Sicma and benefited from a right of first refusal granted by Sicma's majority shareholder, acquired 0.7 per cent of Sicma's share capital on the market prior to launching a recommended takeover bid for the company. At the time of the initial market purchases, the price of the bid had been determined and agreed upon between Zodiac and Sicma. The court held that the purchases were designed to acquire the shares at a lower price than that of the bid in order to reduce the overall price of the transaction. Zodiac was therefore sanctioned for insider trading.

The court held that a bidder's knowledge of the price at which it would launch a bid for the securities of a public company constituted privileged information, even though the actual launch was still subject to conditions and the success of the offer was uncertain; and that the lawfulness of any acquisition of shares made while in possession of such knowledge must be considered in light of the actual goals of the bidder. The court held that 'the acquisition of shares prior to launching a tender offer may be licit if it corresponds to the goal of progressively taking a material shareholding in the target company or of improving one's position to respond to a potential competing bid'.

Accordingly, following the Zodiac case, a prudent approach is to consider that, prior to the filing of a takeover bid, the only legally acceptable acquisitions of shares are acquisitions of material blocks that are instrumental to the acquisition of control of the target company and made at a price equal to that of the offer. In practice, available blocks are acquired either on the day the offer is launched or the day before. Thereafter, the crossing of ownership notification requirement thresholds and the risk of leaks would make market purchases too risky for the bid, due to the risks of competing bids and of the premium disappearing because of market speculation.

During the bid period

Under French takeover regulations, all trades of securities of the target company from the filing of the bid until publication of the final results must be made on the regulated market(s) on which such securities are admitted to trading.

During the bid period, the bidder, the persons acting in concert with it and its financial advisers have the right to acquire securities of the target company. They are, however, prohibited from trading in those securities if the bid is subject to conditions or if the bid includes, in whole or in part, a security component (as indicated below). In the event that the bidder acquires securities at a price exceeding the bid price, the latter is automatically increased to the higher price.

In general, trading in securities relevant to the bid, either as the target company's securities or the securities offered in consideration, is prohibited from the date of filing of the bid with the AMF until the publication of the final results.

Main impact of the Takeover Directive
Pricing rules

The Takeover Directive provides that the equitable price for a mandatory bid is the highest price paid for the same class of securities by the bidder, or by persons acting in concert with it, during a period of no less than six months and no more than 12 months prior to the launch of the mandatory bid.[21] In implementing the Takeover Directive in relation to the minimum pricing provisions for mandatory bids, the French legislature may decide to use a prior acquisition costs approach or may decide to keep the present multi-criteria approach described above.

Defensive measures

In a report issued in June 2005, a working group appointed by the AMF to issue recommendations as to the implementation of the Takeover Directive under French law recommended that France should implement Article 9 of the Takeover Directive – the 'board passivity rule', which is very similar to the current French regime – but should not make Article 11 of the Takeover Directive – the 'breakthrough rule' – mandatory. The working group reasoned that the provisions of Article 11 provide for too strong a restriction on contractual liberty and that the current French approach of disclosing shareholders' agreements already provides sufficient transparency.[22] Finally, the working group recommended that French companies that have opted for Article 11 should be entitled to opt out when subject to a bid from a bidder that does not apply Article 11.

Ten most important points for acquirers in France

- Takeover bids are supervised by the AMF, which is responsible for clearing the bid, approving the offer document and overseeing the orderly conduct of takeovers.
- The acquisition of 33.33 per cent of the share capital or voting rights of a French listed company triggers the obligation to launch a mandatory takeover bid for such company.
- Takeover bids are irrevocable upon filing with the AMF and may be subject only to limited conditions, which may not include financing, due diligence or third-party approval conditions, except for certain regulatory approvals, such as from anti-trust authorities. Bidders may withdraw a bid only in a limited number of circumstances.
- Takeover bids must be made for all the shares and equity securities giving access to the target company's share capital.
- The AMF approves the terms of the bid, including the consideration offered, using a 'multi-criteria analysis' based on several valuation methods.
- The offer document to be approved by the AMF must include a detailed description of the bidder's intentions for the coming 12 months with respect to the industrial and financial policy of the target company, its management, its workforce (including as a result of any contemplated restructuring) and the listing of its securities.
- From the filing of a takeover bid until publication of the final results, all transactions in securities of the target company must be made in the market in which they are traded.
- In the regular takeover bid procedure, tenders are revocable until the last day of the acceptance period and tendered securities are transferred to the bidder following the closing of the acceptance period if the bid is successful.
- The board of directors of the target company must act in furtherance of the company's corporate interest and comply with the principle of board neutrality during takeovers.
- French takeover rules provide for sell-out and squeeze-out procedures whenever a majority shareholder holds 95 per cent or more of the voting rights of the target company.

---

[1] See Article L.433-1 to L.433-4 of the French Monetary and Financial Code.

[2] Pursuant to Article 231-1 of the AMF General Regulations, the AMF may, however, decide to apply its rules to any takeover bid made for the securities of non-French companies that are admitted to trading on a French regulated market. To our knowledge, the AMF has done so only once, in 2001, with respect to a bid for an Ivory Coast company whose shares were admitted to trading only on a French regulated market.

3 Pursuant to Article 231-26 of the AMF General Regulations, when (i) a takeover bid is made for a company whose shares are admitted to trading on a French regulated market as well as on another, non-French market, whether regulated or not; (ii) the AMF does not hold itself competent to supervise the bid; and (iii) an offer document has been prepared for the purpose of the takeover bid and supervised by a competent non-French authority, the AMF may decide that no French offer document is required, provided, however, that the bidder and the target company publish a French press release setting forth the main terms and conditions of the bid, as well as any information that is required to be disclosed in a French offer document and was not included in the offer document prepared for the takeover bid. Upon implementation of the Takeover Directive, offer documents approved by the competent authorities of any EU member state may be recognised and used in other EU member states (see the Takeover Directive, Article 6(2), second paragraph).

4 Stock options, which are not considered securities under French law, need not be covered by the bid.

5 When a bidder acquires, either alone or in concert with others, control of a non-listed company holding more than 33.33 per cent of the shares or voting rights of a listed company, which interest is a material asset of the non-listed company, the bidder is also required to launch a mandatory bid for the equity securities of the listed company.

6 See Articles 234-7 to 234-9 and Article 236-6 of the AMF General Regulations.

7 This penalty may be up to €1.5 million, or ten times the gains realised by the defaulting shareholder.

8 In public-to-private transactions, the acquisition vehicle, which generally finances a significant portion of the acquisition through bank debt, aims at acquiring 95 per cent or more of the share capital of the target for the purpose of tax consolidation with the target. The reduction from 95 per cent to 90 per cent of the squeeze-out threshold should increase the chances that such bidders reach the 95 per cent tax consolidation threshold and may therefore result in more leveraged buyouts with respect to listed companies.

9 In its report, issued in April 2005, the working group appointed by the AMF to make certain recommendations regarding independent financial valuation recommended that, upon implementation of the Takeover Directive, French takeover regulations be amended to allow consideration for a squeeze-out to consist of either cash or liquid securities, at the bidder's option.

10 The AMF has, however, agreed in a few cases to allow securities listed only on a foreign exchange to be offered as consideration requiring, in some of these cases, that foreign brokerage costs on these securities be borne by the bidder.

11 It is notable that the stock price of Legrand's preferred shares was previously about 50 to 60 per cent lower than that of the ordinary shares.

12 See Court of Appeals of Paris, 3 May 2001.

13 In its report, issued in April 2005, the working group appointed by the AMF to make certain recommendations regarding independent financial valuation recommended that the requirement for a fairness opinion be extended to other types of takeover bids.

14 In practice, freeze orders are very rarely granted on any AMF decision in connection with a takeover bid. However, the AMF generally agrees to postpone the closing of the takeover bid until a few days after the Paris Court of Appeals has made a decision on the merits, in order to avoid the risk of a closed bid being cancelled, requiring the unwinding of all related transactions. Legal challenges to the AMF's decisions are common in practice and are seen as an efficient way to gain time.

15 For example, undertakings to tender or not to tender securities to the bid; agreements including a change of control provision; and any clause of any agreement providing for preferred transfer terms, such as pre-emption rights, rights of first refusal, puts or calls.

16 If cash consideration is offered, the cash consideration in any increased bid consisting of an increase in the bid price or in any competing bid must be increased by at least 2 per cent compared to the previous bid.

17 See the competing offers of Saica International and Mondi International for La Rochette in 2002.

18 See the tender offer of Accor Casinos for Compagnie Européenne de Casinos (2002), where the break-up fee was equal to the difference between Accor Casinos' offer price and the price of any competing bid, up to €5 per share, or approximately 10 per cent of the price offered by Accor Casinos.

19 Such by-laws generally provide that every shareholder is limited to voting, typically, 10 or 20 per cent of the total number of voting rights, whatever its actual shareholding in the company, provided, however, that such a ceiling does not apply to any shareholder holding more than, generally, 50 or 66.66 per cent of the company's share capital.

20 However, the defensive value of share buy-backs by the target is limited to the extent that (i) such buy-backs must be carried out under the same conditions (in terms of volume and so on) as before the launch of the bid, and in compliance with the terms of the outstanding share buy-back programme; (ii) any company may hold only up to 10 per cent of its own share capital; and (iii) as treasury shares do not carry voting rights, share buy-backs may actually increase the percentage of voting rights held by the bidder.

PART II: EUROPEAN JURISDICTIONS

[21] See the Takeover Directive, Article 5(4), sentence 1.

[22] See Article L.233-11 of the French Commercial Code, which requires that any agreements providing for the acquisition or sale of listed securities representing more than 0.5 per cent of the share capital or voting rights of a public company, at preferential conditions, be disclosed to the concerned public company and the AMF within five trading days. Failure to comply results in the suspension of the agreements and the contracting parties not being bound by such agreements during any takeover bid.

Chapter 14

Germany

Klaus Riehmer
Cleary Gottlieb Steen & Hamilton LLP, Frankfurt

The German Act on the Acquisition of Securities and on Takeovers (the German Takeover Act, or simply the Act) entered into force on 1 January 2002. It created a statutory framework for takeovers and public bids in Germany. In particular, the Act established reporting standards, requirements for mandatory bids, criteria for the consideration to be offered, the duration of the bid period and conditions under which the target company may employ defensive measures against a hostile takeover. The purpose of the Act is to strengthen and maintain the functionality of German capital markets and to enhance their transparency.

The Act applies to all public offers for shares, certificates in lieu of shares and comparable securities issued by a German-based[1] stock corporation (AG) or company limited by shares (KGaA) that have been admitted to trading on an organised market in Germany or anywhere else within the European Economic Area (EEA).[2] The regime under the German Takeover Act is administered by the Federal Financial Supervisory Authority (BaFin). This Authority is responsible, *inter alia,* for evaluating offer documents and supervising the orderly conduct of public bids under the German Takeover Act. It has been granted legal powers of investigation and intervention to fulfil its role.

Since the German Takeover Act entered into force, there have been more than 130 bids. The overall volume of all takeover transactions amounted to more than €40 billion. This includes, however, the bid for shares in Bayerische Hypo- und Vereinsbank AG (HVB),[3] launched in August 2005. This transaction alone has an overall value of more than €19 billion. With this as an example, it should be noted that some pivotal bids have decisively shaped the takeover activity in Germany over the past years. The 10 largest transactions constituted the bulk of the total volume. Besides the HVB takeover, other important bids included the takeovers of Wella AG by Procter & Gamble,[4] of Degussa AG by RAG[5] and of Stinnes AG by Deutsche Bahn.[6]

The Directive 2004/25/EC on takeover bids (the Takeover Directive) will have an important impact on German takeover law, particularly in the fields of pricing rules, frustrating actions and disclosure. It will also lead to the introduction of a special bid-related squeeze-out regime and a sell-out provision into German law. Implementation of the Takeover Directive is to be completed by 20 May 2006.

Important aspects of the German Takeover Act
Takeover bids, tender offers, mandatory bids and the notion of 'control'
The German Takeover Act distinguishes three types of bids: takeover bids, tender offers and mandatory bids.

PART II: EUROPEAN JURISDICTIONS

Takeover bids are bids made with the intention of gaining control over the target company.[7] 'Control' is defined as the holding of a minimum of 30 per cent of the voting rights in the target company.[8]

Tender offers are bids that are intended, not to gain control over the target company, but simply to increase the bidder's shareholding in the target company.[9] In many cases, they appear in connection with restructuring measures, such as reintegration of a business unit in order to buy out minority shareholders, or in straightforward integration scenarios.[10]

A *mandatory bid* generally must be launched if the bidder has gained control over the target company. The German Takeover Act provides for fundamental sanctions in case of non-compliance with the mandatory bid provisions. Compensation must include interest if the bidder does not comply with its obligation to publish the fact that it has gained control over the target company or does not launch a mandatory bid within four weeks of gaining control.[11] Further, all shareholder rights, including voting rights, attaching to the bidder's shares are suspended during the period in which it fails to comply with the obligation to make the mandatory bid[12] and a significant administrative fine may be levied against the new controlling shareholder in case of non-compliance.

The BaFin may,[13] upon the bidder's written application, exempt the bidder from the obligation to make a mandatory bid.[14] Some provisions of the Bid Regulation[15] contain detailed rules concerning the granting of exemptions from the mandatory bid requirements, which may be made subject to certain conditions. Thus, an exemption may be granted, for example, in certain cases of gaining indirect control[16] or in connection with the reorganisation of the target company by the bidder.

Consideration

As a general rule, the consideration offered in a takeover or a mandatory bid must consist either of a cash payment in euros or of liquid shares admitted to an organised market.[17] Liquid shares need not be shares in the bidder company, nor is the bidder prohibited from offering other kinds of consideration. For example, it may offer unlisted shares, provided that the shareholders of the target company are entitled to either a cash payment or liquid shares as alternative consideration. However, while the bidder is generally free to choose whether to offer a cash payment or liquid shares, cash must be offered if the bidder has purchased a certain amount of shares for cash during a certain period prior to the pre-bid announcement or between the pre-bid announcement and the end of the acceptance period.[18]

Additional measures have to be taken in exchange offers. Above all, in takeover and mandatory bids, shares offered as consideration must be admitted for trading in an organised market.[19] It suffices to meet this requirement, however, that the admission of the shares to stock exchange listing takes effect at the latest at the time of settlement of the offer, that is, when the shares are to be delivered to the shareholders. In practice, however, share offers have proved to be difficult if the shares offered as consideration were not listed prior to the offer. The BaFin's position on this issue has been very rigid. In principle, the bidder must provide evidence that the shares will effectively be listed.

The typical bid procedure

Announcement of the bid and publication of the offer document
After the decision to make a bid has been prepared or once the control threshold has been

exceeded, the decision to make a bid or the fact that control has been reached must be published.[20] The announcement of the offer starts an irrevocable procedure. In accordance with the regulations under the German Takeover Act, an announced bid actually has to be made; neither the announcement nor the offer itself can be withdrawn, at least not without incurring severe sanctions. If a bid is not submitted despite an announcement, the BaFin will prohibit the bid, which may generally lead to the imposition of a fine and a blocking period of one year. Such prohibition might also involve a loss of the bidder's reputation on the market.

Within four weeks following the announcement, the bidder must hand in the offer document.[21] However, this time period may be extended by up to four weeks for cross-border and share-for-share bids.[22] The BaFin then reviews the offer documentation for compliance with the requirements under the German Takeover Act, which generally takes the BaFin 10 to 15 working days. If the BaFin has approved the publication, or if 10 working days have passed since the receipt of the offer document without the BaFin having prohibited the bid, the offer document must be published without undue delay.

Content of the offer document
The offer document, which must be in the German language, must contain the information necessary to make an informed decision regarding the bid. The information must be accurate and complete.[23] The offer document therefore must contain certain minimum details, such as the securities that are the object of the bid, the amount of consideration, the conditions upon which the effectiveness of the bid is contingent or the first and last day of the bid period.[24] The bidder must also provide a written confirmation of adequate financing, if the bid provides for a cash payment as consideration.[25] In share-for-share offers, the 'prospectus' describing the offered shares is part of the offer document.

Duration of the bid
The regular period for acceptance may not be less than four weeks.[26] Subject to extension due to an amendment of the bid[27] or the submission by a third party of a competing bid,[28] the acceptance period may not be longer than 10 weeks. In the case of a takeover bid (but not in the case of tender offers or mandatory bids), an extended period of two weeks for acceptance begins upon publication of the results of acceptances attained during the regular acceptance period. This 'on the fence' or 'wren' rule allows the shareholder concerned to wait and see whether the takeover bid has been successful and to hold or sell its shares accordingly. However, this extended period is not available if a threshold of minimum acceptance stipulated in the offer document is not reached.

Modifications during the bid period
Offers may be modified to only a very limited extent: for instance, the price of the shares offered may be increased or a condition may be waived. Whenever modifications arise, the shareholders of the target company may withdraw their acceptance in order to accept the modified bid.

Conditions

In principle, to achieve flexibility in the composition of the bid and, above all, to tailor the bid according to the particular entrepreneurial objective, a bidder has the option of making a bid contingent on specific conditions. Mandatory bids, however, may generally not be made subject to conditions except as required by law.

The general option to make the bid contingent upon one or more conditions nevertheless is subject to various limitations.[29] Above all, a bid may not be made subject to conditions the fulfilment of which may be brought about only by the bidder or persons close to it. Fulfilment of the conditions may not depend on the sole discretion of the bidder. Permissible conditions include merger control clearance,[30] minimum acceptance requirements,[31] a resolution of the target company's shareholders[32] or, subject to certain limitations, the non-occurrence of a material adverse change.[33]

'Coordinated conduct' – the German version of acting in concert

According to Section 30(2) of the German Takeover Act, voting rights in a target company owned by a third party shall be attributed to the bidder in full if the bidder or its subsidiaries coordinate their conduct, whether by agreement or otherwise, with such third party in respect to the target. Reciprocal attribution for coordinating parties, who together hold a controlling stake, may have significant consequences, since in that case each coordinating party will be obliged to make a mandatory bid.

The definition of 'coordinated conduct' under the German Takeover Act appears to be broader than in the UK City Code on Takeovers and Mergers,[34] which focuses on cooperation through the joint acquisition of shares in order to obtain control. The term 'coordinated conduct' leaves some room for interpretation and has therefore been the subject of discussion in various articles and court cases. Pursuant to recent court decisions, coordinated conduct requires (i) the coordination of membership rights attached to shares of a target company; (ii) leading or attempting to lead to a significant impact on the corporate structure or strategy of the target company; (iii) with such (potential) impact not only producing a one-time effect but resulting in continuing influence over the target company; and (iv) conscious cooperation between the parties amounting to more than merely accidental parallel conduct.[35]

The coordination is not limited to a certain form, such as an explicit agreement in the form of a voting trust. A non-binding gentlemen's agreement may be deemed to constitute coordinated conduct.[36] Parallel share purchases in general, standstill agreements and mutual rights of first refusal, as well as business combination agreements, generally do not lead to the assumption of coordinated conduct. The question of whether cooperation with regard to the election of supervisory board members by various shareholders might constitute coordinated conduct is a controversial one and has recently come to the attention of the public in the case of Deutsche Börse AG. Recent case law has held that such coordination constitutes coordinated conduct if the cooperation has been wilfully agreed upon and leads to a sustainable effect on the target company's management bodies.[37]

The BaFin, according to the general principles of German law, bears the burden of proof as to whether coordinated conduct did or did not occur.[38] The BaFin has some investigative powers, but may not be able to prove coordinated conduct between the parties involved, such as in the cases of Beiersdorf[39] and Pixelpark.[40]

Board neutrality and defensive measures

The target company's management – the management board and the supervisory board – is obliged to issue an opinion on the bid.[41] This statement addresses the consequences of a successful bid and the board's opinion as to the valuation of the target's shares. The reason behind this requirement is to provide the shareholders of the target company with more comprehensive information to help them decide whether or not to accept the bid. The target company's works council (or, if the target company does not have a works council, the individual employees) is granted the right to issue a statement of their own.

As a general rule pursuant to the German Takeover Act, the management board of a target company is subject to a 'duty of neutrality' in takeover bids and mandatory bids.[42] According to this principle, the target's management is generally prohibited from taking any defensive measures after the bidder's pre-bid announcement. However, this rule is subject to certain fundamental exceptions.

The prohibition does not apply to the search for a 'white knight', to measures approved by the supervisory board within the limits of its competence or to any action that a proper and prudent manager would have taken in the absence of the bid. In addition, at a shareholders' meeting, shareholders can authorise the management board to take actions designed to prevent a takeover bid.[43] The resolution of the shareholders' meeting, which requires a supermajority of three-quarters, must specify the proposed authorised actions in detail. Such authorisation may be granted for a maximum period of 18 months, which in practice means that the shareholders must renew any such authorisation at their annual general meeting. Actions that can be authorised at the shareholders' meeting include a capital increase out of authorised capital or the sale of certain assets.

Impact of the Takeover Directive

Supervisory authority and applicable law

In the future,[44] the BaFin will be responsible for the entire scope of bid-related supervision, but only if the target is exchange listed, and not just registered, in Germany. In other cases, a split between supervisory authorities within the various member states connected to the bid may occur. The provisions dealing with the BaFin's competence in the German Takeover Act will have to be adapted accordingly.

Disclosure of target's governance

Pursuant to Article 10 of the Takeover Directive, member states must ensure that all target companies within the meaning of the directive publish detailed information regarding the structure of their capital and their governance principles. The implementation of this provision in German law will require significant amendments to the legislative framework governing annual accounts of German companies. The additional information required under the Takeover Directive is to be included in the MD&A section of the financial statements (*Lagebericht*) according to Section 289 of the German Commercial Code (*Handelsgesetzbuch*).

According to the Bid Regulation,[45] a bidder's offer price in a mandatory or takeover bid must be at least equal to the highest price paid or agreed to by the bidder, or any person acting in concert with it, within the three-month period prior to obtaining control. In addition, the price to be offered must be at least equal to the weighted average domestic stock exchange price of the shares of the target company for the three-month period prior to announcement.

The Takeover Directive provides that the equitable price for a mandatory bid shall be the highest price paid for the same class of securities by the bidder, or by persons acting in concert with it, over a period of no less than six and no more than 12 months prior to the launch of the mandatory bid.[46]

In order to implement the Takeover Directive, the German legislature may decide to base the minimum pricing provisions for mandatory bids on a 'prior acquisition costs' approach or it may keep the present two-pronged approach. In any case, the reference period for determining the equitable price will have to be extended to at least six months.

Squeeze-out/sell-out

In connection with the enactment of the German Takeover Act, the German legislature introduced provisions dealing with the squeeze-out of minority shareholders in stock corporations where the main shareholder directly or indirectly holds at least 95 per cent of the stated capital.[47] This squeeze-out is applicable whether a public offer has led to the necessary threshold or not. Whereas the pricing provisions of the German Takeover Act apply regarding the bid price, the amount paid in the course of a later squeeze-out is calculated on the basis of a corporate valuation, usually leading to higher payments.

The Takeover Directive contains squeeze-out and sell-out provisions[48] that relate these measures to a preceding bid, since these measures may be carried out only within three months of the end of the bid period. These provisions also substantially deviate from the present German squeeze-out rules, since they contain certain price presumptions. The German legislature, however, is not required to cut back on the existing provisions governing squeeze-outs. The legislature will nevertheless be required to implement additional rules regarding post-bid squeeze- and sell-outs.

Frustrating actions

Regarding Articles 9 and 11 of the Takeover Directive (opt in/opt out mechanism), it is expected that Germany will make use of the right to opt out of Article 9(2) and (3) and Article 11, and that the shareholders of future German companies will have to decide whether their company should opt in. Additional legislative activity is still needed in order to provide a framework for companies whose shareholders decide to opt in. The legislature will also need to clarify the requirements for a shareholder 'opt in' resolution, as well as provide a set of rules governing frustrating actions taken by those companies.

Case studies

The following cases serve as examples of important transactions under the regime of the German Takeover Act.

> ### Case study: The UniCredit/HVB merger[49] – the largest cross-border banking merger in Europe
>
> UniCredito Italiano SpA (UniCredit) announced on 12 June 2005 its plan to launch a public offer for HVB. This is the largest cross-border banking merger in Europe to date. It is

also one of the largest takeover transactions in Germany and it is the largest share-for-share offer in Germany since the Vodafone/Mannesmann offer in 1999/2000. The offer period commenced in August 2005. Since HVB owns listed banks in Austria and also (indirectly) in Poland, UniCredit plans to launch public offers in Austria and Poland. These offers will have to be made in compliance with various regulatory regimes. This merger therefore represents the first test of a public multi-jurisdictional transaction in Europe.

Case study: The Blackstone/Celanese takeover[50] – a parallel German/US bid

Blackstone's takeover bid for shares in the German company Celanese AG contained the only parallel US bid that has been launched to date. Because Celanese AG's shares were listed on the New York Stock Exchange, the bid for Celanese was subject not only to the German publication requirements, but also to the reporting requirements of the US Securities Exchange Act 1934.

Shareholders of Celanese who tendered ordinary shares of Celanese, held in book-entry form through the Depository Trust Company or in certificated form in the North American registry, received the offer price in US dollars instead of euros. The actual amount of US dollars received by these shareholders depended upon the WM/Reuters US dollar/euro exchange rate on a specified business day. The offer document contained a variety of explanations pertaining specifically to shares listed in the United States. For example, the document contained specific information on the delisting of shares from the New York Stock Exchange and the fact that tendered shares could no longer be used as collateral for loans in such case. As Celanese shares were regarded as 'margin securities', brokers were permitted to extend credit, taking the securities as collateral.

Further, the offer document indicated that the bidder, in order to reconcile certain areas of conflict between German and US law, intended to request certain specific exemptive or no-action relief from the US Securities and Exchange Commission.

Case study: The Beiersdorf/Tchibo case – the test for 'coordinated conduct'

In October 2003, the German insurance company Allianz disposed of its 32.6 per cent stake in Beiersdorf AG by selling its shares to a consortium formed by Tchibo Holding AG, HGV[51] and TROMA.[52] According to press reports, this transaction was carried out in order to prevent an imminent takeover of Beiersdorf by Procter & Gamble. Tchibo had held a 30.3 per cent stake in Beiersdorf AG prior to the Act coming into force. The BaFin conducted an investigation, which, however, did not conclude that there was any evidence of coordinated conduct among the members of the consortium.[53] According to the BaFin, there was no relevant agreement or understanding regarding the exercise of voting rights in, or influence over, Beiersdorf AG. Further, the BaFin argued that, since Tchibo had held its controlling stake in Beiersdorf AG prior to the Act coming into force, it was not subject to the relevant provisions of the Act. Consequently, Tchibo did not 'gain' control over Beiersdorf in the sense of Section 35(1) sentence 1 of the German Takeover Code, since it was in the control position to bring influence to bear on Beiersdorf AG both before and after the establishment of the consortium.

PART II: EUROPEAN JURISDICTIONS

> **Case study: The Procter & Gamble/Wella takeover[54] – third-party rights**
>
> Procter & Gamble issued a takeover bid for the acquisition of all shares in Wella AG, a German producer of hairstyling and related products. This transaction resulted in a test of third-party rights in takeover scenarios. The price offered for common shares was €27.25 higher per share than the price offered for non-voting preferred shares. Despite this discrepancy, the BaFin approved the offer document. Some holders of preferred shares therefore filed an appeal against the approval. The appeal was dismissed on the basis that the appellants had no standing to submit an appeal or protest.[55] A constitutional complaint also failed.
>
> The court based its legal interpretation on the grounds that the takeover procedure contains no provisions for the protection of individuals' rights that the appellants could have used to support their petition. However, pursuant to the decision of the Federal Constitutional Court, fundamental violations of the provisions of the German Takeover Act might lead to a protected legal position of target company shareholders in some exceptional cases.
>
> Regarding the material issue of differential treatment of share classes in takeover bids, the BaFin accepted this distinction as being in compliance with the law.[56] The principle at stake is the equal treatment of shareholders, which is one of the key concerns of the German Takeover Act. The wording of the relevant provision is indeed very clear. According to the rule, only holders of securities of the target company belonging to the same 'class' shall be treated equally. Different classes of shares may therefore be permissibly treated differently under the German Takeover Act. Subsequent bids in the aftermath of the Wella takeover also treated share classes differently.[57]

---

[1] It is somewhat disputed whether the statutory seat of the target company, the factual place of business or the place of registration is decisive in this context.

[2] See Section 1 of the German Takeover Act.

[3] See the bid announced by UniCredito Italiano SpA to acquire shares in Bayerische Hypo- und Vereinsbank AG (announced on 12 June 2005; see also case studies below for this bid).

[4] See the bid made by Procter & Gamble Germany Management GmbH to the shareholders of Wella AG (published on 28 April 2003; see also case studies below for this bid): €4.65 billion.

[5] See the bid made by RAG Projektgesellschaft mbH to the shareholders of Degussa AG (published on 24 June 2002): €3.63 billion.

[6] See the bid made by DB Sechste Vermögensverwaltungsgesellschaft mbH to the shareholders of Stinnes AG (published on 7 August 2002): €2.38 billion.

[7] See Sections 29 to 34 of the German Takeover Act.

[8] See Section 29(2) of the German Takeover Act.

[9] See Sections 10 to 28 of the German Takeover Act.

[10] See, for example, the bid made by Deutsche Telekom AG to the shareholders of T-Online International AG (published on 26 November 2004).

[11] See Section 38 of the German Takeover Act.

[12] See Section 59 of the German Takeover Act.

[13] See Section 37(1) of the German Takeover Act.

[14] Obligation under Section 35(1) sentence 1 and 35(2) sentence 1 of the German Takeover Act.

[15] Regulation on the Contents of the Offer Document, the Consideration in the Case of Takeover Bids and the Exemption from the Obligation to Publish and Make a Bid.

[16] See the bid made by BNP Paribas SA to the shareholders of Consors Discount Broker AG (published on 12 June 2002).

[17] See Section 31(2) of the German Takeover Act. For further details, see the sub-section on pricing rules in the section 'Impact of the Takeover Directive' below.

[18] See Section 31(3) of the German Takeover Act.

[19] See Section 31(2) of the German Takeover Act.

[20] See Section 10(3) sentence 1 of the German Takeover Act.

[21] See Sections 14(1) sentence 1 and 35(2) sentence 1 of the German Takeover Act.

[22] See Section 14(1) sentence 3 of the German Takeover Act.

[23] See Section 11(1) sentences 2 and 3 of the German Takeover Act.

[24] See Section 11(2) of the German Takeover Act for details.

[25] See Section 13(1) sentence 2 of the German Takeover Act.

[26] See Section 16(1) sentence 2 of the German Takeover Act.

[27] Under Section 21(5) of the German Takeover Act.

[28] Under Section 22(2) of the German Takeover Act.

[29] Established by Section 18 of the German Takeover Act (which is subject to further special requirements, see Section 25).

[30] See, for example, the bid made by RAG Projektgesellschaft mbH to the shareholders of Degussa AG (published on 24 June 2002), the bid made by Robert Bosch GmbH to the shareholders of Buderus AG (published on 8 May 2003) or the bid launched by BCP Crystal Acquisition GmbH & Co KG (Blackstone) to acquire shares in Celanese AG (published on 2 February 2004; see also case studies below for this bid).

[31] See, for example, the bid made by Telco Holding Sàrl (Permira) to the shareholders of Debitel AG (published on 30 April 2004) and the bid made by Körber AG to the shareholders of Winkler + Dünnebier AG (published on 26 August 2004).

[32] See the bid made by GFKL Financial Services AG to the shareholders of ABIT AG (published on 10 October 2003).

[33] See, for example, the bid made by 2016091 Ontario Inc (Open Text) to the shareholders of IXOS Software AG (published on 22 September 2003) or the bid made by BorgWarner Germany GmbH to the shareholders of Beru AG (published on 8 December 2004).

[34] 'Acting in concert' under the City Code on Takeovers and Mergers is defined as, '... persons who, pursuant to an agreement or understanding (whether formal or informal), actively cooperate, through the acquisition by any of them of shares in the company, to obtain or consolidate control of that company'. (See part C. Definitions of the City Code, section 'acting in concert', para. 1.)

[35] See Higher Regional Court of Munich, *Zeitschrift für Wirtschaftsrecht [ZIP]* 2005, pp. 856–57; Higher Regional Court of Frankfurt am Main, *Zeitschrift für Wirtschaftsrecht [ZIP]* 2004, pp. 1309 *et seq.*; Higher Regional Court of Frankfurt am Main, *Zeitschrift für Wirtschaftsrecht [ZIP]* 2003, pp. 1977 *et seq.*; Regional Court of Munich I, *Der Betrieb* 2004, pp. 1252 *et seq.*; Regional Court of Munich I, *Zeitschrift für Wirtschaftsrecht [ZIP]* 2004, pp. 167 *et seq.*; Regional Court of Munich I, Decision of 3 January 2003, *Zeitschrift für Bank- und Kapitalmarktrecht [BKR]* 2003, pp. 810 *et seq.*

[36] See Klaus Riehmer in Haarmann, Riehmer and Schüppen (eds), *Öffentliche Übernahmeangebote* (Heidelberg: Verlag Wirtschaft und Recht, 2002), Section 30, annots 62.

[37] See Higher Regional Court of Munich, *Zeitschrift für Wirtschaftsrecht [ZIP]* 2005, pp. 856–57.

[38] See also Andreas Pentz, 'Acting in Concert – Ausgewählte Einzelprobleme zur Zurechnung und zu den Rechtsfolgen', *Zeitschrift für Wirtschaftsrecht [ZIP]* 2003, pp. 1478 and 1481, and Christoph von Bülow and Thomas Bücker, 'Abgestimmtes Verhalten im Kapitalmarkt- und Gesellschaftsrecht', *Zeitschrift für Unternehmens- und Gesellschaftsrecht [ZGR]* 2004, pp. 669 and 702, for details.

[39] See case studies below for this case.

[40] See Higher Regional Court of Frankfurt am Main, *Zeitschrift für Wirtschaftsrecht [ZIP]* 2003, pp. 1977 *et seq.* (summary proceedings) and *Zeitschrift für Wirtschaftsrecht [ZIP]* 2004, pp. 1309 *et seq.*

[41] See Section 27 of the German Takeover Act for details.

[42] Section 33(1) of the German Takeover Act. See Lars Röh in Haarmann, Riehmer and Schüppen (eds), *Öffentliche Übernahmeangebote* (Heidelberg: Verlag Wirtschaft und Recht, 2002), Section 33, annots 9 and 14; Heribert Hirte in *Kölner Kommentar zum Wertpapier- und Übernahmegesetz* (Cologne: Heymanns, 2003), Section 33, annots 26 *et seq.*

PART II: EUROPEAN JURISDICTIONS

[43] According to Section 33(2) of the German Takeover Act.
[44] Due to Article 4(2)(e) of the Takeover Directive.
[45] Sections 4 to 6 of the Bid Regulation.
[46] See Article 5(4) sentence 1 of the Takeover Directive.
[47] See Sections 327a *et seq.* of the German Stock Corporation Act (*Aktiengesetz*).
[48] In Articles 15 and 16 of the Takeover Directive.
[49] See the bid announced by UniCredito Italiano SpA to acquire shares in Bayerische Hypo- und Vereinsbank AG (announced on 12 June 2005).
[50] See the bid launched by BCP Crystal Acquisition GmbH & Co KG to acquire shares in Celanese AG (published on 2 February 2004).
[51] Hamburger Gesellschaft für Vermögens- und Beteiligungsverwaltung mbH, an investment vehicle owned by the city of Hamburg.
[52] TROMA Alters- und Hinterbliebenenstiftung, Beiersdorf AG's pension fund.
[53] See BaFin's press release dated 23 January 2004.
[54] See the bid made by Procter & Gamble Germany Management GmbH to the shareholders of Wella AG (published on 28 April 2003).
[55] Higher Regional Court of Frankfurt am Main, *Zeitschrift für Wirtschaftsrecht [ZIP]* 2003, pp. 1392 *et seq.* See also Higher Regional Court of Frankfurt am Main, *Zeitschrift für Wirtschaftsrecht [ZIP]*, 2003, pp. 1251 *et seq.* (summary proceedings).
[56] Section 3(1) of the German Takeover Act.
[57] See, for example, the bid made by Turbo Group GmbH (German Equity Partners) to the shareholders of Aktiengesellschaft Kühnle, Kopp & Kausch (published on 7 April 2005).

Chapter 15

Greece

Alexander Metallinos
Karatzas & Partners, Athens

The Greek rules on takeover bids are contained in Decision No. 2/258/5.12.2002 (the Decision) of the Capital Markets Commission (CMC), which replaced Decision No. 1/195/19.7.2000. However, the legal framework for takeover bids is expected to be significantly amended soon through the transposition of Directive 2004/25/EC of the European Parliament and of the Council of 21 April 2004 on takeover bids (the Takeover Directive). Such transposition must take place by 20 May 2006.

Both Decision 2/258/5.12.2002 and Decision 1/195/19.7.2000 were based on Article 19, paragraph 2 of Law 2733/1999, which authorised the CMC to regulate takeover bids. It is doubtful, however, whether such authorisation covers all aspects of the Decision of 2002. In particular, the regulation of mandatory bids is not mentioned at all in the authorising law and therefore the relevant provisions fall outside the scope of the authorisation. Since provisions lacking authorisation are not valid, if there is judicial review of any act of the CMC seeking to enforce them, administrative courts would probably annul such acts. Nevertheless, market participants have, by and large, complied with the Decision and have not attempted to have parts of it declared invalid by the courts.

The problem of lack of proper authorisation for part of the Decision is likely to be solved upon incorporation of the Takeover Directive into Greek law, since a law or a presidential decree implementing the Takeover Directive is likely to replace the Decision.

The Decision applies to takeover bids for companies listed on the Athens Stock Exchange (AthEx), irrespective of whether such companies are governed by Greek law or by the law of another state. Nevertheless, the provisions on mandatory bids apply only to companies governed by Greek law.

The Takeover Directive contains detailed rules concerning the international jurisdiction of supervisory authorities and applicable law:

- if the target company is listed in a market of the EU member state where it has its registered office, the supervisory authority of that member state has jurisdiction and its law governs the tender offer;
- if the shares of the target company are listed in a market of an EU member state different from the one where it has its registered office, (i) the supervisory authority of the member state of trading has international jurisdiction over, and the law of that member state governs matters relating to, the consideration offered and the bid procedure; while (ii) the supervisory authority of the member state of the registered office has jurisdiction over, and

PART II: EUROPEAN JURISDICTIONS

its law governs matters relating to, the information to be provided to the employees of the target company, as well as company law, in particular the percentage of voting rights that confers control and any derogation from the obligation to launch a bid, and also the conditions under which the board of the offeree company may undertake any action that might result in the frustration of the bid.

The Takeover Directive contains detailed rules for the case of a multiple listing of the target company, if none of the markets is located in the member state of its registered office.

Conditionality of offers

According to Article 14 of the Decision, offers may not be subject to conditions other than those relating to any regulatory approvals required, such as anti-trust approvals, or to approvals required for the issuance of securities to be offered in non-cash offers, such as shareholders' approvals for the issuance of shares to be offered in exchange for the target shares.

The offeror cannot set as a condition the absence of a material adverse change in the target. However, in offers other than mandatory offers, the offeror may revoke the offer pursuant to an approval of the CMC if a change in circumstances that is unpredictable and is independent of the will of the offeror renders the maintenance of the offer particularly cumbersome to the offeror. It is crucial that the offeror may not determine itself that there has been such a change in circumstances, but must rely on a decision of the CMC.

The Takeover Directive has left the matter of permitted conditions attached to an offer to be governed by national laws of member states.

Procedure

Takeover bids are launched by informing the CMC and the board of directors of the target, in writing. On the day following such notification, the offeror has to announce the takeover bid to the public by publishing an announcement in the daily price bulletin of the AthEx and in newspapers (as specified in the Decision) containing, *inter alia,* the maximum and minimum numbers of shares to be purchased, the consideration offered and the number of shares already held by the offeror.

The offeror must also prepare an information memorandum, which is submitted for approval to the CMC. The CMC must approve the information memorandum within 10 business days of a complete draft being submitted to it. The information memorandum must also be signed by an adviser to the offeror, who must certify the accuracy of the contents of the information memorandum, and must state in a separate part of the information memorandum his opinion on the methods and procedure for the fulfilment of the offeror's obligations, and on the credibility of the tender offer. This adviser must be a credit institution or an investment services undertaking authorised to provide in Greece the investment service of underwriting.

In cash offers, a credit institution operating in the EU must certify that the offeror has the financial means to pay the entire amount that is payable in cash. In an offer with existing securities as consideration, the credit institution must certify that the offeror has in his possession the securities offered. If the consideration consists of securities created for this purpose, the credit institution must certify that the offeror has taken all appropriate measures in order to be able to fulfil its obligation to deliver the securities.

The offering memorandum must be made available to the public within three business days of its approval by the CMC. The period of acceptance must commence within three business days of the publication of the offering memorandum. Its duration is set by the offeror and may not be shorter than 30 days or longer than 60 days. The period of acceptance may be prolonged by up to 10 days by a decision of the CMC. In competitive offers, the period of acceptance of the initial offer is extended so that it ends simultaneously with the competitive offer.

The offeror must appoint one or more credit institutions and/or investment services undertakings to act as its agents for the receipt of the acceptances (tender agents). Acceptances are revocable, unless it is stated in the information memorandum that they are irrevocable. During the time between the announcement of the tender offer and the end of the acceptance period, the offeror may purchase shares in the market, but is obliged to notify each such purchase to the CMC and the AthEx.

Until five business days before the end of the acceptance period, the offeror may revise the offer, provided that such revision is in no manner to the detriment of the addressees of the offer. Competitive offers may be submitted until seven business days after the end of the acceptance period of the initial offer, but in any case within 40 days after its commencement.

Within two business days after the end of the acceptance period, the offeror must announce the results of the tender offer. If the offer is successful, the shares are transferred off exchange to the offeror. In practice, the acceptance forms collected by the tender agent contain irrevocable powers of attorney to the tender agent to transfer the shares to the offeror. The tender agent pays or, in an offer in kind, transfers the consideration to the accepting shareholders.

Voluntary offers

In voluntary offers, the offeror must seek to acquire a proportion of voting shares exceeding 50 per cent, including any shares that the offeror may already own. He must also specify the minimum number of shares to be tendered in order for the tender offer to be considered successful. If such number is not achieved, the tender offer fails and the offeror cannot acquire any shares tendered. Such number cannot be less than 40 per cent of the shares, including any shares the offeror may already own.

In partial offers, where the offeror seeks to acquire less than 100 per cent of the voting shares of the target company, if the offeror receives acceptances for more shares than those he is seeking to acquire, the acceptances are to be satisfied *pro rata*.

Mandatory offers – the implied concept of control

If a shareholder or a group of shareholders acting in concert acquires more than 50 per cent of a listed company's voting shares, they are obliged to launch a mandatory offer for all the outstanding voting shares of that company within 30 days of crossing the 50 per cent threshold. Contrary to the Takeover Directive, the Decision does not use the term 'control', but implicitly defines control as acquiring more than 50 per cent of the voting shares of a company. The threshold has been set very high, as in a listed company one can certainly exercise control by virtue of holding 50 per cent, but no more, of the shares, or indeed significantly less.

The Takeover Directive provides that a bid must be launched if a party acquires control over a company, but leaves the determination of the percentage that confers control to the national laws of member states.

In addition, the obligation to launch a mandatory offer is subject to a number of exceptions. Specifically, the obligation does not apply in the following cases:

- if the shares, the acquisition of which leads to crossing the 50 per cent threshold, are acquired without consideration;
- if the shareholder acquiring more than 50 per cent undertakes to merge with the company;
- if crossing the 50 per cent threshold is the result of a merger, division or spin-off;
- if the shareholder in question acquires up to 53 per cent and undertakes to dispose of the shares exceeding 50 per cent within one year;
- if crossing the 50 per cent threshold is the result of exercising pre-emption rights in a rights offering;
- if the 50 per cent threshold was crossed through a voluntary offer by virtue of which the relevant shareholder acquired at least 25 per cent of the voting shares;
- if the acquisition of more than 50 per cent is the result of a privatisation;
- pursuant to a decision of the CMC, if the acquisition of more than 50 per cent is the result of a composition of a company in distress with its creditors in the framework of a pre-insolvency composition provided for in Greek law;
- if the acquisition of shares leading to the crossing of the 50 per cent threshold was the result of the performance of an underwriting obligation; or
- if trading in the shares in question has been suspended for at least 12 months.

The combination of the high threshold and these numerous exceptions has made it relatively easy to structure transactions in such a manner that the obligation to launch a mandatory offer is not triggered. By way of example, on three occasions, the acquisition of Saint George Mills, a shell company, by Constantine Balafas, an entrepreneur; the acquisition of Nikas SA, a leading processed food manufacturer, by Global Finance, a private equity fund; and the acquisition of Aluminium of Greece SA by Mytilineos Group of Companies, a metals conglomerate – purchasers in private transactions acquired up to 53 per cent of the shares of a listed company and undertook to dispose of the shares in excess of 50 per cent within one year in order to avoid having to launch a mandatory tender offer. As a result, in practice, mandatory offers have mostly been launched only in cases where the offeror intended anyway to take the company private and would have made an offer even if there were no such obligation.

The Takeover Directive provides for only one exception to the obligation to launch a bid, where the percentage leading to control was achieved through a voluntary bid for all of the target company's shares. Therefore, it will not be sufficient to acquire control through a partial offer, as is the case under current Greek law. This is likely to have the effect of rendering partial bids pointless, since, if a partial bid is successful, the offeror will have to launch a further bid for the remaining shares.

Member states have the right to introduce further derogations from the obligation to launch a mandatory bid, provided that the basic principles of the directive are respected. Therefore, certain of the existing exceptions may be included in the legislation that will incorporate the directive into Greek law.

However, a number of the existing exceptions are incompatible with the principles of the directive and cannot be maintained. For example, the current exception related to privatisation creates a privilege for the state in its capacity as shareholder, which is incompatible with the equal treatment of shareholders provided for in Article 3 of the directive.

Mandatory offers have to be launched at a price equal to the higher of (i) the highest price at which the offeror acquired shares over the last six months prior to the offer; and (ii) the average price of the shares over the last 12 months prior to the offer. The inclusion of the average price as a minimum price can create problems, in particular in falling markets, leading on occasion to the payment of a higher price to minority shareholders compared with the price paid to the majority shareholder. This has increased the incentive to structure transactions in a manner that avoids triggering a mandatory offer. In this manner, a rule that was intended to protect minority shareholders has in fact operated against their interests.

The Takeover Directive provides that mandatory offers have to be made at an equitable price, which is the highest price paid for the relevant securities by the offeror within a period prior to the bid. The period is to be determined by each member state, but must be between six and 12 months. Member states may authorise their supervisory authorities to adjust the equitable price, taking into account, *inter alia,* the average price of the shares over a period of time. Nevertheless, this will have to be determined case by case; the existing hard and fast rule cannot continue to apply after the transposition of the Takeover Directive.

The position of the board of directors of the target company

The Decision regulates the position of the board of directors of the target company in two ways. On the one hand, it provides for an obligation to express an opinion on the tender offer; on the other, it curtails the board's powers during the period of the tender offer.

Within 10 days of the publication of the information memorandum, the board of directors of the target company must express in writing its reasoned opinion on the tender offer. This statement must be accompanied by a detailed report by a financial adviser (a credit institution or investment services undertaking authorised to provide underwriting services in Greece) and must, *inter alia,* express the opinion of the board of directors on the effects of the tender offer on the interests of the company and its employees.

During the period that starts with the notification of the board of directors of the tender offer and ends with the announcement of the result of the tender offer, the powers of the board of directors of the target company are curtailed, so that it is not permitted to use such powers to cause the tender offer to fail. Specifically, the board of directors is prohibited from increasing the target company's capital and from issuing convertible bonds unless it was authorised to do so within the previous 18 months. It is also prohibited from taking any actions that materially change the assets or liabilities of the target company, or that would materially bind its future business policy, unless these actions were decided before the submission of the tender offer.

It is worth noting that, due to constraints imposed by Greek corporate law, many of the usual defences used in other countries against hostile bids are not available to Greek companies:

- Greek company law provides for the 'one share, one vote' principle. The only exception to this principle is the possibility of issuing non-voting preferred shares. Therefore, it is not possible for the articles of association of a company to provide for voting ceilings or shares with multiple voting rights;

- the board of directors cannot decide the distribution of dividends, other than an interim dividend regarding up to 50 per cent of the profits of the part of the relevant financial year elapsed, and therefore it cannot use the distribution of special dividends as 'poison pills';
- the board of directors, even if it is authorised to issue new shares or convertible bonds, does not have the authority to waive pre-emption rights, and therefore the possibility of issuing new shares as a takeover defence is of limited value;
- contracts with members of the board of directors and senior managers require prior shareholders' approval. Therefore, unless 'golden parachutes' are already in place before the bid, the board cannot put them in place during the bid without seeking shareholders' approval;
- shareholders owning 5 per cent or more of a company's capital may cause a shareholders' meeting to be postponed by up to 30 days. Taking into account that a meeting needs to be convened 20 days in advance, it becomes apparent that if the bidder, or a party acting in concert with the bidder, owns 5 per cent or more of the shares, they can effectively stop the board of directors from seeking approval for the takeover defences, which require shareholders' approval.

Accordingly, the main defence that a board of directors may use is to seek a 'white knight'. Indeed, it could be argued that the board of directors has a duty to explore the possibility of a better bid before issuing a positive opinion on a takeover bid.

The Decision as it currently stands already mostly meets the requirements of Article 9 of the directive regarding the obligations of the board of the offeree company. In addition, generally applicable company law is already compatible with the terms of Article 11 of the directive. Therefore it seems unlikely that Greece would make use of Article 12 of the directive, which permits each member state not to apply Article 9(2) and (3) and/or Article 11 to companies registered within its jurisdiction.

Purchase of minority shareholdings

The Decision does not contain provisions on the mandatory purchase of minority shareholdings (squeeze-out) or for the right of minority shareholders to sell their shares to the offeror (reverse squeeze-out). Nevertheless, an offeror that is a Greek company limited by shares may achieve substantially the same result as a squeeze-out by using the procedure of a cash-out merger, which does exist under Greek company law. Under this procedure, a company may absorb another, giving cash instead of shares to the latter's shareholders. If an offeror that is a Greek company limited by shares has acquired two-thirds of the shares of the target company, it can force a decision of the target company's general meeting for a cash-out merger, effectively forcing the minority shareholders to sell their shares. No equivalent procedure exists for a reverse squeeze-out.

The absence of a squeeze-out procedure creates practical problems in cases of successful bids, which the cash-out merger procedure is too cumbersome and time consuming to solve. A company may seek to have its shares delisted upon a decision of its shareholders' meeting with a majority of 95 per cent of all of its shareholders. Such delisting is then decided by the CMC. Successful offerors that acquire more than 95 per cent of the shares of the target company typically cause the target company to decide on delisting. However, as a practical matter, some minority shareholders neglect to accept the offer or, for some reason, fail to transfer their shares to the offeror. This is detrimental both for the offeror, which does not have the flexibility of having a wholly owned subsidiary, and for the minority shareholders, who are left with non-liquid shares.

These problems will be solved through the transposition of the Takeover Directive. This provides for both squeeze-out and reverse squeeze-out if the offeror acquires a minimum percentage of the voting securities of the company or of the shares comprised in the bid. The purchase of the shares has to be done at a fair price. The consideration offered in a voluntary bid will be presumed to be fair where, through acceptance of the bid, the offeror has acquired securities representing not less than 90 per cent of the capital carrying voting rights comprised in the bid. The consideration offered in a mandatory bid will be presumed to be fair.

Major considerations for bidders

Bidders in Greek takeovers should take the following major considerations into account:

- the limited possibility of setting conditions for the success of the takeover and, hence, the risk that the bidder may have to acquire the shares even where there is a deterioration in the business of the target during the offer period (unless the CMC permits a revocation of the offer);
- the possibility of acquiring shares during the offer period;
- the obligation to launch a mandatory tender offer and the various exemptions from this obligation;
- the minimum price in mandatory tender offers;
- the obligation to have available the consideration for the tender offer, in particular, in cash bids financed through debt, the offeror must ensure that the lenders will commit to provide financing, subject only to any permitted conditions of the tender offer;
- the fact that, due to restrictions under the Decision and general Greek company law, the target company's board of directors cannot use most of the takeover defences used in other jurisdictions;
- the requirement of a 95 per cent majority in order to delist the shares;
- the absence of squeeze-out provisions, alongside the possibility of indirectly achieving a squeeze-out through a cash-out merger;
- the absence of a reverse squeeze-out obligation of an acquiring shareholder;
- the possibility that the legal framework will change in the short term due to the pending incorporation of the Takeover Directive.

Chapter 16

Hungary

András Posztl
DLA Weiss-Tessback Horváth & Partners, Budapest

The Hungarian takeover regime does not have a long history. The first 'post-socialist' Companies Act entered into force in 1988, but the first takeover rules entered into force only 10 years later. This is not surprising, since it was only after the first privatisation waves of the 1990s that it became possible to talk about a 'capital/takeover market' in Hungary in any meaningful sense.

The first takeover rules were introduced in 1998, when the Securities Act was amended with a new chapter setting out the rules applicable to takeovers. The incompleteness of the first takeover regime became obvious when Russian and Austrian shareholders of BorsodChem, a major Hungarian listed company, were accused of infringing the takeover rules by 'acting in concert', a concept not known to the takeover rules in effect at the time.

> **Case study: The takeover battle for BorsodChem, 2000**
>
> In 2000, Milford Holdings Ltd, an Irish company under the control of Russian investors, acquired a minority stake of about 25 per cent in BorsodChem, one of the largest Hungarian petrochemical companies listed on the Budapest Stock Exchange (BSE). At about the same time, CE Oil & Gas AG, an Austrian special purpose vehicle belonging to VCP Capital Partners AG, a private equity investment house, also acquired a minority stake in BorsodChem. At the general meeting of BorsodChem held in January 2001, the Russian and Austrian investors voted together on the removal of some of the members of the management board and the supervisory board, and elected new members.
>
> The Hungarian Financial Supervisory Authority (HFSA) commenced an investigation to find out whether infringement of the takeover rules could be established on the basis of the result of the voting. In its resolution, the HFSA concluded that the circumstances were not sufficient to establish that the two groups were acting in concert (the voting in itself was not sufficient for such finding) and, even if it had found that they had acted in concert, the takeover rules at that time provided no legal basis to declare that such a practice violated the takeover rules.

In response to the BorsodChem affair, the Securities Act was amended in 2001 to plug the loophole in the previous system (the so-called 'Lex BorsodChem'). A few months later, the new regime established by the amendment was carried over to Act CXX of 2001 on the Capital Market (the Capital Market Act or CMA), a consolidated act regulating the Hungarian capital market and replacing the Securities Act.

Nature of the takeover rules and enforcement

Currently, the rules relating to takeovers are set out in sections 65–80 of the CMA. Certain provisions of Act CXLIV of 1997 on business associations (the Companies Act) are also relevant in the context of takeovers. Although the CMA expressly authorises stock exchanges to make further rules applicable to listed companies, the BSE has not issued any such rule yet. Thus, the current Hungarian takeover regime is based on mandatory laws.

Unlike certain other takeover regimes, the Hungarian takeover rules apply to all public companies and not only to listed companies.

The takeover rules of the CMA are enforced primarily by the HFSA. Resolutions of the HFSA are subject to judicial review.

Definition of 'control'

In the CMA, both the disclosure obligations and the obligation to make a takeover bid are based on the concept of 'control'. The CMA differentiates three forms of 'control' (*befolyás*).

Acquisition of voting rights

The basic concept of control is linked to the 'acquisition of voting rights enabling the acquirer to participate in the decision making of the target company's general meeting'. According to the CMA, voting rights may be acquired both as a result of the acquirer's deliberate acts, such as purchase agreements, exercise of call options or usufruct agreements on voting rights, and as a result of acts not attributable to the acquirer, such as legal succession, decisions of the target affecting voting rights or purchase of treasury shares.

Voting rights may be acquired not only through the acquisition of the shares of the target company, but also through the acquisition of secondary securities (global depositary receipts or American depositary receipts) issued with respect to the underlying shares.

Control may be acquired directly as well as indirectly, that is, through an 'intermediary company'. In the case of indirect control, the extent of control must be calculated by multiplying the percentages of shares/voting rights held by the acquirer in the intermediary company by the larger of the percentages of shares *or* the percentages of voting rights held by the intermediary company in the target company. If the percentage of shareholding/voting rights held by the acquirer in the intermediary company is higher than 50 per cent, acquisitions through the intermediary company are 100 per cent attributed to the acquirer. When calculating the extent of the control to be acquired, the control to be acquired directly and the control to be acquired indirectly must be aggregated. Similarly, in the case of natural persons, acquisitions by close relatives must be added up for the purposes of the takeover rules.

Control agreements

Under the CMA, control may also be acquired if shareholders of the target company enter into an agreement that entitles a shareholder to appoint and/or remove the majority of the members of the management board or the supervisory board of the target company, or sets out jointly agreed principles to be followed by the contracting shareholders regarding the management/control of the target company.

PART II: EUROPEAN JURISDICTIONS

Concerted action

The CMA expressly provides that control may be acquired via a 'concerted action' among independent persons. However, the CMA does not provide any guidance as to the meaning of 'concerted action', so the concept has been given meaning via the practice of the HFSA (see the discussion of the Zalakeramia case below).

Disclosure of acquisition of control

Disclosure by the acquirer

A party acquiring control must notify the HFSA and the management board of the target company within two calendar days of acquiring control equal to or exceeding 5 per cent. All subsequent acquisitions are subject to the same obligation in 5 per cent stages (that is, on reaching or crossing thresholds of 10 per cent, 15 per cent, 20 per cent and so on) up to 50 per cent control in the target company. The CMA expressly authorises corporations to lower the notification threshold from 5 per cent to 2 per cent. Above 50 per cent, only the reaching of the 75 per cent and 90 per cent thresholds is subject to notification. The rules also apply *mutatis mutandis* to decreases in control.

Under the CMA, the acquirer must also arrange for the publication of its acquisition/disposal of control contemporaneously with making the above notification. Such publication must be made in a national daily, or on the website designated by the HFSA for such purposes, or on the website of the target company or the stock exchange (regulated market) on which the relevant securities are traded.

Contingent acquisitions of control are also subject to the disclosure regime discussed above. Accordingly, even if, pursuant to an agreement, control is acquired only at a later date or if certain conditions are met, the disclosure obligations must be complied with on the date of the agreement. In such cases, the date of, or the conditions precedent to, the acquisition of control must be disclosed.

Until it discharges its notification and publication obligations, the acquirer of control may not exercise its shareholder rights in the target company.

Disclosure by the target company

In addition to disclosure by the party acquiring control, listed companies must issue an extraordinary announcement regarding any event that may have a (potential) impact on their share price, including any changes in their ownership structure exceeding 5 per cent. Such notification must be made to the HFSA within one business day and the relevant stock exchange(s) in accordance with the applicable stock exchange rules.

Further, under the CMA, the target company must also publish a notice of the acquisition of control promptly, but in any case within a maximum of nine days, in all member states of the EU where the shares of the target company are admitted to trading in a regulated market.

Mandatory takeover bids

Under the CMA, as a general rule, acquisition of control in a public company exceeding 33 per cent requires a mandatory takeover bid approved by the HFSA. However, the CMA lowers the mandatory takeover bid threshold to 25 per cent in the case of diffusedly owned companies, that is if no shareholder other than the acquirer holds a shareholding in the target company representing more than 10 per cent of the voting rights.

As a general rule, the bid must be made before the acquirer crosses the bid threshold (*ex ante* bids). However, the CMA specifies four cases where the bid must be made after the acquisition of control exceeding the applicable threshold, so that the mandatory bid is *ex post* if control is acquired:

- otherwise than as a result of the deliberate conduct of the acquirer; or
- as a result of the exercise of a purchase (call) option or a repurchase option, or the completion of a forward purchase agreement; or
- in the course of a privatisation procedure, which is subject to a separate special statutory regime; or
- pursuant to an agreement regarding control over the target company.

In such cases, the acquisition of control must be disclosed in accordance with the general rules and the mandatory takeover bid must be made within 15 days of date of notification by the acquirer of control to the HFSA.

The takeover regime enshrined in the CMA is extremely rigid, as the CMA does not contain any exemption from the obligation to make a takeover bid if the applicable threshold is crossed and does not grant any power to the HFSA to exempt certain transactions from the takeover rules.

When control is to be acquired pursuant to an agreement, the parties to such an agreement must make the takeover bid jointly, unless they agree otherwise as regards the identity of the offeror. However, even if there is such an agreement, all parties to the agreement remain liable for making the mandatory bid. These rules also apply to parties acting in concert.

The mandatory bid must be made to all shareholders and for all the outstanding voting shares of the target company, that is, in the case of mandatory takeover bids, partial bids are not permitted.

The bid may not be made on terms that discriminate among shareholders of the target company as regards the acceptance of the bid. Further, the bid may not be made subject to conditions, except that the offeror may reserve the right to withdraw the bid if its control in the target company is less than 50 per cent after the closing of the takeover procedure.

The CMA describes in detail the actual content of the offer, which must include, among other things, extensive information on:

- the bidder;
- the target company;
- the offer price;
- the acceptance period and the method of acceptance;
- the bidder's business plan for the target company; and
- documentary evidence of the availability of the funds required for the financing of the bid.

Calculation of the minimum offer price

Since the CMA applies to all Hungarian public companies and not only to listed companies, the CMA provides rules for calculation of the minimum offer price in both cases.

PART II: EUROPEAN JURISDICTIONS

As regards listed target companies, the minimum offer price is the higher of the weighted average stock exchange price for the 180-day period preceding the date when the bid was submitted to the HFSA for approval (the 'reference period') and the highest price contracted by the bidder and its affiliates for the transfer of the shares of the target company during the reference period, or – in the case of the exercise of a (re)purchase right – the aggregate of the call price and the option fee.

As regards unlisted target companies, the minimum offer price is calculated in accordance with the above rule, but in such cases the starting point is the weighted average over-the-counter (OTC) price, based on 'OTC fixings', for the reference period.

If, for any reason, the minimum offer price cannot be determined according to the above rules, the minimum price is calculated in accordance with the formulae contained in the bid and approved by the HFSA. The HFSA attempted to interpret this fall-back provision creatively in the Brau Hungária/Heineken case (see below).

Form of the offer price

The bid may provide for the financing of the offer price:

- in cash;
- in Hungarian government securities or government securities issued by other OECD member states; and/or
- by bank guarantee issued by a credit institution with a seat in Hungary or in another OECD member state.

Notwithstanding the foregoing, the bidder must be in a position to pay the total amount of the consideration in cash, since accepting shareholders may always request that the offer price be paid in cash.

Case study: Brau Hungária Rt./Heineken Group (2004)

In 2004, Amstel Rt., a Hungarian subsidiary of Heineken Group, made a takeover bid for the shares of Brau Hungária Rt., a listed Hungarian brewery. A few months earlier, Heineken Group had also acquired the Austrian parent company of Brau Hungária. The purchase price offered for the shares of the Austrian parent company and that offered for the shares of Brau Hungária were different, owing to different legislation being in force and the different stock exchange average prices.

The Hungarian Association of Stock Exchange Minority Investors took the view that the price applied by the Heineken Group in Hungary was unfair, since it was much lower than the price applied in neighbouring Austria. Therefore, the association contested the decision of the HFSA approving the offer.

As a result of the challenge, the HFSA made some corrections to the purchase price, but it was still much lower than that applied in Austria. Following further legal battles and investigation, the HFSA established that the purchase price for the shares cannot be established taking into consideration the weighted average stock exchange price over 180 days, since the circumstances of stock exchange trade were not clear enough. As a result, the HFSA obliged the bidder to establish the purchase price on the basis of the formula set by

> the HFSA. By this resolution, the HFSA set aside the obligation to determine the purchase price on the basis of the weighted average stock exchange price for the previous 180 days, which had previously been standard practice.

Trading prohibition

Up until the closing of the acceptance period, the bidder(s) and its/their affiliates are prohibited from entering into transactions for the transfer or encumbering of the shares subject to the takeover bid. Similarly, the investment service provider acting on behalf of the bidder may not enter into a transaction regarding the shares subject to the bid for its own account until the closing of the acceptance period.

Follow-on acquisitions if threshold is crossed

If, as a result of the bid, the bidder acquires control in the target company in excess of 33 per cent (or 25 per cent, if applicable), it may subsequently further increase its control without having to make a new takeover bid. However, if the acquirer's control later decreases below the takeover bid threshold, crossing the threshold will require a new takeover bid.

Voluntary takeover bids

Under the CMA, it is also possible to make a takeover bid in cases where this is not mandated by the CMA. In such voluntary takeover bids, the rules applicable to mandatory bids apply, with a few exceptions:

- partial bids are permitted – the bidder is free to define the size of the control that it intends to acquire and, if the number of shares offered for sale exceeds the number of shares that the bidder intends to acquire, the offered shares are accepted *pro rata*;
- the management board of the target company is not obliged to provide an opinion on the bid, nor is it not entitled to engage an independent financial adviser at the target company's expense in connection with the assessment of the bid;
- competing offers cannot be made;
- no voluntary takeover bid may be made during a mandatory takeover bid (from the date of publication of the mandatory bid until the end of the acceptance period).

The takeover procedure

Exhibit 16.1 presents an illustrative timeline of a takeover procedure under Hungarian law. In an actual transaction, the dates may vary, owing to the needs of the transaction involving, for example, the length of the acceptance period or publication dates and/or owing to the reaction of the HFSA or the competition authority involved in the bid.

Launch of the bid

The bidder has to employ an investment service provider licensed by the HFSA to administer the offer procedure.

PART II: EUROPEAN JURISDICTIONS

Exhibit 16.1
Illustrative timeline of a takeover procedure under Hungarian law[1]

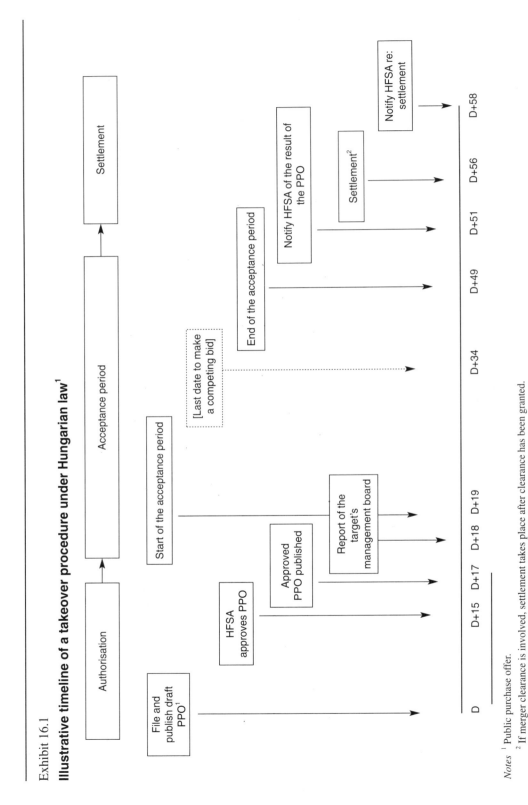

Notes: [1] Public purchase offer.
[2] If merger clearance is involved, settlement takes place after clearance has been granted.

Source: Author's own.

At the launch of the takeover procedure, the bidder must simultaneously submit the takeover bid:

- to the HFSA for approval;
- to the management board of the target company; and
- for publication, expressly indicating that the bid is not yet approved by the HFSA and that the bidder has also applied (where necessary) for competition clearance.

If competition clearance is necessary, it must be filed within 30 days of the first publication of the takeover bid.

The HFSA has 15 days to approve or reject the bid. The HFSA may also require the submission of additional documents from the bidder, which must be done within five days. Following the receipt of such additional documents, the HFSA must decide on the bid within five days. If the HFSA fails to make any decision by the statutory deadline, the bid is deemed to be approved. If the bid submitted to the HFSA is in compliance with the provisions of the CMA, the HFSA may not refuse to approve the bid.

Acceptance period, assessment of the bid, withdrawal of the acceptance

Following the approval of the bid by the HFSA, it must be published once again, with indications of the commencement and closing dates of the acceptance period. The acceptance period may not be shorter than 30 days or longer than 45 days. The first day of the acceptance period may not be earlier than the second day or later than the fifth day following the publication of the final bid. The acceptance period may be extended by 15 days upon the bidder's request, subject to the HFSA's approval. The bidder may not amend/change its bid, except to increase the offer price.

The management board of the target company must give its opinion on the bid and make its opinion available to the shareholders before the commencement date of the acceptance period. In connection with this obligation, the CMA expressly notes that the management board may engage an independent financial adviser for the purpose of evaluating the bid, at the expense of the target company. The adviser's report must also be made available to the shareholders of the target company.

The statements of acceptance by the shareholders of the target company may not be withdrawn, unless the bidder fails to pay the purchase price by the statutory deadline (see below).

Competing bid

A competing bid may be made until the 15th day preceding the closing date of the acceptance period of the initial bid. The provisions relating to mandatory bids also apply to competing bids.

Under the CMA, the HFSA may approve a competing bid only if the offer price contained therein is at least 5 per cent higher than the offer price in the initial bid. Upon approval and publication of the competing bid, the initial takeover bid and the related statements of acceptance become ineffective.

Closing of the takeover procedure

The share purchase agreements between the bidder and the selling shareholders are deemed to be entered into on the closing day of the acceptance period, unless a merger clearance procedure is still pending on that day. In the latter case, the agreements are deemed to be entered into on the date of the merger clearance (if granted).

The bidder must notify the HFSA of the result of the offer within two calendar days after the closing of the acceptance period. The bidder must pay the purchase price to the selling shareholders within five business days after the closing day of the acceptance period (or the date of the merger clearance, if applicable) and must notify the HFSA of the payment within two days. If the purchase price is not paid within 30 days of the due date, the selling shareholders are entitled to withdraw their statements of acceptance.

Squeeze-out and sell-out rights

Squeeze-out right

If, as a result of its takeover bid, a bidder acquires more than 90 per cent of the voting rights in the target company, the bidder becomes entitled to buy out ('squeeze-out') the remaining shares that have not been offered for sale in the takeover procedure. The squeeze-out right may be exercised only within the 30 days following the publication of the result of the bid and only if the offer price has been paid in full to all selling shareholders.

However, owing to the clumsy wording of the CMA, it is questionable whether the squeeze-out right is available if the 90 per cent threshold is crossed otherwise than 'as a result of' a takeover bid – so that, if the bid results in 89 per cent control, then the bidder increases its control to above 90 per cent without making a new bid – or if a second takeover bid already starts from a level of control of 90 per cent plus.

In a squeeze-out, the purchase price of the shares must be the higher of the offer price applicable in the underlying takeover bid and the per-share shareholders' equity of the target company, as indicated in the last audited annual report of the target company.

If the hold-out shareholders of the target company fail to hand over their shares in accordance with the squeeze-out notice, the target company cancels such shares.

Sell-out right

Under the CMA, if a bidder's control in the target company 'following the closing of' the takeover procedure represents more than 90 per cent of the voting rights, the hold-out shareholders have a right to request that the bidder buys out their shares at a price calculated in accordance with the corresponding rules applicable to buy-out rights (see above). The sell-out rights may be exercised only within the 30 days following the closing of the takeover procedure. Owing to the difference in the wording, the sell-out right, unlike the squeeze-out right, is always triggered on crossing the 90 per cent threshold, irrespective of whether that crossing takes place within or outside a takeover procedure.

Defensive tactics

The CMA and the Companies Act are based on the principle of shareholder supremacy as regards defensive tactics. Accordingly, the CMA expressly provides that, as from the receipt of the takeover bid, the management board of the target company is prohibited from making any decision that may 'disturb' the takeover procedure, for example to increase the registered capital or purchase treasury shares. If the board is aware of a takeover bid before its launch, the prohibition applies as from the date on which the board received information on the coming bid. The management board of the target company has very little room for manoeuvre as regards defence.

As regards decision making by the shareholders of the target company, the Companies Act provides that, once the general meeting of the target company has become aware of the takeover bid, all decisions that may 'disturb' the takeover procedure, for example to increase the registered capital or purchase treasury shares, are subject to approval by a supermajority of the general meeting (75 per cent plus). In such cases, restrictions on voting rights provided for in the company's articles of association do not apply.

The Companies Act also provides for a limited 'breakthrough' rule: accordingly, if the articles of association of the target company contain a cap on the maximum number of votes exercisable by a single shareholder, such provision *ipso iure* (by the force of law) becomes ineffective if a bidder acquires control over the target company in excess of 50 per cent.

Sanctions for non-compliance

The takeover provisions of the CMA are primarily enforced by the HFSA. Consequences of non-compliance with the takeover rules include the following:

- *disenfranchisement* – under the CMA, if disclosure obligations are not observed or if control over the target company is acquired without complying with the takeover rules, the party acquiring control cannot exercise its shareholder rights in the target company by force of law;
- *forced transfer* – the acquirer must reduce its control below the applicable threshold (33 per cent or 25 per cent) within 60 days of the decision of the HFSA regarding the forced sale. The acquirer may exercise shareholder rights in the target company only after the completion of forced transfer. In practice, the HFSA also accepts the making of a takeover bid as an alternative to such a forced sale;
- *fines* – if there is a breach of provisions of the CMA relating to disclosure or to takeover bids, the HFSA is entitled to impose a fine, ranging from Ft500,000 (about €2,000) up to Ft100 million (about €400,000), on the party violating these rules. The fine can be imposed repeatedly.

A resolution of the HFSA imposing a sanction on a party that has allegedly breached its disclosure/takeover obligations may be challenged before the Metropolitan Court of Budapest, which has exclusive jurisdiction over such issues. The decision of the Metropolitan Court is non-appealable and becomes immediately enforceable.

Special topics

The concept of 'control'

Under Hungarian law, in the case of registered shares, only shareholders registered in the company's share register are entitled to exercise their votes. The concept of 'control' in the CMA is based on the 'possibility' of the exercise of voting rights.

In light of the foregoing, it is disputed whether it is the acquisition of ownership title to the shares or registration in the share register of the target company that triggers the disclosure/takeover obligations set out in the CMA. The prevailing practice of the HFSA suggests that it is

PART II: EUROPEAN JURISDICTIONS

the acquisition of title to the shares. Accordingly, even if an acquirer does not register itself in the share register, the disclosure/takeover obligation remains applicable nonetheless.

Although the CMA expressly mentions 'concerted actions' as one form of acquisition of control, it fails to provide any guidance as to the actual content of the concept. On the basis of the decisions of the HFSA and judicial review of such decisions, factors of relevance for the purpose of finding a concerted practice are as follows:

- current and/or past links among the relevant parties, such as overlapping ownership or board membership;
- harmonised conduct at the general meeting of the target company, for example, repeated/persistent parallel voting or the persistent absence of a major shareholder from the general meeting, as a result of which another shareholder acquires effective control;
- 'dubious' share acquisitions, as, for example, when an investment services provider acquires a large pool of the target shares and then sells them within a very short period of time via 'pre-arranged trades' with the third parties; and/or
- a common source of financing.

Case study: Zalakeramia/I.G.P.I. and Smilejest (2003)

I.G.P.I. Rt., a Hungarian private company limited by shares, acquired a 26.13 per cent stake in Zalakeramia Rt., a Hungarian tile-making company listed on the BSE, by way of a sale and purchase agreement dated 12 March 2003. An investigation by the HFSA revealed that in the same month I.G.P.I. acquired further shares in Zalakeramia, so that by the end of the month its aggregated control over Zalakeramia reached 32.9 per cent (30.709 per cent direct control and 2.19 per cent indirect control). Meanwhile, on 11 March 2003, Smilejest Ltd, a company registered in the United Kingdom, also acquired a 3.77 per cent stake in Zalakeramia.

In its resolution, the HFSA concluded that I.G.P.I. had acted in concert with Smilejest and, consequently, that the control held by I.G.P.I. and Smilejest had to be aggregated. The aggregate control was above the applicable takeover threshold of 33 per cent, so the parties had breached the CMA by failing to make a takeover bid.

In finding a concerted practice between the parties, the HFSA relied on the following factors:

- similarities in the form, structure and wording of the share sale and purchase agreements entered into by I.G.P.I. and Smilejest;
- the involvement of the same bank as adviser and organiser in both transactions; and
- the financing of both transactions by the same company.

Further, a review of the ownership structure of the companies involved in the case revealed that the ultimate owners of I.G.P.I. and of the financing company were identical.

Vertical ownership and disclosure of acquisition of control

If an acquirer of control is owned by several indirect owners along a vertical ownership chain, there is potential risk linked to the interpretation and practice of the HFSA regarding the question of which entity in the chain must discharge the disclosure obligation. On the one hand, the HFSA claims to require that entities at each level in the ownership chain must comply with the disclosure obligations, even though the wording of the CMA does not support this interpretation. On the other hand, in practice, the HFSA does not seem to require such a multiple disclosure.

The status of depositories: shareholders or proxies?

Under the CMA, entities acting as proxies and registered as 'proxy' in the share register of the target company must be ready to identify the ultimate shareholder if so requested by the HFSA. However, owing to the nature of today's clearing and settlement systems, and the associated multiple layers of shareholders, the depositories are not in a position to be able to identify the actual holder of the shares deposited with them. In such circumstances, the general practice is that the depositories of some depositary receipts programmes register themselves in the issuer's share register as shareholders and not as proxies. However, in order to avoid the triggering of a takeover obligation, these depositories cap their holdings below the applicable takeover threshold.

Repeated crossing of the takeover threshold in a single transaction

If a major shareholder partially sells its stake in a public company and, as a result, its control falls below the applicable threshold, and if, for example, a 'greenshoe' option is involved, it is possible that, after the return of the greenshoe shares to the selling shareholder, its control may rise back above the takeover threshold. As the CMA does not contain any exemptions regarding such cases, the selling shareholder becomes subject to the obligation to make a takeover bid, irrespective of the fact that the transaction, taken as a whole, would obviously decrease its control over the target company.

Impact of the Takeover Directive

The CMA was expressly modelled on the draft Takeover Directive available at the time of the enactment of the CMA. Accordingly, the principles underlying the takeover regime in the CMA are harmonised with the corresponding principles of the directive. Nevertheless, the implementation of the final version of the directive will necessitate the revision of the CMA in several respects. Since the implementation of the directive in Hungary is still at a very early stage, the precise extent and content of the amendments to the CMA is not yet known. It is expected, however, that the implementation of the directive will affect the following areas.

Jurisdictional rules

The CMA currently is not sufficiently sophisticated to provide clear jurisdictional rules (applicable law and supervisory authority) as regards multiple-listed (international) companies. The implementation of the corresponding rules of the directive would therefore be welcome, particularly in view of the fact that in 2004 the shares of two major Hungarian listed companies, BorsodChem and MOL, were introduced onto the Warsaw Stock Exchange immediately triggering uncertainty as to the applicability of the overlapping Polish and Hungarian takeover regimes.

PART II: EUROPEAN JURISDICTIONS

Offer price

Unlike the Takeover Directive, the current version of the CMA does not empower the HFSA to modify the offer price in order, for example, to screen out the effect of market manipulation or insider trading and arrive at an 'equitable' offer price. An amendment is expected to give this power to the HFSA.

Breakthrough rule

Although the Companies Act does contain a limited breakthrough rule, the implementation of the corresponding rules of the Takeover Directive may necessitate further revisions, including as regards compensation of shareholders adversely affected by the breakthrough.

Squeeze-out and sell-out

Implementing the directive would make it clear that squeeze-out is also possible if the 90 per cent threshold is crossed in a takeover procedure and if the acquired control is further increased in a new takeover procedure starting from a level of control of 90 per cent plus.

It is possible that the threshold applicable to sell-out rights will be reduced to 75 per cent.

Employees' information and consultation rights

The Hungarian labour code grants certain information and consultation rights to the trade unions and the workers' council *vis-à-vis* companies in major restructurings. Such rights may be extended to cover the takeover context.

Practical thoughts

Issues that should always be borne in mind when considering a takeover in Hungary include the following.

Incomplete and rigid system

As a result of the forced transformation of Hungary's economic system and its integration into the developed capital markets, the Hungarian capital market tends to develop much faster than the relevant legislative background. Accordingly, it should not be surprising that the Hungarian takeover rules often fail to provide answers as to the legality of a contemplated transaction structure, even if in a more developed capital market the contemplated transaction would be considered a standard deal. Unfortunately, the incomplete statutory background is coupled with a certain rigidity of approach in the CMA, which provides for no exemptions from the takeover obligation if the relevant threshold is crossed and grants no power to the HFSA to exempt certain transactions from the takeover rules.

Lack of settled case law

Although in the past the HFSA has tried to give some guidance to market players by publishing guidance notes/opinions in the area of takeovers, such guidance has been far from coherent.

The outcomes of the judicial review of several decisions of the HFSA have also added to the uncertainty. Currently, the HFSA seems to be rather reluctant to issue guidance notes/opinions, which does not help potential acquirers to structure their contemplated transactions.

Ex ante approval

As a general rule, the Hungarian takeover regime is based on *ex ante* approval. Although acquisition of control in breach of the applicable rules is not void *per se*, such an acquisition may result in substantial fines, disenfranchisement and an order regarding the forced sale of the shares affected by the illegal takeover. Compliance with the takeover rules, therefore, is very important.

Sensitivity of financing arrangements

The financing arrangements related to a contemplated takeover bid are critical as regards compliance with the CMA, from at least two perspectives. First, the CMA substantially restricts the form and type of financing regarding the offer price. Secondly, as regards security/collateral arrangements, including security pledges and voting arrangements, it must always be very carefully considered that the planned arrangement does not make the financing banks themselves subject to the obligation to make a takeover bid.

Increased importance of expertise

With respect to the absence of an active takeover market, the number of professional advisers with substantial experience in this field is rather limited. If the uncertainty surrounding the current Hungarian takeover regime is also taken into account, selection of takeover advisers may easily prove a much more critical decision than it would be in a more developed jurisdiction.

Chapter 17

Ireland

Adrian Benson
Dillon Eustace

The body responsible for the monitoring and supervision of takeovers in Ireland is the Irish Takeover Panel (the 'Panel'), which was established pursuant to the Irish Takeover Panel Act 1997 (the 'Act'). The principal objects of the Panel are to monitor and supervise takeovers and other relevant transactions so as to ensure that the provisions of the Act and any rules made thereunder are complied with in respect of any such transactions.

Relevant statutes and regulations

The Takeover Panel Act and the Takeover Rules

The Irish Takeover Panel Act 1997 Takeover Rules 2001 (the 'Rules') were established to ensure that takeovers and other 'relevant transactions' are conducted in accordance with certain general principles applicable to the conduct of takeovers (the 'Principles') as set out in the Schedule to the Act. These Principles are intended to be applied to ensure that all shareholders are dealt with fairly and treated equally within the context of a takeover.

The Act and Rules apply to public limited companies or any other corporate bodies incorporated in Ireland whose securities are traded on a recognised stock exchange, and also to companies whose securities were traded on such a stock exchange within the five years prior to the relevant transaction. The Minister for Enterprise, Trade and Employment has the power under statute to extend the application of the Act and Rules to any public limited company.[1] The Irish Takeover Panel Act 1997 (Relevant Company) Regulations 2001 clarify the scope of the Act and the Rules to include Irish companies authorised to trade on the London Stock Exchange, the New York Stock Exchange, Nasdaq and Easdaq, and to companies whose securities were traded on one of these exchanges within the five years prior to the relevant transactions.[2]

Other relevant legislation

Other legislation relevant to takeovers in Ireland includes:

- *the Substantial Acquisition Rules* – the Rules are supplemented by the Irish Takeover Panel Act 1997 Substantial Acquisitions Rules 2001 ('SARs'). The SARs impose restrictions on the speed with which a person can increase their holding of between 15 per cent and 30 per cent of the voting rights in a relevant company;

- *the Companies Acts* – the Companies Acts 1963–2005 contain many provisions that are relevant in the context of mergers, takeovers and stake building. They contain, for example, provisions relating to the compulsory acquisition of minority shares, the regulation of schemes of arrangement and reconstructions, the disclosure of interests in shares and insider dealing;
- *the Listing Rules* – the Irish Stock Exchange's Listing Rules impose various continuing obligations on companies listed on the Irish Stock Exchange. Within the context of a takeover, the Listing Rules impose certain disclosure requirements in respect of information to be sent to shareholders, as well as making shareholder approval mandatory in respect of transactions of a certain specified value;
- *EU Merger Control Regulation* – acquisitions and certain joint ventures with a 'Community dimension' are regulated by Council Regulation (EC) No. 139/2004 on the control of concentrations between undertakings (the 'EC Merger Regulation'). If no such 'Community dimension' exists, the takeover/merger may still be subject to the provisions of the Competition Act 2002;
- *Competition Act 2002* – generally, Part 2 of the Competition Act prohibits agreements that prevent, restrict or distort competition and abuses by undertakings of a dominant position. A merger or takeover can be prohibited by these provisions. Part 3 of the Competition Act 2002 provides for the compulsory notification of mergers or acquisitions to the Competition Authority where the worldwide turnover of each of two or more of the undertakings involved in the merger or acquisition (excluding the vendor) exceeds €40 million; each of two or more of the undertakings carries on business in any part of Ireland, including Northern Ireland; and at least one of the companies based in Ireland has a turnover in the state of €40 million or more; and
- *regulated/specific industries* – takeovers and acquisitions of securities in certain industries are subject to additional regulations. These include banks and credit institutions, insurance undertakings, and 'investment business firms' regulated under the Investment Intermediaries Act 1995. A company in one of a number of other industries that require governmental licences to operate may also require approval/clearance from the relevant authorities/minister, depending on the term of any authority or licence under which it operates.

Enforcement

Section 9(1) of the Act gives the Panel statutory authority to make a ruling as to whether any activity or proposed activity as respects a takeover or other relevant transaction complies with the Principles or the Rules.

Section 9(2) empowers the Panel to give directions to any party to the takeover or other relevant transaction to do or to refrain from doing anything that the Panel specifies in its direction. Section 9(3) provides a non-exhaustive list of such directions.

The Panel is also empowered under Section 10 to enquire into the conduct of any person where there are reasonable grounds for believing that a contravention of the Rules or Principles has occurred or may occur.

The Panel may conduct hearings under Section 11 to enable it to properly exercise its powers under Sections 9 and 10. These hearings may be either in public or in private. For the purposes of any such hearing, the Panel has the same powers, rights and privileges as are vested in the High Court or a High Court judge in relation to compelling attendance, examination on oath and compelling the production of documents. A witness before the Panel is also entitled to the same privileges and immunities as a witness before the High Court.

'Control' and other definitions

Section 1(1) of the Act defines a 'takeover' as:

> (a) any agreement or transaction (including a merger) whereby or in consequence of which control of a relevant company is or may be acquired; or
> (b) any invitation, offer or proposal made, or intended or required to be made, with a view to concluding or bringing about such an agreement or transaction.

The term 'control' under the Act:

> means, in relation to a relevant company, the holding, whether directly or indirectly, of securities of the company that confer, in aggregate, not less than 30 per cent (or such other percentage as may be prescribed) of the voting rights in that company.

The term 'security' is defined in Section 1(1) of the Act in relation to a company as:

> (a) any interest in the capital of the company and includes any interest in the nature of a share, stock, debenture or bond, by whatever name called, and irrespective of the rights, if any attaching thereto, of or issued by the company, and
> (b) an interest in a security falling within (a) of this definition.

The term 'voting right' is defined in Section 1(1) of the Act in relation to a company as:

> ... a right exercisable for the time being to cast, or to control the casting of, a vote at general meetings of members of the company, not being such a right that is exercisable only in special circumstances.

The term 'other relevant transactions' is defined in Section 1(1) of the Act as:

> (a) any offer, agreement or transaction in relation to the acquisition of securities conferring voting rights in a relevant company (including a substantial acquisition of securities) which the Panel specifies, in rules under section 8, to be a relevant transaction for the purposes of this act, and
> (b) any agreement, transaction, proposal or action entered into, made or taken in contemplation of, or which is consequent upon or incidental to, a takeover or an offer, agreement or transaction referred to in paragraph (a) of this definition.

Methods of acquiring control

The most common method of obtaining control of a public company is a public takeover offer for its shares. However, there are alternative methods, including:

- schemes of arrangement, which require approval from a court and a majority in number of shareholders representing three-quarters in value of the shareholders voting at a general meeting;[3]
- reverse takeovers, which involve the target company acquiring control of the offeror company to the transaction by way of share-for-share exchange; and
- establishing a new company, which then acquires both the offeror and target companies.

Timing of offers and revisions

Strict time limits are set out in the Rules in respect of certain milestones relating to an offer for shares in a public company. The offer period generally starts with the announcement of a firm intention to make a bid. An offer document must be sent to the target's shareholders within 28 days of the announcement of this firm intention to make an offer.[4]

The offer must initially remain open for acceptance for 21 days following the day the offer document is posted.[5] If a hostile bid has been made, the target has 14 days from the date upon which the offer document was posted to issue its defence document advising its shareholders on the merits and demerits of the offer.[6]

A bid must be conditional on the offeror acquiring shares carrying more than 50 per cent of the target's voting rights. The offeror has up to 60 days from posting the offer document to satisfy this condition unless the timetable is extended by the Panel.

In practice, the offer is usually made conditional on a certain number of acceptances in excess of 50 per cent being obtained. The number of acceptances required is usually set at 80 per cent, as the offeror must obtain this level of acceptances in order to invoke the compulsory acquisition procedure under Section 204 of the Companies Act 1963, which facilitates the acquisition of shares of non-accepting shareholders. If the required level of acceptances is received within the first 21 days of the offer period, the offer must remain open for a further 14 days.[7] This 80 per cent threshold is likely to be amended in the near future in light of Article 15 of the Takeover Directive.

When the acceptance condition has been satisfied, the offeror has a further 21 days to satisfy the other conditions of the offer. This gives a maximum period of 81 days to satisfy conditions, assuming that the acceptance condition is not satisfied before the 60th day. The offeror must send the consideration due to the target shareholders who have accepted the offer within 14 days from the date on which the offer has been declared wholly unconditional.[8]

The terms of the offer can be improved by the offeror, provided that it is not restricted in its ability to do so in the initial offer document. An offeror can revise the terms of its offer up until the 46th day after posting the offer document.

Extensions and revisions of offers

Extensions

Subject to certain exceptions in the Rules, offerors are free to extend the period during which the offer remains open for acceptance at any time. There are, however, two principal restrictions on this right of extension. Rule 31.6 provides that, except with the consent of the Panel, an offer shall lapse unless it has become unconditional as to acceptances by 5 pm on the final closing date, being the 60th day after the posting of the offer document, or an earlier date beyond which the offeror has stated that the offer will not be accepted. The offeror must make

PART II: EUROPEAN JURISDICTIONS

an announcement on the 60th day, or, if applicable, any relevant earlier date, as to whether the offer is unconditional as to acceptances or has lapsed. This announcement should include the details regarding the timing and contents of announcements to the Stock Exchange and the Panel, as required by Rule 17.1, as well as a statement as to the current position in the count of acceptances.

An offeror is not obliged to extend its offer if a condition for its acceptance has not been fulfilled by the closing date.[9] In some cases, the offeror or its directors or advisers may make a statement in relation to the publication of an offer, indicating that the offer will not be extended beyond a specified date.[10] In these circumstances, the offeror is normally bound by the statement, unless a competitive situation subsequently arises, in which case the offeror may choose not to be bound by its statement. Certain conditions must be satisfied before an offeror may deviate from the contents of such a statement:

- the offeror must have reserved the right to do so;[11]
- notice to this effect has been given as soon as possible;
- shareholders have been informed at the earliest opportunity; and
- any target shareholder who accepted the offer on or after the date of the 'no extension' statement is permitted to withdraw his acceptance within eight days of the posting of the notice.[12]

Revisions

Offerors are normally free to revise their offers at any time, subject to certain limitations:

- if an offer is revised, it must be kept open for a period of at least 14 days following the date on which the revised offer document is dispatched to shareholders. This gives the target shareholders sufficient time to consider the revised offer;[13]
- if the offeror or any of its directors, officials or advisers includes in the document dispatched to the shareholders of the target company any statement in relation to the value or type of consideration (a 'no increase statement'), then the offeror is normally bound by that statement and is not permitted to act in a manner contrary to it. Power is reserved to the Panel to consent to a waiver of this restriction;[14]
- however, if a competitive situation arises, the offeror may choose to increase the offer, notwithstanding a 'no increase statement', if it has reserved the right to do so; notice to this effect has been given as soon as possible; shareholders have been informed in writing at the earliest opportunity; and any shareholder of the target company who accepted the offer on or after the date of the 'no increase statement' is permitted to withdraw their acceptance within eight days of the posting of the notice.[15]

Sample timetable for a takeover

The following sample timetable for a takeover in Ireland (Exhibit 17.1) begins on the day of announcement. In the preceding weeks, the offeror will usually have made market purchases of shares in the target and the terms of the offer will have been determined. The timetable is compiled on the basis that no merger control or other issues arise over the course of the takeover.

The deadline for acceptances of the offer that can be counted for the purposes of reaching the 80 per cent threshold pursuant to Section 204 of the Companies Act 1963 is four

Exhibit 17.1

Sample timetable for a takeover in Ireland

Day 1	Announcement of offer
Day 1 + 28 at the latest ('D')	Offer document sent to shareholders (Rule 30.2).
D + 14 at the latest	In the case of a hostile takeover, the defence document is posted to shareholders (Rule 30.3).
D + 21	First closing date – end of the period during which the offer remains open to acceptances.
D + 22	Announcement of the level of acceptances by offeror; announcement that the offer is being extended for a period of (usually) 14 days; offeror commences purchase of target shares in the market.
D + 35	Second closing date.
D + 36	Announcement of level of acceptances and purchases by offeror; possibility of extension of offer.
D + 39 at the latest	Release of new information by the target board (Rule 31.9).
D + 42 at the latest	If the offer is unconditional as to acceptances on day 21, fulfilment of other conditions; if offer is not unconditional as to acceptances, rights of withdrawal become exercisable (Rule 34).
D + 46	Revised offers may not be posted after this date (Rule 32.1).
D + 60	Announcement by offeror as to whether the offer is unconditional as to acceptances and extended indefinitely or has lapsed (Rule 31.6).
D + 81	Deadline for fulfilment or waiver of conditions other than the acceptance conditions above.
D + 102	Deadline for posting of consideration to shareholders, assuming that the offer becomes wholly unconditional on day 81.

months after the date on which the offer document was sent to shareholders. As soon as this level has been reached, the offeror is obliged to immediately give compulsory acquisition notices to the remaining shareholders. In situations where an offer lapses or is withdrawn, Rule 35.1(a) prohibits the offeror, or any person who acted in concert with the offeror, from making another approach to the offeree within a period of 12 months after the date on which the offer lapsed or was withdrawn.

Conditionality of offers

The main purpose of the Rules is to ensure equality of treatment between the shareholders of the company in a takeover situation. A number of Rules set out to achieve this equality, including the following:

- Rule 6.1 provides that the value of consideration per share in the case of a voluntary offer must not be less than that agreed in respect of shares of that class in the target acquired by the offeror (or any person acting in concert with it) within the three-month period prior to the commencement of the offer period and ending at the time of the announcement of the offeror's firm intention to make the offer;

- Rule 10 provides that it must be a condition of every voluntary offer for more than 50 per cent of the voting shares in the target that such an offer will not become unconditional unless the offeror has acquired or agreed to acquire shares carrying (i) over 50 per cent of the voting rights in the target conferred by the equity share capital alone; and (ii) over 50 per cent of the voting rights in the target conferred by the equity share capital and non-equity share capital combined. In practice, it is usual for offers to be made conditional on obtaining acceptances from shareholders holding at least 80 per cent of the shares to which the offer relates. This enables the offeror to compulsorily acquire the shares of those non-accepting shareholders;
- Rule 11(a) requires an offeror to make a cash or cash alternative offer matching the highest price that it may previously have paid for shares in the target company in a number of circumstances;
- Rule 12 provides that any offer to which the Competition Act 2002 applies must be subject to a condition in respect thereof. If an offer would give rise to a concentration with a 'Community dimension' within the scope of the Merger Regulation, a condition of the offer must be that it will lapse if the European Commission either initiates proceedings in respect of the concentration or refers the concentration to a competent authority of a member state before the first closing date of the offer or the date when the offer becomes unconditional as to acceptances, whichever is the later;
- Rule 13 provides that offers must not normally be subject to conditions that depend solely on subjective judgements by the directors of the offeror;
- Rule 14 provides that, except with the consent of the Panel, where the target has more than one class of equity share capital, an offeror cannot make an offer for a class of shares unless a comparable offer is made for every other class of equity share capital, including non-voting shares;
- Rule 15 provides that when an offer is made for equity share capital and the target has outstanding convertible securities, options or other subscription rights, the offeror must make an appropriate offer to the holders of such convertible securities;
- Rule 16 provides that, except with the Panel's consent, during an offer period or when an offer is 'reasonably in contemplation', no special deal can be reached (that is, no arrangement can be made) with any shareholder(s) or intending shareholder(s) with favourable conditions attached that are not being extended to all shareholders.

Break fees and irrevocables

Break fees

Break fees (otherwise referred to as termination, inducement or broken deal fees) are commonly incorporated into negotiations for takeovers in other jurisdictions, in order to indemnify the offeror to some extent if the proposed takeover falls through. However, as arrangements such as these are highly regulated in this jurisdiction, they are less commonplace.

Rule 21.1 prohibits an offeree from entering into any contract to pay compensation to an offeror where this obligation would be contingent in any respect upon the proposed offer lapsing or not being made. The Panel has the power to grant exemptions from this provision, although this is exercised only in limited circumstances. The Panel consents to such arrangements only where they relate to specific quantifiable third-party costs and subject to:

- an upper limit of 1 per cent of the value of the offer; and

- written confirmation from the offeree board and its financial advisers that they consider the arrangement to be in the best interests of the offeree's shareholders.[16]

In addition to the above requirements, the board of the offeree is obliged to undertake an analysis of whether any break fee agreed to would amount to unlawful financial assistance by the company. The Investment Funds, Companies and Miscellaneous Provisions Act 2005 has given some clarity on the matter by providing that the reimbursement by an offeree or by a subsidiary of an offeree of expenses of an offeror pursuant to an agreement approved by, or on terms approved by, the Panel shall not be prohibited.[17]

Irrevocables

A potential offeror is not permitted to contact holders of securities who are not professional investors in order to obtain an irrevocable commitment to accept the offer without the prior consent of the Panel.[18] The financial advisers of the offeror must ensure that these holders of securities are provided with both adequate information and adequate time in order to consider the agreement properly.[19] Such irrevocable commitments are subject to disclosure requirements and details must be contained in the offer document.[20] In addition, a copy of the document evidencing the irrevocable commitment should be made available for inspection from the time when the offer document or the first response circular is published.[21]

Disclosure

The Companies Acts 1963–2005, the SARs, the Rules and the Listing Rules contain provisions with regard to the disclosure of information in connection with the acquisition and/or disposal of shares and interests in shares.

Companies Act 1990

Directors, shadow directors and their families are obliged to disclose their interests in shares or debentures in all Irish registered companies. The Companies Act 1990 further provides that, if a person acquires or ceases to have an interest in shares in a company listed on the Irish Stock Exchange, that person must notify the Irish Stock Exchange of his interest in the shares within five days following the acquisition or cessation, as the case may be, where, following such acquisition or disposal, the percentage level of his interest in the entire share capital of that company exceeds or falls below either 10 per cent, 25 per cent, 30 per cent or 75 per cent.

Part IV of the Companies Act 1990 provides that anyone who acquires or disposes of any shares in a public limited company that results in such person's interests in that company reaching 5 per cent or more of the voting shares in that company must notify the company in writing of the amount of his holding and certain information relating to it within five days. Any further increase or decrease of at least 1 per cent above the existing notifiable level, or a decrease to below 5 per cent, must also be notified.

Substantial Acquisition Rules

The SARs require disclosure of share acquisitions that result in the acquirer holding 15 per cent or more of the voting rights in a company. A person who already holds shares or rights over shares carrying between 15 per cent and 30 per cent of the voting rights of the company, and who makes an acquisition that increases his relevant holding beyond a whole percentage figure, must also disclose this fact to the company, the Irish Stock Exchange and the Panel.[22]

Takeover Rules

Rule 8.1 of the Rules requires all dealings in securities of the target by the offeror or an offeree, or an associate of either of them, within the offer period to be publicly disclosed in accordance with Rule 8.4–8.6. Dealings by anyone owning or controlling 1 per cent or more of any relevant class of securities of the offeror or target company must also be disclosed.[23]

Pursuant to Rule 8.8, stockbrokers, banks and others who deal in securities on behalf of clients during an offer period are obliged to ensure, as far as practicable, that those clients are aware of the disclosure obligations attaching to associates and others under Rule 8 and are willing to comply with these obligations.

Listing Rules

The Listing Rules impose an obligation on each listed company to disclose non-public information in respect of 'major new developments in its sphere of activity' that may lead to substantial movements in its share price.

Acquisitions or disposals of a major interest in shares in a company listed on the Irish Stock Exchange must be notified by such company to the Companies Announcements Office.

The Listing Rules also contain provisions in relation to major transactions involving companies listed on the Irish Stock Exchange. Each transaction must be considered to determine whether it may be classified as a Class 1, Class 2 or Class 3 transaction. The classification of the transaction is determined by assessing its size relative to the size of the listed company proposing to make it. The comparison of size is made by the use of percentage ratios. The percentage ratios are the figures, expressed as a percentage, resulting from a number of calculations in respect of the assets, profits, turnover, consideration to market capitalisation and gross capital of the listed company. The classifications are as follows:

- Class 3 equals a transaction where all percentage ratios are less than 5 per cent;
- Class 2 equals a transaction where any percentage ratio is 5 per cent or more, but each is less than 25 per cent; and
- Class 1 is equal to a transaction where any percentage ratio is 25 per cent or more.

Mandatory offers

Rule 9 of the Takeover Rules provides that, except with the consent of the Panel, an offeror must make a mandatory offer to all holders of each class of equity shares and to all holders of each class of voting non-equity shares in the target company if it, or persons acting in concert with it, does any of the following:

- acquires 30 per cent or more of the target's voting rights;
- already owns less than 30 per cent of the target's voting rights and increases to 30 per cent or more; or

- already owns 30 per cent or more, but less than 50 per cent of the target's voting rights, and increases this by more than 0.05 per cent of the target's voting rights in any 12-month period.

A mandatory offer may only be conditional on acceptances of the offer being received that confer more than 50 per cent of the voting rights in the company on the offeror and any persons acting in concert with it,[24] and/or a condition to the effect that the offer will lapse upon the initiation of proceedings by the European Commission or a reference by it to the Competition Authority.[25] Generally, all other conditions are prohibited.

Subject to the Panel agreeing otherwise, a mandatory bid must be in cash or be accompanied by a cash alternative offer. The price offered must be equivalent to the highest value of the consideration per share paid by the offeror for the target shares in the 12 months before the mandatory offer is triggered.[26] Where securities have been acquired for non-cash consideration during the relevant period, the Rules provide that such acquisition is deemed to be an acquisition of shares at a price equal to the value of that consideration at the time of the acquisition.[27] The value of any such consideration is decided by an independent valuation.

Derogations and dispensations

The Panel has power to issue derogations from an obligation to make a mandatory bid. Situations in which dispensations or derogations may be granted include the following:[28]

- where a person incurs an obligation to make a mandatory offer as a result of an inadvertent mistake, the Panel may waive the obligation to make an offer if sufficient shares are sold within a limited period to an unconnected third party;
- where a company is in such a serious financial position that it can be rescued only by the issue of new shares or the acquisition of existing shares by the rescuer without approval by a vote of independent shareholders, which would otherwise trigger a mandatory offer, the Panel may waive the requirements of Rule 9, paying particular attention to the views of the directors and advisers of the potential target;
- where new securities are issued as consideration for an acquisition or cash subscription and such issue would otherwise result in an obligation to make a general offer under Rule 9, the Panel may waive the obligation where it is 'whitewashed' by independent shareholders at a shareholders' meeting.

Case study: Readymix plc

On 27 September 2004, CEMEX, S.A. de C.V. and RMC Group plc announced that they had reached an agreement on the terms of a recommended acquisition by CEMEX of RMC. This acquisition was to be effected by means of a scheme of arrangement. Just over seven weeks later, RMC and CEMEX announced that at an extraordinary general meeting of the shareholders of RMC all the resolutions proposed had been approved. It was anticipated that the relevant regulatory clearances would be received in due course and the scheme would become effective on 12 January 2005.

RMC held approximately 61.9 per cent of the issued share capital of Readymix plc and thus, in the event of CEMEX's acquiring RMC, it would also acquire control of

> Readymix. CEMEX would then be obliged under Rule 9.1 to extend the offer to the holders of each class of equity share capital and also to the holders of non-equity share capital conferring voting rights in Readymix.
>
> CEMEX made an application to the Panel, which considered the matter on 6 December 2004. The Panel considered the General Principles along with the 'chain principle', which is set out in Note 7 on Rule 9.1. The chain principle provides that a person acquiring control of a company may thereby acquire control of a second relevant company because the first company holds a controlling block of securities in the second company. The Panel considered a number of factors in reaching its decision, including whether the holding in Readymix represented a substantial part of the assets or profits of RMC, or whether one of the main purposes of acquiring control of RMC was to secure control of Readymix. The Panel ultimately decided that neither of these factors was relevant in the circumstances, as the acquisition of Readymix would be an indirect consequence of the acquisition of RMC. Thus, the Panel considered it appropriate to grant a waiver of Rule 9.1.

Acquisition of minority shareholdings

Section 204(1) of the Companies Act 1963 provides that where an offer for all the shares in a target company has been approved by 80 per cent in value of the 'affected shares' within four months of the publication of the terms of the offer, the offeror is entitled to compulsorily acquire the remaining shares in the target. Shares beneficially held by the offeror are excluded from the calculation of the 80 per cent threshold.

However, Section 204(2) provides that if, at the date of the publication of the terms of the offer, the offeror is the beneficial owner of shares in the target to a value greater than 20 per cent of the aggregate value of those shares and the 'shares affected', Section 204(1) will not apply unless the assenting shareholders constitute not less than 75 per cent in number of the holders of those shares.

Conversion of a public limited company to a private limited company

Under Section 14 of the Companies (Amendment) Act 1983, a public limited company may be re-registered as a private company once a special resolution to this effect has been passed by the members. When an offeror has acquired 75 per cent or more of the shares of the offeree, they will be in a position to exercise this power, notwithstanding the fact that they may have failed to reach the 80 per cent threshold required to squeeze-out remaining shareholders under Section 204. However, any threat of conversion to a private limited company or a delisting will more than likely give reason to any dissenting shareholders to reconsider their position regarding any offer, given the consequential reduction of the market for their shares and the effect on the liquidity of the company.

However, the Companies (Amendment) Act 1983 does provide an element of protection against this threat to minority shareholders. Section 15 provides that holders of not less than 5 per cent in nominal value of the company's issued share capital who had not voted in favour of the resolution may apply to the court to have the resolution cancelled.

Board neutrality and defensive measures

Under Irish law, directors have a fiduciary duty to act in the best interests of the company of which they are directors and not to use their powers improperly. Directors must be conscious of their fiduciary duties throughout any transaction. This restricts their freedom when considering whether to recommend or contest an offer, or contemplate taking any actions frustrating an offer.

The Principles also contain provisions relating to directors' duties.[29] The options open to directors of public companies in relation to defensive measures depend upon the stage of the takeover process that has been reached. The power to employ defensive measures is greatly restricted once an offer has been made or is imminent.

Case study: Alphyra Group plc

Alphyra Group plc, an electronic payments solutions group, became the subject of a management buyout (MBO) bid by Rendina Limited, a group of senior executives of Alphyra backed by a US venture capital group, Benchmark Capital. Rendina offered €2.45 per share, which fell below the expectations of most of Alphyra's institutional investors. However, this offer was increased to €2.70 following indications that the Denver-based First Data Corporation was prepared to offer €2.80 per share.

The MBO team, which included the chief executive of Alphyra, indicated that any approach from First Data would be considered 'hostile and unwelcome' and soon afterwards First Data withdrew from the bidding process. Questions were raised as to the appropriateness of the actions of the MBO team and a complaint was lodged with the Takeover Panel raising certain issues in relation to the conduct of the offer by Rendina. It was submitted, first, that Rendina's Rule 2.5 announcement of its offer document did not contain sufficient information on the nature of Alphyra's business, and its financial and trading prospects, to satisfy General Principle 4 and Rule 24.4(c); and, secondly, that circumstances existed that merited an investigation into whether the actions of the MBO team constituted frustrating action, contrary to General Principle 6 and Rule 21.1.

On the first of these points, the Panel ruled that Rule 24.4(c) sets out the detailed financial and other information in respect of an offeree that is required to be disclosed in the offer document. However, there was no specific requirement to disclose the information sought and thus there had been no breach of Rule 24.2(c) and General Principle 4. It was noted that in transactions such as these the independent directors of the offeree and its advisers usually seek to establish procedural practices designed to minimise the extent of any resulting problems. In accordance with Rule 3, two of the directors of Alphyra were appointed as independent directors for the purposes of formulating and communicating advice to Alphyra shareholders: this was enough to fulfil Alphyra's obligation.

On the issue of frustrating action, the Panel, recognising the difficulties that may arise as a result of the 'inherent conflicts of interest' in such situations, noted that two of the directors of Alphyra were appointed as independent directors for the purposes of formulating and communicating advice to the shareholders in accordance with Rule 3. The Panel did consider the comments of the directors, if made, to be inappropriate, but concluded that no sustainable case had been made to justify the submission that there had been a breach of Principle 6 or Rule 21.1.

PART II: EUROPEAN JURISDICTIONS

Defensive measures – pre-bid

Directors may take certain measures in advance of a potential takeover in an attempt to deter any prospective offeror. In these circumstances, the Rules do not apply and consequently directors enjoy a greater degree of freedom of action.

There are several tactics that may be employed by directors wishing to pre-empt any potential bid. These include the following:

- *creation of voting agreements between shareholders* – this occurs where shareholders agree to vote two or more blocks of shares together so that they are not sold separately. This method of obtaining voting power in excess of their shareholding strengthens the position of these shareholders in the event of a hostile takeover. However, parties to agreements such as these may be considered by the Panel to be 'concert parties' pursuant to Section 1(3) of the Act and, if their combined shareholding amounts to 30 per cent or more, there may be repercussions in relation to Rule 9 (the mandatory offer);
- *cross-shareholdings* – where agreements exist between two or more companies to purchase shares in each other that will not be disposed of without consent, each company is assured of a substantial shareholder that will not be prepared to accept any potential hostile offer. However, if any such company holds 5 per cent or more of any class of relevant securities of the offeree, it may find itself subject to the disclosure obligations placed on 'associates'[30] of the offeree by the Rules.[31] The Listing Rules also restrict cross-shareholding in listed companies by requiring that a sufficient number (25 per cent)[32] of shares for which a listing application is made must be in public hands no later than the time of admission. The company is obliged to notify the Stock Exchange if at any time this proportion of shares falls below 25 per cent;[33]
- *obtaining proxy votes* – directors may use votes that have been obtained by their appointment as proxy by shareholders pursuant to Section 136(1) of the Companies Act 1963. This allows directors to use votes obtained in such a manner to support their own stated policies in resisting a potential takeover bid; and
- *creation of non-voting capital and capital with enhanced voting rights* – directors may decide to alter the voting rights attached to shares in order to maintain control by ensuring that a significant proportion of voting shares is in the hands of those who are likely to resist any potential takeover attempt. A company is within its rights to issue shares with weighted voting rights,[34] although the directors must also be empowered to do so by the articles of association. If this is not the case, a special resolution is required. In this situation, pre-emption rights must be considered and may also have to be altered by way of a special resolution. Care must be taken to ensure that the parties whose voting rights are enhanced do not acquire enough control to trigger a mandatory bid under Rule 9.

Defensive measures – post-bid

Once a takeover offer is imminent or has been made, directors of a public company are more restricted with regard to the defensive action which may be taken. This is due to the restrictions contained in Rule 21 and to General Principle 6, which states that the directors of a target company must refrain from conducting the target's affairs in a manner that might frustrate the offer or deprive the shareholders of the opportunity to consider the merits of the offer, without the authority of the shareholders at the general meeting.

One of the defensive measures open to directors is the issuing of new shares to attempt to ensure that the offer is rejected, or to deprive the offeror of control. Where such shares are allotted to a company whose offer would be favoured by the directors of the offeree, this company is described as a 'white knight'. Such action may result in a competitive situation and in these circumstances the Panel may require that the white knight clarifies its intentions within a certain period of time.[35] Failure to do so will result in the white knight's being prohibited from making an offer. Preemption rights may also cause problems in this context, and again it may be necessary to vary these rights in a general meeting. Further, Rule 20.2 provides that the board of the offeree may not favour the white knight in respect of any information to be given to offerors.

The directors may attempt to strengthen the position of the offeree company and discourage the offeror by adopting measures that will result in a substantial increase in the cost of the takeover. Such defensive actions, collectively referred to as 'poison pills', include:

- 'golden parachutes', which require directors of the target to be paid lump sums if the company is acquired or their employment is terminated as a result of an acquisition; and
- the granting of rights to current shareholders to acquire additional shares at a set low price, or debentures that are convertible into equity or that carry a right to subscribe for equity on the occurrence of a takeover offer.

A further option open to directors of a target company is the 'Pac-man defence', whereby the target company launches a bid for the offeror.

The poison pill device is not frequently used in Ireland, as a consequence of the heavy regulation of such defensive actions under the Act and Rules. The Panel's prohibition on frustrating action after a bid is announced[36] precludes any such action without the approval of shareholders. Any similar action taken before the bid is imminent must be justified as being for a proper corporate objective, and directors must always avoid breaching their fiduciary duty to the shareholders and the company.

Section 205 of the Companies Act 1963

Section 205 provides a remedy for minority shareholders claiming that they are being oppressed. In certain relatively limited circumstances, Section 205 is used to limit the ability of directors to adopt certain defensive measures.

Impact of the Takeover Directive

Council Directive (EC) No. 25/2004 on takeover bids (the Takeover Directive) came into force on 21 April 2004. The directive aims to coordinate the laws of the member states of the EU to the extent necessary to afford shareholders a minimum level of protection within the context of a takeover, which should be equivalent throughout the EU.

Member states must implement the Takeover Directive by 20 May 2006. This means that the legislation currently regulating the Panel must be amended to more accurately reflect the provisions of the Takeover Directive. However, these provisions are unlikely to affect the operation of the takeover regime in Ireland to any material extent. This is because many of the provisions are currently provided for under Irish law, whether in primary legislation in the area or in the Regulations made thereunder.

PART II: EUROPEAN JURISDICTIONS

In addition, several of the provisions contained in the directive have been made optional in order to make this directive more palatable for certain member states. The provisions that may be opted out of include Article 9(2) and (3), dealing with defensive measures (discussed below), and Article 11, the 'breakthrough rule', a rule that ensures that an offeror who obtains more than 75 per cent of the capital carrying voting rights in the company after a successful bid is not prevented from obtaining control or amending the articles of association of the company.

It is likely that much of the Companies Acts 1963–2005, the Act and the Rules will remain largely unchanged once the directive has been transposed into Irish law, and it still remains to be seen whether Ireland will choose to opt out of any of the provisions mentioned above.

The main provisions of the directive that are already reflected in Irish law include the following.

Article 5

A mandatory bid must be made where an offeror, as a result of an acquisition of shares by the offeror or persons acting in concert with him, holds securities that directly or indirectly give him a specified percentage of voting rights in the company giving him control of that company. Article 5 does not specify the percentage that constitutes control of the company. This percentage and the method of calculation are to be determined by each member state.[37]

Article 5 requires that mandatory bids be addressed at the earliest opportunity to all shareholders at an 'equitable price'. The definition of equitable price in the directive is similar to that contained in Rule 9, which provides for the maximum period of 12 months, and also makes provision for the method of calculating the percentage that constitutes 'control'.

Article 6

This article sets out the manner in which information concerning bids is to be made public and provides that the relevant supervisory authority be notified of such bids. An obligation is placed on member states to ensure that, once an offer document has been made public, the boards of the target company and of the offeror inform the representatives of their respective employees, or, where no representatives exist, the employees themselves, about the bid.

Subsection (2) obliges member states to ensure that, subject to the prior approval of the supervisory authority, an offeror makes public an offer document containing the information necessary to enable the holders of the target company's securities to reach a properly informed decision on the bid. A comprehensive list of the minimum requirements for information to be included in the offer document is set out in Article 6(3). This list is broadly similar to the list of items to be included in an announcement of a firm intention to make an offer under Rule 2.5 of the Rules.

Article 9

Article 9 prohibits the board of the target company from taking defensive measures, other than seeking alternative bids that may result in the frustration of a takeover bid, without obtaining the prior authorisation of shareholders at a general meeting. Authorisation for any such defensive measure is mandatory from the time the board of the target company receives information concerning a bid until the result of the bid is made public or lapses. Member states are free to require that such authorisation be obtained at an earlier stage, that is as soon as the board of the target company becomes aware that the bid is imminent.

Rule 21.1(a) of the Rules sets out the relevant time period as being 'during the course of any offer or at any earlier time at which the target board has reason to believe that the making of an offer is or may be imminent'. Under Irish law, the approval of the general meeting is already required for defensive measures within this period, along with the consent of the Panel.

Articles 15 and 16

These introduce a procedure for the right of squeeze-out (Article 15) and for the right of sell-out (Article 16). Following a bid made to all shareholders, member states must ensure that an offeror can require the holders of the remaining securities to sell him those securities at a fair price once he holds securities representing not less than 90 per cent of the voting capital carrying voting rights and 90 per cent of the voting rights in the target company, or where, following acceptance of the bid, he has acquired, or firmly contracted to acquire, securities representing less than 90 per cent of the target company's capital carrying voting rights and 90 per cent of the voting rights comprised in that bid. A similar compulsory acquisition procedure is provided for in Section 204 of the Companies Act 1963 (discussed above), but the threshold is currently set at 80 per cent, rather than 90 per cent as provided for in the directive. While member states are given the freedom to set higher thresholds under Article 15, up to a maximum of 95 per cent, lower thresholds are not permitted. Thus, it will be necessary to amend Section 204 accordingly.

---

[1] Irish Takeover Panel Act 1997, Section 2(c).
[2] Irish Takeover Panel Act 1997 (Relevant Company) Regulations 2001, Section 3(a)(i)–(iv).
[3] Companies Act 1963, Section 201(3).
[4] Irish Takeover Panel Act 1997 Takeover Rules 2001, Part B – Principal Rules, Rule 30.2.
[5] Rule 31.1.
[6] Rule 30.3.
[7] Rule 31.2(b)(ii).
[8] Rule 31.8(b).
[9] Rule 31.3.
[10] Rule 31.5(a).
[11] Rule 31.5(d).
[12] Rule 31.5(b)(i) and (ii).
[13] Rule 32.1(a).
[14] Rule 32.2(a).
[15] Rule 32.2(b).
[16] Irish Takeover Panel Notes on Part B – Principal Rules, Notes on Rule 21.1.
[17] Investment Funds, Companies and Miscellaneous Provisions Act, 2005, Section 56(1)(l).
[18] Irish Takeover Panel Act 1997 Takeover Rules 2001, Rule 4.3(a).
[19] Rule 4.3(b).
[20] Rule 2.5(b)(iii)(3) and Rule 24.3(f).
[21] Rule 26(b)(ix).
[22] Irish Takeover Panel Act 1997, Substantial Acquisition Rules 2001, Rule 6(a).
[23] Irish Takeover Panel Act 1997 Takeover Rules 2001, Rule 8.3.
[24] Rule 9.2(b)(i).
[25] Rule 12(a) and (b).
[26] Rule 9.4(a).

PART II: EUROPEAN JURISDICTIONS

[27] Rule 9.4(b).
[28] Irish Takeover Panel Notes on Part B – Principal Rules, Notes on Possible Waivers of and Derogations From Rule 9.
[29] Schedule to the Irish Takeover Panel Act 1997, Principles Applicable to the Conduct of Takeovers, etc. – Principles 6, 7 and 8.
[30] Takeover Panel Act 1997 Takeover Rules 2001, Part A – Preliminary Rules, Rule 2.2(i).
[31] Part B, Principal Rules, Rule 8.
[32] Paragraphs 3.18 and 3.19.
[33] Paragraph 9.37.
[34] Bushell vs. Faith [1970] AC 1099.
[35] Takeover Panel Act 1997 Takeover Rules 2001, Part A – Preliminary Rules, Rule 2.2.
[36] General Principle 6.
[37] Directive 2004/25/EC of the European Parliament and of the Council on Takeover Bids, Article 5(3).

Chapter 18

Italy

Fabio Labruna and Roberto Tallarita
Gianni, Origoni, Grippo & Partners

The Financial Act 1998

The acquisition of equity interests and the takeover of listed companies in Italy are regulated by the Legislative Decree, 24 February 1998, No. 58 governing securities exchange and listed companies (the Financial Act) and the Regulation, 14 May 1999, No. 11971 (the Consob Regulation) issued by the Comissione Nazionale per le Società e la Borsa (Consob), the public authority responsible for regulating the Italian securities market.

The Financial Act provides a set of rules aimed at guaranteeing the transparency of listed companies' ownership and protecting minorities in case of change of control. In particular, the Act requires a bidder, exceeding certain ownership and voting thresholds, to launch a mandatory tender offer for all the outstanding shares of the target company.

As in other jurisdictions, the rationale of such provisions is to protect the rights of minority shareholders by guaranteeing them, in cases of change of control, the opportunity to realise their financial investment at an equitable price. This consideration partially takes into account the per share 'control premium' paid by the bidder for the purchase of the majority stake. In this respect, the Italian legislators tried to mediate the two diverging needs commonly identified in a tender offer scenario: (i) on the one hand, the need for minority shareholders not to be bound to a company that has changed ownership and management, so that they may be allowed to exit while sharing the 'control premium' with the majority shareholder; and (ii) on the other hand, the need for prospective bidders to be able to acquire Italian listed companies without being obliged to pay an identical premium to all minority shareholders.

These aims have been realised, in the legislators' view, by setting out the following main rules:

- a shareholding higher than 30 per cent is considered, for the purposes of takeover regulation only, as a controlling shareholding and therefore triggers, in the basic case, a mandatory bid;
- the mandatory offer price must not be lower than the average between the weighted average market price of the relevant class of shares during the previous 12 months and the highest price paid (or offered) by the bidder for any acquisition of shares of such class during the same period;
- the target's managers are prevented from creating post-bid defences without a shareholders' resolution approved by at least 30 per cent of the outstanding voting shares.

In 2003, as a result of a lengthy debate on the modernisation of the Italian corporate law, Sections 2325 to 2548 of the Italian Civil Code, regulating joint stock companies (*società per azioni*), limited liability companies (*società a responsabilità limitata*) and cooperatives, were significantly amended, effective from 2004, with respect to several material aspects relating to corporate governance, relationships between the company and its shareholders, shares and other special classes of securities, bonds, and financial statements.[1] In accordance with these amendments, certain sections of the Financial Act[2] were amended the following year in order to take account of the newly introduced classes of securities, thereby providing for a new definition of 'participation in the corporate capital', which is referred to, *inter alia,* in the provisions regulating disclosure thresholds and mandatory tender offers.

As a consequence of the above amendment, Section 105 of the Financial Act currently reads as follows:

> ... 'shareholding' shall mean a portion of the capital, held directly or indirectly through trust companies or nominees, represented by shares that give the right to vote in shareholders' meetings on resolutions concerning the appointment, removal or liability of directors or members of the supervisory board. Consob may issue a regulation whereby the relevant capital shall include classes of shares that give the right to vote on one or more different matters taking into account the nature of the influence their exercise, jointly or severally, may have on the management of the company.

Participation in listed companies
Disclosure thresholds

In order to guarantee the transparency of listed companies' ownership, Section 120 of the Financial Act and Section 117 of the Consob Regulation provide that a person (the 'disclosing person') whose participation in the voting capital of a listed company exceeds or falls below certain percentage thresholds must inform the relevant company and Consob.[3] The declaration must be made within five stock exchange business days[4] from the date of the transaction triggering the obligation, regardless of the relevant date of implementation. The relevant disclosure thresholds are 2 per cent, 5 per cent, 7.5 per cent, 10 per cent and subsequent multiples of 5 per cent.

To this end, the calculation of the shareholding must include (i) any shares owned by the disclosing person, even if the voting rights attached to such shares belong or are assigned to third parties; (ii) any shares whose voting rights belong or are assigned to the disclosing person, even though he or she is not the owner of the relevant shares; and (iii) shares owned (or whose voting rights are owned) by nominees, trustees or subsidiary companies of the disclosing person.[5]

In addition, Section 119 of the Consob Regulation provides that, for the purposes of disclosure relating to 5 per cent, 10 per cent, 25 per cent, 50 per cent and 75 per cent thresholds, the calculation of holdings must also include 'potential participation', meaning any issued and subscribed shares that may be acquired or sold (directly or indirectly) at the discretion of the disclosing person, such as by virtue of an unconditional option right. The potential participation deriving from the exercise of conversion rights or warrants must be taken into account only if the acquisition can be made within 60 days.

Notwithstanding the disclosure of a 'potential participation', a new filing must be made where exercising the above rights to buy, sell or convert results in the actual shareholding exceeding or falling below one of the general disclosure thresholds.

As a consequence of infringement of the above provisions, voting rights attached to undisclosed participation may not be exercised and resolutions passed with the casting vote of such undisclosed participation may be challenged under the Italian Civil Code and also by Consob within 180 days of the date of the resolution.

The notion of 'control'

Section 93 of the Financial Act defines the concepts of 'control'. In accordance with this provision, a subsidiary (controlled company) is:

- a company in which another company holds the majority of the voting rights that may be exercised at the ordinary shareholders' meeting;
- a company in which another company holds such a number of voting rights as to exercise a dominant influence over the ordinary shareholders' meeting;
- an Italian or foreign company over which a person has the right, by virtue of a contract or a clause in the by-laws, to exercise a dominant influence, where the applicable law permits; or
- an Italian or foreign company where a shareholder alone controls, on the basis of agreements with other shareholders, enough votes to exercise a dominant influence in the ordinary shareholders' meeting.

Tender offers

An offer to purchase outstanding shares of a listed company (the 'target company') can be either a *voluntary* tender offer or a *mandatory* tender offer. This latter is requested as a matter of law in the event that the bidder exceeds certain thresholds with respect to the participation held in the corporate capital of the target company.

There are four different types of mandatory tender offer:

- *basic case* – if the bidder, as a result of the purchase of the target's shares, holds a participation higher than 30 per cent;
- *downstream tender offer* – if the bidder, as a result of the purchase of shares issued by a holding company (either listed or unlisted), indirectly (or jointly directly and indirectly) exceeds the 30 per cent threshold with respect to the listed subsidiary of such holding company;
- *consolidation tender offer* – if the bidder, holding more than 30 per cent, but less than 50 per cent plus one of the target company shares, increases its participation by more than 3 per cent in 12 months; and
- *residual tender offer* – if the bidder, also as a result of a previous tender offer, holds more than 90 per cent of the target company shares and does not restore a situation of liquid trading.

Mandatory tender offers

Basic case

In the basic case, Italian takeover regulation is aimed at regulating the exit right of the minority shareholders in the event of a change of control. Notwithstanding the specific notion of control contained in the Financial Act, the legislature deemed it appropriate to set the relevant shareholding threshold at 30 per cent of those shares carrying the right to vote in a shareholders' meeting on resolutions concerning appointment, dismissal or liability of directors or of members of the supervisory board. This means that the obligation to launch the offer is not conditional upon the verification of an actual control by the mandatory bidder over the target company, but it is automatically triggered by the crossing of the 30 per cent threshold. This legislative choice was mainly driven by the necessity to identify an objective threshold in order to avoid the legal uncertainty embodied in non-objective criteria, such as the 'dominant influence' criterion.

Thirty per cent threshold

The 30 per cent threshold is calculated with reference to shares carrying the right to vote in a shareholders' meeting on resolutions concerning appointment, dismissal or liability of directors or of members of the supervisory board (relevant shares). However, Consob may indicate other relevant classes of shares to be included in the calculation of the threshold, on the basis of the rights attached to them and the consequent influence that the relevant owners may have upon the management of the company. Consob may also determine by a general regulation when a tender offer must be launched as a consequence of the joint possession of shares and other kinds of securities.

Price

Section 106 of the Financial Act defines the minimum mandatory price for the offer as the average between the weighted average market price of the relevant class of shares during the previous 12 months and the highest price paid or offered by the bidder for any acquisition of shares of such class during the same period. Therefore, the bidder is not obliged to pay the same price both to the majority shareholder and to all other shareholders. Rather, the price paid for the acquisition of the control stake is blended with the average market price of the relevant security. This should ensure both the equal treatment of shareholders and a fair average of the market price over a period sufficiently long to minimise the impact of extraordinary circumstances related to the trading of the securities in the 12 months preceding the offer. Indeed, it is possible that mandatory tender offers may be launched at a price lower than the last trading price preceding the offer.

Downstream tender offers

A downstream tender offer must be launched in the event that the threshold of 30 per cent of the target company's capital is indirectly exceeded as a result of the occurrence of the following conditions:

- the bidder purchases a share participation that leads it to hold more than 30 per cent of a listed company or to control an unlisted company (in both cases, the 'holding');
- the holding holds a share participation in a listed company (the 'participation');
- the aggregate book value of the participation exceeds one third of the holding's assets and is higher than any other holding's fixed assets, or, alternatively, the value of the participation is higher than one-third and is the main element of the price paid to purchase the holding's shares;[6] and

- the transaction leads the bidder to hold, as a result of the sum of such indirect participation and a possible direct participation, more than 30 per cent of the relevant shares of the listed subsidiary.

If the above circumstances occur, the bidder must launch a tender offer on all the outstanding relevant shares of the target company, at a price not lower than the average between the weighted average market price of the relevant class of shares during the previous 12 months and the highest price paid or offered by the bidder for any acquisition of shares of such class during the same period. In this case, the price paid by the bidder must be calculated on the basis of the value attributed to the participation.[6]

Consolidation tender offers

Section 106.3(b) of the Financial Act and Section 46 of the Consob Regulation impose a mandatory tender offer on a shareholder who, already holding more than 30 per cent of the relevant shares, but less than 50 per cent plus one voting shares, increases its participation by more than 3 per cent of all outstanding relevant shares in a period of 12 months.

This provision is aimed at granting an exit right to minority shareholders in the event that a significant shareholder consolidates its participation in such a way as to weaken the power of the minorities.[7]

In particular, as further explained by Consob,[8] the 12 months must be calculated from any share purchase backwards, so as to avoid a situation in which a shareholder consolidates its participation without launching a 100 per cent offer on all the remaining relevant shares, and the 3 per cent increase must be calculated on the basis of the minimum number of relevant shares held in the 12 months. The maximum number of relevant shares that may be freely purchased in a certain day (T_0) is equal to the result of the following formula:

$$(mRS + 3\%RS) - T_0RS$$

where
mRS = the minimum number of relevant shares held between T_0 and T_{0-365};
$3\%RS$ = 3 per cent of the relevant shares; and
T_0RS = the number of relevant shares held at T_0.

Residual tender offers

When a bidder exceeds a threshold of 90 per cent of the relevant shares, he may either restore, within the following 120 days, a number of floating shares sufficient for liquid trading, or he will be subject to the obligation to launch, at a price determined by Consob, a tender offer for all outstanding voting shares.

The above provision also applies in the event that the 90 per cent threshold is exceeded with respect only to a certain class of relevant shares. In such a case, the mandatory offer must be launched for the whole number of shares of that class.

It is worth noting that Consob is empowered to impose a higher threshold on a case by case basis considering the trading history of the relevant listed shares.

The price of the residual offer is set by Consob with reference to:

- the consideration paid for a preceding public tender offer, if any;
- the average weighted market price of the shares over the previous six months;
- the target company's net worth, adjusted on a current value basis; and
- the target company's trend and perspective earnings.

If the threshold is exceeded as a result of a previous 100 per cent tender offer and at least 70 per cent of shares that were the object of such an offer have been tendered, the price for the residual offer will be equal to the price of the previous offer, unless specific different reasons are stated by Consob.[9]

Squeeze-out

If, following the launch of a tender offer for 100 per cent of the outstanding voting shares of a target company, the bidder succeeds in holding a participation higher than 98 per cent in the target company capital, then it is entitled to force the purchase of the remaining shares. This, however, is subject to the condition that the bidder has previously announced to the market in the offering prospectus its intention to exercise such a 'squeeze-out' right.

The price will be determined by an expert appointed by the court, taking into consideration, *inter alia,* the price of the tender offer and the average market price of the target company shares during the previous six months.[10]

Concerted acquisitions (acting in concert)

Section 109 of the Financial Act provides that a mandatory tender offer may also be triggered in the event that the relevant applicable thresholds are jointly exceeded by related persons, or as a result of an autonomous purchase of one of them. This means that, if certain relationships between two or more persons exist, their relevant participation must be jointly considered in verifying whether the applicable threshold has been exceeded. Such relationships are those among:[11]

- the parties to a shareholders' agreement;
- the parent company and its subsidiaries;
- all companies controlled by the same company; and
- the company and its directors and/or general managers.

As a consequence, if a director of a company buys a number of relevant shares of a listed company, he or she will be obliged to launch a tender offer for all outstanding relevant shares of that company, not only where his/her participation is thus increased to more than 30 per cent of the company's relevant shares, but also in the event that the threshold is exceeded on the basis of the sum of the director's participation and the number of relevant shares owned by the company of which he/she is a director.

However, the most significant case of concerted acquisition concerns the parties to a shareholders' agreement. In this case, the legislature has assumed that persons who are mutually bound with respect to the exercise of their voting rights in the shareholders' meeting and/or the transfer of shares act in concert, and, therefore, that their participation must be jointly considered for the purposes of the mandatory tender offer regulation.

In particular, in order to identify which agreements are relevant for the above purposes, Section 109 of the Financial Act expressly refers to Section 122, which regulates duration and disclosure of the shareholders' agreements. Pursuant to Section 122, a shareholders' agreement is any agreement, whatever its form may be, that relates to shares of listed companies and/or of companies controlling listed companies, and that:

- regulates the exercise of voting rights in the shareholders' meeting; or
- imposes a requirement for consultation among the parties before they exercise their voting rights in the shareholders' meeting; or
- restricts the transfer of the syndicated shares or of other securities that grant the right to purchase or subscribe for shares; or
- regulates the concerted purchase and/or sale of company's shares or of securities that grant the right to purchase or subscribe for company's shares; or
- has as its purpose and/or as effect the exercise of a dominant influence over the company.

With reference to shareholders' agreements, the obligation to launch a tender offer is triggered both if the relevant purchase of shares occurs after the execution of the agreement and if the relevant purchase has occurred within the 12 months preceding the execution of the agreement.

On single significant issues, Consob has stated that:

- non-syndicated shares held by the syndicated parties must also be taken into account in the calculation of the applicable threshold, together with the syndicated shares;
- a shareholder's agreement is significant for the purposes of mandatory tender offers only if it is aimed at giving stability to the joint participation and/or coordinating the management of the company – so, for example, lock-up agreements must not be considered in the event that their purpose is to give stability to the market quotation of the shares for a short period after the initial public offering;
- amendments to the relevant shareholders' agreement must be considered only in the event of change of the prevailing party; or
- the simple renewal of a shareholders' agreement is not significant.

For the above purposes, Consob must also take into consideration those agreements that have not been duly disclosed pursuant to Section 122 of the Financial Act. To this end, Consob may carry out a specific investigation aimed at determining whether an undisclosed agreement exists or not. In a recent case, still subject to numerous legal actions, Consob, after carrying out an investigation into the relationship among certain shareholders of an Italian listed bank, deemed that they were mutually bound by an undisclosed shareholders' agreement concerning a dominant influence over the company. As a consequence, Consob challenged the validity of the shareholders' resolution under which the new directors had been appointed, since it was passed with the votes of the parties to the undisclosed agreement (pursuant to Section 122.4 of the Financial Act), and it imposed the launch of a mandatory offer, since the syndicated shareholders hold more than 30 per cent of the relevant shares of the bank.[12]

Mandatory tender offers: exemptions

Consistent with the rationale of the takeover regime, the Financial Act and the Consob

Regulation provide for certain exemptions to the obligation to launch a mandatory bid, in the event that: (i) the purchase leading over the relevant threshold is due to appreciable reasons that are different from the acquisition of the target's control; or (ii) the bidder has already offered to the minority shareholders an adequate opportunity to disinvest equitably.

Section 106.5 of the Financial Act and Section 49 of the Consob Regulation identify the following circumstances as exempting a shareholder who has exceeded the 30 per cent threshold from launching a 100 per cent mandatory offer:

- another shareholder, or other shareholders jointly, control(s) the majority of the voting rights that may be exercised at the ordinary shareholders' meeting of the target company;
- the threshold has been exceeded as a result of the subscription of a capital increase in connection with a plan, notified to Consob and to the market, for the restructuring of the debt of the target company;
- the threshold has been exceeded through intra-group transactions;
- the threshold has been exceeded as a result of the exercise of pre-emptive or redemption or conversion rights relating to the participation that was originally owned by the bidder;
- the threshold has been exceeded by no more than 3 per cent, and the bidder undertakes to sell the exceeding participation within 12 months and not to exercise the relevant voting rights during this period; and/or
- the threshold has been exceeded as a result of merger or demerger transactions approved by the extraordinary shareholders' meeting of the target company on the basis of actual and grounded industrial needs.

Section 106.4 of the Financial Act provides that the obligation to launch a 100 per cent tender offer does not apply if the 30 per cent threshold is exceeded as a result of a previous voluntary tender offer to purchase 100 per cent of the company's share capital, provided that such a preventative offer is in cash or in securities traded in an EU-regulated market.

Further, Section 107 of the Financial Act provides that the above exemption shall also apply in the event of a 'preventive partial tender offer', if the following conditions occur:

- the 30 per cent threshold has been exceeded as a result of a voluntary tender offer for at least 60 per cent of the relevant shares of the target;
- the bidder and/or its 'concerted' parties (pursuant to Section 109 of the Financial Act) has/have not purchased more than 1 per cent of the relevant shares of the target company, either in the 12 months preceding the launch of the above partial offer or during the period of the offer; and
- the partial offer has been approved by as many shareholders as represent the majority of the target's relevant shares, not computing those shares held by the bidder, the majority shareholder (even if a relative majority), to the extent that its participation is higher than 10 per cent, or any concerted party to the bidder and/or to the majority shareholder (pursuant to Section 109 of the Financial Act).

Consob must verify the above conditions and then grant this specific exemption. Note, however, that a 100 per cent mandatory tender offer must be launched if, during the 12 months subsequent to the completion of the preventive partial offer, the bidder acquires more than 1 per cent of the shares (even through a concerted acquisition or forward sales), or if the target company resolves on a merger or a demerger.

The tender offer process

The tender offer process involves different players: the bidder, Consob, the market, Borsa Italiana and the target company. Exhibit 18.1 summarises the main steps needed to launch a voluntary or a mandatory tender offer.

Exhibit 18.1
The tender offer process

	Mandatory offer	*Voluntary offer*
Launch of the offer	The offer must be launched if a purchase leads the bidder to exceed the 30% threshold.	The offer is launched at the bidder's discretion.
Notification to Consob	The bidder must notify Consob of the intention to launch the offer and simultaneously file the relevant prospectus within 30 days from the purchase triggering the obligation to launch the offer.	The bidder must notify Consob of the intention to launch the offer and simultaneously file the relevant prospectus, without a deadline.
Other notifications	The bidder must simultaneously inform the public, the target company and Borsa Italiana of the filing. If the target company is a bank, the bidder must also notify the Bank of Italy of its intention to launch the offer at least seven days before the board of directors meets to decide upon the offer.	
Consob approval	Within 15 days, but clarification and/or supplements may be requested.	
Statement by the target company	To be prepared by the board of directors of the target company and attached to the prospectus or sent to Consob two stock exchange business days prior to the public disclosure (the statement must be publicly disclosed within the first day of the acceptance period).	
Publication of the prospectus	The prospectus must be publicised immediately after the approval by publishing it in newspapers and/or by other adequate means agreed with Consob.	
Acceptance period	15–25 stock exchange business days (subject to extension up to 55 stock exchange business days). If the statement by the target company is not attached to the prospectus, the acceptance period will start at least five days after the publication of the statement.	25–40 stock exchange business days (subject to extension up to 55 stock exchange business days). If the statement of the target company is not attached to the prospectus, the acceptance period will start at least five days after the publication of the statement.
Price	Average between the weighted average market price of the relevant class of shares during the previous 12 months and the highest price paid (or offered) by the bidder for any acquisition of shares of such class during the same period.	The price is decided by the bidder.

(*Continued*)

Exhibit 18.1 (*Continued*)
The tender offer process

	Mandatory offer	*Voluntary offer*
Number of shares	100% of shares carrying the right to vote in shareholders' meetings on resolutions concerning the appointment, removal or liability of directors or members of the supervisory board.	Decided by the bidder.
Conditions	It is not possible to attach conditions.	The offer may be subject to certain conditions, provided that such conditions do not depend on the 'mere will' of the bidder.

Key rules on the conduct of the offer

The prospectus

The prospectus must contain information on the offer, the bidder and the target company. In particular, *inter alia,* the prospectus must include:

- the conditions attached to the offer (if any);
- the intention of the bidder to launch a residual offer (if the 90 per cent threshold is exceeded) and/or to exercise the squeeze-out right (if the 98 per cent threshold is exceeded);
- the structure, group, corporate bodies, business and financial standing of the bidder;
- the corporate capital, business and recent performances of the target company;
- the type, class and number of shares that are the object of the offer;
- the price of the offer, the reasons for the determination of the price and a comparison between the price and certain indices;
- the acceptance period, terms of payment and warranties concerning the payment of the offer price;
- the terms and conditions of possible agreements between the bidder and the target company, or between the bidder and any shareholders and/or directors of the target company; and
- the reasons for the offer and the bidder's future plans regarding the target company.

The statement by the target company

The statement by the target company is to be aimed at evaluating the tender offer and at informing the public whether the target company recommends the offer or is hostile to it. This statement must contain:

- any information that may be useful in evaluating the offer;
- a reasoned judgement of the offer by the board of directors of the target company, indicating the dissenting directors (if any);

- the announcement (if appropriate) of a shareholders' meeting to take defensive measures against the offer;
- an update on public information concerning the shares owned, directly or indirectly, by the target company or its directors, including shares held in companies controlling or controlled by the target company, or regarding any shareholders' agreement entered into in connection with the target company;
- information concerning any significant event not reported in the last financial statements or in the last interim report; and
- fees paid or payable to the directors, auditors and/or general managers of the target.

Conditions attached to the offer

Voluntary offers may be subject to certain conditions, either precedent or subsequent, provided that the occurrence of such conditions does not entirely depend on the bidder's will. The bidder may also waive the conditions, but only by expressly and previously reserving the right to do so in the prospectus.

The conditions most commonly attached to voluntary tender offers include the following:

- *minimum adhesion threshold* – the bidder may make the offer subject to acceptance by as many shareholders as would allow the bidder to reach a certain ownership threshold. This would give the bidder a way out of the offer if it does not receive the necessary majority at a shareholders' meeting;
- *material adverse change* – the bidder may make the offer subject to the non-occurrence of events that are capable of materially modifying the financial or economic situation of the target company and/or of its group;
- *defensive actions* – in this case, the tender offer will be effective provided that the target has not decided upon any defensive actions;
- *negative price variations* – usually, this condition refers to the average share price during the five days immediately before the launch of the offer and provides that the effectiveness of the offer will be nullified by any negative variation in the average share price in any subsequent period of five days running. A significant negative variation could range between 15 per cent and 20 per cent; and
- *public authorisations* – it is very common for tender offers to be conditional upon a favourable decision by the Italian anti-trust authorities and/or other necessary approval by competent authorities.

Fairness and equality of treatment

During the acceptance period, all the entities affected by the offer – the bidder, the target company, the companies belonging to the target group, the directors, the managers and the parties to relevant shareholders' agreements – are obliged:

- to disclose information only by way of official statements sent to Consob and to the public;
- to inform Consob on a daily basis about share dealing, as well as the terms and conditions of such transactions; and
- to observe fair conduct and ensure equality of treatment among shareholders.

In particular, they cannot engage in transactions aimed at influencing acceptance of the offer and/or alter the requirements for the mandatory offer, and they must communicate defensive actions (if any) by way of a clear, complete and fair communication.

Competing offers and increases

The Consob Regulation allows the bidder to revise its offer within three stock exchange business days from the deadline of the acceptance period, although the number of shares subject to the offer cannot be reduced.

Competing offers are permitted, provided that they are aimed at increasing the consideration and/or removing one or more of the conditions attached to the offer. With respect to competing offers, Section 44 of the Consob Regulation provides that:

- the competing offer must be published within five stock exchange business days prior to the expiration of the previous offer and in any case within 50 stock exchange business days after the launch of the previous offer;
- the acceptance periods of all pending offers are to be extended to be made equal to the acceptance period of the latest competing offer, unless such an extension has been waived; and
- the acceptance periods of all pending offers are to be extended by 10 days if the board of directors of the target company calls a shareholders' meeting, to be held during the last 10 days of the acceptance period, to resolve upon defensive measures.

With respect to increasing the consideration of a pending offer, Section 44 of the Consob Regulation provides that:

- increases must be published by means of a notice indicating the amount of the increase and supplementary warranties;
- publication must occur within five stock exchange business days after the launch of a competing offer or of another arising; and
- the last increase may be announced, at the latest, within 10 days from the expiration of the last offer.

After the launch of a competing offer or of an increase in a pending offer, shareholders may withdraw from the acceptance of other offers.

Within five days after the publication of the prevailing offer, securities tendered to other bidders may be tendered to the prevailing offer.

Defensive measures and the passivity rule

The Italian takeover regime limits the power of the directors of the target company to frustrate a tender offer by requiring that defensive measures against a hostile bid must be authorised by a majority of at least 30 per cent of the voting capital at a shareholders' meeting. It is not clear, and is therefore open to question, whether such a quorum must be considered in addition to, or in substitution for, the normal resolution quorum for ordinary and extraordinary shareholders' meetings.

The above rule, which is known as the passivity rule, applies to target companies starting from the date of filing of the prospectus. This provision is a result of the revision of the original Consob Regulation, adopted in 2000, after an adverse judgement by the competent courts in connection with a tender offer on a primary company. This challenged the legitimacy of the provision pursuant to which the passivity rule was effective from the announcement of the bid, even before the filing of the prospectus. As a consequence, the Financial Act and the Consob Regulation currently provide that, after the filing of the prospectus, the target company's directors are prohibited from taking any action that may block the offeror from achieving his purposes, unless such an action is authorised by a resolution passed at a shareholders' meeting by a majority equal to at least 30 per cent of the outstanding voting shares. Directors acting in breach of this provision are punishable by an administrative fine and may also be subject to an action for damages brought by the target company. Further, although the law does not directly address this issue, actions violating the passivity rule might be deemed null and void, as being in conflict with the rule of law.

Consob has indicated three main categories of defensive actions subject to the application of the passivity rule:

- actions aimed at increasing the financial burden to be borne by the bidder in order to complete the offer successfully, such as capital increases, conversion of saving shares or convertible bonds, or buy-back by the target of its own shares;
- actions aimed at modifying the structure of the target, such as mergers or other corporate restructuring, asset stripping transactions (sale of material assets of the target company) or changes in the business plan); and
- actions generally in opposition to the success of a tender offer, such as the launch of a tender offer on the shares of the bidder, amendments to the target's by-laws aimed, for instance, at introducing a limit to the ownership, or the introduction of golden parachutes for the target's managers.

Following the corporate law reform of 2003, the Financial Act allows listed companies to issue special shares whose voting rights are conditional upon the launch of a tender offer. However, the effective granting of such voting rights after the launch of the offer must be authorised by a majority of at least 30 per cent voting in a shareholders' meeting.

Under Italian law, shareholders' agreements do not protect the controlling shareholders from a hostile bid, since Section 123.3 of the Financial Act provides that any party may withdraw from a shareholders' agreement in the event of a public tender offer on the company's shares. Recently, the syndicated parties controlling an influential Italian listed company amended their agreement to try to insert in it a poison pill, which may be seen as aimed at bypassing the regulatory provision. The parties agreed that, in the event of a public tender offer, if a syndicated party intends to accept the offer, each of the other parties has a call option, at the same price as the tender offer price, to purchase the shares of the accepting party, in order to keep such shares within the syndicate. The enforceability of such clauses is uncertain and is currently subject to legal challenge.

The European Takeover Directive

On 21 April 2004, the European Parliament passed Directive 2004/25/EC, aimed at fixing minimum standards that member states of the EU must respect when regulating mandatory and voluntary tender offers. The directive contains certain provisions that are at variance with current Italian regulations, including the following:

- under Article 5, the price of a tender offer must be equal, at least, to the maximum price paid by the bidder to purchase target shares, in a preceding period ranging from six to 12 months, although the national regulator is given substantial discretion in this area;
- under Article 9, defensive actions must be authorised by a shareholders' meeting, although member states may opt out of this rule;
- under Article 11, multiple voting rights and other particular rights in opposition to tender offers are to be neutralised during the tender offer, although member states may again opt out of the rule;
- under Article 15, the squeeze-out threshold must be set between 90 per cent and 95 per cent, but in Italy it is exercisable at the 98 per cent threshold; and
- under Article 16, there is to be a sell-out, but there is no such right under Italian law.

The Italian legislature has not yet implemented the directive, so it is not yet known whether and to what extent the current Italian takeover regime will be modified, and, in particular, whether opt out facilities will be exercised or not.

Case studies

Two key concepts concerning the regulation of Italian listed companies – the notion of control and the mandatory tender offer triggered by a concerted acquisition as interpreted by Consob – can be illustrated by two well-known cases.

> ### Case study: The notion of control: Pirelli, Olimpia and Olivetti (Telecom Italia)
>
> A significant example of Consob's interpretation and enforcement of the notion of control pursuant to the Financial Act arose in the case of Pirelli and Olimpia. These companies were involved, from 2001 onwards, in certain significant transactions concerning the acquisition of Telecom Italia and the restructuring of the relevant group.
>
> Between July and October 2001, Olimpia, a newly incorporated Italian company owned by Pirelli (60 per cent), Edizione Holding (20 per cent), Banca Intesa (10 per cent) and Unicredito (10 per cent), purchased 26.96 per cent of Olivetti SpA, which merged with, and took the name of, Telecom Italia SpA. Scrutinising the transaction from the perspective of competition law, the European Commission maintained that the shareholders' agreement between Pirelli and Edizione Holding constituted a case of joint control over Olimpia. On that basis, and in order to prevent illegal concentration in the telecommunications market, the Commission ordered Edizione Holding to divest certain other overlapping industrial participations.
>
> With reference to a subsequent capital increase by Olivetti, Consob took a completely different approach and requested that the company indicate in the relevant prospectus that Pirelli had sole control of Olimpia which, in turn, had sole control of Olivetti. After Pirelli successfully challenged the decision, and further transactions modifying the ownership structure of both Olimpia and Olivetti (now Telecom Italia) had taken place, Consob issued

a resolution addressing all the main aspects relating to the notion of control contained in the Financial Act.[13] In this resolution, Consob stated that, in order to verify the presence of a controlling position, the following aspects must be examined:

- a shareholding higher than 50 per cent of the share capital may be 'weakened' by a shareholders' agreement or by certain clauses in by-laws giving significant management rights to minority shareholders. In particular, *de jure* control is excluded, notwithstanding the majority of voting rights at the ordinary shareholders' meeting, if a clause in the by-laws or a shareholders' agreement prevents the directors appointed by the majority shareholder from adopting material management decisions without the consent of at least a minority director;
- a minority shareholder is considered as a controlling shareholder if he/she has the majority of the syndicated shares pursuant to a shareholders' agreement and is able to impose material management decisions upon the other parties to the shareholders' agreement;
- *de facto* control must be investigated with respect to the ordinary shareholders' meetings approving the financial statements and the appointment of directors. Analysis of such control must cover an adequate time period in order to ascertain whether the dominant role of a shareholder is an occasional or a regular circumstance.

In consequence, Consob maintained that the shareholders' agreement between Pirelli and Edizione Holding did not 'weaken' the majority position or, therefore, the solitary control of the former, because the 'veto right' of Edizione Holding in respect of certain key management decisions could be by-passed by Pirelli, although Edizione Holding would consequently be entitled to exercise a put option right to sell its Olimpia shares to Pirelli. The put option right of Edizione Holding in case of dissent on key decisions had been considered by the European Commission as evidence, from an anti-trust perspective, of the joint control of Pirelli and Edizione Holding. However, Consob rejected this interpretation, pointing out that the notion of control that is relevant for anti-trust purposes is different from the one applying to financial market matters.

In Consob's view, therefore, Pirelli's ability to have its decisions passed without any consequence, but for the exit right of Edizione Holding, indicated that Pirelli was the sole controlling shareholder of Olimpia. Olimpia, in turn, had *de facto* control of Olivetti, since, on the basis of an examination of an adequate number of shareholders' meetings, it appeared that Olimpia had been able to appoint all the directors on its list and to have the majority in all shareholders' meetings approving the corporate financial statements.

Following the restructuring of the group in 2003, Pirelli no longer has control of Olimpia. In fact, although its participation is still higher than 50 per cent (at 50.40 per cent), Pirelli can appoint only five directors out of 11 and is therefore unable to impose key management decisions on the minority directors.

Case study: Acting in concert – SAI and Fondiaria

In July 2001, while Italenergia was preparing its takeover of Montedison, the insurance company SAI made an irrevocable proposal to buy Montedison's 28.7 per cent participation in La Fondiaria Assicurazioni (Fondiaria), another Italian insurance company. This proposal was accepted by Montedison even before it was made known to the public.

Consob stated that the acquisition by SAI had been concerted with Mediobanca, the second largest shareholder in Fondiaria, and that if and when the acquisition was completed, SAI and Mediobanca would have become jointly and severally obliged to launch a tender offer for 100 per cent of Fondiaria's outstanding shares.[14] Consob maintained, on the basis of its examination of the modalities of the acquisition, that it was possible to infer the existence of a shareholders' agreement, even if not one in writing, between SAI and Mediobanca concerning the purchase. As a consequence, since the joint participation of SAI and Mediobanca would have risen to 44 per cent of Fondiaria's share capital, it would have exceeded the threshold provided by Section 106 of the Financial Act.

The acquisition was not completed and the players tried to restructure the relevant transaction. SAI proposed a merger with Fondiaria that was completed only after a series of intricate financial and judicial decisions involving Consob, the Italian anti-trust authority, the Italian insurance regulator ISVAP, the European Commission, and both administrative and ordinary courts in Italy.

For the purposes of this brief analysis, focusing on the issue of concerted acquisition, it is worth noting that after Consob published its opinion, five new buyers proposed to jointly acquire the 28.7 per cent participation in Fondiaria that could not be purchased by SAI due to the tender offer obligation that would have been triggered. On 17 May 2002, Consob announced that the undisclosed agreement between SAI and Mediobanca seemed to have been terminated. The anti-trust authority carried out an in-depth investigation and concluded that the proposal by the five 'white knights' amounted to an indirect acquisition by SAI itself, due to certain undisclosed put and call option agreements entered into by the parties, coordinated by Mediobanca.

On the basis of the findings of this investigation, which reflected the fact that anti-trust officials have more effective powers than Consob does, Consob[15] compelled Mediobanca and Premafin (the company controlling SAI) to sell all shares in Fondiaria directly or indirectly owned by them above the threshold of 30 per cent of the share capital.

This case highlighted the uncertainties around the form and nature of a shareholders' agreement triggering a joint tender offer obligation under Section 109 of the Financial Act. Both Section 109 itself and Section 122, which lists the agreements to which Section 109 refers, expressly use the term 'agreement', which seems to link the 'concerted' acquisition solely to an express undertaking between the parties, either oral or written. According to this construction, the mandatory bid could not be triggered by an acquisition made by persons acting according to a 'conscious parallelism' and also not by virtue of an express agreement, even one that was not in writing. Although the difference between an express agreement and a 'concerted practice' is often disputed in anti-trust matters, it appears from the terms used in the Financial Act, and from the nature of a shareholders' agreement compared with competition restraints, that Section 109 requires an express agreement, even if concluded by means of tacit acceptance of a written or an oral proposal (involving the performance of the obligation without a previous expression of consent).

Consob did not explain in any detail the grounds for its opinions in this case. It thus failed to resolve the issue.

[1] Legislative Decree 17 January 2003 No. 6.
[2] Legislative Decree 6 February 2004 No. 37.
[3] For companies whose by-laws fix limits on the holdings of their shares, Consob may adopt specific measures laying down different disclosure thresholds.
[4] Intermediaries holding between 2 and 5 per cent for asset management activity may make the declaration within seven days of the publication of the notice of call for the first shareholders' meeting following the acquisition. In such cases, they shall also specify their holding at the date of the declaration.
[5] Pursuant to Section 118.3 of the Consob Regulation, shares registered in the name of or endorsed to trustees, and shares whose voting rights are assigned to an intermediary in connection with collective or individual portfolio management services, shall not be calculated by the persons controlling the trustee or the intermediary.
[6] See Consob Resolution No. DIS/99053857, 12 July 1999.
[7] See Consob Note of 6 March 2000.
[8] See Consob Resolution No. DIS/99093452, 22 December 1999.
[9] See Section 107 of the Financial Act and Section 48 of the Consob Regulation.
[10] See Section 111 of the Financial Act.
[11] See Section 109 of the Financial Act.
[12] See Consob Resolution No. 15029, 10 May 2005.
[13] Consob Resolution No. DEM/3074183, 13 November 2003.
[14] See Consob press release of 10 August 2001.
[15] See Consob press release of 18 December 2002.

Chapter 19

Luxembourg

Laurent Schummer
Linklaters Loesch, Luxembourg

Luxembourg does not currently have any specific legislation on takeovers relating either to companies having their registered office and/or principal establishment in Luxembourg or to companies whose securities are listed on the Luxembourg Stock Exchange (Lux SE). Takeovers have therefore been subject only to the general rules of Luxembourg securities laws governing the public offering of securities in Luxembourg.

This means that any takeover of a Luxembourg company or a company with a listing on the Lux SE that is a public offer to acquire the shares in such target is potentially subject to the *de facto* Luxembourg rules on takeovers. Such regulations actually apply only to exchange offers, whereby the offeror offers securities in exchange for the target's securities. Cash offers are not covered by the Luxembourg securities legislation, although the rules followed with respect to exchange offers have been broadly followed in such cases, on a voluntary basis.

Regulatory authorities and statutory provision

The competent Luxembourg regulatory authorities are the Commission de Surveillance du Secteur Financier (Supervisory Commission for the Financial Sector or CSSF) and the Lux SE.

The law of 23 December 1998 that created the CSSF and the law of the same date on the supervision of financial markets constitute the legal basis of the CSSF competence in relation to takeover review. Under these two laws, the CSSF has a general supervisory power over public offers in Luxembourg, as well as a supervisory authority over the Lux SE.

By a law of 10 July 2005 on the prospectus for securities (the Prospectus Law), Luxembourg implemented Directive 2003/71/EC of the European Parliament and of the Council of 4 November 2003 on the prospectus to be published when securities are offered to the public or admitted to trading and amending Directive 2001/34/EC (the Prospectus Directive), which must be read in conjunction with the Commission Regulation (EC) No. 809/2004 of 29 April 2004 implementing Directive 2003/71/EC as regards information contained in prospectuses, as well as the format, incorporation by reference and publication of such prospectuses, and dissemination of advertisements.

The Prospectus Law has maintained the general competence of the CSSF to supervise public offers that are made by issuers of equity securities having their registered office in Luxembourg. However, the Prospectus Law raises a number of uncertainties with respect to previous takeover practice in Luxembourg, governed mostly by the Grand Ducal Regulation dated 28 December 1990 on the requirements for the drawing up, scrutiny and distribution of the prospectus to be published where transferable securities are offered to the public or of listing particulars to be published for the admission of transferable securities to official stock exchange listing, as amended. These issues will have to be solved case by case until Luxembourg finally implements Directive 2004/25/EC of the European Parliament and of the Council of 21 April 2004 on takeover bids (the Takeover Directive).

One fundamental question is whether the Prospectus Law is still the appropriate legal basis for regulating the content of the prospectus for an exchange and/or cash offer for the purposes of a takeover. The Prospectus Law provides that the offering of securities in connection with a takeover by means of an exchange offer is exempt from the requirements of a prospectus, provided that there is a document containing information that is regarded by the CSSF as being equivalent to that in the prospectus required pursuant to the Prospectus Directive, taking into account the requirements of the Takeover Directive. This seems to confirm the CSSF's past requirement for a takeover prospectus, though still not for cash offers, but the content of such a prospectus remains undefined, unless the Commission Regulation referred to above were to be applied *mutatis mutandis* as the Grand Ducal Regulation of 1990 has been. Some flexibility may be expected from the CSSF as regards the actual content of such a prospectus.

A much trickier question concerns competence for approval and/or recognition of such a prospectus until the Takeover Directive is implemented, notably in relation to share-for-share offers. The Prospectus Law defines new rules on the competent authority to review a prospectus for public equity issues. Whereas a target may often be located in Luxembourg, the offeror is much less often located there, as is shown by the past history of takeovers. The question is whether a foreign authority will accept the task of reviewing a public takeover prospectus targetting a Luxembourg entity, especially in view of the fact that this is not the principle maintained in the Takeover Directive. Again, one may only hope that the CSSF and foreign regulators will show some flexibility, although the CSSF, by default, may wish to be the supervisory entity anyway, continuing its former policy of reviewing without formally approving, in the absence of a legal basis, any such prospectuses that are prepared under its general supervisory competence with respect to the financial markets.

The following description of takeover practice in Luxembourg is based on the situation as it was before the enactment of the Prospectus Law. It may change further as a result of the implementation in Luxembourg of the Prospectus Directive.

Conditionality of offers

Takeover bids on a target may be conditional. Conditions may involve either the obtaining of required approvals under anti-trust legislation and/or the reaching of a certain acceptance rate, or other, unrelated matters, provided that the fulfilment of any condition does not lie exclusively in the hands of the offeror.

Timing and revisions

There has been no mandatory time period for a takeover offer to be open or for any extension of the offer, but offers have generally been open for at least two or three weeks.

PART II: EUROPEAN JURISDICTIONS

The CSSF and the Lux SE have reviewed any prospectuses with respect to takeover bids within about 15 business days. The Prospectus Law now imposes a review period of 10 business days (assuming that this law is to be applied to takeovers).

No specific rules apply as to the time of the announcement of a public tender offer on a Luxembourg target, or as to the disclosure of the acquisition of major shareholdings in a company. Pursuant to the law of 4 December 1992 on the information to be published when a major holding in a listed company is acquired or disposed of, any acquisition of shares in an EU-based issuer listed on the Lux SE must be disclosed to the CSSF if the thresholds of 10 per cent, 20 per cent, one-third, 50 per cent or two-thirds are exceeded. A similar rule is applied with respect to non-EU issuers listed on the Lux SE pursuant to the internal rules and regulations of the Lux SE (Chapter XII – Article 29).

Equal treatment of shareholders not mandatory

Under Luxembourg law, there is no principle or rule that imposes on an offeror under a tender offer a duty to treat all the shareholders of the target equally. Equal treatment of shareholders applies to the issuer, not to the bidder in a takeover.

The absence of such a duty on the offeror has been confirmed in pending litigation involving the Luxembourg issuer, the RTL Group.[1] Appeal proceedings are still pending in this case, in which it is alleged that the Commission recommendation of 25 July 1977 concerning the European Code of Conduct relating to transactions in transferable securities imposes such equal treatment in its General Principle No. 3, as well as in its Supplementary Principle No. 17. So far, however, the Luxembourg courts have held that this recommendation does not have compulsory legal effect in Luxembourg and consequently does not impose any equal treatment requirement on shareholders in, or bidders for, a Luxembourg company. The CSSF has invited offerors under a takeover bid to comply with the principles of the recommendation, but has not taken any injunctive steps to impose equal treatment.

Given the absence of a general principle of equal treatment, different treatment may be reserved under a takeover bid for shareholders of different classes of shares or types of securities. Thus, for example, an offer on shares would not necessarily result in a compulsory offer on convertible bonds.

Minority shareholders have limited rights of protection under current Luxembourg law, since neither securities law nor company law entitles a shareholder to require to be bought out by an overwhelming majority shareholder holding more than a given percentage in a company.

Offer consideration

Luxembourg has seen cash offers, exchange offers and mixtures of the two. No obligation is imposed in exchange offers for a cash alternative, nor is there a requirement that any kind of guarantee for the actual payment of the cash consideration be provided.

The insertion of expert valuations into a takeover prospectus was not always required. Where such a valuation was independently prepared and was considered to be a useful part of the tender offer prospectus, the CSSF usually required its insertion, even if only by excerpt, into the prospectus. However, the CSSF has requested that the method for determining the offer price in a takeover bid is appropriately disclosed in the offer prospectus, in order to allow investors to make a proper assessment of the offer being made to them.

Target securities

Partial bids for shares or other securities in a target have been accepted in the past. There has been no requirement to acquire a minimum controlling stake in the target company, nor has a bidder been obliged to extend an offer for all shares of a target once such a controlling stake has been acquired.

Once takeover bids have had a certain success, they have been extended or renewed in order to increase acceptance of the bids, but on a voluntary basis only. There is no requirement for such a reopening of the offer under applicable Luxembourg legislation, nor has the CSSF or the Lux SE imposed such a reopening.

Offeree neutrality

The CSSF has not imposed the insertion of a report or an opinion by the board of the target company into the takeover prospectus, but it has strongly favoured it. Such a report has usually been inserted by excerpt into the prospectus. The opinion of the board did not have to have a specific content; it was sufficient to state whether or not the board supported the offer, since most tender offers in Luxembourg have been friendly.

Such a report may raise the issue of conflict of interest at the level of the board of directors if, for example, the directors are themselves holders of securities in the offeree company. It is recommended that the solution used in Belgium be adopted, that is, it should be stated that directors are not involved in a conflict of interest when adopting a position on an offer, even if they hold securities in the offeree company, and consequently they may properly participate in discussions of the board's report on the offer.[2]

There has been no requirement to insert into the prospectus the opinion of any other stakeholder in the target company, nor was any independent expert valuation by the target company required.

The directors of target companies have mostly played a neutral or passive role, this too resulting from the friendly nature of most of the tender offers made in Luxembourg.

In the absence of any legislation on takeover bids, there are no specific restrictions on the defensive measures that may be taken by the board of directors of a Luxembourg target company. Any such measures are limited solely by the general principles governing any actions of such a board:

- the board must act in the interest of the company while complying with the appropriate standard of care;
- the directors may not take any action that would result in an abusive use of the assets of the company;
- when the board acts on behalf of the company, it must comply with the principle of equal treatment of shareholders (in contrast with the absence of such a duty on the offeror, as mentioned above);
- if the directors act negligently or fraudulently, they incur a personal liability, pursuant to Article 59 of the law of 10 August 1915 on commercial companies, as amended (the 'Company Act'), and expose themselves to claims by the offeror, the company or the shareholders of the company;
- if the directors dispose of assets in a manner that is not in the company's interest and they do so for personal purposes or for the benefit of another company or undertaking in which

they are directly or indirectly interested, they are guilty of abuse of corporate assets and may be subject to jail terms and fines.

Under Luxembourg company law, authorised capital may be created, pursuant to which a board of directors is entitled to issue shares without further shareholder approval, up to certain limits set out beforehand in the company's articles of incorporation. In respect of such authorised capital, which the shareholders' meeting may put in place for a period not exceeding five years, the board may cancel or limit the preferential subscription right that the shareholders may have in respect of a cash capital increase. The board is not obliged to justify any such cancellation or limitation. It is sufficient for the board to explain at the time of the creation of the authorised share capital the reasons for the granting of such authorised capital and, in particular, to justify the proposed issue price for the shares. Nevertheless, any abusive use of the authorised share capital by the board is subject to the general principles set out above and may lead to personal liability of the directors or, as the case may be, to the invalidation of any abusive use of the authorised capital. On the basis of a Belgian precedent,[3] any use of the authorised capital is permissible as long as such use is made in the interest of the company. Such interest may consist in maintaining a stable shareholding in the company.

In order to fight a hostile takeover, and to the extent that this would prove useful, the board of directors may also repurchase the shares of the target company and may do so, even if the board has not obtained the authorisation by the shareholders that is usually required beforehand, for a certain price range up to an amount of 10 per cent of the share capital and for a period not exceeding 18 months. However, the board must have come to the conclusion that such acquisition is necessary in order to prevent serious and imminent harm to the company. When introducing the relevant legal provisions on share repurchases into the Company Act, the Luxembourg legislature specifically referred to such scenarios.

It is not possible for a Luxembourg issuer to create shares carrying multiple voting rights or limiting the voting rights of the shares in a company at a certain cap. The latter may be achieved only by creating non-voting shares, which are subject to strict Luxembourg regulation, for example, they carry entitlement to a preferred dividend and preferred liquidation proceeds.

Otherwise, actions by the board of directors are mostly unhampered. It is possible to include certain limitations on the powers of the board of directors in the articles of incorporation of a company, but the enforceability and/or validity of such provisions is largely untested, and may, under certain circumstances, be criticised. Nevertheless, the articles could validly provide that shareholders' consent is required for certain actions by the board in response to a hostile takeover attempt.[4]

Squeeze-out and sell-out

Luxembourg securities law does not provide for a squeeze-out of minority shareholders in a listed company. Luxembourg company law, as governed by the Company Act, does not allow a squeeze-out for any other Luxembourg companies.

For the purpose of inducing shareholders to tender in a takeover bid, the only applicable means has been to offer an attractive offer price and/or to threaten the delisting of the relevant issuer from the Lux SE and/or other stock exchanges. Such delisting has been granted by the Lux SE within a relatively short period, depending on the actual threshold reached by the offeror in his takeover bid attempt.

Impact of the Takeover Directive

The Takeover Directive will oblige Luxembourg to introduce legislation on takeover bids for the first time. The Luxembourg government has not yet submitted a formal proposal for the implementation of the Takeover Directive, so it is rather difficult to foresee what form implementation will take. However, Luxembourg has generally implemented EU directives very closely.

Given the RTL Group litigation (referred to above), one may assume that the Luxembourg government will be especially keen to ensure an appropriate level of protection for minority shareholders in target companies, as well as for other stakeholders in the target, such as employees. The Luxembourg legislation will consequently be compliant with the general principles stated in Article 3 of the Takeover Directive, in particular when it comes to the equal treatment of the holders of the same category of shares.

An offeror will have to guarantee the availability of the necessary cash consideration for purposes of pursuing his takeover bid, which has previously not been a requirement in Luxembourg. Article 5 of the Takeover Directive will also be implemented rather closely, in particular with respect to defining the appropriate bid price in a takeover and to imposing a cash alternative for consideration that does not consist of liquid (probably listed) securities.

On the other hand, certain principles to be found in the directive already underlie the policies of the CSSF and the Lux SE in reviewing takeover bids:

- shareholders must have sufficient time to reach a properly informed decision on the bid;
- the board of directors should give its views on the effects of the implementation of the bid;
- the board of the offeree company must act in the interest of the company as a whole.

These and other such principles will merely be 'consecrated' by the implementation of the directive into Luxembourg law.

As regards defensive measures, which are currently subject only to the general principles of company law, it may be expected that, given the great similarities between Belgian company law and Luxembourg company law, the Luxembourg legislature will follow the Belgian legislature and make certain corporate actions by the board subject to prior authorisation by shareholders. This would somewhat limit the target's board freedom of manoeuvre in taking defensive measures.

It may also be expected that Luxembourg will adopt the breakthrough rule provided for in Article 11 of the Takeover Directive, although it is too early to say what form this will take. The cases in which Luxembourg law permits mechanisms justifying the application of breakthrough rules are fairly limited.

One of the major innovations of the Takeover Directive, which will also have an impact on non-listed companies, will be the introduction of squeeze-out rights into the Luxembourg Company Act, following which a majority shareholder holding a given threshold will be entitled to squeeze-out minority shareholders. The threshold may be expected to be set at 90 per cent, similar to the thresholds existing in other EU jurisdictions.

One may also expect the Luxembourg legislature to introduce a right of sell-out for all companies, on the principles stated here, although it may be expected that the threshold for a sell-out will be set a little higher than for a squeeze-out, at 95 per cent.

The supervisory authority for takeover bids will undoubtedly be the CSSF, which is also the regulatory authority with respect to any public offers pursuant to the Prospectus Directive.

PART II: EUROPEAN JURISDICTIONS

Finally, it is to be expected that the CSSF will acquire important injunction powers and/or sanction powers, similar to those created pursuant to the Prospectus Law. Such injunction powers would entitle the CSSF to suspend a public offer, to request further information, to publish its decisions with respect to such public offers and also to impose administrative fines on either an offeror or an offeree that fails to comply with the legislation on the takeover bids.

---

[1] Tribunal d'Arrondissement de Luxembourg (8 July 2003), Conférence du Jeune Barreaux de Luxembourg, *Bulletin d'information sur la jurisprudence,* 8 October 2003.

[2] See Tractebel, Bruxelles, Neuvième Chambre (19 January 2001), *Journal des Tribunaux,* 2001, p. 105.

[3] Serous de Benedetti vs. Société Générale de Belgique, Bruxelles, Première Chambre (1 March 1988), *Journal des Tribunaux* No. 5488, 28 March 1988.

[4] Martin Elvinger, *Les défenses en matière d'acquisition de société, Droit bancaire et financier au Grand Duché du Luxembourg,* Vol. 2, pp. 1001, 2003.

Chapter 20

The Netherlands

Martin van Olffen, Jaap W. Winter and Michael Ch. Schouten
De Brauw Blackstone Westbroek, Amsterdam

Introduction

The Dutch rules on takeovers stem from a variety of sources. For instance, the practical aspects of public offers are regulated mostly by statute, whereas the involvement of trades unions is addressed in the voluntary Merger Code. Under applicable regulations, a number of obligations can arise at different stages of the takeover process. Hence, it is essential for potential market participants to have a basic understanding of their substance and impact. After a brief introduction to Dutch company law, this chapter discusses key features of the regulations that apply to takeovers in The Netherlands.

The typical vehicle for listed companies is the *naamloze vennootschap* (NV), a public company with limited liability, comparable to the German AG. A Dutch *Societas Europaea* (SE) may also be governed by the laws applicable to an NV. The basic corporate structure of an NV is similar to the corporate structure of public companies in most other jurisdictions. Notably, both the management and supervisory boards must act, generally, in the interests of the company as a whole, which includes all stakeholders (for example, shareholders and employees). The members of both these boards are usually appointed, suspended and dismissed by the general shareholders' meeting. The general meeting, in principle, also decides on the adoption of the annual accounts, the issue of shares, distribution of profits, amendments to the articles of association, and dissolution of the company. In addition, there is a statutory requirement of shareholder approval for any board resolution, as a consequence whereof the identity or character of the company is fundamentally altered. Shareholders or depositary receipts holders (discussed below) representing individually or collectively at least 1 per cent of the issued capital have the right to put items on the agenda, which may only be refused by the managing board if these were to jeopardise vital interests of the company. In listed companies, shareholders and depositary receipt holders holding shares or depositary receipts representing a market value of €50 million have the same right.

Notwithstanding the above, in practice, the power of the general meeting is often limited to a significant extent. For instance, the articles of association may stipulate that matters such as the issue of shares, amendments to the articles of association or dissolution can only be decided upon on the proposal of a different body, such as the management board or the supervisory board. Further, a number of companies are subject to the so-called 'structure regime', pursuant to which the powers of corporate bodies are allocated differently. This regime is mandatory to companies that meet certain specific (mostly size related) criteria or that choose to apply the structure regime on a voluntary basis by amending their articles of association accordingly. One key feature of the structure regime is the mandatory institution of a supervisory board, which has the power to appoint and dismiss managing directors (in other words, the general meeting does not have such right). In addition, a number of significant managerial actions require the prior approval of the supervisory board. The general meeting is only entitled to dismiss the supervisory board in its entirety and although the power to appoint supervisory directors is still vested in the general meeting, the supervisory board has the exclusive right to nominate candidates. The general meeting may recommend nominees, while the works council has an enhanced right of recommendation with regard to one-third of the supervisory board members. The general meeting has the right to reject the supervisory board's nominee by a simple majority of the votes cast provided that this majority represents at least one-third of the issued capital.

Methods of acquisition

The typical method of acquisition is by a purchase of shares. Such purchase can be made either by a private agreement or by a public offer, which will be made in the event the target shares are publicly listed. Alternative methods are purchase of assets and effectuating a legal merger, both of which are less common due to their relative complexity; tax considerations often determine this choice. A transfer of assets, in principle, requires the transfer of each individual asset, while different techniques of transfer apply to different types of assets. For instance, the transfer of real estate requires the execution of a deed of conveyance by a civil law notary and transfer tax will be levied. Liabilities need to be assumed, which requires the consent of each creditor concerned. Notably, where a business is acquired through the acquisition of assets and liabilities, the rights and obligations arising from the transferor's employee employment contracts are transferred to the acquirer by operation of law. The transferor and the acquirer are jointly and severally liable for the fulfilment of the obligations arising from these contracts (to the extent such obligations relate to the period preceding the transfer) for a period of one year subsequent to the transfer.

> **Examples: two asset purchase transactions – Equant NV and New Skies Satellites NV**
>
> Equant NV recently entered into a combination agreement worth €1.26 billion with France Telecom SA, its majority shareholder, pursuant to which Equant sold to France Telecom all of its assets, other than (i) the cash consideration to be received by Equant from France Telecom pursuant to the combination agreement; (ii) Equant's rights under the combination agreement; (iii) Equant's employee option plan and the proceeds of any exercise of options thereunder; and (iv) records relating to Equant's corporate organisation. As promptly as practicable after the completion of the asset sale, Equant was liquidated and the proceeds of the asset sale were distributed to the holders of shares in Equant (including France Telecom). Given the nature of this transaction, a major role was reserved for Equant's independent directors.
>
> A similar transaction worth US$1 billion occurred in November 2004, albeit the purchaser (the Blackstone Group) was not an existing shareholder of the company, New Skies Satellites NV After the closing of the asset sale, the transaction contemplated the liquidation of New Skies, pursuant to which two liquidation distributions were to be paid out to New Skies' shareholders.

A legal merger is a technique infrequently used in case of listed companies. In the absence of a specific tax regime, legal mergers can be quite complicated from a tax perspective. Furthermore, cross-border mergers involving an NV are not possible. This is different, however, with respect to the SE, which allows for both cross-border legal mergers and the transfer of a corporate seat to another EU member state without the need to dissolve the SE. The consequence of a legal merger is that the assets of the disappearing company are transferred by operation of law from the disappearing company to the surviving company. Simultaneously, shareholders of the disappearing company acquire shares in the surviving company or, as the case may be, a group company of the surviving company. For obvious reasons, this is different in the event the acquirer is the sole shareholder of the disappearing company. An exception may also apply where shareholders of the disappearing company are offered cash instead of shares, which may be done up to a maximum of 10 per cent of the nominal value of the shares allocated to the shareholders of the disappearing company. This latter technique, if applied correctly, may also constitute a mechanism to squeeze-out minority shareholders of the disappearing company.

Leveraged buy-outs in The Netherlands may be complex due to financial assistance rules. Pursuant to these rules, a company is prohibited from financially assisting a purchaser of its own shares. This includes the providing of security for the debt incurred by the purchaser. There are nonetheless different ways to facilitate leveraged buy-outs. However, it goes beyond the scope of this chapter to discuss these in detail.

Regulatory framework

Employee involvement

The Works Councils Act (*Wet op de Ondernemingsraden*) requires an enterprise which employs more than 50 persons to establish a works council, whose members are elected by, and from, employees. Its purpose is to facilitate a permanent platform for dialogue between employees and management. The act provides, *inter alia*, for mandatory advice procedures with the works councils of Dutch companies that are involved in a merger or takeover. If consultations do not take place in accordance with applicable rules, this may seriously endanger the execution of the anticipated takeover. If the works council's advice is negative and the management of the relevant company nonetheless decides to execute the takeover, the works council has the right to have such decision reviewed by the Enterprise Chamber of the Amsterdam Court of Appeal. The Enterprise Chamber has consistently held that entrepreneurs have large discretion in this respect and will only order a remedy if the entrepreneur could not reasonably have made the decision concerned. In addition to the Works Council Act, the Merger Code (*SER Fusiegedragsregels* 2000) essentially serves to protect the interests of employees by ensuring that the trades unions are timely involved in the process of a takeover by or of a Dutch company. The Merger Code applies where there is a direct or indirect change of control in an enterprise or any part thereof, irrespective in what manner such change was effectuated. A key principle is that the trades unions must be given an opportunity to discuss the acquisition (in so far as it may affect employees' interests) with the parties concerned. Contrary to the works council, the trades unions are not entitled to render advice or to have the decision of the management reviewed by a court. The Merger Code itself does, however, provide for a tribunal and although the Code lacks statutory force, if the tribunal finds that certain acts of the acquirer or the company are not in accordance with the Code, the tribunal may issue a public reprimand.

PART II: EUROPEAN JURISDICTIONS

Merger control in The Netherlands

The Dutch merger control provisions are contained in the Competition Act (*Mededingingswet*), which requires notification to the Dutch Competition Authority (NMa) prior to the anticipated transaction when (i) the companies concerned have a combined worldwide turnover of more than €113.45 million; and (ii) at least two of the companies concerned each achieve a turnover of at least €30 million in The Netherlands. Obviously, where the EU turnover thresholds are met, EU merger control rules apply and the notification should be made not to the NMa, but to the European Commission.

The Dutch merger control provisions are to a large extent similar to the EU provisions. Accordingly, when assessing mergers, the NMa generally follows the principles laid down in the decisions and notices of the Commission and the case law of the European Court of Justice. Notification can take place at such time as it is sufficiently clear that the parties intend to proceed with a proposed transaction. The NMa's investigation procedure has two stages, similar to the EU Phase I and Phase II system. In the first phase, for an initial period of up to four weeks, the NMa will examine whether the notification falls within the scope of the Competition Act and whether a permit could be required for the concentration concerned. A concentration that is found to be within the scope of the merger control provisions can either be cleared or be made subject to the granting of a permit. The NMa will only require that a concentration has a permit if it has reason to believe that a dominant position could be created or strengthened as a result of the concentration which could impede competition within The Netherlands. Accordingly, a permit will be refused if the proposed concentration creates or strengthens a dominant position, as a result of which competition in the Dutch market (or a part thereof) is significantly restricted. The NMa must deliver its Phase II decision within 13 weeks of receipt of the application. The Dutch test mirrors the former EU merger control 'dominance' test. A permit may be issued subject to restrictions and conditions, for example, a concentration may be allowed on the condition that the undertakings concerned agree to certain 'remedies' to deal with anticipated competition problems, such as the disposal of a part of their assets to third parties. In practice, very few cases are investigated at Phase II. It should also be noted that although the Competition Act does not provide for a simplified 'short-form' procedure and there is no separate form, the NMa frequently issues short-form decisions in relatively simple cases.

Public offers

In the absence of a mandatory bid rule, it is, in principle, possible to acquire a majority of shares in a Dutch listed company by buying blocks of shares in private transactions or by gradually buying shares on the stock exchange. However, in practice, this is generally not an alternative, primarily due to disclosure obligations pursuant to the Disclosure Act (*Wet melding zeggenschap in ter beurze genoteerde vennootschappen* 1996). Pursuant to the Disclosure Act, any person who, directly or indirectly, acquires or disposes of an actual or potential interest (such as convertibles or options) in the capital or the voting rights of a public company incorporated under Dutch law with an official listing on a stock exchange within the European Economic Area must give notice of such acquisition or disposal if certain thresholds are exceeded. These thresholds are currently set at 5 per cent, 10 per cent, 25 per cent, 50 per cent and $66^2/_3$ per cent, but will be slightly amended with the implementation of Directive 2004/109/EC (the Transparency Directive). A notification will alert the company and the public that a third party might intend to take control of the company. This will not only be reflected in the stock price, but may also cause the company to pursue defensive measures, effectively prohibiting the gaining of control. A takeover of a listed company will therefore typically take place by means of a public offer.

The offer rules

The Dutch Securities Act (*Wet toezicht effectenverkeer* 1995) and the relevant rules and regulations based thereon (collectively, the Offer Rules) apply to all securities that are either listed on Euronext Amsterdam or regularly traded in The Netherlands and which actually or potentially carry voting rights, including depositary receipts. Both friendly and hostile offers are covered and applicable rules are similar to a large extent, albeit some additional rules apply with respect to hostile offers, as discussed below. Supervision of compliance with the Offer Rules is exercised by The Netherlands Authority for the Financial Markets (AFM), which has a wide range of powers at its disposal to enforce those rules. To facilitate its supervision, a number of disclosure obligations exist *vis-à-vis* the AFM during the process of an offer.

The Offer Rules take as a starting point that a bidder makes an offer for 100 per cent of the securities of the class which he intends to acquire. Such a full offer is called a 'firm' offer (*vast bod*) as it should state the price or exchange ratio offered by the bidder. Alternatively, the Offer Rules also allow for making a partial offer with a view to acquiring a limited percentage of securities of a certain class. Such a partial offer can be made against a fixed price or exchange ratio, or may be made in the form of a tender offer. However, before and subsequent to completion of a partial offer or a tender offer, the bidder's total holdings may not represent more than 30 per cent of the share capital of the target company and the bidder is not allowed to increase his holdings above this level during the first year after the bid. In light of this, in Dutch corporate practice, the partial offer and the tender offer do not occur frequently. An example is the tender offer for Hunter Douglas shares.

> **Case study: Tender offer for Hunter Douglas shares**
>
> In July 2005, a successful tender offer was made for shares in Hunter Douglas NV, a limited liability company incorporated in The Netherlands Antilles. Due to the fact that the shares in Hunter Douglas are traded in Amsterdam, the Offer Rules applied. A tender offer by its majority shareholder, Bergson Holding NV, did not seem feasible, as Bergson already had a shareholding in excess of 30 per cent. However, Hunter Douglas, by issuing a new class of preferred shares to an ING finance entity, diluted Bergson's shareholding sufficiently to allow for a tender offer. Bergson's offer, and the non-intervention by the AFM, were not popular with several minority shareholders, including Franklin Templeton, a US investment fund. The latter, unsuccessfully, brought two legal actions. The first was an administrative law procedure aimed at forcing the AFM to intervene, alleging that Bergson illegitimately deprived them of a takeover premium by not issuing a firm offer. In these proceedings, Hunter Douglas argued successfully that its share issuance was (also) connected to a refinance of existing debts, while the AFM's primary argument was that Bergson acted in compliance with the Offer Rules. Subsequently, Franklin initiated summary proceedings at the Rotterdam District Court.

> In these proceedings, Franklin alleged, in short, that minority shareholders were faced with a prisoner's dilemma, having to offer their shares for a relatively low price to ensure inclusion in the tender offer or face the consequences of an illiquid market after completion of the bid. The District Court, however, did not find a wrongful act present and declined to intervene. It turned out that the alleged downward pressure on the offer price was not as significant as feared by some, as the offer price ultimately reached €44, €2 below the maximum tender price mentioned in the offer.

An important principle of the Offer Rules is that an offer can only be made by publicising a detailed offer document (the offer memorandum) which must comply with applicable rules. If the offer is (partly) made in securities issued by the bidder, a prospectus may have to be included. The offer can be made subject to the fulfilment of certain conditions, such as that (i) at least a certain percentage of securities will be tendered; (ii) there has been no public announcement of an offer by a third party or of the acquisition of a right to have shares issued to such third party; or (iii) no facts or circumstances have occurred since the offer was made, which are so substantial that the bidder cannot reasonably be expected to honour the offer. The Offer Rules require that the offer is extended to all holders of the securities for which the offer is made and that all holders of those securities are entitled to the same consideration. Moreover, the Offer Rules imply that if the bidder, since the initial public announcement of the contemplated offer, has acquired securities as defined in the offer for a consideration that exceeds the price indicated in the offer, all holders of such securities are entitled to a consideration equal to the highest price paid, except if the securities for which a higher price has been paid have been acquired on the stock exchange. If an offer has been honoured, the bidder is, in principle, not allowed to acquire shares in the target company for a higher consideration or on more favourable terms than have been offered to shareholders who tendered their shares in the offer honoured.

Dutch statutory law contains a strict prohibition against providing inside information to third parties and/or trading on such information. The intention to make an offer qualifies as inside information, and the prohibition against trading therefore applies to the target company if it is aware of the intended offer. Consequently, the target company at that point is no longer free to repurchase its shares. This is different for the bidder, who may purchase shares in it or in the target company even if the bidder has the firm intention to make an offer; knowledge of its own intentions does not qualify as inside information. Of course, this is different if the bidder has more specific information regarding the target company which is not publicly available, for example, information pursuant to a due diligence investigation. The prohibition against trading on inside information includes not only listed securities, but also financial instruments, the value of which is determined by the price of listed securities, such as stock options. In practice, major shareholders are regularly contacted prior to the making of an offer in order to gauge their interest in the potential offer and are asked to provide (irrevocable) undertakings to tender their shares. According to policy rules issued by the AFM, a bidder may approach a shareholder or a limited group of shareholders to investigate if, and on what conditions, such shareholders would be prepared to tender their shares. The AFM will accept this approach if it is necessary in order to assess the chances of success of the offer. The bidder would normally enter into a confidentiality and standstill agreement with any shareholder approached. For an irrevocable undertaking to tender shares under an offer to be lawful, the shareholder needs to specify in writing the number of shares tendered and, of course, the insider trading rules may not otherwise be violated.

Timeline

The following offers an overview of the steps and timing that typically apply in respect of a firm (friendly or hostile) offer. With regard to the possible impact of merger control regulation, reference is made to the previous section.

- *Initial contacts between bidder, the target company and/or major shareholder.* It should be noted that in case of a hostile offer, prior to announcing the price or exchange ratio of the offer, a hostile bidder must first notify the management of the target company and invite it to enter into discussions. The Offer Rules require that the management of the target company should be given at least seven days (pursuant to the Merger Code, 15 days) to scrutinise the proposal and respond thereto.
- *Further discussions between intended bidder and target company (and/or major shareholders.* It is standard business practice in The Netherlands to negotiate a letter of intent or merger protocol in which the essentials of the offer are set out and the conditions upon which the management and the supervisory board will support the offer. A due diligence investigation may possibly be performed.
- *Initial and further public announcements.* When an offer is contemplated and the expectation is justified that agreement will be reached between bidder and target, the public, as well as the relevant authorities, must be informed. After an initial public announcement has been made, the Offer Rules require that new developments are announced regarding the offer. In addition, the listing rules require making a public announcement of any fact or circumstance related to a listed company if it is to be reasonably expected that publication of such fact or circumstance would have a substantial effect on the share price. This requirement will become a statutory obligation as a consequence of the implementation into Dutch law of Directive 2003/6/EC (the Market Abuse Directive), which is anticipated in late 2005.
- *Consultations with the works council and trade unions.* The works council and the trades unions should be given the opportunity to express their views on the anticipated merger and at such stage of the transaction that its views may substantially affect the outcome of the merger discussions. In international transactions where the Dutch company to be acquired represents only a small portion of the overall transaction, the practice has been developed that the target and the acquirer conclude a merger agreement subject to the condition that the employee representative bodies in The Netherlands will have been involved and will have been given the opportunity to exercise their rights before closing. Following the implementation of Directive 2004/25/EC (the Takeover Directive), this may also become practice in strictly Dutch transactions. The consultations normally take between two and four weeks.
- *Clarification of the bidder's intentions within 30 days of the initial public announcement.* The bidder will be required to (i) make an offer or at least publicly announce the price or exchange ratio or (ii) renounce the offer or (iii) announce why a decision to make or renounce the offer could not be reached within 30 days and when such a decision is to be expected.

PART II: EUROPEAN JURISDICTIONS

- *Making the offer.* A firm offer can be made either by making an offer memorandum publicly available or by making a public announcement which must include at least the price or the exchange ratio (a summary announcement), in which case, within six weeks of the summary announcement, the bidder should make the offer memorandum publicly available.
- *Tender period of at least 20 days (friendly offer) or 30 days (hostile offer).* An extension of the tender period which results in a postponement of the announcement as to whether the offer will be honoured is only permitted under certain circumstances.
- *General meeting of shareholders.* A general meeting of a Dutch target company must be held. The purpose of the meeting is to discuss the offer with the management and supervisory boards no later than eight days before expiry of the tender period. At least four days prior to that general meeting, the management board of the target company must make available to the shareholders a report setting out its position with respect to the offer. The bidder may also be required to call a general meeting of its shareholders if it is a Dutch company and, as consideration for the securities in the target, issues securities with a total nominal value that exceeds 25 per cent of its issued share capital.
- *Acceptance or rejection of the offer.* A public announcement stating whether or not the offer will be honoured or withdrawn must be made no later than the fifth trading day following the expiry of the tender period. It is customary that a bidder commits itself to settlement within three days after the offer has been honoured.
- *Post-merger squeeze-out.* If the bidder acquired less than 100 per cent, but at least 95 per cent, of the shares of a Dutch target company, Dutch law offers the statutory right to acquire the remaining 5 per cent. If the bidder acquired less than 95 per cent of the shares, the bidder may wish to explore other possibilities, such as pursuing a legal merger or issuing additional shares to raise its interest up to 95 per cent. Dutch law does not contain a sell-out rule that would give a minority shareholder the right to sell its shares to the majority shareholder, but such rule will be introduced pursuant to the implementation of the Takeover Directive (discussed below).
- *Delisting.* Unless the target is also listed elsewhere, Euronext Amsterdam will generally allow delisting solely if either the bidder holds at least 95 per cent of the shares or if Euronext Amsterdam holds the view that trading is so limited that the listing no longer serves any purpose.

Takeover defence

There have been relatively few takeover battles in The Netherlands to date. This is probably due to local business culture, but can probably also be explained by the fact that most listed companies in The Netherlands are well protected against hostile takeovers, deterring potential bidders. This section offers a brief overview of the most common takeover defences and discusses relevant case law. In this respect, it should be noted that the listing rules of Euronext Amsterdam set a limit on the number of takeover defences a company may adopt (that is, two). Nonetheless, listed companies may still adopt various defences which have proven their efficacy throughout the years.

- *Structure regime (discussed above).* By preventing the general meeting from dismissing or appointing managing directors, it is generally felt that the structure regime effectively facilitates management entrenchment.

- *Limited voting rights.* According to Dutch law, voting rights of shareholders may be restricted to a certain maximum irrespective of the number of shares held by a shareholder. However, in practice, this has not become a very popular device. One reason is that such a restriction is fairly easy to circumvent by transferring shares on a temporary basis to other persons or entities which are informally controlled by the shareholder.
- *Priority shares.* Dutch law allows for differentiation in the articles of association between classes of shares and the powers which are attached to such shares. A specific class of shares includes so-called 'priority' shares to which specific control rights can be attached. Approval rights of resolutions taken by the general meeting (including resolutions to amend the articles of association) are quite common, as well as a right to nominate directors (the articles of association may also confer nomination rights upon another corporate body, such as the supervisory board). Such nominations can only be vetoed by the general meeting of shareholders with a majority which can be set at two-thirds of the votes cast representing more than one-half of the issued capital. Priority shares are typically held by a foundation created for such purpose. The listing rules require that no more than half of the board of such foundation may be constituted by managing directors of the company, but do not set any other limits in this respect. Consequently, in practice, the foundation's board may, to a significant extent, be composed of persons who should be considered to have ties to the company.
- *Issue of preference shares.* Many listed companies have created preference shares with financial rights that are limited to a certain percentage of their nominal value and do not share further in the profits of the company. As a result, their economic value is relatively low compared with the ordinary shares. Voting rights, however, are based on nominal values which are usually equal or even higher than the nominal value of ordinary shares, as a consequence of which a package of preference shares may provide the holder with the same voting power as the same number of ordinary shares would against substantial lower costs. In practice, this device is part of contractual arrangements between the company and a foundation created for the purpose. This foundation typically has the right to 'call' the preference shares in the case of a hostile bid. Alternatively, the company may have the right to 'put' those shares to the foundation if such circumstances occur. This assumes that the general meeting has authorised the management board to issue the relevant shares in respect of which such option would be exercisable. Such 'delegation' by shareholders remains conventional, but is becoming increasingly difficult for management to obtain. The listing rules require that the purpose of the foundation should be to further the interests of the company and of all persons involved with the company, including its shareholders and employees. The foundation's articles may include a reference to sustaining the independence and promoting the continuity of the company, but it should be noted that, in practice, the foundations concerned are under increasing pressure to act objectively. The listing rules also require that a majority of the board of the foundation be independent of the company.
- *Issue of ordinary shares.* If preference shares have not been created in the articles of association, the company wishing to protect itself against an unfriendly takeover may not have a choice but to issue ordinary shares to a foundation created for that purpose. As in the case of preference shares, contractual arrangements will be made between the company and the foundation limiting the financial impact, including that the foundation will not invoke its rights to a dividend (except a certain percentage needed to finance the bank loan to be taken out) and the shares will not be transferred to a third party.

- A traditionally fairly common anti-takeover device is the setting up of a voting trust (*certificering*). The shares are issued to a foundation created for that purpose which issues depositary receipts of shares to be traded at the stock exchange. Consequently, the voting rights remain with the foundation while the financial proceeds of the shares are distributed to the holders of depository receipts. The foundation is bound by the same listing rules that apply in respect of a foundation holding preference shares, as discussed above. The articles of association of the company will typically provide that a shareholder may only hold a limited percentage of the shares in the company (typically 1 per cent). The depositary receipts are thus not freely exchangeable for shares and consequently, in the event of a hostile bid on the depositary receipts, the bidder will, in principle, not be able to exercise any voting powers exceeding the limits set in the articles of association. Holders of depositary receipts do have a statutory right to require from the shareholder the granting of a power of attorney to vote in general meetings, but the shareholder is not obliged to grant such power of attorney when the company is facing a hostile bid.

Over recent years, a substantial body of case law on takeover defence has been developing. The prime forum of litigation is the Enterprise Chamber, which has wide-ranging powers to make provisional orders and/or initiate an investigation into the affairs of a Dutch company. In a landmark decision on 18 April 2003, the Dutch Supreme Court reviewed a decision by the Enterprise Chamber regarding certain defensive measures taken by Dutch property group, Rodamco North America NV, which was the subject of an attempted takeover by its competitor, Westfield Ltd. Westfield acquired a 24.5 per cent stake in Rodamco North America and wanted to transfer the management of the property to one of its group companies, without making a general takeover offer. The Supreme Court set out what would be relevant criteria in this case where the anti-takeover defence consisted of an issue of ordinary shares to a foundation on the basis of contractual arrangements, as discussed above:

- an anti-takeover defence may be justified if required in the interest of the continuity of the company and the interests of all its share- and stakeholders;
- an anti-takeover measure should aim to maintain the status quo while further discussing with the bidder its intentions and, to prevent that, prior to reaching a reasonable agreement with the bidder, the composition of the board and/or its policy will be changed in a way which would not be in the interest of the company and all its share- and stakeholders;
- a court would therefore need to test whether or not the board of a target company could reasonably have concluded, and did arrive at that conclusion in a diligent manner, that instituting the anti-takeover defence and maintaining the status quo was necessary in the interests of the company and its share- and stakeholders, pending further discussions with the bidder;
- a court, moreover, has to evaluate whether the anti-takeover measure was adequate and proportionately related to the imminent threat by the bidder and his intentions;
- in the light of the foregoing, it would generally not be acceptable to institute an anti-takeover defence for an unlimited period of time with the sole aim of neutralising the exercise of his rights by a shareholder controlling a substantial shareholding.

Impact of the Takeover Directive

The Dutch government is currently preparing a bill to implement the Takeover Directive, which law should be enacted no later than 20 May 2006. In the first half of 2005, a consultation document was published, the contents of which provide an indication as to how the Takeover Directive may be implemented in The Netherlands. On the basis of this consultation document, this section discusses anticipated changes to the rules that currently apply in The Netherlands, focusing on the key features of the directive.

The mandatory bid

As noted previously, Dutch law currently does not provide for a mandatory bid rule. An issue that is particularly relevant to The Netherlands when introducing such rule is whether depositary receipts will qualify as 'securities' within the meaning of the Takeover Directive and whether the acquisition of depositary receipts could trigger the obligation to launch a bid. Although in the Takeover Directive 'securities' are defined as transferable securities carrying voting rights, the Dutch legislature has proposed to regard depositary receipts as securities within the meaning of the Takeover Directive. Simultaneously, it is proposed that the statutory limitation on the right of holders of depositary receipts to require from the shareholder a power of attorney to vote in general meetings be removed, as a consequence of which such power of attorney should be granted also in the event the company is faced with a hostile bid. Hence, the holding of a certain percentage of depositary receipts should, in principle, imply the capability of exercising an equal percentage of votes.

It is proposed that 'control' over the target which triggers the obligation to launch a bid will be deemed present if the acquirer (i) has the ability to exercise more than the threshold percentage of the votes or (ii) his stake represents more than the threshold percentage of the share capital, whether by holding shares or by holding depositary receipts. The current proposal suggests that control is assumed to be gained by exceeding a threshold of 30 per cent. Although this percentage is in line with applicable thresholds in a number of other EU member states, it should be noted that whether exceeding the threshold will indeed yield control depends largely on the extent to which the company's shares are dispersed. If they are widely dispersed, control may already be gained at a lower percentage. In contrast, the presence of another shareholder representing more than 30 per cent may well prevent the gaining of control by the acquirer. This latter situation is not addressed in the proposed provision stipulating exemptions from the mandatory bid. According to the consultation document, exemptions will, however, be available in the following situations: (i) the target company qualifies as an investment fund; (ii) the acquirer gains control by means of a public offer; (iii) the shares are held on a temporary basis by a special purpose vehicle for takeover defence purposes; (iv) the shares are held by a voting trust foundation which has issued depositary receipts; (v) control is transferred within a group of companies; (vi) the target company has been declared bankrupt or has been granted temporary suspension of payments; (vii) the acquirer has gained control (that is, exceeded the 30 per cent threshold) by acting in concert with the controlling shareholder; (viii) the acquirer has gained control by means of succession; and (ix) the acquirer has gained control (that is, exceeded the 30 per cent threshold) simultaneously with the acquisition of control by another shareholder who can exercise more voting rights than the acquirer. Finally, an exemption will also exist where the acquirer lowers his stake below the 30 per cent threshold within 30 days of exceeding the threshold, provided the shareholder has not exercised his voting rights during that period.

PART II: EUROPEAN JURISDICTIONS

Board neutrality and breakthrough

Article 9 of the Takeover Directive requires that the board of the target company must obtain prior authorisation of the general meeting before taking any action which may result in a lasting impediment to the offeror in obtaining control over the target company. Applicability of such rule will seriously hamper the issue of (preference) shares as a defence mechanism. Although there remains some ambiguity in this respect, it appears likely that the prohibition against frustrating the bid will also prevent the issuing of shares pursuant to the exercise by the foundation of its (option) right to call the shares in the event a takeover is imminent. However, whether companies will indeed be bound to this restriction will depend on its shareholders, as the Dutch legislature appears to have chosen to use the option offered by Article 12 of the Takeover Directive, that is, to not require companies which have their registered office in The Netherlands to apply Article 9(2) and (3) and Article 11 of the Takeover Directive.

In addition, according to the consultation document, companies who choose to apply these articles voluntarily will, nonetheless, be allowed to refrain from adhering to them in the event they become the subject of an offer launched (directly or indirectly) by a company which does not apply these articles (the 'reciprocity rule'). This, *inter alia*, implies that Dutch companies may always set up barriers in the event they become the subject of a bid by non-EU and non-listed bidders, which reduces their apparent exposure to takeovers to a significant extent.

Article 11(2) of the Takeover Directive, in short, provides that, notwithstanding any restrictions in the articles of association or in contractual agreements, securities will be freely transferable to an offeror during the time allowed for acceptance of the bid. A key issue in this respect is whether this article affects the voting trust defence structure. As noted above, in the consultation document, depositary receipts are regarded as securities within the meaning of the Takeover Directive. Consequently, the typical restriction that depositary receipts may be exchanged for shares up to a limited percentage set in the articles of association would be unenforceable against the offeror.

Article 11(3) of the Takeover Directive provides that restrictions on voting rights shall not have effect at the general meeting which decides on any defensive measures in accordance with Article 9 of the Takeover Directive. Although such restrictions are fairly uncommon and multiple voting rights are currently not allowed under Dutch law, Dutch companies may have different classes of shares which may have a different nominal value. Shares with a higher nominal value will carry a number of voting rights equal to a multiple of the shares with the lowest nominal value. It appears that such shares with a high nominal value (and corresponding voting power) do not qualify as multiple voting securities within the meaning of Article 11(3) and would thus be unaffected by this article.

Finally, the consultation documents also provide for implementation of Article 11(4) of the Takeover Directive, containing the 'breakthrough' rule. If, following the bid, the offeror holds 75 per cent or more of the capital carrying voting rights (disregarding shares that have been issued as a takeover defence), *inter alia*, no restrictions on voting rights or any extraordinary rights of shareholders concerning the appointment or dismissal of board members provided for in the articles of association of the target shall apply at the first general meeting following completion of the bid, convened by the offeror in order to amend the articles of association or to remove or appoint board members. It is anticipated that the latter will also affect appointment and dismissal rights conferred upon the supervisory board pursuant to voluntary application of the structure regime.

Implementation of this rule in Dutch law will imply that holders of priority shares will not be entitled to control the dismissal and nomination of board members on the basis of nomination rights. As discussed above, this is already the case under current Dutch law as such nominations can be vetoed by a two-thirds' majority representing more than one-half of the issued capital. However, neither the text of Article 11(4) of the Takeover Directive nor the proposed provision implementing this article touches upon other special rights of holders of priority shares, notably the right to propose or to approve amendment of the articles of association. If such rights indeed were to be left unaffected, this could severely limit the actual exercise of control by the offeror over the target which it has acquired.

Although the fact that Dutch companies will be allowed to opt out of application of Articles 9 and 11 of the Takeover Directive which will leave them substantial room to manoeuvre, interestingly enough, the Dutch legislature has proposed the introduction of an additional provision. This provision reflects its adherence to the 'proportionality between risk-bearing capital and control' principle set forth in the High Level Group of Company Law Experts' report, which provided the basis for the Takeover Directive. According to the consultation document, it is considered undesirable that an offeror who, by means of a public offer, has acquired a stake which represents at least 75 per cent of the share capital would be permanently denied the power to appoint and dismiss directors of the company as a consequence of defensive tactics. Accordingly, it is proposed that in such case the offeror will be entitled to invoke the right to 'break through' when six months have passed after the offer has been made.

It is expected that this will provide a strong incentive to both the board of the target and the offeror to enter into a dialogue. Directors might then be inclined to do so in view of the fact that, after successful completion of the offer, the offeror will probably not hesitate to litigate against directors who, in his opinion, do not fulfil their tasks in accordance with their duties. If this provision is accepted by parliament, then, effectively, the defence against takeover bids in The Netherlands will no longer be foolproof, but will only allow for temporary defence in order to find an alternative, perhaps a white knight competing bid or to negotiate a deal with the bidder.

Chapter 21

Poland

Roman Rewald, Dr. Lukasz Gasinski and Anna Iwaszkiewicz
Weil, Gotshal & Manges, Warsaw

The regulation of takeovers in Poland is currently based on the Law of 21 August 1997 on Public Trading of Securities (referred to as the 'current Law') and the secondary legislation laid down for the implementation of that Law,[1] as well as the Commercial Companies Code,[2] which also applies to public companies.

However, Poland is about to introduce new legislation on the public trading of securities, comprising three laws:

- a Law on Public Offerings and on the Terms of Introducing Financial Instruments to Organised Trading Systems, and on Public Companies;
- a Law on Trading in Financial Instruments; and
- a Law on Capital Markets Supervision.

The new laws are aimed at securing a comprehensive unification of the capital market regulations in a manner consistent with European law. The new legislation is expected to come into force in the beginning of October 2005.

Significant changes in prospect

The new Law on Public Offerings and on the Terms of Introducing Financial Instruments to Organised Trading Systems, and on Public Companies (referred to as the 'draft Law'), will, if passed, implement a number of the provisions of the Takeover Directive in its chapter on significant shareholdings (Articles 69–90), which includes the following significant new provisions:

- new regulations on the launching of bids;
- more effective protection measures for minority shareholders;
- a requirement that more information is issued to investors; and
- a requirement that there be equal access to information on significant shareholders of public companies and on changes in the capital structure of public companies that could influence decisions taken by investors.

In addition, the draft Law:

- specifies the terms on which the minimum price of shares is determined in a bid;

- allows the Polish Securities Exchange Commission (SEC) to intervene in the terms of a bid; and
- removes the currently binding legal requirement to obtain the SEC's permission in order to exceed 25 per cent, one-third and 50 per cent of the total number of votes at a general shareholders' meeting of a public company.

However, it has been already pointed out in the Polish press that the current version of the draft Law does not represent an accurate transposition of the directive into Polish law.[3] Some of the crucial ideas in the directive – notably, the mandatory bid rule, the definition of 'control' and the transparency requirements – have been transposed only in part.

Conditionality of bids

Under Article 77.2 of the draft Law, an offeror will not be able to withdraw from an announced bid except when, after the bid announcement, another entity has announced its own bid pertaining to the same shares. The draft Law goes further than the current Law by providing that a withdrawal from a bid announced for all the remaining shares (shares not included in the original bid) in the offeree company (the company whose shares are subject to the bid) will be possible only when another entity has announced its own bid for all the remaining shares in the offeree company at a price not lower than that stated in the original bid.

This appears to be a remedy for a common practice in which it is not unusual for the offeror to make its withdrawal from the announced bid conditional on the acquisition of an appropriate number of the shares.

Timing

Under the current Law, the period allowed for the acceptance of a bid is defined in the Council of Ministers Regulation of 17 July 2001 on Specimens of Bids to Subscribe for the Sale or Exchange of Public Company Shares, on the Detailed Method of their Announcement and on the Terms of Acquisition of Shares in the Course of Such Bids (the Regulation of 2001).[4] The draft Law provides that, instead of the Council of Ministers, the Minister of Finance will issue an analogous regulation (under Article 81 of the draft Law). It can be anticipated that the regulation will be similar to the one currently in place and will also be consistent with the Takeover Directive's provisions on timing.

The Regulation of 2001 provides that the 'period of a bid' is a period commencing on the day the bid is announced in the press and ending on the day the subscription for the shares covered by the bid is closed. The subscription may not begin sooner than on the seventh day and not later than on the 14th day after the notification of the intention to announce the bid, and no sooner than on the third day after the bid content is published in a national daily newspaper. The time limit for accepting subscriptions must not be shorter than seven business days and not longer than 90 business days from the subscription opening date. However, in cases of subscription for the sale of all the remaining shares in a public company, the time limit for accepting subscriptions is a minimum of 30 business days and a maximum of 90 business days from the opening date. This time limit may be shortened if the objective of the bid has been achieved.

The Regulation of 2001 requires that the content of the bid specifies the time limit for conducting the bid, including the time limit for accepting subscriptions for the shares covered by the bid, with an indication of whether, and subject to what conditions, the time limit for accepting subscriptions will be shortened.

Disclosure of the bid

Certain information requirements are set out in the draft Law. Pursuant to Article 77 of the draft Law, a bid will be announced and conducted by a broker licensed in Poland. At least seven business days before the subscription opening date, the broker will have to simultaneously notify the SEC and the company operating the regulated stock market on which the given shares are listed of the intention to announce the bid. The notification will have to be accompanied by the text of the bid. After the bid has been announced, the broker and the offeree company's management board will have to provide information on the bid, with the text thereof, to the representatives of the company's trade unions (if any) or directly to the company's employees.

Following an analogous solution under the current Law, the draft Law requires that the Minister of Finance issues a regulation on the specimens of the bids, the terms on which shares may be purchased in the course of such bids and the detailed procedure for announcing the bids. The regulation must ensure that the content of the bids enables the appropriate assessment of the terms and conditions of the transaction, and must also determine the terms on which shares may be purchased in the course of bids, in a manner ensuring that the entities responding to such bids have equal rights (Article 81 of the draft Law).

The current detailed requirements on the contents of the bid document are set out in the Regulation of 2001. The Regulation provides that the contents of the bid, as well as information on the establishment of any collateral security, its kind and value, shall be published in the press. In addition, the contents of the bid must be published by the broker conducting the bid in at least one national daily newspaper and also made publicly known in the places where subscriptions for the shares covered by the bid are accepted.

The draft Law provides that three business days before the subscription opening date, at the latest, the SEC may request necessary changes or additions to the content of the bid, or explanations concerning the content, within a specified time not shorter than two days. The opening date will be delayed until the SEC's request has been complied with by the offeror (Article 78).

Mandatory bid rule and definition of 'control'

Under Article 154 of the current Law, any person who has come into the ownership of shares in a public company or of depositary receipts issued in connection with such shares, in a number providing over 50 per cent of the total vote at the general meeting of shareholders, must either:

- announce a bid to subscribe for the sale of the remaining shares of the company; or
- before exercising the voting rights attached to his/her shares, sell the number of shares that would leave him/her with no more than 50 per cent of the total number of votes in the general shareholders' meeting.

The draft Law provides that a shareholder may exceed the threshold of one-third of the total number of the votes in a public company only after the announcement of a bid to subscribe for the sale or exchange of such number of the company's shares as will ensure reaching two-thirds of the total number of the votes (Article 73.1). Further, a shareholder may exceed the threshold of 66 per cent of the total number of the votes in a public company only after the announcement of a bid to subscribe for the sale or exchange of all the remaining shares in the company (Article 74.1).

As a result of the wording of Articles 73 and 74 of the draft Law, no explicit definition of 'control', as required by the Takeover Directive, is included in the draft Law. It remains unclear whether the control threshold is determined by the draft Law at the level of one-third of the total votes, which would be an advisable solution in order to meet the objective of the Takeover Directive objective and compares well with the situation in other EU member states, or rather at the unusually high level of two-thirds. Since a shareholder that exceeds one-third of the total votes is obliged to bid only for the shares constituting two-thirds of the total votes, not for all remaining shares, the draft Law does not allow for exit by minority shareholders from the company when the offeror takes control. Such exit is provided for only when the control constitutes more than two-thirds of the total number of votes.

Under Article 74.3 of the draft Law, a shareholder who, within six months after conducting a bid for all the remaining shares in the company, has acquired more shares in the company in a procedure other than a bid and at a price higher than the price specified in the bid is obliged to pay the difference in the price to all the persons who sold their shares in the course of such bid, within one month from the acquisition.

If all the remaining shares in the offeree company are subject to the bid, the terms of the bid will have to provide the entities responding to the bid with the possibility of selling such shares at a minimum price determined in accordance with the draft Law (Article 76.2).

The draft Law specifies how to determine the price at which the shares covered by the bid are to be purchased (Article 79). If any of the shares in the offeree company are traded in a regulated market, the price may not be lower than the average market price over the six months directly preceding the date of the announcement of the bid, in periods when the shares were traded in the main market, or, if the company's shares were traded on the main market for a period shorter than six months, the average market price over a shorter period.

If the price cannot be determined on the basis of the rules specified above, or the company is in bankruptcy proceedings, the price may not be lower than the fair value of the shares.

In addition, the price for the shares offered in the bids may not be lower than:

- the highest price paid for the shares subject to the bid during the 12 months preceding the bid announcement date by the entity obliged to announce the bid or its dominant parents, or any subsidiaries, or any parties to an agreement with this entity to buy shares; or
- the highest value of goods or rights that the entity obliged to announce the bid, or the associated entities referred to above, expended in return for the shares subject to the bid during the 12 months preceding the bid announcement.

The price offered in the bid may be lower than the price determined in accordance with the rules referred to above only if the shares purchased from a specific person responding to the bid constitute at least 5 per cent of the offeree company's share capital and the entity obliged to announce the bid and such person agree upon such lower price.

Further, the price of the shares offered in the bid for all the remaining shares may not be lower than the mean trading price of the shares in a regulated market within the three months preceding the date of the bid announcement.

The demand to sell the shares may be announced after collateral security has been established with a value of at least 100 per cent of the value of the shares that are to be subject to the bid. The perfection of this security must be confirmed by a certificate from a bank or another financial institution granting the security or acting as an intermediary in granting the same (Article 77.1).

Any violation of the provisions of the draft Law relating to a bid announcement will result in elimination of voting rights. Specifically, a shareholder may not exercise his voting rights attached to:

- shares in a public company that are the subject of a transaction concluded in a violation of the obligations specified in the draft Law, reaching or exceeding a certain threshold of the total number of the votes;
- all shares in a public company if the threshold of two-thirds of the total number of the votes was exceeded in breach of the obligations specified in the provisions on a bid for all remaining shares as specified in the draft Law; or
- shares in a public company acquired in the course of a bid at a price determined in a breach of the provisions on minimum price rules.

Squeeze-out

Article 82 of the draft Law regulates the squeeze-out right. A shareholder in a public company that, independently or jointly with its subsidiaries or dominating entities, and with entities that are parties to agreements on purchasing shares, has reached or exceeded 90 per cent of the total number of votes in the company has the right to require that all the remaining shareholders sell all their shares in the company to such shareholder (forced buy-out). The forced buy-out will occur without any consent from the squeezed-out shareholders and its price will be established in line with the aforementioned rules on minimum price.

The shareholder conducting the squeeze-out may issue a buy-out demand only after establishing a collateral security for at least 100 per cent of the value of the shares to be purchased in the forced buy-out. The perfection of this security must be confirmed by a certificate from a bank or another financial institution that either granted the security or acted as an intermediary in granting it.

A forced buy-out must be announced and conducted through a Polish licensed broker. At least 14 business days before the commencement of the buy-out, the broker must simultaneously notify the SEC and the company operating the regulated stock market where the shares are listed of the intention to announce the squeeze-out bid. The squeeze-out bidder will not be allowed to withdraw from an announced forced buy-out under any circumstances.

Pursuant to the draft Law, the Minister of Finance must issue a regulation providing for the details of squeeze-outs with respect to the manner in which the forced buy-out is announced and the terms of acquisition of shares in the process of any forced buy-out.

Sell-out

Sell-outs are regulated in Article 83 of the draft Law. A shareholder in a public company may issue a written demand that its shares be purchased by another shareholder that has reached or exceeded the threshold of 90 per cent of the total number of votes in such company. As in the case of squeeze-outs, the price of a sell-out may not be less than the price established in line with the aforementioned rules on minimum price. The sell-out demand must be satisfied jointly and severally by the shareholder with 90 per cent or more of the votes, and its subsidiaries and dominating entities, within 30 days of the sell-out demand.

Protecting minority shareholders

Article 84 of the draft Law provides for further measures protecting minority shareholders. A shareholder that holds at least 5 per cent of the total number of the votes in a public company has the power to request that an extraordinary shareholders' meeting is convened in order to adopt a resolution commissioning a special auditor to examine a specific issue connected with the establishment of the company and/or the management of its affairs, at the company's expense, or to include this issue in the agenda for the next general shareholders' meeting.

Board neutrality and shareholders' consent

Acting under Article 12 of the Takeover Directive, Poland has decided to opt out of Article 9 and will therefore not apply the board neutrality rule to companies registered on its territory. Accordingly, there are no provisions in the draft Law that would prohibit the board of the offeree company from taking defensive actions to frustrate bids, even without the prior consent of a general shareholders' meeting.

However, in line with Article 9.5 and 9.6 of the Takeover Directive, Poland will ensure, however, that rules are in force requiring that the management board of the offeree company draws up and makes public a document setting out its opinion on the bid. Under Article 80.1 of the draft Law, the offeree company whose shares are subject to the bid will be obliged to state the formal position of the company's management board on the announced bid not later than two business days before the subscription opening date. The formal position of the company's management board must be notified to the SEC and to the company operating the regulated stock market, and also made public in the press and on the internet. The position of the management board must simultaneously be presented to the representatives of the company's trade unions (if any) or directly to its employees.

The formal position of the company's management board, based on the information provided in the bid by the entity obliged to announce the bid, must contain an opinion concerning the impact of the bid on the offeree company's interests. The opinion must address employment issues, the entity's strategic plans towards the company, and their anticipated impact on employment in the company and the location of its operations. It must also contain the management board's opinion as to whether the price offered in the bid reflects the fair value of the company, provided that the listing price of the company's shares thus far should not be the only criterion on the basis of which such opinion is issued.

The draft Law also requires that, between the date the SEC and the company operating the regulated market are notified, and the date of the closing of the bid, the entity obliged to announce the bid may not:

- purchase shares in the offeree company, except within the bid procedure and subject to its terms;

PART II: EUROPEAN JURISDICTIONS

- dispose of the shares in the offeree company; and
- execute any agreement obliging it to dispose of such shares.

Exemptions

Pursuant to Article 75 of the draft Law, the obligation to announce a bid does not arise upon the purchase of shares:

- introduced to alternative trading systems, which are not subject to an application to admit them to trading in a regulated market or are not admitted to trading in such market;
- from an entity of the same capital group;
- in bankruptcy or in the course of enforcement proceedings;
- pursuant to an agreement for the establishment of financial security executed by authorised entities on the terms specified in the Law on Certain Types of Financial Security;[5] or
- encumbered with a pledge in order to satisfy a debtor entitled under other laws to satisfy its claim by taking over the ownership of the collateral.

In line with Article 90 of the draft Law, the provisions of that article on bids do not apply to shares acquired:

- in a process related to lending through investment companies and trustee banks of securities traded in a regulated market, outside the system protecting the liquidity of such transaction;
- by an investment company in order to perform certain tasks connected with the organisation of a regulated market; or
- as part of a system protecting the liquidity of settling transactions.

Impact of the Takeover Directive

Although the draft Law transposes some of the provisions of the Takeover Directive into Polish law, it does not provide for a comprehensive implementation of the Takeover Directive.

It is important that squeeze-out and sell-out (provided for in Articles 14 and 15 of the Directive, respectively) are to be introduced under the draft Law. This is a significant change from the current situation, in which squeeze-out is regulated under the Commercial Companies Code and hence does not apply in the case of public companies.

In line with Articles 6.2 and 9.5 of the Takeover Directive, respectively, the draft Law requires that the bid and the formal position of the offeree company's management board on the bid are to be communicated to the representatives of its employees or, where there are no such representatives, to the employees themselves.

The method of determining the minimum price as set out in the draft Law is consistent with the provisions on equitable price in the Takeover Directive (Article 5.4).

The draft Law implements Poland's choice to opt out of Articles 9 and 11 of the Takeover Directive. Consequently, there are no rules on board neutrality or on the enforceability of restrictions on the transfer of shares, nor will the breakthrough rule banning multiple voting rights and other voting restrictions be implemented. However, it is worth emphasising that, in line with Article 351.2 of the Commercial Companies Code, the privileges in respect of the right to vote do not apply to public companies. In consequence, it will still not be possible to exercise multiple voting rights in a public company.

As described above, the draft Law, viewed in the light of the requirements of the Takeover Directive, does not explicitly determine the definition of 'control'. As a consequence, it introduces mandatory bids in an ambiguous way.

The draft Law is silent on the transparency requirements set out in Article 10 of the Takeover Directive. There are also no rules defining the competencies of the capital market supervisory authorities of EU member states in relation to bids covering shares admitted to trading in regulated markets in more than one such member states, nor are there any rules on applicable law.

Generally, it must be stated that, although the draft Law implements a number of the detailed solutions provided for in the Takeover Directive, it fails to incorporate some of the crucial ideas in it. However, since the legislature's work on the draft Law has not yet finished, it may be anticipated that certain provisions of the draft Law will be amended and that additional clauses may be added.

---

[1] *Journal of Laws* No. 118, item 754, No. 141, item 945; of 1998 No. 107, item 669, No. 113, item 715; of 2000 No. 22, item 270, No. 60, items 702 and 703, No. 94, item 1037, No. 103, item 1099, No. 114, item 1191, No. 116, item 1216, No. 122, item 1315.

[2] Dated 15 September 2000; *Journal of Laws* No. 94, item 1037.

[3] Oplustil, Krzysztof, 'Sham Harmonisation' in *Rzeczpospolita* No. 114 (2005), p. 4.

[4] *Journal of Laws* No. 86, item 941.

[5] Dated 2 April 2004; *Journal of Laws* No. 91, item 871.

Chapter 22

Portugal

Manuel Costa Salema
Carlos Aguiar, P. Pinto & Associados, Lisbon

with the assistance of Ana Bebiano

After promising signs of economic recovery during 2003, 2004 was a disappointing year for takeover offers in Portugal. The Euronext Lisbon witnessed poor activity, with no major deals taking place other than the bid by Semapa Investments BV for Portucel, a pulp and paper company.

Laws and regulations

The *Código dos Valores Mobiliários* (Securities Code), which came into force on 1 January 2000, is the main source of regulation dealing with takeover offers and includes sanctions for non-compliance. The Securities Code is supplemented by several *Regulamentos* (Regulations) approved by the Comissão do Mercado de Valores Mobiliários (CMVM), including Regulation No. 10/2000, which deals specifically with both public and private takeover offers. Sector-specific regulations are also relevant in industries such as banking and insurance. Finally, if the takeover offer has implications for competition policy, either on the national level or on the EU level, the *Lei da Concorrência* (Competition Act) can also play an important role in the course of a takeover offer.

In addition to the Ministry of Finance, takeovers are primarily supervised and regulated by the CMVM, which has broad powers in the interpretation and application of the regulations. The Banco de Portugal (Bank of Portugal) may also be significantly involved, as too may the Instituto de Seguros de Portugal (Portuguese Insurance Institute), in relation to sector-specific issues, and the Autoridade da Concorrência (Competition Authority), if the takeover offer is covered by competition regulations.

Bidder and target

The bidder is any person or legal entity that decides or is obliged to launch a takeover offer. Such offers can be either partial or general. No distinction is made between Portuguese and foreign bidders.

The target is any company qualified as a *sociedade aberta* (public company) pursuant to the Securities Code, including issuers of shares or other securities granting holders the right to subscribe or acquire shares that are or have been listed on a regulated market in Portugal.

Public offer versus private placement

The Securities Code draws a distinction between public offers and private placements. The former are subject to a more complex regime, involving, among other things, requirements for a preliminary announcement, a launch announcement and a prospectus.

Pursuant to these provisions, an offer addressed to indeterminate recipients is always public, including those addressed to all the shareholders of a public company. Offers solely addressed to institutional investors, including credit institutions and investment firms, are classified as private placements. These are subject to communication to the CMVM for statistical purposes.

Recommended versus hostile offers

Neither the Securities Code nor the CMVM's Regulations draw a distinction between recommended and hostile takeover offers. Both are allowed, although hostile takeover offers are still very rare in Portugal. The course of an offer tends to be longer and more expensive for hostile takeovers than for recommended ones.

The Portuguese market is often subject to rumours of impending hostile bids, but they often remain just rumours. Rumoured potential targets in recent years have included Grupo Media Capital, owner of a major TV station, and the commercial banks Banco Comercial Português (Millennium BCP) and Banco BPI. The sole exception in recent years was the failed hostile takeover bid for Cimpor.

In June 2000, Secilpar, a company controlled by Secil, a Portuguese cement producer, acting in consortium with Holderbank, launched a takeover offer for the entire share capital of Cimpor. On 19 June, Cimpor's board issued an opinion on the bid, stating that the purposes of the bidder were contrary to the best interests of the company, and, indirectly, to the best interests of the shareholders and workers; that the price was clearly insufficient; and, hence, that the takeover was inopportune. At the time, the Portuguese government could veto any shareholder from acquiring a stake in a privatised company, such as Cimpor, representing more than 10 per cent of the share capital. In July 2000, the Ministry of Finance informed Secilpar of its decision not to authorise the intended acquisition.

General versus partial offers

A general takeover offer is an offer for all the shares issued by the target company, as well as all securities granting their holders the right to subscribe or acquire shares in the target. Compulsory takeover offers are always general.

Partial takeover offers are for smaller percentages of the target's share capital above a minimum of 5 per cent.

The bidder in a general takeover offer benefits from certain advantages, provided that the general takeover offer incorporates a price calculated in accordance with the rules governing compulsory takeover offers. These advantages include the following.

First, squeeze-out rights are available only to those reaching the threshold of 90 per cent of the voting rights in the target pursuant to a general takeover offer. If a bidder reaches such a threshold pursuant to a partial takeover, it will need to sell as many shares as will be required to drop below 90 per cent of voting rights and launch a general takeover in order to be in a position to squeeze-out minority shareholders.

Secondly, the compulsory takeover rules are not applicable to bidders that reach the thresholds of one-third or one-half of the voting rights in the target pursuant to a general takeover offer. If a bidder reaches such thresholds pursuant to a partial takeover offer, it will be under a duty to launch a general offer.

In partial takeover offers, the percentage of voting rights is also relevant, as the regime limiting the powers of the target immediately upon receipt of the offer is invoked only if the same is addressed to shareholders holding more than one-third of the voting rights.

Compulsory versus optional offers

Subject to limited exceptions, any person or entity whose holding in a public company, either directly or indirectly, exceeds one-third or half of the voting rights, is immediately obliged to launch a general takeover offer.

This obligation does not apply if the concerned person or entity exceeding the threshold of one-third of the voting rights is able to prove to the CMVM that, notwithstanding its holding, it is not involved in a dominant or group relationship with the target company.

A dominant relationship exists whenever a party, regardless of the location of its headquarters, exercises or is capable of exercising a dominant influence over the target. This will always occur if the concerned person or entity holds more than half of the voting rights, either directly or through a shareholders' agreement, or has the power to appoint or remove the majority of the members of the board of directors or of the audit board.

A group relationship exists whenever, under the terms of the Portuguese Companies Code, the corporate relationship involves the holding of the entire share capital of a company or the existence of a contractual relationship (*contrato de subordinação* and *contrato de grupo paritário*). Once it has been proved that a dominant influence exists, the concerned person or entity immediately becomes obliged to launch a general takeover offer.

Further, if the threshold that has been exceeded is the lower one and the person or entity concerned exceeds, after the initial offer, the higher threshold, it also becomes obliged to launch a general offer. However, the person or entity may either be replaced by another in the fulfilment of this obligation, or suspend the obligation if, by means of a communication sent to the CMVM within five days, it undertakes to end the situation that created the duty within 120 days, by, among other things, the sale of shares in the target company.

Price

The offer price must be the same for each class of shares. However, the bidder is allowed to offer differential pricing for different classes of shares.

In optional takeover offers, the consideration can take the form of a cash payment, securities already issued or to be issued, or a combination of both. The bidder is also allowed to structure the consideration as an option on either cash or securities. Securities must be sufficiently liquid and easily valued. In addition, if the securities have already been issued, they must be listed on a regulated market or be of the same class as shares listed on a regulated market. If they are to be issued, they must be of the same class as existing listed securities. Optional takeovers are not subject to a minimum price.

In compulsory takeover offers, although the price may also take the form of a cash payment, securities or a combination of both under the same conditions as set out above, a cash alternative is always required whenever the price consists of securities. This cash alternative must be of a value equivalent to the securities offered as consideration.

Compulsory takeover offers are subject to a minimum level of price, which cannot be lower than the higher of the following: the highest price paid by the bidder, or any persons or entities related to it, for shares of the same class as the target shares during the six months prior to the publication of the preliminary announcement; and the average market price of the target shares during the six months prior to the publication of the preliminary announcement.

If the price cannot be determined by application of the criteria mentioned in the preceding paragraph, or if the CMVM does not agree to the price offered, it is allowed to ask an independent auditor to calculate the minimum price.

Special rules apply when a competing takeover offer is launched (see below).

Conditional takeover offers

Although the CMVM has become stricter as to which conditions are admissible, takeover offers are usually made subject to the satisfaction of a relatively wide variety of conditions, especially when the takeover offer is optional.

Besides being always subject to the approval of the CMVM, the bidder, when deciding to subject the takeover offer to one or more conditions, must take care that:

- the conditions serve a legitimate interest of the bidder, such interest to be assessed on a case by case basis;
- their fulfilment is not in the bidder's hands or dependent solely on the bidder's subjective judgement;
- they do not adversely affect the market; and
- they are set out in the preliminary announcement (since conditions set out solely in the launch announcement and/or the prospectus are not valid).

Compulsory conditions comprise regulatory approval by the CMVM and, where necessary, the Bank of Portugal, the Portuguese Insurance Institute and/or the Competition Authority.

In addition, it is common to have the following conditions attached to optional takeover offers:

- a minimum tender or level of acceptances from existing shareholders, commonly used by bidders wanting to ensure that they are not obliged to purchase less than a controlling stake. The thresholds usually required are 66.7 per cent of the share capital, giving a qualified majority at the general meeting of shareholders of the target, or 90 per cent of the voting rights, allowing the use of the squeeze-out right;
- provision for material adverse change in the target or issues related to judicial proceedings or breach of contract;
- commercial registration of amendments to the articles of association of the target; and
- whenever the price of the takeover offer includes securities, prior approval by the general meeting of shareholders of the bidder for an increase in its share capital.

Compulsory takeover offers are usually launched without any conditions, with the exception of those related to the registration of the takeover with the CMVM and the authorisation of the other regulatory bodies mentioned above.

When a condition has not been accepted by the CMVM, the bidder is allowed to agree upon the removal of the condition in question while maintaining the course of the takeover offer.

Defence mechanisms preceding a takeover offer

A significant percentage of Portuguese firms listed on the Euronext Lisbon live in the shadow of defence mechanisms that represent an important barrier to those wanting to launch a takeover offer. 'Poison pills' are not common, but other mechanisms are strong enough to discourage hostile takeover offers.

Golden shares still exist, though they are becoming rarer. For example, the state retains special rights over the appointment of directors of Portugal Telecom and also has a right of veto over certain of its material decisions. Multiple share classes are also becoming less common. Accordingly, the most common defence mechanisms in listed companies are:

- voting ceilings, which impose a cap on the percentage of voting rights when these are exercised by a sole shareholder or a group of shareholders acting as a consortium, despite the size of the holding;
- provisions in the articles of association for qualified majorities, higher than those required by law, for the approval of certain key matters, such as mergers and acquisitions;
- change-of-control provisions, which are found in a wide range of agreements, especially credit agreements, although, as the bidder in a hostile takeover has, in principle, no knowledge of the existence of such provisions, their impact as defence mechanisms is relatively limited; and
- shareholders' agreements among key shareholders of a firm, which, under the Securities Code, must be disclosed to the CMVM or, in some cases, to the public, if their purpose is to acquire, maintain or reinforce a qualifying holding in a public company (2 per cent, 5 per cent, 20 per cent, one-third, one-half, two-thirds or 90 per cent), or to secure or frustrate the success of a takeover offer.

Documentation

All documents disclosed in the course of a takeover offer must comply with high standards of accuracy, and the information given must be complete, truthful, up to date, clear, objective and lawful. If that is not the case, the issuers and their advisers may be subject to liability.

In the course of a takeover offer, the bidder must issue a preliminary announcement, a launch announcement and a prospectus. If required, additional disclosures may also occur if the contents of any of these three main documents need to be revised or complemented by new information.

Announcements are required to be published in a mass circulation newspaper and in the *Listing Bulletin*. The prospectus may be published together with the launch announcement and/or made available at the offices of the bidder and of the financial intermediary assisting the bidder.

Finally, the CMVM may also ask the bidder to disclose additional information to ensure that the public is well informed about the takeover offer.

The board of the target company is required to issue a statement to shareholders either recommending or opposing the takeover offer. In hostile takeovers, it is usual to see the target disclosing information contesting the information disclosed by the bidder.

Assistance of a financial intermediary

The Securities Code requires that a financial intermediary shall assist the bidder in the preparation, launching and execution of the takeover offer, providing advice regarding scheduling, pricing and regulatory compliance. It is compulsory for the financial intermediary to be involved in:

- the drafting of the launch announcement and the prospectus;
- the preparation and filing of the registration with the CMVM; and
- the assessment of the declarations of acceptance from the target shareholders at the end of the takeover offer.

However, such assistance is not required:

- in the drafting and disclosure of the preliminary announcement;
- if the bidder is already a financial intermediary authorised to carry out such drafting, preparation, filing and assessment for itself; or
- in relation to the assessment of the declarations of acceptance whenever the assessment is made at a special session of the stock exchange.

Timetable and actions

The key dates in a takeover offer, whether recommended or hostile, are as shown in Exhibit 22.1.

Exhibit 22.1
Timetable of a takeover offer in Portugal

Calendar days	Actions to be taken
- x	Bidder approves the launching of the takeover offer.
0	Bidder sends the preliminary announcement to the target, the CMVM and the Euronext Lisbon.
1	Bidder publishes the preliminary announcement; sends the draft launch announcement and the draft prospectus to the target and to the Euronext Lisbon; deposits the price in a bank account or is issued a bank guarantee and/or blocks any securities to be used as consideration; and applies for the authorisation and/or non-opposition of regulators (as required).
9	Target issues a recommendation to its shareholders.
21	Bidder applies for the registration of the takeover offer with the CMVM.
29	CMVM issues a decision.
37	Bidder discloses the launch announcement and the prospectus.
38	Beginning of the takeover offer period.
53/110	Assessment of the takeover offer at a special session of the stock exchange or by the financial intermediary assisting the bidder; disclosure of the results; physical and financial settlements.

PART II: EUROPEAN JURISDICTIONS

Preliminary announcement

The binding start of a takeover occurs when the bidder issues the preliminary announcement. The Securities Code provides that once the decision to launch a takeover offer has been taken the bidder must send the preliminary announcement to the CMVM, the Euronext Lisbon and the target.

If the takeover offer is compulsory, the preliminary announcement must be published within 30 days after the concerned person or entity has exceeded the thresholds of one-third or one-half of the voting rights. This reflects the regime adopted in the Securities Code, under which a compulsory takeover offer needs to be launched after a concerned person or entity has been allocated voting rights above these thresholds. The rules on compulsory takeovers are no longer based on an *ex-ante* basis, as they were in the previous legal framework in force until 2000.

The bidder is further obliged to publish the preliminary announcement in a mass circulation newspaper.

Launch announcement and prospectus

Between the publication of the preliminary announcement and the application for registration of the takeover offer with the CMVM, no later than 20 days after the publication of the preliminary announcement, the bidder must:

- send the draft launch announcement and the draft prospectus to the target and to the Euronext Lisbon;
- if the price of the takeover offer is in cash or includes a cash payment, deposit the price in a bank account or ask for the issuance of a bank guarantee ensuring the payment of the price, and/or, if the price is a mixture of cash and securities or solely in securities, block such securities in an appropriate account;
- if authorisations and/or non-oppositions are required to be obtained, apply for such authorisations and/or non-oppositions immediately after the preliminary announcement has been published.

Target company's statement

The target's board of directors must, no later than eight days after having received the draft launch announcement, send to the bidder and the CMVM, and publish in the bulletin of the market, a recommendation to its shareholders.

Registration with the CMVM

Within the period of 20 days after the publication of the preliminary announcement, the bidder must apply for prior registration of the takeover offer with the CMVM and deliver an extensive set of documents, including the draft launch announcement and the draft prospectus. The CMVM can require additional information.

The decision of the CMVM to approve or refuse registration of the takeover offer is strictly based on legal criteria. This does not mean that, if granted, the takeover offer will succeed; nor does it mean that the takeover offer cannot be rendered illegal by a judicial decision.

Decision by the CMVM

The CMVM decides within eight days following the receipt of the complete set of documents and other information filed by the bidder. The bidder is always allowed to amend the takeover documents if required to avoid refusal of registration, provided that the situation is reparable.

Once it has been made, the decision of the CMVM is issued to the bidder and disclosed through the CMVM's website (www.cmvm.pt).

Publication of bid documents

During the eight days following the disclosure of the CMVM's decision, the bidder must publish and/or make available the launch announcement and the prospectus. Failure to comply with this obligation may mean that the decision of the CMVM to approve the offer no longer stands.

Offer period

The offer period must be set out in the launch announcement and the prospectus. It may vary between two and 10 weeks. The period usually starts on the working day following the publication of the documents, and ends with the assessment and publication of its results, either at a special stock exchange session organised by the Euronext Lisbon or by the financial intermediary assisting the bidder, followed by the physical and financial settlements.

Revision

The bidder is allowed to revise the conditions of an offer, but only in order to improve the price or if a material change of circumstances occurs.

If the bidder decides to revise the price, either by changing the amount or by changing its nature, the value of the revised price must be increased by at least 5 per cent. A revision of the price is allowed only until the 10th day before the end of the takeover offer period.

A substantial and unpredictable change in circumstances may also allow the bidder to withdraw the offer. However, the bidder needs to demonstrate that, as a result of the change of circumstances, the risks associated with the offer have substantially and unreasonably increased. Withdrawal of the offer is subject to prior authorisation by the CMVM and to judicial review.

Although the CMVM may decide to extend the offer period, either by unilateral decision or following a request by the bidder, such a revision has no impact on acceptances already given by the target shareholders (if any), which remain valid.

Post-bid neutrality

As soon as the target has knowledge of a takeover offer targetting more than one-third of its shares – for example, upon reception of the preliminary announcement – the powers of its board of directors become very limited. From then on, the board may not perform any action likely to cause a relevant change in the target's assets that may harm the intentions disclosed by the bidder. Relevant changes include the issuing of new shares or other securities (poison pills) and the execution of agreements governing the sale of important assets (crown jewels).

However, the following actions are not covered by the limitation: those resulting from the fulfilment of obligations assumed before the target had knowledge of the takeover offer, and those approved by a general meeting of shareholders called after the preliminary announcement of the takeover offer has been disclosed with minimum prior notice of 30 days. Resolutions approved by such a shareholders' meeting, including those relating to interim distribution of dividends or other income, can be approved only by the qualified majority required for a change to the articles of association of the target, being either the two-thirds majority required by the Companies Code or a higher majority set out in the articles.

The ability of the target to set up defence mechanisms is thus very limited. Solutions such as the launching of a competing takeover offer by a white knight, or Pac-man offers, are permitted, but they require approval by a large percentage of the target's shareholders, which may be difficult to obtain in the course of an offer. As a consequence, the recommendation issued by the target's board of directors constitutes the main post-bid defence against hostile takeovers in Portugal.

Squeeze-out and sell-out rights

Following a takeover offer, if a bidder acquires, directly or indirectly, more than 90 per cent of the voting rights in the target, it has the statutory right to acquire minority shareholdings on a compulsory basis, provided that:

- the preceding takeover offer was for all the shares issued by the target, as well as all securities issued by the target granting their holders the right to subscribe or acquire such shares;
- the offer price was calculated in accordance with the rules on compulsory takeover offers;
- the price to be offered to minority shareholders is also calculated under the same rules; and
- the squeeze-out right is exercised within six months following the publication of the results of the preceding takeover offer.

To exercise the squeeze-out right, the bidder must publish a preliminary announcement and send it to the CMVM for registration, and also deposit the price of the compulsory acquisition in a credit institution.

The compulsory acquisition becomes effective upon publication by the bidder of the registration granted by the CMVM. All shares and securities granting rights for subscription and acquisition are immediately delisted, and may not be relisted within the following two years.

If the squeeze-out right is not exercised within the six months mentioned, each of the remaining minority shareholders may ask the bidder to make an offer for acquisition of their shares in the subsequent 30 days. If the offer is not made or not accepted, the minority shareholders are entitled to exercise a sell-out right, which becomes effective once the CMVM has notified the bidder.

To exercise their sell-out right, the minority shareholders must inform the CMVM, indicate a price calculated under the rules for compulsory takeover offers and file a document attesting that their shares are deposited or blocked.

Successive takeover offers

Except as authorised by the CMVM, if a takeover offer fails, the bidder is not allowed, directly or indirectly, to launch a new takeover offer targetting shares of the same class in the 12 months following the publication of the results of the initial takeover offer.

This rule does not apply, however, if the bidder is obliged to launch a compulsory takeover offer.

Competing offers

Competing takeover offers are those launched immediately after the publication of the preliminary announcement and up to the day before the last day on which the initial takeover offer period ends. A competing takeover offer must target at least the same shares targetted by the initial takeover offer and the price must be at least 5 per cent higher than the price offered in the initial takeover offer.

Upon the launching of a competing takeover offer, the initial bidder may:

- revise the conditions of its initial takeover offer – including an increase of at least 5 per cent in the price offered – inform the CMVM and publish an announcement within four days following the launch of the competing offer; or
- do nothing, which means that the initial takeover offer remains valid, with no change in its conditions; or
- revoke the initial takeover offer, publishing the decision to do so within four days following the publication of the preliminary announcement of the competing offer.

The timetable for a competing takeover offer will vary depending on the date of publication of its preliminary announcement. If this is published before the initial offer is registered with the CMVM, the timetable of both takeover offers will be the same. If the preliminary announcement is published later, the competing bidder must apply for registration with the CMVM within eight days following the publication of the preliminary announcement (instead of the usual 20 days) and the target's board of directors must issue a recommendation within four days following the reception of the draft launch announcement (instead of the usual eight days).

Impact of the Takeover Directive

It is not yet clear whether the Portuguese government will opt out of the provisions of the Takeover Directive relating to defensive actions and breakthrough contained in Articles 9 and 11. In any case, the Securities Code will not be substantially modified as a result of any transposition, since the Portuguese legislature, when preparing the Securities Code, already took into account some of the solutions incorporated in the proposal for the Takeover Directive of 1997.

The material impact will mostly occur if the breakthrough rule is fully transposed. As mentioned above, many public companies deploy defence mechanisms that reduce the likelihood of success of hostile takeover offers. Examples include EDP, Portugal's largest electricity provider, as well as PT and Millennium BCP. Due to their market share and their importance in the Portuguese economy, these companies will surely become interesting potential targets for some of the largest European groups.

The readoption of the concept of 'acting in concert' (which was included in the Securities Code of 1991, but was later removed) may also play an important role in relation to the allocation of voting rights under the Securities Code.

Important considerations for bidders

Bidders should take a careful approach when attempting to enter into pre-bid agreements with target shareholders because of the broad discretion of the CMVM in applying and interpreting the takeover rules, especially those relating to the allocation of voting rights in listed companies and to price in compulsory takeover offers.

Bidders should set up a small and reliable team to avoid breach of confidentiality due to the relatively small number of market players usually involved in takeover offers.

Bidders should investigate if the target shareholders are bound by shareholders' agreements (possibly not disclosed to the CMVM) that could frustrate the takeover offer.

If the target is protected by voting ceilings (the most common defence mechanism in Portugal), bidders should be prepared to set up a stake-building strategy instead of a takeover offer (whether friendly or hostile).

Bidders should be prepared to face strong opposition if the takeover offer is hostile, especially in relation to blue chip targets.

Chapter 23

Russia

Scott C. Senecal, Murat N. Akuyev and Yulia A. Solomakhina
Cleary Gottlieb Steen & Hamilton, Moscow

Russia does not have a single statutory code that comprehensively addresses and governs corporate takeovers and related issues. Instead, the regulatory framework for takeovers is created by a number of statutes and other regulatory acts, in particular:

- the Federal Law on Joint Stock Companies, No. 208-FZ, dated 26 December 1995, as amended (the 'Joint Stock Companies Law' or 'JSCL');
- the Law of the former RSFSR on Competition and Limitation of Monopolistic Activity in Commodities Markets, No. 948-I, dated 22 March 1991, as amended (the 'Anti-Monopoly Law'); and
- the Federal Law on the Securities Market, No. 39-FZ, dated 22 April 1996, as amended (the 'Securities Law').

A number of regulatory acts passed by executive bodies implement these statutes.

It should be noted that corporate takeover practice in Russia is a relatively recent phenomenon. Cases where Russian courts have considered corporate takeover matters are few. In recent years, there has been no significant public hostile takeover bid launched on a Russian company, in part because many Russian companies have relatively illiquid share ownership and because the board of directors of the target company is likely to be able to frustrate a hostile bid. Further, many Russian businesses are organised using offshore holding structures, with Cyprus being one traditional jurisdiction for the parent holding company, and takeovers are often implemented at this offshore level.

There have been instances reported where bankruptcy proceedings were aggressively pursued in Russia by creditors or acquirers as a takeover strategy; such tactics are outside the scope of this chapter. Takeovers might also be pursued by way of consolidation, in which a new company is formed by the consolidation of two existing companies, or merger, in which the first company is fully merged into a second company and the first company's legal personality is terminated, but these tactics are not generally pursued.[1]

Takeovers of banks, other credit organisations and insurance companies are subject to specific regulatory requirements.[2] Foreign ownership restrictions also apply for some sectors, such as civil and military aviation, the defence sector generally,[3] and the media.[4]

PART II: EUROPEAN JURISDICTIONS

Anti-takeover provisions of the Joint Stock Companies Law

Scope of the requirements of Article 80

Article 80 of the Joint Stock Companies Law contains two sets of requirements applicable in a takeover context: the prior notification requirement and the tender offer requirement. These requirements apply to any joint stock company that has more than 1,000 shareholders holding its common stock. The sanctions for violating the requirements of Article 80 are limited.

With respect to the notification requirement, Article 80 provides that a person seeking to acquire, individually or together with its affiliates, 30 per cent or more of the issued common shares, including any shares already held by the acquirer and its affiliates, in a joint stock company must notify the company in writing about its intention no earlier than 90 days and no later than 30 days before such acquisition.[5] There are no other specific requirements with respect to such notification. Written notice addressed to the chief executive officer of the company should suffice to satisfy the notification requirement. However, the chief executive officer is not obliged under the Joint Stock Companies Law to inform shareholders of the target company of the offer.

With respect to the tender offer requirement, Article 80 requires that a person that, individually or together with its affiliates, has acquired 30 per cent or more of the issued common shares in a joint stock company must, within 30 days of such acquisition, offer to the other shareholders of the company to buy their common shares and securities convertible into common shares at a price equal to the 'market price' of such shares, but in any case not less than the weighted average price of the shares during the six months preceding the date of such acquisition.[6]

Once the 30 per cent threshold has been reached, each subsequent 5 per cent acquisition of issued common stock is subject to the same Article 80 requirements, both as to notice and as to tender. The requirements of Article 80 do not apply to the initial acquisition of common stock by the founders of the joint stock company during the process of its incorporation.

Russian law does not impose any specific duties on the board of directors or the management of the target company in the takeover context. As a legal matter, the directors and officers are not required to assess the offer or make any recommendations to the shareholders. However, the Federal Commission for the Securities Market (FCSM), the former supervisory authority for the securities market in Russia, recommended in 2002 that the directors inform the shareholders of the target company of their opinion with respect to the takeover.[7] (The FCSM has since been reorganised as the Federal Service for the Financial Markets, or FSFM.)

Types of target companies covered by the requirements of Article 80

As mentioned above, the requirements of Article 80 apply only to joint stock companies with more than 1,000 shareholders holding common stock. Under the Joint Stock Companies Law, a closed joint stock company – a company with a limited number of shareholders, who have statutory pre-emptive rights in case of disposition of shares in the company by its other shareholders – may not have more than 50 shareholders.[8] In practice, therefore, the requirements of Article 80 apply only to open joint stock companies with more than 1,000 shareholders holding common stock and do not apply to such closed joint stock companies.

Notwithstanding the above, the charter of a joint stock company, whether closed or open, and regardless of the number of shareholders, may adopt and implement takeover provisions akin to those set forth in Article 80.[9]

Definition of 'affiliates'

An 'affiliate' under the Joint Stock Companies Law is defined 'in accordance with the requirements of Russian legislation'.[10] In practice, this is generally interpreted as the definition supplied by the Anti-Monopoly Law,[11] under which an 'affiliate' is broadly defined as any natural person or legal entity that is capable of influencing the activities of another legal person or individual entrepreneur. As a matter of regulatory norm and practice, such definition extends to any person being influenced by, or under the common influence of, another person. For a legal entity, 'affiliate' expressly includes:

- any legal entity which has more than 20 per cent of the voting power;
- any person that has more than 20 per cent of the voting power in the legal entity;
- a member of the board of directors (supervisory board) or another management body, a member of the executive body, or a chief executive officer of the legal entity;
- in case the legal entity belongs to a financial–industrial group,[12] members of the boards of directors (supervisory boards) or other management bodies, members of the executive bodies, and chief executive officers of the members of the financial–industrial group; and
- any person that belongs to the same 'group of persons' as the legal entity.

The definition of a 'group of persons' is also broad and overlaps the definition of an 'affiliate'. A 'group of persons' comprises any group of legal entities and/or natural persons meeting one or more of the following criteria:[13]

- with respect to a legal entity, a person or several persons who directly or indirectly have, as a result of agreement (concerted action), more than 50 per cent of the voting power in such legal entity on the basis of sale and purchase agreements, trust arrangements, joint venture agreements, agency or other agreements, transactions, or otherwise;
- with respect to a legal entity, a person, or several persons acting together, having the ability, under an agreement or otherwise, to determine the decisions of such entity, including the ability to determine the terms and conditions of the person's business or to discharge the powers of the person's executive body;
- with respect to a legal entity, a person having the right to appoint the chief executive officer and/or more than 50 per cent of the members of the executive body (such as the management board) of such legal entity, and/or where more than 50 per cent of the members of the board of directors or other management body of such legal entity have been nominated by such person;
- together with a legal entity, a natural person who discharges the powers of the chief executive officer of such legal entity;
- all legal entities where the same natural persons, their spouses, parents, children, siblings and/or the persons nominated by the same legal entity constitute more than 50 per cent of the members of the executive body and/or the board of directors or other management body of such entities, and/or where over 50 per cent of the members of the board of directors or other management body of such entities have been nominated by such persons;
- with respect to one legal entity, another legal entity that has as its chief executive officer a natural person who is an employee of the first legal entity or of an entity belonging to the group of the first entity, or another legal entity whose executive body and/or board of

PART II: EUROPEAN JURISDICTIONS

directors or other management body is more than 50 per cent composed of natural persons who are employees of the first legal entity or of entities belonging to the group of the first entity;
- all legal entities where the same natural persons, their spouses, parents, children, siblings and/or legal entities have, directly or through representatives (attorneys), more than 50 per cent of the voting power in such entities;
- for any two legal entities, where natural persons and/or legal entities have, directly or through representatives (attorneys), more than 50 per cent of the voting power in the first legal entity and, at the same time, the same natural persons, spouses, parents, children, siblings and/or their nominees constitute more than 50 per cent of the executive body and/or the board of directors or another management body of the second legal entity;
- all legal entities that are members of the same financial–industrial group; and/or
- spouses, parents, children and/or siblings of the natural persons cited above.

Accordingly, all the shares held, being acquired or intended to be acquired by a person or its affiliates are to be taken into consideration for the purposes of Article 80.

Tender offer procedure

As stated above, a person that, individually or together with its affiliates, has acquired 30 per cent or more of issued common shares, including the shares that such person already owns, in a joint stock company with more than 1,000 shareholders holding common stock of the company must, within 30 days of such acquisition, offer to the other shareholders of the company to buy their common shares and securities convertible into common shares.[14] According to Article 80(3) of the JSCL, 'an offer to acquire the company's common shares made by a person who acquired the common shares in accordance with this Article must be sent to all common shareholders of the company in writing'.[15] The charter of the target company may provide that the mandatory tender offer to the shareholders must be made through the company and may establish the procedure for such offer. The period for acceptance must be not less than 30 days from the 'moment such offer is received' by respective shareholders.[16] How receipt of such notice by individual shareholders can be assured is not clear. According to Article 80(5) of the JSCL, the offer must contain information regarding:

- the acquirer (name and address);
- the number of common shares the acquirer has acquired;
- the offer price; and
- the period during which the tendered shares must be bought from the shareholders and paid for.

In case the offer is accepted by a shareholder, the tendered shares must be acquired and paid for within 15 days from the acceptance date.

The tender offer procedure is irrevocable and, once the 30 per cent threshold has been reached by the acquirer, whether as the result of one acquisition or as the result of a series of acquisitions by the acquirer and its affiliates, the tender offer rules apply unconditionally. The law does not provide for the possibility of modifying the terms of the tender offer once it has been made.

Consideration

As stated above, the tender offer price must be equal to the market price of the shares and in any case must be not less than the weighted average price of the shares during the six months preceding the date of the acquisition. The Joint Stock Companies Law does not contain an explicit requirement that the mandatory tender offer be for cash consideration only, but the language of Article 80 implies this.[17]

Article 80 does not provide for a procedure to determine the market price of the shares. The FCSM recommended in 2002[18] that the board of directors of the target company should retain an independent appraiser to determine the current market value of the shares and provide such valuation to the shareholders. The FCSM recommended in 2003[19] that the procedure to determine the market value of securities established by Resolution of the FCSM No. 03-52/ps, dated 24 December 2003, be applied to determine the offer price. However, these recommendations are not binding on either the acquirer or the target company.

Opting out of the tender offer requirements of Article 80

The Joint Stock Companies Law allows for any company to opt out of the Article 80 tender offer requirement, but not the notice requirement, by having a provision to that effect in its charter.[20] In addition, the Joint Stock Companies Law allows that the shareholders of a target company may opt out of the Article 80 tender offer requirement by a decision of the general shareholders' meeting passed by a simple majority of the votes of the shareholders present at the meeting, excluding the votes of the acquirer or its affiliates (as opposed to changes to the charter, which require a 75 per cent vote).

However, under the listing rules of the FSFM,[21] which came into force on 15 July 2005, the shares of a joint stock company may not be listed on a Russian stock exchange if the charter of the company has such an opt out provision, unless, in certain cases, the company has undertaken to amend its charter to remove the opt out provision within one year after obtaining the listing. It is unclear how this requirement affects companies listed as of 15 July 2005. The FSFM's listing rules also state that any decision of the shareholders to opt out of the Article 80 tender offer requirement constitutes grounds for delisting the shares.

Consequences of violating the requirements of Article 80

The only express consequence of violating the prior notification requirement and the mandatory tender offer requirement of Article 80 is that shares acquired in violation of the requirements cannot be voted by the acquirer at the general shareholders' meetings of the target company. The violation may not be cured by lapse of time. However, the acquisition of the shares may not be challenged on the basis of non-compliance with Article 80 and the acquirer retains the voting rights with respect to the number of shares acquired in compliance with Article 80. Thus, for instance, if the acquirer has bought a total of 40 per cent of issued common stock of a company and did not meet any of the requirements of Article 80, the acquirer retains the voting rights with respect to 30 per cent minus one share of common stock.[22] Court practice, as reported by secondary sources, indicates that the shares upon resale, other than to affiliates of the 30 per cent acquirer, regain voting rights.

PART II: EUROPEAN JURISDICTIONS

Proposed squeeze-out legislation

In July 2005, the lower house of the Russian legislature, the Duma, passed on a first reading a proposed amendment to the Joint Stock Companies Law under which a holder of 95 per cent plus one share of an open joint stock company could 'squeeze-out' minority shareholders at a price established by an independent appraiser.[23] To become law, the bill needs to pass two further readings by the Duma, then be passed by the upper house of the legislature and signed into law by the president. Not surprisingly, this bill is subject to a lively debate among Russian corporates, investors, market professionals and the press.

Anti-monopoly clearance

Prior approval and subsequent notification requirements

In accordance with Article 18 of the Anti-Monopoly Law, anti-monopoly clearance by the Federal Anti-Monopoly Service of the Russian Federation (FAS) may be required in case of, *inter alia*, acquisition by a person or a group of persons of more than 20 per cent of the voting power in a Russian business entity.[24]

The acquisition requires prior approval of the FAS if:

- the combined balance sheet value of assets of the acquirer, its group and the target Russian company exceeds 30 million 'minimum monthly wages' (about US$104 million as of July 2005); or
- any of the acquirer, its group, or the target Russian company has a market share exceeding 35 per cent, the geographical scope of the relevant 'market' being on a national, regional or municipal basis, depending on the judgement of the FAS.[25]

A list of Russian enterprises having a 35 per cent market share is publicly available. The methodology used by the FAS to determine a 35 per cent market share is not entirely clear. In practice, it seems that the FAS can also deny applications on national security grounds.

In the case of an acquisition of more than 20 per cent of shares in a credit organisation or an insurance company, the prior approval of the FAS is required if the charter capital of the target exceeds R160 million (about US$5.6 million) or R10 million (about US$350,000) respectively.[26]

In addition, the prior approval of the FAS is required in cases of statutory merger or acquisition, or the purchase of 10 per cent of the assets of the target company, when the transaction exceeds the thresholds set forth above.[27]

The acquisition requires subsequent notification to the FAS if the combined balance sheet value of assets of the acquirer, its group and the target Russian company exceeds 2 million 'minimum monthly wages' (about US$6.9 million as of July 2005). If subsequent notification is required, the acquirer may nevertheless choose to apply for prior clearance of the acquisition.

While, as discussed above, the definition of 'affiliate' and the related definition of 'group of persons' under the Anti-Monopoly Law are both very broad, in practice in many cases, no filing has been made with the FAS when a 'group of persons' acquires more than 20 per cent of a Russian business entity. Indeed, it is not unusual for a Russian company with a single ultimate beneficial owner or group of owners to be formally held, in a strategy designed to avoid the FAS filing requirement, by six or more intermediate holding companies, each of which has less than 20 per cent of the voting power in the Russian business entity. Likewise, there is varying practice with respect to FAS filings where a non-Russian parent of a Russian company is acquired. The FAS has taken the position[28] that if, as a result of such acquisition, a Russian company is indirectly controlled[29] by the acquirer, the acquirer should make the appropriate FAS filing; in practice, it is not unusual for an acquirer making an offshore acquisition not to make the filing.

The Anti-Monopoly Law does not provide an exemption from the clearance requirements for intra-group acquisitions. Accordingly, internal reorganisations in a multinational company can formally trigger an FAS filing requirement, even where ultimate beneficial ownership has not changed.

Filing with the FAS

For those acquisitions requiring the prior approval of the FAS, such approval must be obtained by the acquirer prior to the closing of the transaction. The approval remains valid within a one-year period from its issuance and a new approval must be sought if the proposed acquisition is not completed within the one year. Subsequent notification must be made within 45 days[30] after the acquisition.

The documents and information to be submitted to the FAS are generally the same whether the filing requires prior approval or requires only subsequent notification. The filings tend to require more in the way of legal information, rather than market or economic information, such as providing, for each member of the acquirer's corporate group, its legal name, address, products/business, share capital and place in the group structure.[31] Some foreign filers choose in practice to file such information only for those entities in its corporate group that are active in Russia.

In accordance with the Anti-Monopoly Law, the FAS has a statutory 30-day[32] period for the review of the application or notification, but has the right to extend the review period for an additional 20 days and to request additional documents or information. In practice, in particularly complex or contentious acquisitions, the FAS can take longer to reach its decision. The FAS rarely rejects an application on economic grounds.

The Anti-Monopoly Law and the Code of Administrative Violations, No.195-FZ, dated 30 December 2001, as amended (the 'Administrative Code') contemplate two consequences of violating the anti-monopoly clearance requirements: an administrative fine and invalidation of the acquisition. The administrative fine imposed on legal entities ranges between 1,000 and 5,000 minimum monthly wages (about US$3,500 and US$17,500, respectively, as of July 2005). In theory, the FAS can also apply to a Russian court to invalidate the transaction,[33] although apparently this has yet to occur in practice.

Disclosure requirements of the Securities Law

Disclosure by the acquirer

Under Article 30 of the Securities Law, an acquirer of securities, other than debt securities that are not convertible into shares, must disclose, *inter alia*:

- its acquisition of 20 per cent or more of a class of securities of an issuer; and
- as long as the 20 per cent threshold remains exceeded, each 5 per cent increase or decrease of its holding.

The acquirer must make such disclosure to the FSFM, including the acquirer's identity, the type and the state registration number of the securities, the issuer, and the number of securities held by the acquirer, within five calendar days after the acquisition. Article 30 is framed in terms of a single holder of shares, without reference to the holder's affiliates or group.

Disclosure by the target company

Article 30 of the Securities Law provides that an issuer that has registered a securities prospectus[34] is subject to certain continuing disclosure requirements, including the requirement to disclose to the market information about a shareholder holding more than 25 per cent of any type of securities of the issuer. Such information is deemed to be a 'material fact' and must be filed with the FSFM and also published within five calendar days after the date when the entry of such shareholder was made in the shareholder register of the issuer. The publication must be made in the mass media accessible to the majority of the security holders of the issuer.[35]

Separately, a reporting company should report to the FSFM, on a quarterly basis, any shareholder holding more than 5 per cent, as well as any shareholder holding more than 20 per cent, of its charter capital or its common stock.[36]

Violation of disclosure requirements by the target company may result in an administrative fine in an amount between 300 and 400 minimum monthly wages (about US$1,050 and US$1,400, respectively, as of July 2005).[37]

Specific requirements applicable to takeovers of credit organisations

Acquisition of more than 5 per cent of the shares in a credit organisation is subject to post notification to the Central Bank of the Russian Federation (the CBR), whereas acquisition of more than 20 per cent of the same requires the CBR's prior approval.[38] These thresholds, however, apply only to resident buyers; non-resident buyers have to obtain the CBR's prior approval for all acquisitions.[39] The CBR's prior approval needs to be obtained after any FAS proceedings.

---

[1] See Articles 16 and 17 of the JSCL. Consolidations and mergers have generally not been pursued because (i) the acquirer under these tactics would fully and directly assume the liabilities of the target company; (ii) creditors of the target company have the right to demand immediate payment of their debts (Article 15(6) of the JSCL); (iii) shareholders of the target company that do not vote in favour of the transaction (and instead vote against or abstain) have the right to have their shares purchased by the target company at the appraised fair market value of such shares (Article 75 of the JSCL); and (iv) where the acquirer is a Russian company, these tactics would entail additional internal corporate approvals of the acquirer. Nevertheless, at times mergers have been pursued, such as the acquisition of OAO YUKOS by way of absorption merger of OAO VNK in 2002.

[2] See Article 11 of the Law on Banks and Banking Activities and Article 16 of the Law on Protection of Competition in the Financial Services Markets.

[3] See Article 61 of the Air Code of the Russian Federation and Article 12 of the Federal Law on State Regulation of Aviation Development.

[4] See Articles 7 and 19.1 of the Law of the Russian Federation on Mass Media.

[5] Article 80(1) of the JSCL.

[6] Article 80(2) of the JSCL.

[7] Decree of the FCSM No. 421/r, dated 4 April 2002.

[8] Article 7(3) of the JSCL.

[9] Ruling of the Constitutional Court of the Russian Federation No. 255-O, dated 6 December 2001.

[10] Article 93(1) of the JSCL.
[11] Article 4 of the Anti-Monopoly Law.
[12] See Article 2 of the Federal Law on Financial–Industrial Groups No. 190-FZ, dated 30 November 1995. A financial-industrial group is a group consisting of either a parent company and its subsidiaries, or legal entities that have fully or partially integrated their assets on the basis of an agreement on the establishment of a financial–industrial group.
[13] Article 4 of the Anti-Monopoly Law.
[14] Article 80(2) of the JSCL.
[15] Article 80(3) appears to have a drafting oversight, in that under Article 80(2) of the JSCL, an offer is to be made to all holders of common shares and of securities convertible into common shares, but under Article 80(3) only common shareholders are to receive notice.
[16] Article 80(4) of the JSCL.
[17] The tender offer procedure in Article 80 is worded in terms of the sale and purchase of shares. In accordance with the Civil Code of the Russian Federation (Article 454), sale and purchase may be for cash consideration only; any other consideration would lead to the qualification of the transaction as an exchange.
[18] See Clause 1 of the FCSM Order No. 421/r, dated 4 April 2002, and Clause 2.1.2 of Chapter VI of the Code of Corporate Governance introduced by the FCSM Order.
[19] See Resolution of the FCSM No. 03-52/ps, dated 24 December 2003.
[20] Article 80(2) of the JSCL.
[21] See Order of the FSFM No. 04-1245/pz-n, dated 15 December 2004.
[22] Article 80(6) of the JSCL.
[23] A similar bill submitted in July 2004, proposing a threshold of 90 per cent plus one share, was criticised by some representatives of the foreign investment community in Russia.
[24] Under Article 66 of the Civil Code of the Russian Federation, 'business entities' include the following legal entities: open and closed joint stock companies, limited liability companies (*obshestva s ogranichennoi otvetstvennostyu*) and subsidiary liability companies (*obshestva s dopolnitelnoi otvetstvennostyu*).
[25] See Order of the State Committee for Anti-Monopoly Policy No. 169, dated 20 December 1996, as amended.
[26] Article 16 of the Law on Protection of Competition in the Financial Services Markets; Decree of the Government No. 194 of 7 March 2000.
[27] Articles 17 and 18 of the Anti-Monopoly Law.
[28] See, for example, Letter of the State Anti-Monopoly Committee (the predecessor of the Federal Anti-Monopoly Service) No. NF/3919, dated 19 June 1998.
[29] Article 18(2) of the Anti-Monopoly Law.
[30] Although the Anti-Monopoly Law does not specify whether the term is in calendar or business days, the FAS in practice interprets the notification period as being in calendar days.
[31] See Order of the Ministry for Anti-Monopoly Policy No. 276 of 13 August 1999, as amended.
[32] Although the Anti-Monopoly Law does not specify whether the term is in calendar or business days, the FAS in practice interprets the review period as being in business days, in contrast to its view that the subsequent notice period is measured in terms of calendar days (as discussed in footnote 30).
[33] Article 18(9) of the Anti-Monopoly Law.
[34] Articles 19(2) and 27.6 of the Securities Law require an issuer to register a securities prospectus if it makes a public offering, makes a private placement to more than 500 investors or lists its securities in Russia.
[35] A detailed procedure for the disclosure of material facts is set forth by the Order of the FSFM No. 05-5/pz-n, dated 16 March 2005.
[36] See Article 5.5 of the Order of the FSFM No. 05-5/pz-n, dated 16 March 2005 and Clause 6.2 of Annex 11 (Form of the Quarterly Report) to the Order.
[37] See Article 15.19(2) of the Administrative Code.
[38] See Article 11 of the Law on Banks and Banking Activities.
[39] See Article 18 of the Law on Banks and Banking Activities.

Chapter 24

Spain

Alejandro Fernández de Araoz
Araoz & Rueda, Madrid

Spanish takeover rules are embodied in mandatory statutory instruments. Unlike in the United Kingdom, there are no self-regulatory bodies or voluntary codes adopted by market participants. The mandatory rules are interpreted and applied by the Spanish National Securities Market Commission (CNMV), which has broad supervisory and enforcement powers, including the ability to impose substantial fines in the event the rules are breached.

The key statutory instrument in Spain's takeover regime is Royal Decree 432/2003 (RD 432/2003), which became effective on 12 April 2003. It modified Royal Decree 1197/1991 (RD 1197/1991), which contained Spain's existing takeover regulation for public companies. The new legislation has the objectives of protecting the interests of minority shareholders in the event of a change of control, and of improving market efficiency and transparency. The new rules were also intended to tackle the issues raised by a number of controversial takeovers that took place in 2002. They involved acquisitions of equity stakes below 25 per cent (the Spanish mandatory bid threshold) and were structured precisely to avoid having to launch a mandatory bid. Although it was widely perceived that control had changed hands in these cases, minority shareholders were nevertheless denied the benefit of a control premium, which was received only by the controlling shareholders who had sold their stakes to the acquirers. These transactions generated sufficient investor concern to instigate legislative reform.

RD 432/2003 modifies the existing Spanish takeover regime in four fundamental ways: by introducing additional situations requiring mandatory offers, modifying the exceptions to the requirement to make an offer, allowing new types of conditional offers, and modifying the regime applicable to competing bids.

The mandatory bid rule

The Spanish takeover regime, contained in RD 1197/1991 as amended by RD 423/2003, is based on three fundamental principles:

- a 'mandatory bid rule' (MBR) requires that anyone seeking to acquire, in a single transaction or a series of successive transactions, a 'significant participation' (*participación significativa*) in a listed company must do so by means of a public takeover bid (*oferta pública de adquisición* or *OPA*). The key test therefore lies in the concept of a significant participation or stake in the target company. However, an acquirer may be legally obliged

to launch a takeover bid, even if it does not reach the statutory thresholds, when such a stake gives it the ability to appoint a number of directors to the target company's board;
- Spain's MBR is gradual in its effect to the extent that, depending on the percentage of shares the bidder wishes to acquire in the target company, the obligation to extend the bid to a certain percentage of shareholders varies;
- the MBR is applied on an *ex ante* basis: the takeover has to be launched as a prior condition to acquiring shares in the target company, not as a result of such an acquisition.

The Spanish MBR system establishes the basic criteria that trigger the legal obligation to launch a bid. One of these criteria is the acquisition of a certain shareholding percentage in the target company that reaches or crosses the mandatory bid rule threshold. The three different scenarios covered by the concept of a 'significant participation' are as follows:

- the acquisition of 25 per cent or more of the share capital of a company requires an offer for at least 10 per cent of the share capital of the company;
- an acquirer holding between 25 per cent and 50 per cent of the share capital of a company, and intending to acquire 6 per cent or more of the share capital of the company within a 12-month period, is required to make an offer for at least 10 per cent of the share capital of the company. This means that one can acquire up to 5.9 per cent within a year and repeat such a process every subsequent year up to 49.9 per cent; and
- the acquisition of 50 per cent or more of the share capital of a company requires making an offer for 100 per cent of the share capital of the company.

RD 432/2003 has introduced two additional scenarios requiring mandatory offers that are triggered, not solely by the acquisition of a predetermined percentage of a company's shares, but rather by the bidder's ability to appoint a certain number of the target company's board of directors. The new situations requiring mandatory offers are the following:

- the acquisition of more than 5 per cent, but less than 25 per cent, of the share capital of a company, with the power to appoint more than a third of the directors, or, if less than 5 per cent, giving it the right to appoint such a number of directors jointly with those already appointed by the bidder, now requires a mandatory offer for at least 10 per cent of the share capital of the company; and
- the acquisition of more than 5 per cent, but less than 50 per cent, of the share capital of the company, with the power to appoint more than half of the directors, or, if less than 5 per cent, giving it the right to appoint such a number of directors jointly with those already appointed by the bidder, now requires an offer for 100 per cent of the share capital of the company.

In order to determine the percentage of directors representing the interests of the bidder, the rules contain a rebuttable presumption that the following relationships establish a director's appointment by the bidder:

- nomination by the bidder or a related company;
- service as an officer, employee, director or consultant to the bidder or a related company;
- service by the bidder or a related party as a director of the target company;

- nomination with favourable votes from the bidder or a related company; or
- formal recognition in corporate or public documents that the director has been designated by the bidder.

In addition, a public bid must be launched if any of the following events occur:

- a single person becomes the owner of a significant stake as a result of converting convertible bonds, warrants or other securities that entitle their owners to acquire shares, and after all the shareholders have exercised their rights to acquire shares;
- an underwriting agreement is entered into between a public company and a financial institution in the context of a securities offering, as a result of which a significant stake is acquired by a financial entity;
- a public company's by-laws are significantly modified, where the modification is proposed by a shareholder holding more than 50 per cent of the share capital for the first time since it acquired such a stake in the company.

Beyond these criteria, Spanish takeover regulations also cover traditional concepts such as 'acting in concert' and 'group purchases', in which different purchasers are 'consolidated' for purposes of application of the MBR.

It is submitted that linking the MBR to objective thresholds and criteria, instead of to a more elusive and vague concept of 'control', provides a greater degree of legal certainty and predictability to private parties.

Procedural aspects and timetable

Preliminary steps

Provided that a potential bidder keeps its intentions confidential, no official announcements are required until the bidder formally notifies the bid to the CNMV. All bids must be notified to the CNMV for formal clearance. A prospectus explaining the offer and any other relevant documentation should be attached to the formal takeover filing. If the bid is hostile, pre-bid discussions may not have taken place between the bidder and the target, and the target will not be informed of the bid until the CNMV is notified. The target shareholders will first learn about the bid through the press announcement, unless they have been approached before the bid by the bidder to negotiate their support for the bid and to eventually grant irrevocable selling commitments.

Once the bid has been formally notified to the CNMV, the regulator orders a trading suspension of the target's shares until the information has been publicly disclosed and the market has knowledge of it. From this time onwards, the target's directors are obliged to manage the target in the ordinary course of business.

Next, the CNMV issues a resolution clearing or prohibiting the offer, and notifies the bidder and the target of its decision. The bidder must then publish a press announcement in the following publications:

- the *Official Gazette* of the Mercantile Registry;
- the *Stock Exchange Listing Bulletin*; and
- at least two newspapers, including one national newspaper and one widely distributed in the region where the target company has its registered offices.

The press announcement must contain the essential terms and conditions of the offer as stated in the prospectus, as well as the address of the place at which the prospectus and other ancillary documentation are available for inspection.

Mandatory documentation

Once a bid has been authorised by the CNMV, the bidder must announce the offer and immediately afterwards make available to the target's shareholders both the prospectus and certain ancillary documentation.

The prospectus should include, among other things, the following information:

- the bidder's identity and details;
- details of the bidder's group structure (the entities which are part of the same group of companies);
- a list of the target company's shares that are already directly or indirectly held by the bidder, by the bidder's group of companies, or by other persons acting on the bidder's behalf or instruction;
- information on the bidder's activities and financial situation;
- the specific number and class of shares at which the bid is aimed;
- guarantees given by the bidder that it will pay the agreed price to the shareholders who accept the bid;
- the terms for acceptance of the offer; and
- the aim of the bid, expressly stating the intentions of the bidder in relation to the future activities of the target.

The ancillary documentation should include the following information:

- a mandatory bank guarantee, which means that the bid has to be funded ('money good') from the outset;
- any relevant administrative authorisations (clearance from any relevant regulatory or competition authorities as required);
- a draft of the advertisement that announced the offer in the *Official Gazette* and the press; and
- the relevant corporate documentation of the bidder, including the resolution approving the bid, certificates of good standing and audited accounts.

Timetable

The following timetable typically applies:

- the bidder notifies the bid to the CNMV for clearance;
- the CNMV has 15 working days from notification to issue a resolution clearing or prohibiting the bid, although this can be extended if the CNMV requires additional information. In practice, this process will take between four and eight weeks;
- the CNMV orders the suspension of trading in the target's stock immediately after receiving notification from the bidder;

PART II: EUROPEAN JURISDICTIONS

- the bidder has a maximum of five working days after clearance to announce the bid in the *Official Gazette,* the *Stock Exchange Listing Bulletin* and at least two newspapers;
- the bidder needs to make certain information available to the target's shareholders when it makes its offer;
- on notification of CNMV clearance, the target's directors must issue a report on the bid within 10 calendar days;
- the bidder must establish an acceptance period ranging from one to two months from the publication date of the first announcement of the bid;
- if the bid is conditional, the CNMV can extend the above deadlines to allow the target time to hold a general shareholders' meeting. Here, the board can inform the shareholders about the relevant conditions of the bid and any resolutions they need to pass;
- the terms and conditions of the offer can be altered within seven business days before the offer expires. If the terms are altered, the initial time frame is extended by a further seven calendar days; and
- when the period allotted for acceptance has expired, the CNMV must be notified of the result within five calendar days. If the minimum amount of shares stated in the offer has been reached, this is communicated by the CNMV within the following three calendar days from when the CNMV is notified and published in the *Stock Exchange Listing Bulletin* (see Exhibits 24.1 and 24.2).

Finally, it should be mentioned that if the takeover bid fails because the bidder does not achieve the minimum take-up percentage upon which it based the effectiveness of its bid, the bidder is barred from acquiring any additional target shares within six months of the date on which the result of the bid is published, unless through a new public offer.

Exemptions

Mandatory offers are not required in the following four cases:

- purchases of shares by public/governmental institutions in the context of the salvage of a credit institution or insurance company in relation to an insolvency crisis;
- the exercise by governmental authorities of exceptional powers to expropriate pursuant to administrative law;
- significant participations acquired in connection with debt/equity exchanges or capitalisation of credits in the context of an agreement of the company's creditors within insolvency proceedings; and
- unanimous consent by the company's shareholders to sell or renounce the sale of their shares in a public takeover offer.

Nor is a mandatory offer required in cases that are deemed by the Spanish Competition Authority (Servicio de Defensa de la Competencia) to constitute joint control and that meet the following conditions:

- prior to the acquisition, the shareholders exercising joint control owned more than 50 per cent of the shares and appointed more than half of the board;
- the increase in the bidder's shareholding does not exceed 6 per cent in a 12-month period and in any event does not reach or exceed 50 per cent; and

Exhibit 24.1
OPA calendar with no competing bid (with Spanish competition notification)

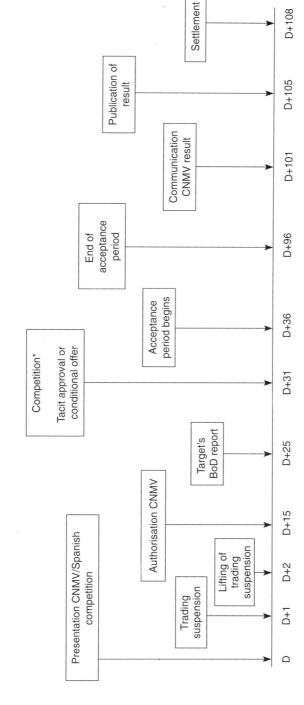

* If second phase is commenced, 90 days should be added to calendar.
Note: This timetable is merely tentative and may be subject to changes depending on specific circumstances

Source: LINKLATERS, *Tender offers in Spain*, April 2004.

PART II: EUROPEAN JURISDICTIONS

Exhibit 24.2
OPA calendar with one competing bid (with Spanish competition notification)

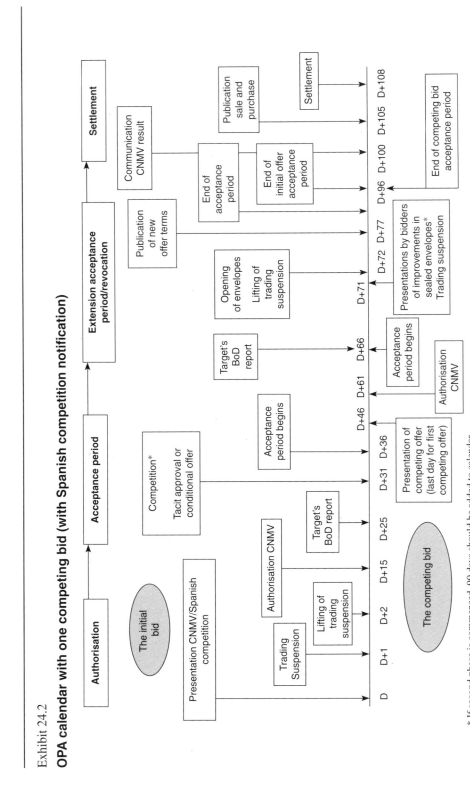

*If second phase is commenced, 90 days should be added to calendar.

Note: This timetable is merely tentative and may be subject to changes depending on specific circumstances

Source: LINKLATERS, *Tender offers in Spain*, April 2004.

- the number of directors appointed by the bidder does not increase as a result of the acquisition.

Despite these new exemptions, certain exemptions present in other takeover regimes are missing from the Spanish regime. These include an exemption for the acquisition of a significant stake as a result of exercising pre-emptive rights when other shareholders do not exercise theirs, and an exemption for contributions in kind that are in the interests of the company.

Defensive tactics and the role of the target company's board

In a pre-bid context, a public company can use classical defensive tactics by including in its by-laws super-majority provisions to approve certain resolutions, staggering its board and/or imposing voting ceilings on individual shareholders. The use of other defensive devices common elsewhere in Europe, such as multiple share classes, is rare in Spain.

However, key shareholders can enter into shareholders' agreements containing voting trust or pooling arrangements, which make contestability of control in the target company much more difficult. Whether Spain opts into or out of Article 11 of the Takeover Directive will be a key consideration, although a grandfathering provision applies to shareholder agreements entered into before the adoption of the Directive.

Once the bid has been formally launched, the target company's board can only take decisions in the ordinary course of business and is barred from taking action that could directly or indirectly frustrate the bid.

Finally, it should be mentioned that the target company's board has to issue a report to the shareholders with its comments and recommendations on the bid. It is increasingly common for a target's board to retain investment banks or financial advisers to produce appraisals or opinions of its recommendation on the 'fairness' of the consideration offered in the bid.

Analysis of the competing bid system

Until the reform of 2003, the Spanish takeover regime included a highly controversial competing bid system whereby the first bidder was the only party allowed to improve its initial bid if it wished to do so, to the detriment of other competing bidders. This generated the undesirable form of opportunistic behaviour known as 'low balling' and prevented the target company's shareholders from extracting the greatest possible value. Additionally, to qualify as such, any competing bid had to provide an improvement in the consideration offered of at least 5 per cent.

From a general economic perspective, the entire subject of auction design and strategy is numbingly complex, with numerous variables coming into play. At any rate, the new system has removed the 'first mover advantage' and will clearly have beneficial effects for target companies' shareholders, as the Aldeasa case suggests (see below).

The new system provides for two phases in the handling of competing bids. In Phase 1, an ascending price auction ('English auction') takes place within 10 calendar days from the beginning of the acceptance period of the previous bid and no later than 30 calendar days from the beginning of the acceptance period of the initial bid. Any bidder is free to launch a competing bid as long as such a bid represents an improvement over the previous one, by, for example, setting a better price, reducing or removing take up conditions, or extending the bid

PART II: EUROPEAN JURISDICTIONS

to a larger number of the target company's shares. In Phase 2, all bidders have an opportunity to submit sealed bids, as long as this new bid offers at least the same consideration as the highest bid in Phase 1 and further represents an improvement over previous bids by extending the offer to a larger number of the target's shares. In addition, improvements no longer have to meet a minimum quantitative level, so that any improvement in the consideration offered now qualifies as such.

However, it is unfortunate that the issues at stake were not further discussed before these new rules were adopted, including, in particular, analysis of whether the second and final round of sealed bids would generate the most efficient outcomes in terms of both shareholder value and the overall dynamics of the takeover process.

> **Case study: The battle for Aldeasa (2005)**
>
> Aldeasa is a group of specialised airport retailing outlets in which Altadis, the Franco–Spanish tobacco company, held a 35 per cent interest. The battle over Aldeasa was highly interesting from a practical standpoint because it was the first test for the new competing bid rules enacted under RD 432/2003.
>
> On 13 December 2004, the Spanish company Gestión de Explotaciones Aeroportuarias (GEA) launched a takeover bid at €29.00 per share for 100 per cent of Aldeasa's share capital. This bid was formally authorised by the CNMV on 18 January 2005. On 24 January, the Swiss group Dufry Holdings launched a competing bid at €31.00 per share and reduced the minimum take up threshold to 50.1 per cent of Aldeasa's share capital. On 28 January, Altadis and Autogrill (controlled by the Benetton family of Italy) launched a joint bid at €33.00 per share, with no minimum take up conditions.
>
> On 14 March 2005, the CNMV announced that, with all three bids having been registered, the deadline for the submission of sealed bids would elapse on 21 March. Once the sealed bids had been opened by the CNMV, the situation was as follows: GEA did not take part in the auction, Dufry maintained the terms of its initial bid and Altadis/Autogrill increased their bid to €36.57 per share.

Taking the company private: mandatory bids in 'public to private' context

When a majority shareholder or group of shareholders decides that there is no longer any point in having a company publicly traded, Spanish law requires that any delisting resolution must be approved by the general shareholders' meeting and that a takeover bid must be launched by the company itself, or by the controlling shareholders, in order to afford minority shareholders a last chance of liquidity and exit from the company. The consideration offered is subject to 'fair price' provisions and has to be formally approved by the CNMV.

Although the takeover rules do not contain specific valuation parameters, in practice, the CNMV requires a 'fairness opinion' in relation to such delisting bids, using standard valuation methodologies such as discounted cash flow models and comparable transactions analysis, in the context of whether the company has been subject to a recent takeover bid.

As a matter of administrative practice, whenever there has been an arm's length bid to delist a public firm, on terms that satisfy the CNMV that the consideration offered is clearly above market value, the regulator has accepted the placement of a standing purchase order with a registered broker-dealer or bank at the offer price, instead of requiring the launching of a second bid. This allows minority shareholders to sell their shares at any time. The measure is most welcome because, while it affords the necessary levels of investor protection, it also dramatically reduces the transaction costs for the bidder; this is now often used by private equity funds in typical 'public to private' transactions.

> **Case study: Telefonica/Terra Networks (2003/2005)**
>
> In November 1999, in the midst of the 'dot com bubble', Telefonica floated its internet and e-business division through an initial public offering (IPO) of 23.6 per cent of the share capital of Terra Networks. The IPO was placed at €11.80 per share. Three months later, the stock was trading at an amazing €141 per share, which meant that Terra's market capitalisation topped €30 billion. Subsequently, Terra acquired the US internet company Lycos, in a deal which diluted Telefonica's stake down to approximately 40 per cent.
>
> At the end of 2000, after the 'bubble' had burst, shares were trading at €11.60 and reached prices as low as €2.77 in September 2004. Further, corporate strategy changed and Telefonica found the need to provide broadband packages to its customers, which directly competed with Terra. On 28 May 2003, Telefonica launched a takeover bid for the 61.6 per cent of the share capital that it did not own for a consideration of €5.52 per share. The offering price sparked the anger of minority shareholders, representing 3 per cent of its share capital, who went as far as to file criminal charges against Telefonica's and Terra's boards of directors. Although the lawsuit was eventually dismissed, the main argument of the minority shareholders was that the IPO at €11.80 per share in 1999, which at the time took into account future profits and the increased value of the services provided by Terra, was a manipulative scheme to artificially increase Terra's price and, subsequently, to take the company private. This disguised the real purpose of the takeover bid in 2003 and thereby allowed Telefonica to elude the 'fair price' provisions applicable to such bids. Finally, the bid, which was conditional on acceptance by shareholders representing at least 36.63 per cent of the share capital, was accepted by 33.6 per cent, which gave Telefonica control over only 71.97 per cent of the share capital, after waiving the minimum percentage of acceptance initially required.
>
> Subsequently, Terra undertook a treasury share buy-back, which increased the Telefonica stake to over 75 per cent. In February 2005, Telefonica proposed a merger with Terra by means of an exchange of nine shares in Terra in exchange for two shares in Telefonica, which represented a premium of 0.73 per cent on the day prior to the announcement, plus a dividend of €0.60 per share. Although in mergers minority shareholders are protected by the appointment by the Mercantile Registry of an independent expert in charge of evaluating the merger price, in this case, Telefonica gained full control over Terra without the requirement of launching a delisting takeover bid. Even after the CNMV stated that the nature of the transaction required its indirect supervision, this transaction was also challenged by Terra's minority shareholders on the same grounds as the takeover bid two years earlier. On 31 May and 2 June 2005, respectively, Telefonica's and Terra's shareholders approved the transaction, although criminal and other judicial proceedings are still pending.

Potential impact of the Takeover Directive on the Spanish regime

In December 2003, after 15 years of negotiations, a political compromise was finally reached that led to the enactment of the Takeover Directive (Directive 2004/25/EC of 21 April 2004). This directive saw the light of day only after a long and acrimonious journey, and on the basis of a highly controversial compromise on two of its key provisions, which were made optional, allowing member states to opt out and firms in these states to opt back in:

- Article 9, which prohibits offeree companies from taking defensive action to frustrate bids without prior shareholder approval; and
- Article 11, which allows offerors to 'break through' certain target company restrictions (such as super-majority provisions or other by-law protections) or other measures that distribute control rights disproportionate to cash flow rights (such as dual-class shares) in order to achieve full control of the target company.

EU regulation is by definition supranational and hence harmonisation is its *raison d'être*. With respect to takeovers, the European Commission advocated harmonisation for the obvious reason that common takeover rules are a key requisite of an integrated market and promote the development of a level playing field for cross-border bids. Obstacles or distortions in cross-border takeovers, caused by differences in national legislation, are undesirable. However, common rules promote a level playing field only if the harmonised jurisdictions are sufficiently similar along other relevant dimensions. Given the considerable variations in ownership and control arrangements within the EU, this condition is far from being satisfied in the case of takeovers and the Takeover Directive has certainly not contributed to promoting the creation of this level playing field, because it will not result in a uniform regulatory framework.

At this stage, it is very difficult to assess the full impact of the directive on the Spanish takeover regime. Since the deadline for implementation of the directive (May 2006) is still relatively far away, there are no draft regulations or bills (at the time of writing) that would allow an analysis of the extent to which Spain will be implementing the directive, including whether it will be opting out of Articles 9 and 11. However, with the exception of the regulation of 'golden shares' in privatised companies, over which Spain was rebuffed by the European Court of Justice (see Commission vs. Kingdom of Spain, Case C-463/00, 13 May 2003), it is probably fair to say that Spain has generally not hampered the free movement of capital. Therefore, its position would probably be more aligned with the Commission or the United Kingdom, viewing the directive as an effective tool with which to subject companies to the market for corporate control and to outlaw obstructive defensive tactics, rather than with those Continental member states that approach capitalism from a larger stakeholder perspective and are more protectionist.

Special topics in takeover practice in Spain

Break-up fees

Break-up fees are a familiar practice in international mergers and acquisitions (M&A), for both public and private companies. The target company's shareholders and/or the target company itself undertake to pay a certain amount to a bidder, in exchange for launching a binding offer, if the offer is subsequently defeated by a higher bid. Break-up fees typically include out-of-pocket expenses incurred by the unsuccessful bidder, such as accounting and lawyers' fees or banking expenses. The rationale is that the target company's shareholders have managed to sell at a higher price because of the effort and cost incurred by the initial bidder, whose bid caused the target company to be put into play in the first place. Hence, the argument runs, it is only fair to reimburse at least the expenses of the bidder whose action lies at the origin of the target shareholders' ability to pocket a hefty premium.

On the other hand, there has been a substantial degree of criticism of break-up fees, particularly in scholarly studies, as it is argued that they act *de facto* as a sort of 'poison pill', which could make a competing bid substantially more expensive. The discussion then moves between those who hold the position that break-up fees paid by the target company should be considered illegal *per se* and those who consider that they are a matter to be decided on a case by case basis, under the business judgement rule and the general duties of care and diligence. The question becomes, essentially, how much is too much?

In Spain, the matter has yet to come before the courts and there had not been an administrative ruling until the CNMV took a stance in the recent CVC/Cortefiel case (2005).

Case study: CVC/Cortefiel (2005)

In the context of its €1.4 billion takeover bid for Cortefiel, a fashion retail business, CVC, a UK private equity house, agreed with the two controlling shareholder families, who jointly held over 57 per cent of the target's common stock, that if a successful competing bid was launched, the target company would pay CVC €3.5 million in break-up fees. The CNMV ruled that this provision was in violation of the principles of the Spanish takeover regime, although the specific grounds for its ruling have not been made public. The prospectus was accordingly modified and the controlling families agreed to assume their commitment directly with CVC.

It is difficult to envisage a judicial challenge in this case, because a decision takes too long and it is widely perceived that players in the M&A market, particularly private equity houses, do not want to antagonise the CNMV on relatively minor issues when their prospectus approval is still pending.

Structuring irrevocables with target shareholders

The general principle established in the existing takeover rules is a shareholder in a target company is automatically released from any tender of his/her shares to a first bidder upon registration of a competing bid. Bidders tend to try to minimise uncertainty in the outcome of the process by building 'toeholds' in the target company and by securing contractual commitments with relevant shareholders of the target company. Both devices reduce the target company's free float, enhance the likelihood of a successful outcome and reduce the likelihood of a competing bid.

A classical topic is the negotiation of an 'irrevocable commitment' with key target's shareholders. While the shareholders in a target company are usually very keen to enter into contractual arrangements of this nature with potential bidders if this prompts the launching of a takeover bid, they normally seek to obtain opting out mechanisms enabling them to obtain release from such contractual commitments if competing bids are launched with sweetened terms, so that they can guarantee that any upside is captured. In practice, this leads to different kinds of irrevocable selling commitments being granted by the shareholders, which may be classified as follows:

- 'strong-form irrevocables' are akin to call options granted to a potential bidder and mean that the shareholder waives any right to sell its shares to any third party. This happened in the EDP-Cajastur/Hidrocantábrico case (2002) when, after failing to secure control of the Spanish utility Hidrocantábrico, TXU granted an irrevocable selling commitment to EDP-Cajastur at a price of €24.00 per share and was forced to forgo two subsequent bids at €26.00 and €27.2 per share. This also happened in the Recoletos bid by Retos Cartera (2005) when Pearson agreed to dispose of its shareholding interest in favour of the vehicle at a predetermined price, as well as in the recent bid launched by INSSEC for CIE Automotive (2005);
- 'semi-strong-form irrevocables' commit the selling shareholder to sell and permit release from that commitment only if a competing bid improves the selling price by a premium of at least x per cent over the agreed price. This was precisely the agreed structure in the recent CVC/Cortefiel case (2005), in which the key shareholding families irrevocably committed themselves to tender to CVC unless a competing bid with an 8 per cent premium over the agreed price was launched;
- 'weak-form irrevocables' involve a commitment to tender to the bidder's offer at a certain price, but release the target's shareholders from any commitment if a competing bid or offer is made.

In all cases, such contractual arrangements have to be disclosed by the bidder in the prospectus. The CNMV carefully scrutinises these arrangements to ascertain whether there are other provisions in these agreements that could breach the fundamental principle of equal treatment of all the target company's shareholders.

Obtaining exclusivity and due diligence from the target company's board

Agreements entered into between the bidder and incumbent shareholders prior to the formal launching of a bid are increasingly common. Typical examples include exclusivity arrangements, due diligence access (Barclays/Banco Zaragozano, 2003; Advent/Parques Reunidos, 2003; Expo-An/Inmocaral, 2005 and WAM/Amadeus, 2005) and even collaboration to ensure an orderly completion of the transaction (Barclays/Banco Zaragozano, 2003).

There is, however, a significant legal loophole that is not easy to resolve when it comes to reconciling the general principles of equal treatment, freedom of contract and necessary confidentiality. Indeed, a potential bidder could also ask the target company's board to provide access to data as a prerequisite for the launch of a competing bid with improved terms. This would place the board in a difficult position. The board has a clear duty to maximise shareholder value and offer the possibility of purchasing the firm to a number of genuinely interested bidders. This was the case in Amadeus (2005) where, once Air France, Iberia and Lufthansa had decided that they would partially sell their stakes in the company, a formal auction period was organised. On the other hand, protecting confidentiality is a key concern, particularly where the potential bidder is a direct competitor. As yet, there are no precedents addressing this issue.

Squeeze-out and sell-out

In Spain, neither the takeover regime nor corporate law envisage the possibility of 'squeezing-out' minority shareholders once a certain threshold in the target company has been achieved by the bidder. This matter will have to be addressed before May 2006, when (as mentioned above) Spain implements the Takeover Directive and, in particular, Articles 15 and 16.

It has been argued that there are ways of achieving a functionally equivalent result through Article 164.3 of the Ley de Sociedades Anónimas (Public Companies Act), which effectively allows a company to reduce its share capital by retiring its own shares as long as the majority shareholders can show there is a legitimate 'corporate purpose' (*interés social*) and the company has the cash to finance this share buy-back. Thus, those minority shareholders who did not tender for different reasons during the bid can be bought out at a 'fair price'. The bid price would presumably be deemed to be fair, although a fairness opinion would be required. The only apparent drawback of this procedure is that it also requires the approval of the majority of shareholders whose shares are subject to the retirement offer, but this can easily be circumvented in practice.

Finally, it should also be mentioned that a target company's shareholders have no 'sell-out' rights under Spanish law.

Conditional bids

Until RD 432/2003 was implemented, takeover bids in Spain could only be conditional on acceptance by a minimum number of shareholders and on approval by the competition authorities. RD 432/2003 permits offers to be conditional on adoption or ratification by the target company, its board of directors or its shareholders' meeting through predetermined resolutions, agreements or plans.

One of the objectives of these new provisions was to facilitate the removal of takeover defences. For example, during its unsuccessful attempt to take over the Spanish electricity utility Hidrocantábrico (2002), TXU publicly stated its wish to condition its offer on the removal by the general shareholders' meeting of provisions in Hidrocantábrico's by-laws (*estatutos*) that limited the voting rights of significant shareholders. However, TXU was unable to do so under the then-existing takeover rules. Such a conditional offer would now be possible.

The right of the offeror to waive the condition that the offer be accepted by a minimum number of shareholders has been maintained. However, it should be stressed that no other conditions are acceptable.

Appealing against decisions of the CNMV

Although the CNMV's decisions are subject to appeal before the Audiencia Nacional – Sala de lo Contencioso (the High Administrative Court), in practice, the right of appeal is almost entirely theoretical, because even provisional decisions could take three to four months to be rendered, which creates an impossible situation of legal uncertainty surrounding a takeover bid. However, in relation to delisting or 'going private' bids, minority shareholders have challenged the 'fair price' agreed to by the CNMV.

PART II: EUROPEAN JURISDICTIONS

Further case studies

Three controversial takeovers (2002)

During 2002, there were three controversial acquisitions of stakes in public companies that, although they were below the 25 per cent threshold that would have triggered the MBR, did *de facto* involve a change of control. These transactions were the following:

- the acquisition in April 2002 by ACS from the Spanish bank BSCH of a 23.9 per cent investment in Dragados, a major construction company, at a 59 per cent premium;
- the acquisition in May 2002 by Sacyr, also from BSCH, of a 24.5 per cent interest in Vallehermoso, a large real estate company, at a 31 per cent premium; and
- the acquisition in June 2002 by Bami from the Spanish bank BBVA of a 23.9 per cent interest in Metrovacesa, a real estate company, at a 75 per cent premium.

In each case, the acquirer appointed a significant number of members to the target company's board of directors in the aftermath of the transaction. As discussed above, under the new regulations enacted in 2003, this is no longer possible.

Case study: Metrovacesa/Quarta Iberica and Astrim (2003)

Following the taking of control by Bami in 2002, Metrovacesa received a takeover offer for 100 per cent of its share capital at a 30 per cent premium from the Italian firms Quarta Iberica and Astrim. The board of Metrovacesa, influenced by Bami, opposed the deal. Accordingly, this hostile bid, which was conditional on 50 per cent of the shares being tendered, ultimately failed.

The CNMV undertook an investigation into Bami and its influence over the board of Metrovacesa, finding that it had violated the MBR in its acquisition of Metrovacesa shares because it controlled more than 25 per cent of the share capital. As a result, the voting rights of Bami in Metrovacesa were suspended.

There have also been in-depth investigations into allegations that Bami had agreed with a number of savings banks and other third parties to buy target shares and hold them with the sole purpose of frustrating the bid launched by the Italian companies. The CNMV could not prove the existence of such warehousing/parking arrangements, which would have triggered 'acting in concert' provisions. This highlights the practical difficulty of proving the existence of certain loose 'gentlemen's agreements', particularly when support is 'paid back' by way of long-term business flow that is entirely legitimate.

Case study: Unwinding joint control – the FCC case (2004)

FCC is one of Spain's largest construction conglomerates, with substantial interests in environmental services, water, cement and real estate. More than 52 per cent of its share capital was held by a holding company in which Esther Koplowitz and Veolia Environnement (formerly Vivendi) shared joint control, although Ms Koplowitz had a dominant say in the vehicle and in the operational subsidiaries. The European Commission cleared Veolia's acquisition and the shareholders' agreements as reflecting a 'joint control' situation.

> When, after a series of disagreements with Ms Koplowitz, Veolia concluded that this partnership had come to an end, it placed its stake in the company up for sale; a group of private investors acquired it, changing the control structure of FCC in the process. Veolia's stake was acquired at a price above the prevailing market price and the transaction was notified to the Spanish Competition Authority on the basis of a change from 'joint control' to 'single control' by Ms Koplowitz. However, the CNMV did not conclude that Ms Koplowitz was under any obligation to launch a takeover to afford the remaining shareholders of FCC the opportunity to share in the control premium paid.
>
> Whether this makes sense or not, one of the key conclusions to be extracted from this case is that the CNMV has refused to automatically apply standard 'control' categories and concepts used by competition lawyers in merger control analysis (joint control, decisive influence and negative control) to takeover law analysis. The case also highlights a potential loophole in the application of the MBR. Changes of control at the private holding company level (in a private/public company pyramid), even when the underlying asset is the control stake in a public company, seem to be exempt from the application of the MBR.

> **Case study: The Amadeus bid (2005)**
>
> Amadeus is a leading global distribution system and technology provider for the global travel and tourism industries. Controlled by Air France, Iberia and Lufthansa, Amadeus is a Spanish company whose shares are traded on the Madrid, Paris and Frankfurt stock exchanges. Sensing a strong appetite in the market for the business operated by the company, the three airlines organised a limited auction in which they accepted different offers from interested parties, finally choosing as partners BC Capital and Cinven Partners, which had submitted binding offers at €7.35 per share. Since the airlines wanted to retain significant stakes in the company, this was a complex deal in which the airlines were simultaneously sellers and bidders, because they joined the private equity investors in a Luxembourg holding company that in turn owned the Spanish bidding vehicle.
>
> This bid is particularly interesting for the following reasons:
>
> - the way the auction process was managed;
> - the complex roll up structure agreed between the airlines and the private equity investors, which gave the airlines the option of reinvesting part of their cash proceeds in the vehicle;
> - the firm's listing on three stock exchanges (Madrid, Paris and Frankfurt), which raised complex cross-border issues for the various supervisory authorities involved, compounded by publication/disclosure requirements and language issues; and
> - the fact that only certain target shareholders (the airlines) were offered the chance to 'roll up' (reinvest part of the cash received in the bidding vehicle), which raised interesting issues as to whether this breached the target shareholder parity treatment principle and whether all target shareholders should have been offered the same opportunity.

PART II: EUROPEAN JURISDICTIONS

Some practical thoughts on takeovers in Spain

First, it is important to keep in mind that the MBR is a precondition for acquiring a significant stake in a public company and not an *ex-post* requirement. Overstepping the thresholds without having launched a bid could be legally considered as a serious securities infringement and give rise to not only the suspension of voting rights on the shares acquired, but also a significant fine.

Secondly, entering agreements with target shareholders prior to a bid requires a careful analysis to establish whether such agreements exclusively plan to structure irrevocables and/or if they attempt to regulate long-term shareholders' agreements in a post-bid scenario. In this regard, it is important to emphasise that shareholders' agreements (*pactos parasociales*) in public companies have to be fully disclosed to the CNMV and to the target company.

Thirdly, Spain is a relatively small market, in which takeovers tend to be financed by banks in Madrid or Barcelona, and the number of financial advisers and law firms involved in these transactions is relatively small. Hence, it is not always easy to achieve confidentiality of negotiations and potential bids. Organising small and reliable teams is crucial.

Fourthly, launching a bid in Spain requires that the bidder be fully funded from the outset, since a bank guarantee has to be deposited at the CNMV with the complete file. This is a major problem in some cases, for example those involving UK public companies, for which the bid could be a 'class 1' transaction requiring shareholder approval. Since conditional bids 'subject to funding' or to 'shareholder approval' are not permissible, this may require some sort of bridge funding, which is not always easy to obtain and could be expensive.

Finally, within the boundaries of the applicable takeover rules, the CNMV has broad discretion to apply and interpret such rules on the basis of general principles, such as investor protection, fairness and equal treatment of a target company's shareholders. There is no point in attempting to challenge a ruling of the CNMV before the courts, since the timing of judicial review is incompatible with the market and financial constraints of a takeover.

Chapter 25

Sweden

Thomas Wallinder and Patrick Marcelius
Mannheimer Swartling, Stockholm

The main source of takeover regulation in Sweden is the Rules Concerning Public Offers for the Acquisition of Shares (the Takeover Rules) issued in 2003 by a non-statutory organisation, the Swedish Industry and Commerce Stock Exchange Committee (the NBK). The Takeover Rules are binding on companies listed on the Stockholm Stock Exchange and constitute good practice on the Swedish securities market.

One of the objectives of the Takeover Rules is to ensure fair and equal treatment of the shareholders of the target company. The Takeover Rules are to be interpreted so as to achieve their underlying purpose. Both the wording and the spirit of the Takeover Rules must be observed. The Takeover Rules are based on a number of general principles that encapsulate the essential spirit of the Rules and offer guidance on how to interpret them.

Under the Takeover Rules, the Swedish Securities Council is empowered to issue statements and rulings on points of interpretation of the Rules, as well as to grant dispensations from them. In addition, the body of past statements and rulings by the Securities Council offer guidance on the interpretation of the Takeover Rules.

There are also other sets of rules relevant to takeovers, including:

- the listing agreement with the Stockholm Stock Exchange, which contains, among other things, a requirement to inform the Exchange about a potential public offer and rules on selective disclosure of price-sensitive information;
- the Companies Act, which contains a number of relevant provisions, particularly those relating to exchange offer documents and compulsory acquisition of minority shareholdings;
- the Market Abuse Act, which contains, among other things, provisions on insider trading that make certain dealings in securities with inside information and certain forms of dissemination of inside information criminal offences;
- the Financial Instruments Trading Act, which sets out rules dealing with prospectus requirements and disclosure requirements for acquisitions and transfers of shareholdings; and
- the Rules Concerning the Disclosure of Acquisitions and Transfers of Shares, etc. (the Disclosure Rules), issued in 1994 by the NBK, which contain provisions requiring disclosure of acquisitions and transfers of shareholdings.

Bid preparation, timing of offers and revisions

The timing and planning of a takeover offer depend on a number of factors, particularly on whether the offer is likely to be friendly or hostile. Bid preparation often includes a number of steps leading up to the announcement of the offer. While there is no requirement to put an offer to the target board before the offer is announced, the offeror often contacts the chairman of the board or the managing director of the target in order to determine the target's attitude to the potential offer.

In relation to friendly takeovers, it is common for offerors to carry out due diligence on the target. Pre-takeover due diligence in Sweden is normally limited in scope and more limited than due diligence on a private acquisition.

Further, under the listing agreement, the target company and the offeror are required confidentially to inform the Stockholm Stock Exchange about the potential bid, in order to enable the Exchange to monitor movements in the price of the target company's shares. If information about the bid is leaked, resulting in untoward movements in the share price, the Exchange may suspend trading in the shares.

Irrevocable undertakings

In order to increase its chances of success, an offeror often seeks acceptance undertakings from key target shareholders before making the offer. Such undertakings are usually made conditional on the offer being declared unconditional and institutional shareholders often insist that their undertaking (if any) ceases to apply in the event of a higher offer. Sometimes, such undertakings contain a 'long stop date' or a requirement that the offer must be announced and/or declared unconditional before a certain date. Undertakings do not usually contain many other provisions. In particular, they usually do not include representations and warranties.

The press release announcing the offer must contain information regarding the extent to which the offeror has received undertakings from target shareholders to accept the offer. There is no clear consensus among practitioners as to whether irrevocable undertakings are covered by the Disclosure Rules. In the absence of any statement or ruling by the Securities Council, any analysis of whether irrevocable undertakings are covered by the Disclosure Rules should be made on a case by case basis.

Exclusivity

Exclusivity agreements, whereby the target agrees not to negotiate with any other potential offeror, are not common in Sweden. It may be argued that the Takeover Rules impose limitations on the target's capacity to agree to an exclusivity agreement, as the target is expected under the Takeover Rules to apply the rules on due diligence in the same way in relation to all potential offerors. The Takeover Rules are also based on the principle that it is for the shareholders to decide on the merits of an offer. Against this background, any analysis of exclusivity agreements must be made on a case by case basis, taking into account, among other things, the type of offer, particularly if the offer is a 'merger of equals', and any qualifications to exclusivity, such as 'fiduciary outs'. The offeror may, however, seek to obtain similar results by entering into exclusivity agreements with the key shareholders of the target company, although such agreements are likely to be relatively unusual.

Break fees

Break fee arrangements, whereby the target undertakes to pay a fee to the offeror if the transaction is not complete, have been agreed in some public offers, but they are not common practice in Sweden. The Takeover Rules do not specifically address the issue of break fees, nor is there any case law or clear consensus among practitioners on them.

Break fees would give rise to a number of difficult legal issues. In general, both the Companies Act and the principles underlying the Takeover Rules arguably impose limitations on the target company's agreeing to break fees. In particular, the Takeover Rules are based on the principle that it is for the target company's shareholders to decide on the merits of the offer. A break fee agreed in favour of the offeror would also require an analysis of the target board's potential liability towards the company and its shareholders. Against this background, any analysis of break fees must be made on a case by case basis, taking into account, among other things, the type of offer, particularly if the offer is a 'merger of equals'; any qualifications to the break fee, such as 'fiduciary outs'; the 'payment triggers'; the size of the break fee and whether the break fee is a genuine pre-estimate of loss.

Key dates

Exhibit 25.1 sets out an indicative timetable for a cash offer. Most of the dates may be varied depending on the circumstances in each case.

Revisions of the offer

The offeror is entitled to increase the offer price at any time after the announcement. An increase in the offer price is obligatory where the offeror acquires shares during the course of the offer, whether on the market or otherwise, at a price in excess of the offer price. An increase in the value of the bid does not automatically have an effect on the acceptance period. However, the target shareholders must be given sufficient time to consider and assess the revised offer, particularly where there are competing offerors. The offeror may be required as a result to extend the acceptance period, where the value of the bid is increased towards the end of the acceptance period.

Further, the Financial Supervisory Authority has taken the view that an increase in the offer price requires a supplement to the offer document, which must be registered with and/or approved by the Authority. The acceptance period may therefore need to be extended.

Conditionality of offers

An offeror is not allowed simply to reserve a right to withdraw the offer once it has been made. However, a voluntary takeover offer is usually made subject to the satisfaction of a number of conditions, which must be objective – it must be possible to determine objectively whether or not a condition has been satisfied – and must not, except where a condition relates to regulatory approvals such as anti-trust clearances, give the offeror a decisive influence over their fulfilment.

Under the Takeover Rules, the offeror is obliged to announce the offer immediately after a firm decision has been made. Once the offer has been announced, the offeror is not allowed to withdraw the offer unless:

- the offer contains an acceptance condition or a condition regarding any necessary resolutions by the general meeting of the offeror or the target, and it is clear that this condition has not been, or cannot be, satisfied;

PART II: EUROPEAN JURISDICTIONS

Exhibit 25.1

Indicative timetable for a cash takeover offer in Sweden

Day	Action
Before the announcement day	Under the listing agreement, both the target and the offeror confidentially inform the Stockholm Stock Exchange about the potential offer; relevant competition authorities may also be confidentially informed about it (if applicable).
Announcement day	Once the offeror has made a firm decision to make an offer, the offeror must immediately announce the offer by means of a press release.
Announcement day + 2 business days	Filings are made with the relevant competition authorities (if applicable).
Announcement day + up to 5 weeks	The offer document is posted and the acceptance period starts.
Announcement day + 5–6 weeks	Approvals are obtained from the relevant competition authorities (if applicable).
Announcement day + 5–7 weeks	The acceptance period expires; under the Takeover Rules, the offer must stay open for at least three weeks.
Expiry of acceptance period + 3–5 business days	Announcement of the result of the offer, and declaration that the offer is unconditional, as soon as possible after the expiry of the acceptance period (in practice, as soon as the acceptances tendered have been counted, typically within five business days, depending on the number of shareholders).
Expiry of acceptance period + 7–9 business days	Payment of the consideration.
Expiry of acceptance period + 2 weeks	The squeeze-out procedure is initiated by the offeror sending a letter to the target board requesting that the squeeze-out procedure be settled by arbitration.
Expiry of acceptance period + 4 weeks	Delisting of the target company, often on the basis of a timetable agreed with the Stockholm Stock Exchange earlier in the process.
6–8 months after initiation of squeeze-out procedure	The offeror is granted 'advance title' to the minority shareholdings.
12–18 months after initiation of squeeze-out procedure	The squeeze-out procedure is completed, unless the arbitration award has been challenged.

- the offer has been made conditional on the absence of a higher competing offer and such an offer is made; or
- the offer has been made subject to any other condition and it is clear that this condition has not been, or cannot be, satisfied, and this is of material importance to the offeror's acquisition of the target company.

Although a voluntary offer may be made subject to conditions, it is quite difficult to terminate an offer for non-fulfilment of most conditions. The Takeover Rules provide that a bid can be terminated only if the relevant breach of condition would be of material importance to the offeror's acquisition of the target, unless the condition in question is:

- the acceptance condition;
- a condition relating to necessary resolutions by the general meeting of the offeror or the target; or
- a condition relating to the absence of a higher competing offer.

The more general a condition (other than one of these three) is, the harder it is for the offeror to withdraw the offer on the basis that the breach of the condition is of material importance to the offeror's acquisition of the target. In practice, the offeror in most cases needs to consult the Securities Council before terminating the offer.

Material adverse change conditions: the Rambøll case (2003)

On 17 February 2003, the Danish company Rambøll Hannemann & Höjlund A/S announced a public offer for Scandiaconsult AB. The financing of the offer was made conditional on the non-occurrence of anything beyond Rambøll's control that could not reasonably have been foreseen and that either affected 'Rambøll's or Scandiaconsult's liquidity or earnings adversely' or caused 'serious disturbance in the Nordic capital market or the Nordic market for contribution and technical consultants'. The Securities Council ruled that a public offer may be made subject to a material adverse change condition if the material adverse change is capable of being verified objectively and the condition is not so wide that in practice it would be very difficult for the shareholders to understand the implications of the condition. However, a 'serious disturbance in the Nordic capital market or the Nordic market for contribution and technical consultants' did not satisfy this test.

Stake building

An offeror may wish to increase the likelihood of a successful bid by building a stake in the target through off-market or on-market purchases before making the offer. This stake building is possible, but there are a number of applicable restrictions and such purchases may also have an impact on the offer price, as well as on the form of consideration offered in the bid. The acquisition of a large or controlling stake may also trigger an obligation to make a mandatory bid.

The Takeover Rules provide that, if the offeror carries out due diligence on the target and receives non-public price-sensitive information from the target, the offeror must not make any on-market or off-market dealings in shares of the target until such information has been made public. In practice, this rule often prevents the offeror from dealing in target shares once the offeror has commenced a due diligence exercise. The insider trading provisions in the Market Abuse Act may also be relevant to stake building, but they do not prevent the offeror from acquiring shares in the target before the announcement of the offer where the inside information relates only to the offeror's intention to make an offer.

Stake building can also give rise to disclosure obligations. The Disclosure Rules provide that any acquisition that takes a shareholding to 5 per cent of the total number of shares or voting rights in a Swedish company listed on a Swedish stock exchange or authorised marketplace, and any subsequent percentage that is a multiple of five up to and including 90 per cent, must be disclosed. This requirement also applies if the holding falls below any of these thresholds. The Financial Instruments Trading Act also contains disclosure requirements relevant to stake building where the voting rights attached to a shareholding reach or exceed any of the following thresholds: 10 per cent, 20 per cent, one-third, 50 per cent or two-thirds.

Mandatory bids

The Takeover Rules do not contain a definition of 'control', but require a person who, alone or together with a concert party, acquires shares carrying 30 per cent or more of the voting rights in the target company to make a public offer for the remaining shares in the target company, on the basis that a 30 per cent holding would typically give *de facto* control. Where the target company holds its shares in treasury, these shares are included for the purposes of the threshold calculation. In other words, share buy-backs do not have any effect on the mandatory bid threshold.

The rules requiring a mandatory bid do not apply to the mere holding of rights to acquire shares. Accordingly, the obtaining of irrevocable undertakings or the acquisition of call options, warrants or convertible debt instruments would not trigger the obligation to make a mandatory bid. The mandatory bid requirement is not triggered until the acquisition is final and the acquirer can exercise the voting rights for the shares.

An indirect acquisition may also trigger a mandatory bid under the Takeover Rules. This may occur where an offeror acquires shares in another company (Company A) and Company A itself already holds shares in the target company (Company B). Where the acquisition of shares in Company A results in the offeror becoming the parent company of Company A, their shareholdings in Company B are aggregated and, if the total shareholdings reach or exceed the 30 per cent mark, the offeror is required to make a mandatory bid for Company B.

The Securities Council may waive the requirement to make a mandatory bid, for instance where the holding arises as a result of a gift, inheritance, a 'rescue operation' for a company that is in serious financial hardship or the company's issuing of new shares as consideration for the acquisition of a company or a business. The Securities Council may also waive the mandatory bid requirement where there has been no *de facto* change of control, for instance where a corporate group is restructuring or where the company is controlled by a family and a new generation of family members is taking over the control of the company.

Consideration

In general, an offeror making a voluntary bid is free to offer whatever price it wishes, although, unless the offer price is at some premium to the current market price of the target's shares, it is unlikely to be a successful bid. In addition, under the Takeover Rules, the offer price must not be less than the highest price paid by the offeror for shares in the target within six months of the announcement of the offer or during the course of an offer.

The offeror must offer all holders of shares of the same class identical consideration per share. However, in special circumstances, certain shareholders may be offered consideration in another form, but with the same value, for instance, where the target company has a very large number of shareholders. In such cases, there may be practical reasons for offering cash for small blocks of shares, despite other shareholders being offered consideration in some other form.

Where a company has more than one class of share, the offeror may offer consideration that differs both in form and value. However, shareholders of each class must always be treated fairly and any premium, calculated as a percentage of the value of the shares, must be the same for all classes of share, unless there are special reasons that justify different premiums. Commercial and market reasons may justify different premiums, for instance, where the different classes of share carry different voting rights. However, differences in the treatment of different categories of owners must never be unfair. In three recent rulings, the Securities Council has stated that it is a widespread view in the securities market that holders of a non-listed class of share carrying more votes than a listed class of share should normally not be offered a price that is more than 10 per cent higher than the price for the listed class of share. However, a price difference of more than 10 per cent may not necessarily be unreasonable, depending on the reasons for the price difference. In two of the cases, the Securities Council ruled that a 12 per cent price difference between a listed share and a non-listed share carrying more votes than the listed share was not unreasonable, based on the facts of the case. Despite these rulings by the Securities Council, the Swedish Shareholders' Association (an independent lobby organisation supporting the interests of smaller shareholders) and certain institutional shareholders seem to take a more restrictive view on price differences and certain price differences may therefore be a sensitive issue.

If an offer is made to both shareholders and holders of call options on shares, the aggregate consideration for a share and an outstanding call option on the share must not exceed the consideration for other shares of the same class that do not constitute the underlying asset of a call option.

There are generally no restrictions on what sort of consideration may be offered in a Swedish voluntary bid. However, in practice, the consideration in voluntary offers invariably consists of cash, securities or a combination of the two.

A mandatory bid must always be accompanied by a cash alternative. Further, if the offeror has acquired more than 10 per cent of all the shares in the target for cash within six months of the announcement of the offer, the offer must be accompanied by a cash alternative. This requirement also applies where the offeror has acquired more than 10 per cent of all the shares in the target for cash during the course of an offer.

Hostile bids

What the directors of a target company have to consider on receiving a hostile bid

The defensive measures available to the board of the target are restricted by the board's duty to act in the interests of the company and all shareholders. As a result, the board of the target may be in breach of the directors' duties if it carries out actions with a view to frustrating a potential bid.

The Takeover Rules provide that, once the target company has good reason to assume that a serious offer is about to be made or the offer has already been made, the target company must not take any action that would typically be likely to undermine the bases for making and implementing the offer or its implementation, unless the action is approved by the shareholders at a general meeting.

The Takeover Rules do not contain any list of actions that are to be regarded as 'frustrating actions'. The overriding consideration is whether the action would normally be likely to undermine the bases of the offer. However, frustrating actions generally include issuing shares on a non-pre-emptive basis, acquiring or disposing of material assets, carrying out share buy-backs, or making a bid for the offeror or another company. The launch of any counter-bid for the offeror is also likely to qualify as a 'frustrating action' under the Takeover Rules and would require the shareholders' approval.

In addition, Swedish shareholders may be expected to resist anything that could prevent an offer being made for the companies in which they have an interest. They are therefore unlikely to vote for anything that might have this effect. Accordingly, it is unusual to put any actions that count as frustrating actions to a vote of the shareholders.

Protection against a hostile takeover offer

If a company is aware that it might be subject to an offer, it may decide to carry out various preparatory steps in advance of receiving an actual bid. For example, directors could be made aware of their duties in a takeover situation and of the provisions of the relevant regulations that are most likely to be relevant. All appropriate advisers, primarily financial advisers and lawyers, may also be contacted.

Structural protection is not usually something that Swedish companies would put in place. Nevertheless, certain measures can be taken in advance of an announcement of an offer or the commencement of negotiations with an offeror.

The articles of association may provide that *different voting rights* are attached to different classes of shares. Under the Companies Act, the voting rights of a share must not exceed the voting rights of another share by more than 10 times. As of 2003, 53 per cent of Swedish listed companies had issued shares with multiple voting rights and, on average, the controlling shareholder(s) held 25 per cent of the shares and 41 per cent of the voting rights in such companies. As a result, depending on the structure of shareholdings, a bid may require the support of the controlling shareholder(s) to enable the offeror to squeeze-out the minority shareholders and to pass resolutions for the alteration of the target's articles following the bid. Such resolutions typically require a majority of two-thirds of the votes cast, as well as two-thirds of all shares present or represented at the general meeting.

Listed companies can hold *mutually supportive cross-holdings* in each other, thereby making it more difficult for a potential offeror to gain control and/or preventing a potential offeror from acquiring more than 90 per cent of the shares and voting rights in these companies. Further, shareholders with substantial holdings in such companies can enter into agreements giving the other parties to such agreements a right of first refusal with respect to the sale of shares covered by the agreement.

A company's articles of association may contain provisions conferring *pre-emption rights* on transfers of shares in favour of existing shareholders. However, classes of shares that are listed must not be subject to any such restriction. The articles of association may also provide for the *capping of the number of votes* a shareholder may exercise at a general meeting. Such provisions may prevent an offeror from gaining control of the target, unless the offeror acquires the number of shares and votes necessary to alter the target's articles of association.

Under the Takeover Rules, the target board is required to announce a reasoned opinion of the offer within a reasonable time before expiry of the acceptance period. The target board is not required to seek independent financial advice in relation to its opinion, although a 'fairness opinion' from an independent financial adviser is often obtained. However, in management buy-outs, the target board must obtain a fairness opinion.

An offer that becomes 'hostile' will have been rejected by the target board, in some cases on the basis of a fairness opinion. The usual arguments are that the offer undervalues the target and its prospects, and/or that the offer carries an insufficient premium for control and that, by keeping their shares, the shareholders will reap the rewards of improved future prospects, rather than letting the offeror take them. In order to back these arguments up, the target board will seek to present the performance of the target in the most favourable light and may release new information about future plans, or profits or asset valuation. Where the offeror is offering its own securities as consideration, the target board may also seek to attack the value of the offer by focusing on the offeror's financial condition or operational performance.

Where an offer has been notified to the Swedish Competition Authority or the European Commission, the relevant regulatory authority may request (or even use its legal powers to require) information from the target as to the competitive and other effects of the merger. The target should not therefore be prevented from producing information in response to such requests that is unhelpful to the offeror's case and that, accordingly, results in the offer not being cleared by the relevant authority, provided that the target's views are valid and correct. However, the target should take care to ensure that the information provided is not misleading or intended to mislead.

Even before the 'frustrating actions' provisions of the Takeover Rules come into play, the directors of a company, given their duties to shareholders, must be careful about building provisions into contracts that effectively prevent or severely hinder the making of an offer. However, where the underlying transaction is in the best interest of the company and the provisions are a condition of the other party's proceeding, the target should generally be free to agree to the provisions.

There should generally be no legal objection to a target board seeking a third party (a 'white knight') to make an alternative offer for the target. However, the directors of the target should be aware that dissemination of information about a potential offer may be a criminal offence under the Market Abuse Act, that selective disclosure of price-sensitive information may be contrary to the listing agreement, and that, unless the white knight enters into a confidentiality agreement, such selective disclosure may trigger an obligation to disclose the information.

However, the target would generally be prevented from seeking a 'white squire' to build up a protective stake in the target, given that issuing new shares in the target and/or selling treasury shares to the white squire would normally qualify as 'frustrating actions', unless the 'frustrating action' has been approved by the shareholders at a general meeting.

What a hostile offeror should bear in mind

Hostile takeovers are relatively uncommon in Sweden. Making a hostile offer may require more strategic planning than making a recommended offer. If the offeror offers cash, it must justify the price to the target shareholders without suggesting to its own shareholders that it is 'overpaying'. If the offeror offers its own shares, it exposes its own operational track record to criticism by the target and also exposes its own share price to possible downturn pressure in the market. In turn, the hostile offeror must remember that it must always comply with all relevant standards in making its 'pitch' to the target shareholders. In addition, the hostile offeror may also have to explain why its offer is better than that of a competing offeror, which adds yet another dimension and, possibly, extra strains on the offeror's share price.

A hostile offeror should also bear in mind that there may be protective structures in the articles of association of the target, which may prevent the offeror from gaining control of the target or restrict the offeror's freedom of action following the bid, unless the offeror acquires shares representing more than two-thirds of the shares and votes in the target, and thus becomes free to amend the articles of association. Certain alterations in articles of association may require a super-majority of more than two-thirds, under either the Companies Act or the articles of association themselves.

The articles of association of the target may also provide for shares with multiple voting rights. Depending on the structure of shareholdings, a bid may thus require the support of the principal shareholder(s) to enable the offeror to squeeze-out the minority shareholders and to pass resolutions for the alteration of the target's articles following the bid.

Further, where an unfriendly shareholder controls a significant stake in the target, the shareholder may have appointed board members of the target. Even if such board members are in the minority, they may take actions that are damaging to the offer, such as publicly questioning the offer. In a ruling in November 2004, the Securities Council stated that a member of the target board is free to publicly express his/her opinion about the offer, whether or not that board member is also a shareholder in the target, if, in his/her capacity as director, he/she believes that to do so would be in the best interests of the target shareholders.

If there is more than one offeror

A competing offeror may make a bid at any time. There is no requirement that it should be at a higher price, but it is obviously unlikely to be successful if it is not.

A competing offer does not have any automatic effect on acceptances of the original offer that have already been tendered. However, where the original offer is subject to any unfulfilled condition at the time when a competing offer is made and the original offeror has reserved the right to withdraw or modify any such condition, shareholders in the target company who have accepted the original offer are free to withdraw their acceptances. As a result, in order to be successful, a competing offer should in practice be made well before the original offer has been declared unconditional.

The original offeror and the competing offeror are free to increase their offers. If the offer price is increased, the offeror is not required to make a new offer, but may be required to extend the acceptance period.

The impact of a competing offer was illustrated in the takeover battle for the Swedish internet service provider Song Networks. On 14 September 2004, the Danish company TDC announced a public offer of Skr70.00 per share for Song Networks. The offer received the backing of Song Networks' board and about one-third of its shareholders. However, on 22 September, Tele2, Sweden's second largest telephone company, decided to place a higher competing bid of Skr75.00 per share for Song Networks. On 28 September, TDC decided to increase its offer to Skr82.50 per share and, on 29 September, Tele2 responded by increasing its offer to Skr85.00 per share. On 27 October, TDC increased its offer to Skr95.00 per share, which eventually became the winning bid. The takeover battle for Song Networks gave rise to a Securities Council statement to the effect that the target shareholders must be given sufficient time to consider and assess a revised offer, particularly where there are competing offerors.

Acquisitions of minority shareholdings and delisting

Compulsory acquisition of minority shareholdings

The Companies Act allows the offeror to acquire minority shareholdings on a compulsory basis if, whether alone or together with any of its subsidiaries, it owns more than 90 per cent of the shares and voting rights in the target. Where the 90 per cent mark is exceeded, a minority shareholder also has a right to be bought out by the offeror. If a target company holds its own shares in treasury, such shares are disregarded for the purposes of this calculation.

The squeeze-out procedure is settled by arbitration under the Arbitration Act. However, unlike other arbitration awards, the award in a squeeze-out procedure may be challenged by the parties on both procedural and substantive grounds.

In a squeeze-out procedure, the offeror typically requests the transfer of title to the minority shareholdings ('advance title'). If the offeror provides satisfactory security for the price of the shares, including interest, the minority shareholders must accept that the offeror is granted advance title to their shareholdings and that the offeror thereby becomes the sole shareholder of the target. Ultimately, it is the arbitration panel that determines whether or not the security is satisfactory.

Once the offeror has been granted advance title to the minority shareholdings, the squeeze-out procedure concerns only the price for the shares. The Companies Act provides that, if the greater part of the offeror's shareholding in the target has been acquired by a public offer, the price for the remaining shares must be equivalent to the value of the offer consideration, unless there are any special reasons for a different price, such as when a long time has passed since the offer was completed, or a material change in the circumstances affecting the value of the consideration has occurred. If this rule does not apply, the price must reflect the real value of the minority shareholdings at the time of the initiation of the squeeze-out procedure. Further, the fact that such shares represent a minority holding must be disregarded. Following a cash offer, the arbitration panel often determines the price on the basis of the stock market price of the target shares at the time when the squeeze-out was initiated.

Delisting

Any resolution to apply for delisting typically lies with the board of the target. The application for delisting must generally be granted by the Stockholm Stock Exchange, but, if the Exchange considers the delisting of the target inappropriate, it may refuse to grant the application, though, arguably, only for an interim period.

Delisting of the target is straightforward following an offer where the offeror has become the owner of more than 90 per cent of the shares and voting rights in the target. In such cases, the board of the target typically submits an application to the Stockholm Stock Exchange to delist the target two or three weeks after the initiation of the squeeze-out procedure.

However, where the offeror has not become the owner of more than 90 per cent of the shares and voting rights in the target, the issue of delisting becomes more complex. The Securities Council appears to have taken the view that the shareholders in a listed company have normally invested in the company on the assumption that there will be a functioning market in the shares until the continuing listing requirements for the distribution of shares are no longer satisfied. In particular, under the current listing rules of the Stockholm Stock Exchange, a company listed on the 'A-List' must have, among other things, at least 25 per

PART II: EUROPEAN JURISDICTIONS

cent of the shares and 10 per cent of the votes distributed to the public; these are continuing obligations. It seems that where these listing requirements are satisfied following a takeover offer, it would generally be contrary to good market practice for the target board to apply for delisting at the request of the offeror.

Impact of the Takeover Directive

A White Paper addressing the implementation of the Takeover Directive (2004/25/EC) was published in June 2005. The White Paper introduces certain changes to the current takeover regime, the most important of which are set out below. It is proposed that the changes take effect on 20 May 2006.

Statutory underpinning of the Takeover Rules

The White Paper proposes the introduction of statutory underpinning for the Takeover Rules. Under the proposed legislation, Swedish stock exchanges and authorised marketplaces would have to lay down rules in accordance with the Takeover Directive. An offeror would be under a statutory duty to comply with these rules. The proposed legislation would also provide that an offeror is under a duty to make a mandatory bid where the offeror acquires shares carrying 30 per cent or more of the voting rights in the target company. While the proposed legislation would not prevent the NBK (or other self-regulatory body) from continuing to prepare and put forward changes to the Takeover Rules, the stock exchanges and the authorised marketplaces would be responsible for ensuring that the Takeover Rules comply with the Takeover Directive.

Changes to substantive provisions

The implementation of the Takeover Directive will also require changes to substantive provisions. Under the proposed legislation, the scope of the Takeover Rules would be widened to offers for shares in Swedish companies listed only on a 'regulated market' in an EU member state other than Sweden, in which case only certain provisions of the Takeover Rules, such as the provisions relating to mandatory bids and actions taken by the target board, would apply. However, where the offer is for shares in a foreign company listed on a 'regulated market' in Sweden, the Takeover Rules would be amended so that they apply only if the shares are not also listed in the member state where the company has its registered office, in which case only certain provisions of the Takeover Rules, such as the provisions on the consideration of the offer, the contents of the offer document and the procedure of the bid, would apply.

The White Paper also introduces a wider definition of concert parties that would include 'natural or legal persons who cooperate with the offeror or the offeree company on the basis of an agreement, either express or tacit, either oral or written, aimed either at acquiring control of the offeree company or at frustrating the successful outcome of the bid'. Further, the scope of the definition would be widened to cover parties acting in concert with the target, rather than, as in the current definition, only parties acting in concert with the offeror.

Under the current Takeover Rules, the offer must stay open for at least three weeks, but there is no restriction on the maximum time an offer can stay open. The implementation of the Takeover Directive will require changes to the Takeover Rules, as the Takeover Directive provides that the acceptance period may not be longer than 10 weeks. However, member states are allowed to provide that the period of 10 weeks may be extended on condition that the offeror gives at least two weeks' prior notice of its intention to close the bid. Accordingly, the White Paper contains a proposal that the acceptance period may be extended beyond 10 weeks on condition that the offeror gives at least two weeks' prior notice of its intention to close the bid.

The proposed implementing measures also include additional requirements that trade unions be informed about a public offer. It is proposed that the offeror and the target would be under a duty to inform the relevant trade union(s) about the offer as soon as the offer has been announced. The White Paper also proposes changes relating to the target board's response, as the Takeover Directive requires that the response includes information on the target board's views on the effects of the offer and the offeror's strategic planning for the target, and the likely repercussions for jobs and business locations.

Under the proposed legislation, the offeror would also be under a duty to inform the Financial Supervisory Authority about the offer and the offeror's undertaking towards a stock exchange or an authorised marketplace to comply with the relevant Takeover Rules no later than when the offer is made.

Under the proposed legislation, the annual reports of listed companies would have to include information about protective structures and other arrangements that may be relevant to a potential offeror, including:

- the structure of the share capital;
- restrictions on the transfer of securities;
- significant direct and indirect shareholdings;
- restrictions on voting rights;
- rules governing the appointment and replacement of board members; and
- material agreements that may be terminated on a change of control of the company.

It is proposed that Sweden opts out of the breakthrough provisions in the Takeover Directive, so that the breakthrough provisions are not likely to be made mandatory in Sweden. As a result, the implementation of the Takeover Directive is likely to require changes to the Companies Act to allow Swedish companies to adopt breakthrough provisions in their articles of association. The White Paper proposes to reject the 'reciprocity' principle in the Takeover Directive on the basis that the utilisation of this principle would add too much complexity to the implementing provision and that it is unlikely Swedish companies would adopt breakthrough provisions in their articles of association anyway. As a result, any breakthrough provisions in the articles of association would combine to apply even if the offeror is from a country where there are no such provisions.

Lastly, it is proposed that the Financial Supervisory Authority be designated as the 'competent authority' in Sweden under the Takeover Directive, with increased powers to supervise public offers and enforce compliance with the proposed legislation.

Important points for offerors to keep in mind

Institutional shareholders account for more than 85 per cent of the total market capitalisation of the Stockholm Stock Exchange. As a result, gaining the support of institutional shareholders is often key to the success of public offers in Sweden.

While structural protection is not usually something that Swedish companies would put in place, the articles of association of the target may provide that different voting rights are attached to different classes of shares. As a result, a bid may, depending on the shareholder structure, require the support of the controlling shareholder(s) to enable the offeror to squeeze-out the minority shareholders and to pass resolutions for the alteration of the target's articles of association following the bid.

The Takeover Rules provide that if the offeror carries out due diligence on the target and receives non-public price-sensitive information from the target, the offeror must not make any on-market or off-market dealings in shares in the target until such information has been made public. In practice, this rule often prevents the offeror from building up a stake in the target until the price-sensitive information has been made public.

The Takeover Rules do not contain a definition of 'control', but they do require a person who, alone or together with a concert party, acquires shares carrying 30 per cent or more of the voting rights in the target company to make a public offer for the remaining shares in the target company, on the basis that a 30 per cent holding would typically give *de facto* control. An indirect acquisition may also trigger a mandatory bid under the Takeover Rules.

Break fees and exclusivity agreements are not common practice in Sweden. Arguably, both the Companies Act and the principles underlying the Takeover Rules impose limitations on the target company's agreeing to break fees and exclusivity undertakings. As a result, an offeror may find it difficult to protect itself against third-party involvement.

Although a voluntary offer may be made subject to conditions, it is quite difficult to terminate an offer for non-fulfilment of most conditions. The Takeover Rules provide that a bid can be terminated only if the relevant breach of condition would be of material importance to the offeror's acquisition of the target, unless the condition in question is the acceptance condition; a condition relating to necessary resolutions by the general meeting of the offeror or the target; or a condition relating to the absence of a higher competing offer.

In a squeeze-out procedure, the offeror typically requests 'advance title' to the minority shareholdings. On the grant of advance title, the offeror gains complete control over the target by becoming the sole owner of the target. An offeror should be aware that it may take some time to obtain advance title to the minority shareholdings, typically between six and 12 months following the initiation of the squeeze-out procedure.

Part III:

United States

Chapter 26

An ocean of difference on takeover regulation

John Armour
Faculty of Law and Centre for Business Research, University of Cambridge

David A. Skeel, Jr
University of Pennsylvania Law School

The return of the hostile takeover market in the United States, after several years of slumber, is raising familiar issues about US takeover regulation: can a target company pick a lower value bid over a higher offer, as MCI recently did? Can it simply shoo away an unwanted bid, as PeopleSoft tried to do in 2004? Many Americans would be astonished to learn that these questions would not even be asked if the bidding contest took place on UK soil. In the United Kingdom, a target company's management is prohibited from taking any action that might have the effect of frustrating a takeover bid without the consent of the company's shareholders. This means that the target's shareholders are the ones who decide which bid they prefer, not its managers, who may be more concerned about protecting their turf than making the best decision for the target company.

At least as striking are differences in the mode of takeover regulation in the United States and the United Kingdom. US takeovers are regulated by a combination of mandatory federal securities law, which oversees tender offers, and Delaware state court judges, who decide whether the resistance of the target company's directors is acceptable. The Takeover Panel, which polices takeovers in the United Kingdom, does not rely on judges or statutes at all. The Panel itself is staffed largely by business and financial experts, on secondment from City firms. The Panel's guidance is crystallised in the form of the City Code, a set of 'soft law' rules, which for most of its history has been enforced solely through the threat of public censure. In this chapter,[1] we compare and contrast these aspects of the two systems, in the belief that each may have lessons not only for the other, but for jurisdictions elsewhere in the world that may be considering how best to structure their systems of takeover regulation.

The content of takeover regulation in the United Kingdom and the United States

US regulation gives the bidder complete flexibility to bid for as small or as large a percentage of the target company's stock as the bidder wishes. US law has never imposed a 'mandatory bid' rule, requiring bidders that acquire a large block of target shares to make an offer

PART III: UNITED STATES

for all the target company's shares. US tender offer regulation does require, however, that the bidder pays the same price for all the shares it acquires; that the bidder purchases a *pro rata* amount of the shares of each shareholder that tenders shares; and that it keeps the bid open for at least 20 days.[2] The US regulations thus protect shareholders against 'Saturday night special' bids, kept open for only a short time and made available only to the first shareholders who tender, in order to create pressure on shareholders to rush to tender. However, they do not guarantee shareholders that they will be able to sell all their shares if a bidder takes control of the company.[3]

While US regulation of tender offer bidders is quite shareholder-friendly, the treatment of target managers' responsibilities in the face of an unwanted takeover bid is anything but. Managers of a target company are permitted to use a wide variety of defences to keep takeover bids at bay. The most remarkable of the defences is the 'poison pill' or shareholder rights plan, which is designed to massively dilute a hostile bidder's stake if the bidder acquires more than a specified percentage of target stock, usually 10 or 15 per cent. Poison pills achieve this effect – or, more accurately, they would if they were ever triggered – by, among other things, inviting all the target's shareholders except the bidder to buy two shares of stock for the price of one. The managers of a company that has both a poison pill and a staggered board of directors have significant discretion to resist an unwanted takeover bid.[4]

In addition to poison pills and staggered boards, US targets are also permitted other defences, such as break-up fees and other lock-up provisions, that are designed to cement a deal with a favoured bidder while keeping hostile bidders at bay.[5] The discretion vested in target managers is not absolute. They are sometimes required to remove takeover defences, as when the managers have tilted the playing field towards one bidder in the heat of an actively contested takeover battle.[6] Yet target bidders have extensive discretion, particularly if they wish just to 'say no' to any bid to acquire the company. Moreover, nearly every state has enacted anti-takeover legislation, designed to slow down unwanted takeovers.[7] Under Pennsylvania's anti-takeover law, for instance, managers are permitted to take non-shareholder interests into account and a bidder who acquires 20 per cent or more of the target's stock must disgorge any profits made on the stock within the next 18 months.[8]

In contrast to the United States, UK takeover regulation has a strikingly shareholder-oriented cast. The most startling difference comes in the context of takeover defences. Unlike their US counterparts, UK managers are not permitted to take any 'frustrating action' once a takeover bid has materialised.[9] This rules out the exercise of poison pills and also any other defensive tactic that would have the effect of impeding target shareholders' ability to decide on the merits of a takeover offer, such as buying or selling stock to interfere with a bid, or agreeing to a lock-up provision with a favoured bidder.[10]

The UK rules governing the making of offers are largely consistent with the goal of giving shareholders an unfettered choice whether to accept or reject a takeover bid. As in the United States, bidders are subject to an equal treatment rule that requires them to pay the same price to everyone who tenders into a tender offer, although the UK rule sets the price at the highest at which the bidder acquired the shares during the previous year, as opposed to the period of the tender offer as is stipulated in the United States. Almost the only provision that can be viewed as discouraging takeovers is the United Kingdom's mandatory bid requirement.[11] The mandatory bid provision requires a bidder that acquires 30 per cent or more of a company's shares to keep going and to make an offer for all the shares. In effect, this prohibits partial bids and thus chills at least some takeover offers by forcing bidders to raise enough money to acquire the entire company. Yet this rule serves the important function of minimising the coercive effect of partial bids on target shareholders, who may feel pressured into accepting for fear of otherwise being left with a minority stake worth considerably less than the bidder is offering. Concerns with coercive bids are one of the justifications for the use of defensive tactics in the United States.[12]

To be sure, the United Kingdom's City Code becomes relevant only when a bid is on the horizon. Up to that point, managers' conduct is regulated by a combination of their common law fiduciary duties and the UK Listing Rules. It might be thought that managers seeking to entrench themselves would take advantage of this less stringent *ex-ante* regulation to 'embed' takeover defences well before any bid comes to light.[13] Such 'embedded defences' could range from the fairly transparent, such as the issuance of dual-class voting shares, the use of 'golden shares' or generous golden parachute provisions for managers, to the more deeply embedded, such as provisions in bond issues or licensing agreements for acceleration or termination on a change of control. Yet in practice, such defences are rarely observed on anything like the scale they occur in the United States.

A combination of self-regulatory rules, market norms and other rules of UK company law restricts directors' ability to entrench themselves before a bid appears. First, directors are subject to stringent restrictions regarding the issuance of new shares. They are required by company law to seek approval from the general meeting for authority to issue new shares,[14] which power is usually granted only subject to guidelines formalised by institutional investors.[15] Moreover, pre-emption rules provide that directors must offer any new shares first to existing shareholders *pro rata* with their holdings.[16] Dual-class voting shares are not prohibited by the UK Listing Rules, but they are strongly frowned upon by institutional investors,[17] to the extent that a company that seeks to issue them suffers a severe price penalty in raising capital.[18] More generally, amendments to corporate constitutions, such as 'golden shares', which might be used to entrench managers against the threat of shareholder removal,[19] would almost certainly be voted down by institutional investors if management were to seek to introduce them.

In sum, then, the UK regime facilitates shareholder choice, in comparison with the board discretion model adopted in the United States. This is reflected in the empirical evidence on the frequency of bids. Completed takeovers in the United Kingdom account for a larger share of the country's GDP than do those in the United States.[20] Perhaps most significantly for our purposes, hostile bids are far more likely to succeed in the United Kingdom than in the United States.[21]

Overall, therefore, UK takeover law is far more shareholder-oriented than the rules in place in the United States are. As the authors of *The Anatomy of Corporate Law*, a prominent new book on comparative corporate law, put it, '[d]espite the commonality of the issue, the United Kingdom and the United States have made almost diametrically opposed choices'.[22]

The divergent modes of regulation

The differences in the mode of takeover regulation are, if anything, even more striking than the substantive differences between the two countries' regulatory regimes.

US takeover regulation is the domain of courts and regulators. The tender offer itself is regulated by the Securities and Exchange Commission (SEC), which assesses compliance with the disclosure and process rules. Managers' response to a takeover bid, by contrast, is regulated primarily by state courts, which usually means Delaware's chancery judges and its Supreme Court. When a takeover bidder believes that the target's managers are improperly stymieing its bid, the bidder generally files suit in the Delaware chancery court. The suit argues that the target managers have breached their fiduciary duties – that the managers' resistance is beyond the pale – and that the managers should be forced to remove their defences so that the takeover can be considered by the target's shareholders.[23]

The key players in the drama are lawyers and courts. Each of the relevant parties is advised by lawyers and contested takeover battles nearly always make their way to the courts. In Delaware, the most sophisticated and efficient corporate law arbiter of all the states, this generally means a week or two, but sometimes substantially longer, in the chancery court. To give just one example, the recent battle by Oracle to take over PeopleSoft required a trial that unfolded over several weeks while the parties bargained, as vice chancellor Leo Strine has put it, 'in the glare of the vice chancellor's bald head'. The PeopleSoft battle ended when PeopleSoft's managers agreed to the takeover, which obviated the need for either a written opinion or an appeal to the Supreme Court, but many of the most hotly contested takeover issues are finally resolved after another round of lawyers' arguments in the Supreme Court.

In the United Kingdom, the influence of lawyers is much less pronounced.[24] When a hostile bidder launches a takeover effort and believes that the target's managers are interfering with the bid, the bidder lodges a protest with the Takeover Panel. Originally housed in the Bank of England, the Takeover Panel is now located in the London Stock Exchange building. The Takeover Panel, which includes representatives from the Stock Exchange, the Bank of England, the major merchant banks and institutional investors, administers a set of 'soft law' rules known as the City Code on Takeovers and Mergers.[25] The Panel provides guidance to parties about conduct consistent with the Code, and assesses complaints and issues rulings regarding possible breaches of the Code, both in 'real time'.

Oversight by the Panel differs from the US framework for regulating takeovers in at least three important respects. First, as just noted, the Takeover Panel addresses takeover issues in real time, imposing little or no delay on the takeover effort. It is important not to overstate this point. The Delaware courts provide an extraordinarily prompt response to takeover challenges, often deciding the case as soon as the parties have completed their oral arguments. Nevertheless, the combination of SEC oversight of the tender offer and a judicial process for addressing challenges to the target's response adds up to at least limited delay. The informality of the Takeover Panel, by contrast, enables it to respond almost immediately. In the words of one commentator:[26]

> The reputation of the Panel in the City depends considerably on the efficiency of the Panel executive in dealing promptly, fairly and decisively with the large number of queries that pour into the office every day ... If the point is a difficult one, the Panel executive may ask for time to consider, but this is thought of in terms of hours rather than days.

Secondly, because the Panel relies on soft law rather than hard law, it can continuously update its oversight of takeover activity. The Panel is actively engaged with the parties, which enables it to adjust its response both to the particular parties before it and to the changing dynamics of business within the City of London.

Finally, as already noted, lawyers play relatively little role in the Panel's oversight. The Panel's members come from the principal shareholder and financial groups, and the staff consists primarily of business and financial experts, rather than lawyers, due to a determination from the beginning 'that the Panel executive should for the most part be staffed by temporary secondments from City firms'.[27] The Panel is thus business-oriented rather than legalistic in its approach. The culture could hardly be more different from the 'lawyers with briefcases' approach that characterises US takeover regulation.

Conclusion

The very different outcomes of the MCI takeover battle in the United States and Malcolm Glazer's recent bid for Manchester United plc in the United Kingdom vividly illustrate the difference an ocean makes. Because MCI was able to prevent Quest from taking its offer directly to MCI's shareholders and because it was not clear whether the Delaware courts would force MCI to make way for the higher Quest bid, MCI's directors seem to have succeeded in imposing their preference for Verizon's lower-value bid on MCI's shareholders. With Manchester United, by contrast, it was the target's shareholders who made the choice.

We do not mean to imply that the United States should ditch its current approach to takeovers in favour of a Takeover Panel and a 'soft law' code. The success of the Panel depends in part on conditions that are not present in the United States, such as the fact that the principal UK shareholders, banks and exchange are all located within a few blocks of each other in the City of London. Professionals who know one another and constantly rub shoulders are more likely to adhere to the Panel's informal guidance than relative strangers are. In addition, the limitations of a more legalistic approach are counteracted in important respects in the United States by the efficiency and sophistication of Delaware's courts. By judicial standards, Delaware is astonishingly fast.

While one can imagine lessons that US regulators could learn from the UK approach and vice versa, we believe that the greatest relevance of the contrast is for emerging economies both in Continental Europe and elsewhere in the world. Reformers have too often assumed that top-down, mandatory regulation, together with courts, is the only way to regulate corporate transactions in emerging economies. Yet the success of the UK Takeover Panel suggests that this assumption is seriously flawed. The US approach requires an effective governmental regulator, together with an efficient court system. In many emerging economies, one or both of these elements is missing. In some, the parties that are most directly affected by corporate regulation – large shareholders, banks and exchanges – are located in close proximity to one another, and they have a direct financial stake in the success of the regulatory framework. In this context, informal self-regulation might prove more effective than the US combination of formal statutes and courts. The UK strategy will not invariably be the best, any more than the US approach will be, but reformers and law makers should keep in mind that there at least two ways to regulate takeovers, not just one.

---

[1] This chapter draws upon a larger work in progress. See J. Armour and D.A. Skeel, Jr., 'Who Writes the Rules for Hostile Takeovers, and Why?', Working Paper, University of Cambridge/University of Pennsylvania Law School (2005); and a shorter commentary, J. Armour and D. Skeel, 'Transatlantic Lessons on Takeovers', *Financial Times*, 22 June 2005, p. 13.

PART III: UNITED STATES

[2] The principal US tender offer regulations were enacted in connection with the Williams Act of 1968, which amended the Securities and Exchange Act of 1934. For a brief summary of the regulations, see M.A. Eisenberg, *Corporations and Other Business Organizations: Cases and Materials*, eighth edition (New York: Foundation Press, 2000), pp. 1136–40.

[3] Eschewing a mandatory bid rule can be seen as shareholder-friendly, even though it means that some of each shareholder's shares may not be acquired, because mandatory bid rules have a chilling effect on takeovers.

[4] This point is made most forcefully in L.A. Bebchuk, J.C. Coates IV and G. Subramanian, 'The Powerful Antitakeover Force of Staggered Boards: Further Findings and a Reply to Symposium Participants' (2002) 55 *Stanford Law Review* 885. Some commentators believe that the Delaware courts may soon limit the ability of companies that have both a staggered board and a poison pill just to 'say no' to unwanted bids, but even if Delaware takes this step, US takeover law would still remain far more manager-friendly than UK regulation.

[5] See, for example, D.A. Skeel, Jr., 'A Reliance Damages Approach to Corporate Lockups' (1996) 90 *Northwestern University Law Review* 564.

[6] See, for example, *Revlon, Inc. vs. MacAndrews & Forbes Holdings, Inc.*, 506 A.2d 173 (Del Supr. 1985).

[7] The first generation of state anti-takeover statutes was struck down in *Edgar vs. MITE Corp.*, 457 U.S. 624 (1982), largely because they purported to govern any corporation doing business in the state. State law makers subsequently revised their anti-takeover statutes to apply only to companies incorporated in the state. The second generation statutes were upheld in *CTS Corp. vs. Dynamics Corp, of America*, 481 U.S. 69 (1987).

[8] See, for example, Pennsylvania Consol. Stats. An. sec. 1715 (consideration of other constituencies); sec. 2575 (disgorgement).

[9] City Code on Takeovers and Mergers, General Principle 9.

[10] See, generally, L. Rabinowitz, *Weinberg and Blank on Takeovers and Mergers*, fifth edition and updates (London: Sweet & Maxwell, 2005), Section 20.

[11] The prohibition on the giving by companies of financial assistance for the acquisition of their shares was formerly a significant restriction on the feasibility of leveraged buyout transactions in the United Kingdom. However, with the introduction of the 'whitewash' procedure for private companies in 1981, such transactions are now readily facilitated by the expedient of taking the company private before the financial assistance is given. See Companies Act 1985, Sections 151–58.

[12] The most persuasive and consistent advocate of this position has been Martin Lipton, who is widely credited with the invention of the poison pill. See, for example, M. Lipton, 'Takeover Bids in the Target's Boardroom' (1979) 35 *Business Lawyer* 101; M. Lipton, 'Pills, Polls, and Professors Redux' (2002) 69 *University of Chicago Law Review* 1037.

[13] J. Arlen and E. Talley, 'Unregulable Defenses and the Perils of Shareholder Choice' (2003) 152 *University of Pennsylvania Law Review* 577.

[14] Companies Act 1985, Section 80.

[15] See, for example, Association of British Insurers, *Guidance on Directors' Powers to Allot Share Capital and Disapply Shareholders' Pre-emption Rights* (May 1995).

[16] UK Listing Rules, 4.16–4.21. The Companies Act 1985 also provides a pre-emption rights regime (Sections 89–96), but the protection for investors found in the Listing Rules is stronger. See E. Ferran, 'Legal Capital Rules and Modern Securities Markets – The Case for Reform, as Illustrated by the UK Equity Markets', in K. Hopt and E. Wymeersch (eds), *Capital Markets and Company Law* (Oxford: Oxford University Press, 2003), pp. 115, 131–33. The pre-emption rights regime may be relaxed with shareholder approval, but institutional investors will permit this only in limited circumstances. See, for example, Association of British Insurers, *Pre-emption Group Guidelines* (October 1987).

[17] G.P. Stapledon, *Institutional Shareholders and Corporate Governance* (Oxford: Oxford University Press, 1996), pp. 58–59; L. Rabinowitz, *Weinberg and Blank on Takeovers and Mergers*, fifth edition and updates (London: Sweet & Maxwell, 2005), paragraph 4-7077.

[18] For example, non-voting shares typically trade at a discount of 10–20 per cent: L. Rabinowitz, *Weinberg and Blank on Takeovers and Mergers*, fifth edition and updates (London: Sweet & Maxwell, 2005), paragraph 4-7073.

[19] See *Bushell vs. Faith* [1970] AC 1099.

[20] S. Rossi and P.F. Volpin, 'Cross-Country Determinants of Mergers and Acquisitions', 74 *Journal of Financial Economics* (2004), pp. 277, 281, report statistics on the rate of takeover activity across countries during the period 1990–2002, as shown on the Thomson Financial SDC Platinum database. Rossi and Volpin define this as the proportion of listed firms targetted in a completed deal during the sample period. In the United Kingdom, the proportion

was 53.65 per cent and in the United States it was 65.63 per cent. However, the market capitalisation of listed firms in the United Kingdom accounted for a larger proportion of GDP than did those in the United States. See, for example, A. Demirgüç-Kunt and R. Levine, 'Stock Market Development and Financial Intermediaries: Stylised Facts', World Bank Policy Research Working Paper 1462 (May 1995), p. 33: between 1986 and 1993, the ratio of market capitalisation to GDP in the United Kingdom was 0.92, compared with 0.64 in the United States. When the takeover rates are scaled for the respective size of the stock markets compared to the size of the national economy, this reveals that the United Kingdom had a larger proportion of its GDP subject to takeover activity than the United States, at 49.36 per cent compared to 42.00 per cent in the United States.

[21] W.D. Schneper and M.F. Guillén, 'Stakeholder Rights and Corporate Governance: A Cross-National Study of Hostile Takeovers', Wharton School Working Paper (2004), p. 55, report that the SDC Platinum database of M&A transactions shows 219 hostile bids in the United Kingdom during the period 1988–98, of which 99 were successful, compared with 429 in the United States during the same period, of which only 97 were successful.

[22] R. Kraakman *et al.*, *The Anatomy of Corporate Law: A Comparative and Functional Approach* (Oxford: Oxford University Press, 2004), p. 164.

[23] Once the bidder has filed suit, other target shareholders often file 'piggyback' litigation. The Delaware courts usually address the various suits together.

[24] See, generally, Lord Alexander of Weedon, 'Takeovers: The Regulatory Scene' [1990] *Journal of Business Law* 203 (1990); T.P. Lee, 'Takeover Regulation in the United Kingdom', in K. Hopt and E. Wymeersch (eds), *European Takeovers: Law and Practice* (London: Butterworths, 1992), p. 133; L. Rabinowitz, *Weinberg and Blank on Takeovers and Mergers,* fifth edition and updates (London: Sweet & Maxwell, 2005), Part 9.

[25] The Takeover Panel, *City Code on Takeovers and Mergers* and the *Rules Governing Substantial Acquisitions of Shares,* seventh edition and updates (London: Bowne International, 2002). A regularly updated version of the City Code can be viewed at www.thetakeoverpanel.org.uk.

[26] A. Johnston, *The City Takeover Code* (Oxford: Oxford University Press, 1980), p. 125.

[27] *Ibid.*, p. 127.

Chapter 27

US takeover law and practice

Introduction

The following examines the duties of the board of directors faced with a takeover offer in the US context. It is presented to underline the differences in the legal landscape of merger regulation between Europe and the United States. As discussed in Chapter 1, there has been limited federal regulation of M&A transactions since the introduction of the Williams Act in 1968, and its further amendment in 1970, which primarily dealt with timing and disclosure issues. There is no 'federal corporation law' in the United States, in part because of a number of US Supreme Court decisions that have confined potentially expansive provisions of the US securities law to disclosure problems rather than substantive conduct or fiduciary duty.

Prior to the implementation of the Williams Act, there were no major information disclosure requirements to target shareholders imposed on bidders. The Act amended the Securities Exchange Act of 1934 and extended the disclosure requirements contained in the 1933 Securities Act (which related to equity issuance) to tender offers. The main regulations of the act are:

- **Section 13(d):** Requires disclosure through the filing of the form schedule 13D with the Securities and Exchange Commission (SEC) when a 5 per cent ownership threshold is passed. This must be done within 10 days of exceeding the threshold. Individuals acting in concert are treated as a single entity for the purposes of this section, which also applies to 'stock parking' carried out by banks and brokers acting in the interest of an acquirer. Parties who have filed a 13D must provide an update after any material change. However, if 5 per cent of beneficial owners have not acquired more than 2 per cent in the following year and have no interest in launching a takeover bid, they can subsequently file a schedule 13G.
- **20-day opening:** The bidder's tender offer must be open for 20 business days before he can start to acquire the target's shares. This allows a longer period in which target shareholders can assess the offer, and was a response to short coercive offer periods previously put forward by bidders. It also gives time for competing bidders to come forward and, if necessary, the board to search for a 'white knight'. Once a new offer is tabled, any existing offers must be extended to at least 10 days from the date of the new offer.
- **Equality of shareholder treatment:** Since partial bids are theoretically allowed in the United States, the bidder is required to treat all shareholders equally. If more shareholders tender than are required to meet the offer threshold, the bidder must purchase shares *pro rata* from all shareholders to prevent preferential treatment of any particular group.

Subsequent to the Williams Act, the Court of Chancery and the Supreme Court of the state of Delaware, where 60 per cent of S&P 500 firms are incorporated, have been the primary influence in shaping US merger regulation. It should be noted that there are no federal regulations on mandatory bid thresholds, squeeze-outs and sell-outs, and nothing equivalent to a breakthrough rule in the United States. Therefore, this chapter concentrates on judicial review and judge-made law in the United States, particularly in relation to the duties of the board of directors examining an M&A transaction. It is the board of directors, within the legal framework established by state statutes, previous cases and its own fiduciary responsibilities to shareholders, which must approve a takeover offer. These latter duties are defined primarily by three cases:

- **Dodge vs. The Ford Motor Company (1919):** This case established the business judgement rule which protects directors from personal liability in discharging their duties if they have acted in good faith, with due care and within their authority. It also highlights directors' primary duties toward shareholders. Later, in CNLBS vs. Philip K. Wrigley (1968), the Delaware courts reiterated these principles stating, 'courts of equity will not interfere in the management of the directors unless it is clearly made to appear that they are guilty of fraud or misappropriation of corporate funds, or refuse to declare a dividend when the corporation has a surplus of net profits which it can, without detriment to its business, divide among its stockholders'.
- **Unocal Corp. vs. Mesa Petroleum Corp. (1985):** The Delaware Supreme Court declared that general defensive tactics used by Unocal here were 'reasonable in relation to the threat that the board rationally and reasonably was posed by Mesa's (the raider) inadequate and coercive two-tier tender offer'. In justifying the decision, the court stated that the business judgement rule applied to directors' duties in relation to takeover defences. In essence, this meant that directors will not incur liability in taking the decision to reject a takeover bid as long as there are no conflicts of interest on their part, and they discharged their duty of care. However, the court subjected directors to an enhanced duty of care and a test of reasonableness in relation to the threat faced.
- **Revlon Inc. vs. MacAndrews & Forbes Holdings, Inc. (1986):** The board of the cosmetics manufacturer Revlon rebuffed a takeover offer from corporate raider Ronald Perelman, opting instead for a counter-offer from Forstmann Little. The Delaware Supreme Court extended directors' duties in a sale of control situation to maximise shareholder value. Under the Revlon test, once the directors have decided to sell control of a company, '[t]he directors' role change[s] from defenders of the corporate bastion to auctioneers charged with getting the best price for the stockholders at a sale of the company'.

If the directors decide to reject an offer, a wide range of defensive tactics is open to them, including the issuance of new equity with special rights to selected parties (poison pill), a manoeuvre forbidden in most European jurisdictions. However, the strength of directors' fiduciary responsibilities to shareholders in the United States and the ability of shareholders to enforce these via the courts and the removal of the board in a proxy contest, entail that the interests of all parties are weighed in the balance.

Jeremy Grant

PART III: UNITED STATES

The following extended excerpt on US takeover defences was kindly provided by Watchell, Lipton, Rosen and Katz.

US takeover preparedness and responding to unsolicited offers

A corporation that carefully employs advance takeover measures can improve its ability to deter coercive or inadequate bids or secure a high premium in the event of a sale of control of the corporation.

Rights plans in particular are the most effective device yet developed to deter abusive takeover tactics and inadequate bids. Economic studies have concluded that, as a general matter, takeover premiums are higher where rights plans or modern anti-takeover statutes are in effect than in the absence of such provisions, and that a rights plan or similar protection increases a target's bargaining power. In addition, numerous studies have concluded that the negative impact, if any, of adoption of a rights plan on a company's stock price is very small (less than 1 per cent over the period immediately preceding and following adoption of the plan) and is likely not statistically significant.

Advance preparation for defending against a takeover may also be critical to the success of a preferred transaction that the board has determined to be part of the company's long-term plan. A decision to enter into a business combination transaction does not necessarily obligate a board to serve merely as auctioneer. In the case of a merger or acquisition not involving a change of control, the board may retain the protection of the business judgement rule in pursuing its corporate strategy. As a practical matter, of course, an unsolicited offer involving a substantial premium over the market price may be difficult to ignore or ultimately avoid.

In addition to making good business sense, advance planning for an unsolicited takeover makes good legal sense. The courts have recognised that the business judgement rule is applicable both to preplanned strategies and to responses to a bid, but have held that defensive measures taken in response to a bid will be subject to a higher level of judicial scrutiny.

The Delaware Supreme Court's landmark Time decision illustrates the absolute necessity for a company that desires to maximise its ability to reject a hostile takeover bid to consider periodically its long-term business and acquisition strategies. In Time, both the Delaware Court of Chancery and the Delaware Supreme Court were influenced heavily by the documented history of Time's long-term business and acquisition strategies and Time's prior consideration and rejection of Paramount as a merger partner. Under Time, Delaware's courts respect and defer to a company's long-term plans and will not force a company to accept a hostile takeover bid if its board determines to reject the bid and pursue the long-term plans.

Rights plans

Rights plans are the most effective device yet developed in response to abusive takeover tactics and inadequate bids, and have become a central feature of most major corporations' takeover preparedness. The first version of the rights plan was developed in 1984. Today, over 2,300 companies have adopted rights plans that are in effect.

Rights plans do not interfere with negotiated transactions, nor do they preclude unsolicited takeovers. The evidence is clear, however, that rights plans do have the desired effects

US TAKEOVER LAW AND PRACTICE

of both forcing an acquiror to deal with a target's board and ultimately extracting from an acquiror a higher acquisition premium than would otherwise have been the case. The issuance of share purchase rights has no effect on the capital structure of the issuing company; rather, its only immediate effect is on the balance of negotiating power between a would-be acquiror, on the one hand, and a target and its stockholders, on the other hand. If an acquiror takes action to trigger the rights, however, dramatic changes in the capital structure of the target company and/or the acquiror can result.

A rights plan carefully drafted to comply with state law and a company's charter remains the basic and most effective protective device to prevent coercive offers and disruption of a company's long-term business strategy.

The basic design

The key features of a rights plan are the 'flip-in' and 'flip-over' provisions of the rights, the effect of which, in specified circumstances, is to impose unacceptable levels of dilution on an acquiror. The risk of dilution, combined with the authority of a target's board to redeem the rights prior to a triggering event (generally an acquisition of 15 per cent or 20 per cent of the target's stock), gives a potential acquiror a powerful incentive to negotiate with the target's board rather than proceeding unilaterally.

A rights plan should also provide that, once the triggering threshold is crossed, the target's board may exchange, in whole or in part, each right held by holders other than the acquiror for one share of the target's common stock. This provision avoids the expense of requiring rights holders to exercise their flip-in rights, eliminates any uncertainty as to whether individual holders will in fact exercise the rights, producing the intended dilution, and provides the board additional flexibility in responding to a triggering event. In cases where the acquiring person holds less than 50 per cent of a target's stock, the dilution caused by implementation of the exchange feature is substantial and can be roughly comparable to the dilution caused by the flip-in provision, assuming all eligible rights holders exercise their rights. The exchange also allows the board to control the amount of dilution since these provisions typically provide that the rights may be exchanged in whole or in part.

Chewable pills

In order to satisfy activist stockholders, some companies have resorted to a rights plan that does not apply to a cash offer for all of the outstanding shares of the company. Recent versions of this exception have limited its scope to cash offers containing a specified premium over the market price of the target's stock. While a so-called 'chewable pill' rights plan has some limited utility and may avoid a proxy resolution attack, it is not effective in most situations, and may create an artificial 'target price' for a company that does not maximise shareholder value.

Basic case law regarding rights plans

There is currently no doubt as to the legality of rights plans. Rights plans, properly drafted to comply with state law and a company's charter, typically survive judicial challenge, including under a Unocal analysis. The 'flip-in' feature of rights plans was held, in some early cases, to violate state corporate law. These rulings, however, have now been overruled, either judicially or by legislation explicitly authorising the flip-in. Furthermore, courts have recognised rights plans as important tools available to boards to protect the interests of a corporation.

Therefore, almost all litigation concerning rights plans now focuses on whether or not a board should be required to redeem the rights in response to a particular bid. In this respect, courts applying Delaware law have upheld, or refused to enjoin, determinations by boards not to redeem rights in response to two-tier offers, or inadequate 100 per cent cash offers, as well as to protect an auction or permit a target to explore alternatives.

On the other hand, some decisions, such as Macmillan, City Capital Associates Ltd. Partnership vs. Interco, Inc. ('Interco') and Grand Metropolitan Public Ltd. vs. Pillsbury Co. ('Pillsbury'), have held that the rights may not interfere with shareholder choice at the conclusion of an auction, or at the 'end stage' of a target's attempt to develop alternatives.

Importantly, both Pillsbury and Interco involved circumstances in which a board, rather than 'just saying no', had pursued a restructuring that was comparable to the pending all-cash tender offer. In its opinion in Time, the Delaware Supreme Court criticised some of these cases as reading Unocal to permit 'substituting [the court's] judgement as to what is a "better" deal for that of a corporation's board of directors'.

Case law regarding a board's obligation to redeem rights plans essentially follows the logic of the Delaware courts' sale of control/non-control transaction case law, as well as the basic Unocal standard. Thus, a board engaged in the sale of control of a company may not apply a rights plan in a discriminatory manner favouring one change in control transaction over another, but, in the non-change of control context, it may implement or strengthen an existing rights plan, including favouring a preferred strategic merger, as part of a business strategy to remain independent. In the context of a response to an unsolicited offer, a board adopting a rights plan is well advised to consider the adequacy of the unsolicited offer and its impact on the company's long-term business strategy. A board may also benefit in the Unocal analysis from an investment banker's inadequacy opinion, although courts have not required such opinions in the context of a 'just say no' response to an unsolicited offer.

Renewal of rights plans, shareholder proposals and the economic evidence
Rights plans have generally been adopted with initial 10-year lives. In view of the demonstrated success of rights plans in avoiding coercive and abusive takeover tactics and in protecting a board's right to 'just say no' to a low bid or a bid not consistent with the company's long-term strategy, renewal of rights plans is sensible and warranted. Renewal of a rights plan does not require stockholder approval, unless the plan itself provides otherwise. Renewal also provides a board with an opportunity to amend a rights plan to reflect developments included in later-generation rights plans, as well as in the applicable state corporate and case law.

Shortly after rights plans became popular with major companies, activist institutional shareholders, such as CREF, sponsored precatory resolutions attacking rights plans as so-called 'poison pills'. Today, many institutions routinely vote for such resolutions. Their voting is generally performed by policy committees, not investment analysts, and is typically based on predetermined published principles, rather than a case-by-case analysis. The number of shareholder proposals to redeem and/or require a vote on rights plans between the years 1999 and 2004 is set forth in Exhibit 27.1.

Exhibit 27.1

Number of shareholder proposals related to rights plans, 1999–2004

	No. of anti-poison pill proposals	*Average support (%)*	*No. receiving majority vote*	*Majority vote proposals as a % of the whole*
2004	50	62	39	78
2003	84	60	63	75
2002	50	60	39	78
2001	23	57	17	74
2000	26	58	20	77
1999	27	62	22	81
Average	42	59	32	77

Source: Investor Responsibility Research Center.

The responses of companies confronted with successful stockholder proposals used to be to maintain the status quo and retain the rights plan, but this has changed in recent years. According to the Council of Institutional Investors, none of the eight companies whose shareholders supported by a majority a proposal to redeem the company rights plan took action in 1998; in 2002, eight of the 28 companies (29 per cent) to receive majority-supported anti-rights plan resolutions redeemed or otherwise modified their rights plan; and in 2003, 22 of the 40 companies (55 per cent) with a rights plan that received majority resolutions on the topic elected to eliminate their plan through redemption or amendment. While all of the data for the 2004 proxy season is not yet available including, in particular, the company responses to stockholder votes, as of 1 February 2005, of the 56 companies that included a proposal regarding the redemption of a rights plan or mandatory stockholder approval prior to the adoption of a new rights plan in their 2004 proxy, 33 proposals received majority approval by stockholders who voted at each company's annual meeting. In certain instances, companies have sought to placate individual activist and institutional stockholders by implementing so-called TIDE (triennial independent director evaluation) provisions or 'chewable pill' features (for example, permitting a transaction that would otherwise trigger the rights to proceed if it meets certain fair price or similar requirements).

The fact that a company does not have, and has not announced an intention to adopt, a rights plan does not prevent such stockholder proposals. Companies such as Boeing, Exxon Mobil, Mattel and Sears have faced stockholder proposals regarding termination and/or constraints on adoption of rights plans, even though they had neither a rights plan nor an announced intention to adopt one. Institutional Investor Services (ISS) recommended that its clients withhold votes from nominees for 3M's board (including its CEO) on account of rights plan-related stockholder proposals. In 3M's situation, ISS took the view that the company failed to implement a stockholder proposal supported by a majority in 2002 and 2003 that would require the board to seek stockholder approval for any future rights plan. ISS's view was surprising given that 3M did not have a rights plan and it had adopted a policy requiring prior stockholder approval of a future rights plan, subject to limited exceptions. ISS's recommendation notwithstanding, the directors from whom ISS recommended stockholders withhold their votes were reelected by an approximately 80 per cent vote. Faced with a withhold vote recommendation by ISS in a similar context, Monsanto Company recently engaged in an active proxy solicitation in favour of its director nominees, which similarly ended with the reelection of its directors.

Many institutional investors have come to recognise that a rights plan can be an effective negotiating tool for a responsible board. That fact notwithstanding, in its 2005 US and global policy update, ISS announced that it would begin to recommend withholding votes from all directors (except from new nominees) if a company has adopted or renewed a rights plan without stockholder approval since the company's last annual meeting, does not submit the rights plan to a vote at its upcoming annual meeting or adopts a rights plan with no requirement to submit the plan to a vote within 12 months of its adoption. ISS's policy change will be applied prospectively and rights plans adopted prior to the policy change will not be considered. If a company that triggers this policy commits to submitting its rights plan to a stockholder vote within 12 months of its adoption, ISS will not recommend a withhold vote.

Since the invention of rights plans in 1984, economists and market analysts have debated the economic impact of rights plans on the market price of a company's stock, as well as on takeovers and takeover premiums. Although a 1986 study by the SEC comparing the market prices of companies' stock prior to and immediately after an announcement of the adoption of a rights plan found a 'statistically significant' reduction in market price of 0.66 per cent in some circumstances, every major investment bank that studied the matter has concluded that the adoption of a rights plan has no effect on the stock prices of companies that are not the subject of takeover speculation. The analysis of Comment and Schwert, who used the same methodology as the SEC study, but with a database four times the size of the SEC study, indicated that the adoption of a rights plan has no meaningful price effect on a company's stock price. A study of 341 rights plans adopted between 1 January 1998 and 31 October 1998 concluded that 'the announcement of the adoption of a stockholder rights plan had no effect on the average company's stock price.'

Moreover, a 1988 Georgeson & Company Inc. study demonstrated that companies with rights plans received substantially higher premiums than companies without rights plans. This conclusion has been reaffirmed by other studies, including that by Comment and Schwert. They concluded that rights plans are 'reliably associated with higher takeover premiums'. According to one published report based on analysis by a major investment bank of 245 deals between 1988 and 1995, each with a market value in excess of US$500 million, the median premium for a company with a rights plan was 51 per cent, compared with 35 per cent for companies not having rights plans. Another Georgeson study that analysed 319 takeover transactions completed between 1992 and 1996, found that premiums paid for companies with rights plans averaged 8 percentage points higher (a 26 per cent increase in the premium paid) than premiums for companies without rights plans. The Georgeson study also found that the presence of a rights plan neither decreased the likelihood that a company would become a takeover target nor increased the likelihood that an announced takeover bid would not be completed.

More recently, a study jointly released in February 2004 by Institutional Shareholder Services (ISS) and Georgia State University found that companies with rights plans and other takeover defences outperformed companies without such defences. Strong takeover defences were found to be correlated with: (i) higher shareholder returns over three-, five- and 10-year periods; (ii) stronger profitability measures (return on equity, return on assets, return on investment and net profit margin); (iii) higher dividend payouts and dividend yields; and (iv) higher interest coverage and operating cash flow to liability ratios.

In terms of overall stockholder proposals relating to corporate governance in 2004, Georgeson Shareholder records a decline in the number of proposals of approximately 3 per cent from 2003. Proposals related to executive compensation and to seeking the ability to nominate candidates for directors were particularly prominent in 2004. Despite the reduced number of proposals overall, the number of proposals that were submitted, but subsequently omitted or withdrawn, increased significantly by approximately 22 per cent. This increase in withdrawn or omitted proposals is attributable at least in part to increased dialogue between companies targetted by these proposals and the shareholder proponents or proxy advisory firms. Moreover, the possibility that proxy access rules could be adopted by the SEC provided an increased incentive to companies to discuss governance changes rather than face a stockholder proposal that would run the risk of being approved by either a majority of votes cast or a majority of outstanding shares. A reduction in the number of 'withhold vote' campaigns in 2004 also reflects increased preemptive action on the part of companies.

'Dead hand' pills and 'shareholder rights' by-laws

Dead hand pills

In the face of a 'just say no' defence, the takeover tactic of choice has become a combined tender offer and solicitation of proxies or consents to replace a target's board with directors committed to redeeming outstanding rights under a rights plan to permit the tender offer to proceed. The speed with which this objective can be accomplished depends, in large part, upon other defences that a target has in place. In Delaware, a bidder can act by written consent without a meeting of stockholders, unless such action is prohibited in the certificate of incorporation, and can call a special meeting between annual meetings if permitted under a target's by-laws. Conversely, if a target has a staggered board, a bidder can generally only replace a majority of the target's board by waging a proxy fight at two consecutive annual meetings.

Thus, if a target's charter does not prohibit action by written consent and does not provide for a staggered board, a bidder can launch a combined tender offer/consent solicitation and take over the target as soon as consents from the holders of more than 50 per cent of the outstanding shares are obtained. Even if its charter prohibits action by written consent and precludes stockholders from calling a special meeting, a target without a staggered board can essentially be taken over once a year by launching a combined tender offer/proxy fight shortly before the time of the target's annual meeting. In contrast, a target with a staggered board may well be takeover proof until the second annual meeting.

Within this framework, a target in the first category cannot rely on an ordinary rights plan to give much protection in the face of a combined tender offer/proxy fight. The predicament faced by such targets has spawned variants of the so-called 'continuing director' or 'dead hand' pill.

'Pure' dead hand pills are rights plans which permit only directors who were in place prior to a proxy fight or consent solicitation (or new directors recommended or approved by them) to redeem the rights plan. Once these continuing directors are removed, no other director can redeem the pill. The Cordis board adopted such a pure continuing director redemption provision in 1995 when faced with a consent solicitation to replace its board with the nominees of Johnson & Johnson ('J&J'). J&J challenged the Cordis rights plan under Florida law, but the parties agreed to a merger before the litigation reached any conclusion.

Modified dead hand provisions come in a variety of forms. So-called 'non-redemption' or 'no hand' provisions typically provide that no director can redeem the rights plan once the continuing directors no longer constitute a majority of the board. This limitation on redemption may last for a limited period or for the remaining life of the rights plan. Another variant is the 'limited duration' or 'delayed redemption' dead hand pill. This feature can be attached to either the pure dead hand or no hand rights plan. As the name indicates, these rights plans limit a dead hand or no hand restriction's effectiveness to a set period of time, typically starting after the continuing directors no longer constitute a majority of the board. These rights plans delay, but do not preclude, redemption by a newly elected board. The rights plan that Marvin Davis confronted in his attempted takeover of Northwest Airlines provided that a newly elected board could not redeem the pill for a period of 180 days after the meeting.

Some dead hand rights plans broaden the concept of continuing directors to include more persons than the pure dead hand pill does, creating a milder form of dead hand pill. Rights plans define such continuing directors to include not only directors who were members of the board at the time of the rights plan's adoption (or who were recommended or approved by such persons), but also directors who were elected by a supermajority vote of the stockholders. Such adaptations leave open the possibility that, before a potential acquiror purchases enough shares to trigger a rights plan, it could conduct a proxy contest or consent solicitation to replace the board with its slate of directors who could then redeem the rights without being subject to the dead hand limitations.

> **Case study: Quickturn Design Sys. vs. Shapiro (1998) – striking down dead hand provisions**
>
> The validity of dead hand provisions depends in large part upon the state law that applies. In the case of Quickturn Design Sys., Inc. vs. Shapiro ('Quickturn'), Delaware has made clear that dead hand provisions – even of limited duration – are invalid. At issue in Quickturn was a no hand pill provision of limited duration that the Quickturn Design Sys. board had adopted in the face of a combined proxy fight and tender offer by Mentor Graphics. The provision barred a newly elected board from redeeming the rights plan for six months after taking office if the purpose or effect would be to facilitate a transaction with a party that supported the new board's election. The Delaware Court of Chancery struck down the delayed redemption no hand provision of the rights plan on fiduciary duty grounds. Applying the Unocal standard, the lower court found that this particular rights plan, which effectively barred transactions only with Mentor, was an impermissibly disproportionate response to the threat posed by the bidder.
>
> On appeal, the Delaware Supreme Court reached the same result, but on different grounds. The court held that the dead hand feature of the rights plan ran afoul of Section 141(a) of the Delaware corporation statute, which empowers the board with the statutory authority to manage the corporation. Relying on the requirement in Section 141(a) that any limitation on a board's power must be stated in the certificate of incorporation, the court found that dead hand provisions would prevent a newly elected board 'from completely discharging its fundamental management duties to the corporation and its stockholders for six months' by restricting the board's power to negotiate a sale of the corporation. The reasoning behind the Quickturn holding leaves little room for dead hand provisions of any type in Delaware.

Nothing in the Quickturn decision undercuts the validity or usefulness of traditional rights plans or the readoption of rights plans in anticipation of the expiration of a company's rights plan. Indeed, the Quickturn decision expressly relied in its analysis on the reasoning in previous cases that upheld the board's authority to adopt rights plans. The Quickturn decision does suggest that Delaware corporations with dead hand provisions in their rights plans should proactively seek counsel regarding amendment of their plans before stockholder litigation arises.

Not all states have come down against dead hand rights plans. In a test of the validity of a pure dead hand pill under Georgia law, Invacare Corporation vs. Healthdyne Technologies ('Invacare'), a federal court upheld such a provision. The Invacare decision rejected the offeror's contention that a dead hand pill impermissibly restricts the power of future boards, including a board elected as part of a takeover bid to redeem a rights plan. The court relied upon the 'plain language' of a Georgia statute that expressly grants a corporation's board the 'sole discretion' to determine the terms contained in a rights plan.

In the context of AlliedSignal's contest for control of AMP in 1998, a Pennsylvania federal court validated a no hand rights plan under Pennsylvania law. Faced with a combined consent solicitation and tender offer by AlliedSignal, the AMP board replaced a pure dead hand provision in its rights plan with a no hand provision preventing redemption until the expiration of the rights plan some 14 months later. The federal district court reviewing the AMP board's action concluded that the adoption of the no hand rights plan was within the authority granted to the board pursuant to a Pennsylvania statute that, like the Georgia statute in Invacare, bestowed upon a board considerable latitude in selecting the terms of a rights plan.

As indicated above, rights plans that provide for redemption only by 'continuing directors' can be critical in takeover situations where the target company lacks a staggered board and, following Invacare and AMP, may become more attractive to companies incorporated in states such as Georgia and Pennsylvania which have adopted pill validation statutes confirming a board's ability to design the terms of a rights plan.

However, Delaware cases have long made clear that the responsibility of responding to a takeover lies with the board and may not be delegated to stockholders. The statutory grounding of the Quickturn decision supports this reading of Delaware law. If a proposed by-law amendment is contrary to applicable law, the shareholder proposal for such by-law amendment can be excluded from a corporation's proxy statement under Exchange Act Rule 14a-8. While this issue has not been fully addressed by the Delaware courts, the SEC has permitted the exclusion of such a purportedly binding by-law amendment shareholder proposal from a proxy statement based upon an opinion of Delaware counsel that such a by-law amendment would be invalid.

Defensive charter and by-law provisions

Defensive charter and by-law provisions typically do not purport to, and will not, prevent a hostile acquisition. Rather, they provide some measure of protection against certain takeover tactics and allow a board some additional negotiating leverage. Provisions of this kind include the following:

- classified or staggered board provisions;
- provisions which eliminate stockholder action by written consent;
- cumulative voting provisions;
- provisions affecting the ability of shareholders to remove directors without cause and to alter the size of a board;

PART III: UNITED STATES

- 'fair price' provisions (which require that stockholders receive equivalent consideration at both ends of a two-step bid, thus deterring coercive two-tier, front-end loaded offers); and
- by-law procedures governing stockholder nominations for directors and submission of stockholder proposals at meetings.

Classified boards and fair-price charter provisions require stockholder approval to be implemented and, due to general institutional investor opposition to such provisions, few companies have put forth new proposals in recent years. By-law provisions governing the calling of, and the business to be addressed at, stockholder meetings can be adopted without stockholder approval in Delaware. Such provisions should be reviewed periodically to ensure that they are consistent with recent case law and SEC developments.

By-law provisions regarding the business to be conducted at, and the manner of presenting proposals for, annual and special meetings, as well as stockholder action by written consent, can be especially helpful in protecting against an unexpected proxy contest for control of the board of directors. Typical provisions include:

- **Nominations and stockholder business:** By-law provisions requiring stockholders to provide advance notice of business proposed to be brought before, and of nominations of directors to be made at, stockholder meetings have become common. These provisions generally set a date by which a stockholder must advise the corporation of the stockholder's intent to seek to take action at a meeting and fix the contents of the notice, which can include information such as beneficial stock ownership and other information required by Regulation 14A of the federal proxy rules. Failure to deliver proper notice in a timely fashion usually results in exclusion of the proposal from stockholder consideration at the meeting.
- **Stockholder meetings:** If, as in Delaware (see 8 Del. Code Ann. § 211(d)), the state corporation law permits elimination of the calling by stockholders of special meetings, such a by-law provision may be helpful in regulating stockholder meetings. Where state law does not so permit, corporations should consider adopting by-law provisions to regulate the ability to call special meetings.
- **Scheduling annual meetings:** Many by-laws specify a particular date for an annual meeting. This should be amended to authorise the board to set an alternative date.
- **Postponements:** A board should be authorised to postpone previously scheduled annual meetings upon public notice given prior to the scheduled annual meeting date.
- **Adjournments:** The chairman of the stockholder meeting should be specifically authorised to adjourn the meeting from time to time whether or not a quorum is present. Adjournments and postponements may help prevent premature consideration of a coercive or inadequate bid.
- **Vote required:** To approve a proposal, except for election of directors (which requires a plurality of the quorum), the required stockholder vote should not be less than a majority of the shares present and entitled to vote at the meeting (that is, abstentions should count as no votes for shareholder resolutions). For Delaware corporations, § 216 of the Delaware General Corporation Law dictates this result unless the charter or by-laws specify otherwise.
- **Procedures for action by stockholder consent:** If the corporation's charter does not disallow action by stockholder consent in lieu of a meeting, the by-laws should establish procedures for specifying the record date for the consent process, for the inspection of consents and for the effective time of consents. Although Sections 213 and 228 of the

Delaware General Corporation Law contemplate such procedures, Delaware courts have closely reviewed these provisions to determine whether their real purpose is delay and whether the procedures are unreasonable.

> **Case study: SoftKey vs. The Learning Company**
>
> Delaware courts have affirmed a board's ability to adopt reasonable by-law amendments in response to a hostile offer. In litigation arising out of the unsolicited bid by SoftKey International to acquire The Learning Company ('TLC'), the Delaware courts upheld the TLC board's decision to amend a by-law in order to delay a special TLC stockholder meeting demanded by SoftKey. SoftKey demanded the meeting under TLC's existing by-law, which authorised holders of 10 per cent or more of the shares to call a special meeting on 35 days' notice. SoftKey sought to replace the TLC directors in order to redeem TLC's rights plan and implement SoftKey's takeover. In response, the TLC board amended the by-law to require a minimum of 60 days' notice. That delay enabled TLC to schedule the vote on its previously announced stock merger with Broderbund Software approximately 30 days in advance of the SoftKey removal meeting. The board's action was defended on the basis that the delay gave the board a reasonable period of time to seek better alternatives to SoftKey's offer in the event the stockholders were to reject the Broderbund merger. Without the by-law amendment, the SoftKey initiated removal meeting would have occurred two days after the then scheduled meeting on the Broderbund merger. The Delaware Court of Chancery upheld the by-law amendment. The court tested the amendment under the Unocal reasonable proportionality test, and found SoftKey's tactics to constitute a threat to legitimate stockholder interests inasmuch as SoftKey's goal was to 'circumven[t] the current board's negotiating power'. The Delaware Supreme Court affirmed the decision.

Although more difficult to effect and subject to stockholder approval, amendments to a company's charter can also support a board's efforts to remain independent. Charter amendments related to the voting rights of common stockholders are infrequent, but have been upheld in court. Under a 'tenure voting' provision, newly transferred shares of stock lose their super voting characteristic until held by one beneficial owner for a set time, typically two to four years. Such charter provisions can deter creeping acquisitions of a large voting block and also generally encourage investors to become long-term holders of a company's stock. A tenure voting structure may adversely affect the valuation and liquidity of a company's stock, and must comply with stock exchange and NASD rules relating to disparate voting rights. A board considering such a voting structure should receive the advice of investment bankers and legal advisors prior to presenting the proposal for stockholder approval. In addition, companies seeking to implement defensive charter amendments will need to address the general opposition of institutional investors to such measures.

Change of control employment agreements

Change of control employment and other benefit arrangements should be reviewed to ensure that senior executives and other employees will be properly protected in the event of a merger or other business combination. In the event of a takeover involving a change of control or a strategic merger, senior executives typically face a great deal of pressure, including uncertainty concerning their own future, and such arrangements help assure their full cooperation in the merger negotiation process.

Appropriately structured change of control employment agreements are both legal and proper. Careful attention must be paid to tax, regulatory and other legal concerns. Although there is little case law relating to the adoption of such change of control employment agreements, they have typically been found, absent a conflict of interest, enforceable and consistent with directors' fiduciary duties.

Companies may also wish to consider so-called 'tin parachutes' for less senior executives in order to formalise company policies regarding severance, as well as the appropriate treatment of stock-based compensation plans in the event of a change of control.

Companies, however, can expect increasing shareholder scrutiny of change of control employment arrangements. For instance, recently, CALPERS, which owned approximately 0.5 per cent of WellPoint Health Networks Inc., opposed the US$16.4 billion merger between WellPoint and Anthem, Inc., not on the basis that the transaction was contrary to the shareholders' best interest, but only citing 'excessive pay packages to be given to top WellPoint executives' as the reason for its opposition.

Passive responses to unsolicited offers: just say no

The developments in strategic mergers and related case law do not undercut the 'just say no' defence to an acquisition proposal. Indeed, unless the target has otherwise subjected itself to Revlon duties (for example, by having previously agreed to enter into an acquisition involving a change of control, as in QVC), it seems clear that the target may, if it meets the relevant standard, just say no to an acquisition proposal.

Targets of unsolicited offers have been successful in rejecting such proposals in order to follow their own strategic plans. In response to a hostile bid by Moore, Wallace Computer Services relied on its rights plan and long-term strategy, rather than seeking a white knight, initiating a share repurchase programme, or electing another 'active' response to Moore's offer.

When Moore challenged the rights plan in a Delaware federal district court, Wallace was able to satisfy the refusal to redeem the pill under the Unocal standard. Although 73 per cent of Wallace's stockholders tendered into Moore's offer, the court found that the Wallace board had sustained its burden of demonstrating a 'good faith belief, made after reasonable investigation, that the Moore offer posed a legally cognisable threat' to Wallace. The evidence showed that the favourable results from a recently adopted capital expenditure plan were 'beginning to be translated into financial results which even surpass management and financial analyst projections'. As the Moore decision illustrates, where the target of a hostile bid wishes to consider rejecting the bid and remaining independent, it is critical that the board follows the correct process and has the advice of an experienced investment banker and legal counsel.

Moreover, ArvinMeritor's recent attempt to acquire Dana Corporation illustrates the continuing viability of a 'just say no' defensive posture. ArvinMeritor's premium-priced all-cash tender offer, Dana's widely disbursed shareholder base and the absence of a staggered board at Dana appeared to make Dana an easy target. However, weaknesses in ArvinMeritor's bid allowed Dana to conduct a classic, business logic-based defence. Dana essentially put the burden on the bidder to explain how it planned to address the absence of financing for the tender offer, the high level of post-transaction leverage that would be at the combined company and anti-trust issues raised by the takeover. In addition, Dana proactively explained its side of the story, describing its ongoing restructuring programme and improving financial results. After a four-month attempt to acquire Dana, ArvinMeritor quit the field.

While QVC does not limit the ability of a company that has entered into a strategic stock merger that is not a sale of control (but that may involve a premium to the seller's stockholders) from deciding to cancel (or continue) such merger after the appearance of a third-party hostile bid and reject the hostile bid, as a practical matter, the seller's stockholders may pressure the company into accepting one or the other bid, or putting itself up for auction. This reality underscores the importance of careful planning prior to pursuit of even friendly stock-for-stock business combinations.

Active responses to unsolicited offers

White knights and white squires

A white knight transaction, namely a merger or acquisition transaction with a friendly acquiror, can be a successful strategy where the white knight transaction provides greater economic value to target company stockholders than the initial hostile offer. In some contexts, however, white knight transactions, because of required regulatory approvals and related procedures, are more difficult to accomplish. For example, in a banking or telecommunications acquisition, a white knight will require the same regulatory approvals as are required by the hostile acquiror and, to the extent that the white knight commences the approval process after the hostile acquiror does, the white knight will suffer a timing disadvantage. Certain target companies may also be constrained by a scarcity of available acquirors, depending upon applicable regulatory restrictions and anti-trust considerations.

A white squire defence, which involves placing a block of voting stock in friendly hands, may be more quickly realised. The 1989 decision of the Delaware Chancery Court upholding the issuance of convertible preferred stock by Polaroid Corporation to Corporate Partners, in the face of an all-cash, all-shares tender offer, marks the most significant legal test of the white squire defence. Although the technique of a white squire defence combined with a self-tender offer at market or a slight premium to market was used defensively by Diamond Shamrock and Phillips-Van Heusen in 1987, neither instance prompted a legal challenge by the would-be acquiror. The Polaroid decision confirmed the prevailing line of cases upholding the issuance of stock to a white squire as a defensive measure when the result was not to consolidate voting control in management or employee hands. Such sales to 'friendly' parties should be carefully structured to avoid an unintended subsequent takeover bid by the former 'friend'. Voting and standstill agreements may be appropriate in this context.

Restructuring defences

Restructurings have been driven in part by the threat of hostile takeovers. The failure of a company's stock price to reflect fully the value of its various businesses has provided opportunities for acquirors to profit by acquiring a company, breaking it up and selling the separate pieces for substantially more than was paid for the entire company. A primary goal of any restructuring is to cause the value of a company's various businesses to be better understood and, ultimately, to be better reflected in its stock price.

Like many forms of takeover defences, a restructuring is best initiated well before a company is actually faced with a bid. In most cases, a restructuring will only be possible if there has been careful advance preparation by the company and its investment bankers and counsel. Arranging for a friendly buyer of a particular asset, for example, and restructuring a business to accommodate the loss of the asset are time consuming, costly and complicated endeavours and are difficult to effect in the midst of a takeover battle.

Restructuring defences have been successfully implemented in a number of prominent transactions. During the course of First Interstate's effort to take over BankAmerica, BankAmerica announced a corporate restructuring programme which involved selling businesses that were not essential to BankAmerica's strategy and reducing its work force. ITT also used this strategy as part of its response to Hilton Hotels' unsolicited offer for the company.

In addition to asset sales, a stock repurchase plan, such as that pursued by Unitrin in response to American General's unsolicited bid, may be an effective response to a takeover threat. Buy-backs at or slightly above the current market price allow stockholders to lock in current market values and reduce a company's available cash, which may be critical to any leveraged acquisition bid. Companies may also initiate such buy-backs when they choose not to pursue other publicly announced acquisitions in order to prevent a deterioration in the stock price and/or to reduce vulnerability to unsolicited offers. A principal benefit of stock buy-backs is that they may be quickly implemented. The CBS buy-back announced in August 1994, shortly after CBS stated that it would not pursue its previously disclosed merger with QVC (which had received an unsolicited offer from Comcast), is one example of the speed with which a buy-back may be implemented following the termination of merger discussions.

Corporate spin-offs and split-ups
Target companies have used spin-offs to enhance shareholder values and frustrate hostile acquisition attempts. One means of focusing stock market attention on a company's underlying assets is to place desirable assets in a corporation and sell off some of the shares in an initial public offering. Another means of boosting the share price of a company is to deconglomerate and sell off businesses which no longer fit the company's strategic plans or split the company into logically related units.

In either case, a company tries to focus the market's attention on its individual businesses which, viewed separately, may enjoy a higher market valuation than when viewed together.

There is often institutional pressure on multi-industry companies to spin-off or sell underperforming divisions that sell at low price earnings multiples and are perceived (rightly or wrongly) as dragging down the market valuation of the high-multiple business. Major companies such as AT&T, Baxter, Dun & Bradstreet, Monsanto and W.R. Grace have undertaken complex spin-offs.

In addition to potentially increasing target company valuations, spin-offs may produce tax consequences that discourage takeover attempts. Commercial Intertech used this defence to thwart an unsolicited offer by United Dominion. The spin-off of the profitable Cuno filtration business to CIC stockholders created a tax 'poison pill'. Had United Dominion acquired either CIC or Cuno following the spin-off, the acquisition could have generated a prohibitive tax liability. A similar technique was employed by ITT in response to the hostile bid by Hilton.

Use of an ESOP or SECT as a takeover defence
The issuance of common stock to a newly formed Employee Stock Ownership Plan (ESOP) or Stock Employee Compensation Trust (SECT) may be a valid response to a hostile offer. In

recent years, this response has not been used, although companies with ESOPs already in place may gain support from them when responding to an unsolicited offer. The existence of an ESOP makes consummation of a tender offer or a successful proxy fight by a hostile bidder more difficult. The trust agreement for the ESOP may provide that the unallocated stock will be voted proportionately to the votes cast by employees with respect to the allocated shares and that unallocated shares will be tendered into a tender or exchange offer in the same proportion as allocated shares.

Regulatory action

In addition to anti-trust regulation, which may itself provide an important ground for disputing the feasibility of a hostile offer, many companies are subject to other regulatory authorities that must approve a change of control. In industries such as telecommunications and banking, federal (and sometimes state) regulators may be receptive to arguments made on behalf of a target (or by a target itself) maintaining that a merger is not consistent with the policies and practices of the relevant agency. A company subject to such regulation may take full advantage of any rights it may have to file protests and comments with such agencies. However, in view of the ongoing oversight of such agencies and the importance of maintaining strong relationships with regulators, companies should avoid filing dilatory or frivolous comments. Concerns regarding anti-trust, financing, management resources and relevant public policy interests may properly be brought to the attention of regulators.

As with other defensive responses, a seller already committed to one transaction must be careful in responding to the third-party bid with regulatory objections, since regulatory issues relating to one offer may well be applicable to the preferred merger partner's bid.

Appendix I:

Directive 2004/25/EC of the European Parliament and of the Council of 21 April 2004 on Takeover Bids

DIRECTIVE 2004/25/EC OF THE EUROPEAN PARLIAMENT AND OF THE COUNCIL OF 21 APRIL 2004 ON TAKEOVER BIDS

DIRECTIVE 2004/25/EC OF THE EUROPEAN PARLIAMENT AND OF THE COUNCIL
of 21 April 2004
on takeover bids

(Text with EEA relevance)

THE EUROPEAN PARLIAMENT AND THE COUNCIL OF THE EUROPEAN UNION,

Having regard to the Treaty establishing the European Community, and in particular Article 44(1) thereof,

Having regard to the proposal from the Commission (¹),

Having regard to the opinion of the European Economic and Social Committee (²),

Acting in accordance with the procedure laid down in Article 251 of the Treaty (³),

Whereas:

(1) In accordance with Article 44(2)(g) of the Treaty, it is necessary to coordinate certain safeguards which, for the protection of the interests of members and others, Member States require of companies governed by the law of a Member State the securities of which are admitted to trading on a regulated market in a Member State, with a view to making such safeguards equivalent throughout the Community.

(2) It is necessary to protect the interests of holders of the securities of companies governed by the law of a Member State when those companies are the subject of takeover bids or of changes of control and at least some of their securities are admitted to trading on a regulated market in a Member State.

(3) It is necessary to create Community-wide clarity and transparency in respect of legal issues to be settled in the event of takeover bids and to prevent patterns of corporate restructuring within the Community from being distorted by arbitrary differences in governance and management cultures.

(4) In view of the public-interest purposes served by the central banks of the Member States, it seems inconceivable that they should be the targets of takeover bids. Since, for historical reasons, the securities of some of those central banks are listed on regulated markets in Member States, it is necessary to exclude them explicitly from the scope of this Directive.

(5) Each Member State should designate an authority or authorities to supervise those aspects of bids that are governed by this Directive and to ensure that parties to takeover bids comply with the rules made pursuant to this Directive. All those authorities should cooperate with one another.

(6) In order to be effective, takeover regulation should be flexible and capable of dealing with new circumstances as they arise and should accordingly provide for the possibility of exceptions and derogations. However, in applying any rules or exceptions laid down or in granting any derogations, supervisory authorities should respect certain general principles.

(7) Self-regulatory bodies should be able to exercise supervision.

(8) In accordance with general principles of Community law, and in particular the right to a fair hearing, decisions of a supervisory authority should in appropriate circumstances be susceptible to review by an independent court or tribunal. However, Member States should be left to determine whether rights are to be made available which may be asserted in administrative or judicial proceedings, either in proceedings against a supervisory authority or in proceedings between parties to a bid.

(9) Member States should take the necessary steps to protect the holders of securities, in particular those with minority holdings, when control of their companies has been acquired. The Member States should ensure such protection by obliging the person who has acquired control of a company to make an offer to all the holders of that company's securities for all of their holdings at an equitable price in accordance with a common definition. Member States should be free to establish further instruments for the protection of the interests of the holders of securities, such as the obligation to make a partial bid where the offeror does not acquire control of the company or the obligation to announce a bid at the same time as control of the company is acquired.

(10) The obligation to make a bid to all the holders of securities should not apply to those controlling holdings already in existence on the date on which the national legislation transposing this Directive enters into force.

(11) The obligation to launch a bid should not apply in the case of the acquisition of securities which do not carry the right to vote at ordinary general meetings of shareholders. Member States should, however, be able to provide that the obligation to make a bid to all the holders of securities

---

(¹) OJ C 45 E, 25.2.2003, p. 1.
(²) OJ C 208, 3.9.2003, p. 55.
(³) Opinion of the European Parliament of 16 December 2003 (not yet published in the Official Journal) and Council decision of 30 March 2004.

relates not only to securities carrying voting rights but also to securities which carry voting rights only in specific circumstances or which do not carry voting rights.

(12) To reduce the scope for insider dealing, an offeror should be required to announce his/her decision to launch a bid as soon as possible and to inform the supervisory authority of the bid.

(13) The holders of securities should be properly informed of the terms of a bid by means of an offer document. Appropriate information should also be given to the representatives of the company's employees or, failing that, to the employees directly.

(14) The time allowed for the acceptance of a bid should be regulated.

(15) To be able to perform their functions satisfactorily, supervisory authorities should at all times be able to require the parties to a bid to provide information concerning themselves and should cooperate and supply information in an efficient and effective manner, without delay, to other authorities supervising capital markets.

(16) In order to prevent operations which could frustrate a bid, the powers of the board of an offeree company to engage in operations of an exceptional nature should be limited, without unduly hindering the offeree company in carrying on its normal business activities.

(17) The board of an offeree company should be required to make public a document setting out its opinion of the bid and the reasons on which that opinion is based, including its views on the effects of implementation on all the company's interests, and specifically on employment.

(18) In order to reinforce the effectiveness of existing provisions concerning the freedom to deal in the securities of companies covered by this Directive and the freedom to exercise voting rights, it is essential that the defensive structures and mechanisms envisaged by such companies be transparent and that they be regularly presented in reports to general meetings of shareholders.

(19) Member States should take the necessary measures to afford any offeror the possibility of acquiring majority interests in other companies and of fully exercising control of them. To that end, restrictions on the transfer of securities, restrictions on voting rights, extraordinary appointment rights and multiple voting rights should be removed or suspended during the time allowed for the acceptance of a bid and when the general meeting of shareholders decides on defensive measures, on amendments to the articles of association or on the removal or appointment of board members at the first general meeting of shareholders following closure of the bid. Where the holders of securities have suffered losses as a result of the removal of rights, equitable compensation should be provided for in accordance with the technical arrangements laid down by Member States.

(20) All special rights held by Member States in companies should be viewed in the framework of the free movement of capital and the relevant provisions of the Treaty. Special rights held by Member States in companies which are provided for in private or public national law should be exempted from the 'breakthrough' rule if they are compatible with the Treaty.

(21) Taking into account existing differences in Member States' company law mechanisms and structures, Member States should be allowed not to require companies established within their territories to apply the provisions of this Directive limiting the powers of the board of an offeree company during the time allowed for the acceptance of a bid and those rendering ineffective barriers, provided for in the articles of association or in specific agreements. In that event Member States should at least allow companies established within their territories to make the choice, which must be reversible, to apply those provisions. Without prejudice to international agreements to which the European Community is a party, Member States should be allowed not to require companies which apply those provisions in accordance with the optional arrangements to apply them when they become the subject of offers launched by companies which do not apply the same provisions, as a consequence of the use of those optional arrangements.

(22) Member States should lay down rules to cover the possibility of a bid's lapsing, the offeror's right to revise his/her bid, the possibility of competing bids for a company's securities, the disclosure of the result of a bid, the irrevocability of a bid and the conditions permitted.

(23) The disclosure of information to and the consultation of representatives of the employees of the offeror and the offeree company should be governed by the relevant national provisions, in particular those adopted pursuant to Council Directive 94/45/EC of 22 September 1994 on the establishment of a European Works Council or a procedure in Community-scale undertakings and Community-scale groups of undertakings for the purposes of informing and consulting employees [1], Council Directive 98/59/EC of 20 July 1998 on the approximation of the laws of the Member States relating to collective redundancies [2], Council Directive 2001/86/EC of 8 October 2001 supplementing the statute for a European Company with regard to the involvement of employees [3] and Directive 2002/14/EC of the European Parliament and of the Council of 11 March 2002 establishing a general

---

[1] OJ L 254, 30.9.1994, p. 64. Directive as amended by Directive 97/74/EC (OJ L 10, 16.1.1998, p. 22).
[2] OJ L 225, 12.8.1998, p. 16.
[3] OJ L 294, 10.11.2001, p. 22.

DIRECTIVE 2004/25/EC OF THE EUROPEAN PARLIAMENT AND OF THE COUNCIL OF 21 APRIL 2004 ON TAKEOVER BIDS

framework for informing and consulting employees in the European Community — Joint declaration of the European Parliament, the Council and the Commission on employee representation ([1]). The employees of the companies concerned, or their representatives, should nevertheless be given an opportunity to state their views on the foreseeable effects of the bid on employment. Without prejudice to the rules of Directive 2003/6/EC of the European Parliament and of the Council of 28 January 2003 on insider dealing and market manipulation (market abuse) ([2]), Member States may always apply or introduce national provisions concerning the disclosure of information to and the consultation of representatives of the employees of the offeror before an offer is launched.

(24) Member States should take the necessary measures to enable an offeror who, following a takeover bid, has acquired a certain percentage of a company's capital carrying voting rights to require the holders of the remaining securities to sell him/her their securities. Likewise, where, following a takeover bid, an offeror has acquired a certain percentage of a company's capital carrying voting rights, the holders of the remaining securities should be able to require him/her to buy their securities. These squeeze-out and sell-out procedures should apply only under specific conditions linked to takeover bids. Member States may continue to apply national rules to squeeze-out and sell-out procedures in other circumstances.

(25) Since the objectives of the action envisaged, namely to establish minimum guidelines for the conduct of takeover bids and ensure an adequate level of protection for holders of securities throughout the Community, cannot be sufficiently achieved by the Member States because of the need for transparency and legal certainty in the case of cross-border takeovers and acquisitions of control, and can therefore, by reason of the scale and effects of the action, be better achieved at Community level, the Community may adopt measures, in accordance with the principle of subsidiarity as set out in Article 5 of the Treaty. In accordance with the principle of proportionality as set out in that Article, this Directive does not go beyond what is necessary to achieve those objectives.

(26) The adoption of a Directive is the appropriate procedure for the establishment of a framework consisting of certain common principles and a limited number of general requirements which Member States are to implement through more detailed rules in accordance with their national systems and their cultural contexts.

(27) Member States should, however, provide for sanctions for any infringement of the national measures transposing this Directive.

(28) Technical guidance and implementing measures for the rules laid down in this Directive may from time to time be necessary, to take account of new developments on financial markets. For certain provisions, the Commission should accordingly be empowered to adopt implementing measures, provided that these do not modify the essential elements of this Directive and the Commission acts in accordance with the principles set out in this Directive, after consulting the European Securities Committee established by Commission Decision 2001/528/EC ([3]). The measures necessary for the implementation of this Directive should be adopted in accordance with Council Decision 1999/468/EC of 28 June 1999 laying down the procedures for the exercise of implementing powers conferred on the Commission ([4]) and with due regard to the declaration made by the Commission in the European Parliament on 5 February 2002 concerning the implementation of financial services legislation. For the other provisions, it is important to entrust a contact committee with the task of assisting Member States and the supervisory authorities in the implementation of this Directive and of advising the Commission, if necessary, on additions or amendments to this Directive. In so doing, the contact committee may make use of the information which Member States are to provide on the basis of this Directive concerning takeover bids that have taken place on their regulated markets.

(29) The Commission should facilitate movement towards the fair and balanced harmonisation of rules on takeovers in the European Union. To that end, the Commission should be able to submit proposals for the timely revision of this Directive,

HAVE ADOPTED THIS DIRECTIVE:

Article 1

Scope

1. This Directive lays down measures coordinating the laws, regulations, administrative provisions, codes of practice and other arrangements of the Member States, including arrangements established by organisations officially authorised to regulate the markets (hereinafter referred to as 'rules'), relating to takeover bids for the securities of companies governed by the laws of Member

---

[1] OJ L 80, 23.3.2002, p. 29.
[2] OJ L 96, 12.4.2003, p. 16.

[3] OJ L 191, 13.7.2001, p. 45. Decision as amended by Decision 2004/8/EC (OJ L 3, 7.1.2004, p. 33).
[4] OJ L 184, 17.7.1999, p. 23.

APPENDIX I

States, where all or some of those securities are admitted to trading on a regulated market within the meaning of Directive 93/22/EEC (¹) in one or more Member States (hereinafter referred to as a 'regulated market').

2. This Directive shall not apply to takeover bids for securities issued by companies, the object of which is the collective investment of capital provided by the public, which operate on the principle of risk-spreading and the units of which are, at the holders' request, repurchased or redeemed, directly or indirectly, out of the assets of those companies. Action taken by such companies to ensure that the stock exchange value of their units does not vary significantly from their net asset value shall be regarded as equivalent to such repurchase or redemption.

3. This Directive shall not apply to takeover bids for securities issued by the Member States' central banks.

Article 2

Definitions

1. For the purposes of this Directive:

(a) 'takeover bid' or 'bid' shall mean a public offer (other than by the offeree company itself) made to the holders of the securities of a company to acquire all or some of those securities, whether mandatory or voluntary, which follows or has as its objective the acquisition of control of the offeree company in accordance with national law;

(b) 'offeree company' shall mean a company, the securities of which are the subject of a bid;

(c) 'offeror' shall mean any natural or legal person governed by public or private law making a bid;

(d) 'persons acting in concert' shall mean natural or legal persons who cooperate with the offeror or the offeree company on the basis of an agreement, either express or tacit, either oral or written, aimed either at acquiring control of the offeree company or at frustrating the successful outcome of a bid;

(e) 'securities' shall mean transferable securities carrying voting rights in a company;

(f) 'parties to the bid' shall mean the offeror, the members of the offeror's board if the offeror is a company, the offeree company, holders of securities of the offeree company and the members of the board of the offeree company, and persons acting in concert with such parties;

(g) 'multiple-vote securities' shall mean securities included in a distinct and separate class and carrying more than one vote each.

2. For the purposes of paragraph 1(d), persons controlled by another person within the meaning of Article 87 of Directive 2001/34/EC (²) shall be deemed to be persons acting in concert with that other person and with each other.

Article 3

General principles

1. For the purpose of implementing this Directive, Member States shall ensure that the following principles are complied with:

(a) all holders of the securities of an offeree company of the same class must be afforded equivalent treatment; moreover, if a person acquires control of a company, the other holders of securities must be protected;

(b) the holders of the securities of an offeree company must have sufficient time and information to enable them to reach a properly informed decision on the bid; where it advises the holders of securities, the board of the offeree company must give its views on the effects of implementation of the bid on employment, conditions of employment and the locations of the company's places of business;

(c) the board of an offeree company must act in the interests of the company as a whole and must not deny the holders of securities the opportunity to decide on the merits of the bid;

(d) false markets must not be created in the securities of the offeree company, of the offeror company or of any other company concerned by the bid in such a way that the rise or fall of the prices of the securities becomes artificial and the normal functioning of the markets is distorted;

(e) an offeror must announce a bid only after ensuring that he/she can fulfil in full any cash consideration, if such is offered, and after taking all reasonable measures to secure the implementation of any other type of consideration;

(f) an offeree company must not be hindered in the conduct of its affairs for longer than is reasonable by a bid for its securities.

(¹) Council Directive 93/22/EEC of 10 May 1993 on investment services in the securities field (OJ L 141, 11.6.1993, p. 27). Directive as last amended by Directive 2002/87/EC of the European Parliament and of the Council (OJ L 35, 11.2.2003, p. 1).

(²) Directive 2001/34/EC of the European Parliament and of the Council of 28 May 2001 on the admission of securities to official stock exchange listing and on information to be published on those securities (OJ L 184, 6.7.2001, p. 1). Directive as last amended by Directive 2003/71/EC (OJ L 345, 31.12.2003, p. 64).

DIRECTIVE 2004/25/EC OF THE EUROPEAN PARLIAMENT AND OF THE COUNCIL OF 21 APRIL 2004 ON TAKEOVER BIDS

2. With a view to ensuring compliance with the principles laid down in paragraph 1, Member States:

(a) shall ensure that the minimum requirements set out in this Directive are observed;

(b) may lay down additional conditions and provisions more stringent than those of this Directive for the regulation of bids.

Article 4

Supervisory authority and applicable law

1. Member States shall designate the authority or authorities competent to supervise bids for the purposes of the rules which they make or introduce pursuant to this Directive. The authorities thus designated shall be either public authorities, associations or private bodies recognised by national law or by public authorities expressly empowered for that purpose by national law. Member States shall inform the Commission of those designations, specifying any divisions of functions that may be made. They shall ensure that those authorities exercise their functions impartially and independently of all parties to a bid.

2. (a) The authority competent to supervise a bid shall be that of the Member State in which the offeree company has its registered office if that company's securities are admitted to trading on a regulated market in that Member State.

(b) If the offeree company's securities are not admitted to trading on a regulated market in the Member State in which the company has its registered office, the authority competent to supervise the bid shall be that of the Member State on the regulated market of which the company's securities are admitted to trading.

If the offeree company's securities are admitted to trading on regulated markets in more than one Member State, the authority competent to supervise the bid shall be that of the Member State on the regulated market of which the securities were first admitted to trading.

(c) If the offeree company's securities were first admitted to trading on regulated markets in more than one Member State simultaneously, the offeree company shall determine which of the supervisory authorities of those Member States shall be the authority competent to supervise the bid by notifying those regulated markets and their supervisory authorities on the first day of trading.

If the offeree company's securities have already been admitted to trading on regulated markets in more than one Member State on the date laid down in Article 21(1) and were admitted simultaneously, the supervisory authorities of those Member States shall agree which one of them shall be the authority competent to supervise the bid within four weeks of the date laid down in Article 21(1). Otherwise, the offeree company shall determine which of those authorities shall be the competent authority on the first day of trading following that four-week period.

(d) Member States shall ensure that the decisions referred to in (c) are made public.

(e) In the cases referred to in (b) and (c), matters relating to the consideration offered in the case of a bid, in particular the price, and matters relating to the bid procedure, in particular the information on the offeror's decision to make a bid, the contents of the offer document and the disclosure of the bid, shall be dealt with in accordance with the rules of the Member State of the competent authority. In matters relating to the information to be provided to the employees of the offeree company and in matters relating to company law, in particular the percentage of voting rights which confers control and any derogation from the obligation to launch a bid, as well as the conditions under which the board of the offeree company may undertake any action which might result in the frustration of the bid, the applicable rules and the competent authority shall be those of the Member State in which the offeree company has its registered office.

3. Member States shall ensure that all persons employed or formerly employed by their supervisory authorities are bound by professional secrecy. No information covered by professional secrecy may be divulged to any person or authority except under provisions laid down by law.

4. The supervisory authorities of the Member States for the purposes of this Directive and other authorities supervising capital markets, in particular in accordance with Directive 93/22/EEC, Directive 2001/34/EC, Directive 2003/6/EC and Directive 2003/71/EC of the European Parliament and of the Council of 4 November 2003 on the prospectus to be published when securities are offered to the public or admitted to trading shall cooperate and supply each other with information wherever necessary for the application of the rules drawn up in accordance with this Directive and in particular in cases covered by paragraph 2(b), (c) and (e). Information thus exchanged shall be covered by the obligation of professional secrecy to which persons employed or formerly employed by the supervisory authorities receiving the information are subject. Cooperation shall include the ability to serve the legal documents necessary to enforce measures taken by the competent authorities in connection with bids, as well as such other assistance as may reasonably be requested by the supervisory authorities concerned for the purpose of investigating any actual or alleged breaches of the rules made or introduced pursuant to this Directive.

5. The supervisory authorities shall be vested with all the powers necessary for the purpose of carrying out their duties, including that of ensuring that the parties to a bid comply with the rules made or introduced pursuant to this Directive.

Provided that the general principles laid down in Article 3(1) are respected, Member States may provide in the rules that they make or introduce pursuant to this Directive for derogations from those rules:

(i) by including such derogations in their national rules, in order to take account of circumstances determined at national level

and/or

(ii) by granting their supervisory authorities, where they are competent, powers to waive such national rules, to take account of the circumstances referred to in (i) or in other specific circumstances, in which case a reasoned decision must be required.

6. This Directive shall not affect the power of the Member States to designate judicial or other authorities responsible for dealing with disputes and for deciding on irregularities committed in the course of bids or the power of Member States to regulate whether and under which circumstances parties to a bid are entitled to bring administrative or judicial proceedings. In particular, this Directive shall not affect the power which courts may have in a Member State to decline to hear legal proceedings and to decide whether or not such proceedings affect the outcome of a bid. This Directive shall not affect the power of the Member States to determine the legal position concerning the liability of supervisory authorities or concerning litigation between the parties to a bid.

Article 5

Protection of minority shareholders, the mandatory bid and the equitable price

1. Where a natural or legal person, as a result of his/her own acquisition or the acquisition by persons acting in concert with him/her, holds securities of a company as referred to in Article 1(1) which, added to any existing holdings of those securities of his/hers and the holdings of those securities of persons acting in concert with him/her, directly or indirectly give him/her a specified percentage of voting rights in that company, giving him/her control of that company, Member States shall ensure that such a person is required to make a bid as a means of protecting the minority shareholders of that company. Such a bid shall be addressed at the earliest opportunity to all the holders of those securities for all their holdings at the equitable price as defined in paragraph 4.

2. Where control has been acquired following a voluntary bid made in accordance with this Directive to all the holders of securities for all their holdings, the obligation laid down in paragraph 1 to launch a bid shall no longer apply.

3. The percentage of voting rights which confers control for the purposes of paragraph 1 and the method of its calculation shall be determined by the rules of the Member State in which the company has its registered office.

4. The highest price paid for the same securities by the offeror, or by persons acting in concert with him/her, over a period, to be determined by Member States, of not less than six months and not more than 12 before the bid referred to in paragraph 1 shall be regarded as the equitable price. If, after the bid has been made public and before the offer closes for acceptance, the offeror or any person acting in concert with him/her purchases securities at a price higher than the offer price, the offeror shall increase his/her offer so that it is not less than the highest price paid for the securities so acquired.

Provided that the general principles laid down in Article 3(1) are respected, Member States may authorise their supervisory authorities to adjust the price referred to in the first subparagraph in circumstances and in accordance with criteria that are clearly determined. To that end, they may draw up a list of circumstances in which the highest price may be adjusted either upwards or downwards, for example where the highest price was set by agreement between the purchaser and a seller, where the market prices of the securities in question have been manipulated, where market prices in general or certain market prices in particular have been affected by exceptional occurrences, or in order to enable a firm in difficulty to be rescued. They may also determine the criteria to be applied in such cases, for example the average market value over a particular period, the break-up value of the company or other objective valuation criteria generally used in financial analysis.

Any decision by a supervisory authority to adjust the equitable price shall be substantiated and made public.

5. By way of consideration the offeror may offer securities, cash or a combination of both.

However, where the consideration offered by the offeror does not consist of liquid securities admitted to trading on a regulated market, it shall include a cash alternative.

In any event, the offeror shall offer a cash consideration at least as an alternative where he/she or persons acting in concert with him/her, over a period beginning at the same time as the period determined by the Member State in accordance with paragraph 4 and ending when the offer closes for acceptance, has purchased for cash securities carrying 5 % or more of the voting rights in the offeree company.

Member States may provide that a cash consideration must be offered, at least as an alternative, in all cases.

6. In addition to the protection provided for in paragraph 1, Member States may provide for further instruments intended to protect the interests of the holders of securities in so far as those instruments do not hinder the normal course of a bid.

DIRECTIVE 2004/25/EC OF THE EUROPEAN PARLIAMENT AND OF THE COUNCIL OF 21 APRIL 2004 ON TAKEOVER BIDS

Article 6

Information concerning bids

1. Member States shall ensure that a decision to make a bid is made public without delay and that the supervisory authority is informed of the bid. They may require that the supervisory authority must be informed before such a decision is made public. As soon as the bid has been made public, the boards of the offeree company and of the offeror shall inform the representatives of their respective employees or, where there are no such representatives, the employees themselves.

2. Member States shall ensure that an offeror is required to draw up and make public in good time an offer document containing the information necessary to enable the holders of the offeree company's securities to reach a properly informed decision on the bid. Before the offer document is made public, the offeror shall communicate it to the supervisory authority. When it is made public, the boards of the offeree company and of the offeror shall communicate it to the representatives of their respective employees or, where there are no such representatives, to the employees themselves.

Where the offer document referred to in the first subparagraph is subject to the prior approval of the supervisory authority and has been approved, it shall be recognised, subject to any translation required, in any other Member State on the market of which the offeree company's securities are admitted to trading, without its being necessary to obtain the approval of the supervisory authorities of that Member State. Those authorities may require the inclusion of additional information in the offer document only if such information is specific to the market of a Member State or Member States on which the offeree company's securities are admitted to trading and relates to the formalities to be complied with to accept the bid and to receive the consideration due at the close of the bid as well as to the tax arrangements to which the consideration offered to the holders of the securities will be subject.

3. The offer document referred to in paragraph 2 shall state at least:

(a) the terms of the bid;

(b) the identity of the offeror and, where the offeror is a company, the type, name and registered office of that company;

(c) the securities or, where appropriate, the class or classes of securities for which the bid is made;

(d) the consideration offered for each security or class of securities and, in the case of a mandatory bid, the method employed in determining it, with particulars of the way in which that consideration is to be paid;

(e) the compensation offered for the rights which might be removed as a result of the breakthrough rule laid down in Article 11(4), with particulars of the way in which that compensation is to be paid and the method employed in determining it;

(f) the maximum and minimum percentages or quantities of securities which the offeror undertakes to acquire;

(g) details of any existing holdings of the offeror, and of persons acting in concert with him/her, in the offeree company;

(h) all the conditions to which the bid is subject;

(i) the offeror's intentions with regard to the future business of the offeree company and, in so far as it is affected by the bid, the offeror company and with regard to the safeguarding of the jobs of their employees and management, including any material change in the conditions of employment, and in particular the offeror's strategic plans for the two companies and the likely repercussions on employment and the locations of the companies' places of business;

(j) the time allowed for acceptance of the bid;

(k) where the consideration offered by the offeror includes securities of any kind, information concerning those securities;

(l) information concerning the financing for the bid;

(m) the identity of persons acting in concert with the offeror or with the offeree company and, in the case of companies, their types, names, registered offices and relationships with the offeror and, where possible, with the offeree company;

(n) the national law which will govern contracts concluded between the offeror and the holders of the offeree company's securities as a result of the bid and the competent courts.

4. The Commission shall adopt rules for the application of paragraph 3 in accordance with the procedure referred to in Article 18(2).

5. Member States shall ensure that the parties to a bid are required to provide the supervisory authorities of their Member State at any time on request with all the information in their possession concerning the bid that is necessary for the supervisory authority to discharge its functions.

Article 7

Time allowed for acceptance

1. Member States shall provide that the time allowed for the acceptance of a bid may not be less than two weeks nor more than 10 weeks from the date of publication of the offer document. Provided that the general principle laid down in Article 3(1)(f) is respected, Member States may provide that the period of 10 weeks may be extended on condition that the offeror gives at least two weeks' notice of his/her intention of closing the bid.

APPENDIX I

2. Member States may provide for rules changing the period referred to in paragraph 1 in specific cases. A Member State may authorise a supervisory authority to grant a derogation from the period referred to in paragraph 1 in order to allow the offeree company to call a general meeting of shareholders to consider the bid.

Article 8

Disclosure

1. Member States shall ensure that a bid is made public in such a way as to ensure market transparency and integrity for the securities of the offeree company, of the offeror or of any other company affected by the bid, in particular in order to prevent the publication or dissemination of false or misleading information.

2. Member States shall provide for the disclosure of all information and documents required by Article 6 in such a manner as to ensure that they are both readily and promptly available to the holders of securities at least in those Member States on the regulated markets of which the offeree company's securities are admitted to trading and to the representatives of the employees of the offeree company and the offeror or, where there are no such representatives, to the employees themselves.

Article 9

Obligations of the board of the offeree company

1. Member States shall ensure that the rules laid down in paragraphs 2 to 5 are complied with.

2. During the period referred to in the second subparagraph, the board of the offeree company shall obtain the prior authorisation of the general meeting of shareholders given for this purpose before taking any action, other than seeking alternative bids, which may result in the frustration of the bid and in particular before issuing any shares which may result in a lasting impediment to the offeror's acquiring control of the offeree company.

Such authorisation shall be mandatory at least from the time the board of the offeree company receives the information referred to in the first sentence of Article 6(1) concerning the bid and until the result of the bid is made public or the bid lapses. Member States may require that such authorisation be obtained at an earlier stage, for example as soon as the board of the offeree company becomes aware that the bid is imminent.

3. As regards decisions taken before the beginning of the period referred to in the second subparagraph of paragraph 2 and not yet partly or fully implemented, the general meeting of shareholders shall approve or confirm any decision which does not form part of the normal course of the company's business and the implementation of which may result in the frustration of the bid.

4. For the purpose of obtaining the prior authorisation, approval or confirmation of the holders of securities referred to in paragraphs 2 and 3, Member States may adopt rules allowing a general meeting of shareholders to be called at short notice, provided that the meeting does not take place within two weeks of notification's being given.

5. The board of the offeree company shall draw up and make public a document setting out its opinion of the bid and the reasons on which it is based, including its views on the effects of implementation of the bid on all the company's interests and specifically employment, and on the offeror's strategic plans for the offeree company and their likely repercussions on employment and the locations of the company's places of business as set out in the offer document in accordance with Article 6(3)(i). The board of the offeree company shall at the same time communicate that opinion to the representatives of its employees or, where there are no such representatives, to the employees themselves. Where the board of the offeree company receives in good time a separate opinion from the representatives of its employees on the effects of the bid on employment, that opinion shall be appended to the document.

6. For the purposes of paragraph 2, where a company has a two-tier board structure 'board' shall mean both the management board and the supervisory board.

Article 10

Information on companies as referred to in Article 1(1)

1. Member States shall ensure that companies as referred to in Article 1(1) publish detailed information on the following:

(a) the structure of their capital, including securities which are not admitted to trading on a regulated market in a Member State, where appropriate with an indication of the different classes of shares and, for each class of shares, the rights and obligations attaching to it and the percentage of total share capital that it represents;

(b) any restrictions on the transfer of securities, such as limitations on the holding of securities or the need to obtain the approval of the company or other holders of securities, without prejudice to Article 46 of Directive 2001/34/EC;

(c) significant direct and indirect shareholdings (including indirect shareholdings through pyramid structures and cross-shareholdings) within the meaning of Article 85 of Directive 2001/34/EC;

(d) the holders of any securities with special control rights and a description of those rights;

(e) the system of control of any employee share scheme where the control rights are not exercised directly by the employees;

(f) any restrictions on voting rights, such as limitations of the voting rights of holders of a given percentage or number of

DIRECTIVE 2004/25/EC OF THE EUROPEAN PARLIAMENT AND OF THE COUNCIL OF 21 APRIL 2004 ON TAKEOVER BIDS

votes, deadlines for exercising voting rights, or systems whereby, with the company's cooperation, the financial rights attaching to securities are separated from the holding of securities;

(g) any agreements between shareholders which are known to the company and may result in restrictions on the transfer of securities and/or voting rights within the meaning of Directive 2001/34/EC;

(h) the rules governing the appointment and replacement of board members and the amendment of the articles of association;

(i) the powers of board members, and in particular the power to issue or buy back shares;

(j) any significant agreements to which the company is a party and which take effect, alter or terminate upon a change of control of the company following a takeover bid, and the effects thereof, except where their nature is such that their disclosure would be seriously prejudicial to the company; this exception shall not apply where the company is specifically obliged to disclose such information on the basis of other legal requirements;

(k) any agreements between the company and its board members or employees providing for compensation if they resign or are made redundant without valid reason or if their employment ceases because of a takeover bid.

2. The information referred to in paragraph 1 shall be published in the company's annual report as provided for in Article 46 of Directive 78/660/EEC (¹) and Article 36 of Directive 83/349/EEC (²).

3. Member States shall ensure, in the case of companies the securities of which are admitted to trading on a regulated market in a Member State, that the board presents an explanatory report to the annual general meeting of shareholders on the matters referred to in paragraph 1.

Article 11

Breakthrough

1. Without prejudice to other rights and obligations provided for in Community law for the companies referred to in Article 1(1), Member States shall ensure that the provisions laid down in paragraphs 2 to 7 apply when a bid has been made public.

(¹) Fourth Council Directive 78/660/EEC of 25 July 1978 on the annual accounts of certain types of companies (OJ L 222, 14.8.1978, p. 11). Directive as last amended by Directive 2003/51/EC of the European Parliament and of the Council (OJ L 178, 17.7.2003, p. 16).
(²) Seventh Council Directive 83/349/EEC of 13 June 1983 on consolidated accounts (OJ L 193, 18.7.1983, p.1). Directive as last amended by Directive 2003/51/EC.

2. Any restrictions on the transfer of securities provided for in the articles of association of the offeree company shall not apply vis-à-vis the offeror during the time allowed for acceptance of the bid laid down in Article 7(1).

Any restrictions on the transfer of securities provided for in contractual agreements between the offeree company and holders of its securities, or in contractual agreements between holders of the offeree company's securities entered into after the adoption of this Directive, shall not apply vis-à-vis the offeror during the time allowed for acceptance of the bid laid down in Article 7(1).

3. Restrictions on voting rights provided for in the articles of association of the offeree company shall not have effect at the general meeting of shareholders which decides on any defensive measures in accordance with Article 9.

Restrictions on voting rights provided for in contractual agreements between the offeree company and holders of its securities, or in contractual agreements between holders of the offeree company's securities entered into after the adoption of this Directive, shall not have effect at the general meeting of shareholders which decides on any defensive measures in accordance with Article 9.

Multiple-vote securities shall carry only one vote each at the general meeting of shareholders which decides on any defensive measures in accordance with Article 9.

4. Where, following a bid, the offeror holds 75 % or more of the capital carrying voting rights, no restrictions on the transfer of securities or on voting rights referred to in paragraphs 2 and 3 nor any extraordinary rights of shareholders concerning the appointment or removal of board members provided for in the articles of association of the offeree company shall apply; multiple-vote securities shall carry only one vote each at the first general meeting of shareholders following closure of the bid, called by the offeror in order to amend the articles of association or to remove or appoint board members.

To that end, the offeror shall have the right to convene a general meeting of shareholders at short notice, provided that the meeting does not take place within two weeks of notification.

5. Where rights are removed on the basis of paragraphs 2, 3, or 4 and/or Article 12, equitable compensation shall be provided for any loss suffered by the holders of those rights. The terms for determining such compensation and the arrangements for its payment shall be set by Member States.

6. Paragraphs 3 and 4 shall not apply to securities where the restrictions on voting rights are compensated for by specific pecuniary advantages.

7. This Article shall not apply either where Member States hold securities in the offeree company which confer special rights

APPENDIX I

on the Member States which are compatible with the Treaty, or to special rights provided for in national law which are compatible with the Treaty or to cooperatives.

Article 12

Optional arrangements

1. Member States may reserve the right not to require companies as referred to in Article 1(1) which have their registered offices within their territories to apply Article 9(2) and (3) and/or Article 11.

2. Where Member States make use of the option provided for in paragraph 1, they shall nevertheless grant companies which have their registered offices within their territories the option, which shall be reversible, of applying Article 9(2) and (3) and/or Article 11, without prejudice to Article 11(7).

The decision of the company shall be taken by the general meeting of shareholders, in accordance with the law of the Member State in which the company has its registered office in accordance with the rules applicable to amendment of the articles of association. The decision shall be communicated to the supervisory authority of the Member State in which the company has its registered office and to all the supervisory authorities of Member States in which its securities are admitted to trading on regulated markets or where such admission has been requested.

3. Member States may, under the conditions determined by national law, exempt companies which apply Article 9(2) and (3) and/or Article 11 from applying Article 9(2) and (3) and/or Article 11 if they become the subject of an offer launched by a company which does not apply the same Articles as they do, or by a company controlled, directly or indirectly, by the latter, pursuant to Article 1 of Directive 83/349/EEC.

4. Member States shall ensure that the provisions applicable to the respective companies are disclosed without delay.

5. Any measure applied in accordance with paragraph 3 shall be subject to the authorisation of the general meeting of shareholders of the offeree company, which must be granted no earlier than 18 months before the bid was made public in accordance with Article 6(1).

Article 13

Other rules applicable to the conduct of bids

Member States shall also lay down rules which govern the conduct of bids, at least as regards the following:

(a) the lapsing of bids;

(b) the revision of bids;

(c) competing bids;

(d) the disclosure of the results of bids;

(e) the irrevocability of bids and the conditions permitted.

Article 14

Information for and consultation of employees' representatives

This Directive shall be without prejudice to the rules relating to information and to consultation of representatives of and, if Member States so provide, co-determination with the employees of the offeror and the offeree company governed by the relevant national provisions, and in particular those adopted pursuant to Directives 94/45/EC, 98/59/EC, 2001/86/EC and 2002/14/EC.

Article 15

The right of squeeze-out

1. Member States shall ensure that, following a bid made to all the holders of the offeree company's securities for all of their securities, paragraphs 2 to 5 apply.

2. Member States shall ensure that an offeror is able to require all the holders of the remaining securities to sell him/her those securities at a fair price. Member States shall introduce that right in one of the following situations:

(a) where the offeror holds securities representing not less than 90 % of the capital carrying voting rights and 90 % of the voting rights in the offeree company,

or

(b) where, following acceptance of the bid, he/she has acquired or has firmly contracted to acquire securities representing not less than 90 % of the offeree company's capital carrying voting rights and 90 % of the voting rights comprised in the bid.

In the case referred to in (a), Member States may set a higher threshold that may not, however, be higher than 95 % of the capital carrying voting rights and 95 % of the voting rights.

3. Member States shall ensure that rules are in force that make it possible to calculate when the threshold is reached.

Where the offeree company has issued more than one class of securities, Member States may provide that the right of squeeze-out can be exercised only in the class in which the threshold laid down in paragraph 2 has been reached.

4. If the offeror wishes to exercise the right of squeeze-out he/she shall do so within three months of the end of the time allowed for acceptance of the bid referred to in Article 7.

5. Member States shall ensure that a fair price is guaranteed. That price shall take the same form as the consideration offered

DIRECTIVE 2004/25/EC OF THE EUROPEAN PARLIAMENT AND OF THE COUNCIL OF 21 APRIL 2004 ON TAKEOVER BIDS

in the bid or shall be in cash. Member States may provide that cash shall be offered at least as an alternative.

Following a voluntary bid, in both of the cases referred to in paragraph 2(a) and (b), the consideration offered in the bid shall be presumed to be fair where, through acceptance of the bid, the offeror has acquired securities representing not less than 90 % of the capital carrying voting rights comprised in the bid.

Following a mandatory bid, the consideration offered in the bid shall be presumed to be fair.

Article 16

The right of sell-out

1. Member States shall ensure that, following a bid made to all the holders of the offeree company's securities for all of their securities, paragraphs 2 and 3 apply.

2. Member States shall ensure that a holder of remaining securities is able to require the offeror to buy his/her securities from him/her at a fair price under the same circumstances as provided for in Article 15(2).

3. Article 15(3) to (5) shall apply *mutatis mutandis*.

Article 17

Sanctions

Member States shall determine the sanctions to be imposed for infringement of the national measures adopted pursuant to this Directive and shall take all necessary steps to ensure that they are put into effect. The sanctions thus provided for shall be effective, proportionate and dissuasive. Member States shall notify the Commission of those measures no later than the date laid down in Article 21(1) and of any subsequent change thereto at the earliest opportunity.

Article 18

Committee procedure

1. The Commission shall be assisted by the European Securities Committee established by Decision 2001/528/EC (hereinafter referred to as 'the Committee').

2. Where reference is made to this paragraph, Articles 5 and 7 of Decision 1999/468/EC shall apply, having regard to Article 8 thereof, provided that the implementing measures adopted in accordance with this procedure do not modify the essential provisions of this Directive.

The period referred to in Article 5(6) of Decision 1999/468/EC shall be three months.

3. Without prejudice to the implementing measures already adopted, four years after the entry into force of this Directive, the application of those of its provisions that require the adoption of technical rules and decisions in accordance with paragraph 2 shall be suspended. On a proposal from the Commission, the European Parliament and the Council may renew the provisions concerned in accordance with the procedure laid down in Article 251 of the Treaty and, to that end, they shall review them before the end of the period referred to above.

Article 19

Contact committee

1. A contact committee shall be set up which has as its functions:

(a) to facilitate, without prejudice to Articles 226 and 227 of the Treaty, the harmonised application of this Directive through regular meetings dealing with practical problems arising in connection with its application;

(b) to advise the Commission, if necessary, on additions or amendments to this Directive.

2. It shall not be the function of the contact committee to appraise the merits of decisions taken by the supervisory authorities in individual cases.

Article 20

Revision

Five years after the date laid down in Article 21(1), the Commission shall examine this Directive in the light of the experience acquired in applying it and, if necessary, propose its revision. That examination shall include a survey of the control structures and barriers to takeover bids that are not covered by this Directive.

To that end, Member States shall provide the Commission annually with information on the takeover bids which have been launched against companies the securities of which are admitted to trading on their regulated markets. That information shall include the nationalities of the companies involved, the results of the offers and any other information relevant to the understanding of how takeover bids operate in practice.

Article 21

Transposition

1. Member States shall bring into force the laws, regulations and administrative provisions necessary to comply with this Directive no later than 20 May 2006. They shall forthwith inform the Commission thereof.

APPENDIX I

When Member States adopt those provisions, they shall contain a reference to this Directive or shall be accompanied by such reference on the occasion of their official publication. The methods of making such reference shall be laid down by the Member States.

2. Member States shall communicate to the Commission the text of the main provisions of national law that they adopt in the fields covered by this Directive.

Article 22

Entry into force

This Directive shall enter into force on the 20th day after that of its publication in the *Official Journal of the European Union*.

Article 23

Addressees

This Directive is addressed to the Member States.

Done at Strasbourg, 21 April 2004.

For the European Parliament
The President
P. COX

For the Council
The President
D. ROCHE

Appendix II:

Comparison of national takeover provisions*

*Accurate as of October 2005.

COMPARISON OF NATIONAL TAKEOVER PROVISIONS

Country:	Austria	Belgium	Denmark	France
Disclosure threshold:	5%–50% in multiples of 5% steps, 75%, 90%; company may change thresholds in its articles of association.	5%, 10%, 15%. Multiples of 5%. Companies may lower to 3%.	5% and 5% intervals between 10 and 100 as well as 1/3 and 2/3.	5%, 10%, 15%, 20%, 25%, 33.3%, 50%, 66²/₃%, 90% and 95% of shares or voting rights. Companies may lower to 0.5% and multiples thereof.
Disclosure timing:	9 calendar days.	2 working days.	Immediately, ie, same trade day.	5 trading days.
Mandatory bid threshold (MBT):	Rebuttable presumption at 20% but no definitive threshold – power to exercise dominant influence on the target (shareholders' meeting board of directors).	No threshold – power to exercise a decisive influence on board and managers.	33% of the votes and able to exercise a controlling influence.	33.3% of shares or voting rights.
Offer pricing:	Average market price during the last 6 months and no higher discount than 15% as compared to the highest consideration granted by the bidder during the last 12 months.	Price must exceed the market price.	Highest price paid by the bidder within last 6 months (up to 12 months in exceptional circumstances).	'Multi-criteria analysis' based on several valuation methods (ie, volume-weighted average trading price, purchase price paid by bidder prior to launching the bid, DCF, net asset value).
Post bid defences:	Board neutrality – post bid defences are legitimate if approved by shareholders' resolution or based on board's obligations incurred before the bid.	Board neutrality – must act in the best interests of the company. Post bid defences outlawed – except for redemption of shares up to 10% of capital.	Yes, but board must act in the interest of the shareholders. Shareholders may restrict board defences.	Board neutrality – post bid defences are subject to prior approval of general meeting of shareholders.
Squeeze out:	90%.	95%.	90%.	95%.
Sell out:	No.	No.	90%.	95%.
Offer acceptance period:	20–50 trading days (subject to extension).	10–20 working days.	Min 4 weeks – max 10 weeks.	25–35 trading days (subject to extension).
Revisions to offers:	Yes, during the acceptance period in favor of the shareholders.	Yes, but only to improve the offer for the securities holders.	Yes, prior to expiry of offer period.	Yes, in limited circumstances including by improving initial bid within 5 trading days of the deadline.
Competing offers:	Yes; shareholders may withdraw from any previous declarations of acceptance with regard to another bid.	Yes, within 2 working days of deadline. Counter offer must be at least 5% higher.	Yes, prior to expiry of offer period.	Yes, within 5 trading days of the deadline.
Breakthrough rule (BTR):	No.	No.	Limited BTR if resolved by the shareholders at a general meeting.	No.

393

APPENDIX II

Country:	Finland	Germany	Greece	Hungary
Disclosure threshold:	5%, 10%, 15%, 20%, 25%, 1/3, 1/2, 2/3 (and 90%).	5%, 10%, 25%, 50%, 75% (or in case of price relevance).	5%, 10%, 20%, 1/3, 50% and 0.66% Also holders of more than 10% must disclose any change of more than 3% (or 1.5% during the first year after listing).	5%, 10%, 15%. Multiples of 5%. Companies may lower to 2%. Above 50% only thresholds are 75% and 90%.
Disclosure timing:	Without undue delay	7 calendar days; immediately in case of price relevance.	Next day.	2 calendar days.
Mandatory bid threshold (MBT):	2/3 of the votes.	30% of the voting rights.	50%.	33%. However, the threshold is 25% for widely-held companies.
Offer pricing:	*Voluntary offers*: not regulated. *Mandatory offers*: at market value (generally the volume-weighted average price paid in public trading during the 12 months preceding the triggering of the offer obligation or any higher price paid by the offeror during this 12-month-period).	The higher of (i) the highest price paid, or agreed to be paid, by the bidder (or persons acting in concert with it) in the three-month period prior to the publication of the offer document and (ii) the weighted average stock exchange price of the target shares in the 3-month-period prior to the announcement of the bid.	Not less than weighted average of the average price of last 12 months and highest price paid by the acquirer during the last 6 months.	The higher of the weighted average stock price of the prior 180 days or the highest price paid by the bidder.
Post bid defences:	Board neutrality – obligation to act in the best interests of the company, with particular regard to the interest of the shareholder collective.	Management board of the target must not take any frustrating action after the announcement of the bid, except for (i) actions that a prudent manager of a company not subject to a bid would have taken; (ii) the search for a competing bidder; (iii) actions taken with the approval of the target's supervisory board; and (iv) actions taken by the management board (with supervisory board approval) which fall within the competence of the shareholders' meeting and to which the shareholders' meeting has authorised the management board to take by resolution adopted prior to the announcement of the bid.	Board neutrality – post bid defences subject to special approval by the general meeting.	Board neutrality – post bid defences are subject to a 75% supermajority of the general meeting.
Squeeze out:	90%.	95% of the stated capital.	No, but possibility of a cash out merger.	90%.
Sell out:	90%.	No.	No	90%.
Offer acceptance period:	*Voluntary offers*: not regulated, FSA recommendation 2 weeks – 3 months. *Mandatory offers*: 1 month.	4–10 weeks; possible extension in case of target general meeting, competing bid, or revised bid; additional extension of 2 weeks in certain cases of takeover bids.	30–60 calendar days.	30–45 working days.
Revisions to offers:	Not regulated.	No specific limitations.	Until 5 working days prior to end of acceptance period.	Yes, until deadline on the conditions that (i) the offer price is higher and (ii) the revision will have been published by the deadline.
Competing offers:	Not regulated.	Revision is limited to certain issues ie, price increases; offer an option for other consideration; lower or waive a minimum acceptance threshold; waive conditions; no mandatory time limit.	Until 7 working days prior to end of acceptance period.	Yes, within 15 calendar days of deadline. Counter offer must be at least 5% higher.
Breakthrough rule (BTR):	No.	No.	No voting ceilings allowed under Greek company law.	Limited BTR – breakthrough voting ceiling with 50% of share capital.

COMPARISON OF NATIONAL TAKEOVER PROVISIONS

Country:	Ireland	Italy	Luxembourg	The Netherlands
Disclosure threshold:	5%, 10%, 15%, 25%, 30% and 75%, above and below, depending on the relevant legislation.	2%, 5%, 7.5%, 10%. Multiples of 5%.	10%, 20% 0.33%, 50% and 0.66%.	5%, 10%, 25%, 50% and 66.6% (to be slightly amended with the implementation of Directive 2004/109/EC).
Disclosure timing:	In general, 5 days from the date the obligation to disclose arises. Dealings during the offer period and acquisitions which result in a holding of 15% or more of the voting rights or which increase a 15–30% holding beyond a whole percentage figure must be disclosed not later than 12.00 noon on the business day following the transaction.	5 working days.	7 calendar days.	2 working days.
Mandatory bid threshold (MBT):	Generally, once 30% or more of the targets voting rights have been acquired.	30%.	No rule.	Not applicable (to be introduced with the implementation of Directive 2004/25/EC, expected threshold 30%).
Offer pricing:	The price must be equivalent to the highest value of the consideration per share paid by the offeror for the target shares in the 12 months before the mandatory offer is triggered.	Not less than weighted average of the average price of last 12 months and highest price paid by the acquirer.	No rule.	No general minimum offer price (to be introduced with the implementation of Directive 2004/25/EC).
Post bid defences:	Board neutrality – but some defences are available which are very heavily regulated and are subject to shareholder approval.	Yes, but with consent of 30% of the share capital.	Board to act in company's best interest.	Yes.
Squeeze out:	80%.	98%.	Not available.	95%.
Sell out:	No.	No.	Not available.	No (to be introduced with the implementation of Directive 2004/25/EC, expected threshold 95%).
Offer acceptance period:	21 days (first closing date) to 35 days (second closing date) and subject to further extension.	15–40 working days (subject to extension to 55).	No rule.	At least 20 days (friendly offer) or 30 days (hostile offer).
Revisions to offers:	Yes, up until the 46th day after the posting of the offer document, provided the offeror is not restricted from doing so in the initial offer document.	Yes, within 3 working days of the deadline.	Possible.	No.
Competing offers:	Yes, subject to the provisions of Rules 31, 32 and 33 of the Takeover Rules.	Yes, within 5 working days of the deadline.	Possible.	Yes.
Breakthrough rule (BTR):	No.	Limited BTR – breakthrough voting ceiling if a takeover offer is launched for the entire share capital.	No rule.	No (possibly to be introduced with the implementation of Directive 2004/25/EC).

APPENDIX II

Country:	Poland	Portugal	Spain	Sweden
Disclosure threshold:	5%, 10%, 20%, 25%, 33%, 50%, 75%.	2%, 5%, 10%, 20%, one third, half, two thirds, 90%.	5% and multiples thereof, whether upon purchase or upon disposals.	5%, 10%, 15% (multiples of 5% up to and including 90%).
Disclosure timing:	7–14 days after the notification but no sooner then on the third day after publishing.	3 calendar days.	7 working days.	09.00 a.m. on the first subsequent business day.
Mandatory bid threshold (MBT):	33%.	One third and half.	25%, 50%. Special rules apply for purchases between 25%–50%. Below such thresholds as long as more than 5% is acquired, special rules apply if power to appoint a certain number of directors to target board.	30% (votes).
Offer pricing:	Not less than average stock price of the last 6 months.	The highest of the following prices: price paid by the bidder for shares of the same class as the target shares; average market price of the target shares during the 6 months prior to the publication of the Preliminary Announcement.	No restrictions apply to consideration offered to target shareholders (bid price could even be below market price) except if 'fair price' pro-visions apply in the following contexts: – going private or delisting bids; and – material amendment of by-laws if shareholder owns more than 50% of share capital.	The offer price must not be less than the highest price paid by the offeror for shares in the target within 6 months of the announcement of the offer.
Post bid defences:	Board must act in the interest of the Company.	Very limited with the board being prevented from performing any action likely to cause a relevant change in the target's assets capable of harming bidder's intentions.	Board neutrality – must act in the best interests of the company. Post bid defences are outlawed.	Outlawed, unless approved by the target shareholders in general meeting.
Squeeze out:	90%.	90%.	No.	90% of shares and votes.
Sell out:	90%.	90%.	No.	90% of shares and votes.
Offer acceptance period:	7–90 working days (sale of all remaining shares in a p.c. 30–90 days).	2–10 weeks.	Minimum 1 month – maximum 2 months.	Not less than three weeks.
Revisions to offers:	No.	Only to improve the price or if a material circumstance occurs.	Yes, within 7 working days of the deadline.	Yes, but may require an extension of the acceptance period and a supplement to the offer document.
Competing offers:	Yes.	Yes; up to the day before the last day on which the initial offer ends. Must increase the price by at least 5%.	Yes, within 10 working days from the beginning of the acceptance period of the prior bid but no later than 30 working days from the beginning of the acceptance period of the initial bid, if applicable.	Yes.
Breakthrough rule (BTR):	No.	No.	No.	No.